Japanese Women:
New Feminist Perspectives
on the Past, Present, and Future

Edited by Kumiko Fujimura-Fanselow
and Atsuko Kameda

The Feminist Press
at The City University of New York
New York

Published 1995 by The Feminist Press at The City University of New York,
365 Fifth Avenue, New York, New York 10016
www.feministpress.org

12 11 10 09 08 07 06 05 04   7 6 5 4

Library of Congress Cataloging-in-Publication Data
Japanese women : new feminist perspectives on the past, present, and
   future / edited by Kumiko Fujimura-Fanselow and Atsuko Kameda.
      p.   cm.
   "Selected bibliography of works in English on and by Japanese
women": p.
   ISBN 1-55861-093-6 (cloth). — ISBN 1-55861-094-4 (paper)
   1. Women—Japan. 2. Feminism—Japan. I. Fujimura-Fanselow,
Kumiko, 1947–   II. Kameda, Atsuko.
HQ1762.J38   1995
305.42'0952—dc20   95-1166
                                                                            CIP

The Feminist Press would like to thank Mariam Chamberlain, Joanne
Markell, and Genevieve Vaughan for their generosity.

Cover design: Lucinda Geist
Text design: Tina R. Malaney
Cover art: "Tsuzukimono" (Serial) by Ito Shoha, 1916. Courtesy of Fukutomi
Taro Collection. Reprinted with the permission of Ito Masako. "Shimbun"
(Newspaper) by Domoto Insho, 1950. The National Museum of Modern Art,
Kyoto. Photo provided by Ashahi Shimbun Newspaper Company. Reprinted
with the permission of Domoto Insho Commemoration and Promotion
Foundation.

Typeset by Mod Komp Corp.

Printed in the United States of America on acid-free paper

To our mothers
Fujimura Ayako   *Kameda Chiyoko*

Contents

Part Three: Marriage, Family, and Sexuality: Changing Values and Practices

Part Four: Women at Work

Part Five: Women's Future: Asserting New Powers

Preface

A rich and abundant body of scholarship both on the history of Japanese women as well as contemporary issues concerning women has developed over the past twenty years as an outgrowth of the feminist movement that emerged in Japan. Simultaneously, there has been a great deal of attention and curiosity among Japanese concerning women in other countries, with the result that a considerable body of scholarship and literature from abroad has been translated and made available to Japanese readers. In fact, translated works by American, British, French, and other scholars served as an important stimulus for Japanese scholars in the initial phase of the growth of feminist research, which began in the early 1970s. The intervening years have given birth to numerous and diverse writings about Japanese women by Japanese women.

Interest in books written by and about women in other countries remains high, and we have access to a continuing flow of information from abroad. Unfortunately, however, there has not been a reciprocal flow of information about Japanese women to readers abroad. The main barrier is undoubtedly language. Until very recently Japanese has not been a language that has been studied widely; at the same time, while most Japanese scholars read English, relatively few possess a similar competency in writing. Consequently, firsthand observations and research on various aspects of Japanese society have not been made widely available to non-Japanese reading audiences. It is probably fair to say that, aside from the small minority of students and scholars who are engaged in a specialized study of Japan, most non-Japanese are quite uninformed about current Japanese society beyond clichés and about the current situation of Japanese women in particular, except in the form of superficial reports.

Recently, in the United States, for example, there has been more reporting about Japanese women in the mass media. But such journalistic reporting, often confined to a few minutes or a few pages, often tends to focus on the uniqueness or peculiarity of its subject matter and thereby to present a distorted, exaggerated, or stereotypical picture to the average reader. Japanese women are often portrayed as suffering from oppression in a society that, though "Westernized" and modern in many respects, still retains traditional and even feudalistic values and practices, particularly with regard to women. At the extreme are writers, both Japanese and non-Japanese, who claim that it is wrong to apply so-called Western standards and measures in judging the situation of Japanese women and who claim most Japanese women are, in fact, quite happy with their lives, even though they may not necessarily enjoy the same level or nature of equality with men that women from other countries might find desirable. This view of Japanese society and culture, whether it focuses on the educational or employment system or the status of women, is all too common in much that is presented to readers abroad.

A 1992 *Los Angeles Times* article reported that, for each Japanese book translated into English, the Japanese publish 35 to 40 titles from the United States and Europe.[1] In the same article we are told that in 1990 Japan published an estimated 4,000 titles in translation, more than 3,000 of them from English. But the United States published only 82 titles translated from Japanese—compared to 321 titles translated from French, 202 from German, 145 from Russian, and 23 from Latin, according to a *Publishers Weekly* study. In addition, articles that appear in Japanese magazines and scholarly journals are rarely available in English translation. The unfortunate result, as a leading Japan scholar, Chalmers Johnson, is quoted as saying in the article, is that there is a persistent gap between what the Japanese write at home and what the world reads abroad.

This volume is intended as a contribution toward closing this gap. The essays within it provide an introduction to current Japanese feminist scholarship on Japanese women. These essays endeavor to present a description and analysis, from a feminist perspective, of the current status of Japanese women and the various forces and factors that have shaped and continue to shape it. They examine the issues and problems women confront in the family, the workplace, schools, and the cultural and political arenas. At the same time, and more importantly, they highlight the changes in attitudes and consciousness which are taking place among Japanese women themselves. And they underline the struggles women are undertaking as active agents in this ongoing process of social change, both individually and collectively, to bring about greater equality and to make available more opportunities and choices for women.

While it is true that certain aspects of Japanese society and culture—including values, traditions, and structures—pose a particular set of restrictions and obstacles to women's advancement within various spheres of society, it is just as important to recognize the commonalities that characterize women and the issues they confront across societies. Many of the issues and problems that Japanese women confront are shared by women in other societies. Moreover, in this highly interdependent world in which countries are closely connected by economic, political, and cultural ties and the flow of news and information is almost instantaneous, issues that come to the forefront in any one society inevitably become subjects of attention in other societies, and strategies devised by one society for dealing with a particular issue are closely scrutinized and sometimes even adopted by other societies.

In the case of Japan developments and pressures from overseas have been a particularly potent force in compelling the government to face up to and deal with issues that Japanese women themselves have attempted to bring to public attention, and therefore an understanding of developments concerning women in other countries and of what women in other countries are thinking, doing, and fighting for have been instructive and crucial for Japanese feminists. We feel that, similarly, a fuller understanding of Japanese women and how they view various issues and how they are responding to problems and pressures can provide valuable perspectives for women in other societies.

The essays included here are all written by Japanese women who have researched and written extensively about Japanese women.[2] A considerable volume of significant research on Japanese women has been produced by non-Japanese, particularly American, female scholars over the last twenty years. Our decision to focus exclusively on works by Japanese researchers in no way reflects negative evaluation of research done by non-Japanese. We simply wanted to focus specifically on current writings by Japanese women themselves, partly to make their research accessible to a wider audience. We also feel that they might be able to contribute different and perhaps invaluable perspectives and insights in their capacities both as researchers observing and studying about Japanese women and also as Japanese women themselves, drawing on their own lifelong, day-to-day experiences as daughters, sisters, wives, mothers, and professionals living and working in Japanese society and experiencing firsthand the various social pressures, rules, and expectations that bear on women.

The contributors to this volume are from a wide range of backgrounds; the majority are academics, but also among the group are journalists, a former high school teacher turned politician, a free-lance writer, and a woman who identifies herself primarily as a feminist-activist. Nearly all of them have lived, studied, worked, and done research in the United States and other countries for varying lengths of time, and so they are able to bring a comparative perspective to their writing. Most of the essays have been written specifically for this volume.

As noted, an abundance of writings about women is available in Japan today. This volume by no means presents a comprehensive treatment or picture of Japanese women. It is designed to present one sample of contemporary research on selected issues concerning Japanese women. Our decisions regarding what subjects to include in this volume were based primarily on what topics we determined were important to present and, second, on the availability of contributors who would be able to write on those particular topics—at least in draft form—in English. Inevitably, compromises had to be made: some topics had to be dropped since we could not find appropriate people to write about them in English; about one-third of the essays were submitted in Japanese and translated into English; many of the other essays required considerable editing, both in terms of the English as well as to make them more readily understandable to those who do not have a great deal of knowledge and familiarity with Japan in terms of its history or contemporary situation.

This book, then, is directed at readers interested in studying and learning about the current status of women in Japan. It does not assume sophisticated prior knowledge of Japan. We envision the book serving as a valuable text in women's studies courses in English-speaking countries at the undergraduate and graduate levels designed to provide a cross-cultural perspective on issues concerning women as well as in courses on Japanese society within departments of Japanese studies at colleges and universities in English-speaking countries. Many of our colleagues in Japan have also expressed interest in using the book in women's studies courses offered at junior colleges and universities in which texts written in English are frequently used.

As a final note, when we first conceived the idea of putting together this book, we immediately decided to approach Florence Howe at The Feminist Press. This desire reflected our deep respect for the many years of commitment Florence Howe has demonstrated to feminism and the goals of expanding knowledge about women from many different cultures and promoting the teaching of women's studies and our strong identification with that commitment and those goals. We are deeply grateful to Florence Howe for giving us the opportunity to publish our book with The Feminist Press. In addition we are grateful to Mariam K. Chamberlain, President Emerita of the National Council for Research on Women, for her invaluable advice and comments on the manuscript. Finally, we would like to thank Neeti Madan and Alyssa Colton, our editors at The Feminist Press, for their continuous support, and to Elizabeth Gratch, for her meticulous copyediting.

Following Japanese practice, Japanese family names precede given names in the text, except when the names of this book's editors and contributors appear. The reference lists at the end of each essay and the Selected

Bibliography follows American custom, with authors listed in alphabetical order by family name with American punctuation.

Kumiko Fujimura-Fanselow
Atsuo Kameda

NOTES

1. Efron, Sonni. 1992. "A Bilateral Imbalance in the Book Trade." *Japan Times*, 25 May, 23; reprinted from the *Los Angeles Times*, 21 May, 1992.

2. The chapter "The Changing Portrait of Japanese Men" includes contributions by two men, a Japanese journalist and an American scholar who is a longtime resident in Japan.

Introduction

Kumiko Fujimura-Fanselow

"The Era of Women"

The Image

"Onna no jidai," or "the era of women," is a catchphrase heard often these days in Japan. The implication is that, having attained a large measure of equality in a highly affluent society, Japanese women today are able to choose freely from a variety of options in their pursuit of an active and fulfilling life. At the same time, women are portrayed as being more vibrant, more independent, more in tune with new ideas and new values, and enjoying a happier, longer, more balanced lifestyle in comparison with their male counterparts, who are often portrayed as holding on to old-fashioned views on everything from marriage to the environment and tied to the dull, stultifying routine of the salaried white-collar worker, or *salariman*.[1]

Recent advances in the area of politics, employment, education, and culture as well as marriage and family are cited in support of this notion of the era of women. On the cultural front an impressive number of women writers have appeared in recent years, and an increasing number of them have become recipients of prestigious literary awards. On the political front is the growing presence of female politicians, exemplified most prominently by the appointment of Doi Takako as leader of Japan's largest opposition party, the Socialist Party, in 1986, as well as the successful election of a record high of twenty-two female candidates in the 1989 election for the House of Councilors of the National Diet. Women have increasingly become visible in local politics also: female representation in local (prefectural, municipal, town, and village) assemblies grew from 1 percent in 1976 to 3.3 percent in 1992 (Nihon Fujin Dantai 302, table 109), and the first female mayor was elected (in Ashiya) in 1991. A quick glance at educational statistics reveals a higher percentage of female as compared to male high school graduates entering colleges and universities—46 versus 41 percent in 1994. The overwhelming majority of female college and university graduates, over 80 percent, are taking up employment and doing so in a wider range of fields than in the past. Better education and the availability of more job opportunities have increasingly made it possible for women to look upon marriage as an option rather than a prescribed lifestyle. Data indicate that college-educated women are choosing to continue working and to postpone marriage. A report released by the Management and Coordination Agency in July 1992 showed that 56.2 percent of women aged twenty-five to twenty-nine with at least a bachelor's degree were unmarried in 1990, up 15.7 percentage points from 1980, and the work force rate for women aged twenty-five to twenty-nine gained 7.1 percentage points to 61.2 percent ("Educated women" 1992, 2).

Looking specifically at developments on the employment front, we can point to the passage of the Equal Employment Opportunity Law (EEOL) in 1985, which, among other things, opened up the previously all-male career track within Japanese companies to university-educated women, and also the Child Care Leave Law of 1991, which requires companies to grant unpaid leave to either parent until the child reaches the age of one. We see signs of women shedding traditional stereotypes and going into a variety of traditionally male occupations and professions. For example, in the years since the first female news co-announcer appeared on NHK (Japan's government-sponsored television network), in 1979, female newscasters have become a presence on nearly all news programs.

A dramatic development has been the advancement by married women, including those with children, into the labor force. Even in the cases of those who choose not to work outside the home, very few remain content to be housewives exclusively. Instead, they seek a life outside the home through a variety of activities, including study at privately run "culture centers," which offer courses in everything from foreign languages, literature, and law to traditional arts, handicrafts, cooking, and sports. Others take up classes offered at local government facilities or at one of the more than a hundred women's centers that have been established throughout Japan, some of which help housewives acquire skills for reentering the job market. Housewives have also become enthusiastically involved in a variety of community-related activities, including volunteer work, establishment of consumer cooperatives, efforts to protect the environment, political movements, peace movements, and campaigns against political corruption. Whereas not so long ago married women were expected to stay at home most of the time, today we typically see groups of middle-aged women playing tennis or swimming together, going shopping, eating out, and traveling and sightseeing both within and outside the country.

The Reality: Persisting Inequalities

The evidence, which tends to portray Japanese women as having gained access to a wide range of options and opportunities and quite contented with their lives, must be balanced against a range of other indicators that show women are still far from having achieved real, substantive equality in nearly every sphere of life—the family, schools, the workplace, the media, and politics. Women are still conspicuously absent in the top ranks of business and government. Thus, for example, while more and more women who take up employment are remaining on their jobs for ten or more years (the figure was 27 percent in 1992 compared to just 19 percent in 1980) (Rodosho fujinkyoku, app. p. 28, app. table 23), a mere 1 percent of employed women occupied administrative-managerial positions (compared to 7.4 percent in the case of males), and women made up just 8 percent of all those occupying such positions in 1992 (app. p. 17, app. table 11). In the case of firms with more than one hundred workers, just 1.7 percent of company directors and managers were women, up only slightly from the figure of 1 percent in 1982 (app. p. 28, app. table 24). At the national political level, as of 1993, there were only 14 women in the House of Representatives out of a total of 511 members, representing a gain of just 7 women since 1975. Although a woman was first appointed to the cabinet (as minister of Health and Welfare) back in 1960, since then women have only intermittently occupied positions in the cabinet, and the highest number of women appointed to a cabinet thus far has been three, which took place under the short-lived prime ministership of Hosokawa Morihiro in 1993–94.

In the academic realm the marked progress made by women as students has hardly been matched by women's advancement as faculty and administrators in higher education: women constitute 31 percent of the student body of four-year universities, yet only about 4 percent of university presidents and less than 10 percent of university faculty are female (Mombusho 1994). Finally, although the concept of gender equality has, in principle, been accepted by most Japanese—and there is certainly less tolerance for overt display of sexual discrimination than was the case in the past—at the same time, it is not at all uncommon to see and hear sexist attitudes and behavior, both in private and in public, in the home, schools, workplaces, on television, in political settings, and elsewhere.[2]

How women themselves actually perceive their current status in Japanese society is very difficult to gauge. Individual perceptions inevitably vary according to such factors as age, socioeconomic status, educational background, and level of consciousness about issues concerning women. In one national survey conducted in 1992 which looked at perceptions of the extent to which men and women enjoy equality in the home, the workplace, education, the political arena, legal provisions, and in terms of social attitudes, customs, and conventions, women responded that they thought men received superior treatment in all areas, with the exception of education, in which they thought there was equality. The study yielded a number of other interesting findings: one was that men were more likely to believe that both sexes enjoyed equality in all of these areas, and the other was that there was not much change in terms of women's responses from similar surveys that had been done starting in 1975 (with the exception that their perception of equality in the workplace had increased, which was probably due to the enactment of the Equal Employment Opportunity Law in 1985), which seems to indicate that many women do not feel a great deal of progress has been made in promoting gender equality in the intervening years (Nihon Fujin Dantai 1993, 216, fig. II-74, 217, fig. II-75).

To cite one other example, in a similar survey conducted in 1981–82 in Japan, the United States, Sweden, West Germany, England, and the Philippines, Japanese women's perception of equality ranked the lowest overall (217–18, fig. II-76). This was true even with respect to their assessment of gender equality in the household, which, in fact, as some would claim (see, e.g., Iwao 1993), is a sphere in which Japanese women enjoy dominant status. Most Japanese wives probably do assume a major role in the day-to-day management of household affairs and expenses—supervising the children's schooling, making sure the monthly bills get paid, and so on. Yet, when it comes to making decisions about major purchases or choice of college, the authority of the husband is apt to be given more weight. Moreover, there is an underlying attitude on the part of many housewives that they are, after all, supported by their husbands and financially dependent on them and, on the part of many husbands, that they are "the breadwinners" and therefore somehow superior to their wives. This kind of attitude is reinforced, for example, by the designation of the husband as the "head of household" on various governmental and private sector forms. The growing evidence of the widespread incidence of domestic violence also serves to raise doubts about the degree of gender equality in the home.

The view presented in this volume is that many women are pleased, with some good reason, by the significant strides they have made toward securing greater rights and opportunities in the home, workplace, and schools. But, at the same time, an increasing number of women are becoming not only aware of but also frustrated and angered by the persisting constraints on their ability to participate more fully and equally with men in many spheres and activities and by the gap they perceive between their status and position and that of women in many of the other industrialized countries.

Legal and Formal Constraints on Women's Progress

As we try to understand why actual, substantive equality for women has yet to be more fully realized in Japanese society, we find that the obstacles stem both from formal policies, legal constraints, and overt discrimination as well as from a variety of social structures and attitudinal constraints.

Reforms initiated by the Allied (in practice, U.S.) Occupation following

Japan's defeat in World War II, and later voted into law by the Japanese Diet and embodied in the Japanese Constitution promulgated in 1946 and the revised Civil Code, secured the legal rights and guarantees of constitutional, civil, and educational equality which Japanese women had for so long struggled to achieve. The Fundamental Law of Education enacted in 1947 provided for equality of educational opportunity and the establishment of coeducation at all levels, and the Labor Standards Law of 1947 stipulated equal treatment for women in the workplace and equal pay for equal work. More recent legislative developments, such as revisions of certain provisions in the Civil Code and the enactment of the Equal Employment Opportunity Law and the Child Care Leave Law, have further strengthened and secured additional legal rights for women in the family and the workplace. Yet even these new laws fall short of eliminating various forms of sex discrimination and facilitating further progress toward the attainment of equality, independence, and autonomy.

The EEOL certainly had a positive impact in terms of expanding employment opportunities for female university graduates in the latter part of the 1980s, which, it so happened, was a period of booming economic growth and prosperity accompanied by a labor shortage. In the wake of the recession that Japan has faced since 1991, however, discrimination against women has resurfaced, and many employers have once again cut back on the hiring of female graduates. This has not surprised those feminists who recognized the serious limitations of the EEOL from the very beginning.

In addition, as Yoko Kawashima points out in "Female Workers: An Overview of Past and Current Trends," the EEOL has had little impact in terms of improving the situation faced by the large proportion of female workers who fall into the category of the peripheral labor force. As noted earlier, one of the major developments over the past thirty years has been the entry by married women into the labor market: today 53 percent of all married women are in the labor force; married, divorced, and widowed women make up two-thirds of all employed female workers (Rodosho fujinkyoku 1993, app. p. 25, app. table 18). But a closer examination reveals that 31 percent of all employed women are part-time workers, defined as those who work fewer than thirty-five hours per week (app. p. 68, app. table 66). Women as a whole represent about 68 percent, and married women alone make up 65 percent of all part-time employees (40). Most of these women work for low wages in smaller firms; they are frequently denied retirement benefits and housing and family allowances as well as opportunities for skills training and promotion, and they are not enrolled in health, employment, or welfare annuity insurance programs. Moreover, they lack job security since their employment is subject to changes in economic conditions.

Although it is generally said that many married women choose part-time employment because it is more compatible with the demands of family responsibilities, and many claim to work not out of financial necessity but, rather, to supplement family income and for other reasons such as "to make use of free time" or "to take part in society, find a life purpose," a fact that cannot be overlooked is that for most middle-aged women who have been out of the labor market for several years and who lack specialized skills, part-time work (or home-based work) is the only option available to them. Many employers will not hire women beyond a certain age for full-time positions. In a 1990 survey by the Ministry of Labor only 15 percent of the companies surveyed indicated that they hired women seeking re-employment on a full-time basis (Rodosho fujinkyoku, app. p. 58, app. table 55).

Also significant in terms of sustaining this pattern of employment among many married women are current policies pertaining to taxation and social welfare as well as company policies regarding pay and provision of dependency allowances for spouses and children and other benefits, which are premised on a social arrangement whereby the wife basically stays home and is supported by the husband. Disadvantages accrue to a couple should the wife earn in excess of one million yen (or roughly ten thousand dollars) per year, and for this reason many women limit their work hours and earnings. In 1989, 63 percent of female part-timers were earning under one million yen.

The fact is, women's participation in the labor market, whether it be on a full- or part-time basis, is becoming increasingly indispensible and unavoidable, not only because it is increasingly difficult for couples with children to maintain desired levels of living standards on one salary but also because a growing number of women are finding themselves in the position of having to support themselves, and often their children, as a result of divorce and widowhood or because they have chosen to remain single. What this points to is a need for a reassessment and modification of existing policies and practices based on an acknowledgment of women as a core labor force, rather than simply a peripheral or supplementary one. There will need also to be an acknowledgment of the individual, rather than the family, as the basic economic unit in society.

Opportunities for women to assume a more equal role in various spheres are constrained by official policies with respect to provision of child daycare facilities and welfare services and facilities for the elderly and bedridden. Since the mid-1970s the policy of the Japanese government has been increasingly directed toward shifting the burden of meeting various social service needs from the central government to local bodies and to individual families (the so-called Japanese-style welfare system). With the shrinking size of Japanese families (which was 2.99 persons in 1992, compared to 5 persons in 1953), this inevitably means those burdens and responsibilities will fall increasingly on wives, daughters, and daughters-in-law. At the same time, few companies and municipal offices provide family care leave to employees. A 1990 survey by the Ministry of Labor of companies with thirty or more employees found that fewer than 14 percent provided such leave (Nihon Fujin Dantai Rengokai 155, table II-38). Another survey by the Labor Ministry in 1991 revealed that, of those companies, 45 percent provided for a maximum of one year's leave; only 9 percent allowed for more than a year's leave, while the rest allowed for less than one year's leave (155, table II-40).

With regard to child care leave, though the Child Care Leave Law went into effect in 1992 and requires companies to allow parents of both sexes to take a leave of up to one year until the child reaches the age of one, the law does not require employers to pay workers while they are on leave, and, in fact, only one-third provide salary and other payments to such workers (Nihon Fujin Dantai Rengokai 281, fig. 58). The implications of such policies and practices in terms of women's ability, on the one hand, to combine and balance individual needs and goals, including career goals, with family-related responsibilities, and, on the other hand, to lead secure and independent lives in their old age are extremely serious. Child care and care of the ill and elderly are, in fact, the factors most frequently cited by women as impediments to women's ability to continue working (Sorifu 1989).

Norms and practices associated with the corporate system present another major set of obstacles to the realization of greater progress for women outside the home and more equal sharing of responsibilities in the home. Japan's often touted "miraculous" economic growth over the last thirty years has been made possible precisely because employers have been able to count on wives to be at home tending to household matters and caring for the children almost single-handedly while the men have devoted themselves to their jobs. In addition to being expected to spend excessively long hours at work, company employees are frequently transferred to different posts both within Japan and overseas. Although workers may, theoretically, refuse transfers, their future promotion may be jeopardized if they do so.

In recent years we have seen a dramatic rise in the numbers of workers moving to their new posts in a distant workplace and leaving their families behind. These so-called single transfers *(tanshin funin)* have been preferable for a variety of reasons, such as reluctance to have children transfer schools (particularly at the high school level where admission is based on entrance examinations), hesitancy about vacating homes on which loan payments are still being made, a growing desire on the part of working wives to continue their jobs, and the need to care for aging parents. Understandably, the hardships entailed in continuing such a living arrangement for four or five years or even longer are numerous and burdensome for both husbands and wives. Thus far "single transfers" have typically been men, since relatively few women have occupied positions that entail transfers. In fact, many companies have rejected female candidates, using the argument that because of their family responsibilities women cannot be counted on to accept transfers. As the ranks of women occupying responsible positions increase, this issue will likely become even more serious.[3]

So long as the current culture and practices of the male-centered workplace, which are incompatible with the demands of home and family, dominate and so long as women who wish to pursue professional careers and be accorded equal treatment with men must conform to that culture, the majority of Japanese women will continue to be automatically excluded; most will choose to settle for part-time work or seek a different outlet for their talents, for example, community and volunteer activities. Substantive equality for women at home and in the larger society cannot be achieved without fundamental changes in laws and official policies as well as in management and personnel policies and practices—beginning with a reduction in working hours and improvement in provisions and facilities for the care of children and the sick and elderly—so that both women and men can more comfortably combine family responsibilities with outside commitments.

Normative and Attitudinal Constraints on Women's Progress toward Equality

The kinds of obstacles to women's attainment of greater equality and opportunity are, to an important degree, sustained and buttressed by norms, values, attitudes, and expectations pertaining to gender roles which persist in the consciousness of many Japanese, including women. Moreover, as several of the chapters in this volume attempt to show, those norms and values continue to be reproduced and passed on to the younger generation of Japanese in the home and through schools and the mass media.

While the popularity of the traditional view that "men should work and women should stay home" has declined in recent years, as evidenced by the results of national public opinion polls conducted over the past twenty years, it still enjoys considerable support, though to a lesser extent among females than males—46 percent versus 66 percent in a 1992 survey (Nihon Fujin Dantai Rengokai 1993, 219, fig. II-77). As a consequence, many women continue to feel compelled to restrict their activities outside the home, including employment. Similarly, despite the general trend toward liberalization in attitudes regarding women's employment, only a minority of either women or men endorse the view that women should continue to work after they have children. Instead, in congruence with dominant attitudes with respect to the mother's role in child rearing, most feel women should leave employment to care for children and return to work when the children have grown (at which point part-time employment is the most realistic option). Another normative expectation, namely that caring for parents in their old age is a woman's duty and responsibility, especially in the case of daughters-in-law, compounded by the lack of sufficient public resources and facilities for the care of the elderly, exerts strong pressures on women to curtail their outside involvements and in many cases to withdraw from the workplace when a parent or in-law becomes frail or ill.

It is also generally accepted that women bear the total responsibility for maintaining a home and caring for the children. Even when husbands support their wives' work outside the home on a part-time basis—often because the extra income is needed to make the mortgage payment or to pay for children's private lessons or college tuition—their "approval" often comes with the condition that wives continue to perform all of the necessary household/domestic chores so that husbands need take on no additional responsibilities. The result, of course, is that working wives end up taking on a double burden. Several studies bear out the findings of a survey conducted by the Management and Coordination Agency in 1991 which found that, among working couples, the husbands spent an average of just twelve minutes on housekeeping, shopping, and child care on weekdays (Rodosho fujinkyoku 1993, app. p. 63, app. table 61).

Portents of Change

There are, however, many signs of changes in values and attitudes on the part of the Japanese, particularly the younger ones, regarding not only gender roles but also work and other matters. As Masanori Yamaguchi points out in his essay on Japanese men, many men are beginning to question, if not reject, the type of work-centered, structured lifestyle typified by the corporate *salariman* (salaried workers) which has been accepted as the norm. In this respect it is interesting to note that two conditions young men and women seeking employment often cite as important criteria in choosing a firm are, one, that they not be required to work overtime and, two, that they get both Saturday and Sunday off. For these young people, who have grown up in an affluent consumer society, having "private time" to pursue leisure activities, take vacations, and spend time with friends and family is as important, if perhaps not more so, than working and getting ahead. In other words, they are apt to view work as but one aspect of their lives and a means of enabling them to live full lives, in contrast to an earlier generation for whom the work ethic and company loyalty and commitment were significant motivating factors. A number of recent surveys also indicate that young people are much less likely to aspire to enter a major company and stay with that company throughout their working lifetimes. A new phenomenon among Japanese women, similar to that which can be seen among American women, is the rise in the number who have started their own businesses at which they can work on terms that are more compatible with their needs.

Simultaneously, women's attitudes toward marriage and divorce are also undergoing transformation. Thus, many women, particularly those with university degrees, are postponing marriage. They are doing so not only because they are busy pursuing careers but also because, with the ability to be financially independent, they are unwilling to settle simply for marriage with any man. The kind of husband many seek is one with whom they can establish an equal partnership. Changes in women's expectations, together with their advancement into the paid labor market, which has enabled more women to achieve some measure of financial independence, are also reflected in the growing incidence of divorce, 70 percent of which are now initiated by women.[4] Particularly significant has been the rise in the proportion of divorces occurring among couples who have been married fifteen years or more and who have two or more children. In spite of the financial difficulties entailed in supporting themselves and their children—due in part to inadequacies in child support and other provisions—in more than 70 percent of the cases, women take custody of the children. This rising incidence of divorce among Japanese women in their forties and fifties is but one manifestation of the kind of "strange stirring, a sense of dissatisfaction, a yearning" that Betty Friedan identified among many American women in the early 1960s. Whereas in the past, as Kyoko Yoshizumi notes in her essay on marriage and the family, a man was judged to be a good husband and father so long as he provided adequate financial support for his family, many women, including those in their middle years, are beginning to yearn for something more from their marriage, that is, emotional support and understanding. One may view the involvement of married women in various endeavors outside the home as part of their search for self-definition beyond the traditional identity as wife and mother.

In addition to changes in attitudes and expectations, demographic, economic, and other changes are also having important impact on women's lives and their role in society. For example, on the employment front, although sex biases in hiring and promotion are still very prevalent at the large, well-established corporations, which continue to attract ample pools of male graduates from the most prestigious universities, the smaller companies, which are considered to be less attractive, are turning to qualified female graduates. This trend can be expected to become more prominent as the pool of young Japanese workers declines in the years to come and, at the same time, the current generation of men making personnel and management decisions gives way to one less bound by gender stereotypes and biases. The increasing need to augument the labor force with women can be expected to force government and employers to make greater efforts to improve child day care and other provisions and facilities. Another significant development is that, while growing numbers of married women have been entering the labor market, the financial contribution of wives to the household has assumed added importance in recent years, since Japan entered a period of severe economic recession in 1991, which has been accompanied by salary reductions, bankruptcies of many smaller companies, and layoffs of middle-level management personnel and cutbacks on overtime work (which has been an important source of supplementary income) at many of the large corporations. One consequence of wives assuming this kind of added role may well be a gradual altering of the power relationship between wives and husbands.

Domestic and International Pressures for Promoting Women's Equality

The developments I have described and the issues I have outlined have been brewing over the period of the last fifty years, since the launching of the supposedly new era for Japanese women which began following the end of

World War II and the birth of democracy. Yet it is within the last twenty years or so that those issues have gained recognition and become subjects of debate in society as a whole and among women in particular.

As was the case throughout the industrialized societies, the years following the end of World War II brought rapid and far-reaching changes in the lives of Japanese women, including life cycle changes associated with a dramatic decline in the average number of children born (from 5 per woman before World War II to 1.46 in 1993), rise in levels of educational attainment, later marriages, and a lengthening of the average life expectancy (to 82.2 years—the highest in the world in 1993). At the same time, rapid economic growth during the 1960s, accompanied by a growth in jobs in wholesaling and retailing and in the service industries, led to an expansion in demand for female workers. Increasingly equipped with university degrees, the younger women sought access to careers formerly closed to women. Married women, whose burden of housework was eased by labor-reducing devices and the trend toward nuclear families and fewer children, and who were released from the daily demands of child care by their late thirties, also sought to work outside the home.

While women's aspirations became heightened, employers' policies continued to be shaped by the dominant norms, which stipulated women's place and role as primarily in the home, so that university-educated women continued to be subjected to discrimination in hiring and promotion, while married women who reentered the labor force could still only obtain low-paying, part-time employment. Meanwhile, in the home, social conventions, supported by the policies of the conservative government, continued to dictate that women bear the full burden of household responsibilities, including the care of the increasingly large cohort of elderly parents and in-laws, even when these women engaged in paid employment.

The women's liberation movement that emerged in the early 1970s reflected the growing frustrations felt by many, particularly young, well-educated women, about the persistent manifestations of gender inequality and discrimination in a society that had, in principle, become thoroughly democratized and reached an advanced stage of economic development. At the same time, it owed much to the women's movement that had sprung up in the United States in the late 1960s. While this *"uman ribu"* (the Japanese pronunciation of *women's lib*) marked the dawn of the second phase of feminism in Japan, as well as elsewhere in the world, initially the movement failed to gain wide support among women and was mostly ignored by the government (see the essay by Kazuko Tanaka, "The New Feminist Movement in Japan, 1970–1990").

Much more influential and significant in terms of attracting the attention of a wider audience of Japanese to issues concerning women, of bestowing legitimacy on demands for women's equality, and of forcing the Japanese government to take administrative actions to promote equality were developments on the international front. These included the designation of the

International Women's Year in 1975, the adoption of the World Plan of Action at the conference held in Mexico City outlining measures for implementing the objectives of the International Women's Year, the launching of the UN Decade for Women 1976–85, and the adoption of the Convention on the Elimination of All Forms of Discrimination against Women by the UN General Assembly in 1979. It was clear that, while Japan had already attained some of the goals of the World Plan of Action, such as eliminating illiteracy and guaranteeing legal equality for both sexes, it fell short of reaching other goals, such as gender equality in the workplace and participation by women in policy-making. At the same time, Japan's outstanding economic success drew increasing interest from the international community in Japanese economic structure and employment and management practices and, inevitably, growing criticism of its discriminatory treatment of Japanese women. Japan's political and economic leaders were highly sensitive to these pressures from abroad.

In the fall of 1975 the government established the Headquarters for the Planning and Promotion of Policies Relating to Women, which was given the task of formulating concrete domestic policies for implementing those goals. At the same time, the Advisory Council on Women, reporting to the prime minister, was established. In 1980 the Japanese government became a signatory to the UN Convention on the Elimination of All Forms of Discrimination against Women, thereby entering into a legally binding commitment to work to end discrimination in the family, education, media, employment, and other areas. Women from a range of professional fields, including journalists, teachers, academics, and lawyers, became involved in an increasingly public and widespread debate about and criticism of gender inequality in all spheres of Japanese society. These developments served to bestow legitimacy on the debate over feminist issues and the demand for women's equality.

Outside pressures, together with pressures brought to bear by broadly based women's movements and by challenges, including lawsuits, brought forth by individual women, resulted in the enactment of several pieces of legislation aimed at eliminating remaining remnants of sexual discrimination. Issues pertaining to women have gradually entered the consciousness of nearly all Japanese women as well as many men. This is due in large measure to the attention given to these issues by the mass media; indeed, almost daily one finds an article pertaining to women in each of the national daily newspapers. Also significant is that this development has been accompanied by a heightened attention to other human rights issues, including the rights of children, the disabled, and workers from foreign countries.

The Roots of Current Feminist Scholarship

The flourishing of new research about, and mostly by women, in a wide range of disciplines over the last twenty years, a sample of which is represented in this volume, is an outgrowth of the developments previously described. A vital source of influence on the growth of this scholarship, particularly in the earlier years, was the works of feminists in the West, particularly the United States. In the beginning translations of feminist writings by American, British, and other scholars constituted the bulk of books published in the field of women's studies. Since the latter part of the 1970s, however, works by Japanese researchers and scholars have become increasingly dominant, although publications from abroad continue to be translated and widely read. The dissemination of the growing volume of works by and/or about women has been promoted by the establishment of women's bookstores, including one in Kyoto called Shoukadoh, started in 1982, and one in Tokyo called Ms. Crayon House, started by Ochiai Keiko, a noted novelist and advocate of children's and women's rights, in 1989, as well as through the establishment of women's centers at the national, prefectural, and local levels, which also sponsor lectures, seminars, and workshops on various issues concerning women. In addition, study of and research on women has gradually achieved a degree of academic recognition, as evidenced by the growing number of junior colleges and universities offering courses in women's studies and related fields.

The examples of the current feminist scholarship presented in this volume reflect the social, political, cultural, and other developments and challenges women have confronted over the last twenty or more years and the new consciousness that has emerged among women. It should be pointed out, however, that research on issues pertaining to women appeared much earlier, at the turn of the twentieth century. As has been the case in the United States, for example, there has been a new appreciation of previous scholarship on women, and some of the older studies have become the focus of renewed attention as younger scholars have discovered common threads between concerns of feminists today and the arguments that were raised by earlier writers.

The first major debate that ensued prior to World War II was that carried on primarily by three prominent feminists of the time, Hiratsuka Raicho, Yosano Akiko, and Ichikawa Fusae. This so-called Debate over the Protection and Support of Motherhood, which began in 1918, revolved around the issue of how best to enable women to achieve equality and economic independence and the question of whether or not it was in the interest of women to have the government accord protection and special treatment to them in their capacity as mothers (e.g., protective legislation in the workplace). It is, in fact, an argument that has resurfaced time and again, most recently during the drafting stage of the recently enacted Equal Employment Opportunity Law. The Housewife Debate, which started in the mid-1950s, concerned the question of whether homemaking by itself constituted a legitimate endeavor for women or whether women as well as men had a duty as well as the right to engage in outside work. (Brief descriptions of these controversies are presented in Mioko Fujieda and Kumiko Fujimura-Fanselow's essay on women's studies.)

In more recent years we have seen discussions and arguments among feminists espousing such diverse positions as those of ecological feminism, socialist feminism, radical feminism, and postfeminism (see Ehara 1990). Many of these debates have taken place primarily among feminist theorists and academicians and have had little impact on those outside academe. One issue that has continued to be debated and has drawn the attention of ordinary Japanese women, housewives as well as career women, has been that of whether the liberation of women is to be attained through participation in the labor market or by rejecting the values of competition and exploitation associated with capitalist industrial society and cultivating, instead, those values associated with the home, the community, and the environment. This harks back to earlier debates about motherhood and the role of housewives. More recently, attention has gradually turned to such previously neglected issues as sexual harassment, lesbianism, and the various forms of gender-based violence, including domestic violence.

Organization of the Book

Japanese Women: New Feminist Perspectives on the Past, Present, and Future attempts to analyze the complex and often contradictory situation in which Japanese women find themselves today, drawing on current feminist research about or on the historical, religious, social, political, economic, and cultural dimensions of women's lives both past and present. The book is organized into five parts, beginning with a section that provides a historical and cultural context for women's present-day status, moving on to an examination of sexism in the educational process, both past and present; continuity and change in the social institution of marriage and family; and issues centering around women and work. The book concludes with a section that looks at efforts made by Japanese women both in the past and today to resist restraints imposed upon them and to struggle for autonomy and equality. The volume represents an initial effort to convey, through the vision and scholarship of Japanese feminists, deeper insights into the challenges facing Japanese women today, the changes, the progress, and the problems still to be solved.

Part 1

Part 1 provides a historical, social, and cultural context for understanding how women's lives and images have been shaped and defined by ideological and religious beliefs as well as through the family system, language, and culture. The Meiji period (1868–1912) was one in which Japan established itself as a centralized nation-state and embarked on a program of modernization, eventually emerging on the world stage as a military and industrial power. The hierarchical, patriarchal social order based on rule by the emperor was duplicated at the family level and given legal support by the Meiji Civil Code of 1898, which established the family, or *ie*, system and reinforced the legal authority of the household head, who was usually male. Women were not only confined to a separate and subordinate role within the family and denied legal rights, but they were also excluded from voting and participation in politics.

As Sachiko Kaneko's essay demonstrates, even in this period, Japanese women did not totally acquiesce to the narrow status allowed to them or to the ideology of the "good wife and wise mother" which was promoted through the state-controlled educational system. Kaneko describes the efforts undertaken by women from the early part of the Meiji period through the end of World War II to bring about reforms of the political and family system and to seize political rights, including suffrage, for themselves.

While the legal basis for the subordination of women and for their exclusion from various spheres of social activities was established in the Meiji period, going back further in history, religion—which in the Japanese case includes the native Shinto religion as well as the imported religions Confucianism and Buddhism—has also been a major force in providing a foundation for and maintaining the concept of separate gender roles and the patriarchal social order. Focusing specifically on Buddhism, which was brought into Japan through China and Korea in the sixth century, Haruko Okano describes the process whereby, following the establishment of a national system of administration in the seventh century, Buddhism, increasingly under state control, came to function as a political instrument of the state. Nuns were gradually excluded from the performance of important religious functions, a development that paralleled, in fact, the fate of women in the secular world. She also describes how certain concepts contained in the Mahayana sutras, mixed with the indigenous Japanese idea of ritual purity and blood as a source of impurity, led to the establishment of the view that women were sinful and could not obtain salvation.

Of particular interest is Okano's description of the family structure of Buddhist temples, in which men, who headed the temples, lived atop the holy mountains and conducted various religious affairs, while their female family members resided in a separate religious space at the foot of the mountain, performing their separate, assigned support tasks—sewing, washing, and cooking for the monks. Also significant is Okano's assessment that sexism is very much inherent in the so-called new religions that have come into being during the last one hundred years—despite the fact that women are more numerous among their adherents. Like the more traditional religions, they are characterized by a fixed division of gender roles, with men in charge of the bureaucratic functions and women performing various daily routines at the local chapters.

Orie Endo treats language, another vital aspect of culture which has functioned to define society's perception of women and their status. She addresses both Japanese expressions that overtly denigrate or belittle women as well as those that, used by many women, serve to elevate the status of men in relation to women. Endo also looks at gender differences in the language used by men and women and the existence of a distinctive "women's language," which even today girls are taught to use through family socialization and schooling. She explains that women's language was deliberately promoted as part of an education aimed to produce girls who would be obedient and submissive to their husbands and in-laws. Endo also highlights the fact that, reflecting changes in various aspects of women's lives in recent years, women, particularly the young, have begun to deviate from prescribed language norms and to adopt patterns of speech formerly associated with men, while at the same time, growing sensitivity to issues of gender equality have led to efforts by the government and the mass media to alter certain offensive linguistic terms used.

The essays by Chieko M. Ariga and Midori Wakakuwa describe the severe restrictions placed on women's literary and artistic production by a patriarchal system that confined women to domestic life and denied them educational opportunities as well as the material and psychological freedom needed for artistic creation. The three nineteenth-century-born artists described in Wakakuwa's essay succeeded as accomplished artists precisely because they were outside the confines of the paternalistic family system. Two of them left Japan to go abroad to study and paint, and the third was raised in a fatherless family and forced to support herself and her mother. The two essays also emphasize that male domination of literary and artistic institutions in Japan has made it extremely difficult for women to gain recognition for their work without the support of male patrons and unless, as illustrated in the example of the writer Amino Kiku, their work conforms to the established category of "female" literature and thereby receives validation by male critics. Both Ariga's and Wakakuwa's work represent a pioneering effort by feminist scholars to rediscover and reevaluate Japanese female artists and their contributions.

The theme of male cultural domination is also the subject of Midori Fukunishi Suzuki's essay on television's perpetuation of gender stereotyping and sexism. The television industry itself is characterized by gender inequality: there are very few female producers, directors, and scriptwriters. Suzuki describes the growth of networks of feminists who, in cooperation with similar groups in other countries, have begun to campaign for reform of the television industry itself as well as to raise the consciousness of the viewing audience to issues of sexism on television.

Part 2

The essays in part 2 evaluate education both as an instrument of oppression that restrains women, locking them into sexually defined roles, and discourages their participation in public life as well as a force for liberating women and equalizing their opportunities. Kimi Hara's historical review and analysis of the nature and development of female education from the Meiji period forward demonstrates how the state-controlled, sex-segregated educational system of prewar Japan, based on the ideology of "education for good wives and wise mothers," was designed to maintain a conservative social order and to keep women in a separate and inferior role within the family and society. At the same time, Hara's account of her own experiences at a girls' high school whose philosophy and practices reflected those of the New Education Movement—launched during the period of so-called Taisho democracy, in opposition to the existing nationalistic education and bearing the influence of the latest educational ideas and methods from Europe and the United States—attests to the efforts of many educators who sought to resist efforts to circumscribe the education of young women.

The series of educational reforms instituted under the influence and direction of the Allied Occupation following the end of World War II established the legal basis for guaranteeing equality of educational opportunity to women; the earlier policy of education for good wives and wise mothers was henceforth to be replaced by one that would seek to promote gender equality and women's participation in all spheres of public life. Atsuko Kameda in her essay argues that the achievement of these latter goals has been hampered by the fact that, while the legal and structural bases for equality have been achieved, sexism and gender stereotyping continue to be reproduced and perpetuated both through family socialization and through the knowledge, values, and expectations transmitted through the formal as well as the hidden curriculum—textbooks, teaching practices, tracking, counseling and guidance programs, male dominance in the teaching profession, teacher-student interactions, and school rituals. These are issues that have only recently come to be addressed.

Kumiko Fujimura-Fanselow's essay focuses on women in higher education, examining the reasons for persisting gender differences in patterns of college attendance, changing patterns of employment among female graduates, and the attitudes of college women regarding their future, including employment, marriage, and family. Her analysis shows that, while, on the one hand, the expansion of educational opportunities for women as well as opportunities for highly educated women to make use of their training in various fields of employment have greatly expanded in recent years, on the other hand, biases against women in the workplace, which have become more pronounced since the recent downturn in the economy, lack of adequate child care facilities, and lingering traditional norms and expectations regarding women's role in the home and society operate to create considerable ambivalence among young women over issues of career, marriage, and family.

A major new and potentially promising development in the area of women's education has been the growth of women's studies. While the number of Japanese colleges and universities offering courses in women's studies has increased considerably over the past fifteen years, as Mioko Fujieda and Kumiko Fujimura-Fanselow note in their essay, women's studies continues to exist on the periphery of academe. At the same time, academic scholars in the field of women's studies face the challenge of forging closer links both with female activists outside of academia and with women's studies scholars and activists in neighboring Asian countries.

Part 3

The family was the cornerstone of the government's political, economic, and social policy in prewar Japan. The Meiji Civil Code of 1898, which gave legal support for the patriarchal family system, severely restricted women's rights in matters pertaining to marriage, children, property, and divorce. The new Constitution and the Civil Law enacted after World War II abolished this patriarchal family system and secured legal equality for men and women in matters pertaining to marriage and the family. While the family system has been formally abolished, Kyoko Yoshizumi notes in her essay, which looks at marriage and the family in contemporary society, that psychological and cultural as well a legal residues of that system persist, thereby restricting women's freedom of choice and independence and hindering the realization of a truly egalitarian relationship between wives and husbands. One important aspect of Yoshizumi's article is that she refutes the notion, frequently advanced by both Japanese and Western writers and based on the low divorce rate in Japan, that Japanese housewives are generally happier with their lot than their counterparts in the West. She points to the growing evidence that women are increasingly demonstrating their dissatisfaction, in the case of middle-aged and elderly women by initiating divorce and among younger women by choosing alternative lifestyles beyond the traditional one of marriage.

Masami Ohinata discusses the various social, political, and economic functions that have been bestowed on motherhood over the last one hundred years. She argues that the continued emphasis on motherhood, particularly the idea that mothers possess an innate aptitude for child rearing and that they should devote themselves exclusively to their children until the children reach a certain age, restricts women from fully participating in society and securing equality with men. Another deeply held norm and expectation based on the ideology of the patriarchal family system is that parents have the right to depend on children in old age and that women, particularly daughters-in-law, should assume the role of caregiver for elderly parents and in-laws. This notion, reinforced by the current Japanese government's policy over the last twenty years of cutting back on funds allocated for elderly (as well as child) care and shifting this burden to the family, has, as Takako Sodei points out in her essay, posed tremendous strains on women concerning their positions as they seek to assume new roles outside the home.

A slightly different perspective on marriage and the family in contemporary Japan is provided in the discussion by Charles Douglas Lummis, a long-time American resident and scholar/educator in Japan, Satomi Nakajima, and the volume's two editors. They treat the impact of the women's movement and changes in women's aspirations and roles over the past twenty years on Japanese men and their view of women as well as their attitudes toward their roles as husbands, fathers, and wage earners. Factors impeding greater participation by men in domestic activities, including various aspects of the Japanese employment system and dominant attitudes about masculinity, are also explored. The dialogue is followed by a response by Masaki Yamaguchi, of the *Yomiuri shimbun* newspaper, who has been reporting on changes in the family over the last several years. His reflections, based on many hours of conversation with men in various parts of the country and in many differing walks of life, offer valuable insights into the ongoing process of self-questioning and redefinition of the male role which is under way among a yet small but growing number of Japanese men today.

Finally, the chapters by Kuniko Funabashi and Aiko Hada focus on various aspects of an issue that has thus far not received adequate attention either by social and governmental bodies or by Japanese feminists, namely gender-based violence. Hada's piece on domestic violence directed against women and the findings of a survey conducted in 1992 by the Domestic Violence Action and Research Group, of which she is a member, provides one of the few available sources of data on an issue that, though pervasive, has tended to be concealed and overlooked. Funabashi examines the pornographic culture in Japan today as expressed in mass-produced visual media—specifically, comic magazines, advertisements, and videos. She also analyzes how the false mystique about sex and notions of femininity and masculinity as presented in these media have shaped sexual awareness and behavior and promoted sexual violence against women.

Part 4

Part 4 explores several aspects of the disparity between the place and role of women and men in the Japanese labor market. Yoko Kawashima provides an overview of both historical and contemporary trends in women's labor force participation and shows how, despite the growing presence of women, including married women, in the paid labor force today, the assumption that women's place is in the home and that they should be supported by men leads employers to view women as supplementary workers in the workplace and secondary breadwinners in the household and to treat them accordingly. At the same time, the male-centered culture of the workplace and the gender division of household labor in the home lead women themselves to have ambivalent attitudes toward work. Kazuko Tanaka's analysis of the life cycle employment patterns and occupational distribution of women in relation to educational background reveals that, while access to both educational and employment opportunities has rapidly increased, education has not been fully translated into career advancement for Japanese women, due largely to the limited employment opportunities for married women, especially those seeking to reenter the labor market after having left it because of household and child care responsibilities.

Yayori Matsui is a renowned journalist who has investigated and written about issues confronting Asian women. She is also cofounder of the Asian

Women's Association, which has taken up action on several issues, including campaigns against sex tours in Asia. Her essay deals with a phenomenon that has accompanied the postwar rise in economic prosperity and one that various women's groups have endeavored to bring to national and international attention—that is, the expanding sex industry that has exploited both Japanese women and those who come to work in Japan from various other Asian countries. Matsui describes the various factors, both on the supply side and the demand side, which support and maintain this industry and emphasizes how the demand for "hostesses" who cater to Japanese businessmen in bars, nightclubs, and other establishments is inextricably tied to Japan's employment and management system as well as to deeply rooted sexist and patriarchal attitudes that date back several centuries. At the same time, Matsui locates this issue within the larger context of a global economic system marked by growing inequality among nations and resultant victimization of women.

Part 5

While all of the essays presented in the volume portray women not simply as victims of externally imposed restraints and the influence of social institutional values but also active agents, demonstrating resistance and seeking change, the essays in the final section deal specifically with efforts by women, both in the past and today, to struggle against injustices imposed on women by the prevailing political, economic, and social system and to demonstrate and assert their energies and strength in a variety of nontraditional ways. Mioko Fujieda profiles some of the key figures in Japan's first phase of feminism, which flourished in the late nineteenth and early twentieth centuries, many of whom were inspired and encouraged by the struggles and achievements of early feminists in the West. Kazuko Tanaka looks at the second phase of feminism in Japan, tracing its growth and changes in terms of direction, goals, strategies, and main actors, from the women's liberation movement of the early 1970s to the current decade. The UN Convention on Elimination of All Forms of Discrimination against Women rallied strong pressures on the part of women to address the many forms of sexual discrimination and legal inequities which had remained despite the various reforms that had been legislated following the end of World War II. Kiyoko Kinjo examines recent efforts by women, both individually and through organized group efforts, to secure legal rights in the areas of employment, marriage, and abortion.

Women have also begun to assert their power and influence in the political sphere. For the first time since the immediate postwar period, when women first gained the right to vote and run for political office, we have seen a major increase from the mid-1980s in the number of female candidates both running for and getting elected to political office. Yoko Sato, like Matsui a veteran journalist and author, chronicles the recent political debut of housewives and the process by which they have begun to channel their concerns with issues that have tended to receive little attention from male politicians, such as those pertaining to women, children, the elderly, and the environment, into political involvement, including electoral politics. Sato's essay is supplemented by profiles of two female politicians who were elected to local city assemblies in 1987, Aokage Takako, a housewife from a recently established, locally based political party affiliated with a major consumer's cooperative association, and Mitsui Mariko, from the Socialist Party. The profiles, the first written by Naoko Sasakura and the second by Emiko Kaya, reveal two women struggling to pursue their unique agendas in an institution that represents *the* most staunchly male bastion of power and—admittedly slowly—beginning to show success in making their influences felt.

NOTES

1. This is the point of view set forth by Sumiko Iwao in *The Japanese Woman: Traditional Image and Changing Reality* (New York: The Free Press, 1993).

2. To cite a very recent example, in April 1994 Ozawa Ichiro, a leading power broker and former representative secretary of the (now defunct) coalition party, the Shinseito, made the remark, "Whose business is it what woman a man sleeps with?" in connection with reports that the socialists were considering withdrawing from the coalition party. When criticized for displaying a contemptuous attitude toward women, rather than apologizing, Ozawa vigorously attacked the press, in particular the *Asahi shimbun* newspaper, for printing the remark in the first place since it had been made, so he claimed, off the record.

3. Several individuals have brought suits challenging employers' right to force workers to accept transfers. Others, such as two couples who recently filed a lawsuit against their employer, All-Nippon Airways, have charged that companies have forced employees to accept single transfers as a means of sexual harassment, that is, in order to get women who work for the same company as their husbands to take "early retirement" ("Tanshin funin shigonen nagasugiru," *Asahi shimbun*, 17 May 1994, 16).

4. Although Japan's divorce rate is still relatively low in comparison to that in the United States and Western European countries (1.45 per 1,000 people in the population in 1992, compared to 4.96 in the United States, 3.20 in England, and 2.37 in Sweden in 1985), the number has nearly doubled in the period between 1970 and 1993, from 96,000 to 189,000. The actual number is much greater if we were to include what is commonly called "domestic divorce" and "latent-disintegration" families, or those in which husband and wife continue to remain legally married in spite of the fact that a conjugal relationship no longer exists and in some cases the couple lives apart (see "Marriage and Family: Past and Present," by Kyoko Yoshizumi in this volume).

REFERENCES

"Educated Women in 20s Pick Jobs over Families." 1992. *Japan Times*, 25 July, 2.

Ehara, Yumiko, ed. 1990. *Feminizumu ronso—nanajunendai kara kyujunendai e* (Controversies within feminism—from the 1970s to the 1990s). Tokyo: Keiso shobo.

Iwao, Sumiko. 1993. *The Japanese Woman—Traditional Image and Changing Reality.* New York: The Free Press.

——— and Hiroko Hara. 1979. *Joseigaku kotohajime* (Introduction to women's studies). Tokyo: Kodansha.

Mombusho (Ministry of Education). 1994. *Mombu tokei yoran* (Digest of educational statistics). Tokyo: Mombusho.

Nihon Fujin Dantai Rengokai, ed. 1993. *Fujin hakusho* (White paper on women). Tokyo: Popuru shuppan.

Rodosho fujinkyoku (Ministry of Labor, Women's Bureau). 1993. *Hataraku josei no jitsujo* (Status of working women). Tokyo: Rodosho.

Sorifu (Prime Minister's Office). 1989. *Josei no shugyo ni kansuru ishiki chosa* (Survey of women's attitudes regarding work). Tokyo: Sorifu.

"Tanshin funin shigonen nagasugiru" (Four to five years of single transfer is too long). 1994. *Asahi shimbun* (Asahi newspaper). 17 May, 16.

❖ 1 ❖
Women's Place: Cultural and Historical Perspectives

A woman casting her vote in the first general election for the House of Representatives held following the end of World War II in which women voted for the first time in Japanese history. Of the roughly twenty million women qualified to vote, 67% cast their ballots on election day, April 10, 1946, and of the 79 women candidates running for seats, 39 were elected. Mainichi Shimbun Newspaper, April 11, 1946. *Courtesy of Mainichi Shimbum Newspaper Information Service Center, Tokyo.*

The Struggle for Legal Rights and Reforms: A Historical View

❖ ❖ ❖

Sachiko Kaneko

apanese women had few individual or political rights before World War II. Under the prevailing *ie*, or family, system, which was the foundation of prewar Japanese society, the proper place for women was considered to be within the home, under the authority of the male family head. Any type of involvement by women in political activities was thought to be contradictory to natural physiological and psychological laws and to the traditions and customs of Japanese society.[1] Yet, in the face of such prevailing attitudes, many women struggled for their rights.

Women's Place

The Political Situation

In the mid-nineteenth century, in the face of pressures from Western countries as well as changes taking place within the country itself, Japan was forced to abandon its policy of seclusion, which dated back nearly three hundred years. With the Meiji Restoration of 1868 Japan began a process of transformation from a feudal to a modern, unified national state. The new government, in order to guarantee the nation's independence and to achieve self-sufficiency, worked to build its power and national wealth through economic and military development, based on knowledge, ideas, and skills from the West, particularly the United States and Europe.

The government, however, shifted away from its Western-oriented policies in 1874, when the Popular Rights Movement was born and people began to call for the establishment of a national assembly. Several women took part in this political cause.[2] On the island of Shikoku in 1878 Kusunose Kita, a forty-five-year-old woman, argued that she should have the right to vote because she had been paying taxes as the household head since her husband's death in 1872. She was called the "grandma of people's rights." Kishida Toshiko lectured and wrote about equal rights for women beginning in 1882. Kageyama (later Fukuda) Hideko was influenced by one of Kishida's speeches, joined the Popular Rights Movement, and later became a socialist. At that time women could still attend political meetings and organize political groups.

The government suppressed the Popular Rights Movement, while promising to establish an assembly by 1881. It sought to create a national polity as soon as possible in order to build a modern country that could compete with other nations. In 1889 the Meiji Constitution was proclaimed, establishing a constitutional monarchy with the emperor as sovereign head of state.

During the next year three important events occurred. The first took place when the National Diet, Japan's national assembly, convened with members of the Lower House who had been elected on the basis of a limited franchise. Only men who paid a certain amount in taxes had the right to vote. Second was the adoption of the Imperial Rescript on Education, based on Confucian ideas, which emphasized loyalty to the emperor and filial piety to parents. The goal of education was to create subjects willing to serve the nation and the emperor, and pupils were indoctrinated with this family-state ideology. Japan was to be regarded as a family-state and the emperor the head of the Japanese family. Finally, the government issued the Meeting and Political Organization Law in 1890, which restricted all political activities.

Women's political participation became still more difficult under the Police Security Regulations of 1900, which succeeded the Law of 1890. Article 5 prohibited women and minors from joining political organizations, holding or attending meetings in which political speeches or lectures were given, and initiating such meetings.[3] Women were denied all political rights at both local and national levels.

In 1905, a group of women from a small socialist group called the Commoners' Association (Heiminsha) petitioned for a revision of Article 5. They gathered hundreds of signatures and went to the Diet every year until 1909, though without any success.[4]

The *ie*, or Family, System

In 1898 the Civil Code established a family network of relationships known as the *ie* system. According to this code, the patriarchal head of the family (usually the eldest son) held an unquestioned authority over the rest of the family. Together with the privilege of primogeniture, he had an obligation to support the family financially. He could designate the areas where the rest of the family could reside; if they protested, he did not have to support them.

4

Women under twenty-five and men under thirty needed the consent of the head of the family before marrying.

A woman had very few legal rights. When she married she entered her husband's family (and the family register), and control of her property was transferred to her husband. Custody of children was held by the father exclusively. A husband's illegitimate sons (if any) had prior rights to the family estate over legitimate daughters. For this reason women were expected to produce male heirs.

In the event of divorce there was also severe discrimination. A wife's adultery constituted grounds for divorce, and she could be punished under the new Criminal Code of 1880. In the case of the husband, only if he committed adultery with a married woman and was sued by her husband and punished would the wife be granted divorce. Adultery was also defined differently for men and women. Although concubinage was officially abolished in 1880, licensed prostitution still existed, and a polygamous attitude was prevalent across all strata of Japanese society.

Following Japan's victory in the Sino-Japanese War (1894–95) the government promoted girls' education designed to lend support to the family system and the place of women within that system. The Girls' High School Law, issued in 1899, aimed to educate girls to become "good wives and wise mothers." The number of women's secondary schools increased as time passed. However, women were expected to support their husbands, raise children, and not work outside the home.[5]

The Struggle for Political Rights

The New Women's Association (Shin fujin kyokai)

The death of the Meiji emperor marked the beginning of the Taisho period (1912–26). After World War I the universal manhood suffrage movement emerged, and *demokurashii* (democracy) became a key word to characterize the Taisho period. Hiratsuka Raicho formed the New Women's Association—the first organization of female citizens to be established on a nationwide scale—with Ichikawa Fusae in 1920.[6] It had 331 members that first year. During the next year the Red Wave Society (Sekirankai), the first socialist women's organization, was founded in Tokyo by Yamakawa Kikue.

Hiratsuka called for the reconstruction of society. Motherhood, she insisted, should be esteemed, and she criticized the patriarchal *ie* system and demanded rights for women and children. The association called for women's right to political participation through a revision of the Security Police Law, Article 5. It also petitioned the Diet to enact a law to restrict marriage for men with venereal diseases.[7]

The New Women's Association held meetings and lectures across Japan. The group collected more than two thousand signatures for the revision of Article 5. Hiratsuka and Ichikawa visited legislators, asking for cooperation and support, from early morning to late evening. At the same time, in order to move around and work more efficiently, they took to wearing Western clothes when they went out, instead of the traditional kimono, with its wide sleeves and tight sashes. Hiratsuka and Ichikawa worked diligently, but personal conflicts and differences ended their work together. Hiratsuka withdrew from the movement, and Ichikawa went to the United States in order to observe the women's movement and labor movement there.

Oku Mumeo became the new leader of the movement. In 1922 she visited the infamous Baron Fujimura, who had been a strong opponent of Oku's group. He was impressed by the young mother, who had a baby on her back during the visit. His image of the suffragettes changed, and he thereafter supported the movement. Later in 1922 the petition was approved, and Article 5 was revised. Women were now able to organize and participate in political meetings.

Female schoolteachers and housewives supported this political reform. The most cooperative group was the Japan Woman's Christian Temperance Union (WCTU) (Kirisutokyo fujin kyofukai), originally organized in 1874 in the United States to work for the prohibition of alcohol. Mary Leavitt, of the U.S. organization, gave a series of lectures in Japan, one of which impressed Yajima Kajiko. In 1886 Yajima, president of a girls' missionary school, began organizing for the WCTU in Japan. She was particularly interested in the issue because she had divorced a drunken husband. The members decided to name the group Kyofukai (Reform Society) and to work for specific reforms because they thought Japanese society was in need of purification. They regarded the polygamous attitude within Japanese society as a social evil and thought concubinage and prostitution should be abolished. They insisted on monogamy and petitioned for a revision of the Civil Code and the Criminal Code. They supported the abolition of licensed prostitution, and they built a shelter for prostitutes who had run away from brothels.[8]

In 1916 the WCTU began a two-year campaign against building prostitution quarters in Osaka but failed. Kubushiro Ochimi, a successor of Yajima, realized the necessity of securing women's rights and declared that suffrage was indispensable for the success of their cause.

The Women's Suffrage League (Fusen kakutoku domei)

After the Great Kanto Earthquake of 1923, women's groups worked together to help victims, and the Federation of Women's Association in Tokyo (Tokyo rengo fujinkai) was formed. Kubushiro saw this as an opportune time to organize a national women's suffrage organization. Universal male suffrage was drawing near (it was approved in 1925). Ichikawa Fusae worked at the Tokyo International Labor Organization after spending several years in the United States. While working in the United States, she had visited Hull House, founded by Jane Addams, and spoken with various union leaders. She had also met Alice Paul, a leader of the National Women's Party, who encouraged her to work for women's suffrage in Japan.[9]

In 1924 Kubushiro and Ichikawa established the League for the Realization of Woman Suffrage (Fujin sanseiken kakutoku kisei domeikai). During the next year the organization changed its name to the Women's Suffrage League (Fusen kakutoku domei). After Kubushiro's withdrawal Ichikawa became the general secretary and was regarded as the central figure in this struggle.

The league issued the following manifesto:

> Women, who form one-half of the population of the country, have been left entirely outside the field of political activity, classified along with males of less than 25 years of age and those who are recipients of relief or aid from State or private organizations. We women feel ourselves no longer compelled to explain the reasons why it is at once natural and necessary for us, who are both human beings and citizens, to participate in the administration of our country. . . . We women must concentrate our energies solely on one thing, namely, the acquisition of the right to take part in politics, and cooperate with one other regardless of any political, religious and other differences we may have.[10]

Membership in the league increased each year. There were about 200 members at the beginning, 483 in 1927, and 1,762 in 1932. In the western part of Japan the All-Kansai Federation of Women's Association (Zen kansai fujin rengokai) supported the league. Together they collected fifty-six thousand signatures and sent them to the House of Representatives in 1927. By 1931 the government was on the verge of granting franchise to women at the local (from village to city) level. It appeared that the acquisition of women's suffrage was imminent.

Family Life—Women's Problems

Taisho Period (1912–26)

While some women became active outside the home, for example, joining the suffrage movement, others were facing family problems inside the home. This is evident in the number of women's magazines and women's columns in newspapers which appeared. Women's issues became popular early in the Taisho period. *Seito* (Bluestocking) (1911–16) was published by Hiratsuka Raicho, and in 1914 *Yomiuri shimbun*, a national newspaper, established a column for women. Two important women's magazines, *Fujin koron* (Women's review) in 1916 and *Shufu no tomo* (Friends of housewives), began publishing in 1917. These publications were widely read by women; the percentage of girls entering school had reached 96 percent by 1907.[11]

Fujin koron was directed at intellectuals and dealt with theoretical issues of women's liberation such as the famous, ongoing "dispute over the protection of motherhood."[12] Yosano Akiko, a well-known poet, advocated the economic independence of married women. Hiratsuka was more concerned, however, with the protection of motherhood. She had been influenced by the ideas of Ellen Key, the Swedish thinker and author of *Love and Marriage* (1903). Hiratsuka emphasized the incompatibility of work outside the home

7

and raising children inside the home. Then Yamakawa Kikue argued from a socialist point of view that the important thing was to change economic relations in the existing society. This dispute reflected the fact that increasing numbers of women—including married women—were working outside the home in silk reeling and cotton spinning mills, contributing to the economic development of their country.

On the other hand, *Shufu no tomo* dealt with various problems women faced managing the family in their daily lives.[13] Thrift and savings were emphasized. During the Taisho period the number of people in the middle class increased as industrialization and urbanization progressed. Nuclear families emerged, consisting only of the husband, wife, and children, and young housewives of this class were particularly attracted to *Shufu no tomo*. It was supported by a wide range of women and obtained the largest circulation among all magazines in 1920, reaching about 600,000 in 1931 and 1,800,000 in 1941.

Shufu no tomo listened to women's voices; letters from readers were welcomed and printed. Eventually, an advice column, or *minoue sodan*, was instituted to serve the readers. The letters pointed to some of the common problems women faced. In a typical letter a housewife wrote about how she suffered from her husband's extramarital affairs and drinking, which led to the family's poverty. In addition, her husband had infected her with a venereal disease. Another letter dealt with divorce, from a bride who was expected to work hard but could not satisfy her parents-in-law and was driven out of the family. Her in-laws had forced her to divorce her husband and leave their children behind. There were other letters from single women who suffered from the prospect of forced marriages arranged by parents or relatives.[14]

The Early Showa Period (1926–45)

The early Showa period saw an increase in social insecurity brought about by the economic depression and the Manchurian Incident of 1931 (which marked a significant step in Japan's expansion into China). Advice columns were also popular at this time. *Yomiuri shimbun* published an advice column from 1931 to 1937 with Kawasaki Natsu as one of the columnists. She was an educator and later became director of the action committee for the first Mother's Congress (Hahaoya taikai) in 1955.[15] Of the 1,248 letters that appeared between 1931 and 1937, Kawasaki answered 954 (76.4 percent), most of them submitted by young women, roughly half of whom were married and the other half single.[16]

Women's problems varied; some were economic, some emotional, and others physical. The largest number of letters from married women were about their husbands' extramarital affairs. The next largest number were about loveless marriages. Single women sought advice about love and marriage: they wanted to marry men whom they loved, but their parents tended to force "arranged" marriages. Many also suffered from rape or sexual harassment. The following is a typical letter from a married woman:

> Age: 22. I was forced to marry at the age of 19. My husband is selfish and drinks a lot. I was mistreated by my mother-in-law so that I lost weight and my breast milk stopped. I came back to my own parents' home, but my parents-in-law refused to allow my child to come to me. (1934.5.3.)

Under the *ie* system filial piety and obedience were demanded of women. A bride had to serve her parents-in-law first, then her husband. The parent-child relation was much more important than the relationship between wife and husband. Many women could not even consider divorce, since they were economically dependent on their husbands. After a divorce the custody of children was granted to the father according to the Civil Code.

Kawasaki's advice, generally, was as follows: she didn't ignore or deny filial piety but limited its meaning. Instead of passive self-sacrifice, women should find their own way, which would eventually comfort their parents. She told young women not to abandon the hope of love in marriage and to try to persuade parents of its benefits. She advised that married women reside separately from in-laws, because the basis of the family should be the husband and wife. She suggested couples trying to live together for the children instead of considering divorce. Economic independence was particularly difficult for divorcees. Finally, Kawasaki believed women's problems could be solved not by women's awareness alone but also by changes in the social system. She supported a revision of the Civil Code and the protection of motherhood as well as adequate vocational training and sex education.

These letters indicate not only the conflicts that existed under the *ie* system but also that the system itself did not work. Ironically, the *minoue sodan* column in *Yomiuri* was terminated in 1937 when the fighting in China turned into a war.

The Difficulties of War

Japan had taken the first step toward war with the Manchurian Incident of 1931. Militarism swept the country. The government suppressed the growing labor movement and arrested socialists. Those with more liberal ideas found it difficult to speak and write freely in public.

In 1932 the Women's National Defense Association (Kokubo fujinkai) was established and was supported by the army. There was also a group called the Women's Patriotic Society (Aikoku fujinkai), which had been formed in 1901 and played an active role during the Russo-Japanese War (1904–5). These two groups saw soldiers off at train stations and prepared comfort bags for the war effort. Their activities were similar in nature, and they soon became competitive in seeking to increase their memberships. By the end of 1935 the membership of the Defense Association stood at 2.5 million and outnumbered that of the Patriotic Society (2.2 million).[17]

Japan's militaristic policies affected the activities of Ichikawa's group too. Attainment of suffrage became more difficult, and membership rapidly decreased from 1,762 in 1932 to 690 in 1939. The group had to change its course in order to survive. Instead of suffrage, members emphasized local consumer problems and a reform election campaign for the Tokyo Municipal Assembly. They demanded passage of the Protection of Mother-and-Child Bill in 1934. This bill was approved in 1936 because the government saw an increase in population as a way to help the war effort. It commended mothers for having a large number of children.

Ichikawa felt depressed when the war with China began, and she wrote: "Under these circumstances, the attainment of suffrage becomes much harder. Yet, our purpose of suffrage is to cooperate with the government and men in order to make a contribution to our nation and society."[18] When she came home to Aichi Prefecture to visit her mother, Ichikawa attended a local meeting of the Women's National Defense Association. Many women, young and old, seemed happy to leave their homes to hear lectures by local veterans. She felt that this was a kind of "emancipation." Women in rural villages had never had time of their own in the past, but now they could attend a meeting free from their chores for half a day.

It is ironic that, while Japanese women had no political rights, their social participation was encouraged at the grassroots level. The Women's Suffrage League had disbanded in 1940. But in 1942, after Japan's attack on Pearl Harbor, the Great Japan Women's Organization (Dai-Nippon fujinkai) was established, and all women's groups were consolidated under the control of government authorities. Awkwardly, the government emphasized that a woman's place was in the home, but at the same time accepted the fact that, because of the war, women began to work outside the home in factories. Thus, the *ie* system, previously insisted upon by the government, collapsed under war conditions.

Postwar Reforms

Japan was defeated and accepted the Potsdam Declaration on 15 August 1945. Ichikawa Fusae established the Women's Committee on Postwar Countermeasures (Sengo taisaku fujin iinkai) on 25 August and once again demanded women's suffrage. It was possible to organize a sizable group in a short time because of women's history of struggle in the prewar period and the existence of the former network.

On 9 October 1945 a new Cabinet came into power, with Shidehara Kijuro as prime minister. On 10 October the group held a conference and decided to enfranchise women.[19] On 11 October the Supreme Commander for the Allied Powers, General Douglas MacArthur, called on the Japanese government to institute five basic reforms in the social order, including the emancipation of women through their enfranchisement and the liberalization of education. His aim was to democratize Japan as to well as to pacify and stabilize the country. By the end of 1945 women's suffrage was approved under a revision of the election law, and in the following year thirty-nine women were elected in the first national general election.

The new Japanese Constitution was proclaimed in 1946. It clearly outlined Japan's renouncement of war and respect for fundamental human rights. Article 14 stated that all people are equal under the law and that there would be no discrimination in political, economic, or social relations because of race, creed, sex, social status, or family origin. Article 24 prescribed that marriage would be based only on the consent of both individuals.

With the new Constitution it was necessary to revise certain laws. The government set up the Judiciary and Legislative Council, and revision of the Civil Code was discussed. A heated controversy ensued about whether to abolish the *ie* system. Then, Kawasaki, a member of the council, gave an impressive speech in support of the new system. She explained women's prewar experiences based on her experience with *minoue sodan:* "I have received as many as 70,000 letters, 90 percent of which were from women. These letters pointed out women's miserable lives. Some suffered because of economic problems, others because of family troubles. All these problems derived from the 'ie' system."[20] Kawasaki said that women would raise joyful voices if the *ie* system were to be revised, and she urged council members to listen to those voices. The revised Civil Code was issued in 1947, and Japanese women became free from the patriarchal *ie* system.

Conclusion

It was not until after World War II that Japanese women finally attained the right of suffrage and legal equality in marriage. Yet, as I have described here, many women actively struggled to seize those rights for themselves from the very beginning of the Meiji period, when Japan embarked on its program of modernization. The welfare and interests of women were constantly subordinated to the interests of the nation-state and the *ie* system. The new Constitution, based on democratic ideals of equality and respect for individual human rights, which was proclaimed following Japan's defeat in World War II, finally granted political rights to women. At the same time, the abolition of the *ie* system allowed women to enjoy equality within marriage and in the home. Women, who had suffered bitter experiences under the traditional system and had fought so long for these reforms, welcomed these changes.

Once women had at last achieved legal equality, the remaining challenge was to bring about actual, substantive equality. It is a challenge that has proven to be much more difficult, requiring, as it does, fundamental changes in individual and social attitudes regarding gender roles.

NOTES

1. See Baron Fujimura Yoshiro's speech in 1921 before the House of Peers, in Ichikawa Fusae, *Ichikawa Fusae jiden, senzen hen* (Autobiography of Ichikawa Fusae, the prewar period) (Tokyo: Shinjuku shobo, 1975), 94. In Japanese mythology, however, the Sun Goddess, Amaterasu, ruled the Heaven and commissioned her grandson to govern the Earth—the islands of Japan. According to Chinese historical sources, Queen Himiko ruled a part of Japan around A.D. 250. In the seventh and eighth centuries several empresses engaged in social and political activities. For a brief history of Japanese women in the premodern period, see Dorothy Robin-Mowry, *The Hidden Sun: Women of Modern Japan* (Boulder, Colo.: Westview Press, 1983), 5–29.

2. For some individuals in the women's movement during the Meiji period, see Mioko Fujieda's article, "Japan's First Phase of Feminists," in this volume; and Sharon L. Sievers, *Flowers in Salt: The Beginnings of Feminist Consciousness in Modern Japan* (Stanford, Calif.: Stanford University Press, 1983).

3. Translation of Article 5 from Robin-Mowry (*Hidden Sun*, 64), with English slightly changed by the author.

4. Kodama Katsuko, *Fujin sanseiken undo shoshi* (A short history of women's suffrage movement) (Tokyo: Domesu shuppan, 1981), 29–34.

5. For a discussion of women's education in the Meiji period, see Kimi Hara's article, "Challenges to Education for Girls and Women in Modern Japan," in this volume.

6. Hiratsuka became involved in the women's movement after she published *Seito (Bluestocking)*, a literary magazine for women, and advocated the appearance of female "geniuses" in 1911.

7. Hiratsuka Raicho, *Genshi josei wa taiyo de atta: Hiratsuka Raicho jiden* (In the beginning woman was the sun: autobiography of Hiratsuka Raicho), (Tokyo: Otsuki shoten, 1973), 2:38–213.

8. See Nihon kirisutokyo fujin kyofukai, ed., *Nihon kirisutokyo fujin kyofukai hyakunenshi* (A centennial history of the Japan Woman's Christian Temperance Union) (Tokyo: Domesu shuppan, 1989); and Kaneko Sachiko, "Kindai nihon ni okeru josei kaiho no shiso to kodo—Yajima Kajiko to Nihon Kirisutokyo Fujin Kyofukai" (Japanese women's liberation: Yajima Kajiko and the Japan Woman's Christian Temperance Union), *Ajia bunka kenkyu*, extra issue no. 2 (November 1990): 203–17.

9. Ichikawa, *Ichikawa Fusae jiden*, 118.

10. Katayama Sen, "The Political Position of Women," *Japanese Women* 2, no. 6 (November 1939): 2 (with English slightly changed by the author).

11. Fukaya Masashi, *Ryosai kenbo shugi no kyoiku* (Education for "good wives and wise mothers") (Tokyo: Reimei shobo, 1966), 212.

12. See Kochi Nobuko, ed., *Shiryo: bosei hogo ronso* (Materials: the dispute over the protection of motherhood) (Tokyo: Domesu shuppan, 1984).

13. Shufu no tomo sha, ed., *Shufu no tomo sha no gojunen* (Fifty years of Shufu no tomo sha) (Tokyo: Shufu no tomo sha, 1967), 41–56.

14. Kaneko Sachiko, "Taishoki *Shufu no tomo* to Ishikawa Takeyoshi no shiso" (The thoughts of Ishikawa Takeyoshi and Friends of Housewives in the Taisho period), *Rekishi hyoron*, no. 411 (July 1984): 48–50.

15. See Hayashi Hikaru, *Hahaoya ga kawareba shakai ga kawaru: kawasaki natsu den* (If mothers change, society will change: a biography of Kawasaki Natsu) (Tokyo: Sodo bunka, 1974).

16. The following examples of *"minoue sodan"* are from Kaneko Sachiko, "'Minoue

sodan' ni miru kachi ishiki henkaku no kokoromi—1931–37 nen, Kawasaki Natsu no kaito o chushin ni" (Transformation of the Value Concept of Japanese women—*"minoue sodan,"* 1931–37), *Ajia bunka kenkyu,* no. 10 (November 1978): 111–13.

17. Fujii Tadatoshi, *Kokubo Fujinkai: hinomaru to kappogi* (The Women's National Defense Association: the rising sun and cooking aprons) (Tokyo: Iwanami shoten, 1985), 95.

18. Ichikawa, *Ichikawa Fusae jiden,* 434.

19. Horikiri Zenjiro, "Fujin sanseiken wa Makkasa kara no okurimono dewa nai" (Women's suffrage was not given by MacArthur), in Fujin sansei jusshunen kinen gyoji jikko iinkai zanmu seiri iinkai, ed., *Fujin sansei jusshunen kinen gyoji jikko iinkai kiroku* (The record of the acting committee for the commemorative event of the tenth anniversary of women's suffrage) (September 1959), in *Seiji* (Politics), vol. 2 of *Nihon fujin mondai shiryo shusei* (Compiled materials on Japanese women's issues), ed. Ichikawa Fusae (Tokyo: Domesu shuppan, 1977), 677–78.

20. Wagatsuma Sakae, ed., *Sengo ni okeru minpo kaisei no keika* (The process of revising the Civil Code after the war) (Tokyo: Nihon hyoronsha, 1956), 83.

REFERENCES

Fujii, Tadatoshi. 1985. *Kokubo Fujinkai: hinomaru to kappogi* (The Women's National Defense Association: the rising sun and cooking aprons). Tokyo: Iwanami shoten.

Fujin sansei jusshunen kinen gyoji jikko iinkai zanmu seiri iinkai, ed. 1959. *Fujin sansei jusshunen kinen gyoji jikko iinkai kiroku* (the record of the acting committee for the commemorative event of the tenth anniversary of women's suffrage). In *Seiji* (Politics), vol. 2 of *Nihon fujin mondai shiryo shusei* (Compiled materials on Japanese women's issues), ed. Ichikawa Fusae. Tokyo: Domesu shuppan, 1977.

Fukaya, Masashi. 1966. *Ryosai kenbo shugi no kyoiku* (Education for "good wives and wise mothers"). Tokyo: Reimei shobo.

Hayashi, Hikaru. 1974. *Hahaoya ga kawareba shakai ga kawaru: Kawasaki Natsu den* (If mothers change, society will change: a biography of Kawasaki Natsu) Tokyo: Sodo bunka.

Hiratsuka, Raicho. 1973. *Genshi josei wa taiyo de atta: Hiratsuka Raicho jiden* (In the beginning woman was the sun: autobiography of Hiratsuka Raicho), vol. 2. Tokyo: Otsuki shoten.

Ichikawa, Fusae. 1975. *Ichikawa Fusae jiden, senzen hen* (Autobiography of Ichikawa Fusae, the prewar period). Tokyo: Shinjuku shobo.

Kaneko, Sachiko. 1978. "'Minoue sodan' ni miru kachi ishiki henkaku no kokoromi—1931–37 nen, Kawasaki Natsu no kaito o chushin ni" (Transformation of the value concept of Japanese women—*"minoue sodan,"* 1931–37). *Ajia bunka kenkyu,* no. 10.

———. 1984. "Taishoki *Shufu no tomo* to Ishikawa Takeyoshi no shiso" (The ideas of Ishikawa Takeyoshi and Friends of Housewives in the Taisho period). *Rekishi hyoron,* no. 411.

———. 1990. "Kindai Nihon ni okeru josei kaiho no shiso to kodo—Yajima Kajiko to Nihon kirisutokyo fujin kyofukai" (Japanese women's liberation: Yajima Kajiko and the Japan Woman's Christian Temperance Union). *Ajia bunka kenkyu,* extra issue no. 2.

Katayama, Sen. 1939. "The Political Position of Women." *Japanese Women* 2, no. 6.

Kodama, Katsuko. 1981. *Fujin sanseiken undo shoshi* (A short history of the women's suffrage movement). Tokyo: Domesu shuppan.

Kochi, Nobuko, ed. 1984. *Shiryo: Bosei hogo ronso* (Materials: the dispute over the protection of motherhood). Tokyo: Domesu shuppan.

Nihon kirisutokyo fujin kyofuka, ed. 1989. *Nihon kirisutokyo fujin kyofukai hyankunenshi* (A centennial history of the Japan Woman's Christian Temperance Union). Tokyo: Domesu shuppan.

Robin-Mowry, Dorothy. 1983. *The Hidden Sun: Women of Modern Japan*. Boulder, Colo.: Westview Press.

Shufu no tomo sha, ed. 1967. *Shufu no tomo sha no gojunen* (Fifty years of Shufu no tomo sha). Tokyo: Shufu no tomo sha.

Sievers, Sharon L. 1983. *Flowers in Salt: The Beginnings of Feminist Consciousness in Modern Japan*. Stanford, Calif.: Stanford University Press.

Wagatsuma, Sakae, ed. 1956. *Sengo ni okeru minpo kaisei no keika* (The process of revising the civil code after the war). Tokyo: Nihon hyoronsha.

Women's Image and Place in Japanese Buddhism

❖ ❖ ❖

Haruko Okano

*Translated by Kumiko Fujimura-Fanselow
and Yoko Tsuruta*

In Japan today, there are still certain designated places that by tradition are barred to women. For example, women are not permitted to climb certain so-called holy mountains *(reizan)* such as Omine Mountain in Nara. Similarly, there is a taboo against women setting foot at the site of a tunnel under construction based on the superstition that, if she does so, the mountain goddess will become angry or jealous and cause an accident.[1] And in 1989, attention was focused on the sumo wrestling association when it refused to allow a female government minister to present an award at the closing ceremony because that would have entailed her stepping up to the sumo ring, which also has traditionally been restricted exclusively to men. On the other hand, some Japanese claim, half-jokingly, that the fact that women's colleges are allowed to exist while previously all-male universities were made coeducational following post–World War II educational reforms is an example of discrimination against males. While at a glance all of these may be seen as manifestations of sexual discrimination, my own view is that, eventually, compromises and solutions will be worked out as we begin to see more women who insist they want to be sumo wrestlers or men who express a desire to study at a women's university. What is of critical importance is to build and establish a foundation and a social climate that will give emergence to and support individuals who will not feel inhibited or restricted from expressing such liberated aspirations.

Sexual discrimination cannot be measured simply by the extent to which women are excluded from various spheres of life; more often, dis-

15

crimination is hidden and, therefore, difficult to assess. The assigning of predetermined gender roles as a matter of course in, for example, social organizations such as schools and workplaces, functions to limit women's freedom as well as their abilities. In Japan, as in many other societies, religions—in this case Shinto, Buddhism, and Confucianism—have contributed significantly to the development and maintenance of separate gender roles and of gender inequality. These religions have encouraged people to accept a notion of ethics which proclaims that people are born with differing abilities and into different statuses within society, thereby serving to maintain the prevailing social order. In so doing, religions have served to promote unequal sex roles. This idea, within the context of a patriarchal social system, served to give rise to a distorted image of the relationship between the sexes and the view that women are subordinate to men. For example, every newly ordained head of a temple in the Jodo Shin sect, one of the Japanese Buddhist sects, is given a copy of the manual *Jushokudo* (The way of the religious leader), which states, "The husband is the lord and the wife is the servant" (Inoue 1989, 115). In recent years these traditional religions have come under severe criticism by feminists for having accepted and legitimatized unequal gender relationships within society.

Similarly, many newer religions, such as Rissho Koseikai and Jissenrinrikoseikai, which have gained adherents among those who have been unable to find satisfaction in the traditional religions, also maintain the traditional idea of unequal sex roles, their ideal women being wives who obey their husbands. Yet, ironically, these new religions have more women than men both among their leaders or teachers and their followers. In comparison to Western societies, it is often very difficult to discern the presence of gender discrimination in Japanese society. In fact, many of the issues related to sex discrimination in Japan cannot be analyzed through the lens of Western feminism.

Though Shinto, Buddhism, and Confucianism have all played a historically significant role in the formulation, justification, and enforcement of national ideology and state power,[2] this essay focuses on Buddhism as the most influential of the three in shaping the image and role of women and supporting sexism in Japanese society. Following my discussion of Buddhism and its effects on women's position in society, I will examine the history of the salvation of women in religions and clarify the influence these religions have had on the history of women's struggle for liberation in Japan.

Women in Early Buddhism and Mahayana Buddhism

The most important goal in the Buddhist religion is the achievement of satori, or enlightenment. One who reaches the state of enlightenment is called a buddha, and, according to the original teachings of Buddhism, becoming a Buddhist priest means giving up all of one's personal possessions and renouncing the worldly life. Thus, Buddhism in its original form was an ascetic religion. This characteristic seems to suggest that Buddhism has from the first manifested a fear of sexuality and, therefore, certain antifemale characteristics (Okano 1988, 410–26). As we know from historical records, Gautama Buddha himself was ambivalent in his views toward women. While the Pali canon, a collection of sutras from the fourth to third centuries B.C. written in the Pali language, includes various statements ascribed to Buddha which express the common sex discriminatory ideas of the Indian society of his time, he at the same time clearly states that women need to and can be saved. He admitted women into his own religious order as nuns. The various sects of Buddhism which were established after the death of Gautama Buddha follow his sacred teachings in different ways. All of these sects, which fall within the larger category of Theravada Buddhism, however, share the notion that Nirvana—the final, ultimate state of bliss—can be achieved by death and that it is possible only through the renunciation of the worldly life. Originally, then, it was possible for both men and women to become buddhas if they lived accordingly and underwent rigorous religious training. In the first century B.C. a new movement arose among the masses in rebellion against Theravada Buddhism. This movement, which came to be called Mahayana Buddhism, declared that salvation is open to everyone. Mahayana Buddhism spread and became dominant in China, Korea, and Japan.

According to the principles of the Buddhist religion, a buddha is an entity that is sexless. Yet, since it came to be deified in Mahayana Buddhism, thirty-two characteristics came to be attributed to this entity. One of these characteristics was a hidden penis, which is obviously contradictory to the established sexless nature of a buddha. As a result, the idea that a buddha, including the historical figure Gautama Buddha, must be male became entrenched within the religion. In light of this it is interesting to note that in China and Japan, Avalokiteśvara, the *bosatsu*, or Bodhisattva of compassion, which was originally male, has been represented in female figures (e.g., Hibo Kannon); this was presumably done to balance the masculine-oriented Buddhist pantheon. A Bodhisattva is a personage in an intermediary stage in the evolution of an ordinary person into a buddha. Characteristically, a Bodhisattva tries to answer the appeals of the struggling faithful without asking for anything in return. Such a manifestation of generous love, much akin to that associated with a mother, probably led people to cast these saints in the figure of female statues.

Yet, if buddha were defined as male, then how could women achieve salvation? Yet to deny the possibility of salvation for women was contradictory to the notion of universal salvation preached by Mahayana Buddhism. The possibility of salvation for women was further diminished by the concept of the "five hindrances" stated in the Lotus Sutra, which refer to the five existences that women can never achieve: the four Indian Gods (Brahma, Shakra

[Indra], Mara, and Cakravartin) and buddha. To get around this contradiction, the notion of a "metamorphosed male" was introduced, meaning that women could become a buddha after becoming a male.

Similarly discriminatory are the "three obediences" for women: "Women must obey their father as a daughter, once married obey their husband, and when widowed, obey their son. Women must not become independent" (Manu Hoten, chap. 5, 148). The idea of three obediences was brought into Japan in the Mahayana sutras, and, hand in hand with a Confucian teaching of a similar nature, crucially influenced women's education in Japan. The Mahayana sutras are not, however, entirely antifeminist. Some of them guarantee equality between the sexes in the process of becoming a buddha, an idea that goes back to the original teaching by Gautama Buddha. A religion based on an egalitarian concept of human beings would have raised the questions posed in the Chinese sutra: "How could a man achieve Satori if a woman could not?" and "Can there be any difference between the sexes in terms of one's desire to achieve Satori?" (Hai-lung-wang-ching, bk. 3 [A.D. 414], qtd. in Iwamoto 1980, 75). The idea, however, that women and men are essentially equal did not become part of the mainstream of Buddhist doctrine.

Acceptance of Buddhism and Rejection of Female Priests by a United Japan

In the middle of the sixth century Mahayana Buddhism was brought to Japan by the scholar Wani, an envoy of the king of the Korean kingdom of Paikche, together with other features of Chinese civilization, including Confucianism and the Chinese writing system. In 584 Buddhist nuns first made their appearance, and soon thereafter the temple Sakuraiji was built in Nara for these nuns. It was not until twenty years later that the monastery Kentsuji was built for monks. This twenty-year gap is interesting in terms of how it signified Japanese attitudes toward Buddhism at the time. When these first Japanese Buddhist nuns were selected, there was an expectation or hope that they would have the kind of shamanic and charismatic powers that had been found in Himiko and other queens of ancient Japan. The nuns were regarded as priestesses or conductors of religious ceremonies.

In 624 all Buddhist monks and nuns were placed under the central control of the Emperor and the government. There is no concrete evidence indicating discrimination between monks and nuns until the middle of the Nara era (646–794). Thus, for example, nuns and monks were allowed to recite sutras in the same place. The Japanese view of women in Buddhism had not been affected by the discriminatory statements found in the Mahayana sutras.

This changed during the eighth century, as more women became nuns and more temples were built for female Buddhists. In Kinai (within the capital district) thirteen nunneries were built, and provincial temples were built for monks as well as for nuns by order of the Shomu emperor and the Komyo empress consort. In this era each monastery had a partner nunnery; Todaiji and Hokkeniji, for example, were treated as a "pair temples," as were Saidaiji and Sairyuniji. There seems also to have been an economic link between the partners: monasteries were in charge of the finances of nunneries. The nunneries had such a dependent status that they were referred to as "the laundry room of monasteries" in the *Nihon sandai jitsuroku*, a record from the ninth century. It seems that nunneries were subordinate to monasteries, and nuns were expected to serve monks and secular men in their everyday life. Thus, the relationship between a monastery and a nunnery, in the eighth century, seems to have been parallel to that between men and women in the secular world.

As Buddhism came increasingly under state control and was used to promote and protect the nation, it became increasingly patriarchal. While priests became functionaries of the state, nuns were regarded as less and less welcome. After the year 730 nuns were gradually banned from chanting in the court and in other official Buddhist ceremonies. In the mid-ninth century, for a period of time women were restricted from entering religious life. These developments parallel the history of women's gradual expulsion from important functions within the Shinto religion in the previous era.

Concept of Female Impurity

In the Heian era the notions of five hindrances and three obediences repeatedly mentioned in the Mahayana sutras, mixed with the indigenous Japanese idea of ritual purity and blood as a source of impurity, led to the establishment of the view that women were sinful and could not obtain salvation. "Blood impurity" refers to the fact that menstruation and childbirth were seen as sources of uncleanliness and, therefore, a cause of ceremonial impurity.

It is debatable when this idea began and whether it originated in Shinto or in Buddhism. In any case there seem to have existed in early Japanese history, special "monthly huts" *(tsukigoya)* and "parturition huts," isolated sheds to which women withdrew during menstruation and childbirth. Some say that the reason for this was to avoid defilement by blood, while others, including Orikuchi Shinobu, feel that it was an expression, instead, of the awe of blood and its sacred power (1955, 466f.). Women's bleeding has been viewed ambivalently in many cultures; as a source of life and power, it has been both worshiped and feared. What is clear is that the idea of blood impurity is not found in *Kojiki* or in *Nihon shoki*, which chronicle the beginnings and earliest history of Japan. In the mid-Heian era (ninth to twelfth centuries) "female bleeding" came to be regarded as a source of defilement, and since that time women have been prohibited from taking part in Shinto ceremonies while menstruating.[3]

Following the establishment in the seventh century of a national sys-

19

tem of administration, women became excluded from posts in major religious institutions. In Shinto, however, women were not thought to be impure or sinful beings but, rather, impure only during menstruation and puerperium. Today it may appear as if Shinto is free from sex discrimination, since women are able to perform the same religious duties as men within Shinto institutions. Yet the idea of blood impurity is still very much present. Thus, for example, female staff members are required to take hormone pills and control their menstruation schedule in order to avoid polluting religious ceremonies.

Among Buddhists it was thought in ancient India that human birth was defiled because it originated from the parents' sexual pleasure (Nagata 1986, 677). Yet, fairly old Buddhist sutras such as *Choagon Kyo* (Dirghâyama) and *Ashukubukkoku Kyo* (Aksobhyasya tathâgatasya vyûha [A.D. 147]) deal with women's body and childbirth in a positive way, mentioning a possible painless childbirth in the ideal paradise. More ascetic sutras written for monks such as the Lotus Sutra and the Sukavativyuha Sutra (dating back roughly two thousand years), in contrast, inheriting the original Indian idea, state that being born through the vagina involves impurity. Therefore, an ideal birth was a supernatural one. Bodhisattvas, Buddhas, and other religious entities were supposed to have entered their mother's womb through the help of God and to have been born from her right armhole.

Concept of Woman as the "Sinful" and "Unsalvable"

An admixture of the two ideas blood impurity and "impure women" led to the establishment of the belief that women are sinful and cannot attain salvation. Honen (1133–1212), for example, the founder of the Jodo, or Pure Land, sect, regarded women as "being too sinful and facing too many obstacles to acceptance by any of the Buddhist paradises" (Kasahara 1984, 58). This negative view of women is found in writings of women themselves. The mother of General Udaisho Michitsuna (tenth century), writing in her diary, *Kagero nikki*, talks about her conflict with her husband, describes herself as "sinful," and relates how she repeatedly made up her mind to become a nun, confining herself for periods of time in different temples. Even Izumi Shikibu, who is known for her unusually liberated thinking, complains in her diary (ca. 1004) about not being admitted to Mount Hiei because of women's sinfulness. In one of her poems she expresses the wish that she were a flower on the hat of a monk so that she could go on the holy Mount Hiei. Murasaki Shikibu, in her novel *The Tale of Genji* (ca. 1011), analyzes the reasons for women's lack of virtue and unsalvability. She makes the criticism that it is because women only wish to depend on others, and therefore lack the ability to take leadership, that they are said to be lacking in virtue. She seems to have meant to say that a woman should not depend so much on the conditions of her father, husband, and sons that she could not be secure, but rather, she should be independent, just as men were. Her appeal for women's independence seems so insightful that it still is one of the key points in today's feminism.

Concept of Metamorphosis

The image of women as "defiled" and "sinful" grew not only out of the concept of impurity by blood but also from the notions of the three obediences and five hindrances. It was in order to provide a means for women to overcome these obstacles to the attainment of buddhahood and salvation that the notion of "metamorphosis" was proposed. According to this idea, a woman could become a buddha and be reborn again in the Pure Land after first being changed to a man. This principle, which is prominent in the Lotus Sutra and in the three great Amida Sutras (second to fifth centuries A.D.), has, since the Heian era, represented the only means through which women might obtain salvation.

The idea of metamorphosis became more important in the Muromachi era (fourteenth to fifteenth centuries) with the introduction from China of the folk belief in the Ketsubon Sutra that all women who have given birth to a child will go to the hell of blood. This belief held that blood shed in the process of childbirth polluted the earth, which in turn polluted the rivers, which could eventually pollute monks if they unwittingly took the water for their tea. In the Edo era (seventeenth to nineteenth centuries) the idea of blood pollution was expanded to include menstrual bleeding, so that it came to be believed that all women would go to the hell of blood after death. Despite a general skepticism about the orthodoxy of such a belief, this Chinese idea became widely spread in Japan and thereby functioned to promote negative attitudes toward women.

Exclusion of Women from Buddhist Temples

This belief regarding the impurity and sinfulness of women became manifested in the phenomenon whereby women were excluded from certain of the state Buddhist temples. In some cases, such as the temple at Mount Koya and at Mount Hiei, the temple as well as the entire mountain on which it stood were closed off to women, whereas in other cases, such as Todaiji, Yakushiji, Horyuji, and Zenkoji temples, only the innermost sanctuary of the temples were made off limits to women.

Originally, temples excluded women to keep monks free from sexual distractions. In other words, the rejection of women by Buddhist temples was introduced for the purpose of maintaining the religious order. A legend that was passed on to support the orthodoxy of this practice of rejecting women at Mount Hiei and Kinpusen temples goes thus: when a nun, Toran, tried to enter the sanctuary, a horrible disaster occurred, and she was destroyed because of her impurity, and the sanctuary was thereby saved. This legend and its variants can be read, from a feminist viewpoint, to be paradoxical; the

21

real force of the religion was revealed only when confronted by the impurity of women (Abe 1989, 188). Thus, the exclusion of women, which was originally practiced as a means of maintaining the discipline of monks, became established as a method of giving added power and authority to the temples. The temples that followed this practice were precisely those that were closely connected with the ruling power, which looked to religion as a means of control.

Criticism of Women's Exclusion

What is clear regarding this practice of female exclusion which served religious and political functions is that, whatever the rationale, it was created by men. There were some attempts to oppose this absurd practice as early as the tenth century. Besides the nun Toran, who tried to enter a sanctuary, additional examples are found in literature such as in the Noh plays *Sotoba no Komachi*, by Kan'ami, and *Tatatsu no Saemon*, by Zeami (Abe 1989, 189). These cases, however, were exceptional. Even radical thinkers, such as the founders of the new Buddhist sects of the Kamakura era (twelfth to thirteenth centuries), Honen, Shinran (1173–1262), Nichiren (1222–82), and Myoe (1173–1232), did not criticize the exclusion of women by the temples.

The only exception was the Zen patriarch Dogen (1200–1253). In a chapter of his *Shobogenzo* entitled "Raihaitokuzui" he clearly criticized the exclusion of women by ancient Buddhism, claiming that it was an evil practice and had no grounding in actual religious principles. He even criticized, implicitly, the five hindrances to women's attainment of salvation mentioned in the Lotus Sutra. In this respect Dogen may deserve the title of feminist. However, after he moved to Eihei Temple in Echizen in 1243, he began to claim that leaving the worldly life was sacrosanct and became more supportive of the practice of female exclusion by the temples. Dogen appears to have felt the same ambivalence that Buddha held. And their ambivalence seems to exemplify the dilemma frequently encountered in religious life between asceticism and sexuality. It was not until the seventeenth century that the liberal ideas expressed by Dogen in his earlier years reappeared.

The *Ie* Structure of Religious Organizations

In order to understand why it took so long for another liberal philosopher such as Dogen to emerge and why the practice of female exclusion persisted so tenaciously, we need to examine another critical factor, which has to do with the characteristically Japanese-style *ie* (household, or family) social organization of these temples. While the monks lived atop the holy mountains conducting various religious affairs in service of the nation, their wives, mothers, and sisters resided in a separate community called a *satobo* at the foot of the mountains under the protection of the monks, leading a religious life and performing their assigned roles—sewing and washing the monks' clothing and preparing their meals. A *satobo* also functioned as an asylum for women who lacked protection and as a new home for those who had abandoned the worldly life (Nishiguchi 1987, 54). A *satobo* represented the closest connection a woman could have to the religious sanctuary of the mountaintop. Many of these *satobo* originated with the mothers of some famous monks. Legends tell of elderly mothers who lived religious lives under the protection of their sons, who led spiritual lives atop the mountains and eventually died, watched over by their sons, and were believed to be reborn in the Pure Land. Tales of mothers of great monks such as Saicho, Kukai, and Ennogyoja have been loved by the local people, and these women have come to be worshiped as patron saints of safe delivery and nursing.

What we find, then, is that while, on the one hand, the religious sanctuaries atop the mountains were restricted only to men, on the other hand, a separate religious space *(ie)* was created for their female family members. The ultimate wish of these women was to die with their men beside them and be buried at the top of the holy mountain, which represented paradise. Women could reach the top of the holy mountain only after death.

It has been a normal Buddhist practice since the feudal age for a priest to serve at a temple supported at the same time by his own *ie*, or family. In particular, the Jodo Shin sect has had an *ie* within the organization from the very beginning of its history. However, the status of the wives, who functioned as the main support within the *ie*, has always been low, and women have never been allowed to become head of a temple, a tradition that is now severely criticized by feminists. Even in the Jodo Shin sect, despite the importance of the *ie* in its philosophy, Shinran, Zongaku, Rennyo, and all the other priests espoused the idea of differentiated gender roles and supported the notion of metamorphosis. This contradictory fact has recently attracted critical attentions of male researchers (Endo 1989).

Women, through their role within the *ie*, have been a source of support behind the development of various Buddhist sects in Japan in greater or lesser degrees.[4] The fact that, in spite of this, women's status has been held down and their freedom of thought restricted is due in large degree to the importance given, at least in principle, to the Buddhist concept of "leaving the worldly life." In reality this idea has been distorted in the process of undergoing assimilation in the Japanese setting, as demonstrated in the discussion of women's presence within the *ie* attached to the monasteries. Japanese Buddhist groups must now undertake a reexamination of how this distortion came about and reconsider the status and position of women.

Sexism in the "New Religions"

Buddhism was imported to Japan, and it became diffused within the population from the top down. On the other hand, the so-called new religions,[5] to which I will now turn, are indigenous to Japanese society. They, too, however, are characterized by sexism.

What is collectively called "new religions" vary considerably in terms of length of existence. Among the older ones membership dates back several generations; others came into being in the period immediately following World War II, amid the social upheaval that prevailed in postwar Japanese society; while the most recent ones were established in the 1970s. These new religions also differ in terms of their belief systems. Yet they also share many characteristics in common. One of them is that their religious authority is derived from the traditional religions, such as Shinto, Buddhism, and Christianity. In this respect, all the new religions can be said to be another sect or offshoots of the traditional ones. A second common characteristic is that these new religions have created a pseudofamily, that is, an organization just like the *ie*, with the founder as the "parent" and the religious community leaders as elder siblings. This characteristic seems to provide a feeling of security to those who might lack the support of a real family and have not found help through traditional religions or from social service organizations. A third common feature shared by these new religions is that most of them have actively sought to play an influential role in national politics.

These religions show a similarity to the traditional religions of Japan such as Shinto and Buddhism in terms of their historical development and structure. The case of Rissho Koseikai, an offshoot of the Nichiren sect of Buddhism, is a good illustration (see Osumi 1989). Rissho Koseikai was originally founded in 1936 by a woman possessing shamanistic charisma, assisted by a man who was in charge of the establishment of laws and doctrines. In the early period following its establishment seven out of eight leaders were women. After the death of the shamanic woman following the war, however, the group began to emphasize systematizing the religious doctrines and building its organization. Today the key figures consist exclusively of men, and there is a fixed division of gender roles within the organization, with men in charge of the bureaucratic functions and women performing the various daily routines at the local chapters.

The concept of unequal sex roles is widely accepted within the new religions. Moreover, their followers are encouraged to emulate this concept in their own family lives, with the husband assuming the role of leader and the wife that of subordinate. For example, Sokagakkai, founded in the 1930s, upholds a domestic role for women, based on the teaching of Nichiren, founder of the Nichiren sect of Buddhism, that "a woman, while subordinating herself to all (including men), is able to control all (including men)" (Inoue 1988, 286). Although a woman must subordinate herself to her husband, an exception is made in the case in which a husband opposes the wife's membership in the religious organization. Another new religion, Jissenrinrikoseikai, which was founded immediately following World War II, compares the roles of the husband and wife to those of the engine car, performing the dominant, active role, and the trailed car, which is subordinate and passive. In these religious organizations women are repeatedly taught to cultivate obedience rather than to be clever, and the religious magazines carry many stories showing how an obedient wife successfully manages to resolve family problems (Numata 1988, 236). The hierarchical distinctions derived from Confucianism, too, are widely accepted among these new religions.

To summarize the ideas common among new religions, the role of women is perceived as that of maintaining the family by taking care of the spirits of ancestors and stillborn children and caring for elderly parents, while the role of men is to contribute toward the maintenance of national prosperity through their work in industry. This picture coincides with the welfare policy of Japan's ruling political party, the Liberal Democratic Party. The new religions thus provide ethical support for the maintenance of the present system of Japanese society, which retains a central role for the *ie*.

What reason(s) account for the fact that the new religions attract so many female followers? According to Inoue (1988) and Numata (1988), the answer can be found in the fact that these religions perform the following types of functions:

1. They offer help and advice on problems housewives commonly confront (mothers-in-law, husbands, children's education).

2. They provide companionship as well as activities for women to fill the void left by husbands who are busily caught up in their work and children who have grown and gone off on their own.

3. Housewives can find a sense of purpose by participating in religious-affiliated activities within their communities.

4. The notion of "obedient wife and responsible mother," espoused by these religions, provides a measure of stability and peace, superficial though it may be, within the family.

5. They provide opportunities for women to engage in self-expression and gain experience in the larger society by allowing them to assume positions of responsibility and leadership within the organization, for example, presiding over or speaking before large groups of followers.

Incidentally, with regard to this last point, giving women opportunities to perform various executive-type functions helps to veil the sexism that is in fact characteristic of these religious organizations.

Conclusion

The women of Japan today constitute a highly diverse population both in terms of the values they hold and the lifestyles they lead. Are either the traditional religions or the new religions capable of responding adequately to the emotional sufferings experienced by these diverse types of women—housewives who suffer from loneliness in spite of living with their families, single women, married but childless women, unmarried mothers, women who are caught in a dilemma between career and family life? What must be done—what changes must be undertaken—in order that women can be truly liberated *as* women, rather than *from* being a woman?

One of the obstacles that has been preventing Buddhism and the new religions from recognizing the various values that women hold is their adherence to a family-like structure. The Constitution, which was enacted in 1947 following World War II, contained several provisions aimed at abolishing the traditional family system and securing equality of the sexes within the family. The sexism inherent in Japanese religions will continue to prevail so long as the family system is maintained. The function and meaning of this family system and the role of women within that system, particularly the domestic functions performed by them, must be reexamined and reevaluated in order for women to achieve a solid status within the sphere of organized religion.

There is another factor that has prevented feminist issues from being clearly perceived in Japanese society—namely, a lack of individual consciousness and a sense of individuals making decisions for themselves and taking responsibility for themselves. In Western societies one tends to regard things in terms of dichotomies, for example, between sacred and secular, right and wrong, or superior and inferior, and then to proceed to do away with those elements that are seen as negative. In Japan, however, there is a tendency to accept and try to harmonize both the good and the bad rather than to seek to make clear the differences. Within this milieu individual qualities and abilities are often ignored. Social pressures encourage people to be as similar to others as possible and to maintain the status quo rather than seek to change it.

This kind of society, which tends to accept everything without analysis or criticism and to embrace all of its members indiscriminately so long as they stay within the social order, has been labeled a "maternal society" by the psychologist Kawai Hayao (1976). In such a society individuals are not required or encouraged to decide matters for themselves. By extension, in such a society individuals are unlikely to think seriously about feminist issues and to raise such questions as "Who is wrong?" and "Who are the enemies of feminism?" Men, too, are robbed of their autonomy in the social organizations in which they work and are therefore also victims.

Our society is structured in such a way that all Japanese, of both sexes and at all levels, are forced to surrender their freedom for the sake of maintaining harmony and order within the larger social organization, that is, the nation. The pursuit of feminist issues within the Japanese context inevitably leads to consideration of other fundamental issues. One of these is the responsibility incumbent on those of us who have tended to entrust everything to organizational structures such as the nation, industry, and educational institutions to cultivate our own wills and personalities and to mature into individuals who can exercise independence and initiative in directing our lives.

NOTES

1. In March 1992 the technical chief of a local Construction Ministry site became the first female field officer to enter a tunnel being built by the government. In October 1990 a female reporter for a Japanese newspaper had been banned from attending a ribbon-cutting ceremony for a tunnel in Yamagata Prefecture ("Woman defies taboo, enters tunnel," *Japan Times*, 22 March 1992, 3).

2. Christianity was introduced to Japan in 1549 by the Jesuit priest Francis Xavier. While it was initially tolerated and even encouraged under the rule of Nobunaga, following the ascension of Hideyoshi various edicts were issued banning it, and under Ieyasu persecution of Christians became more intense. Christianity vanished from the scene, although it continued to be practiced secretly by converts. It was not until 1873 that complete religious freedom was granted. At present Christians constitute just 1 percent of the total Japanese population. There are several complex reasons that have been set forth to explain why Christianity has not gained a significant foothold in Japan, and it is beyond the scope of this chapter to go into these explanations. One important factor, however, is that the Christian concept of a spiritual, non-blood-related brotherhood or family could not compete against the concept of the traditional family system, with its emphasis on the primacy of ties based on blood.

3. See, for example, *Engishiki* (Institutes of the Engi Period), a collection of codes of laws completed in 927, and *Kinpisho*, a book written by Emperor Juntoku and completed around 1221, which records the history and origin of imperial court ceremonies and sets forth the rules and etiquette for carrying out such ceremonies.

4. It should be mentioned that in the seventeenth century temples were established by nuns to which women seeking to sever a marriage (which was extremely difficult for a woman to do) were able to flee.

5. This section is a translation of part of an essay written in German by the author entitled "Weiblichkeitssymbolik und Sexismus in alten und neuen Religionen Japans" (Feminine symbolism and sexism in old and new religions of Japan), in *Japan—ein Land der Frauen?* (Japan—a women's country?), ed. Elizabeth Gössmann (Munich: Iudicium Verlag, 1991), chap. 5, pp. 124–29.

REFERENCES

Abe, Yasuro. 1989. "Nyonin kinsei to suisan" (Prohibition of women and self-imposition). In *Miko to megami* (Maidens and goddesses), ed. Kazuo Osumi et al. Tokyo: Heibonsha.

Endo, Hajime. 1989. "Bomori izen no koto" (The origin of marriage for priests of the Jodo Shin Sect). In *Shinjin to kuyo* (Faith and service for the dead), ed. Osumi Kazuo et al. Tokyo: Heibonsha.

Inoue, Setsuko. 1989. "Bukkyo no josei sabetsu ni tachiatta onnatachi (Women who criticized sexism in Buddhism). *Shukyo joho* (Religious News), no. 32 (June): 115.

————. 1988. *Shufu o Misuru shin shukyo* (The new religions that charm housewives). Tokyo: Tanizawa shobo.

Iwamoto, Yutaka. 1980. *Bukkyo to josei* (Buddhism and women). Tokyo: Daisan bunmeisha.

Kasahara, Kazuo. 1984. *Bukkyo ni miru Nihon josei kaiho-shi* (History of women's liberation as seen in Buddhism). Tokyo: Hoso daigaku kyoiku shinkokai.

Kawai, Hayao. 1976. *Bosei shakai Nihon no byori* (The pathology of Japan's maternal society). Tokyo: Chuokoronsha.

Manu Hoten (Laws of Manu). 1991. Trans. Nobuyuki Watase. Tokyo: Chuokoronsha.

Nagata, Mizu. 1986. "Butten ni miru boseikan" (View of motherhood in Buddhist scriptures). In *Bosei o tou* (Questioning motherhood), vol. 1, ed. Wakita Haruko. Tokyo: Jinbun shoin.

Nishiguchi, Junko. 1987. *Onna no chikara* (The power of women). Tokyo: Heibonsha.

Numata, Kenya. 1988. *Gendai Nihon no shin shukyo* (New religions in contemporary Japan). Tokyo: Sogensha.

Okano, Haruko. 1990. "Nihon josei no shukyojo no ichi" (The status of Japanese women in religion). In *Nihon-Doitsu: josei no atarashii uneri* (Japan and Germany: the new surge of women), ed. Tokyo doitsu bunka senta. Tokyo: Kawai shuppan.

————. 1988. "Himmel ohne Frauen" (Heaven without women). In *Das Gold im Wachs* (The gold in wax), ed. E. Gössmann and G. Zobel. Munich: Iudicium Verlag.

Orikuchi, Shinobu. 1955. *Oguri Hangan-ron no keikaku* (The plan for a study on Oguri Hangan). *Orikuchi Shinobu zenshu*, vol. 3. Tokyo: Chuokoronsha.

Osumi, Kazuo. 1989. "Shin shukyo ni miru josei no katsudo" (The activities of women as seen in the new religions). In *Shinjin to kuyo* (Faith and service for the dead), ed. Kazuo Osumi et. al. Tokyo: Heibonsha.

"Woman Defies Taboo, Enters Tunnel." 1992. *Japan Times*. 22 March.

Aspects of Sexism in Language

❖ ❖ ❖

Orie Endo

Translated by Kumiko Fujimura-Fanselow

I n looking at women and language in the Japanese context we can identify two issues, both of which reflect the differential status of women and men in Japanese society. The first has to do with how women are defined or characterized through the language—the kinds of words and expressions used to refer to or to describe women. There are, in Japanese, many expressions within general usage that treat women in very different ways from men and in many cases overtly denigrate or belittle women and refer to them in a highly derogatory manner based on physical appearance, marital status, and so on. In addition, women themselves continue to use expressions that elevate the status of men in relation to women, and men accept such expressions as a matter of course.

The second issue concerns a feature of Japanese that has been a subject of considerable interest and curiosity to non-Japanese—namely, gender differences in the language used by men and women and the existence of a distinctive "women's language," or *onnakotoba*. There is a cultural tradition that prescribes the appropriate behavior expected of Japanese women, and included within this tradition is a "feminine," or *onnarashii*, speech style, which is characterized by, among other features, politeness and tentativeness and the use of special vocabulary (including verb forms) and sentence structures as well as by a distinctive tone of voice and carriage. Even today, girls are taught from the time they are small, through family socialization and schooling, to use *onnarashii* forms of speech and expression. At the same time, however, reflecting changes in various other aspects of women's lives in recent years, many women have begun to deviate from the norm in many situations, and there has been a gradual convergence in the speech forms of females and males. These issues have only recently come under debate in Japan as feminist scholars have come to recognize the various ways in which language reflects and perpetuates differential status for women and men.

Words and Expressions That Denote Differential Status for Women and Men

The very word for *female* or *woman*, *onna*, unlike the word for *man*, which is *otoko*, contains a strong and often negative sexual connotation (Nakamura 1990). *Onna* can be substituted for many sexually related terms, such as mistress or prostitute. Thus, for example, in the sentence "Yasushi wa otoko ni natta," which literally means "Yasushi has become a man," the general implication is that of a man becoming an independent person (e.g., as a result of completing a difficult task), but if we substitute the male name Yasushi with that of a female, the same sentence now refers to the female subject's first experience of menstruation or sexual intercourse. Similarly, whereas the expression "*ii otoko*" (a good man) can denote both a sexually attractive man, when spoken by women, and a socially competent or reliable man, when said by a speaker of either sex, "*ii onna*," which is spoken only by men, carries only the sexual connotation of "a sexy woman." The expression "*onna o shiru*" (to know a woman), as in "He still doesn't know a woman," also carries a purely sexual connotation, meaning "He still hasn't had a woman" or "He's still a virgin," while to say "He has a woman" ("Kare ni wa onna ga iru") implies the existence of a mistress.

In addition, several of the Chinese characters that have the character *onna* as a component likewise carry a negative meaning. The Chinese character, formed by combining two characters, for *woman* is *memeshii* and is used to describe a man who is timid and irresolute, or "sissy." Putting three characters for *woman* yields the word *kashimashii*, which means "noisy." Thus, we have the expression "Get three women together, and you get noise." The character for *woman* is also a component of the characters for "servant" and "jealousy."

Most of the grossly sexist and insulting words and expressions used either to describe women or which make reference to women refer to the marital status, age, or the so-called feminine or unfeminine personality or characteristics of women:

• *urenokori* (unsold merchandise)—a reference to a woman who remains unwed past the so-called marriageable age of twenty-five or so; *ikiokure* (late to go) and *oorudo misu* (old maid), taken from the English *old Miss*, convey a similar meaning.

• *busu, okame* (literally, a fawning turtle), and *chinkusa* are all terms of insult hurled at women, meaning "uglies."

• *otokomasari*—literally meaning "superior-to-man," used to describe a spirited or spunky woman or one who excels over men in some way, physically or intellectually. The term implies a lack of femininity.

• *shokuba no hana* (office flowers)—used to refer to young female office workers who serve as decorations for brightening the predominantly masculine office environment. "Office flowers" are characterized by their short-lived blossoming, since most of them stay on the job for just a few years until they get married.

• *onna no kusattayo na* (literally, like a rotten woman) is a term of insult directed at men perceived as sissies or wimps.

• *memeshii*—written by repeating the Chinese character for *woman* twice, means "effeminate," "unmanly" or "sissy."

• *yome ni yaru* (give away in marriage), *yome ni iku* (to go as a bride), and *yome o morau* (to receive the bride)—*yome* means "daughter-in-law" as well as "bride." All of these terms, still widely used, are an inheritance of the traditional system of marriage whereby the bride entered the family of the groom.

• *rojo* or *roba* means "old woman."

In recent years, as is the case with words and expressions that violate human rights or are discriminatory toward persons with handicaps, words that clearly express bias against women have come under scrutiny at the governmental level and by the mass media and educational institutions. Thus, several of these expressions—such as "office flower," "give away in marriage," "unsold merchandise," and "old woman"—are no longer used in official documents or in the mass media. In place of *old woman*, for example, newspapers are more apt these days to use the term *elderly person (rojin)* or else to spell out "a woman of such-and-such age." In day-to-day conversations, however, we continue to hear such expressions. Apart from the such overtly sexist words and expressions, there are many other expressions in general usage that belittle women and place them in a position of inferiority vis-à-vis men.

Shujin

Within the past decade or so there has been much debate in Japanese newspapers and magazines over the usage of *shujin*, the term most commonly used by married women in reference to their husbands. (When referring to someone else's husband the honorific prefix *go* is added, so that one says "*goshujin*.") The two Chinese characters used to write this word have the meaning "lord" or "master." In olden times this word, which literally means "master," was used in the context of master-servant relationships. It was not until the turn of the twentieth century that the word came to be used as a referent for one's husband, but usage of the term to refer to one's husband was limited to women of the upper class and intellectual circles. After World War

II, however, *shujin* took firm root as more and more women appropriated the term, gradually overtaking the more neutral term for husband, *otto*, in popularity. At a meeting of the Mothers Association (Hahaoya taikai) held in 1955 a call was issued to the women of Japan to use the term *otto* (rather than *shujin*) to refer to their husbands as part of an effort to do away with feudalistic practices and ways of thinking and to encourage women to live not as subordinates but as equals with their husbands, as set forth in the provision in the postwar Japanese Constitution that marriage must be based on the principle of equal rights for husbands and wives and on mutual cooperation (Endo 1987, 36).

Despite such efforts, however, *shujin* has continued to be popularly used. In various surveys conducted in recent years (NHK 1982; Endo 1985; Yoneda 1986; NHK 1990) at least 60 percent of married women surveyed responded that they use the term *shujin* when talking about their husbands. While such a finding is somewhat disconcerting, at the same time, we ought not thereby jump to certain conclusions regarding the consciousness of Japanese married women with respect to their status vis-à-vis their husbands. These results show merely what women *said* was the term they used in talking about their husbands; they are not based on observations of actual behavior. Therefore, it is possible that in actuality women use other terms more frequently and that they are giving the answer that they think is the norm. We also cannot tell from these results how women actually feel about using the term *shujin*. In other words, we cannot conclude from these figures that the majority of married Japanese women wholeheartedly embrace this usage.

There are several possible reasons why women use this term *shujin*: some may see it as the most standard term; others may use it because they don't know any other appropriate terms; still others use it simply as a convenient code; while for some women the word accurately represents the relationship between themselves and their husbands. When asked their feelings about using this word, some women said they realized that it implies they are in a subordinate position relative to their husband and, therefore, they don't like the word, but that they use it because there doesn't seem to be a good alternative: *danna* and *teishu* also imply a master-servant relationship and sound informal; *otto* is another possible word that is very neutral, but they hesitate to use it because, they believe, people might think they were putting on airs; and while the word *tsureai*, which is another word for *spouse* that has been in use for over three hundred years, means "partner" or "the person one keeps company with" and therefore carries no connotations about superiority or inferiority, to many people it sounds somewhat old-fashioned. Others justify using this term, insisting that their relationship with their husbands is one of equality, not master and servant, and that they use the term *shujin* simply as a convenient symbol. What is very clear is that *shujin* is not used as naturally and without hesitation by the Japanese in the way that the words for "father," "daughter," or "son" are used. Feminists in Japan generally shun the use of the word *shujin* and instead refer to a husband as *otto, tsureai,* or the English word *partner,* pronounced *paatonaa.* When it comes to talking about someone else's husband, however, one has little choice but to use the word *goshujin,* unless one refers to him by first name, which is very uncommon, except among close friends.

It is interesting to consider how those studying Japanese as a foreign language feel about the usage of the term *shujin* to refer to one's husband. Japanese textbooks used by foreigners studying Japanese generally use *shujin.* In my teaching experience, Chinese students, who of course use Chinese characters in their own native language, as well as many of the Korean students who also know the Chinese characters, immediately grasp the meaning of the term when it is written out. These students are generally very surprised by the usage of such an anachronistic term to refer to the husband-wife relationship. They, who have come to a country that is at the forefront in terms of modern, up-to-date technology and economic development, have been led to assume that the society itself and the status of women and men is also modern and up-to-date. After living in Japan for some time, however, these people come face to face with various aspects of social life which are, in fact, premodern or are not in line with the laws; the status of men and women and husbands and wives is one of those aspects.

A student of mine from South Korea lamented: "In my country, too, women over the age of forty refer to their husbands as *shujin,* but that term is no used by younger women. I never dreamed that this word was still used in Japan, which is economically more advanced than Korea. I don't want to use this word, but I do so because if I use some other word Japanese people will think that I don't know Japanese well." A Chinese woman who teaches Japanese and is married to a Chinese who also teaches Japanese told me that in her country both the husband and the wife use the same word, *airen,* to refer to each other. Yet when she and her husband use Japanese, she refers to him as *shujin,* and she felt that this had the effect of making her husband feel that he is indeed the master.

Kanai

While the most popular word used by women to refer to husbands has the meaning "master," *kanai,* which is the term many husbands use in talking about their wives, is written with Chinese characters for "house" and "inside." The meaning conveyed, thereby, is of one who remains (or *should* remain) inside the home, premised on the idea that it is the husband who works outside the home and earns money. Such an image, however, very much contradicts social reality today, since many married women are engaged in a variety of community-related, leisure, and study activities and more than half work either full- or part-time outside the home.

In a study by Yoneda Masato (1986) in which he asked husbands how they referred to their wives in a telephone conversation, the responses differed somewhat according to age as well as the nature of the relationship between the respondent and the person on the other end of the phone: when talking with one's former teacher, men were found to be most likely to use the term *kanai*, whereas when talking with a friend they used the wife's name; at the same time, *kanai* was found to be more popularly used by older men, while younger men tended to refer to their wives by name.

While *kanai* is a term of reference for one's own wife, *okusan*, or "Mrs. Interior" in Cherry's translation (1987, 66), is the most common term for referring to or addressing other men's spouses or, more generally, all married women. *Okusan*, or *okusama*, originally referred to married women of the ruling aristocratic class in feudal society who, unlike the majority of women who had to toil in the fields, lived cloistered in the far interior of their mansions. In the early part of the twentieth century the term came to be applied to wives of white-collar workers, while still later it came to designate all married women. Many women dislike being addressed as *"okusan"* and prefer, instead, to be called by their names, for example, Tanaka-san.

Mibojin

Mibojin, the Japanese word for "widow," is another word that, although commonly used, in fact has very negative connotations. The Chinese characters used to write out the word literally have the meaning "the one who is not yet dead." The term for "widower" is totally different and carries no such implication. At one time the word was used by widows to refer to themselves and the implication was: "My husband has preceded me in death. Although I should have been buried with him, here I remain, a bad woman who has yet to die." It is based on the idea that a loyal retainer should be willing to follow his master to the grave. This concept is very much akin to the Hindu custom of *sati* (self-immolation, usually on a husband's funeral pyre). The word *mibojin* has come to be used not only by widows to refer to themselves but by others as well.

Nyoboyaku

Individuals who perform a supporting role for a person in some important position—such as a prime minister, a company president, or a star baseball pitcher—are often referred to as the *nyoboyaku*, or "the one performing the wifely role." The implication is that, just as the wife serves or supports the husband, the *nyoboyaku* is one who remains close to the other person as an aide, helping out in various ways. The issue, then, is why such a supportive function is defined as constituting a wifely function. Surely the relationship between married couples in contemporary Japan is no longer one in which the wife is in a subordinate, supportive position vis-à-vis the husband.

Terms That Place Women in the Same Category as Children

There are several words and expressions in Japanese that place women in the same category as children. One of these is *shijo*, a word meaning "children" written with the Chinese character for "child" and that for "female" and used in such expressions as *kikokushijo*, which means "returnee children" (i.e., children who have returned to Japan after having been brought up abroad). Another example is *fujoshi*, which means "women and children," written with the Chinese characters for *woman, female*, and *child*. This term was frequently used during the Persian Gulf War of 1990–91 in reporting about women and children who were released by the Iraqi authorities in Kuwait and allowed to return to Japan. Likewise, at the various levels of government we inevitably find that matters relating to women are handled in the "women's and minor's bureau." Another example is the frequent use of the term *onna no ko* (female child) to refer to adult women, whereas *otoko no ko* (male child) is used only to refer to male children. Referring to female workers in an office as "girls" clearly reflects the view that they are seen as occupying a lower position and status vis-à-vis their male coworkers.

Personal Titles and Gender Marking

Unlike in the case of English in which personal title differs according to gender (as well as marital status in the case of women, unless *Ms.* is used), in Japanese the same suffix, *-san*, is appended to the first or last name (e.g., Suzuki-san) for both men and women, irrespective of marital status. In this respect there is no gender differentiation. While this is, in fact, the general practice in speech, when it comes to writing some differences become apparent. Newspapers will often refer to both men and women in various positions by title, such as Prime Minister So-and-So or Committee Chair So-and-So or else use *-san*. Yet when several women and men from various professional or occupational backgrounds are being referred to—as, for example, in the case of participants at a meeting or conference—very often the suffix *-san* is applied to women's names, and *-shi* is applied to men, although more recently there is a tendency to use one or the other suffix for persons of both sexes. A very clear distinction in usage is still apparent in the case of newspaper articles dealing with announcements of death: *-san* is always used in the case of women, while *-shi* is reserved for men. There is a difference in the degree of respect or esteem that these two suffixes imply, with *-shi*, a Japanese term of Chinese origin that is more formal than *-san*, connoting a higher degree of respect and formality.

A related point is that in Japanese society such forms as *female lawyer, female reporter*, and *female police officer* are commonly used. Identifying a subclass of a group such as lawyers, reporters, or police officers as female, of course, carries the implication that the group itself is basically male. In the case of teachers, this is not the case. This undoubtedly has some relation to the fact that women now make up more than 50 percent of all elementary school teachers. In the 1982 NHK study one out of three respondents (both male and female) indicated that they did not think it was particularly necessary to put in *female*. Among the younger female respondents the percentage was higher: 45 percent of females in their twenties and 41 percent of those in their thirties.

Fujin versus *Josei*

As mentioned, there has been some effort in recent years at the governmental level and by the mass media to examine and alter certain linguistic terms used in reference to women that are either offensive to women or present an inaccurate or distorted image of women today. One example of this is the switch in recent years—from the use of the word *fujin*, which conjures up the image of a somewhat older married woman with a family, to *josei*, which means "woman" or "womankind"—in the names of various governmental offices that handle matters related to women, for example, *Josei kikaku-ka*, or Women's Planning Bureau. As one Tokyo ward government office explained the reason for deciding to make this change, '*Fujin*' is generally used as a pronoun for married women; but the resolution of problems faced by women entails dealing with women of all ages—from infants to the elderly. Moreover, there is no word comparable to '*fujin*' for men." Starting in April 1992 the term *fujin* was changed to *josei* in the titles of all Tokyo municipal offices containing the term, although it was retained in the case of *fujin keisatsukan*, or "female police officer." One interesting and rather tricky stumbling block to the use of *josei* comes up in the expression "*josei mondai*." Although the literal meaning of the term is "women's problems or issues," ever since the mass media used the same words to refer to the sex scandal surrounding Prime Minister Uno in 1989, which forced his resignation from office, it has unfortunately also taken on the connotation of "problems faced by men as a result of a sexual relationship with a woman."

Male-Female, Father-Mother, Husband-Wife

In compound words such as *danjo* (male and female), *fufu* or *fusai* (husband and wife), and *fubo* (father and mother), the male character almost inevitably is placed first. While this practice is now taken for granted—and, indeed, the same words written in the reverse order, such as *jodan* or *saifu*, are not recognized as real words today—what is interesting is that this has not always been the case throughout Japanese history.

An examination of *Manyoshu*, a collection of native Japanese poetry composed by men and women of all classes dating from the fifth to the eighth centuries, which was completed in the eighth century, reveals, for example, instances in which the word *mother* is written before that of *father* (Endo 1990, 87–91). Likewise, *woman* sometimes precedes *man* in writings contained in the *Manyoshu* as well as in some works dating to the Edo period of the seventeenth to the nineteenth centuries (97–100). *Meoto*, with the character for *wife* written before that for *husband*, can also be found in writings from the Edo period. My own feeling on this matter is that we ought to recover some of the flexibility that existed in these earlier periods and allow people to say (or write) *mother* before *father*, or

vice versa, depending on the occasion and whether one wants to emphasize one word or the other.

"Women's Language" as a Feature of Japanese

The other major aspect of Japanese we must consider in talking about gender
and language is the existence of a women's language. Written descriptions of
the Japanese language as well as instructors of the Japanese language never
fail to note that differentiation in the language used by females versus males
is one of the characteristic features of the Japanese language. Women's language is said to be characterized by the usage of exclusively female expressions; the avoidance of formalistic words, including words of Chinese origin,
as well as coarse and vulgar expressions; abundance of expressions convey-
ing respect, politeness, and courtesy; a manner of speaking that is respectful
and polite as well as roundabout and tentative; a high-pitched voice; repetitive speech; abundant use of adjectives; frequent use of honorifics that are
appended to certain nouns; and special verb forms and sentence construc-
tions used by all Japanese in polite situations. In addition, women are apt to
adopt a distinctive tone of voice, carriage, and behavior.

We ought to keep several points in mind in thinking about Japanese
women's language. One is that Japanese is by no means unique in this
respect. Differences in male and female speech patterns occur in several languages, including English. Another important point to keep in mind is that,
while a "woman's language" does in fact exist, it is not something that developed out of any "natural" differences—biological or otherwise—in female
versus male inclinations, nor something women themselves decided they
wanted to use. Rather, it was consciously and deliberately taught and
diffused—or more strongly, imposed—on women and girls through the
process of education over the period of several centuries. Thus, it is important to understand the historical development of this phenomenon and to recognize that the language prescribed for usage by women has served in turn
to define and regulate appropriate behavior and actions for women. Finally,
we need to recognize that, while gender differences in language usage do
still exist, those differences are becoming much less marked in present-day
Japanese society. Increasingly, Japanese women, particularly the young, are
adopting patterns of speech formerly associated with men; conversely, and
equally important, several words and expressions that fall under the category
of women's language turn up frequently in men's speech, particularly among
the younger generation.

The Historical Development of Women's Language

Evidence of sex-exclusive features in Japanese can be found in literary works
dating quite far back in history, such as the *Manyoshu*, and in the many works
written by the noble court ladies of the Heian period (ninth to the twelfth
centuries), the most famous of which is *The Tale of Genji*, written by Lady

Murasaki and considered to be the world's first novel. Such differences were not, however, significant. As research by Mashimo Saburo (1969), Sugimoto Tsutomu (1967), Kunida Yuriko (1964), and Matsumura Akira (1986) has demonstrated, it was during the feudal Muromachi period (fourteenth to sixteenth centuries) that a distinctly female language called *nyobo kotoba* evolved. *Nyobo kotoba* developed initially as the language of court ladies residing within women's quarters and involved a special vocabulary for various foods, utensils, and other household items. As *nyobo kotoba* came to be regarded as refined, graceful, and feminine language, it gradually spread to the temples, the homes of the great lords and the warriors, the wealthy merchant families, and, finally, to the general townspeople, becoming established as a language of women in general.

Later, in the Edo period, another unique variety of women's language came into being that consisted of language used commonly by court ladies, women who worked in the service of the court and ruling warrior class families, and by prostitutes. In describing the process by which words and expressions developed by these women became incorporated into the language of women in the larger population, Mashimo Saburo (1966) and Yuzawa Kokichiro (1964) emphasize the important point that it did not take place naturally or spontaneously but, rather, was deliberately promoted and diffused through educational channels. Training in the use of "proper," "feminine" language was in fact closely tied to the education of girls and young women in general over the span of several centuries, which can be seen by examining the many training manuals written for girls widely used as texts in schools in the Edo period. The primary aim of female education in those days was regarded as that of bringing up girls who would be obedient and submissive to their husbands and in-laws, and these manuals echoed such a theme. The following excerpt from Kaibara Ekken's classic statement of proper behavior for the well-bred woman, *The Greater Learning for Women*, written in 1672, is an apt illustration:

> More precious in a woman is a virtuous heart than a face of beauty. The vicious woman's heart is ever excited; she glares wildly around, she vents her anger on others, her words are harsh and her accent vulgar. When she speaks, it is to set herself above others, . . . to outdo others—all things at variance with the "way" in which a woman should talk. The only qualities that befit a woman are gentle obedience, chastity, mercy, and quietness. . . . Never set thyself up against thy husband with harsh features and a boisterous voice! . . . A woman should be circumspect and sparing in her use of words. (Passin, 1965, 174 and 176)

Other manuals instructed girls to speak in soft, low, gentle voices, much as if one were talking to a small child, and to refrain from using any sharp, mean, annoying, "masculine" words or expressions. Schools were not the only sites in which training in appropriate feminine behavior was carried out. From the latter half of the Edo period the homes of the warrior class (samurai) came to serve as a kind of finishing school for daughters of the merchant or farming classes who went there to work as servants and learned at the same time the manners, taste, and speech of samurai women.

In the modern period, heralded by the establishment of the new Meiji government in 1868, the ideology of gender equality and equal education for girls and boys enjoyed support initially, but, with the ascendancy of the more conservative forces, an increasingly sex-differentiated education was promoted within the state-controlled system of public education that persisted right up through World War II. Emphasis on moral education and education for "good wives and wise mothers" served to maintain the value placed on the proper usage of a distinctively women's language.

Women's Language Today

To what extent do Japanese women continue to use a uniquely feminine language? The liberation of Japanese women following Japan's defeat in World War II and the establishment of a democratic society based on the principle of sex equality theoretically implied that women were freed linguistically from the restrictions that had bound them from feudal times. The fact that discussions about women's language continue to be pursued and that many parents and teachers persist in correcting children—girls, in particular— who use forms of speech thought to be reserved for the other sex, even today, suggests that control over women through language is still significant, that the existing framework of a women's language exerts social pressures on women to speak in a prescribed feminine way and limits their freedom of expression.

As with the use of the term *shujin*, or "master," to refer to one's husband, we can identify several different motivations to account for the use of women's language by Japanese women. There are undoubtedly many women who regularly use women's language as a matter of course and without any hesitancy and for whom speaking in such a manner comes quite naturally as a result of many years of socialization and practice. Other women may have strong skepticism and even resistance to doing so yet use it primarily as a strategy for achieving certain goals—namely, getting one's male listeners to listen to what they have to say within the context of certain social situations in which, were they to speak like men, they would be seen as threatening and dismissed even before they could be heard. As Ide Sachiko (1991) explains, no matter how rational or logical a woman's reasoning may be, there is a strong likelihood that male audiences will be turned off from the beginning if her manner of speaking and presenting her views are not couched in the female style of speaking expected of her as a woman. In other words, "Say whatever you have to say, but say it in a soft, gentle, nonthreatening tone." While such a strategy is understandable, we have to ask whether by adopting such a strategy we are not helping to perpetuate the notion that women must speak and behave in a certain way.

Although women's language continues to be a dominant aspect of Japanese, at the same time, as women have advanced into various spheres of social, professional, political, and educational life, the linguistic forms they use have inevitably changed. One problem has been that most descriptions of women's language have tended to be based on rather vague and impressionistic data rather than on a scientific analysis of actual speech patterns as seen among various samples of women in a variety of settings and interactions.

Recent studies that have looked systematically at gender differences in speech (Kawaguchi 1987; Endo 1989, 1990) point to a gradual convergence in the linguistic forms used by women and men. This trend is particularly marked among today's youth. In a survey of junior and senior high school girls conducted by the Japan Broadcasting Company (NHK Television 1988), 59 percent of the former and 50 percent of the latter said that they sometimes used "men's language." In their view the use of men's language enabled them to get across their message to the listener more clearly and directly. While these changes are clearly evident, not surprisingly, opinions about whether this is a desirable development or not vary among different segments of the population.

Unquestionably, there is a relationship between the fact that more and more women are becoming active and prominent in various spheres of society in which women's language is abandoned and the fact that young girls' speech patterns have become "less feminine," for, by rejecting "feminine" speech forms, they are also rejecting a style of speech and behavior that has restricted the ability of their mothers and grandmothers to break out of the narrow definition of appropriate feminine behavior. Equally interesting is the fact that many men, particularly younger men, seem to be abandoning the use of certain words and verb forms associated with masculine speech forms that might be described as "rough" or "swaggering," and which are commonly used by men in their sixties or older, and are adopting, instead, the politer "feminine" speech forms. They, too, may be rejecting the restrictive definition of masculinity that has hitherto constricted the behavior of men as well as that of women. It may well be that we will gradually see the evolution of a more or less "neutral" language that is seen as acceptable for both sexes.

For the present many women seem to adopt different forms of speech according to time, place, and occasion and the particular place in which they find themselves: thus, a female business executive or academic may be seen using a straightforward form of speech at a business meeting or academic conference yet using women's language in a more informal social gathering. Some use women's language as a conscious strategy in certain situations in which they feel they are more likely to have their views listened to if they are presented in a nonthreatening women's speech style rather than in a more blunt and straightforward style.

Teaching "Women's Language" to Students of Japanese as a Foreign Language

To conclude, I would like to reflect on the issue of sexism and women's language within the context of teaching Japanese as a second or foreign language. In recent years, as Japan has become a dominant economic and trading power, there has been a heightened interest in learning Japanese as a foreign language in many countries. As Japanese—like English, French, or Spanish—increasingly becomes a language not only of the Japanese people but of a larger community, we need to confront various issues. One of these concerns the validity of teaching students of Japanese to use women's language.

A large majority of those who teach Japanese to non-native speakers are women—72 percent, in the case of Japan—and many of these teachers diligently teach female students to use women's language. Whether or not a particular female teacher prefers to use women's language in her own speech is a matter of personal choice and values. Within the classroom, however, teachers should, in my view, try to use language that is as close to "neutral" as possible. Moreover, they should not force students to learn or use women's language either on the basis of a particular preference or from a belief that teaching students to speak and behave in a "properly" feminine way will help them make a smoother entry into Japanese society. Such an act of "goodwill," I would argue, represents an act of serious oppression.

The choice of whether to use women's language or not should be left with each student. At the same time, those who elect to adopt women's language in their own speech ought to be made aware of the kinds of images and messages they communicate when they speak in this register. Similarly, while many textbooks routinely teach the words *shujin*, for *my husband* (or *goshujin*, for *your husband*) and *kanai*, for *my wife*, actual usage among native speakers of Japanese varies considerably according to such factors as the speaker's social class background, age, occupation, and the nature of his or her relationship to the other party, so that learners should be presented with a range of possible alternatives to choose from.

REFERENCES

Cherry, Kittredge. 1987. *Womansword—What Japanese Words Say about Women.* Tokyo, New York, and London: Kodansha International.

Endo, Orie. 1991a. "Josei Nihongo kyoshi no kadai" (Problems confronting female teachers of Japanese). *Language Teacher—Special Issue—Feminist Issues in Language Teaching* 15, no. 7 (July): 7–11, 52.

———. 1991b. "Kotoba to josei" (Language and women). *Kokubungaku kaishaku to kansho* (Japanese literature: interpretation and appreciation). (July): 28–37.

———. 1987. *Kininaru kotoba—Nihongo saikento* (Troubling words—A reexamination of Japanese). Tokyo: Nan'undo.

———. 1985. "Haigusha o yobu kotoba" (Words for referring to one's spouse). *Kotoba* (Language) 6:20–49.

———, ed. 1992. *Josei no yobikata daikenkyu* (Research on how women are addressed). Tokyo: Sanshodo.

Endo, Orie et al. 1990. "Dansei no hanashi kotoba" (The spoken language of men). *Kotoba* (Language) 11:1–88.

———et al. 1989. "Josei no hanashi kotoba" (The spoken language of women). *Kotoba* (Language) 10:1–84.

Ide, Sachiko, and Naomi Hanaoka McGloin, eds. 1990. *Aspects of Japanese Women's Language*. Tokyo: Kuroshio Publishers.

Ide, Sachiko, Tamura Suzuko and Orie Endo. 1991. "Kotoba no kenkyu to josei" (Study of language and women). *Kokubungaku kaishaku to kansho* (July): 13–27.

Kawaguchi, Yoko. 1987. "Majiriau danjo no kotoba" (Mixing of men and women's language). *Gengo seikatsu* (Linguistic life), no. 429 (July): 34–39.

Kunida, Yuriko. 1964. *Nyobo kotoba no kenkyu* (A study of *nyobo kotoba*) Tokyo: Kazama shobo.

Mashimo, Saburo. 1969. *Fujingo no kenkyu* (A study of women's language). Tokyo: Tokyodo.

———. 1966. *Yurigo no kenkyu* (A study of the language of the gay quarters). Tokyo: Tokyodo.

Matsumura, Akira. 1986. *Nihongo no tenkai* (Development of the Japanese language). Tokyo: Chuokoronsha.

Nakamura, Momoko. 1990. "Woman's Sexuality in Japanese Female Terms." In *Aspects of Japanese Women's Language,* ed. Sachiko Ide and Naomi Hanaoka McGloin. Tokyo: Kuroshio Publishers.

NHK (Nihon hoso kyokai [Japan broadcasting corporation]). 1990. "Kotoba ishiki no shoso" (Aspects of attitudes regarding language). *Hoso Kenkyu to chosa* (August): 26–41.

———. 30 January 1988. "Doshite tsukau 'otoko kotoba'" (How and why we use 'men's language'). Television program.

———. 17 September 1982. "Nihongo saihakken" (Rediscovering Japanese).

Passin, Herbert. 1965. *Society and Education in Japan*. New York: Teachers College Press, Columbia University.

Sugimoto, Tsutomu. 1967. *Kindai Nihongo no shinkenkyu* (New research on modern Japanese). Tokyo: Ofusha.

Yoneda, Masato. 1986. "Fufu no yobikata" (Forms of address among married couples). *Gengo seikatsu* (Linguistic life), no. 416 (July): 18–21.

Yuzawa, Kokichiro. 1964. *Kuruwa kotoba no kenkyu* (A study of the language of the pleasure quarters). Tokyo: Meiji shoin.

Who's Afraid of Amino Kiku?
Gender Conflict and the Literary Canon

❖ ❖ ❖

Chieko M. Ariga

Amino Kiku (1900–1978) seems to have disappeared from the scene of Japanese literature today. A writer born in turn-of-the century Japan, she was a contemporary of Miyamoto Yuriko (1899–1951), and, like other women writers of her day, wrote semi-autobiographical fiction ("I-fiction," or *shishosetsu*). During her long and prolific writing career, which spanned nearly sixty years, Amino received wide public recognition and many literary prizes and awards. Her works were acclaimed for their detached observations and her style for its unadorned plainness by the critics and writers of her time.

Given this profile, it is curious that Amino is not treated as a major author in literary history books and guides to Japanese literature published today. Most of the books on Japanese authors which have been published in Japan in recent decades do not even mention her name. For example, in *Nihon kindai bungaku no shiso to jokyo* (Ideology and circumstances of modern Japanese literature [Odagiri 1971]), only two women writers, Sata Ineko and Tsuboi Sakae, are represented. In *Nihon no kindai bungaku* (Modern Japanese literature, [Wada 1982]) Amino's name does not appear, while other women writers contemporary to her—such as Okamoto Kanoko (1889–1939), Miyamoto Yuriko, Uno Chiyo (b. 1897), Hayashi Fumiko (1903–51), Hirabayashi Taiko (1905–71), Tsuboi Sakae (1900–1967), Sata Ineko (1904–present), and Nogami Yaeko (1885–1985)—are all mentioned. Likewise, in *Kindai joryu bungaku* (Modern Japanese literature by women, 1983) the works of Okamoto Kanoko, Hayashi Fumiko, Hirabayashi Taiko, and Sata Ineko are detailed.

There is no question about the artistry of the women writers included, but why is Amino excluded from the canon of Japanese women authors? This essay will maintain that Amino's exclusion from the canon of both male and female Japanese authors stems from the fact the women she depicted in her fiction did not conform to the patriarchal definition of "woman."[1] In the course of this discussion, I will reveal the mechanism of ideological control and exclusion operating in the Japanese literary institution.[2]

Japanese Women's Literature Defined by the Patriarchal Institution

Before the Meiji period (1868–1912), few women produced literature, except during the Heian period (794–1192), known as "the flourishing age of literature by court ladies." A host of court ladies at the imperial palace—including Murasaki Shikibu, Sei Shonagon, Izumi Shikibu, Michitsuna's mother, and Sugawara no Takasue's daughter—left diaries and fictional tales depicting the lives of the royal family and aristocrats centered around love relationships between men and women. The most well-known works are Murasaki Shikibu's *Genji monogatari (The Tale of Genji)* and Sei Shonagon's *Makura no soshi (The Pillow Book)*, both assumed to have been written in the early eleventh century. In subsequent periods, writing by women disappeared for the most part a consequence of having a military government whose political foundation was Confucianism.[3] The social order was based upon the Confucian family system in which women's roles were defined solely as those of wife and mother. This left little opportunity for them to participate in the world of letters. It was not until the Meiji period that women started writing again.

In the Meiji period the most recognized women writers were Higuchi Ichiyo (1872–96), who left fictional pieces on the life of an ordinary woman, and the poet Yosano Akiko (1878–1942). The other writers followed, including Miyamoto Yuriko and the writers of her generation, who actively wrote semi-autobiographical fiction in the Taisho (1912–25) and Showa (1925–89) periods. The works of Enchi Fumiko (1905–86) and Koda Aya (1904–90) became popular after World War II. In the 1950s the so-called first wave of women writers emerged. Writers like Sono Ayako (b. 1931), Ariyoshi Sawako (1931–84), Kurahashi Yumiko (b. 1935), and Setouchi Harumi (b. 1922) were followed by a second wave of writers: Kono Taeko (b. 1926), Tanabe Seiko (b. 1928), Tsumura Setsuko (b. 1928), Oba Minako (b. 1930), Takahashi Takako (b. 1932), Tomioka Taeko (b. 1935), Kanai Mieko (b. 1947), and Tsushima Yuko (b. 1947).[4] In the works of these postwar writers, the subject matter expanded to include hatred of motherhood, womanhood, or women's bodies; some wrote on social and political issues, unlike the prewar writers.[5]

In recent years the number of Japanese writers who are women has grown, partly because "women's literature" is now being promoted commercially, sometimes involving lucrative film or television adaptations. The recipients of the prestigious Akutagawa and Naoki literary awards include more and more women. If one includes such contemporary best-selling writers as Hayashi Mariko, Yamada Eimi, and Yoshimoto Banana, it indeed appears that women are flourishing on the Japanese literary scene.

Yet to conclude from this evidence that women occupy a prestigious position in the Japanese literary establishment would not be quite correct. Even though many of them have excellent reputations, their literature is still largely relegated to the confines of women's literature. Compared with men's literature, women's literature occupies only a secondary status in the orthodoxy of the Japanese literary establishment. In fact, as in the West, women's works are almost always classified by Japanese literary scholarship as *joryu bungaku* (female-school literature), which treats subjects peculiar to women, as opposed to *bungaku* (literature), which treats subjects considered universal, serious, and important (Hijiya-Kirschnereit 1986, 11). The arrangement of typical *bungaku zenshu* (complete works of literature series) well proves this point. Women's works are customarily put together in separate volumes, regardless of their differences in style or the time in which they lived.

As pointed out by many female writers and scholars, such categories are clearly a product of male culture.[6] Of course, for generations the very nature of literature that all but excluded women ensured that the pre-Meiji works by women were appropriated by male scholars and philologists. This tradition has continued into present-day literary scholarship. Works after the Meiji period are often divided into *kindai Nihon bungaku* (modern Japanese literature) and *gendai bungaku* (contemporary Japanese literature); the evaluation of these, too, has remained exclusively in the hands of male writers and critics. Among those active in the elite Tokyo coterie *(bundan)* in the Taisho and early Showa periods were naturalist *(shizenshugi)* writers and the White Birch *(shirakabaha)* group. Centering around small-scale literary journals circulated among a small number of literature lovers, these people actively wrote and set the standard of the literature of their day (Fowler 1988, 131–32).

The Tokyo coterie eventually dissipated as political pressure forced them to cooperate with the wartime effort. Also, commercialism gradually took over in the Showa period. Publishers became interested in selling more copies of books, rather than small-scale journals and magazines written by specialists (ibid., 141). Next came the age of postwar *bundan*, which includes the established writers and critics, some free-lancers, and others belonging to academic institutions. This group includes people such as Kobayashi Hideo, Ito Sei, Hirano Ken, Nakamura Mitsuo, Kato Shuichi, Maruya Saiichi, Eto Jun, and Karatani Kojin, to name a few.

Looking over the past one hundred years of Japanese literary culture, however, one has a hard time finding women who were included in the mainstream literary criticism. In fact, the sheer numbers of Japanese women writers recognized in this century tend to obscure the fact that women have hardly been represented in the evaluative body of the core Japanese literary institutions. In the words of the feminist critic Ueno Chizuko (1993, 5):

> The predominance of men in literature has been fostered and perpetuated by well-entrenched patterns in publishing, reviewing, and marketing literary works. There is only a handful of female critics, leaving men to virtually monopolize the field as well as the screening committees for the major literary prizes given to works considered "superior."[7]

It is normally the case that the critical commentary and introduction attached to a literary work or volume are written by major *bundan* male critics, as is most typically observed in the *bungaku zenshu* published by Chuokoron, *Nihon no bungaku* (Japanese literature, 1964–1970). Even in the eight volumes of *Gendai no joryu bungaku* (Modern women's literature, 1974–1975), published by the Mainichi Newspaper company and edited by women writers, Enchi Fumiko and Sata Ineko, the critical essays about the works are all written by male critics. The most glaring example is *Gendai nihon bungaku zenshu* (Complete works of contemporary Japanese literature, 1956–1959), which includes three volumes containing major critical essays by literary critics from the Meiji period to the 1950s: out of a total of eighty-six critics, there is not a *single* woman.

Books on female-school literature are also often written and edited by male critics and scholars: for example, *Shintei Meiji joryu sakkaron* (A newly revised account of Meiji women writers) (1983) and *Monogatari joryu bundanshi* (An anecdotal history of women writers, vol. 2, 1977.)[8] Almost all book reviews on Japanese literature in major newspapers and magazines are done by *bundan* male critics as well. Even though the recent rise of feminist scholarship is gradually challenging and changing this situation, still, as far as the mainstream literary criticism is concerned, women's participation is extremely limited.[9]

Women's works are evaluated and institutionalized as female-school literature in this heavily male-dominated literary milieu, meaning that, if a writer is not recognized as one of the major writers by *bundan* male critics, she is more than likely not to be included in the canon of Japanese literature.[10] In what follows I will explore Amino's exclusion from the literary canon by examining the representation of women in her works—women who defy the established category of "woman." For a comparison, I will also look at the representation of women in the works of women writers contemporary with Amino who are considered to be major—namely, Hayashi Fumiko, Hirabayashi Taiko, Miyamoto Yuriko, Tsuboi Sakae, and Uno Chiyo. The investigation will reveal that the major difference between their works and Amino's works is that, in the former case, women are always constructed in relationship to men. The conclusion suggests that the implication in Amino's work of the "woman alone" and the "female grotesque" in the context of compulsory heterosexual economy has much to do with Amino Kiku's exclusion from the Japanese literary canon.

A Profile of Amino Kiku

Amino Kiku was born to the family of a self-employed harness manufacturer in 1900.[11] Her mother was from Tatsuno in Nagano prefecture. Amino's childhood was full of turmoil. Having had an affair with a younger man, her mother was abandoned by her family and later publicly accused of adultery in a lawsuit pressed by her father, when Amino was seven. Then three stepmothers came one after another, all of whom either died or disappeared. Her biography says that, when the second mother died and the third mother was to come, Amino attempted suicide. Her childhood often became the subject of her writings. Even though her upbringing was not a happy one, at least her father's business was going well, especially after the Russo-Japanese War (1904–5), when war supplies such as harnesses became in great demand. Amino was allowed to take lessons in classical Japanese singing and guitar.

After finishing girls' high school, she was to take sewing lessons, but, because she was a good student, her parents reluctantly gave her permission to go to a women's college. In 1916 Amino entered Japan Woman's University (Nihon joshi daigaku) to study English literature. Miyamoto Yuriko was her classmate. After graduating in 1920, she started publishing her work while serving on the editorial staff of the university alumnae newsletter. Her first published work was *Aki* (Autumn, 1920). Between 1922 and 1925 she attended lectures in the Russian Department at Waseda University. On the recommendation of Shiga Naoya (1883–1971), Amino's lifetime mentor and friend, her two works, *Ie* (The Family, 1925) and *Mitsuko* (1926), were published.

In 1930 Amino married and went to Manchuria with her husband. In 1938 they divorced. This experience is depicted in *Tsumatachi* (Wives, 1943). During World War II she produced such collections of stories as *Wakai hi* (Youth, 1942), *Itoko* (Cousins, 1943), and *Yuki no yama* (Snowy Mountains, 1943). Representative works after the war include *Tsukimono* (Possessed by Evil Spirits, 1946) and *Kin no kan* (The Golden Casket, 1947), for which she received the Women Writers' Award. From time to time she also translated Russian and English works, including children's stories, such as *Hi no tori* (Firebirds, 1955) and *Semushi no kouma* (A Hunch-back Pony, 1957). She also wrote a biography of Charlotte Brontë (*Sharotto Bronte den*, 1942).

Amino's works received more and more public recognition, especially after *Sakura no hana* (Cherry Blossoms, 1961), which brought her yet two more literary awards. The succeeding works, *Yureru ashi* (Blown Reed, 1964) and *Ichigo ichie* (The Crucial Encounter, 1967), which received the Yomiuri Literary Award, were also successful. The following year she received the Japan Art Academy Award. She continued to write until her death. Her later works include *Enzan no yuki* (Snow in the Distant Mountains, 1971), *Hi no sasu heya* (A Room with Sunlight, 1975), and a collection of essays, *Kokoro no saigetsu* (Years in My Heart, 1972). She died in 1978 at the age of seventy-eight.

Representations of Women in Writings by Amino's Contemporaries

We will now look at the literary representation of women in the works of female-school writers contemporaneous with Amino—namely, Miyamoto Yuriko, Hayashi Fumiko, Hirabayashi Taiko, Tsuboi Sakae, and Uno Chiyo. They provide a good comparison, since they all were born at the turn of the century and, like Amino, wrote semi-autobiographical fiction in one form or another. For this analysis I have selected those works with a reputation for being fairly representative of each author. Let me note at the outset that it is not my intention here to devalue the merits of works by these authors; separate levels of analyses of their works are certainly important. For the purpose of this essay, however, I must risk reducing their texts for representational analysis.

Let us first look at the women in the texts of Miyamoto Yuriko and Hirabayashi Taiko, both of whom were successful proletarian writers. Miyamoto, probably the best known of all, is remembered for her leftist activity in political movements against the dictatorial military government of the prewar period. Despite the active revolutionary "proletarian writer" label put on Miyamoto, the women she constructed in her texts are often faithful and dedicated to the men who are the center of their lives.

For example, *Banshu heiya* (Banshu plain, 1947),[12] considered to be one of her most successful works, is about the life of a woman, Hiroko, during World War II. It is said to be a political work, envisioning a positive future for communism in Japan. Yet a close reading reveals it to be as much a study of the main character's struggle to be a good, loyal wife and daughter-in-law in a male-centered family system.

Hiroko's husband, Jukichi, is jailed for his leftist activities during the war. Hiroko, herself an active member of the proletarian movement, is a good caretaker who supports her husband and his family both financially and morally during his twelve-year absence. Frequent visits to his prison, more than a thousand letters written to him, and her care for his family matters attest to her devotion as a patient and enduring wife who waits for her husband with heroic martyrdom.

A theme showing the helplessness of women is repeated throughout the text. For example, while helping the husband's family after they are victimized by a flood, the heroine sighs, thinking that, if only her husband or his brothers had been there, the family would not have suffered so. The household of women without men is physically and emotionally vulnerable. In spite of the fact that Hiroko is such a reliable, strong woman, she thinks that it would be difficult to live without her husband. The hope that her husband will be released from prison someday is the only thing that sustains her. She admits, however, that her loyalty and love toward her husband are probably pretty one-sided, because her husband does not need her as much as she needs him: "Hiroko could not think of life without Jukichi. But she knew well that Jukichi would live the kind of life he chose, whether or not she was with him. Hiroko realized this more than once during those hard enduring years" (Miyamoto 1975, 7:346). After the Peace Preservation Law is abolished,[13] the news of the release of political prisoners is announced. Hiroko excitedly sets out on her journey east to see her husband who is returning from a penitentiary in Abashiri, Hokkaido.

Fuchiso (The weathervane plant, 1947), obviously a continuation of *Banshu heiya*, is about Hiroko and her husband, Jukichi, who has now been released from jail. After a period of recuperation Jukichi returns to his leftist political activity. The book ends with a depiction of a communist meeting, with moving scenes of the release of leftist prisoners, including Jukichi. This text is viewed as another installment in Yuriko's ardent expression of excitement at building a proletarian society in the new Japan, yet, when one focuses on the interaction between Hiroko and Jukichi, the book seems as much about the relationship and power struggle between a husband and wife.

In fact, most of the episodes that unfold after Jukichi's release clearly show his attitude as the head of a family and Hiroko's puzzlement. One day, for example, the two go out, and, while riding on a train, Jukichi criticizes Hiroko for being "widowlike," for working too hard and losing her femininity. Hiroko's feelings are deeply hurt, and she cries. She has been battling with life alone during his absence; it has been hard to survive and support not only her husband but also his family. She feels she should be appreciated, not criticized. Later, however, she thanks him for pointing out her shortcoming, something she says she did not notice.

In spite of her doubts, outwardly Hiroko never argues, never explains, and certainly never takes issue with him; instead, she simply accepts whatever her husband says to keep peace at any cost. What emerges here is a power play between a husband, who tries to put his wife under his control, and his wife, who struggles to be good and obedient and to submit to him.[14]

Hirabayashi Taiko is another proletarian writer who wrote about her life with a husband engaged in leftist politics. Her noted novel *Seryoshitsu* (At a clinic, 1927) is about a sick and pregnant protagonist in Dalian, China, shortly before World War II. She, her husband, and his group are arrested and charged with the terrorist activity of bombing trains. She suffers from beriberi, from her pregnancy, and can hardly move. In a basement room at a clinic of a hospital filled with humidity and odor, unattended like a stray dog, she gives birth. The baby soon dies of malnutrition. Though having gone through all these sacrifices, she thinks to herself:

I will not blame my husband. It was obvious to me that such terrorist activities would certainly result in this kind of messy imprisonment. At the time of planning, my husband and three members laughed at my hesitation, saying that it was the timid conservatism of a pregnant woman. But the outcome is just what I anticipated. Still, if we cannot accomplish anything without terrorism, I guess

> I must do as they say. That's the obligation of political activists. It is also the duty of a wife to her husband. Hence, I have no regrets. (Hirabayashi and Ohara 1969, 48:8)

A woman protagonist in *Hitori iku* (Walking alone, 1946) is incarcerated for outlawed activities together with her husband. She has been relocated to a prison in the suburbs of Tokyo from the prison where she was kept with him, because she always looked in the direction of her husband's cell. The new prison is cold, and she suffers from tuberculosis. The only thing that occupies her mind is her sickly husband; she worries about his health and well-being more than her own. A husband to her is a father and child, both at the same time. She says: "I cannot possibly leave my husband and die, a husband who is like my only son and yet like my own father. Thinking this and that about my husband, I really started believing that he is the child I gave birth to" (Ibid., 67).

The women Hirabayashi wrote about are, like Yuriko's, political activists, intellectual women who write and publish. And yet a closer examination shows them to be loyal and faithful women who believe that following their husband is "the way of a wife." To them political interests are often secondary to their concern and preoccupation with their husbands, so much so that they adjust themselves to their husbands' ideas and ways even against their wills. At times doubts do occur to them about their subordinate roles, but they immediately give them up in the name of "feminine virtues." These women are also dedicated, nurturing mothers, lovingly taking care of their husbands, whom they treat as their own children.

In a different view of womanhood Hayashi Fumiko and Uno Chiyo wrote about a woman's intense jealousies toward the "other woman" in love triangles. The story in Hayashi's noted *Ukigumo* (Drifting clouds, 1951) is about a woman's obsession and suffering in a relationship with a nihilistic and emotionally unavailable man.[15] The heroine, Yukiko, a typist, meets Tomioka, a specialist sent by the Ministry of Agriculture and Forestry in French Indochina during World War II. Their passionate love affair takes place in the utopian village in which they live unaffected by the war. But their promised life is no longer the same after they return to Japan. In the confusion after the war Tomioka has no job and a wife and parents to support. He lacks the courage and passion to divorce his wife and start a new life with Yukiko. They go through several attempts to separate from each other, including affairs with different partners, but Yukiko is obsessed with this self-destructive man and cannot let him go. The only way out is to commit suicide, but they lack courage for this. When his wife dies, and his other mistress whom he met at a hot spring is killed, he decides to live on a small isolated island, Yakushima, south of Kyushu. Yukiko, though not wanted by Tomioka, clings to him and follows him like a beaten dog in the hope that he will eventually marry her. On the way she becomes ill and dies.

What guides the plot of *Ukigumo* is a woman's masochistic love for a cold and emotionally abusive lover. Tomioka is prone to dangerous affairs: to begin with, he snatches his wife from another man, impregnates a native woman, has an affair with Yukiko, and steals the wife of a tavern owner. He is addicted to a never-ending self-destructive love triangle. Yukiko is constantly jealous of his other women and yet cannot let him go. She is obsessed with this man as much as he is obsessed with the thrill of illicit love affairs that lead nowhere. This fixation ultimately leads to her destruction.

Uno Chiyo's jealous women are often on the other side: wives who suffer from their jealousies for their husband's other woman. In *Sasu* (To stab, 1966) the narrator and her husband have a successful publishing business right after World War II.[16] Because the narrator is older than her husband, she is constantly threatened by and jealous of younger women dancers with whom her husband associates, and she takes dance lessons to compete with these girls. Even though she finds that he is having an affair with another woman, afraid to face the truth, she busies herself with a new business venture and with designing their house. When she is on a trip to France, her husband writes that his affair has ended, but he soon begins others. She suffers from burning jealousies and spends sleepless nights in agony. Although they no longer communicate, each living in opposite ends of the house, she does not have the courage to bring up the subject. She cannot confront her husband because of her fear that the marriage would break up if she did. The story ends when her husband finally asks her for a divorce and decides to move out.

In *Ohan* (1957) Uno depicted a very different woman, an all-forgiving, eternal woman who has no feelings of jealousy and thinks only of the happiness of her man.[17] Unlike other works, the story is narrated by Ohan's husband in the manner of flashbacks. At the beginning Ohan and her dissipated husband separate when he has a geisha as a mistress. Some years later they happen to meet on the street, and their relationship is rekindled because of their son. He promises Ohan that they will reunite. When the boy is drowned in a river on a rainy day, however, Ohan disappears, leaving a letter. In it she says that she does not want to disturb the happiness of his life with his mistress and that she has been made extremely happy just by knowing that she was loved by him. She concludes that she only hopes he will continue to care for his mistress. Ohan is a selfless martyr wife, who thinks only of her husband's happiness at the expense of her own life.

This figure leads to the next category, the cultural ideal of the eternal mother, and no writer portrays this ideal womanhood as eloquently as Tsuboi Sakae. In her popular *Nijushi no hitomi* (Twenty-four eyes, 1952),[18] the protagonist, the teacher Oishi, is a newly appointed elementary schoolteacher at a small branch school in a village along a cape on Shodoshima Island. At first her students and their parents dislike her and treat her coldly, but after a while they begin to understand her genuine love and concern for their children and change their attitude. One day Oishi injures her leg, and, when commuting becomes difficult, she is transferred to the main branch school in a nearby town. Several years later the village children start commuting to the main branch school, and Oishi's contact with her students resumes.

Soon World War II breaks out, and a hard and enduring wartime life begins. Oishi loses her mother, husband, and a child and is left with her two sons. The whereabouts of her students are unknown. When the war finally ends Oishi returns to work at the old branch school in the village. The story ends when her former students come back and a class reunion is held.

Teacher Oishi's love for her students fits the ideal of a nurturing mother. She cries at her students' troubles, and she tries to help them with their family difficulties and financial problems. Oishi represents the all-giving selfless mother-woman who will do anything for her students/children.

Representation of Women in the Writings of Amino Kiku

Unlike the women in the texts of these authors, whose lives largely revolve around men, Amino's women are not in relationships with men, which means they are out of circulation among them.[19] Her early piece, *Umibe* (By the seaside, 1942), for example, tells a story of two young women on a trip to a nunnery by the quiet seaside. Teiko and Haruko, students in a women's school, visit this nunnery to finish their school theses. There are other female students, their teacher (a woman), and a runaway wife staying there as well. The narration advances by contrasting the quiet life of the nuns and the wishful and yet unsettled lives of young women. Currently, all of these women have little to do with men. Teiko seems to have some interest in men, but nothing is happening in her life; Haruko has several suitors but never takes them seriously. Her housemates, two students and their teacher, are passionately involved in the pursuit of knowledge and the change of women's status in Japan. The runaway wife, a piano teacher, wants to break away from her husband, who does not support her career. And, of course, the nuns carry on a quiet life out of touch with the world of men. The nunnery is a utopian shelter for single women.

Amino's women often express discontent with life centered around a man and marriage. In *Tsukimono* (Possessed by evil spirits), for example, the heroine, Hiro, has four different mothers (one real mother and three stepmothers). When her father marries for the fourth time, Hiro talks to herself as follows:

A year later, Hiro's father married again. Hiro herself, under stress, unwillingly married. This marriage made her realize the constant toil expected of a wife in a Japanese family. About a year after Hiro's marriage, her father and his fourth wife had a baby girl. Looking at the face of the new-born infant, Hiro felt sorry for her, thinking "this baby too will have to go through various hardships in life as a woman." (Nogami and Amino 1965, 337–38)

In *Wakare* (*Separation*, 1940) Yoshino cannot bear a child and expresses her discontent at the idea of living with her husband's family.[20] This event is in a sharp contrast with Hiroko in Miyamoto's *Banshu heiya* (The Banshu plain), who tries financially and emotionally to help her husband's family for twelve years during his absence.

Likewise, Amino depicts the internal consciousness of a single woman without children, who is outside of the patriarchal family system. In *Tsumetai kokoro* (Cold heart, 1946),[21] the heroine's indifference to a sickly kitten is depicted in a detached manner. Ume moves into a small shack, which used to be a henhouse. She does not like cats, but, fearing rats, she decides to keep one. The kitten she has received from an acquaintance demands constant care, but Ume pays little attention to it, and, eventually, the kitten dies. She feels guilty and thinks of a comment by her former mother-in-law: "Childless women are cold." She does not deny it and thinks that it is indeed due to her childlessness that the kitten has died.

In *Hitorigurashi* (Living alone, 1959), the heroine, Yoshiko, feels a little lonely thinking about her own future when hearing about a writer, Nagai Kafu, who died alone. A cleaning lady found him in the morning. Yoshiko suspects that there might be no one with her when she herself dies, yet she feels encouraged by Kafu, who disliked people and, like her, favored solitude. She takes each day as it comes and lives a quiet, peaceful life.

Above all what uniquely characterizes Amino's women is that they have real bodies—bodies that are not aesthetic or sensual but, rather, bodies that may be injured or diseased, bodies that excrete and menstruate. For example, in *Mitsuko* (1926), which is about the difficult relationship between the heroine, Mitsuko, and her stepmother, the stepmother is hospitalized because of typhoid fever. When Mitsuko visits her in the hospital, a nurse is attending her stepmother. The stepmother does not quite like this nurse, who is not very gentle. When the nurse tries to comb the mother's hair, she cries hysterically, "Stop it, stop it, please!" After a while she says she has to have a bowel movement and asks for a portable toilet. Mitsuko tries not to look at what the nurse is doing, pretending she has no interest. The stepmother, with her eyes closed, appears to have no will to resist and quietly lets the nurse do what she must.

> "I have felt like a movement since this morning, but I couldn't quite . . . ," said the mother in a low voice.
> Mitsuko, with a show of cheerfulness, said, "Yes, I understand. You are just not used to this."
> When the nurse finished cleaning up, the mother said more than once, "Was it OK? Did I do it all right?" Mitsuko asked the nurse.
> She said immediately, "Yes, that's fine."
> Mitsuko told the mother, "Your nurse said that's fine," but she did not have enough kindness to check it herself. (Amino 1969, 1:64)

Keiko, the protagonist of *Kin no kan* (The golden casket, 1947), suffers from a type of fungal infection.

When she began her translation work, the fungus on her hands and feet spread. Also for some unknown reason her face puffed up like a drowned body. Not only could she not work but she could not do her hair or wear a sash because of the bandage on her hands. She barely survived with the help of a young maid at her father's house. . . . By the end of August her hands healed a little, but the condition of her feet worsened because she had stood for over two hours at the funeral of her friend, a senior woman writer. Keiko applied gauze with ointment to the wound along with oil paper, and then put a thick bandage over it. Still the pus dripped down and it was very unpleasant to her. . . .

Keiko and her stepmother did not stay for Takayoshi's wake. Keiko did not go to the seventh day service either. It was partly because of her infected feet which left ugly pus marks on the clean floor of Miyoko's house. (Nogami and Amino 1965, 385 and 394)

In *Akai kaaneishon* (Red carnations, 1950) the heroine, Yoshiko, is close to her sister, Umeko. This beautiful sister has a disease and goes through an operation for an intestinal obstruction. Umeko's physical condition after the operation is described in great detail:

Feeling wet and uncomfortable, Umeko asked for a bandage change. A nurse told her to just leave it, but Umeko repeated the request. The nurse and Yoshiko undressed the wound.

A bad smell suddenly attacked their nostrils. What they found was that excrement that should be discharged from the anus had come from the old wound [in the stomach].

"Oh, Good! You must feel clean now. I'm sure gas was released too. It's good that all the body waste is gone," said Yoshiko to Umeko. (Ibid., 417)

Umeko was concerned that it was the time for the last penicillin shot of the day. The assistant went out of the room to call a duty nurse.

Umeko said to Yoshiko, "Bad timing, my period just started . . ."

"Oh? Even after that big operation? I thought when one is seriously ill, the period normally stops. Well, but, that must mean you are in good physical condition. You cannot eat right now, but the blood transfusion probably is giving you nourishment." So Yoshiko consoled her, while, at the same time, thinking to herself, "What bad timing this is. Even a healthy person becomes weak during a period." (424)

As these examples show, the woman's body in Amino's texts is cast directly and boldly. In the texts of Hirabayashi, too, the woman's body is detailed, but this body is that of a pregnant mother or a wife welcoming her husband. The woman's body of Amino is not for men: it is not the body of a virgin or of a sensual, grown-up woman, nor is this body for reproduction.

According to the theories of body politics as developed in the past decade, the image of the disorderly woman or the bodily grotesque is subversive (Mikhail Bakhtin, 1968; Natalie Z. Davis 1975; Julia Kristeva 1982; Peter

Stallybrass and Allon White 1986; Miriam Silverberg 1991).[22] It is possible to view the bodies of Amino's women as subverting the body of the woman tamed and appropriated by the dominant ideology of patriarchy. Amino's women assert the otherness of their existence through their bodies, which produce excess, blood, and defecation, having nothing to do with the seducer or the container of penis (Hite 1988, 133–34). Their "grotesque bodies" exist for the benefit not of men but, rather, of themselves. This body demystifies and degrades the idealized femininity prescribed by the patriarchal symbology. As the entity outside the system, it cuts through male codes and rules and therefore has a destabilizing power.

Conclusion

For the past decade the cultural meaning of "single women" in literature and history has been explored by scholars and theorists in conjunction with the critique of patriarchy and compulsory heterosexual economy.[23] In this emerging new discourse the heterosexual system, which has long been considered "natural" and "normal," is increasingly looked at as a cultural construct that marginalizes and excludes from effective participation certain groups of people, including single people beyond an acceptable marriageable age (particularly women), homosexual men, and lesbians. Those groups of people have been often labeled as deviant, abnormal, dangerous, and threatening and have been excluded from society because compulsory heterosexuality must be maintained and enforced at all costs in order to maximize continuing patriarchal control.

Unlike the women commonly portrayed in the works of her contemporaries, Amino's women clearly belong to an excluded group, the category of single women. They are unattached to men; they have no romantic expectations about men; they are disillusioned and disappointed by marriage; they do not want to live with the husband's family; and they have no children. Furthermore, they have life-sized adult bodies that are not sensual or aesthetic nor organized for reproduction. Their bodies are infected, and they menstruate and produce bodily wastes. Amino's women do not fit smoothly into the culturally defined signifiers of acceptable "women"; their very existence and presence subverts and threatens to nullify the patriarchally dictated gender distinctions. These women are self-representations from inside the marginal/woman's territory. Here lies the primary reason for the exclusion of Amino from the female-school literary canon.

The admission of literary works as "major" is a result of "successful critical promotion" (Robinson 1985, 105), and not any single event. It reflects literary sensibilities, values, and ideologies of certain periods and places. The female-school literature canon in Japanese literature is clearly a cumulative product of a patriarchal culture; it is a "gentlemanly artifact" (106). It is a site in which the hegemonic power is covertly manifested in the form of academic classification of literary knowledge.

One sometimes hears a comment about Amino as a writer who is *"jimi"* (down to earth, subdued), as opposed to *"hade"* (gay, splashy), because she did not write about matters in terms of gender. This comment seems true, but only on the surface: it does not take into account the underlying subversive nature of her works. Thus, it is no accident that Amino, inconvenient to the patriarchal discourse, has come to be valued less and less as the *bundan* version of the history of modern Japanese literature continues to be told. Amino needs to be brought back into the literary mainstream and to be promoted continuously. Such an endeavor will surely lead to the remapping of the canon of Japanese literature, past and present.

NOTES

This chapter is based on the author's Japanese essay "Kafuchoseika no josei bungaku: Amino Kiku wa doko e," *U.S.-Japan Women's Journal*, no. 8 (1990): 83–100; and her English essay "Who's Afraid of Amino Kiku? Gender Conflict and the Literary Canon in Japanese Literature," *International Journal of Social Education*, 6, no.1 (1991): 95–113. Permission to reprint has been granted by the publishers, the U.S.-Japan Women's Center, Palo Alto, California, and the Indiana Council for Social Studies, Muncie, Indiana. Some revisions have been made for the present version.

1. There are many definitions of the word *patriarchy*. I use the term here as Teresa L. Ebert (1988:19) defines it: "The organization and division of all practices and signification in culture in terms of gender and the privileging of one gender over the other, giving males control over female sexuality, fertility, and labor." Though it is said that patriarchy exists transhistorically and globally, it is not one universalizing system; it takes diverse forms and manifestations depending on time and location. The patriarchy in present-day industrial Japan, for example, is intricately intertwined with the development of capitalism. See Ueno 1990.

2. In *L'ordre du discours* (1971) Foucault states that the discursive formation is based upon control and economizing by excluding. It involves external control, internal control, and the control of agents. Within the second category he lists an academic discourse controlled under the name "scholarship" (Uchida 1990:164–66). In all of his writings Foucault targeted the critique of the notion of "humans beings" in the modern West, but he rejected any notion of identity politics which replaces "human beings." It is my position that we should learn from the insight of Foucault and other poststructuralist critics who put the subject into critical interrogation, but my essay, which is a feminist analysis of the Japanese literary institution, presupposes a female identity. Of course, noncritical self-identification without a consideration of the marginalized spaces within must be avoided, but I believe that essentializing (identity politics) is a necessary tool for any political movement against oppression. For a feminist critique of Foucault from the perspective of identity politics, see Horowitz 1987 and Hartsock 1990.

3. Female poets such as Abutsuni, who wrote a well-known travelogue *Izayoi nikki* (1277) in the Kamakura period (1192–1333), and *Kaga no Chiyo* (1703–75) in

the Edo period (1603–1869) were two of the better-known exceptions. The women who gained any prominence in letters during those periods were generally poets.

4. See Yamada 1985, 10–16. For a bibliography on the works of Japanese women writers in English translation, see Mamola 1989.

5. The works of leftist writers such as Miyamoto Yuriko, Hirabayashi Taiko, and Sata Ineko, however, necessarily involve social issues.

6. One female writer, Saegusa Kazuko (1984), however, thinks that *joryu bungaku* is a positive category for women.

7. This scarcity of women in literary criticism in Japan is partly due to the fact that there have been far fewer women in academic institutions. Even today many feminist scholars and researchers are not full-time instructors.

8. *Kindai joryu bungaku* (Modern women's literature, 1983), edited by Nihon bungaku kenkyu shiryo kankokai, is a collection of essays by both male and female researchers, but women account for only 30 percent of the contributors.

9. For the state of art on feminist criticism and research on women's literature in Japan, see Kitada 1991.

10. My project is situated within the emerging feminist discourse in Japan to bring back the female writers buried or forgotten in the patriarchal literary canon. See Kitada 1991.

11. The following sources were used as reference for Amino's life: "Amino Kiku," in Nogami and Amino 1965, 44:515–44); and Nihon Kindai Bungakukan 1977. Her book, *Yureru ashi* (Blown Reed, 1964), is an autobiography of her life.

12. For an English translation of *Banshu heiya*, see Miyamoto 1963, 1986.

13. The Peace Preservation Law, originally enacted in 1887, was amended from time to time over the years. The new Peace Preservation Law of 1925, designed to suppress communist activities, prohibited groups that harbored dangerous thoughts or might advocate a change in Japanese political forms or the private property system. It remained in effect until it was abolished in October 1945, following Japan's defeat in World War II.

14. Miyamoto wrote about different kinds of women in other works: her most well-known, *Nobuko* (1926), for example, is about the heroine's difficult growth process through marriage and divorce, toward independence.

15. For an English translation of *Ukigumo*, see Hayashi 1957.

16. For an English translation of *Sasu*, see Uno 1991.

17. For an English translation of *Ohan*, see Uno 1961.

18. For an English translation of *Nijushi no hitomi*, see Tsuboi 1983.

19. These authors, however, have some works that do not fit this characterization.

20. For an English translation of *Wakare*, see Amino 1991.

21. This is the date Amino completed *Tsumetai kokoro*. This short story appears in Nogami and Amino 1965, but the date of the first publication is not clear.

22. For a general introduction to the subject and references, see Russo 1986.

23. See, for example, Auerbach 1982, special issue of *Journal of Family History* 1984; Vicinus 1985; Doan 1991; special issue of *Rekishi hyoron* (1992). For a critique of heterosexuality from a lesbian perspective, see Rich 1980.

REFERENCES

Amino, Kiku. 1991. "Separation" (Wakare). Trans. Chieko M. Ariga. *Manoa: A Pacific Journal of International Writing* 3, no. 2 (Fall).

————. 1969. *Amino Kiku zenshu* (The complete works of Amino Kiku). 3 vols. Tokyo: Kodansha.

Auerbach, Nina. 1982. *Woman and the Demon: The Life of a Victorian Myth.* Cambridge, Mass. and London: MIT Press.

Bakhtin, Mikhail. 1968. *Rabelais and His World.* Trans. Helene Iswolsky. Cambridge, Mass. and London: MIT Press.

Davis, Natalie Zemon. 1975. *Society and Culture in Early Modern France.* Stanford, Calif.: Stanford University Press.

Doan, Laura L., ed. 1991. *Old Maids to Radical Spinsters: Unmarried Women in the Twentieth-Century Novel.* Urbana and Chicago: University of Illinois Press.

Ebert, Teresa L. 1988. "The Romance of Patriarchy: Ideology, Subjectivity, and Postmodern Feminist Cultural Theory." *Cultural Critique* 10:19–57.

Fowler, Edward. 1988. *The Rhetoric of Confession: Shishosetsu in Early Twentieth-Century Japanese Fiction.* Berkeley, Los Angeles, and London: University of California Press.

Hartsock, Nancy. "Foucault on Power: A Theory for Women?" In *Feminism/Postmodernism*, ed. Linda J. Nicholson. New York and London: Routledge, 1990.

Hayashi, Fumiko. 1964. *Nihon no bungaku*, vol. 47: *Hayashi Fumiko* (Japanese literature, vol. 47: Hayashi Fumiko). Tokyo: Chuokoronsha.

————. 1957. *Floating Cloud* (Ukigumo). Trans. Yoshiyuki Koitabashi. Tokyo: Information Publications.

Hijiya-Kirschnereit, Irmela. 1986. "Joryu bungaku ga bungaku ni naru hi" (The day when women's literature becomes "literature"). *Asahi shimbun*, 2 September, 11.

Hirabayashi, Taiko and Tomie Ohara, 1969. *Nihon no bungaku*, vol. 48: *Hirabayashi Taiko, Ohara Tomie* (Japanese literature, vol. 48: Hirabayashi Taiko and Ohara Tomie). Tokyo: Chuokoronsha.

Hite, Molly. 1988. "Writing—and Reading—the Body: Female Sexuality and Recent Feminist Fiction." *Feminist Studies* 14 (Spring): 121–42.

Horowitz, Gad. 1987. "The Foucaultian Impasse: No Sex, No Self, No Revolution." *Political Theory* 15:61–81.

Iwaya, Daishi. 1977. *Monogatari joryu bundanshi* (An anecdotal history of women writers), vol. 2. Tokyo: Chuokoronsha.

Joryu bungakushakai. 1975. *Gendai no joryu bungaku* (Contemporary women's literature), vol. 7. Tokyo: Mainichi shimbunsha.

Journal of Family History. 1984. Special issue (Winter).

Kitada, Sachie. 1991. "Feminizumu bungakuhihyo no genzai: Nihonhen" (Japanese feminist literary criticism: state of the art). *New Feminism Review* 2:162–71.

Kristeva, Julia. 1982. *Powers of Horror: An Essay on Abjection.* Trans. Leon S. Roudiez. New York: Columbia University Press.

Mamola, Claire Zebroski. 1989. *Japanese Women Writers in English Translation: An Annotated Bibliography.* New York and London: Garland Publishing.

Miyamoto, Yuriko. 1984a. "Banshu Plain" (Banshu heiya, excerpt 1). Trans. Brett de Bary, *Bulletin of Concerned Asian Scholars* 16, no. 2 (April–June): 40–45.

————. 1984b. "The Weathervane Plant" (Fuchiso, excerpt). Trans. Brett de Bary. *Bulletin of Concerned Asian Scholars* 16, no. 2 (April–June): 46–47.

————. 1975. *Gendai no joryu bungaku* (Contemporary women's literature), vol. 7. Tokyo: Mainichi shimbunsha.

————. 1969. *Nihon no bungaku* (Japanese literature), vol. 45: *Miyamoto Yuriko* (Tokyo: Chuokoronsha.

———. 1963. "Banshu Plain" (Banshu heiya, excerpt 2). Trans. Yukiko Sakaguchi and Jay Gluck. In *Ukiyo*, ed. J. Gluck. New York: Vanguard Press.

Nihon bungaku kenkyu shiryo kankokai, ed. 1983. *Kindai joryu bungaku* (Modern Japanese literature by women). Tokyo: Yuseido.

Nihon kindai bungakukan. 1977. *Nihon kindai bungaku daijiten* (Comprehensive dictionary of modern Japanese literature), s.v. "Amino Kiku."

Nogami, Yaeko, and Kiku Amino. 1965. *Nihon no bungaku*, vol. 44: *Nogami Yaeko, Amino Kiku* (Japanese literature, vol. 44: Nogami Yaeko and Amino Kiku). Tokyo: Chuokoronsha.

Odagiri, Hideo. 1971. *Nihon kindai bungaku no shiso to jokyo* (Ideology and circumstances of modern Japanese literature). Tokyo: Hosei daigaku.

Rekishi hyoron. 1992. Special issue on "Rekishi no naka no shinguru" (Singles in history), no. 503 (March).

Rich, Adrienne. 1980. "Compulsory Heterosexuality and Lesbian Existence." *Signs* 5, no. 4: 631–60.

Robinson, Lillian. 1985. "Treason Our Text: Feminist Challenges to the Literary Canon." In *New Feminist Criticism: Essays on Women, Literature, and Theory*, ed. Elaine Showalter. New York: Pantheon Books.

Russo, Mary. 1986. "Female Grotesques: Carnival and Theory." In *Feminist Studies, Critical Studies*, ed. Teresa de Lauretis. Bloomington: Indiana University Press.

Saegusa, Kazuko. 1984. *Sayonara otoko no jidai* (Good-bye to the age of men). Tokyo: Jinbun shoin.

Sata, Ineko, and Sakae Tsuboi. 1968. *Nihon no bungaku*, vol. 49: *Sata, Ineko, Tsuboi Sakae* (Japanese literature, vol. 49: Sata Ineko and Tsuboi Sakae). Tokyo: Chuokoronsha.

Shioda, Ryohei. 1983. *Shintei Meiji joryu sakkaron* (A newly revised account of Meiji women writers). Tokyo: Bunsendo.

Silverberg, Miriam. 1991. "The Modern Girl as Militant." In *Recreating Japanese Women, 1600–1945*, ed. Gail Bernstein. Berkeley, Los Angeles, and Oxford: University of California Press.

Stallybrass, Peter, and Allon White. 1986. *The Politics and Poetics of Transgression*. Ithaca, N.Y.: Cornell University Press.

Tsuboi, Sakae. 1983. *Twenty-Four Eyes* (Nijushi no hitomi). Trans. Akira Miura. Rutland, Vt. and Tokyo: Tuttle.

Uchida, Ryuzo. 1990. *Misheru Fuko* (Michel Foucault). Tokyo: Kodansha.

Ueno, Chizuko. 1993. "The Rise of Feminist Criticism." *Japanese Book News*, no. 2 (Spring): 5, 20.

———. 1990. *Kafuchosei to shihonsei: Marukusushugi feminizumu no chihei* (Patriarchy and capitalism: a horizon for Marxist feminism). Tokyo: Iwanami shoten.

Uno, Chiyo. 1991. "To Stab" (Sasu). Trans. Kyoko Iriye Selden. In *Japanese Women Writers: Twentieth Century Short Fiction*, ed. Noriko Mizuta Lippit and Kyoko Iriye Selden. New York: M. E. Sharpe.

———. 1969. *Nihon no bungaku*, vol. 46: *Uno Chiyo, Okamoto Kanoko* (Japanese literature, vol. 46: Uno Chiyo and Okamoto Kanoko). Tokyo: Chuokoronsha.

———. 1961. "Ohan. " In *The Old Woman, the Wife, and the Archer: Three Modern Japanese Short Novels*, ed. and trans. Donald Keene, 51–118. New York: Viking Press.

Vicinus, Martha. 1985. *Independent Women: Work and Community for Single Women, 1850–1920*. Chicago and London: University of Chicago Press.

Wada, Shigejiro. 1982. *Nihon no kindai bungaku* (Modern Japanese literature). Tokyo: Dobosha.

Yamada, Yusaku. 1985. *Joryu bungaku no genzai* (The current status of women's literature). Tokyo: Gakujutsutosho shuppansha.

Yoshida, Seiichi, ed. 1969. *Joryu bungakushi* (History of female-school literature). Tokyo: Dobun shoin.

Three Women Artists of the Meiji Period (1868–1912): Reconsidering Their Significance from a Feminist Perspective

❖ ❖ ❖

Midori Wakakuwa

Translated by Naoko Aoki

Women artists have been recorded in the history of art of Western Europe since the times of ancient Greece, increasing in number and quality during the sixteenth century. Although the sexist ideology characteristic of Christianity had decisive influence on the absence of women in the history of art, Renaissance humanism produced many women artists, to the extent that Giorgio Vasari (1568) felt obliged to describe some of them in his very well-known book.

The number of women artists in modern times is innumerable. Their works and lives, however, have never been given the place in the history of art which they justly deserve. Linda Nocklin (1992) declared the absence of "great" women artists in her memorable thesis, and spurred a reevaluation of these artists. All subsequent publications in the field, including the only example in Japan by the present author (Wakakuwa 1985), are in line with Nocklin's thesis.

Japan has had far fewer women artists than Western Europe. The primary reason is that patriarchal power has always had a more pervasive and persistent influence on every aspect of society in Japan. In the Western world the birth of humanistic thought, which recognized the concepts of dignity and freedom, contributed to the development of the idea of equality among human beings, including women, although it did not directly effect change in women's position in society and the family. This humanistic thought had an important influence on the development of democratic political ideals in modern Western societies. In the Japanese case, however, prior to the Meiji period there was no such countervailing force against the persistent patriarchal system and its ideology because a rigid feudalistic structure was fundamentally sustained by this ideology. Another factor that affected the situation of Japanese women in the Edo, or Tokugawa, period (1603–1867) was the influence of Confucian ideology. Confucianism is a philosophy that prescribes as its moral basis a hierarchical order—such as a ruler and his subjects, a father and his children, a husband and his wife. It is basically an organizational prescription of male order in society.

There had been, as a matter of fact, some women artists in the Edo period, such as, for example, the poet-painter Ema Saiko. The emergence of a bourgeois class and its own cultural power led to the flourishing of a new culture called *chonin bunka* (bourgeois culture) *within* the feudalistic-Confucian paradigm. As in Europe in the sixteenth and seventeenth centuries, there were more opportunities for women to become artists than in the medieval period. These women, however, were almost exclusively daughters of artists, who were able to acquire the necessary professional training in a master's studio. I have enumerated several examples, from the Italian painter Artemisia Gentileschi (ca. 1597–after 1651) to the French painter Rosa Bonheur (1822–99) in *Lives of Women Artists* (Wakakuwa 1985). The case of Ema Saiko, which has been described in detail by Patricia Fister (1991), is, however, a very exceptional one. She was, as Fister notes, a *bunjin*, a term that denotes a pedant, or gifted amateur; she was not a professional painter who had trained professionally and received payment for her work.

The Meiji Restoration of 1868 had two contradictory aspects: one, modernization, represented by the destruction of the feudalistic system and the establishment of a modern bureaucracy and a capitalistic economic system in which the bourgeoisie gained power; and, at the same time, retrogressive movement, represented by the restoration of the emperor system and imperialism. The emperor system, headed by a hereditary male "god" who has inherited mythic power since ancient times, was retained as symbol of patriarchal ideology. The Meiji revolution, then, did not signify the destruction of Japan's long-standing gender system.

The Meiji era (1868–1912) nevertheless produced three admirable women painters. One was Yamashita Rin (1857–1939), who left many fine icons in Russian Orthodox churches in Japan. Rin was one of the first Japanese women to have studied abroad. She studied the works of Raffaello Sanzio (Raphael) and Guido Reni at the Hermitage Museum in St. Petersburg and mastered orthodox oil painting techniques. Ragusa Tama (1861–1939) married the Italian artist Vincenzo Ragusa, who was invited by the Japanese government to teach at their newly established academy. Tama went to Italy with her husband and achieved fame as a painter there. Uemura Shoen (1875–1949) came out of the traditional world of ukiyo-e[1] and developed a new genre of Japanese paintings. She was a single mother.

One common characteristic among the three is that they miraculously succeeded in escaping from the strong paternalism of Japanese society and becoming artists. Yamashita and Ragusa physically escaped by leaving the country. Uemura was brought up in a fatherless family and had children outside marriage, seemingly, therefore, escaping patriarchal power. This essay will examine the lives of these three artists.

Yamashita Rin

Yamashita Rin was born to a family of lower-class samurai, or warriors, in Kasama, Ibaraki Prefecture, in 1857. The Tokugawa feudalistic regime that had ruled Japan for about two hundred and sixty years collapsed in 1868, and substantial political power was restored to the imperial family. This marked the birth of a modern imperialist and capitalist nation that was to compete with the rest of the world. The restoration brought drastic reforms in politics, economics, society, and culture in modernizing the country.

One of the most important historical events in Rin's life was the establishment of the policy known as Haihan-Chiken, in 1871. The Tokugawa regime had ruled the country by dividing it into political and geographical units called *han*. Each *han* was governed by a daimyo, or lord, appointed by the government. Everyone who belonged to the samurai class served a daimyo under a feudalistic ruler-subject relationship. With the new policy the Meiji government abolished these *han* and set up prefectures, which were also geographical and political units but of a more centralized and bureaucratic nature. Many of the samurai in Japan lost their jobs, including those in Rin's family. Where Rin lived, daughters of the lower samurai class without any means of livelihood were forced to marry farmers in order to reduce the number of family members the fathers had to support. Before the restoration daughters of the samurai class, which was at the top of the feudalistic social hierarchy, never married farmers. Rin, reportedly, had heard of a samurai woman, who, unable to adapt herself to the lifestyle of her farmer husband's family, killed her children and herself. When Rin learned, therefore, that she herself would be forced to marry a farmer, she decided to leave her family and become financially independent.

Rin ran away from home at the age of fifteen. This tells us two things. The first is that Rin, even then, refused to live a traditional Japanese women's life. Japanese women in feudal times obeyed their fathers' will and followed their husbands when married. A maxim for women which originated in Confucian thinking says, "Women have no home in any of the three worlds." Similarly, the "three obediences" for women contained in the Mahayana Buddhist sutras, which were brought into Japan from China, teach women to "obey your father as a daughter," "once married obey your husband," and "when widowed obey your son." Second, as she says in her autobiography, Rin left home with the explicit intention of becoming independent by pursuing training as a painter, which she had determined was her calling (Oda 1977, 10). Rin's drive to leave home and seek an independent life is quite natural for women in our time, but it was a near impossible decision in feudal

Japan. Rin's act of leaving home itself was one of the first examples of the new ways of living for women which emerged in the early stages of Japan's modernization. It goes without saying that, with no money or connections, her choice was an extremely risky one.

Yamashita Rin started her training as a live-in maid and apprentice at the home of a ukiyo-e painter in Tokyo. We find a fairly large number of copies from ink pictures done in this period. The drawings of prostitutes' lives among them are, of course, far from realistic, and the techniques are manneristic. Although this kind of training was at variance with her natural talents as a painter, it can also be thought to have formed the basis of her extraordinary talent for painting icons, which consist of a set of stereotyped line drawings.

Later Rin was attracted by the newly imported Western realism and went to Nakamura Seijuro for instruction. Fortunately, the Meiji government was trying to introduce technologies from the more highly developed countries as a means of implementing its policies of industrialization and *fukoku-kyohei* (enrich the nation, strengthen the army). As part of this effort, it established an art school in the department of technology of the Imperial University in 1876. Rin applied and was accepted.

The government invited the Italian painter Antonio Fontanesi to teach at the school. He introduced the academic spirit and techniques of Western paintings to Japan for the first time. According to Aoki Shigeru (1986), Fontanesi brought many materials with him and started energetically teaching his Japanese students the techniques and ideas that had been accumulated since the Renaissance period. Fontanesi found it difficult to convey such ideas as perspective, anatomy, and shading, partly because his students lacked basic knowledge in mathematics, geometry, and medicine and partly because he had to depend on an extremely poor translator. Everyone in the class, however, was greatly impressed by "the refined theory of paintings and the refined reference materials," according to Matsuoka Hisashi, one of Fontanesi's students, who later studied in Italy (Oda 1977, 39). We can still see in Rin's sketches of plaster busts and copies proof of Fontanesi's professional teaching.

Rin was a very good student. Her works clearly show talent, a keen eye for observation, sophistication in drawings, and an ability in composition. On one piece of paper for wrapping I found some notes written in India ink taken during a lecture on drawing. Rin wrote, "There are two kinds of drawings; one copies the skeleton of things, the other comes from one's soul." The source is obviously Giorgio Vasari's theory of drawing (1568, 177).

Fontanesi's lectures afforded a unique and valuable opportunity to plant the ideas and techniques of orthodox Western painting in modern Japanese society, but he was obliged to return to Italy due to ill health in 1878. Prospero Ferucci, his successor, failed to gain the trust of the students, and they all quit the school at the same time. Rin had lost the best teacher in her life, and she quit, too.

Rin had become a believer of the Russian Orthodox Church at the urging of a friend. Around the time that she left the art school, Father Nikolai, who was the first propagator of the Russian Orthodox Church in Japan, was feeling the need for new churches and skilled painters. Father Nikolai was planning to send a female friend of Rin's to a convent in St. Petersburg as the first Japanese student of icon painting. However, the woman married just before her departure and gave up her career. Rin was chosen as her replacement. It can be thought that Rin accepted the offer only for personal reasons; she had lost her financial and educational basis. In order to live, paint, and be independent, she had no other choice than to stay with the Russian Orthodox Church. It is true that Rin was a professional icon painter, but it is unlikely that religion was more important than art for her.

This choice had one crucial contradiction. Icons in the Russian Orthodox Church are essentially the anonymous art of the Middle Ages, which does not require artistic originality. It is obvious, however, from her talent and her way of life that Rin possessed a strong individuality. She had put herself in the flow of Western realism and acquired orthodox techniques and theories of Western modern painting through Fontanesi. She was also influenced by Fontanesi's personal style, as shown in her studies of landscape, which are similar to the works of the Fontainebleau School. If she could have worked as her nature directed, her works would not actually have been Byzantine icons. With money and support Rin could have been an Asai Tadashi, another student of Fontanesi's who developed the early Japanese Western landscape under his influence. Being extremely poor and a woman, which made it difficult to obtain support from the community, Rin had to detour from her original goal. This contradiction would reveal itself in a rather tragic way in St. Petersburg.

In 1880 Yamashita Rin left for St. Petersburg. She worked as a babysitter for a diplomat on the boat. She was full of hopes, but her expectations of life in the Occident were soon destroyed. She did not find herself in the Occident but, instead, in a convent. Living there damaged her both physically and mentally. Rin spent three years in the convent learning manneristic icon production. She was supposed to be there for six years, but she left early because of ill health. In addition to communication problems caused by Rin's poor Russian, the painting assignments were unconvincing for an apprentice who had already studied Western realism. She became absolutely desperate. In a diary she kept in St. Petersburg as a consolation for the solitary mind, Rin criticizes "the ghostly paintings from Greece" given to her as a model (22 December 1881; qtd. in Oda 1977, 121). She also showers abuse on the nuns who, she says, were "simply incompetent." Her pride in her talent as a painter seems to have aroused her colleagues' antipathy. She always felt that everyone was nasty to her and that they were making fun of her. It was probably at this stage in her life that she started drinking. "What seemed to be a hope is now an entrance to despair," she wrote on 7 July 1881 (qtd. in ibid., 82).

Among the monotonous pages in her diary which show us the apprentice silently drawing icons, there is one brilliant, dynamic passage that describes the day she happened to go into the Hermitage Museum. Raphael. Rembrandt. Guido Reni. Tintoretto. Andrea del Sarto. Rin saw their work for the first time in her life. She was delighted. The palace was full of the Occidental tradition that she had dreamed of. She got a leave from the rector and permission to copy the paintings at the museum, which took half an hour by horse-drawn cart to reach. The days she went to the museum were supreme bliss. Rin's diary has a series of statements about them. "Went to the Hermitage" and "Went to the Hermitage again. Copied a head all day. Beard is very difficult" (5 December 1881; qtd. in ibid., 122). For some reason, however, the rector forbade her from going to the museum, as if the Renaissance war against Byzantine paintings was not over yet. Italian paintings were considered harmful influences on painters of traditional icons. Rin was strictly forbidden from painting in her own way. She spent the rest of her days in Russia in despair and melancholy and was sent home, sick and disappointed.

Yamashita Rin's relations have allowed the display of three oil paintings at Nichido Gallery in Kasama. One of them is the head of a saint with a beard. It is obviously the one Rin wrote about in her diary, but it is not just a simple copy. The painting is a combination of two paintings of saints by Guido Reni in the Hermitage Museum. The origin of another painting of the Holy Mother and Child and John, set against a landscape, is unknown. The color tone called "changing" is a characteristic of sixteenth-century Tuscan paintings. The child is close to the ones by Andrea, and the background has the air of late manneristic paintings conserved in the Hermitage Museum. It is a very unique case that a Japanese painter in the late nineteenth century was influenced by sixteenth- and seventeenth-century Italian painting, because of the overwhelming influence of French modern painting, introduced by Kuroda and Fujishima, which became the official mainstream style in Japan. Rin must have been satisfied with these three paintings. She kept them for life.

Rin returned to Japan in 1882 and spent thirty-five years in a convent established by Father Nikolai, painting one hundred and fifty icons for Russian Orthodox churches. Her unsigned icons are still found in churches in the central and northern parts of the country. They are valuable artworks, incomparably unique in style. Her works tell us an interesting fact. Rin's Maria is Byzantine in form, but her style and techniques are baroque. They especially remind us of the humanistic and emotional tone of Guido Reni, Raphael, and Annibale Carracci. Within the constraints imposed by the conventional iconography of Byzantine icons, Rin expressed her own love of Western paintings of the Renaissance and Baroque periods, using an effective play of light and shade with brilliant colors and giving her figures a vivid expression. In her icons we can see the traditional iconography of sacred figures, yet the style is more that of Guido Reni, or at times Raffaello Sanzio (Raphael) and Tintoretto, which are preserved in the Hermitage Museum.

Her depictions of the "Virgin and Child" are represented full of life with humanized expressions, and the biblical scenes are composed in a much more dramatic way than is found in any other Byzantine painting. The art of the mother country of her beloved teacher, Fontanesi, is there with the splendor of passion and humanity.

After the Russian Revolution in 1917 Rin lost her job and went back to her hometown, Kasama. She never painted again. She spent a quiet retired life in the company of flowers and a young son of her nephew. This child, Ogawa Hideo, later wrote a biography of Yamashita (Oda 1977) and is a caretaker of her work. According to Ogawa, Yamashita was in the habit of having tea and a small amount of alcohol. Her later years were spent in clear and bright solitude. From what I know of her, I feel the taciturn peace of a person who did her best to swim across the stormy sea during an age of great change. She never gave up. She must have had no regrets.

Ragusa Tama

Ragusa Tama married Vincenzo Ragusa, an Italian architect who was invited, like Fontanesi, by the Japanese government to teach at the art school of the Imperial University. Her situation may look completely different from Yamashita's, but for both an encounter with a Westerner triggered their self-liberation.

Ragusa Tama was born to a middle-class family and started sitting for Vincenzo at his earnest request. Ragusa had become acquainted with Tama in the large flower garden kept by her parents which he had visited in order to find motifs for his students to paint. Ragusa was collecting Japanese handicrafts of high artistic value and also asked Tama, who had a talent in painting, to sketch the collected pieces for a record. Ragusa taught her the accurate art of Western drawing and the canon of painting mythological and historical themes. Tama acquired the advanced techniques of oil painting in private lessons.

Ragusa Tama lived in Palermo, Sicily, as a successful painter from 1881 to 1933. On her fortieth birthday in 1901 her friends in Palermo gave her a splendid party. There Gaetano Finocchiaro, an Italian poet, dedicated a poem to her which expressed admiration for a beautiful white water lily blooming in unfamiliar soil. Tama's works had received awards at Italian expositions from 1889 forward. In 1910, she not only was invited to exhibit at the International Exposition in New York, representing Italian women painters, but she also received the highest prize in the women artists category. Later she won first prize at the International Exposition of Art in Venice. The Carusos, one of the wealthiest families in Palermo, commissioned Tama to paint the ceiling of a hall. *Apotheosis of Heavenly Music* is painted in baroque style. Tama also taught at a school of art and handicrafts established by her husband.

In spite of her fame in Italy, Tama remained totally unknown in Japan.

The fact can be explained by two factors that played important roles in Japan's modernization process. First, there was a major change within Japanese painting circles. Although Japan, especially the government, was keen on introducing traditional Italian Renaissance into academe and invited Italian artists as "foreigners in government service" in the very early stages, nationalistic tendencies advocated by Ernest Francisco Fenollosa, an American philosopher and art historian, and Okakura Tenshin, a leader of the Japanese art world, soon severely hindered Westernization efforts. Fenollosa and Okakura founded the Kanga-kai in order to encourage the creation of a new style of Japanese painting and to reject the reception of any European manner of painting. This movement had two meanings. Fenollosa fully recognized the high quality of traditional Japanese art and advised Japanese artists to reject the invasion of foreign influences in order to conserve it. His motivation was akin to that of some Westerners who have favored trying to conserve the purity of Asian cultures from Western contamination. Okakura, on the other hand, sought to give new life to the traditional art form in order to assert national identity, which, he felt, faced a crisis from the deluge of Western culture. Their nationalistic tendency triumphed when the Tokyo Bijutsu Gakko (National Academy) was established in 1889 with only the faculties of Japanese painting and Japanese sculpture.

Second, there was a shift in the reception of Western painting. In the first stage, when the government founded Kobu Bijutsu Gakko (National Art School) in 1876, it had invited the Italian painter Fontanesi to Japan to teach an academic and naturalistic style of painting. His students soon gained fame for their realistic representations. Yet Fontanesi left Japan in 1878, after getting beriberi, and in the same year Fenollosa came to Japan. Kobu Bijutsu Gakko was abolished in 1883. It is noteworthy that this school allowed women to enter, whereas its later successor, the Tokyo Bijutsu Gakko, was reserved for men only. There was a nationalistic resurgence that was manifested in various aspects of Japanese social and political life which accompanied the consolidation of imperialism.

The second stage was marked by the return of Kuroda Kiyoteru from Paris in 1882. Kuroda, who had studied under the eclectic (impressionism mixed with academism) painter, Raphael Collin, introduced to Japan a manneristic impressionism whose new technique better fitted the Japanese mentality of the Meiji era than the academic realism that had been brought by the Italians. Kuroda became the first president of the newly founded Tokyo Bijutsu Gakko in 1892. He also organized the Hakuba-kai, which became the most influential artists' group and gained a prominent position in the first Bunten (Official Exposition of Arts) held by the minister of education in 1907.

It is not surprising, therefore, that Tama's style, which developed through the teaching of an Italian architect was, like Yamashita's, seen as outside the major current. Tama's anonymity in Japanese art history was determined when Japan decided to follow France.

Two large paintings by Tama named *Gogatsu no bara* (Roses in May) and

Haru (Spring), now owned by the Tokyo National University of Arts, were done with accurate academic techniques; no postimpressionist techniques were used. Many landscapes and genre paintings produced in Palermo show technical perfection, but many of the themes are of a sentimental literary nature, and, seeing them, I could not help feeling the limitation of the times.

What is important is that Tama concentrated on Western themes to help her husband with his school, out of love and respect for him. Until his death in 1927 Tama felt no contradiction between Japan and Italy. Vincenzo was her world and her entire art world. She went to Italy because that was her husband's country. When he died Tama had no reason to stay there. Naturally, she went to the Japanese Embassy in Rome and applied for permission to return to Japan, but it was denied. As the country was rapidly becoming ultranationalistic, Tama was regarded as a traitor, or immoral woman who had had intercourse with a foreigner. The Japanese administrator in Rome rejected her application. "I was astonished as if I had slipped off the earth into hell. I could not stop crying to think that my connection with Japan had been cut even though I myself had never forgot it." This shock made her forget her native language. When she finally returned to Japan in 1933, according to her niece, she was not able to speak a word of Japanese.

Tama returned to Japan during the Manchurian Incident (1931–37). In 1937 Japan started war against China, which ended with its defeat in World War II in 1945. Tama spent those years in Karuizawa, a resort town in the mountains which was popular among high society in Japan. She spent her time painting plants, never people or historical events. Her paintings of flowers in her later years are almost pure Japanese paintings. We find no trace of the baroque ceiling painting.

Ragusa Tama was a typical woman painter in the sense that she became a painter through her husband. She took his country as her own and pursued her career as a mainstream Western painter. When he died she returned to Japan and to Japanese painting, yet her identity was in the will of the man she loved.

Uemura Shoen

Uemura Shoen was awarded an Order of Cultural Merit by the Japanese government in 1948, the highest honor in Japanese painting circles. Her life, however, was not at all an easy one.

Shoen was born in Kyoto and started learning Japanese painting at the Kyoto Painting School. Later she studied under Suzuki Shonen. In the Kyoto Painting School the training of young painters was conducted in a medieval-style *bottega*, in which apprentices learned techniques in the house of their master. Female apprentices were not rare even in those days, but it was extremely difficult in many ways for them to achieve independence as artists, not the least of which was the custom of almost obligatory marriage, which forced women to give up their careers. Shoen's father died when she was quite young, and her mother worked hard to care for her. Unlike many of the women in Kyoto, Shoen was able to concentrate on her painting without the business of housekeeping and nursing, because her family did not have a patriarch. Her mother, Nakako, to whom Shoen devoted many pages in her autobiography, *Seibisho* (n.d.), managed the housekeeping and, after Uemura had an illegitimate child, took care of the child.

Uemura was the "man" in the family: she was the head of the family and the breadwinner. Cases like hers are fairly common in the history of Western art, though rare in Japan. For example, Angelika Kauffmann and Marie Elisabeth Louise Vigee Lebrun, who were well known in eighteenth-century European painting circles, supported their families. Marie Laurencin and Suzanne Valadon, born "illegitimate," were thus also without a father as head of the family. My own research (Wakakuwa 1985) on twelve female painters, eight European, and four Japanese—ranging from the Italian painter Artemisia Gentileschi to the contemporary Japanese artist Tada Minami—has revealed that the women who were able to pursue their artistic careers were without a patriarch to make decisions about their lives. When the ruling power of the family was not in the hands of a man, daughters were not forced into marriage. They may actually have been discouraged from marriage in order to keep a breadwinner in the family.

Yet Uemura, like most young women, wanted marriage. She once explained that one of her early works, *Jinsei no hana* (Life's bloom), in which she painted a bride dressed for the wedding, was the dream of her youthful days. She also often painted mothers and children. In these paintings a married woman with her eyebrows freshly shaved happily nurses her baby. Although the models were her mother and her child, Uemura painted them as any mother and child in an ordinary family. In *Niji o miru* (Looking at a rainbow) a contented married woman looks out of a window at a rainbow with her baby in her arms. This is actually the happy family with the father which Uemura dreamed of. Father and husband were the missing factors in her life as well as the determining factors that enabled her to realize her career as a painter.

Kyoto was a city completely dominated by men. Japanese painting circles, too, were male dominated. Shoen became pregnant several times by her teacher and secretly bore his children. She put one of them out to nurse, but the child died quite young. Another was brought up by her mother. Shoen's sufferings as a woman are well known. Shoen and her teacher may have loved each other, but their relationship was basically one in which the man dominates the woman. To contemporary eyes it may seem a form of sexual harassment that women could not refuse male desire in order to survive. In fact, women artists were and still are not considered as possible subjects for a lawful marriage. They are thought to be sexually deviant and immoral by the standard of popular ethics. Without a father or a suitable guardian to support her financially, a woman artist had to accept a teacher or an art dealer as her patron. The social environment in which Shoen lived was one characterized by sexual discrimination. She told a person close to her near the end of her life, long after she had gained prominence and respect, that everyone around her was an enemy.

Uemura Shoen produced many stereotypical paintings steeped in the aesthetic convention of "Bijinga" in the middle period of her career. Bijinga is a genre of Japanese painting which deals exclusively with the beauty of women, a typical example of which is ukiyo-e. For example, one painting entitled *Honoo* (Flame), owned by the National Museum of Tokyo, depicts a well-known jealous wraith featured in a Noh play and conveys an unearthly quality. This work, together with *Hanagatami* (Flower keepsake) and *Kinuta* (taken from the title of a Noh play by Zeami, in which a woman is depicted beating a cloth on a *kinuta*, or fulling block, as she yearns for the return of her long-absent husband), both of which portray insane women, give full expression to Shoen's feelings of lost love and jealousy. The object of her jealousy was not her teacher but, instead, an ordinary townsman with whom she was seriously in love, perhaps for the first time in her life. Their plan for marriage was broken off because of her situation, and the man later married a woman who was considered appropriate. Shoen was driven to the threshold of insanity, deprived of a seemingly last opportunity to take part in ordinary family life.

Shoen successfully turned her passion to creating a life worth living through her paintings. The themes and main subjects in all her paintings are women. Moreover, the women depicted in her paintings of this period are decisively different from those that appear in paintings done by men in the tradition of the Kyoto school of Bijinga, whose tradition dates back several hundred years. The major characteristic of women in the paintings before Shoen was that they were treated as the object of men's sexual interest. Shoen painted working women for the first time in the history of Japanese painting. One of the masterpieces along that line is *Yugure* (Dusk). Here a middle-aged woman opens the paper-covered sliding door of her room to get enough light to thread a needle. Her plain kimono, the needlework, and the weak sunlight of the dusk impressively create an atmosphere of daily life. Japanese painting portrayed the reality of working women for the first time through Shoen's works. They are as significant as the works of Millet, who painted working women instead of bourgeois women. In the late 1930s Uemura painted another middle-aged woman shown repapering a door to prepare for the coming winter in *Banshu* (Late autumn). In another painting in a series titled *Yuki no naka* (In the snow), she described women walking in the severe cold with heavy snow on their umbrellas. The clean, sharp, uncompromising lines of her drawing supported by her accurate drawing ability and the use of just a few colors clearly show the painter's integrity of mind. It took Shoen a long time to reach this heightened state. Shoen received a great many awards for her noble and innovative art.

Shoen continued to support her mother and her fatherless son. Her son, Shoko, grew up to be a successful painter like his mother. Both Shoen's own success and her son's made her later years peaceful and glorious ones. In her last painting, which shows silently falling snow in a garden, however, I see the intense solitude of a woman who was not allowed to pursue her true happiness in the feudal Japanese painting circles of the Meiji era.

Conclusion

It used to be seriously believed that the absence of women in art history proved the innate lack of creative ability in women. It was claimed that we had no female Michelangelos or Leonardos because women did not have the ability. Research by feminist scholars, however, has located another explanation: the exclusion of women from all formal education, including art. In the Japanese case women were not allowed to enter the national art universities until after World War II.

In the 1970s American art historians made an effort to rediscover and reevaluate women artists in the past to refute the mythology of women's innate inability by pointing out the talented female artists in history. Another aim of their efforts was to find out the general conditions that enabled women to be artists by examining their lives in detail and to clarify how these few women could develop and actualize their abilities in male-dominated societies and still be unable to become "great" artists. All the women artists studied fell into one of three categories. Some were born to a painter's family and had early professional training. Others were born to a family that had no sons; their fathers raised them as they would raise their sons. Still others did not have fathers; they had to support the family in place of a man in the family. In short, these women were, like men, raised, educated, and treated to engage in art. The reason they nevertheless did not become "great" was that they were never commissioned to execute projects that might be considered socially significant.

The work of rediscovering women artists has not been undertaken out of nostalgia. It has had a significant importance in terms of helping understand the social context in which the potential of most women has been destroyed or thwarted.

The three Japanese women painters discussed here are no exception. Yamashita Rin and Ragusa Tama were able to realize their potential through the help of Westerners; these are specific examples that also suggest the Japanese situation in the late nineteenth century, when the country was forced to open its doors to Western influence. Uemura Shoen shared a common feature with Western female painters in that she was the head of her family.

In some respects the lives of all three, however, were tragic. Yamashita Rin remained an unknown painter of icons all through her life, and even recent dictionaries of art do not record her name, whereas her male classmates left their names in history. Ragusa Tama was discriminated against as a foreigner's wife and dissociated herself from the formal painting circles. She is considered a nonprofessional and not highly valued. Uemura Shoen, on the other hand, was awarded the highest honor, the Order of Cultural Merit, as a renowned painter of Nihonga, or Japanese-style, painting, which has occupied the highest position in Japan's artistic world since the time of Fenollosa and Okakura. Her personal life, however, was not a happy one. At the end of her life she confessed to a friend that she had always been surrounded by enemies: she suffered sexual harassment from her master and was forced to give up her first child, and unable to marry the man she loved most, Shoen had to support her family and bear the stigma of her illegitimate children.

NOTE

1. Ukiyo-e is a Japanese art movement that flourished from the seventeenth to the nineteenth centuries and produced paintings and prints depicting the everyday life and interests of the common people.

REFERENCES

Aoki, Shigeru, ed. 1986. *Meiji yoga shiryo* (Reference materials of Western paintings in the Meiji era). Tokyo: Chuokoronsha.

Fister, Patricia. 1991. "Female bunjin: The Life of Poet-Painter Ema Saiko." In *Recreating Japanese Women, 1600–1945*, ed. Gail Lee Bernstein. Berkeley, Los Angeles, and Oxford: University of California Press.

Nocklin, Linda. 1971. "Why Have There Been No Great Women Artists?" *Art News*, no. 9.

Oda, Hideo. 1977. *Yamashita Rin*. Tokyo: Nichido shuppan.

Uemura, Shoen. N.d. *Seibisho*. N.p.p.

Vasari, Giorgio. 1971 (1568). *Le Vite dei piu eccellentii Pittori, Scultori e Architetti* (The lives of the most eminent painters, sculptors, and architects), ed. L. Ragghianti, vol. 1. 2d ed. Milan: Rizzoli.

Wakakuwa, Midori. 1985. *Josei gaka retsuden* (The lives of women artists). Tokyo: Iwanami shinsho.

"Dusk" by Uemura Shoen. Owned by Kyoto Furitsu Oki Kotogakko (Kyoto Prefectural Oki Senior High School). Photo provided by New Color Shashin Insatsu Corp., Kyoto. Reprinted with the permission of the Japan Artists' League.

Women and Television: Portrayal of Women in the Mass Media[1]

❖ ❖ ❖

Midori Fukunishi Suzuki

The first television broadcast in Japan took place in 1953. In the forty years since then, the relationship between television and people's lives has changed greatly. In the early days a television set was revered as one of the "three sacred treasures" of Japanese families (a refrigerator and a washing machine were the other two); owning one was a status symbol. In the 1960s television became more widespread as the economy grew, and its function in people's daily lives increased in importance. One consequence of the booming economy was that the husband stayed at the office until late at night, leaving the television set to take his place as the companion of his wife and children and, eventually, to become the center of the family circle.

By 1975 television had become the dominant medium in terms of yearly advertising revenue, beyond even newspapers. Television's influence on the household and on society as a whole spread. The so-called new media, such as communication satellite and cable television, made their appearance in the 1980s, ushering in the "information age." Even with the rise of such media, however, television's function as a transmitter of information has become stronger and its hold on people's lives more tenacious, to the extent that it has become integrated into people's environments.

As television becomes more and more a part of the everyday environment, it becomes as indispensable to people as air. In most cases, however, people are not consciously interacting with television. Programs and commercials stream into homes incessantly, yet—even though some of the information broadcast may well be worthwhile—most people do not consciously think about the content or objectively consider whether or not it is really useful to them. Most people, likewise, make no effort to learn how the information that is broadcast is chosen and processed, to learn about the production processes going on behind the screen, or to judge the content of the information broadcast.

Integrally related to this issue concerns the ways women are portrayed on television, which tend to be highly stereotyped and biased. Most women, however, are not aware of this, so that the influence of television on their thinking and behavior, both consciously and unconsciously, is all the more extensive. As television becomes ever more a part of the environment, discrimination against women becomes a part of daily life, and related problems become greater and deeper. The following discussion deals with these points and, additionally, looks at recent efforts by women to try to influence the television media and to combat sexism on television and bias against women in the television industry.

Women as Television Viewers: Estranged from Real Information

Daily routines and activities start with the morning news. After waking up, one turns on the TV and listens to a succession of news reports, each of which lasts about a minute or two. People get dressed, wash up, and eat breakfast to this staccato rhythm then leave for work or school.

After the wife and mother sends everyone off, she clears away the breakfast things and starts her housework, but she will most likely not turn the TV off. The women's magazine–style shows (called "wide shows" in Japanese), which are information programs aimed at female audiences broadcast daily in the morning and afternoon, come on, providing her with steady information. She probably absorbs most of it without being conscious she is doing so.

Problems become apparent when we carefully consider the content and volume of this information. A 1984 study analyzed all the morning news programs and women's magazine–style shows broadcast by all the networks in the Tokyo area during a particular week that year (FCT 1985). Topics covered on news programs included politics, economics, general events in society, sports, and topics pertaining to daily life. The topics were virtually the same as those covered by the newspapers, except that they were dealt with in about as much depth as newspaper headlines, and the same stories were repeated over and over.

The number of topics on a given women's magazine–style show covered but two or three specific areas. The most common topic and the one taking up the largest amount of time was the entertainment world, accounting for up to 32 percent of broadcast time. The next most frequently broadcast topic related to items of practical benefit: TV shopping and offers for free gifts, cooking and food tips, household tips, health and beauty advice, and information on hobbies (listed in order according to amount of time taken up). Almost half the time on some programs was spent on this information, actually serving the same purpose as commercials: the promotion of products and services. Presenting commercial information is now a daily occurrence, as is the broadcasting of information on the entertainment world and the inclusion on news programs of information on travel and scenic and historical sites. Murders are also common topics of women's magazine–style shows. Some programs will depict a criminal case in dramatic form.

One can only conclude that morning programs—women's magazine-style shows, at least—offer virtually nothing to a woman which would help her manage her daily affairs independently. These programs offer scandals involving personalities in the entertainment world, contrived cases of murder, and "practical tips" that are really consumption-promoting commercials. Moreover, if women think that the morning television programs really inform them about world affairs and provide them with information useful to their daily lives, they may lose sight of the fact that some information *cannot* be imparted by television. Thus, as most women live their lives in the so-called information society—rather, *because* they are living in that society—they are actually separated from information and are confined to a world of discrimination and prejudice.

This problem is exacerbated by the fact that the majority of women (as well as men) who regularly view television do so uncritically and undiscriminatingly. In 1985 the Research Group on Women and Mass Media Culture was asked by the Tokyo Metropolitan Government to carry out a research study on female residents in Tokyo ages sixteen to sixty-nine with regard to television (Tokyo Metropolitan Government 1986). To the question, "Can you tell from TV news what is going on in the world?" 82 percent of the respondents replied "yes" or "I guess so." Asked whether they could trust television news, 89 percent responded with one of these two answers. The same survey questioned women about commercials; a mere 17 percent indicated, "I watch commercials but realize that there are problems with them"; 38 percent said they watched them with interest, 31 percent that they watched without thinking, 7 percent said commercials made them want to buy the product. The younger age groups, especially, lacked critical ability regarding commercials: the percentage of respondents answering, "I watch commercials with interest" was 48 percent for teenagers, 53 percent for women in their twenties, and 40 percent for women in their thirties.

Women in their thirties and younger have been brought up watching television. During childhood they probably watched cartoons daily, most of which were broadcast during prime time on commercial networks.[2] Thus, they spent about 20 percent of their viewing time watching commercials. A 1990 study reports that, among the five commercial networks, an average of 63 commercials taking up 635 seconds were aired per day per network during the prime time slot (from 7 to 9 P.M.). This means that a person who watched television every day during a one-week period would spend 74 minutes viewing 441 commercials; over a whole year the figures would come to 450 hours and 23,000 commercials (FCT 1991).

The lack of a critical perspective regarding commercials seems only natural under the circumstances. Most women in this age group, and women in their forties and older as well, have probably had no lessons in critical viewing of any programs, in choosing what to watch and what not to. All this is the result of the fact that education, centered around the written word, has neglected the audiovisual media, notably those such as television which have permeated our lives. Recently, there is finally talk of education in "reading, writing, and expressing oneself" through television and other electronic media. More time will be necessary, however, before a place is made for such education in the public school system.[3]

How Japanese Television Portrays Women

Research on the portrayal of women in television programs and commercials has paralleled the striking progress of the women's movement, and it is continuing, particularly in Europe and North America. In Japan, as well, a great deal of research has accumulated over the past ten years (see, e.g., Muramatsu 1979; FCT 1987; Muramatsu 1990). As I present the data from Japanese research, I will attempt to show from two standpoints—gender stereotyping and the commercialization of sexuality—how the depiction of women on television relates to sexism in general.

Gender Stereotyping

Studies done both in Japan and abroad consistently show that on the average, for every woman depicted on a television program, there are two men. This, of course, does not reflect the situation in the real world, in which women and men are found in approximately equal proportions. The ratio varies somewhat by kind of program: on Japanese television women and men appear about equally on home comedies and women's magazine–type shows; on action-drama programs and cartoons, however, there are about three to five times as many males as females. There is, likewise, some variation among commercials, depending on the product being advertised and the target audience. In commercials for alcoholic beverages and fast foods men outnumber women two to one. Commercials for pharmaceutical products show women and men more or less evenly. Commercials employing children or depicting families generally use far more females than males, irrespective of the product being promoted (FCT 1986, 1983).

The age range of men who appear on television is substantially wider than that of women, the range for women being primarily from the late teens to the early thirties. As a result, men on television are on the average ten years older than women. Seventy percent of the women who appear regularly on morning news programs and women's magazine–type shows, for example, are in their twenties; a woman over forty is a rarity (FCT 1985). The age range of men on news programs is much wider: 80 percent are in the thirty- to fifty-year range; of these, the majority are in their forties. For women's magazine–type shows the figure for men of this age range is 60 percent.

The reason that women in lower age brackets are used is that the highest value accorded women in Japan is that they be young and "cute" or "beautiful." Any other type of women is usually depicted in a negative way. In variety programs or programs involving audience participation, for example, women considered ugly *(busu)* or older women (derogatorily referred to as *oban* or *babaa*) are treated disparagingly and are often the objects of laughter and ridicule. The criteria for selecting women for television appearance are youth and looks; those for men are social standing, experience, and education. The roles women and men play are thus out of balance. Returning to the example of news programs, main newscasters and commentators are usually men, while assistant newscasters and reporters are women, reflecting in a most obvious manner the traditional discriminatory division of labor between the sexes.

These traditional values are deeply rooted in television and are frequently exhibited in dramas and cartoons as well. Married women characters, whether depicted as employed outside the home or not, are shown in their "places": in housekeeping roles—cooking, shopping, laundering—and as the caretakers of husbands and children. Although a husband may occasionally be shown doing housework, the wife is generally portrayed as feeling sorry for the husband in such cases, as in NHK's "Shufu Monogatari" (The tale of a household). If this is not the case, the couple is portrayed as being highly unusual, and the portrayal is comical, as in TBS's "Papa wa Newscaster" (Papa is a newscaster).

Commercials even more than programs are apt to depict women in the role of housekeeper and child rearer. In an analysis of characters' behaviors in 749 commercials portraying families, mothers were depicted as being absorbed in cooking, shopping, and laundering and in taking care of their husbands and children; only rarely were they shown associating with others or engaging in activities outside the home. Any portrayal of their being employed was nonexistent (FCT 1983). In the same study daughters depicted in commercials with mothers were usually found doing housework. When shown with fathers, however, their role was as the father's young "lover" or cute plaything and did not involve housework.

In this way women are from childhood bound to the traditional view of the sexual division of labor. In an analysis of 449 commercials employing children, gender stereotyping was evident in 41 percent of them (FCT 1986). Specifically, girls were pictured as dependent, cute, and sexy and as an encouragement to boys. In another study of 185 toy commercials, warm colors such as red, pink, and yellow appeared in the background, and the theme song or background music was romantic or fairy tale–like when girls appeared in the commercials. In the case of boys, on the other hand, the colors were cold—black, gray, or blue—and the background music was fast, modern, and electronic (FCT 1980).

The results of these analyses of commercials are the same as those derived from analyses of women's personalities as depicted on television programs. A series of analytic studies made in 1981–85 by the Forum for Citizens' Television (FCT) of evening dramas and cartoons showed that female main and supporting characters were usually depicted as being dependent, emotional, romantic, cute, tender, warm, dedicated, submissive, cheerful, and peaceful; these are generally regarded as positive characteristics for women to possess (FCT 1981; see also FCT 1983, 1986). This evaluation, however, is based on the traditional view of "femininity." This way of looking at women is thus being affirmed and reinforced through television. By contrast, those traits considered as expressions of "masculinity" are activeness, intelligence, ability to think, plan and control, creativity, courage, and violence. In the analysis it was clear that females were only rarely shown possessing these traits.

Women are also characterized as exhibiting negative traits—as being materialistic, perverse, and vain. Such traits, however, are usually possessed by peripheral characters, usually older women, such as a mother-in-law who torments her daughter-in-law or a meddlesome female neighbor.

In recent years dramas whose main character is a woman with a career, such as NHK's year-long series "Inochi" (Life), have been appearing more than before. Although this is in itself a favorable trend, gender stereotyping is still apparent, as it is in the case of the main character, a female doctor, on "Inochi," a show in which the heroine, despite being a professional, is portrayed as often reacting emotionally rather than rationally.

Stereotyping is not limited to women but also occurs with minority groups, the elderly, people with disabilities, children, and others easily placed in a socially powerless position. Stereotyping has an ideological side to it: it does more than simply deny these groups the possibility of variety and individuality; it affirms already-existing prejudices and discrimination and legitimatizes them (Seiter 1986). This aspect of stereotyping must not be overlooked. We must not take the naively optimistic view that if women are portrayed on television as having careers, the problems will disappear.

The Commercialization of Sexuality on Television

In the past six or seven years there has been an increase in the portrayal of sexuality on television programs—drama, cartoons, variety shows, and talk shows—broadcast during the hours of the evening when families, including children, are watching. There is, of course, nothing wrong with discussions of sexuality. In an age when pornographic films and videotapes flood the marketplace and sports newspapers, weekly magazines, and comic books are overflowing with more of the same, women and men need to have a thorough, correct understanding of sexuality if they are to understand one another and build relationships based on equality. There would be no problem if television provided a vehicle for doing so. This is hardly the case, however: the insulting, prejudicial view that a woman is her genitals is no longer limited to late-night shows but has also permeated morning and daytime women's magazine–style shows and evening programs aimed at general audiences.

On variety programs pornographic magazines and the like are often used as the basis of comic routines; elements of the sex business, such as topless bars, form the scene of a skit, and young female stars are made to appear in bunny suits or as bar hostesses (FCT 1982; also FCT 1986). In such scenes the camera usually moves in on the chest or abdomen or the skirt.

The depiction of sex on dramas involves marital unfaithfulness and illicit love affairs. A study in the United States showed that in the early 1970s sexually suggestive behavior increased on television and that 70 percent of portrayals of sex involved illicit affairs or a relationship with a prostitute (National Institute of Mental Health 1982). That this trend came to Japan about five years later is evident in the Japanese programs of the 1980s. While there are now more light situation comedies than before, their greatest concern is with sex: whether a husband or wife, married person or single, all adults talk about sex in a frivolous way or are involved in extramarital affairs. A wife involved in such a tryst is often depicted bragging about it to the other women in the neighborhood. Men are not the only ones commercializing sexuality; women commercialize themselves as well.

Although there is no exact data telling how much commercialization of sexuality there is on television as a whole, it certainly exists to a very extensive degree. In a 1981 analysis of commercials for alcoholic beverages, 30 percent of the 58 sake commercials in the study expressed the idea that "sake and women are men's things" (FCT 1981). A 1987 FCT study found that 26 percent of the 207 soft drink commercials used young women in bikinis as eye-catching devices (FCT 1988). A 1986 monitor study by the Women's Liaison Council on Buraku Liberation (founded in 1983 in Osaka as a coordinating organization to fight discrimination) pointed out furniture, underwear, and soap commercials in which women appeared either naked or dressed only in underwear. Examples of commercials for just about any product can be found in which the camera takes an extreme close-up of a woman's lips, upper body, or abdomen (she may be clothed) or in which a woman uses her body to entice a man.

Adults are not the only ones depicted unclothed in commercials. Some commercials use naked babies and fifth- and sixth-grade girls. Although it is easy to excuse this by saying that naked children are cute, we must not overlook the fact that children are being made to undress for commercial purposes for extended periods of time. The roots of this denying of children their rights are the same as those that commercialize women's sexuality. In reality pornography in Europe and North America often includes children as well as adult women; this has become a major social problem. I believe this problem also exists in Japan. Thus, to put an end to this obnoxious practice

81

as well, women must strenuously protest advertising that commercializes sexuality.

The Deep-Rooted Patriarchy

On 7 January 1989 Emperor Hirohito, who had reigned for sixty-three years, passed away. The following day a series of ceremonies took place bringing forth the Crown Prince Akihito as the new emperor.

It is well-known that Emperor Hirohito was a fascist leader who was praised as a living god during the period of Japanese militarism, when Japan invaded the Chinese continent, and during the world war that ensued. After its defeat in World War II Japan was reborn as a democratic nation. With the formal demotion of the emperor to a mere "symbol" under the new Constitution, Hirohito was deprived of any formal role in national politics. But, as the same individual who had ruled throughout the prewar and wartime years, his existence continued to cast a spell over the consciousness of the Japanese people. Any criticism of the emperor, therefore, was considered taboo.

With the death of the man who had survived such a drastic transformation, it was only natural that the Japanese felt deep emotions: the event marked the end of an era. Nonetheless, the content presented by the mass media to the public during these two days was somewhat excessive. It would not be an exaggeration to say that newspapers and television stations featured nothing but events concerning the present and past of the emperor. Particularly disturbing was the uninterrupted television coverage of the emperor and the imperial system, which continued for forty-three hours on the national public station, NHK, and forty-four hours on all the commercial networks. The daily lives of the nation's citizens were smothered by these monoperspective visuals as if for the sole purpose of asserting an autocratic reality.

Furthermore, it can also be said that the two-day television broadcasts symbolized the depth and stability of the patriarchy (with the emperor at its head) and, at the same time, strongly emphasized the status of women and other subordinate individuals. In addition to the continuous series of imperial ceremonies, from which women were noticeably absent, all commercials were banned, so that the end result was the disappearance from the screen of any visual depictions of young and lively women. This complete disappearance of women from the pictures proved that females, who had supposedly succeeded in bringing the so-called era of women, were in actuality only used as products and an eye-catcher for selling services, as well as product labels and wrappers, to be "sold" along with other products on a daily basis.

Following this there have been several occasions on which "royal family reports" have received blanket coverage for long periods of time. In 1990 the engagement (in January) and marriage (in June) of Prince Akishino to Kawashima Kiko and the coronation in November of the Emperor Akihito ensured that wonderful royal family reports continued for most of the year.

Then, in 1993, in the few months between the engagement and June marriage of the crown prince and Owada Masako, the breathless coverage exceeded even that of Prince Akishino's marriage. The event was treated as a matter of first national importance.

Put simply, the style of reporting could only be described as "royal family promotion." Having become new members of the royal family through marriage, Masako and Kiko were marked as "new stars" and hounded by the press like media personalities. Moreover, basing their standards on traditional female virtues, reporters have praised to the skies the appearance and fashion—as well as the gentleness, grace, and reserve—of the pair. Their academic achievements, including the fact that Masako had graduated from Harvard, were mentioned at times, but never as more than a condition of eligibility, and since the marriage there has been no mention of these facts.

By claiming that promotion of the royal family through images of pomp and ceremony bring the royal family closer to the public, the press creates the illusion of a democratized Imperial House. The Imperial House, however, is based on the system of primogeniture—the very embodiment of patriarchy. This discriminatory system is hardly ever discussed in the mass media. The mere mention of the subject, in fact, is generally considered taboo, especially on television. Moreover, the new stars on the imperial stage, who are shown as fulfilling traditional female roles, are portrayed as ideal images, thereby obscuring the deep-rooted patriarchy. Thus, the television audience, including many women, is unknowingly enlisted to support and strengthen the system that denies female equality from its very core (see Suzuki 1992a).

Issue of Women' Representation in the Television Industry

As a UNESCO report on the world's women and the communication media has emphasized (Gallagher 1986), the hiring of women by the media is also an important concern within the general issue of promoting equality of women and men on television. In Japan, since around 1980, more women have appeared as newscasters, and in 1986 female emcees began to be used on women's magazine–style shows. Female producers and directors of dramas and documentaries—some of them now well-known—also exist, as do female scriptwriters. On the whole, however, the proportions of women and men employed by the television industry, as well as the newspaper industry, are far from equal. As table 1 shows, women constitute only 6 percent of the total work force of NHK and 18.5 percent of the commercial broadcasting companies in Japan, and most of them are in subordinate positions in the business, programming, operations, and announcer divisions.

Studies conducted in the United States show that the portrayal of women on television does not necessarily improve as more women are hired by the mass media. In Japan sexual inequality is extremely pronounced in the television business, and it is very difficult for female employees of television broadcasting stations to express their views or work with movements against sexual discrimination. Even though the results of affirmative action on sexual

Table 1
Women Employed in the Mass Media, 1990

	Total	Number of Women	Women as Percentage of Total
Newspaper companies	65,304	4,914	7.5
(All employees)			
Reporters		915	1.4
Private broadcasting companies	28,469	5,276	18.5
(All employees)			
Reporters		107	0.4
Directors		212	0.7
Announcers		633	2.2
NHK (Japan Broadcasting Corp.)	14,654	860	5.9
(All employees)			
Reporters		22	0.2
Directors		154	1.1
Announcers		33	0.2

Sources: Compiled from Inoue Teruko and Ebara Yumiko eds., *Women's Data Book.* (Tokyo: Yuhikaku, 1991), 217, figs. 90-1, 90-2, and 90-3. Original data from Nihon Shimbun Kyokai (Japan Newspaper Association), *Shimbun romu shiryo* (Newspaper labor data) (annual); survey by Nihon Minkan Hoso Renmei; survey by NHK.

inequality in broadcasting stations in the United States, Canada, Australia, and various European countries have not yet been fully successful, at least affirmative action exists. In Japanese broadcasting stations no one even brings up the need for such a policy.

Efforts by Women to Influence the Television Media and Combat Sexism

While these many issues confront us, fortunately, we have witnessed over the past fifteen years or so a gradual increase in the number of Japanese women and men who are starting to take action concerning media issues.

Women Who "Talk Back" to Television

The 1985 survey by the Research Group on Women and Mass Media Culture found that 37 percent of women in their thirties, fifties, and sixties and 28 percent of women in their forties named morning and noontime women's magazine–style shows as programs they watch regularly. By occupation slightly less than one-half of full-time housewives and one-third of self-employed women and those employed part-time said they regularly watched these programs. When asked if they had ever tried directly to influence the media, including broadcasters, for example, by writing a letter to a newspaper or magazine, less than 3 percent said they had; the figure among women in their twenties, fifties, and sixties was less than 1 percent (Tokyo Metropolitan Government 1986).

Looking at such statistics, one might conclude that the situation is difficult to salvage. Yet, if we look at the problem more closely, it becomes clear that there are women intimately involved in these issues, a fact not discernible from simply looking at a general survey. The number of women who criticize television and other media, who "talk back" to the media, has been increasing, and their activities are becoming more diverse and more organized.

The earliest example of women criticizing and "talking back" to television and other mass media was that of the efforts of the Women's Action Group, formed in 1975. That year House Incorporated aired a television commercial that stated, "I [the boy] do the eating" and "I [the girl] do the cooking." Interpreting this as a case of gender stereotyping and bias against women, the group initiated a protest movement to get the commercial taken off the air immediately. The movement caused a rather big stir in the mass media, but few within the media understood or reported on it correctly. The same group requested that NHK, the public television network, portray women and men equally in its broadcasts and protested that network's 1975 New Year's Eve singing contest (Kohaku uta gassen) by posting leaflets and handing them out to members of the audience entering the NHK Hall. The leaflets stated, "Stop singing songs that depict women as possessions!" (Nakajima 1986). Since then the group has repeatedly protested against newspapers, women's magazines, and advertisements on public transportation which depict women in a discriminatory manner.

The Women's Liaison Council on Buraku Liberation protested in 1983 against the Maruhachi Mawata Company's commercialization of women's sexuality in its television commercial. In 1986 the member women's organizations of the council cooperated in monitoring the portrayal of women on television. Their study encompassed all the programs and commercials (divided into morning, daytime, and nighttime periods) broadcast by the seven channels available in the Osaka area during a three-day period in April. The key word of the Buraku Liberation Movement is human rights. Therefore, when women activists in the movement turned their attention to the media, they readily grasped the issues involved, bringing a feminist perspective to those issues. They have now come together as a group of media professionals, organizing media literacy workshops to increase awareness on media issues.

The Forum for Citizens' Television

In 1977 the Forum for Citizens' Television was established as an independent "citizens' forum to reform television" made up of media "senders," audiences, and researchers acting in their individual capacities. Originally founded as the Forum for Children's Television, *Citizens'* was added to its title at the time of its tenth anniversary, and then *Children* was omitted at the time of its fifteenth anniversary. Since its establishment, FCT has conducted a series of investigative research and held regular forums. FCT's original concern was children's television; however, because children's problems are closely related to women's problems, and because since its second year of activity more women than men became involved as office staff in its work, FCT chose the portrayal of women on television as the object of its first study, in 1978. Since then one of FCT's concerns has been with television and women's issues, and its annual content analysis studies have been conducted from women's perspectives. The results of the studies are published in a series of reports. Based on its 1986 report, FCT presented a statement on television and children's rights to television stations, the National Association of Commercial Broadcasters in Japan, and large advertising agencies. One of the points of this was the need for a reform in the gender stereotyping seen on commercials in which children appear.

Recent Movements to Reform the Broadcast Industry

The movement toward taking action on media issues peaked with the promotion of equal rights on the bicentennial of the French Revolution and the fortieth anniversary of the United Nations Declaration of Human Rights, both of which were celebrated in 1989. The problem of the relationship between mass media and equal rights thus gained an aspect of social importance, and movements focusing on women's rights were reviewed from their basic premises.

Various new movements proposing radical reforms on the part of the broadcasting industry have been started, supported by the unceasing efforts of women. Efforts are being made to transform the consciousness of the viewing audience as a whole, rather than acting on a case-by-case basis, such as trying to ban sexist advertisements, as was done in the past.

One example of this reformist movement is the establishment of the Women's Network in Broadcasting (WNB), a gathering of women working for commercial broadcast stations. The members of this group are building their association on a premise of equality, disregarding position and corporate affiliation. The object of the group is to "make it an association that allows for participation by everyone interested in broadcasting" ("Hoso women ga network" 1989) and is calling for participation by the general public. It took three years for this group, which is looked to as a catalyst for many positive changes by women outside the media, finally to come into being, as the women working in the media were somewhat reluctant to take action. This is probably due to the fact that a majority of these women are young and unmarried and, therefore, unaware of this discrimination.

A second movement concerns the efforts of the Women's Committee of the Japan Federation of Commercial Broadcast Workers' Unions. In 1989, three years after the Equal Employment Opportunity Law was enacted, this committee surveyed women working in commercial broadcasting and announced the results, which made apparent their severe working conditions. In addition, the women of the committee also attended the FCT-sponsored forum, at which they reported the results of their survey, promoted exchange of ideas, and clarified the common ground between themselves and their audience ("Terebi to josei hyogen" 1989).

Yet a third movement, organized by FCT, which created a network called "The Mass Media and Human Rights Network," proposed "A Petition Advocating Equality between Women and Men in Broadcasting" to NHK, the National Association of Commercial Broadcasters in Japan, and various commercial broadcasters. The character and values of the FCT citizens' forum was clearly and well represented by the seventy-five participants, half of whom were men, and included broadcasting/publishing journalists, editors, mass communications researchers from various universities and research organizations, and citizen activists.

The same network called on the broadcast industry of Japan, a country that has ratified the UN Convention on the Elimination of All Forms of Discrimination against Women (CEDAW), to "investigate its organizational structure and the content of programming" and for each station to "take reformist steps to remedy the situation so that the rights of women would be honored in accordance with CEDAW." The following specific suggestions were made:[4]

I. Amend the NHK Domestic Broadcast Programming Code and the Broadcast Regulations of the National Association of Commercial Broadcasters in Japan by adding the following articles about the rights of women so that:
   1. There will be no expressions which violate the rights of women or further discrimination against them.
   2. The interests and opinions of women are reflected in broadcasts in harmony with the basic tenets of the UN's CEDAW.

II. NHK and commercial stations, in all levels of their operations, including decision-making on overall policies, program production, news reporting, technology and personnel matters, should increase women's participation, should strengthen affirmative action, and take measures to enable women to continue working.

III. Each NHK and commercial broadcasting station should establish a section or person to be responsible for promoting the equality of women and men in broadcasting, carrying out inspections of broadcasting content, and checking on personnel matters with regard to hiring practices, work assignments, promotions and opportunities for continuing education.

Conclusion

Technologically speaking, Japanese broadcasting stations are world leaders; the first Japanese satellite is a reality, as is high-definition television, and the nation's technology, unprecedented and superior, has made satellite news broadcasts a daily affair. The actual content, organizational structure, and corporate stance of the stations, however, tell a different story. The Japanese broadcasting industry is incredibly slow in reflecting change. Moreover, its members are completely separated from the broadcast industries around the world, which are undergoing rapid changes, resulting from the constant challenges of feminist activities.

The myth of male superiority is deeply rooted in the Japanese broadcast industry, and yet it is exceptional that an international organization is able so thoroughly to ignore feminist ideas and ideals. Generally speaking, in the Japanese broadcast industry there are still only a few men who can clarify the reason why it is wrong to depict women in fixed gender roles. Mass media constantly throws out the catchphrase "the era of women" and strikes a pose of approval toward equal rights for women. But this trend is based purely upon the commercial, and inhumane, calculation that healthy women "sell" as products and in no way promotes true liberation for women.

Currently, the catchphrase "the era of women" is being uttered often and insistently, but the problems related to fixed gender roles remain fundamentally misunderstood. The fact that such a phrase is becoming popular is hardly ideal for women. On the contrary, the situation is extremely dangerous; the advertising industry excels at transforming anything and everything into a product, suppressing women while also denying their basic, equal rights. In fact, by closely observing recent trends in mass media, we can see that they are both boosting the female as a symbol and handling her as an object. I say this because mass media are subtly indicating pornographic philosophies, in which women are ruled by means of violence. Further, these expressions are being used with increasing frequency.

Television has grown into a powerful and agile equal rights restraining device. As long as there is no increase in the number of people who both recognize this fact and are sufficiently alarmed to take action, this device will not only remain intact but will grow yet more powerful.

The feminist network acting against sexism in the media is beginning to grow and spread throughout Japan. We also see an increase in the number of Japanese women attending international conventions proposing themes related to the problems of discrimination in broadcasting. In addition, more Japanese women representing activists are holding and being invited to symposiums and forums. I personally have close relationships with feminists who are keenly concerned about this issue in Sweden, Canada, the United States, and many Asian countries. These women are committed to numerous media reform activities. For several years I have also been participating in the Asian Network of Women in Communication (ANWIC), funded by the World

Association for Christian Communication (WACC), holding media awareness workshops for women in Asian nations.[5]

The borderless waves of broadcast communication media were said to have acted as catalysts for the political reforms in Eastern Europe. We can also anticipate that our feminist activities will cross national boundaries and make equality between women and men a reality. We believe that this ideal can only be realized through global unification on the matter. With this belief as our fundamental support, Japanese women will definitely continue to make progress, but at times we may well be stuck with a feeling of exasperation due to the very slow pace of change and progress.

NOTES

1. Parts of this essay have appeared in *Women and Media in the Asian Context*, ed. World Association for Christian Communication (WACC) and People in Communication (PIC) (Quezon City, Philippines: PIC, 1991).

2. Public television and commercial television coexist in Japan. NHK (Japan broadcasting corporation, which is public, has two nationwide channels and two satellite channels. Five Tokyo-based commercial broadcasters function as national networks. All channels except the NHK educational channel broadcast almost twenty-four hours daily.

3. To educate the public on the media the Television Environmental Research Society published a media awareness workshop handbook entitled *Terebino mikata, tsukaikata* (Viewing and interacting with television) in 1987. See also Midori F. Suzuki, "Media kyoiku to josei" (Media education and women), in *Masumedia bunka to josei ni kansuru chosa kenkyu*, ed. Tokyo Metropolitan Government, 1986.

4. The English-translated document in its entirety is reprinted in *Asian Media Alert*, no. 2 (Spring 1990): 8–9. Contact: c/o AVACO, 2-3-8 Nishiwaseda, Shinjuku-ku, Tokyo.

5. The Women's Desk of ANWIC publishes a quarterly magazine, *IMPACT* (CISRS House, 14 Jangpura B, Mathura Road, New Delhi 110014, India). Also, see Suzuki 1992b.

REFERENCES

Forum for Citizens' Television (FCT). 1991. *Terebi ga utsushidasu "gaikoku" to Nihon no kokusaika* (How Japanese television views the world: is Japan truly internationalized?). FCT's seventh diagnostic and analytic survey report. Tokyo: Forum for Citizens' Television.

———. 1988. *Terebi wa do shogyo-ka sareteiruka* (How television is commercialized). FCT's sixth diagnostic and analytic survey report. Tokyo: FCT.

———. 1986. *Terebi to kodomo no jinken* (Television and children's rights). FCT's fifth diagnostic and analytic survey report. Tokyo: FCT.

———. 1985. *Joho-ka suru asa no terebi to shufutachi* (Information-oriented morning television and women). FCT's fourth diagnostic and analytic survey report. Tokyo: FCT.

———. 1983. *Terebi to kazoku* (Television and the family). FCT's third diagnostic and analytic survey report. Tokyo: FCT.

———. 1982. *Terebi to kodomo no kenko* (Television and children's health). FCT's second diagnostic and analytic survey report. Tokyo: FCT.

———. 1981a. *Kodomo ga miteiru bangumi to CM* (Programs and commercials that children watch). FCT's first diagnostic and analytic survey report. Tokyo: FCT.

———. 1981b. *Kodomo no miteiru iyakuhin CM, arukoruinryo CM* (Pharmaceutical and alcoholic beverage commercials that children watch). Tokyo: FCT.

———. 1980. Terebi komasharu to kodomotachi (Television commercials and children: an analysis of toy commercials). Tokyo: FCT.

Gallagher, Margaret. 1986. *Communication in the Service of Women: A Report on Action and Research Programmes, 1980–1985*. Paris: UNESCO.

"Hoso women ga network" (Networking of women in broadcasting industry). 1989. *Asahi shimbun* (Asahi newspaper), 11 November, 19.

Muramatsu, Yasuko. 1990. "Of Women by Women for Women?" *Studies of Broadcasting*, no. 26 (March): 86–104.

———. 1979. *Terebi dorama no joseigaku* (Women's studies on television dramas). Tokyo: Sotakusha.

Nakajima, Satomi. 1986. "Masukomi eno undo" (Movements against mass media). *Nihon fujin mondai konwakai kaiho*, no. 45: 38–43.

National Institute of Mental Health. 1982. *Television and Behavior*. Washington, D.C.: US Government Printing Office.

Seiter, Ellen. 1986. "Stereotype and the Media: A Re-evaluation." *Journal of Communication* 2 (Spring): 14–26.

Suzuki, Midori F. 1992a. "Don't Be Afraid to Be Critical: A New Direction in Japan's Media Education." In *New Directions: Media Education Worldwide*. London: British Film Institute.

———. 1992b. *Television: darenotameno media ka* (Television: whose medium is it?). Tokyo: Gakugei shorin.

———. 1986. "Media kyoiku to Josei" (Media education and women). In *Masumedia bunka to josei ni kansuru chosa kenkyu*, ed. Tokyo Metropolitan Government.

Television Environmental Research Society. 1987. *Terebino mikata, tsukaikata* (Viewing and interacting with television). Workshop handbook.

"Terebi to josei hyogen" (Television and women's representation). 1989. *FCT Gazette*, no. 34 (August): 1–5.

Tokyo Metropolitan Government, ed. 1986. *Masumedia bunka to josei ni kansuru chosa kenkyu* (Survey research on mass media culture and women). Tokyo: Tokyo Metropolitan Government.

Women's Liaison Council on Buraku Liberation. 1986. "Terebi to josei" (Television and Women). *Buraku kaiho kenkyu* (Bulletin of the Buraku Liberation Research Institute), no. 52 (October).

❖ 2 ❖

Education

Women students in a class in applied physics and chemistry at Japan Women's University in the early 1900s. This subject was made a requirement for all students from the time of the university's inception in 1901. Courtesy of Mainichi Shimbun Newspaper Information Service Center, Tokyo.

Challenges to Education for Girls and Women in Modern Japan: Past and Present

❖ ❖ ❖

Kimi Hara

ducation frees the human spirit." How often have I been struck by and reminded of the significance of this inscription inside the entrance of Judd Hall at the University of Chicago. Education, in the true sense of the term, helps develop human potential, emancipating us from all bindings and restrictions. Education regenerates one's heart and mind and thereby influences the social and cultural forces and institutions within a society. At the same time, education is a sociocultural product, reflecting the kind of society and culture in which women and men struggle to survive.

In this essay I present a historical review and analysis of the nature and development of education for girls and women in Japan in the modern period and the social and cultural forces and factors that have shaped that education. Female education in Japan prior to the end of the World War II can, by and large, be characterized as gender segregated, gender stereotyped, inferior, and less valued compared to that of males. The essay examines why female education in Japan has been treated in this manner and the consequences of such a distorted type of education as well as the changes that have taken place since the end of World War II and the impact of those changes.

Women's Education prior to the Meiji Period

Prior to the establishment of a nationwide system of education under the Meiji government in 1872, the type and level of education available to the Japanese people depended on their social class as well as gender. In the three

93

hundred years of the Tokugawa (or Edo) period that preceded the Meiji Restoration of 1868, sons of the samurai, or the ruling military class, were educated in the domain schools (hanko) which were maintained by each of the roughly 280 feudal domains (han) into which the nation was divided. Very often attendance requirements as well as type of curricula provided differed for different ranks of the samurai. *Gogaku* (local schools) developed rapidly after the middle of the nineteenth century, starting out as a "branch" of the main domain school or soon turning into one. By the end of the Tokugawa era some of these schools included students of both samurai and commoner class (Passin 1965, 19). In addition to these schools, there was also a wide variety of private academies, or *shijuku*, which were institutions of higher education largely for the samurai but, in many cases, also admitted commoners. "By the end of the end of the Tokugawa period," writes Passin, "it would be fair to say that practically all the children of the *samurai* class (and of the much smaller court nobility) attended some kind of school for some period of time" (1965, 43). This statement applied, however, only in the case of males. In the case of the daughters of the samurai class, they were usually kept at home and given tutoring either by the family or an outside tutor.

The primary institution for the education of commoners, who constituted the overwhelming majority of the population, were the *terakoya*, which were small, private educational establishments started by public-minded individuals. Teachers—often samurai, priests, or doctors—taught the "3Rs" to groups of thirty to forty pupils in "schools" housed in shrines, temples, vacant buildings, or private homes. By the end of the Tokugawa era the ratio of female to male teachers reached 55 to 100 (Osada 1961, 123). Besides the 3Rs, the basic curriculum included instruction in morals and manners. In accordance with the teachings of Confucianism, from the age of seven boys and girls were seated separately. Osada informs us that the ratio of female to male pupils at *terakoya* was about 1 to 4; attendance was particularly low in the more conservative, rural areas of the country, while in cities like Edo (present-day Tokyo) and other urban areas the proportion of female pupils was much higher, in fact little below that of boys (124). While girls were taught the 3Rs, beyond that the emphasis was on teaching the basic skills required for running and maintaining a household—namely, sewing, weaving, spinning, etc. In some cases instruction was also given in tea ceremony, flower arrangement, and painting. From the middle of the eighteenth century on, slightly higher-level educational institutions corresponding to the middle-school level began to be established for the children of the commoner class. Apart from formal education, domestic service was another vehicle of female education of a more informal variety. Many young women of the farming and merchant classes received training in manners and in skills required for running a household by becoming domestic servants in the homes of samurai families for a couple of years.

The major strain of thought underlying the education of females was the Confucian conception of the role of women, which confined them to childbearing and child rearing and which held that learning was not only unnecessary but, indeed, harmful for women, a thought exemplified in the following statement by Matsudaira Sadanobu, the shogunal chancellor from 1786 to 1793: "It is well that women should be unlettered. To cultivate women's skills would be harmful. They have no need of learning. It is enough if they can read books in *kana* [the Japanese syllabary, as distinct from the more difficult Chinese characters]. Let it be that way" (Karasawa 1956, 105; qtd. in Passin 1965, 46). Notwithstanding the restrictions imposed by such attitudes toward women, in the Tokugawa period quite a few women managed to acquire literacy, and, indeed, as research by feminist historians in recent years has unveiled, many literary works of various genres—diaries, essays, poetry, historical tales—were produced not only by women of the noble class but also by those of the commoner class (Kuwabara 1990, 180–96). In the case of the majority of women, however, the social definition of the women's role which confined them to the realm of the household afforded women little opportunity for applying their education in the larger, social realm.

Women's Education from the Meiji Period to the End of World War II

The Development of Education from the Meiji Period

In the face of social, intellectual, and economic pressures from within as well as threats from the United States and other Western powers, the Meiji Restoration of 1868 marked the emergence of Japan from a feudal society, long isolated from the rest of the world, into a modern nation-state under the monarchical rule of Emperor Meiji. In the words of Beasley, "[It] has something of the significance that the English Revolution has for England or the French Revolution for France; it is the point from which modern history can be said to begin" (1972, 1–2).

The Meiji Restoration also marked the first educational reform in modern Japan. Two main streams of educational thought were evident: one was *bunmei kaika*, or "civilization and enlightenment" (Kaigo 1961, 108–12). Education was to be one of the keys to meeting the challenges posed by the Western countries by providing skills required for military and economic development, promoting a common sense of nationhood, and opening the way to the full realization of the intellectual resources of the country. The other stream of thought was a conservative one based on Confucian philosophy which emphasized loyalty to the emperor. The former was based on the idea of equality of all people and breaking up the existing hierarchy of classes (warriors, farmers, artisans, and merchants). Thus, whereas it had formerly been regarded as unnecessary for girls and women to go to school, under the influence of those espousing "civilization and enlightenment," equality in educational opportunities for both sexes was, in principle, at least partially established.

The nation's leaders were eager to eliminate illiteracy among the people in order to modernize the country and to catch up with the advanced nations of the West. In l871 the Ministry of Education was established, and in the following year the Fundamental Code of Education was promulgated, making four years of elementary schooling compulsory for all children, irrespective of sex or social status. Plans were announced for the establishment of 53,760 elementary schools, 256 middle schools, and 8 universities.

School buildings had to be constructed anew, but neither the government nor the local districts had the necessary financial resources to build them.[1] By 1879 only 52 percent of the planned number of elementary schools had been built. In 1882 the rate of girls' attendance was less than one-half that of boys. Even boys' attendance was only 40 percent of the appropriate age group (Karasawa 1968, 16–17). In the northern prefectures remote from Tokyo there could hardly be seen a single girl in a school. As Karasawa (1968, 41) notes, this reflected the continued dominance of the notion that females need not be literate or learned and that childbearing and child rearing were the only activities worthy for them. Obedience was considered to be a woman's greatest virtue. If girls and women became educated and enlightened, they would be able to think for themselves, thereby causing much trouble and inconvenience to the prevailing social order; such was the generally held view. Therefore, females were discouraged from becoming critical minded and confident. The following statement made in 1887 by Mori Arinori, the first minister of education as well as a great promoter of "civilization and enlightenment," is an expression of these very views regarding women's education:

> The fundamental basis for an enriched country lies with education, whose basis is with *women's* education. The success or failure of the country depends upon women's education. This must not be forgotten. In the process of educating girls and women, we must put across the idea of serving and helping their country. The models for women are a mother nurturing her child; a mother teaching her child; her son coming of age and being conscripted to go to war and leaving his mother with a good-bye; a son fighting bravely on the battlefield; and a mother receiving a telegram informing of her son's death in the war. (Morosawa 1978, 23–24)

Mori recommended that those pictures be posted in classrooms because they symbolized the essence of the spirit of women's education.

The Ideology of Japanese Education prior to World War II

The ultimate purpose of education, as envisioned by the Meiji leadership, was "to enrich the country and strengthen the army." In order to consolidate the foundation of the country against threats posed by the Americans, English, and Russians, who demanded that Japan open its doors to the world, the Japanese government adopted the slogan "Enrich the country and strengthen the army" *(fukoku kyohei)* This can be restated as making the country (not the people) rich by means of building a strong army. This slogan infiltrated and penetrated into all spheres of Japanese life—political, legal, economic, social, cultural, and educational. Adoption of this slogan as the basis of national policy must be viewed in the sociopolitical context of the extraordinary national crisis that existed at the time.

The political indoctrination of militaristic ideas and thoughts to the younger generation was most effectively carried out by means of the educational system. As Reischauer points out, "In classrooms and army barracks the young Japanese was taught to glory in Japanese military traditions" (1964, 129). Thus, Japanese were taught to sacrifice themselves for the sake of the emperor in order to enrich their country, but not the people themselves.

For girls and women the basic principle was "Education for good wives and wise mothers" *(ryōsai kenbo kyōiku)*, which restricted their role primarily to the home and family. In fact, to be a good wife and wise mother was seen as the other side of the coin of "Enrich the country and strengthen the army." It was for men to enhance the wealth of the country and maintain its strength by becoming hard workers and brave soldiers, while women's duty was to serve their men and families and maintain the continuity of the Japanese patriarchal family system.

These ideals were embodied in the Imperial Rescript on Education, which was promulgated in 1890. It was based on a nationalistic ideology that focused on worship of the emperor as the embodiment of the spiritual unity of the nation. The Rescript stressed the importance of such virtues as loyalty to the emperor, filial piety, cooperation and consideration among brothers and sisters, harmony between spouses, trust among friends, and love toward the masses. It is clear that the Rescript was not based upon the principle of universal human rights or the dignity of human beings; rather, it aimed at promoting the interests of the nation-state. A copy of the Rescript, which was considered a sacred document, occupied a prominent place within each school and was read out loud by the principal to the teachers and the student body on ceremonial occasions. This document was the heart of prewar Japanese education, and for nearly fifty years it served as a tool of the state for molding a loyal and nationalistic citizenry.

The Dawn of Women's Education

With respect to the education of girls and women, in 1871, immediately following the Meiji Restoration, when Japan was just opening its doors to the world, a phenomenal event took place. In the early years of the Meiji period thousands of young men were sent abroad or went on their own, to Europe and the United States, in order to study and bring back knowledge and skills that could be put to use in the new society. In 1871 a group of five young girls were included among fifty-nine students sent to the United States and Europe. An account of how this came about is given by Tsuda Umeko, one of the five girls, who later founded a college for women:

It is said that when Count Kuroda was in America he was struck with the position and influence of women in the country and found that it was because the American women as well as the men receive education. The desire to have Japanese women equally enlightened made him take the step which led to our being sent abroad. It therefore was decided by the Government, through his advice, to send over a number of girl students and the five chosen may have included all those who applied or desired to go. (Tsuda 1980, 77–78)

As noted in Tsuda's account, Kuroda Kiyotaka proposed to Mori Arinori, the high commissioner to the United States, that the government officially send a group of young women to the United States for study. The plan called for a ten-year period of study, with expenses for the journey, tuition, and school costs; living expenses to be guaranteed; and an annual provision of eight hundred dollars for incidental expenses. Initially, there were no parents interested in sending their young daughters to the United States, but a second attempt at recruitment produced five candidates, Yoshimasa Ryoko (aged fifteen), Ueda Sadako (also fifteen), Yamakawa Sutematsu (twelve), Nagai Shigeko (nine), and Tsuda Umeko (eight). Tsuda Umeko's father was a very progressive man who had studied Dutch and English and had accompanied a group led by Fukuzawa Yukichi to Europe and the United States in 1867. He had been much enlightened by the impact of Western culture.

Tsuda Umeko and the others departed for San Francisco on 23 December 1871, accompanied by government officials who were traveling to the United States and Europe in order to negotiate treaties with various governments (the so-called Iwakura Mission). After living in the United States for more than ten years with an American family and later going back again to the United States and graduating from Bryn Mawr College, Tsuda established a small women's college in Tokyo in 1900 called Women's English College (later Tsuda College). Although it was not a mission school, it was based on Christianity and placed high value on the spirit of the Bible. Her vision and ideals were profound and high. She aimed at providing Japanese women with professional, academic training and helping them develop all-round personalities. This was quite different from the prevailing concept of education for "good wives and wise mothers." Emphasis was placed also on providing a thorough and individualized education in small groups, particularly in the teaching of English. Tsuda's ideal has been inherited from generation to generation at Tsuda College. Who would have dreamed of such a woman educator emerging out of the Iwakura Mission? Through Tsuda Umeko a new Western wave was introduced to innovate Japanese higher education for women. (For further discussion of Tsuda, see Oba 1986, 1990; and Furuki 1991).

It is important to note the important role played by Christian missionaries in promoting female education during the Meiji period (see Karasawa 1968, 59–65). Although the Fundamental Code of Education had initially provided for coeducation at all levels, following the Education Act of 1880, which called for the abolishment of coeducation beyond elementary school, women were formally excluded from public middle schools. In fact, as a rule, girls and boys were thereafter segregated after the third year of elementary school.

Christian missionaries pioneered in establishing high schools for girls, such as the Ferris Seminary (1870), Kobe Jogakuin (1875), and others such as Aoyama Gakuin, Joshi Gakuin, Kassui, and Iai in various parts of Japan. The missionary teachers came from the United States, Canada, and Great Britain. It was not until the 1880s that the government took steps to set up secondary schools for girls, and, as late as 1894, only eight public girls' high schools existed throughout Japan (Nihon Joshi Daigaku 1967, 201, table 2). The rapidly expanding industrial economy led to a growing need for female workers not only in factories but also as telephone operators, office workers, teachers, and receptionists, which in turn spurred demand for more education for girls. The Sino-Japanese War (1894–95) also had a significant impact. The plight of women left widowed and forced to find employment pressed home the need to provide greater education and occupational training for women. The Girls' High School Law, promulgated in 1900, called on local governments to establish at least one girls' high school in each prefecture with a four-year course of study, and in 1920 five-year secondary schools for girls opened which offered more practical and technical subjects. As years went by, these schools spread rapidly, from 156 public and 53 private girls' high schools in 1912, to 487 public and 176 private schools by 1926, and in the 1920s and 1930s both the number of girls' high schools and their enrollment caught up with and surpassed the number of boys' middle schools and their enrollment. The principle underlying secondary education for girls was, again, primarily that of training them for their role as homemakers and instilling feminine virtues.

Women were denied admission to universities, yet, as in the case of secondary schools, several girls' colleges were established by the private sector. The first of these was the Women's English College, established in 1900 by Tsuda. The same year saw the opening of a women's medical school in Tokyo, followed by a school of fine arts and Japan Women's University in 1901. By 1937 forty-two private women's colleges offered three-year courses. The majority of these institutions were, however, in large cities such as Tokyo, Kyoto, and Osaka, so that women residing in rural areas had little access to them. Two national women's higher normal schools were established by the government for the purpose of training teachers for girls' high schools and women's normal schools, and six public or prefectural colleges were established prior to World War II. All of these institutions of higher education for women were regarded as inferior to men's colleges and universities. In other words, women's education was placed not within the mainstream but, rather, on the periphery.

According to a survey conducted by the Ministry of Education in 1925, roughly 15 percent of the appropriate age group entered girls' high schools of various types. Enrollment in institutions of higher education was considerably lower: in 1920 only 1.2 women out of 1,000 were enrolled in such institutions, though by 1935 the ratio had increased almost fourfold.

An Ad Hoc Educational Council was convened from 1917 to 1918 in order to make preparations for meeting changes brought about as a result of World War I. It proposed, among other things, the need for placing greater emphasis on moral education in elementary schools, teacher education and practical education for girls, and the establishment of higher professional institutions for women (see Osada 1961, 241–44). The council emphasized that the content of the Imperial Rescript on Education must be taught carefully so that girls would grow up to become "good wives and wise mothers" who were instilled with patriotic feelings. The actual changes that came about following World War I, however, had profound influences on the thinking of many young girls, who, transcending the traditional image, tried to move in a new direction toward self-reliance.

Democratic Influences on Women's Education in the Taisho Period

In the second decade of the twentieth century, which marked the start of the new Taisho era (1912–26), there surfaced in Japan a ferment of democratic and liberal thought, which was manifested in many forms: a movement for universal manhood suffrage; the emergence of *demokurashii* (democracy) as a key word; the appearance of numerous women's organizations that espoused various causes, including socialism, political rights for women, and the abolition of prostitution; as well as the development of new schools of educational thought. The so-called New Education Movement that was launched in this period in opposition to the existing nationalistic education reflected the influence of educational ideas and methods that found their way to Japan from Europe and the United States. A number of educational leaders—such as Sawayanagi Masataro of Seijo Gakuen, Ohara Kuniyoshi of Tamagawa Gakuen, and Higuchi Choichi, influenced by Ellen Key (1849–1929), Paul Nartorp (1845–1924), and John Dewey (1859–1951)— became interested in child-centered education and freedom-oriented education and introduced the Dalton Plan, the Project Method, and other educational ideas and methods to Japan (Karasawa 1953, 259–62). Not only did numerous existing schools, public as well as private, adopt one or another of these concepts and methodologies into their curriculum, but in addition new schools were founded based on those principles, such as Seijo Gakuen and Jiyu Gakuen (Freedom School), a private high school founded by Hani Motoko, who was one of the first graduates of the First Girls' High School, established in Tokyo in 1888 as the first government-sponsored girls' high school. The outbreak of war marked by the Manchurian Incident in 1931 and subsequent growing ultranationalism put an end to these efforts.

My experiences at the First Girls' High School of Tokyo, which I entered in 1928, exemplify many of the ideas and principles advocated by this New Education Movement. The principal of my high school, Ichikawa Genzo, had traveled throughout the world in order to observe new educational practices, and he served as chairman of the National Association of Principals of Girls' High Schools for many years. The high school consisted of five grades, seventh through eleventh. Each grade consisted of five classes of forty-eight girls. The total number of students was around twelve hundred. Competition for entry into this high school was very keen; generally, there were five to six applicants for each student accepted. Since the school was a public, government-run school, the monthly tuition was quite low—four yen, fifty sen. Nevertheless, in terms of social class background, the students were predominantly from the upper and upper-middle classes.

The symbol of the school was a tower of hope named Almond Tower, soaring high in the sky. The entire building was heated by steam, and the toilets were Western style. The science classrooms (which included physics, chemistry, botany, biology, and zoology), music room, painting and drawing room, history and geography rooms, gymnasium, playground, library, and auditorium were equipped with modern facilities. Each classroom was provided with all the needed dictionaries and books for self-study. A hot lunch program was provided as well. There were also special Etiquette Rooms, one Japanese and the other Western, in which girls learned how to behave in their daily lives. In the Japanese Room students sat straight on the tatami mat floor and practiced repeatedly how to sit, stand, walk, and bow according to the Japanese style. Also, they learned how to behave when invited as guests and how to entertain guests as hostesses as well as how to drink green tea and eat Japanese cakes. The etiquette teacher had been a dancing teacher for the empress and was very strict in training the girls. In the Western Room we were taught how to sit in a chair, how to serve and to drink English tea, and how to greet and carry on conversations. We were also taught Western table manners.

Self-government, self-study, and self-reliance were stressed at this school. Each school day, from Monday to Friday, consisted of six forty-five-minute periods, including one period for self-study. On Saturdays there were only four periods. During the self-study period, which was scheduled just before the lunch hour, students were allowed to go to the library if they wished to. Silence was observed as a rule. Students could prepare for afternoon classes as well as review what had been studied in the morning. The classroom teachers were there to help students and answer questions as needed.

The principal and the teachers placed great confidence in the young women's abilities and characters. Students were expected to learn and to behave. As people tend to behave as expected, the girls enjoyed school and strove hard to achieve no less than boys. Unlike girls' high schools generally, these students were never treated as not equal to boys. For instance, in English classes two teachers, who were native speakers of English, Mrs. Okamura from Hawaii and Mrs. Tanaka, an American who had graduated from the University of Chicago, taught us English conversation during the extracurricular hour.

The principal was an enthusiastic advocate of women's rights and conducted special classes for the eleventh grade in which discussions were held on current topics of interest to the students. I can remember discussing such topics as suicide, women and smoking, women's suffrage, women's professions, and marriage. In each grade students studied a different religion or belief: Bushido (Way of the samurai), Shintoism, Confucianism, Buddhism, and Christianity. The principal's goal was to expose the students to all types of religions so that they could choose their own freely in later years.

Even though the days of militaristic regimentation were approaching and Japan's economic conditions were getting tighter, what went on in these classrooms was challenging and enjoyable. Students were never forced to emulate the virtues of "good wife and wise mother"; instead, they were inspired and challenged to think about and solve problems. Through such an opportunity for diversified, experiential learning, my classmates and I gained a sense of righteousness and a sense of dignity as women.

The principal and teachers also made special efforts to encourage their female students to enter higher educational institutions. In 1935 only 4.6 females out of 1,000 females in the age group pursued education beyond high school, a figure representing a mere one-tenth of the rate among males. At this high school, however, as many as one out of two went on to higher education with the aim of becoming teachers, medical doctors, dentists, pharmacists, writers, artists, or musicians, a figure that surpasses today's.[2]

World War II and Its Impact on Female Education

As the nation endured war for nearly fifteen years, until Japan's defeat in World War II on 15 August 1945, most adversely affected was education for young people. Militarism and ultranationalism were the main thrusts in education (see Kaigo 1961, 148–49). Indoctrination and regimentation were practiced as ways of disciplining the young hearts and minds of students. With the start of World War II in December 1941, educational activities were severely restricted or else suspended. In 1941 students were graduated from institutions of higher education four months earlier than scheduled; in 1942 the length of studies was reduced by six months and in 1943 by twelve months. The same practice was applied to secondary schools as well.

In 1944, when American air raids on Japanese cities became intense, schoolchildren were evacuated with their teachers to the countryside, where they lived in shrines and temples. Discipline was strict, indeed militaristic; youngsters were forced to obey the orders of teachers and upper-class students without question. Some children died of illness and hunger.

Nearly three million girls and young women were mobilized to replace men in different posts in society at the sacrifice of their education (Fujii 1971, 23). In addition, half a million women worked on farms in place of fathers, husbands, brothers, and sons who had been drafted in the war.

Educational Reforms following World War II

Out of the terrible ruins wrought by World War II and Japan's defeat, the women of Japan were at last able to obtain equality of educational opportunity as a result of a series of educational reforms that were instituted under the influence and direction of the Allied Occupation. In March 1946 the United States Education Mission, consisting of twenty-seven members and headed by chairman George D. Stoddard, arrived in Japan to recommend educational reforms to the Supreme Commander for the Allied Powers, General Douglas MacArthur. Prior to their arrival, at the recommendation of General MacArthur, a committee of twenty-nine Japanese scholars and educators had been organized, headed by Tokyo University President Nambara Shigeru.

The Education Mission from the United States was determined to liberate Japan's education from militaristic and ultranationalistic influences and to bring about decentralization and democratization as well as to remove discrimination against women. The Japanese Education Committee, headed by Nambara Shigeru, also discussed and debated important issues pertaining to the reorganization and democratization of Japanese education. The report, which was submitted to the Education Mission as well as to the Japanese government, was in agreement with the Report of the Education Mission in both spirit and content (Osada 1961, 294–95). Based on the recommendations of the Education Mission, equality of educational opportunity for women was guaranteed in several provisions in the new Japanese Constitution, enacted in 1946, and in the Fundamental Law of Education, established in 1947.

Article 26 of the Constitution defines the basic right of all boys and girls to receive education and the obligation of adults to make sure that they receive such education. The Fundamental Law of Education set forth in more detail the aims and principles of education in accordance with the spirit of the Constitution and provided for nine years of free, compulsory education for both boys and girls; coeducation, which was formerly limited to the elementary school, was now recognized by law and extended to all levels. A common curriculum for both boys and girls was instituted in schools, and women were now allowed to attend the same schools and go on to the same universities as men. Under the new system of higher education which went into effect in 1949, thirty-one of the women's higher educational institutions in existence—two national, three municipal, and twenty-six private—were elevated to the status of college or university. Many of the other existing higher institutions were given the title "short-term college" *(tanki daigaku),* or junior college.

In the 1960s Japan pushed headlong toward rapid industrialization, a process that transformed social structures as well as human relations. As technological innovations advanced, economic growth accelerated. It was, in fact, the invisible work of women employed as cheap labor which sustained the Japanese economy from the bottom to bring about this growth, as it has ever since the Meiji Restoration (Hara 1984, 190–91).

As industrialization and economic growth progressed, there was a concomitant rise in the educational levels attained by the Japanese people. The percentage of girls within the appropriate age group entering upper secondary school (tenth through twelfth grade) doubled within a mere twenty-five-year period, from 47.4 percent in 1955 to 95 percent in 1979. Within the same period the percentage of young women studying at junior colleges increased eightfold and those in four-year universities grew sixfold.

Conclusion

The process of the development of women's education in Japan is none other than a long history of struggle against bondage toward the emancipation of women as individual human beings. In pre–World War II society little attention or respect was accorded to the dignity, personal autonomy, independence, and freedom of choice of women. Instead, the family and the nation were always given priority and exercised dominance over women.

Through the educational reforms that were instituted under the influence of the Allied Occupation following Japan's defeat in the World War II, the long-established sex-discriminatory system of education was, at least in principle, destroyed almost overnight. In contrast to the earlier policy of education for "good wives and wise mothers," women were henceforth to be encouraged to develop their potentials as individuals and as contributing citizens to society.

In spite of the advances that have been made in women's education, there are still several impediments to the realization of full equality in the sphere of education for Japanese women. Moreover, the prewar concept of gender-differentiated education and the ideology of education for "good wives and wise mothers" has resurged from time to time over the postwar period. Thus, for example, back in the mid-1960s, when rising numbers of women began to enter four-year universities, some educators denounced this trend, charging that it would lead to the demise of the country, since women did not utilize their education for the benefit of society, and urging that the numbers of women admitted to universities be limited. This became a subject of much debate in the mass media (Hara 1976, 62).

Another example is that in September 1969 the basic principles of an "education suited for the special aptitudes and abilities of females and males" were issued by the Ministry of Education, as a result of which general home economics was made a required subject in upper secondary schools for female students only. At the time, the director of the Bureau of Elementary and Secondary Education of the Ministry of Education was quoted as saying: "This undoubtedly aims at educating women as good wives and wise mothers. No one dares to oppose it" (*Mainichi Shimbun*, 1 October 1969). This measure was put into effect in 1973; not until 1989 was the policy reversed, requiring both sexes in upper secondary school to study home economics beginning in 1994.

There is, among many Japanese, a sense of complacency that equality of educational opportunity for women has now been fully achieved. *Japanese Women Today,* a report issued by the Office of the Prime Minister, explains efforts to improve and advance the status of Japanese women following the United Nations (UN) women's decade. It states, "Specifically, Japan must eliminate persistent, stereotyped concepts based on traditional sex roles and provide a climate conducive to women's full participation in society" (1990). The report, however, does not sufficiently point out the backwardness of women in terms of, for instance, their rate of entry into four-year universities. The fact is, however, women are twenty-five years behind men in terms of rates of entry into four-year universities. Moreover, women are mostly oriented toward private, expensive junior colleges, which have very little linkage to four-year universities. Miscellaneous schools, culture centers, and centers for social education, which have sprung up in large numbers over the recent years, are regarded as suitable learning sites for women.

In these and many other ways Japanese women are still on the periphery rather than in the mainstream of education . Unless women are given full equality of educational opportunity, they cannot hope to participate in society on an equal footing with men. Particularly since the UN Decade for Women, women's education has been oriented toward a global perspective. It is hoped that Japanese women, with enlightened hearts and minds, will utilize their varied experiences, knowledge, and technical skills toward the solution of problems that confront not only their own immediate society but also the global society that transcends national boundaries.

NOTES

1. At the age of sixteen Watatsuki Reijiro, a future prime minister of Japan, taught children, as a substitute teacher, in a makeshift classroom atop a cow shed. He received only 1.5 yen per month in salary. He recalled cows mooing downstairs, while his pupils made a great fuss upstairs (Karasawa 1968, 15).

2. It was most unfortunate that a few years after our graduation the principal was forced to resign from his post due to pressures from the militaristic government because he was considered to be too progressive and liberal. In 1935 some of the alumnae of the First Girls' High School established a private girls' high school named Oyugakuen and invited him to be the principal so that he could bring to realization his high ideals.

REFERENCES

Beasley, W. G. 1972. *The Meiji Restoration*. Palo Alto, Calif.: Stanford University Press.

Fujii, Harue. 1971. *Korekara no josei to joshi kyoiku* (Women and women's education in the future). Tokyo: Sekaishoin.

Furuki, Yoshiko. 1991.*The White Plum, a Biography of Ume Tsuda*. New York and Tokyo: Weatherhill, 1991.

Hara, Kimi. 1984. "Women Workers in Textiles and Electrical Industries in Japan." In *Women on the Move: Women in a World Perspective*. Paris: UNESCO.

———. 1976. "Joshi kyoiku no tenkai to shakai hendo" (Development of women's education in relation to social change). In *Shakai hendo to kyoiku* (Social change and education), ed. Yoshihiro Shimizu. Tokyo: Tokyo University Press.

Kaigo, Muneomi. 1961. *Kyoiku-shi* (History of education). In *Gendai Nihon shoshi* (A short history of modern Japan), ed. Tadao Yanaihara. Tokyo: Misuzu Books.

Karasawa, Tomitaro. 1968. *Meiji hyakunen no kyoiku* (One hundred-year history of education since Meiji). Tokyo: Nikkei shinsho.

———. 1956. *Kyoshi no rekishi* (History of teachers). Tokyo: Sobunsha.

———. 1953. *Nihon kyoiku-shi* (History of Japanese education). Tokyo: Seibundo shinkosha.

Kuwabara, Megumi. 1990. "Kinseiteki kyoyo bunka to josei" (Modern culture and women). In *Nihon josei seikatsushi* (A history of the lives of Japanese women), vol. 3: *Kinsei* (Modern period), ed. Josei-shi sogokenkyukai. Tokyo: Tokyo daigaku shuppankai.

Morosawa, Yoko. 1978. *Onna to kyoiku* (Women and education). Tokyo: Heibonsha.

Nagai, Michio. 1961. *Nihon no daigaku* (Japanese universities). Tokyo: Chuko shinsho.

Oba, Minako 1990. *Tsuda Umeko*. Tokyo: Asahi shimbunsha.

———. 1968. "Tsuda Umeko—joshi kyoiku no senkakusha" (Tsuda Umeko, a pioneer in women's education). *Joshi kyoiku mondai* (Issues in women's education). (January): 69–76.

Osada, Arata. 1961. *Nihon kyoiku-shi* (A history of Japanese education). Tokyo: Ochanomizu shobo.

Passin, Herbert. 1965. *Society and Education in Japan*. New York: Teachers College Press, Columbia University.

Prime Minister's Office (Tokyo). 1990. *Japanese Women Today.*

Reischauer, Edwin O. 1964. *Japan Past and Present*. Tokyo: Charles E. Tuttle.

Tsuda, Umeko. 1980. *Tsuda Umeko bunsho* (Writings by Tsuda Umeko). Tokyo: Tsuda College.

Sexism and Gender Stereotyping in Schools

❖ ❖ ❖

Atsuko Kameda

*Translated by Kumiko Fujimura-Fanselow
and Atsuko Watanabe*

T he notion that much of the gender differences we perceive are the product not of biological factors but, rather, the result of socialization and
education that occur in the home, the school, and other institutions
within society is one that is now widely accepted. Based on the view that
gender is a social and cultural construct, in recent years we have begun to
reevaluate and reconsider many of the dominant conceptions worldwide
regarding gender.

Changes in these directions have been visible in Japan as well. Some
years ago a slogan that read "Individuality (or individual differences) transcends gender differences" appeared in a pamphlet on women distributed
by the Office of the Prime Minister. That this was a rather novel and uncon-
ventional notion to many Japanese at the time is attested to by the considerable attention given to it by the popular press. As in many other societies,
however, the feminist movement of the 1970s and 1980s and the various
efforts undertaken throughout the world, beginning with the United Nations
International Women's Year (1975), to eliminate discrimination against
women, have had a significant impact in terms of bringing about changes in
traditional notions regarding what are, or ought to be, "appropriate" roles,
behaviors, education, and lifestyles for women versus men.

In terms of schooling, the long history of education based on the premise
of preparing women for the domestic role of "good wife and wise mother" is
approaching an end, to be replaced by one that seeks to promote gender
equality. To achieve this goal, however, requires looking beyond the issue

merely of equality at the systemic level, that is, equality in terms of access to educational opportunity and curriculum. It is also necessary to examine how the inner structure of schooling reproduces and perpetuates sexism and gender-based inequality, through, for example, existing teaching materials and methods, guidance and career counseling practices, the hidden curriculum, daily classroom practices, and school rituals.

Many Japanese have tended to take it for granted that while business enterprises in Japan are still male-dominated, in the sphere of education, equality between women and men has truly been achieved. The impetus for trying to understand and point out the many respects in which education in Japan continues to be male-dominated has come in large part from the growth of women's studies since the mid-1970s. In the ensuing years an effort to promote non-sexist education aimed at bringing about greater equality in the relationship between women and men, liberated from traditional conceptions of gender roles, has become increasingly visible in both the practice of and research in education (see, for example, Amano 1986; Kameda and Tachi 1987).

Gender Role Socialization

Before we turn to issues of sexism and stereotyping in the formal educational system, let us look briefly at some aspects of gender socialization that take place within the more informal setting of the family. From the time children are born many Japanese hold very different expectations of them, depending on their sex. Fortunately, we are much less likely today to hear the comment, "Oh, too bad it's not a boy!" when a daughter is born, but other comments—such as "Daughters are much easier to bring up," "With sons you have to worry about getting them into good colleges, but with daughters you don't have such worries," and "You must have great expectations for your son's future"—are still commonly heard. In addition, there is a considerable emphasis on the notion of "femininity" and "masculinity" and on instilling what are viewed as gender-appropriate behaviors in children.

In the 1980s, many countries, including Japan, undertook various measures to promote equality between women and men. Yet the results of an international comparative study conducted by the Office of the Prime Minister in 1982 show some distinct differences between the attitudes of Japanese and other peoples, as shown in table 1. A considerably higher proportion of Japanese—nearly 63 percent—indicated they were in favor of bringing up their children in conformity with notions of femininity and masculinity.

The levels of education Japanese parents desire for their children also seem to vary considerably for daughters as opposed to sons—more so, in fact, than among parents in other societies, as we can see from table 2.

More than 70 percent of the Japanese respondents aspire to a university-level education or higher for sons; the comparable figure in the case of daughters is less than 30 percent. The results of the 1988 survey are almost the same. These outcomes reflect a continuing and a pronounced tendency among many Japanese to distinguish men and women along a variety of dimensions. Moreover, this tendency persists among women themselves, so that its implications in terms of shaping attitudes, expectations, and practices

Table 1

Attitudes Regarding Socialization for Daughters and Sons, in Percentage

	Favor Sex-Differentiated Socialization	Favor Bringing Up Boys and Girls the Same	Other/ Don't Know
Japan	62.6	34.4	3.0
United States	31.3	61.9	6.8
Philippines	28.1	67.4	4.5
England	20.1	76.3	3.6
West Germany	19.9	74.5	5.6
Sweden	6.0	92.0	1.9

Note: The sample includes females ages twenty and above.

Source: Sorifu (Office of the Prime Minister). 1982. *Fujin mondai ni kansuru kokusai hikaku chosa* (Comparative international survey on women's issues). Tokyo: Sorifu.

Table 2

Level of Education Women Desire for Male versus Female Children, in Percentage

	University/ Graduate School		Junior College		Vocational/ Technical School		High School		Lower Secondary School	
	M	F	M	F	M	F	M	F	M	F
Philippines	87.3	84.5	3.2	3.4	5.8	6.6	2.5	4.0	0.2	0.2
United States	68.9	65.8	2.9	6.0	7.1	5.0	9.4	11.3	0.2	0.3
Sweden	31.1	30.8	27.4	29.2	13.0	11.4	4.2	4.3	—	—
West Germany	19.6	14.3	—	—	15.0	15.1	25.7	23.1	13.4	21.6
England	48.1	44.1	—	—	23.3	25.7	14.9	16.3	0.1	—
Japan	73.0	27.7	1.2	28.9	5.0	6.0	9.6	26.3	0.1	0.2
Japan (1988)	78	33	9	45	—	—	11	20	0	0

Note: The sample includes females ages twenty and above.

Source: Sorifu (Office of the Prime Minister). 1982. *Fujin mondai ni kansuru kokusai hikaku chosa* (Comparative international survey on women's issues) Tokyo: Sorifu.
Figures for Japan (1988), from NHK. 1988. *Nihonjin no ishiki chosa* (Survey on the consciousness of the Japanese). Tokyo: NHK.

with respect to child rearing and planning for children's education and careers are great.

Although some changes are taking place, parental attitudes on child rearing have been shown to differ markedly according to the child's sex. Kashiwagi, for example, has reported that Japanese boys are frequently brought up with the expectation that they will be "active, brave and strong," while girls are brought up to be "obedient, polite, and non-argumentative" (1973). A 1985 comparative survey of parent-child relationships in the United States and Japan (Nihon Seishonen Kenkyujo 1986),[1] in which this writer took part, found that Japanese mothers seemed to feel that they bore a major responsibility for the home and family and at the same time that daughters ought to be brought up to be good housewives. On the other hand, American mothers tended not to expect either adults or children to conform to the notion of division of roles based on gender. This seemed to have an impact on actual child rearing, so that these mothers were not especially concerned about raising their daughters to be good wives and mothers.

Messages about gender-appropriate behavior are conveyed to children not only through parental upbringing but through the mass media as well. To give just one example, recently cooking programs on television directed at children have become popular in Japan. While such programs are good in the sense that it is important for children to learn basic skills necessary for daily life, the problem is that the children who appear on these programs are inevitably girls, thereby reinforcing the notion that "girls do the cooking, boys do the eating."

Achievement of Legal and Structural Basis for Gender Equality

Turning now to the educational system, this section examines the extent to which gender equality has been achieved in formal education in terms of guaranteeing access to educational opportunities and establishing a common curriculum.

Prior to World War II separate tracks existed for males and females beyond the elementary school, and females were denied access to universities, with the result that women lagged behind men in levels of educational achievement. Postwar reforms in the educational system, embodied in the School Education Law and the Fundamental Law of Education, established the necessary legal and structural basis for gender equality in terms of access to educational opportunity. Schools became coeducational at all levels, and women were granted access to universities.

Since that time remarkable progress has been made in terms of enrollment at various levels of schooling, especially among females. While education is compulsory only through lower secondary school (i.e., grade 9), as many as 98 percent of females and 96 percent of males now go on to upper secondary school (see table 3).

Table 3

**Percentages of Graduates from Lower Secondary
School Attending Upper Secondary School,
Selected Years, 1950 to 1994**

Year	Females	Males
1950	36.7	48.0
1960	55.9	59.6
1970	82.7	81.6
1980	95.4	93.1
1990	96.2	94.0
1994	97.5	95.6

Note: These figures represent the number of students going on to upper
secondary school, including those combining high school attendance
with employment, divided by the total number of students who
graduated from lower secondary school in a given year, multiplied by
100.
Figures for 1990 and 1994 include those enrolled in the correspondence
program.

Source: Mombusho (Ministry of Education). *Gakko kihon chosa* (School
basic survey) (for each year shown).

It is also noteworthy that, since 1989, the percentage of females entering
postsecondary institutions has exceeded that of males; in 1994 the figures
were 46 percent versus 41 percent. These figures, however, conceal important
gender differences, in that more than 50 percent of the women entered junior
colleges as opposed to four-year universities, whereas among men 95 percent
entered four-year universities.

With regard to curriculum the postwar educational reforms mandated
that all students pursue a common, uniform curriculum at all levels of education. As part of this policy, home economics was made a mandatory subject
for both girls and boys at the elementary and secondary levels. At the lower
secondary schools level, a course called "industrial arts and homemaking"
was newly established in 1958, and boys were taught industrial arts and girls
homemaking. Subsequently, in 1977, the Ministry of Education's Course of
Study (which sets forth the curriculum for elementary and secondary
schools) was revised, making it possible for girls to take some industrial arts
subjects and boys some subjects in homemaking in lower secondary schools
starting in 1981. A more recent revision of the Course of Study in 1989 provided for further movement in having boys and girls study both homemaking
and industrial arts beginning in 1993. At the upper secondary school level,
"general home economics" was established as a course of study principally
for girls in 1960. In 1969 requirements were altered making four credits of
general home economics mandatory for girls only starting in 1973.

Various women's groups as well as organizations comprised of teachers, including the Kodo suru onnatachinokai (Women's action group) and the Kateika no danjo kyoshu o susumerukai (Association for the promotion of the study of homemaking by both sexes) carried out a vigorous campaign to bring about a change in this requirement. The immediate impetus for a change in this policy came when Japan became a signatory to the United Nations Convention on the Elimination of All Forms of Discrimination against Women in 1980. The Ministry of Education was forced to take up this issue as part of the task of establishing a uniform curriculum for males and females, as called for in Article 10 of the convention. Under the revised Course of Study for Upper Secondary Schools announced by the Ministry in 1989, general home economics was made a required subject for both sexes in upper secondary school, starting in the 1994 academic year. In addition, changes were made in the field of physical education, so that, while previously boys had taken martial arts such as judo or kendo (Japanese-style fencing), and girls dancing, students were now given the choice of selecting either martial arts or dance.

Even though home economics has become a required subject for both sexes in high school, this has not been implemented in many schools due to a variety of reasons: lack of qualified teachers and/or lack of necessary facilities and equipment, resistance on the part of some local boards of education based on the view that it is unnecessary for male students to study this subject, as well as resistance on the part of many schools (and parents) who view this as taking valuable time away from preparation in those subjects on which students are tested in university entrance examinations.

Examining Sexism and Gender Stereotyping in Textbooks

Roughly four hundred million copies of textbooks are printed each year for use by elementary and lower secondary school students in Japan. Although the textbooks are put out by private publishers, they undergo rigorous inspection by the Ministry of Education prior to publication. Gender issues are not taken into account in this inspection procedure, however, and gender biases continue to permeate school textbooks.

An analysis of textbooks used in elementary schools and lower secondary schools made by a women's group in 1975 revealed several significant facts (Fujin mondai konwakai 1975, 1976). The majority of figures and main characters who appeared in the Japanese language arts textbooks were male; there were some sixth grade texts in which none of the main characters was a female. The overwhelming majority of the textbook authors were male. Scattered throughout the text were illustrations that depicted traditional gender roles. In the social studies texts women were often portrayed in the role of homemakers; the occupational roles in which they were shown were limited to those of nurses, teachers, waitresses, and other female-dominated jobs. Finally, in the case of English textbooks, sentences that dealt with activities such as baking and washing dishes consistently used the pronoun *she* or a female proper name for the subject.

Subsequently, representatives from many women's groups met with textbook publishers and sought their cooperation in eliminating gender stereotyping in textbooks and bringing in, as textbook writers and editors, women and men who were sensitive to the need for promoting gender equality. Over the years we have seen a slight, if contradictory, improvement. Textbooks today are more likely to include illustrations and pictures of fathers grocery shopping or preparing meals and women working in a variety of occupations. When the League of Japanese Lawyers conducted a study in 1989, however, to examine the extent to which gender discrimination had been eliminated in textbooks, it found that, unfortunately, not a great deal had changed over the previous ten years (Owaki 1991). For example, while more males were likely to be depicted in texts used in home economics classes, they were more likely to be pictured in the role of "overseer," examining or inspecting the work of others, in contrast to females, who were pictured actually doing laundry or cooking. Thus, while the fact that males are appearing in such texts represents a step forward, the ways in which they are depicted only serves further to buttress existing ideas regarding gender roles. The League of Japanese Lawyers has issued this warning: "Texts, pictures and illustrations that instill and reinforce rigid attitudes toward gender roles must be revised. Instead textbooks should be written that are based on the principle of gender equality and from which students can learn about a variety of ways of living based on both men and women living as independent human beings."

Recently, many teachers themselves have begun to call into question sexism and gender stereotyping found in textbooks and other teaching material and to seek changes. In addition, while they have not gone so far as to establish a clear policy regarding gender equality, as some U.S. publishers such as McGraw-Hill and Scott, Foresman have done, a number of Japanese publishers are beginning to show sensitivity in this respect. A very much related point is the fact that issues of gender are not taken up in the training of prospective teachers. Textbooks used in psychology and education courses in teacher training programs do not talk about how gender roles are changing in contemporary society or the growing aspirations among women for independence. Thus, in addition to improving textbooks used in elementary and high schools, textbooks used in teacher preparation programs need to be examined and improved.

Examining School Practices

Many of the practices that go on in schools and classrooms are not determined by any institutional regulations but, rather, are done as a matter of custom. Repeated over and over again in the course of daily school life, however, these customary practices often reinforce established attitudes regarding gender. Such practices have recently been scrutinized.

Differentiating the Sexes: Calling the Roll

One of the pervasive features of Japanese schools, and of Japanese society as a whole, one might say, is the tendency to distinguish the two sexes in a variety of ways. The school bags carried by elementary school pupils are almost invariably black in the case of boys and red in the case of girls; the set of paints that are often purchased through the school come in a blue box for boys and a red box for girls; likewise, in some cases boys are given black or blue library cards, while girls get red or pink ones. Boys and girls are lined up separately, and boys are paired up with boys and girls with girls for a variety of activities. Also, girls and boys are often placed in separate teams for sports and other competitive activities.

One such practice that is almost universally followed by Japanese teachers in classrooms at all levels, and one that has become a subject of controversy in recent years, is that of having separate registers for boys and girls and, moreover, consistently calling the boys' roll first. The same order is often followed when returning test results, giving out report cards, and reading out students' names at school entrance and graduation ceremonies. A survey of elementary schools in the Tokyo metropolitan area showed that a mere 0.5 percent of the schools followed the practice of mixing girls' and boys' names ("Yatta!! danjo kongo meibo" 1991). A group of Japanese women who attended the International Women's Conference in Nairobi in 1985 conducted an informal survey of representatives from nine countries to find out whether such a practice was followed elsewhere. What they found was that, apart from Japan and India, the usual practice was to list girls and boys together according to alphabetical order. Upon their return to Japan these women brought this matter to the attention of the mass media, and in recent years it has attracted growing attention. Various schools have started to experiment with alternative approaches that do not entail separating girls and boys—for example, mixing the sexes and calling the roll by alphabetical order or, as in some elementary schools, according to the children's date of birth. The issue is currently under consideration by school boards and city councils throughout the country. In the city of Sakai, near Osaka, a decision was made by the city council in 1990 to institute mixed-sex listing of students', as well as teachers' names, from kindergarten through lower secondary school. A councilwoman named Yamaguchi Ayako was instrumental in pushing through this reform (Sasakura and Nakajima 1990, 65–68).

A high degree of bureaucratic control and regulation is characteristic of Japanese schools, and maintaining a distinction between male and female students is but one manifestation. Even if the formal setting of schools and classrooms is coeducational, as is the case at the compulsory education level in Japan, daily exposure to the kinds of gender bias practiced in schools is likely to instill in many youngsters a consciousness of gender differences and male superiority. This is not to say, of course, that sex-role socialization is always or necessarily "successful." As happens quite frequently in all societies (see, e.g., Walker and Barton 1983; Weiler 1988), there are many girls (and boys) who resist the dominant messages regarding sex-role appropriate attitudes and behaviors, and there are also teachers at all levels who strive to convey very different kinds of messages to their students. Thus, many of us have encountered women in our college classes who resisted efforts by their high school teachers to discourage them from applying to college or who possessed the critical capacity to question such taken-for-granted practices and regulations as that which requires girls in lower and upper secondary school to wear skirts to school.

Participation in Student Councils and Club Activities

As in many countries, each Japanese school has a self-governing student council or association that makes decisions regarding such matters as rules of student conduct and budgets for club activities. The chair, vice chair, treasurer, and secretary are elected by the student body from among those running for office. Theoretically, any student can run for office, but there seems to be a common understanding that, while it is all right for a girl to run for vice chair, treasurer, or secretary, the very top office should be occupied by a boy. Even in the absence of any formal regulations, a girl who seeks the top position is likely to be accused by her classmates of "trying to put on airs" or of "lacking in feminine appeal."

Turning to club activities, one of the biggest activities in high school is the biannual national baseball tournaments. The fact that only boys participate in the tournament is itself an issue, but there are other problems as well. Membership in baseball clubs includes girls, but they participate as "managers," whose role is to put away equipment, wash uniforms, and prepare meals and snacks for the players. In short, they perform a support role for the male players. Managers are not allowed to set foot on the grounds or the benches at the national tournaments. Of course, these girls volunteer to become managers, but one cannot help but wonder if they are, in fact, practicing to be housewives. Schools spend enormous amounts to support baseball teams, yet they offer opportunities only to the boys to develop their skills and potential in the sport. At the same time, the fact that what is expected of girls is merely to fulfill housekeeping roles illustrates just how deeply the ideology and practices of gender role differentiation so characteristic of Japanese society have infiltrated the schools and the lives of students.

The view that the role of leader or group representative ought to be occupied by a male is, of course, reflected in adult society, in which men clearly dominate the top positions in politics, business, and other spheres. Even community volunteer groups and parent-teacher associations are often headed by men, in spite of the fact that usually women are the ones who do the actual work within these organizations. One cannot help thinking that schools bear a certain degree of responsibility for continuing to reproduce this state of affairs.

On the other hand, changes are under way. For example, we hear of instances in which female students have run for student council president and been elected, with the result that other female students have been encouraged to take a more active role in various aspects of school life. Some teachers have proposed that student council offices be occupied by an equal number of female and male students.

The growing attention now being paid to everyday practices that go on in schools and classrooms is beginning to yield a better understanding of how sexism and gender stereotyping are embodied in and reproduced through not only the formal but also the hidden curriculum. This awareness has, in turn, given rise to efforts at change and reform.

Sexism in Faculty Organization—The Position of Female Teachers

Compared with other professions, teaching has long been a profession open to women, and it includes a considerable number of women. The Meiji government began training women as elementary school teachers in the latter half of the nineteenth century based on the notion that women were good with small children as well as because women could be hired at a much lower salary than men. Because teaching is a public sector profession, women have have been able to secure a comparatively stable position within the profession.

The history of female teachers has not, however, been easy or smooth. Thus, for instance, in the Meiji period daughters who wished to enter a normal (i.e., teacher training) school were thought to bring shame to the family, based on a highly negative attitude in Japanese society toward women working outside the home. Opposition to female teachers has long existed, based on such notions as "a woman should stay home and raise her own children" and "it is unnatural for a woman to have a profession and work outside the home." In addition, the very idea of women possessing formal knowledge was not acknowledged, as the case of Kono Yasui illustrates. Yasui, born in 1880, became a teacher at the age of twenty-two after graduating from the government-run Tokyo Women's Higher Normal School (now Ochanomizu Women's University). She wrote a textbook on physics, but the governmental officials refused to grant it authorization, saying, "A woman could not have written such a textbook." In 1914, when she applied for a government permit to go to the United States in order to study physics, the words "for study of homemaking" were added to the permit by officials. Subsequently, in 1927, Yasui became the first woman in Japan to be awarded a doctorate in science, and she continued to pursue her research. Her experience illuminates how difficult it was for a woman to gain recognition for work outside the domestic sphere.

Table 4
Representation of Women in Teaching and Administrative Positions at Various Levels of Education, 1993, in Percentage

Elementary school	Principals	7.2
	Head teachers	16.7
	All teachers	60.4
Lower secondary school	Principals	1.2
	Head teachers	4.1
	All teachers	38.4
Upper secondary school	Principals	2.5
	Head teachers	2.0
	All teachers	21.8
Junior college	Presidents	11.7
	Full professors	26.2
	Associate/assistant professors	38.6
	Instructors	47.0
	Assistants	78.1
	Total faculty	38.7
Four-year university	Presidents	4.0
	Full professors	5.5
	Associate/assistant professors	9.1
	Instructors	13.2
	Assistants	15.3
	Total faculty	9.9

Source: Mombusho (Ministry of Education). *Gakko kihon chosa* (School basic survey). 1994.

The teaching profession today guarantees the benefits of gender equality in terms of pay and retirement age as well as maternity and child care leave. Thus, since there is much less overt discrimination in teaching than in jobs in private industry, teaching continues to be popular among women who aspire to long-term careers. The actual position female teachers occupy within the educational structure, however, needs to be looked at more closely.

We can see from table 4 that the proportion of females among teachers becomes smaller as one moves up the educational ladder. Japanese women occupy a smaller proportion of public elementary and secondary school teachers compared to those in England and France.

When we look at the numbers of women who occupy the position of school administrator (see table 4), we find the figures to be extremely low: a mere 7.2 percent of elementary school principals are female; the corresponding figures at the lower secondary and upper secondary schools are, respectively, 1.2 and 2.5 percent. These low figures attest in part to the difficulties female teachers, like other working women, face in trying to advance in their careers while at the same time having to bear the major share of household responsibilities. Another factor is that there is an unwritten regulation in some places that, in cases in which both spouses are teachers, only one of them is eligible to be a principal.

Males are also more likely to be found in other positions that allow for participation in the process of decision making, such as that of head teacher or grade leader. The functions served by female teachers, on the other hand, tend to be congruent with women's traditional gender role; for example, they are more likely to teach younger children, and they are often expected to serve tea at faculty meetings. There is a common tendency within schools to assign a lower evaluation to female teachers based on the assumption that their own family and household responsibilities prevent them from giving as much time and commitment to their work as men might. For this reason male teachers are also more likely to be assigned as advisors to clubs and sports teams.

At the college level more women teach in junior colleges than in universities. Looking again at table 4, we see that women make up 38.7 percent of all faculty members in junior colleges and less than 10 percent of four-year university faculty. Among faculty in graduate schools the figure is about 5 percent. Moreover, the higher the professional rank, the smaller is the proportion of females. In addition, within universities women's representation is higher at the private than at the national universities, at all-female than at coeducational universities, and at the more recently established ones than at the older, more prestigious institutions. As of 1982, women represented a mere 1.1 percent of the faculty at the former imperial universities, which include Tokyo and Kyoto universities, the most prestigious universities in the country (Kano 1984, 194, table 7). To take another example, at Waseda University, which is one of the oldest and most prestigious of the private coeducational universities, in 1991 there were forty full-time female faculty at the instructor/assistant professor level and above, representing just 4 percent of the total. Women employed as assistants and adjuncts accounted for 11 percent of the total (Ishido 1992, 31).

Women's underrepresentation in college and university faculties is a manifestation of the highly rigid and closed organizational nature of Japanese universities, particularly the national universities. Positions are rarely announced publicly, so that women do not have an opportunity to compete openly for a university teaching or research position. Faculty members and research staff tend to be recruited from particular networks through a patronage system, and women are generally excluded from those networks.

At the same time, there are few networks that function as a source of recruitment for women. There are, moreover, no affirmative action programs designed to promote the hiring of women and to redress gender imbalances. As a consequence, fewer women than men are able to obtain employment following completion of master's and doctoral degree programs. In 1992, about 4,500 women completed the master's degree program (compared to roughly 25,000 males); 19.5 percent of these women (and 15.6 percent of the men) went on for further study, while less than 50 percent (compared to 75 percent of the men) obtained employment. Of the 879 women (compared to about 5,600 men) who completed the doctoral degree program the same year, again, just 51 percent found employment, in contrast to 69 percent of men (Mombusho 1993, 96–99).

Many women continue teaching as adjuncts on a yearly contract basis at two or three institutions without ever obtaining a full-time position. A factor that further aggravates this problem is that job transfers are very common within Japanese companies, so that a female academic married to a businessman faces the prospect of having to give up a position in order to accompany her husband to another location. The various forms of discrimination that exist in academia are likely to prove much more difficult to attack than those found in business and industry (see Bando et al. 1981; Kano 1984, 1988; Michii 1982; and Saruhashi and Shiota 1985, for further discussion of female academics in Japan).

Despite the fact that the teaching profession (at least up to secondary school) provides, in theory, equal opportunities for women and men, like other structures in Japanese society, it is highly male-centered, and women still occupy a marginal position. Assumptions and criteria upon which promotion or job assignment are based commonly result in excluding women. Thus, as noted, for example, female teachers with families are assumed to be too busy with family responsibilities to be able to function as administrators, and men who have had experience as members of sports clubs in college are thought to be more qualified than women as advisors for school sports teams. Such forms of systemic discrimination prevail in many fields of work, of course, but it is an issue that needs to be explored further with regard to the teaching profession.

Integrally related to the issue of male dominance in the teaching profession is that of the role played by teachers in shaping students' attitudes and future aspirations. Female students study, participate in other school activities, and make choices regarding future schooling under the direction primarily of male teachers. There are some male teachers and guidance counselors who hold the view that it is not so important for a young woman to strive for admission to a four-year university or that, if she wants to go to college, then literature or home economics is the most appropriate field. The usual argument is, "It's a waste of both time and money for girls to go to a university, since they're going to end up getting married in a couple of years anyway." Sexist comments and attitudes exhibited in the process of teaching,

119

guidance and counseling, and extracurricular activities, needless to say, have a very strong impact on students.

Very few institutions engaged in teacher training provide courses dealing with women's studies or issues of gender inequality in their curricula. There is an urgent need to provide opportunities for teachers to reexamine their own sexist attitudes and assumptions. Recently, seminars for teachers based on the theme of promoting gender equality have been conducted in various parts of Japan—for example, in Tokyo and in Kanagawa Prefecture—and teaching materials, such as videotapes, are beginning to be developed.

The Emergence of Women's Studies

Courses in women's studies have become more widespread in Japanese colleges and universities as well as in adult education programs. In 1992, 24 percent of all junior colleges and universities offered at least one course in women's studies (Kokuritsu Fujin Kyoiku Kaikan 1994). Although the number is still small, some teachers in lower and upper secondary school are beginning to take up women's studies in their classrooms as well. For example, in teaching history, there has been an attempt to correct the imbalance found in most textbooks, in which usually no more than ten female historical figures appear, by incorporating the findings of recent research by scholars in the field of women's history.

To give another example of efforts being undertaken by teachers at the high school level, Yoshida (1988) has reported on her attempt in her Japanese language arts classes to get female students to reflect on themselves by having them write about their thoughts regarding their future educational goals, careers, and gender roles. Her analysis of the students' writings reveals that many young women have conflicting feelings about their futures; on the one hand, they are eager to be involved in society and to have careers, yet, on the other hand, often they feel that they ought to devote themselves to caring for their children while they are small. Yoshida followed this up by having students read materials dealing with the issue of child rearing from various social perspectives. In this way, by incorporating the theme of women's lifestyles into Japanese language arts lessons, this teacher was able not only to work on the skills of reading and writing but also to provide an opportunity for students to think about their own future lives.

In a survey of roughly two thousand kindergarten, elementary, and secondary school teachers conducted by the Tokyo Metropolitan Educational Research Center, the respondents mentioned the following among the efforts they are making in an effort to promote gender equality in education:

• in social studies classes, making students realize that housework is not exclusively a woman's job

• presenting material that portrays men performing housework

• talking to male students about the importance of assuming household responsibilities and to female students about the importance of taking an active part in society

• avoiding the use of such expressions such as "act in a feminine (or masculine) manner" in attempting to guide student behavior

• encouraging male students to participate in dance and female students to participate in martial arts in physical education classes

• striking an even balance in the number of male and female figures who appear in language arts and mathematics problems

• using the personal pronoun *she* more often than *he* in making up sentences in English, since examples that appear in English language textbooks are apt to use *he* more often than *she*.

(Toritsu kyoiku kenkyujo 1992)

These are examples of guidelines that individual teachers have thought up and tried to apply in their own classrooms.

Recently, we are beginning to see more organized efforts to bring about changes in classroom teaching materials and teaching practices. For example, just a few years ago a number of feminist researchers and elementary school teachers put together a textbook directed at third- and fourth-grade elementary school students aimed at promoting gender equality, entitled *Why Do We Make Distinctions?* (Yokohama-shi 1992). The title refers to the kinds of gender distinctions that are commonly made in schools and in society at large. The textbook addresses such questions as "Are there such things as 'boys' colors' and 'girls' colors'?" and "What do you want to be when you grow up?" and presents interviews with a female bus driver and a male nursery school teacher; it is designed to provide examples that encourage children to develop their abilities and make plans for the future unencumbered with preconceived notions about what is gender appropriate. Another interesting example is an illustrated children's book published by the planning section of the Setagaya ward office in Tokyo, entitled *Why, Mother?* based on an essay written by a boy in reaction to his mother's constant admonition "Because you are boy . . ." (Tokyo-to 1990).

Efforts to make education in Japanese schools free from gender biases have only just begun, and most teachers are still struggling to find ways to realize this goal. In the future we need to develop more teaching materials and manuals for teachers. Simultaneously, workshops and training programs need to be set up so that teachers can explore different ways of utilizing and applying such materials in their day-to-day teaching. Infusing a new, gender-free perspective into curricula and teaching methods and practices may be one step toward bringing about a more general reform of the educational process. Thus, for instance, if schools cease to track students into certain fields of study or types of schools based on the socially and culturally constructed categories of gender, then perhaps we can realize the goal of developing the potential of each individual student without reference to any biological categories.

Looking to the Future

An issue that has not received much attention, yet is extremely vital, concerns the process of gender-tracking in Japanese education. Lower and upper secondary school teachers often report that in the conference that takes place in the presence of the student and his or her parents in order to discuss which high school or college the student should apply to, the critical decision is reached much more quickly in the case of female students. What happens very frequently is that the very fact of being a female functions to "cool off" aspirations in the eyes of young women themselves, their parents, and teachers. Thus, even if a male and female student have roughly the same grades, the female student is apt to get steered to a less competitive high school or college, while male students are encouraged to aim for the best schools.[2]

In this way tracking takes place along the dimensions of both gender and levels of achievement (as represented by grades). What on the surface appears to be a choice freely made by a young woman reflects, in many instances, the end product of a long process of socialization and education through which she has internalized certain messages and self-images. If we are to alter the current situation whereby many women go into junior colleges rather than four-year universities and are underrepresented in the physical and social sciences, we need to look more seriously at gender-based tracking at the precollege level.

Thus far, little attention has been paid to making conscious efforts, through guidance or career counseling, to encourage young girls to go into fields of study or occupational spheres that have traditionally been male dominated. Currently, technical courses in high school vocational programs and the science and engineering faculties in universities consist predominantly of male students. If we are really committed to altering this situation, then we need to take more aggressive steps to recruit young women into these fields, through, for example, career training and guidance, as has been done in the United States and the United Kingdom.

Since the 1980s the number of women both within and outside academia engaged in research in various areas of women's studies has increased greatly, as have course offerings in women's studies in colleges and universities. What is required now is to bring to bear on the educational system and its practices the results of various research findings that relate to women's education. We have only just embarked on this undertaking. It is urgent that researchers engaged in women's studies link up with elementary and secondary teachers and jointly develop necessary materials and practices for the classroom. Through this endeavor to reconstruct education based on the principle of liberating students from the confines of established gender roles, we can, it is hoped, pass on a valuable legacy to the next generations of Japanese women.

NOTES

1. In this survey, fifty-two Japanese and thirty American couples with two-and-a-half-year-old children were given questionnaires to complete and were interviewed.

2. One of the reasons high school teachers tend to track female students into less competitive schools is that, as recent evidences have shown, some public high schools practice discrimination in their admission procedures. In Tokyo, for example, it has been revealed that the top public high schools, which, under the prewar educational system, were boys' middle schools, require a higher score on the entrance examinations for girls and maintain a quota for admitting girls ("Danjo byodo e undo" 1988). In addition, there have been reports from other parts of Japan of administrators at coeducational high schools urging their counterparts in lower secondary schools to discourage female students from applying to their schools and to send more boys instead ("Onna seito yori danshi o" 1987).

REFERNCES

Amano, Masako, ed., 1986. *Joshi koto kyoiku no zahyo* (The coordinates of women's higher education). Tokyo: Kakiuchi shuppan.

Bando, Masako, Michiko Noguchi, and Yoko Shinyama, eds. 1981. *Josei to gakumon to seikatsu—fujin kenkyusha no raifu saikuru* (Women, study, and life—the life cycle of women researchers). Tokyo: Keiso shobo.

"Danjo byodo e undo—toritsuko no boshu teiin" ("Movement for gender equality—quotas on admissions at Tokyo metropolitan high schools). 1988. *Asahi shimbun* (Asahi newspaper), 20 May.

Fujin mondai konwakai. 1976. *Fujin mondai konwakai kaiho, 24—kyokasho wa danjo byodo o sodatenai* (Twenty-fourth report of the Fujin mondai konwakai association—textbooks do not promote sexual equality). Tokyo: Fujin mondai konwaki.

———. 1975. *Fujin mondai konwakai kaiho, 22—Kyokasho no naka no danjo sabetsu* (Twenty-second report of the Fujin mondai konwakai association—gender discrimination in textbooks). Tokyo: Fujin mondai konwakai.

Ishido, Tsuneyo. 1992. "Josei daigaku kyoju koyo no susei" (Trends in the employment of female university professors). *IDE,* no. 334 (April): 29–33.

Kameda, Atsuko, and Kaoru Tachi. 1987. "Gakko ni okeru sexism to danjo byodo kyoiku" (Sexism in schools and equal education). In *Onna no me de miru: koza joseigaku 4* (Seeing through women's eyes: lectures on women's studies, vol. 4). Tokyo: Keiso shobo.

Kano, Yoshimasa. 1988. *Academic women: josei gakusha no shakaigaku* (Academic women: sociology of women academics). Tokyo: Toshindo.

———. 1984. "Nihon no josei kenkyusha—sono genjo to rekishiteki hendo" (Women researchers in Japan—their current status and historical changes). In *Daigaku kyojushoku no sogoteki kenkyu—Academic profession no shakaigaku* (A comprehensive study of the college academic profession—sociology of the academic profession), ed. Michiya Shimbori. Tokyo: Oga shuppan.

Kashiwagi, Keiko. 1973. "Gendai seinen no seiyakuwari no shutoku" (Acquisition of gender roles among contemporary youth). In *Gendai seinen no sei ishiki* (Consciousness of gender among contemporary youth), ed. Shin Ida. Tokyo: Kaneko shobo.

Kokuritsu Fujin kyoiku kaikan (National Women's Education Centre). 1994. *Koto kyoiku kikan ni okeru joseigaku kanrenkamokuto no genjo—heisei gonendo chosa hokoku* (Status of women's studies and related courses in institutions of higher education—report of the 1993 survey). Saitama-ken: Kokuritsu fujin kyoiku kaikan.

"Kyoiku gemba no danjo kubetsu o tou, kenkyu shukai de hokoku aitsugu" (Teachers question gender differentiation in schools; successive reports made at a research gathering). 1992. *Yomiuri shimbun* (Yomiuri newspaper), 28 January.

Michii, Takako. 1982. "The Chosen Few: Women Academics in Japan." Ph.D. diss., State University of New York at Buffalo.

Mombusho (Ministry of Education). 1994. *Mombu tokei yoran* (Digest of educational statistics). Tokyo: Daiichi mombusho.

Nihon seishonen kenkyujo. 1986. *Yojikino nichibei oyako kankei chosa* (Survey of parent-child relations among American and Japanese during childhood). Tokyo: Nihon seishonen kenkyujo.

"Onna seito yori danshi o—chugakko ni juken yosei" (Calling on junior high schools to send male rather than female applicants). 1987. *Asahi shimbun* (Asahi newspaper), 20 March.

Owaki, Masako. 1991. *Kyokasho no naka no danjo sabetsu* (Sex discrimination in textbooks). Tokyo: Akashi shoten.

Saruhashi, Katsuko, and Shobei Shiota, eds. 1985. *Josei kenkyusha* (Women researchers). Tokyo: Domesu shuppan.

Sasakura, Naoko, and Satomi Nakajima. 1990. *Onna ga seiji o kaeru* (Women bringing about change in politics). Tokyo: Shinsensha.

Tokyoto Setagaya-ku kikaku (Setagaya Ward Office, Planning Section), ed. 1990. *Okasan, nandeya* (Why, mother?). Tokyo: Gakuyo shobo.

Toritsu kyoiku kenkyujo (Tokyo Metropolitan Institute of Educational Research). 1992. *Danjo byodo kyoiku ni kansuru kenkyu* (Research on education based on gender equality). Tokyo: Metropolitan Institute of Educational Research.

Walker, Stephen, and Len Barton. 1983. "Gender, Class and Education: A Personal View." In *Gender, Class, and Education*, ed. Stephen Walker and Len Barton. Barcombe, U.K.: Falmer Press.

Weiler, Kathleen. 1988. *Women Teaching for Change*. New York, Westport, Conn., and London: Bergin and Garvey.

"Yatta!! danjo kongo meibo" (We did it!! Mixed-sex class rosters). 1990. *Asahi shimbun* (Asahi newspaper). 23 February.

Yokohama-shi kyoiku iinkai (City of Yokohama Board of Education), ed. 1992a. *Doshite wakeruno?* (Why do we make distinctions?). Yokohama: Board of Education.

———. 1992b. *Doshite wakeruno?—Katsuyo no tebiki* (Why do we make distinctions?—Teachers' manual).

Yoshida, Kiyomi. 1988. "Onna no ikikata o kangaeru—koko kokugo de no jugyo jissen" (Thinking about women's lives—women's studies in a high school language arts class). *Nihon joseigakkai joseigaku nempo* (Annual report of the Women's Studies Society of Japan), no. 9: 74–83.

College Women Today:
Options and Dilemmas

❖ ❖ ❖

Kumiko Fujimura-Fanselow

I n contrast to fifty years ago, when fewer than one out of a hundred young Japanese women went on to college or some other institution of postsecondary education, today that figure exceeds one out of three. The overwhelming majority of female college graduates—80 percent of university and 87 percent of junior college graduates in 1992—take up employment following graduation. Moreover, growing numbers of graduates are taking on jobs or positions that were once closed to them. These changes parallel and reflect major developments in society over recent years, such as the rise in prosperity among the Japanese people, the growth in labor force participation by women, and transformations in attitudes and aspirations among women which have occurred in part as a result of the women's movement of the last fifteen to twenty years.

The expansion of educational and employment opportunities for Japanese women has made it possible for young Japanese women to exercise a wider range of choices and options in planning their lives. At the same time, however, that freedom of choice is greatly circumscribed by a variety of social structural as well as attitudinal constraints, among them persisting biases against women in the workplace, lack of adequate child care facilities, and lingering traditional norms and expectations regarding women's role in the home and society. New options seem to coexist with persisting barriers, and today's college women appear to be caught in a dilemma, at once awakening to new aspirations and possibilities for their future yet, at the same time, often deterred from testing out those opportunities by persisting obstacles and the weight of tradition and custom.

This essay explores the changing portrait of college women today and their attitudes regarding their future role in society. I will be drawing on data from various studies as well as on observations based on my experiences over the last five years teaching courses in women and education as well as a required introductory course in women's studies to entering first-year students at a women's university near Tokyo. What I hope to demonstrate is the spirit and desire on the part of young women today to seize new opportunities and make use of their education and talent, combined with a widespread feeling of ambivalence and confusion over issues of career, marriage, and family which is based on a sober assessment of the difficulties entailed in balancing and combining these.

Change and Continuity in Patterns of Participation in Higher Education

As Kimi Hara describes elsewhere in this volume, in prewar Japanese society higher education was available to women only at the two national women's higher normal schools and the forty or so private women's colleges, none of which was accredited as a university. On the eve of World War II about 10 percent of girls graduating from elementary school went on to girls' high schools, and of those graduating from high school fewer than one out of ten went on to some type of postsecondary institution. As might be expected, the family backgrounds of women who pursued higher education in the prewar days were far from average. These women tended to come from rather affluent families and to have parents who were better educated than most Japanese. Prevailing social opinion strongly disapproved of women acquiring higher education. The argument that academic study would make a young woman *"namaiki"* (conceited, impertinent, forward) and therefore make it difficult for her to find a husband and that, even if she married, she would be disliked by her husband for her "pride" and "conceit," was frequently put forward.

By the eve of World War II, however, upper-class families had gradually come to look with favor upon higher education as a means of providing their daughters with general cultural enrichment, which would enhance their position when it came to marriage. This view was expressed in the notion of *ryosai kenbo kyoiku*, or "education for good wives and wise mothers." Education, however, that led to a clear occupational objective, such as training for the teaching profession, continued to be frowned on by many. This reflected the general norm that women's place was in the home and a disapproval of women going out into the world and working, irrespective of the type of occupation.

Educational reforms undertaken following the end of World War II established the principles of equal educational opportunity and coeducation at all levels. University status was granted to many of the existing women's colleges, while universities that had previously admitted only men were made coeducational. In the ensuing years levels of educational attainment have risen to the point that in 1993 over 96 percent of girls went on to and graduated from high school following nine years of compulsory schooling. At the same time, the proportion of females in the relevant age group entering colleges and universities has risen from just 5.5 percent in 1960 to 45.9 percent in 1994, overtaking males since 1989. These seemingly very positive developments need to be balanced, however, against conspicuous gender differences that have persisted in patterns of educational participation and achievement.

• A majority of females pursue higher education in junior colleges rather than four-year universities. In 1994, for example, 54 percent of females entering college went into junior colleges; among males, on the other hand, 95 percent went on to four-year universities. The rate of female entry into four-year universities today—21 percent in 1994—is about what it was for males in the early 1970s (see table 1).

• Females accounted for 31 percent of all university undergraduate students in 1994; on the other hand, females made up nearly 92 percent of all junior

Table 1

Percentages of Females and Males of the Appropriate Age Group Entering Junior Colleges and Four-Year Universities, for Selected Years, 1955 to 1994

| Year | Junior College | | University | |
	Females	*Males*	*Females*	*Males*
1955	2.6	1.9	2.4	13.1
1960	3.0	1.2	2.5	13.7
1965	6.7	1.7	4.6	20.7
1970	11.2	2.0	6.5	27.3
1975	19.9	2.6	12.5	40.4
1980	21.0	2.0	12.3	39.3
1985	20.8	2.0	13.7	38.6
1990	22.2	1.7	15.2	33.4
1994	24.9	2.0	21.0	38.9

Note: These figures represent the number of students going on to either junior college or four-year university divided by the total number of students who graduated from lower secondary school three years prior to each year (which represents basically the total of all those in the eighteen-year-old age group), multiplied by 100.
Source: Mombusho (Ministry of Education), *Gakko kihon chosa* (School basic survey) (Tokyo: Mombusho), annual.

college students (see table 2). Women who enter four-year universities tend to be a much more select group than their male counterparts both in terms of social class and academic ability (Tomoda 1972; Kyoto Daigaku Kyoikugakubu 1982: 37, fig. V-2).

• The comparatively low rate of female enrollment at four-year universities means that women continue to constitute a small minority in graduate schools. Only 3.7 percent of all women graduating from university went on to graduate school in 1992, compared to 8.8 percent among males (Mombusho 1993, 38–39); women constituted just 18.5 percent of students enrolled in master's degree programs and 16.6 of those in doctoral degree programs (82–83).

• A substantial proportion of women are clustered in traditionally female fields of study—humanities and education in four-year universities and humanities and home economics in junior colleges—while relatively few receive training for business and professional careers, except in fields such as teaching or pharmacy (see table 3).

• The ratio of women majoring in law, political science, or economics has risen considerably even just within the past five to six years, from 16 percent in 1986 to 21 percent in 1990, but still very few are found in engineering (2.7 percent) or science (2.3 percent).

Table 2

Percentages of Females among All Students Enrolled in Universities and Junior Colleges, for Selected Years, 1955 to 1994

Year	University	Junior College
1955	12.4	54.0
1960	13.7	78.7
1965	16.2	74.8
1970	18.0	82.7
1975	21.2	86.2
1980	22.1	89.0
1985	23.5	89.8
1990	27.4	91.5
1994	31.3	91.8

Source: Mombusho (Ministry of Education), *Gakko kihon chosa* (School basic survey) (Tokyo: Mombusho), annual.

Table 3

Percentage Distribution of Female Students at Universities and Junior Colleges in Various Faculties and Departments, for Selected Years 1965 to 1993

Four-Year Universities			
	1965	1980	1993	(1993—Males)
Humanities	45.2	35.9	33.9	7.6
Social sciences	5.2	14.7	24.2	47.1
Natural sciences	2.3	2.2	2.3	4.0
Engineering	0.5	1.3	4.0	26.5
Agriculture	0.8	1.7	3.1	3.3
Medicine/Dentistry and other health-related fields	8.6	8.9	7.4	4.4
Home economics	9.4	8.1	5.6	0.0
Education	20.1	18.1	11.9	4.2
Art	6.6	7.1	5.3	1.1
Other	1.3	2.6	2.1	1.7

Junior Colleges			
	1965	1980	1993	(1993—Males)
Humanities	26.6	23.7	28.9	6.4
Social sciences	4.3	6.5	12.0	33.2
Engineering	0.6	0.5	1.6	40.1
Agriculture	0.3	0.2	0.9	5.2
Health	0.5	4.3	5.6	7.0
Home economics	52.1	30.0	25.3	1.3
Education	11.9	27.1	16.2	1.7
Art	3.6	5.5	4.6	4.8
Other	0	2.2	5.5	0.3

Source: Figures compiled from Mombusho (Ministry of Education), *Gakko kihon chosa* (*School basic survey*) for each year.

Why These Gender Differences?

Social Attitudes Regarding Women's Education

The various manifestations of gender discrepancies in patterns of participation in higher education are attributable to several related factors. They reflect, first of all, certain cultural norms and attitudes regarding the role of women in society and the purposes of higher education for women within this culturally defined role. Such notions as "a man should be better educated than his wife," "too much education will make a woman too proud and therefore unfit to be a good wife," and "the goal of women's education should to be produce good wives and wise mothers," old-fashioned though they may sound, are at the basis of many Japanese people's attitudes regarding education for women.

Nationwide public opinion surveys conducted over the past several years reveal that while there has been a general rise in the levels of education that the Japanese desire for children of both sexes, parents continue to assign higher priority to the education of sons. Most parents want their daughters to receive at least a high school education, but beyond that they are likely to think in terms of a junior college for their daughters and a four-year university for their sons. In a 1988 national opinion poll by NHK (Japan Broadcasting Corporation), 33 percent of the respondents indicated that they wanted daughters to receive a four-year university education (45 percent wanted them to go to a junior college), in contrast to 78 percent in the case of sons. These results are similar to those derived from a survey of third-, fifth-, and eighth-graders and their mothers in Tokyo, in which 68 percent of the mothers indicated they wanted a four-year university education for sons, as compared to just 37 percent in the case of daughters (Takeuchi 1985, 25). Those parents with more education and a higher socioeconomic level who reside in large urban centers are more likely to want a university education for their daughters. Yet it remains true that at every level Japanese parents exhibit lower aspirations for daughters than for sons. Parents are apt to approach the subject of their sons' education much more seriously from an early age. Thus, for example, they are more likely in the case of sons to start sending them to private *juku*, or tutorial schools, after school or on the weekend from around the fourth grade in order to get supplementary academic instruction and prepare them for entrance exams for one of the better secondary schools, which in turn are thought to prepare students for the top universities.

Discussions with some of the students at the women's university where I teach confirm these data and observations. The majority of students at this university come from well-to-do families who more or less took it granted that their daughters, as well as sons, would attend university. Yet there are cases in which one or the other parent or some other relative thought it was a waste of time and money for young women to attend college for four years and felt, instead, that a junior college education was sufficient. Others have mentioned that, while in the case of their brothers, the parents were very keen on having them go to a top-ranking university and were even willing to allow them to spend a year or two as a *ronin* studying at "cram schools" devoted to teaching of techniques for passing university entrance exams in order to gear up to retake the college entrance examinations, rather than settle for a lower-ranking institution, in their own case the parents were not nearly as particular about which university they entered. Moreover, they were certainly not willing to spend resources to support a *ronin* daughter, so that few of them even applied for admission to one of the top-rated (coeducational) universities.

These attitudes concerning the relative importance of higher education for women are intimately tied to considerations about the role of women both within the family and in other institutions of society. Thus, the tendency on the part of most Japanese parents to place lower priority on the education of daughters than sons is a reflection in large part of the assumption and norm that women will marry and have children and not take up careers following completion of their education. The following comments by two students illustrate this point:

> Parents expect much of sons. Parents expect sons to enter a good school and enter a good company, but to daughters they say, "After all, you will marry one day. Find a good husband."

> Now on the surface, there is equality of the sexes in Japanese society, but there is sexual discrimination in the home. Girls are taught that they should be quiet by their parents as well as teachers. Girls who are active and self-assertive are said to be tomboys and pushy. Even if girls have great dreams, they are told that they should be "normal" married women by their parents.[1]

As table 4 shows, the view that "men should work and women should stay at home" has only recently come to be questioned by a substantial proportion of women themselves, while among men it continues to have considerable support.

Most parents have sought for daughters the kind of education which would provide general cultural enrichment in preparation for their future

Table 4

Attitudes toward Gender Roles, in Response to: "How do you feel about the idea that men should work and women should stay at home?"

	Women in Percentage		Men in Percentage	
	1987	1990	1987	1990
Agree	36.6	25.1	51.7	34.7
Disagree	31.9	43.2	20.2	34.0
Neither	29.3	29.1	26.4	29.7

Source: Sorifu (Office of the Prime Minister), *Fujin ni kansuru yoron chosa* (Public opinion survey on women), 1987 and 1990. Tokyo: Sorifu.

roles as wives and mothers. Many have viewed two years at a junior college as sufficient for these purposes; those able to and wanting a four-year university education for daughters have, for these same reasons, preferred to send them to women's universities (which numbered 94, out of a total of 534 universities, in 1993) rather than coeducational, universities. In addition, teachers and guidance counselors often further reinforce these tendencies by steering young women to less competitive high schools and colleges while encouraging male students to aim for the prize institutions (see the essay by Atsuko Kameda in this volume for a further discussion of this point). Changes in such attitudes are certainly discernible, especially in the large urban centers. They are reflected in the fact that, for example, among young women who graduated from high schools in the Tokyo metropolitan area in 1994, the percentage advancing to four-year universities exceeded that going to junior colleges for the first time, 24.3 to 23.7 percent ("Yonensei e shingaku . . ." 1994). The education of daughters has taken on greater importance to parents as a result also of the fact that more and more of them are having only one or two children.

Aspects of the Educational System

In addition to cultural and attitudinal factors, we can point to certain features of the structure of higher education itself which have given rise to and reinforced existing sex disparities in patterns of participation at higher institutions. First of all, one major reason why so many women have been enrolled in junior colleges over the past thirty years is that, in the absence of a concerted government effort to expand opportunities for women to pursue higher education at universities, it is the private junior colleges that have been most aggressive in establishing facilities catering almost exclusively to female clientele (see Fujimura-Fanselow 1985, 478–81, for further discussion of this point).

Similarly, female students' overrepresentation in the humanities, home economics, and education and their underrepresentation in fields such as science, engineering, law, economics, and other social sciences are in large part a consequence of the fact that the range of study options offered at most private women's universities (which enroll roughly one-fourth of all women studying at four-year universities) and junior colleges is extremely limited. In the case of women's universities, except at a handful of institutions, the humanities and home economics faculties are the only ones available. Traditionally male professional subjects such as engineering, accounting, economics, and law are almost totally absent from their curriculum. This bias in curricula offerings is even more pronounced at the junior colleges. Most women simply have not been given an opportunity to choose nontraditional study options. In this way, instead of preparing women to assume the same roles as men, the institutions serving women have tended both to reflect and to reinforce differential expectations concerning the uses of education.

Restrictions in Employment Opportunities for Female University Graduates

Sex disparities in educational participation are attributable not only to cultural attitudes and the educational system but also to prevailing inequalities in the labor market. Except in a few professions in which women have long been visible, employment opportunities for university-educated women in Japan have been extremely limited, both in comparison to male graduates and also to graduates from junior colleges, and this factor too has served to steer women away from four-year universities.

The practice among employers has been to hire young women straight out of school for various jobs, based on the assumption that they will work up until they get married or, at most, until they have a child. Women have been excluded from the traditional systems of lifetime employment and of promotion and wages based on length of consecutive service within a particular company. (For a detailed discussion of the status of women in the labor market, see the essay by Yoko Kawashima in this volume.) High school or junior college graduates have been hired as "OLs," or "office ladies," to perform routine clerical work, but graduates from four-year universities have not been taken on for such positions because they are more expensive and presumably have fewer years remaining until they leave their jobs. At the same time, most employers have been reluctant to hire these women to perform tasks comparable to those assigned to male university graduates. Many companies have had a policy of not recruiting female university graduates, and for this reason, until very recently, employment rates among female university graduates have been lower than those among junior college graduates. Until just a few years ago the differential in starting pay for women and men was greater among university graduates than among high school and junior college graduates.

Various legal and social changes have resulted in modifying this situation somewhat. The major legal step has been the passage of the Equal Employment Opportunity Law in 1985. More companies began to hire female four-year university graduates, in some cases for management track positions, prompting in turn a trend away from junior colleges and toward four-year universities and from women's universities to coed universities, which offer a greater variety of study options in more directly job-related fields. Yet the downturn in the Japanese economy in the 1990s has served to diminish once again employment opportunities for university-educated women, as they have fallen victim to efforts by companies to cut back on new hiring. In addition, the obstacles that confront women in the workplace are still such that many or even most young women continue to feel—and rightfully so—a great deal of uncertainty and apprehension about planning for long-term careers.

Attitudes of Young Women Regarding Their Future

Motivations for Pursuing Higher Education

As mentioned earlier, under the highly elitist system of education which existed in prewar Japanese society, a mere 1 percent of the relevant age group of women received education beyond high school. These women usually had a clear motivation for pursuing higher education, which was either to pursue knowledge and learning or else to enter one of the professions that were open to women and do something useful for society. The same was true of women who entered colleges and universities in the immediate postwar years and in the 1950s.

In this day and age, however, when college attendance has become accessible to a much wider and more diverse population of young women (and men)—and, in fact, increasingly come to be viewed as a matter of course for those of the middle class—female students hardly constitute a homogeneous group. Today's young women express a variety of motivations for going to college, and very often several different motives are at work within an individual: "to pursue scholarly learning," "to gain cultural enrichment," "to acquire specialized training and skills in preparation for future career," "to make friends and enjoy myself," "to enjoy a period of moratorium before going out into the work world," "because everyone around me is going to college," "to kill time before getting married and settling down," and "because I want to get married to a man with a university education" (see Nihon Rikuruto Senta, annual). Males, too, give different reasons for going to university, but the basic underlying reason is commonly understood to be because a university degree or credential is indispensable for finding good employment, and the more prestigious the university, the better the chances of getting into one of the larger companies, which provide good pay, benefits, and security.

Various studies in the past have shown that women who attend coeducational universities and major in the more male-dominated fields—law, economics, political science, engineering, etc.—as well as those from less well-to-do families are apt to have stronger career motivations for attending college compared to those from more affluent homes those who go to a junior college or a women's university and major in one of the traditionally female fields. In reality, however, the picture is much more complex. Even at the women's university where I teach, which is generally categorized as a "finishing school for young women from well-to-do homes," the students express varying motivations for pursuing higher education as well as varying degrees of career aspirations. Increasingly, though, it has become common for young women to at least pay lip service to the claim that one reason they are in college is to get training for future careers, regardless of whether or not they really plan to pursue long-term careers.

Some Type of Employment after Graduation

Based on the evidence, it is not surprising to find that today it is both a common and socially accepted practice for women to work following college graduation. Employment rates among females graduating from four-year universities has risen markedly in recent years, from around 60 percent twenty years ago to more than 80 percent in recent years. Their rate of employment has also gradually caught up with that of graduates from junior colleges. While nearly all women anticipate taking a job after finishing college, their attitudes and motivations toward work and their long-range career plans vary considerably.

As a matter of fact, what is interesting as one observes Japanese college women of today is their striking resemblance to American college women of fifteen or twenty years ago, for it was precisely in the mid-1970s that American coeds began to make inroads into the hitherto male-dominated law, business, and medical schools and to develop a strong career orientation. This time lag reflects, of course, the fact that opportunities for women in these fields have become open to women only very recently. Thus, today, as various studies have shown, 80 to 90 percent of female American college seniors aspire to marry, have children, and have a career, in many cases in the lucrative, male-dominated professional and technical sector. Japanese college women, on the other hand, are just now, and in many cases very hesitantly, beginning to consider the possibility of pursuing long-term careers, and even then few seem to aspire to high-paying and challenging professional jobs. The idea of combining career, marriage, and family is viewed as a much more remote and unrealistic—though, for many, attractive—possibility. Due in large part to the Japanese mass media, which has greatly played up the themes of "the age of women" and *kyaria uman* (career women), today's young women are well aware that there are indeed many women "out there" who manage to "have it all." These images and messages, however, compete with others they receive when they look at women who are immediately around them—for example, their own mothers, who for the most part either work part-time or are full-time housewives—or when they read and hear about the continuing discrimination faced by women in the workplace and the burdens faced by full-time working mothers.

We can discern a typology of attitudes, motivations, aspirations, and levels of commitment with regard to work among Japanese college women today. As one would expect, these differences are intricately tied to attitudes regarding women's role in society and in the home.

At one end of the spectrum are those who, though they plan to take a job following graduation, look upon work primarily as a way of gaining some experience in society and also enjoying themselves with the money they earn while living at home with their parents before settling down to the "real" business of getting married and raising a family. Because they view work as a temporary activity lasting three or four years, such women tend not to be very choosy, therefore, about the actual content of the work for which they are hired; they're willing to settle for a clerical job as an OL or "Office Lady." But they do show a preference for the large, big-name corporations, partly because of the pool of eligible men they offer. These women intend to stop working when they marry or else when they have a child and to stay home while the children are small, though many of them consider the possibility of going back to work once the children are older.

The second category, made up of those whom Amano (1985, 12) classifies as "bread-earners," regard work primarily as a means of earning their own livelihood and being financially independent. These women dislike the idea of being supported by their parents—or their husbands. Because they anticipate working on a long-term career basis, they don't want to settle for a dead-end job that involves just routine clerical or support-level work. Instead, they aspire to a more specialized type of work. They're not particularly interested in working for a "brand-name" company but, rather, in one that is willing to assign women positions of responsibility and allow them to work even after marriage or childbirth.

Another category that Amano (1985, 12–13) has identified consists of women whose prime motivation for wanting to take up a career is to seek "self-realization." These women want to develop and realize their talent and potential through their work; therefore, they are very careful in choosing the type of job or company they go into. Imbued with a "pioneer spirit," they aspire to break into professions that have traditionally been dominated by males or into one of those fields that has been newly opened up in recent years—for example, electronics and computers. Because they see their work as a path to their own self-development, they would like to be able to continue work on a long-term basis. Yet because, unlike the second group, who regard work as more or less a necessity, those who fall into this group place priority on being able to find enjoyment and fulfillment in their work, they are quite often willing to abandon their plans for a career working altogether if they fail to find the "right" kind of work with the "right" company and to look for self-fulfillment elsewhere (such as marriage) or else to join the first group and plan to work for just a few years in a routine clerical job.

There is, in addition, an emerging group of extremely able and ambitious young women—admittedly small as yet—who aspire to professional careers demanding a high level of both skills and commitment. In some respects they may overlap with those in the previous category. Of the women in this category who I have encountered among the students at the university where I teach, the majority plan to attend graduate school either in Japan or else abroad (usually in the United States) in order to acquire the training and qualifications necessary for going into such fields as psychological counseling, international relations, and the teaching of Japanese as a foreign language either in Japan or abroad or for working for international organizations such as the United Nations. It is interesting to note that, among this particular group of students at my institution, nearly all are very skilled in English;

some, in fact, lived abroad at some point. These women appear to view marriage and children as something very far down the road.

Over recent years there seems to have occurred a gradual shift in the proportions of women falling under these various categories, with those who regard work as simply a means of gaining social experience showing a decline relative to the other groups. Nevertheless, this group, together with those who seek employment primarily as a means to self-realization, overshadow those who, like most males, look upon work as a simple matter of course, necessary for one's survival as an independent adult. While the assumption that women will work for some time following graduation has become the general norm, the majority of young women do not, at this point, envision pursuing work on a continuous and long-term—that is to say, career—basis. Instead, they tend to view their continued involvement in work as very much contingent upon a host of factors—including the type of work they are able to find, working conditions, and, above all, marriage and childbirth.

At this point most college-educated women tend to show a relatively short-term commitment to their jobs. A survey of women employees at 172 companies listed on the Tokyo exchange who were hired in the spring of 1986 found that the percentage of female college graduates (from both universities and junior colleges) who remained on the job after five years was roughly one-half (50.4 percent), a figure somewhat lower than that found among female high school graduates (54.2) and considerably lower compared to that among male college graduates (84.5 percent) ("Tekireiki wa kigyo no teki" 1991). Something else that I have found from talking with female students at my universities is that, even among those who plan to pursue careers, very few seem to aim for high-paying, high-prestige careers. Thus, for example, those who are skilled or are interested in foreign languages are apt to mention careers in interpreting, translating, teaching English at a private tutorial school or in their homes, or becoming a flight attendant, tour conductor, or a secretary to a diplomat, but not teaching foreign languages at a university or actually going into the foreign service and becoming a diplomat. The following section explores some of the factors that shape and give rise to these attitudes.

Factors Shaping Women's Future Aspirations and Expectations

Of course, not all college women fit neatly into one of these three categories. What is important to understand is how young women's career motivations and expectations fit in with or relate to their attitudes, goals, and aspirations with respect to the future as a whole and the forces and factors that shape those attitudes and aspirations. Significant among those is the fact that today's generation of college women were born into a society that was well into an era of economic prosperity and were brought up for the most part in well-to-do families, so that they have neither had to nor been encouraged to think about working as a matter of financial necessity. At the same time, they have lacked role models to whom they could look in formulating alternative, nontraditional career plans.

Lack of Knowledge and a Long-Term Perspective

An overriding impression I have gained from talking with young women just entering college and from listening to their reactions to various issues I have brought up in class in regard to women is that in most cases these women, and probably most eighteen- and nineteen-year old women, have not given much serious thought to their long-term futures, investigated different career options, or thought about concrete plans of action and how their education might be tied to those plans, nor have they been encouraged or helped to do so.

In my introductory freshmen women's studies course each semester there are a few students who have had a teacher in high school who brought up one or another issue having to do with women; however they are the exception. The curricula in Japanese schools, which are designed and carefully controlled by the Ministry of Education, make no provisions for dealing with gender-related issues (see the essay by Atsuko Kameda in this volume, for a more detailed discussion of the treatment of gender issues in public schools). In the course evaluation form I have students complete at the end of my course, several students have made comments such as: "Until I entered this college I never questioned or doubted women's position in society" and "It is only since entering this university that I have come to think about women's lives." The lack of a long-term perspective regarding one's own future came across pointedly in the opening sentence a young woman wrote for an assignment in which I asked the students to describe the kind of lives they expected to be leading when they were forty years old: "Frankly, I am put off because I have never thought of my future beyond a few years." This was, in fact, a typical opening line.

The students I have come in contact with have a very limited knowledge or understanding of the current situation of women in Japanese society, the changes taking place in their lives—for example, life cycle changes, growth in employment among housewives and mothers, the increase in options that are becoming available to them, or the problems that continue to confront women in the home and the workplace, including a growing instability within marriages which is evident despite Japan's relatively low rate of actual divorce.

What knowledge they do have tends to be based on images they have absorbed from the mass media or from their immediate environment, and so they tend to have a skewed, either overly optimistic or overly pessimistic, picture. The majority seem to be pessimists, resigned to what they perceive is a status quo in which women are greatly handicapped by various obstacles to women's full participation in society and feeling that it is not within their power to shape their own lives and futures. Many of these women decide that it is more realistic and smarter to settle for a clerical job at some big company and work for a few years than to try to get a management-track position.

Many young women plan to stop working when they have children and to resume work again when their children reach a certain age. It is true, of course, that it is now a very common practice for married women with children to enter or reenter the labor market. In general, however, opportunities for a woman in her thirties and forties who has once withdrawn from the labor market to return to a full-time job with prospects for career advancement are extremely limited, even if she has a university degree. Even for part-time positions there are age limitations on hiring, with forty-five years the upper limit. A shortage in labor has intensified the demand for the labor of married women, but, even with that, the average hourly pay for female part-timers stands at a mere 700 yen, which is under US$7.00 (Rodosho Fujinkyoku, 1991, app. p. 78, app. table 78). Few students are aware of these facts.

A Shortage of Role Models

As noted, most young women are not given an opportunity in schools to explore issues concerning women or to think about and plan for their futures. Compounding this shortcoming has been the absence of diverse role models who young women can readily look to, identify with, and aspire to emulate. Many young women today are drawn to the image of the career woman, but they find it very difficult to identify truly with that image, to see themselves in that role. One reason for this is that the models most young Japanese women see when they look at the women who are in their immediate environment—namely, their own and their friends' mothers—are full-time homemakers or else women who work on a part-time basis.

> Japanese children imagine their future by looking at their parents. They see the father working very hard and coming home late and taking few holidays and the mother doing the housekeeping. So I think Japanese children imagine their future like this and they can't have any big dreams.

> The fact that there are relatively few active, working women around children has an influence on their views regarding marriage. Children's views of marriage is dominated by what they see in their own homes and in fairy tales they read.

> For my part, I want to work, and I think it should be an important job. Somewhere in my mind, though, I think that since I'm a woman, if I encounter some problem my parents will help me, and also when I marry I can rely on my husband even if I have a job. This is humiliating for me, because I want to be independent, but in fact, this consciousness have taken root in my mind deeply. One of the reasons is that for me, the closest woman is my mother, and she is a wife, so I think it is natural way of living for women.

As indicated above, Japanese women who attend four-year universities

139

today tend to come from rather well-to-do homes in which the father usually earns sufficient income to support the family so that the mother does not have to work for financial reasons. Moreover, while many of the mothers of today's students attended either a junior college or university (the figure was 55 percent among first-year students surveyed at my university in 1994), in those days—that is, the 1960s—not only was it considered much less socially acceptable for women to work—especially after marriage, but also job opportunities for female graduates were extremely limited, so that relatively few women of their generation pursued careers. Even in the case of those with prior work experience, many reason that they are better off staying home rather than taking a part-time job that is not very interesting to them and pays very little.

While full-time homemakers bear most of the responsibilities for child care and housekeeping, at the same time, those who are married to university-educated men employed by one of the bigger companies have the financial resources to pursue, in their leisure time, various activities that afford some degree of fulfillment, whether it be attending classes at a culture center, playing tennis and golf with friends, engaging in volunteer activities (e.g., the PTA, local food cooperatives, politically oriented groups). At my college, about half of the students' mothers are full-time homemakers; the rest have mothers who engage in some type of work, but more than half of these mothers work only part-time, as translators, English teachers in a private school or private tutors of English, piano, the tea ceremony, etc., or in a family business. Some of the students have been encouraged to prepare for lifelong careers by mothers who have expressed regret over not having had the opportunity to do something more with their own lives. Many of the students, however, see their mothers' lives as generally happy and fulfilling: "When I am forty years old, I will be a mother of many children. I want to be a mother like my own mother. She doesn't have a job, but she has hobbies and enjoys herself. I want to find my own pleasure and I want to have a lovely family." In fact, their lives seem to be much more attractive compared to that of their fathers, who are for the most part salaried white-collar workers who have to commute long distances on congested trains, work long hours, rarely take vacations, and not have much of a life apart from their work.

The unarticulated assumption underlying the thinking of most of these young women is that they will marry and stay happily married so that they need not become financially independent. Moreover, they envision that, once married, they will be able to enjoy the same standard of living and lead the same kind of comfortable lifestyle as their mothers, not having to work for financial reasons. In thinking so, however, they are assuming that the Japanese economy will continue to grow and function at an equally high level over the next twenty years and that a single income will be sufficient to maintain the same standard of living. Many see themselves with two or three children, living comfortable lives, being able to afford vacations abroad a couple of times a year, and taking part in sports and hobbies.

About the only immediate role models of career women that these women have encountered prior to entering college have been their elementary and secondary schoolteachers, but, as a couple of the students commented, they tend to look upon these women only as "teachers," rather than as women who in most cases combined careers with families. At the college level women made up 38 percent of the faculty in junior colleges and 10 percent of four-year university faculty (see table 4 in Kameda's chapter).

Today a new potential role model of a career woman is presented by university-educated women who have begun to venture into the hitherto male-dominated management-track positions within Japanese corporations. As yet, however, there have not been enough successful models to convince young women that the extra effort will indeed result in promotion along the way and that such a demanding career can be successfully combined with marriage and family. They are, instead, more likely to read or hear about those who have quit their jobs out of frustration and/or exhaustion.

The Pull of Marriage and Motherhood

Very much related to these points in terms of shaping young women's career aspirations is the powerful pull of marriage and motherhood on their consciousness. Kyoko Yoshizumi (see her essay in this volume) makes the point that the notion that women's happiness lies in marriage and the strong social pressures on all women to marry and to do so by a certain age have become greatly moderated in recent years. The average age of women's first marriage has risen to nearly twenty-six, and much is reported in the press about how more and more women are postponing marriage and choosing the single life. While this is indeed the case, at the same time, the notion that it is "natural" and "normal" for everyone to marry (and have children) is still quite pervasive in Japanese society. Moreover, marriage is seen very much as a means of conferring legitimacy and status to both men and women. Thus, for example, many single men talk about wanting to get married so that they will be regarded as stable and trustworthy by their employers.

Certainly, among young, college-age women—eighteen- to twenty-two-year-olds—marriage continues to hold a very strong attraction. Nearly all of them assume they will get married, stay married, and live "happily ever after" with a man who will provide for them. In fact, they have not given much thought to their futures beyond marriage; the assumption is that somehow things will fall into place. The "Cinderella syndrome" is very much a part of their consciousness. Other matters, including their continued involvement in a career, are seen as contingent upon the man they marry, and, consequently, they seem reluctant about making major career commitments: "I'm reluctant to make any big career plans for the future, anything that involves a lot of training or commitment, because I don't know whether I'll be able to continue my career once I get married. That's why I'd rather aim for a more limited, low-level career. . . . Then, even if I have to give it up for marriage, I won't feel that I'm making a big sacrifice or that I'm throwing away something important."

With regard to children, data point to a gradual decline in birthrate—to a record low of 1.46 in 1993, compared to 1.91 in 1975. While many different factors are behind this trend, certainly one of them is the fact that more women are choosing careers over families; another is that it has become at least somewhat more socially acceptable for a woman to say that she simply does not want to have children. At the same time, however, Japanese peoples' attitudes in this regard have not shifted nearly to the extent of that of, say, Americans, particularly among those living outside the major cities. There is still a very strong consensus that it is "normal" for people to get married and raise children. Moreover, people tend to assign responsibility for the care and upbringing of children to the mother. A lot of young women I have spoken with cite having children as "a woman's unique privilege." On the whole, even those who plan on careers show an unquestioning willingness to accept the responsibility for child care almost single-handedly. The question of how the two goals—having a career and being a perfect wife and mother—are to be reconciled is not something these young women have seriously considered. In this respect, again, they are perhaps not so different from many or even most American coeds today (Machung 1989). These sentiments are expressed in some of the things my students wrote for an assignment in which they were asked to write about their lives at age forty:

Recently, people say that women should have a job, but I don't think so. I think that women who get married should bring up their children *perfectly*. And so, I will be a full-time housewife when I am age forty.

When I am forty, I will have my life work. I want to become a marketing consultant. To be able to engage in the kind of work I want to do will be the happiest thing for me. [She also goes on to say:] Then I will get married, and I will have two or three children. The biggest dream of mine is to become a good mother.

I want to be working when I'm forty. If I should not make the most of my studies at the university, all my efforts would come to nothing. My parents and my relatives are expecting a lot from me, so I can't let them down. The coming times will be better for working women. I don't want to simply make copies and serve tea. I want to work as hard as men. . . . I will probably also be married and have children. I want to be a good wife and mother. Some women say, "I want to work hard, so I don't want children," but *I want children because I think it is a woman's privilege to have children*. It is hard to be successful at both work and housework, but there are women who manage both perfectly, so I ought to be able to do so. (My emphasis)

I want to be a psychologist. . . . When I'm forty I will be married, and I will have some children. When my children are small, I won't work, but when they grow up, I will work again. I think that a mother must take care of her children, and I think that taking care of children is the real mother's job. If a mother is very very strong, she need not give up her job and continue working, but I couldn't, since I'm not strong.

These statements can be better understood in terms of the dominant Japanese conception of motherhood described by Masami Ohinata (see her essay in this volume) and the great symbolic importance attached to mothers. As Ohinata explains, mothers are seen as having an innate aptitude for child rearing and the primary responsibility for bringing up children. This responsibility entails a total devotion to one's children, spending as much time as possible with them, doing everything for them and catering to all of their needs—indeed, sharing a sense of oneness with one's children—and at the same time a willingness to sacrifice one's own plans and desires for the sake of the children's well-being.

Such a notion, which assigns an all-important role to the mother in the life of the child and emphasizes motherly love as the key to a child's development and education, inevitably leads many women to feel strong internal motivations and pressures, as well as external pressures, to give up their careers when they have children. There is a strong consensus that a mother should stay home with her children at least until they reach the age of three.[2] In various opinion polls a majority of women as well as men have supported the view that women should discontinue working for a few years after marrying or giving birth. Thus, while employment rates among females ages twenty to sixty-four have been increasing, the familiar "M" curve continues to be prominent, showing a marked dip among the thirty- to thirty-four-year olds. If we look at the female population as a whole, in 1992, 56 percent of all women with children were in the labor force. Looking only at those employed in the nonagricultural sector the figure was 42 percent. The figure varies according to the age of the youngest child: among mothers whose youngest child is between zero and four only twenty-one were employed. The percentage goes up to 37 percent among those with a child between ages four and six, 48 when the child is between seven and nine, and over 53 to 57 among those whose youngest child is between ages ten and seventeen. A closer look, however, reveals that of all the employed mothers, only 54 percent were working thirty-five hours or more per week—that is, on a full-time basis—while 45 percent worked fewer than thirty-five hours per week (Rodosho Fujinkyoku 1993, app. p. 25, app. table 18).

These dominant attitudes regarding the responsibilities of motherhood and the anticipation that they will want to or that they must give up their careers once they have children lead many young women to refrain from even considering taking up careers involving responsibility and long-term commitment. At the same time, most of these women do not give much consideration to their lives twenty or thirty years ahead, to what their wants and needs might be at that point, and what they ought to do to plan for that future.

Impediments to Women's Pursuit of Careers

I have described some factors related to the socialization process which influence how today's Japanese college women look upon their future and think about careers, marriage, and family. The fact remains, however, that, even if young women set high career goals for themselves, their ability to carry forth those goals is likely to be restricted severely by a variety of forces and factors that continue to play a significant role—including biases against women in the workplace, social attitudes pertaining to gender roles, and problems entailed in reconciling the dual demands of career and family. Thus, many women today are skeptical or even pessimistic as they look to the future.

Obstacles within the Workplace: Persisting Biases and Overly Demanding Workload

The Equal Employment Opportunity Law (EEOL), which went into effect in 1986, has to some degree opened up more opportunities to women, especially four-year university graduates, but the results have been uneven. In a survey of 1,134 corporations by the Ministry of Labor, the percentage of businesses that reported hiring female university graduates has increased since the enactment of EEOL, from 55.3 percent in 1987 to 59.2 percent in 1988 and 61.9 percent in 1989. Among very large companies—that is, those with one thousand or more employees—the figure was even higher, over 80 percent (Takano 1991, 206). On the other hand, whereas in 1989 roughly 71 percent of businesses reported recruiting female as well as male graduates for administrative and sales work, less than 48 percent said they recruited women for technical positions, while 50 percent said they recruited exclusively males for such positions (207, table II-68). Still, it is a fact that the door has opened somewhat more for female graduates, and there is a greater diversification in terms of the types of work they are entering today as compared to ten years ago, most noticeably an increase in the number of women going into technical and sales work. These developments should not, however, be interpreted as a direct result of the passage of EEOL. The enactment of the law coincided with a period of labor shortage in a prospering economy, and it was this that helped promote the realization of the goals contained in the law.

The downturn in the economy since 1991, however, has virtually wiped out the gains made by female university graduates in the late 1980s: the employment rate among these women, which had reached 86 percent in 1991, fell to 80 percent in 1992, and even lower, to about 76 percent, in 1993. A survey of two thousand companies listed on the stock exchange found the number of female university graduates hired in 1994 to be 71 percent of the figure for the previous year. One out of three companies did not hire any female university graduates ("Daisotsu saiyo" 1994).

Turning to another aspect of the problems faced by university-educated women in obtaining employment, much has been made of the fact that, since the passage of EEOL, an increasing number of companies have opened up to female graduates access to management-level positions by introducing the two-track system—the "comprehensive" track (traditionally reserved for male university graduates), so named because employees are rotated to various departments with the purpose of giving them broad-based experience and knowledge, and the "general," or clerical, track (the traditional women's track, entailing support-level clerical work) (see the essay by Yoko Kawashima in this volume, for a fuller discussion).

Thus far the number of women who have actually been hired for the comprehensive track has been very small. In 1990, for example, Tokyo Marine and Fire Insurance Company, which ranked at the top in terms of the numbers of female university graduates it hired, took on 14 women out of a total of 294 employees for the comprehensive track and 422 women for the general track. To cite another example, All-Nippon Airways, another popular company among young women, started recruiting women for the comprehensive track in 1987, yet, as of 1990, it had taken on a total of just 12 women for this track. In the case of Japan Air Lines just three women, as compared to 139 men, were hired for the comprehensive track ("Arata na danjo 'kuwake' mo" 1990).

The fact of the matter is that a great many employers continue to practice various forms of discrimination. It has been reported that, even though companies may allow women to apply for management-track positions, they in fact often have a separate, much lower hiring quota for women than men. Very frequently a company will go through the motion of interviewing women when, in fact, many of the available positions have already been filled by men through an "old boy" network. Some companies may specify that a prospective female applicant "must live at home" or "must live within a ninety-minute commuting distance." This is because many companies do not want to have to provide dormitory facilities for women employees; also, employers feel more reassured about employing young women who are living under the supervision of their parents. Among college women I have talked to there seems to be a general understanding that connections are especially important for women when it comes to landing a good position. It has also been reported that during job interviews young women are frequently asked such questions as whether or not they plan to continue working after they marry or have children, whether they would be willing to accept job transfers and job assignments abroad, and even whether they would have any objections to being asked to serve tea as part of their work. (Recently many women working in private companies as well as in government offices have begun to raise objections against forcing women to perform this function.) As Kawashima points out in her essay, even after being hired, women continue to confront differential treatment in terms of job assignment, opportunities for specific on-the-job training, and promotion. The responsibilities entailed in working in a comprehensive track position— the many hours of overtime work, plus frequent business trips and periodic transfers—are almost impossible to reconcile with marriage, let alone motherhood, given the heavy responsibilities that most Japanese wives and mothers continue to bear. Increasingly, we read about women joining the ranks of men among the victims of so-called *karooshi*, or "death resulting from overwork."

Problems Entailed in Combining Career and Family

Even if a woman succeeds in getting hired for a management-track position, she faces an even greater challenge when she attempts to combine career with marriage and family. A major problem for women who wish to continue in their careers even after they marry, and particularly after they have children, is that so often they are forced to take on almost single-handedly the double burden of career plus housekeeping, child care, and, increasingly (as Takako Sodei's essay in this volume discusses), care of the elderly. One aspect of this problem has to with persisting attitudes, assumptions, and norms regarding women's role which result in forcing working women to bear a double burden; another has to do with inadequacies in the availability of child care facilities and in provisions within the employment structure and in the workplace for accommodating the demands of child care.

Attitudes and Norms Regarding Women's Role

> I don't think it's true that Japanese girls lack confidence or pride. We know the reality of Japanese society and accept it and give up trying to change it. Actually, we do have hopes for our future, but in Japan, women's success is prevented by the social system and its traditions. If Japanese women want to keep working after marriage, many husbands don't help with housework, and if they have a child, the women have to bring up the child, do housework, plus work. But it's very hard for us, so we choose either marriage or work.

In spite of the fact that more than half of all married women now work in some capacity outside the home, one still has a very strong sense that women's employment is not really taken for granted. Instead, the concept of a sex-based division of labor and the views that "women's place is in the home" and housework and child care are "women's work" remain firmly implanted in the consciousness of many Japanese. As mentioned, national public opinion polls conducted over the years seem to point to a gradual abandonment of the traditional view that "men should work and women should stay home" (see table 4). Yet we cannot rely on the results of such general surveys alone to gain an accurate picture of changing attitudes. A comment one often hears from men is: "It's fine for wives to work, *so long as they continue to perform all of the necessary household chores and take care of children so that I don't have to take on any of those responsibilities."*

In fact, however, not only men but also most women seem to share this view. In a 1989 poll by the Prime Minister's Office 61.6 percent of the men and 69.0 percent of the women felt women should work only to the extent that her job does not interfere with her family responsibilities, and 18.4 percent of the men and 9.9 percent of the women felt women should not work at all, because it would be impossible to meet the demands of the home if they do (Bando 1991, 21–22). In a nationwide poll undertaken in 1990 by the Prime Minister's Office on the sharing of household chores among working couples, 42 percent of all respondents said that the woman should take on the bulk of the work and the man should provide a helping hand when he can, while 35.4 percent said that the spouse who has a free hand should perform the task. Only 16.6 percent felt that the burden of housework and child care should be shared equally by women and men. More women than men indicated that men should shoulder at least part of the responsibility; there was, however, little difference in the percentages of full-time homemakers and working women who support this view (Bando 1991, 22).

These attitudes are translated into practice, so that even when married women have full-time jobs, they frequently bear the bulk of the responsibility within the home. A national survey by the Management and Coordination Agency in 1991 found that, among working couples on weekdays, the wife spent an average of four hours on housekeeping, child care, and shopping, compared to the husband's average of just twelve minutes (Rodosho Fujinkyoko 1993, app. table 61). In another, smaller study of roughly 130 full-time working mothers in New York and in Tokyo conducted by Sanwa Bank Home Consultants, more than 58 percent of the women in the Tokyo sample said that they performed nearly all of the chores having to do with housekeeping and child care by themselves, while roughly 38 percent said they shared these responsibilities with their husbands. The comparable figures among the respondents in the New York sample were 25 percent and 68 percent ("Shigoto yori katei" 1992, 16). Japanese working mothers are also much less likely compared to their counterparts in many other countries to have their children help out with household tasks (Fukaya 1991, 19, table 4).

Problems Associated with Child Daycare

Reinforcing these social pressures on mothers to stay home and care for their children is the lack of satisfactory alternatives, either in the form of adequate facilities for child daycare or for provisions for child care leave for employees. When asked in a 1989 poll conducted by the Prime Minister's Office to name the biggest obstacle to continuing work, 59 percent of the female respondents cited child care and 49 percent mentioned care of the aged or sick (Bando 1991, 22). While Japan has had a relatively good system of public child daycare, the number of public daycare facilities has been on a decline in recent years, despite an increase in the number of working mothers with small children. This is not simply attributable to the decline in birthrate, as the government would claim, but to a policy decision on the part of the national government since the beginning of the 1980s to devote greater resources to a buildup of the national military at the expense of promoting social welfare and to shift the burden and responsibility for the provision of social services from the national government to the regional government bodies and to the private sector. This has meant that the availability of such facilities is now much more dependent on the financial resources of local governments, with the consequence that the provision of facilities has become more uneven across regions and local communities. The total number of daycare centers has been declining since reaching a peak in 1984 (Nihon Fujin Dantai Rengokai 1991, 155, table II-44).

A major problem for working mothers is the severe lack of facilities for infants under the age of one as well as those that stay open into the evening (past 6:00 P.M., which is when most daycare centers close). This gap has become increasingly filled by "baby hotels," unlicensed facilities that are open longer hours and accept infants. These unlicensed centers have come under fire for their inadequate facilities and high children-to-staff ratios. In an attempt to cope with this situation the Health and Welfare Ministry decided to have two thousand child care centers around the country open from 7 A.M. to 10 P.M. beginning in April 1991. The ministry also decided to begin providing subsidies at the end of 1991 for child-care facilities that have entered into special contracts with restaurants, mass media organizations, department stores, airline companies, and other businesses that require employees to work late at night, on weekends, or over consecutive days. It has also advocated the establishment of daycare facilities within companies. While some of these moves can be seen as positive, as Kurokawa Toshio (1991, 15) points out, they ought also to be viewed with some skepticism as an effort simply to make it easier for companies to require women, as well as men, to work overtime, late at night, and on weekends and to take on nightshifts.

Inadequacy in Provisions for Child Care Leave

Up until the passage of the Child Care Leave Act in 1991 only female nurses in public institutions and teachers in public schools were entitled to take unpaid leave until the child is one year old. Although the Equal Employment Opportunity Law had encouraged employers to provide parental leave, as of 1988 only 19.2 percent of all businesses had set up such a system (Rodosho fujinkyoku 1991, app. p. 84, app. table 91). What finally prompted the introduction of a child care leave act was a sharp decline in the average number of children born to women between ages fifteen and forty-nine to 1.57 children in 1989 and 1.53 in 1990.

The Child Care Leave Law, which came into force in 1992, requires all businesses to provide either the father or the mother a fixed period of leave until the child is a year old if an employee requests such a leave. The law represents a major new step in that it allows men to take advantage of child care leave. On the other hand, it contains several deficiencies: it does not require employers to provide pay during the period of leave or to get a substitute for the position of the employee on leave, nor does it guarantee that an employee will be able to return to his or her previous position or be legally protected against being placed at a disadvantage in terms of salary and promotions as a result of taking leave, and, finally, the law did not apply to businesses with thirty or fewer employees until 1995.

These shortcomings in the law make it highly unlikely that, among working couples, men will, in fact, take such leave, since in most cases the husbands earn a higher income than the wives and thus the costs of taking a leave would be greater. Of course, improving the provisions of the law will not alone help to encourage fathers to take child care leave. The prevailing attitudes regarding gender roles will also have to be overcome before we find a substantial number of men taking advantage of such a provision. Even in the case of women, however, the climate in many workplaces, in which the assumption is that women will or should quit their jobs when they marry or have children, is certainly not conducive to making them feel comfortable and secure about taking advantage of child care leave, even if they can receive full or partial pay during their leave. The important point, then, is that in addition to improving the law on child care leave, we need to undertake an effort to alter various attitudes pertaining to issues of gender roles, women's rights in the workplace, the joint responsibility and rights of women and men in the matter of child care, and so on.

Thus, women face very real difficulties when they attempt to pursue the dual goals of a successful career with marriage and family. The findings of a survey that focused on the status of women in administrative and managerial positions illustrate these points very clearly. The survey found, first of all, that only 24.9 percent of all companies had women in positions of section chief or higher; in 62.7 percent of these companies women made up less than 1 percent of all those placed in those positions. It further revealed that nearly 60 percent of all women in these positions were single and that 80 percent were forty years old or older. Among those who were married, divorced, separated, or widowed, 36 percent had no children. Of those who did have children, roughly 72 percent reported that a grandparent had cared for their children while they were small (Nijuisseiki Shokugyo Zaidan 1990).

Prospects and Challenges for the Future

The hurdles that face college women today who contemplate pursuing careers on an equal basis with men are indeed numerous. The prospect of having to confront those obstacles serves to deter many young women from planning for careers. Many women who have undertaken the challenge have abandoned their efforts, frustrated by the biases they encounter or worn out by the pressures of their heavy workloads and/or the burdens and pressures arising from their home lives. These examples have, in turn, been used by employers as a rationale for persisting gender inequalities in the workplace. The employers insist that it is women themselves who must change their attitudes and become more fully committed to their careers if they want to achieve equality. It is clear, however, that real equality in the workplace cannot be achieved without, first of all, eradicating the still existing forms of sexual discrimination in hiring and other practices as well as radically altering current employment patterns, beginning with a reduction in working hours, so that both women and men can work in full-time positions and still have time for their families. Beyond this must come further improvements in the system of child care and child care leave as well as changes in attitudes pertaining to women and their roles as wives, mothers, and workers.

At the same time that debates and discussions on these issues are taking place, little by little, changes in several areas are under way: the average number of years that women stay in a single job is increasing—from 4 years in 1960 to 6.1 years in 1980 and 7.4 years in 1992 (Rodosho Fujinkyoku 1993, app. p. 27, app. table 21), partly because more women are postponing marriage and because more of them are continuing to work after marriage and childbirth; employers, in an effort to retain or rehire qualified female workers, are adopting a variety of schemes, such as granting extended child care leaves and allowing former workers to return as full-time employees after a long period of absence; in cases in which working wives earn an income that is sufficiently large so as to make a real contribution to the family, many husbands are becoming increasingly receptive to the idea of having their wives work and more willing to cooperate in matters of housekeeping and child care.

Those involved in the education of young women have a potentially vital role to play in this process in terms of helping them to be aware of the changes under way in society and in women's lives which are likely to shape their futures, to help them think about and plan their futures, to prepare and train them to be able to take advantage of rising career opportunities and options, and to confront and deal with the problems they are likely to face in the process. Courses in women's studies, which have become gradually more visible in junior colleges and universities, particularly in women's schools, can serve a vital function in this respect, as the following comments written by some of my students at the end of the introductory course on women's studies show:

> Before I entered this university and studied about women, I didn't doubt the thoughts around me; I accepted them—that the best life for a woman was to marry, have children, be a good mother and live a peaceful life. But after I entered this university and met and talked with a lot of women about different issues, I realized that there were different viewpoints, and I started to doubt my thinking up to then.

> Until I entered this college I didn't question or have doubts about women's position in society. And I think students who don't take women's studies are not aware of these problems. I think women who have no opportunity to think about these issues will be puzzled when they enter society. I wish not college students, but high school students would have a chance to think about them.

As these comments suggest, and my experiences bear out, even though many young Japanese women enter college with little awareness of women's issues and often have a very limited and stereotyped vision of their futures, they are very much open to the challenge of alternative viewpoints and new possibilities.

Another important task for those of who teach and work with women students in Japanese colleges and universities is, as Adrienne Rich (1979) puts it, to "take them seriously." There is a tendency within Japanese society, especially within the mass media, to refer to *joshidaisei,* or "female college students," in a somewhat derogatory way, as caring more about fashion and enjoying themselves at the expense of their parents' pocketbook than about their studies and as going to college simply to kill time until they get married. I have detected these same attitudes among many faculty members, women as well as men, who therefore expect and demand less of women students and do not encourage them to prepare for professional careers. "Let's face it, most of these young women are here for cultural enrichment and most of them will simply get married and raise families, so let's give them that kind of education rather than trying to provide specialized training." Some professors refrain from failing women students and running the risk of making them repeat a course and delay their graduation because such a mark of failure would hurt their chances of "making a good marriage." Students have related to me similar comments made to them by professors which implied a lack of seriousness toward their studies and/or a lack of ability to absorb difficult material or to produce high-level work. Of course, there are also those professors, including men, who try to encourage their students. One quite elderly male professor at my university regularly tells incoming students: "Don't look upon marriage as an escape. Take responsibility for your own life."

My own observation is that women are, in fact, more serious about their studies than men are. This is backed up by studies such as that conducted in 1990 by the Ministry of Education, which found that women students are more likely to attend class, to spend more hours studying either in the library or at home, to read more books, and to indicate that they understand the content of lectures (Mombusho, *Gakusei* 1990). What's more, many of today's college women are extremely intelligent and capable. Yet these same women exhibit a surprising lack of confidence in themselves and in their abilities and, as a result, set very limited goals for their future. A full and satisfactory explanation of why this is so is beyond the scope of this discussion.

Today we are seeing a very clear and definite decline in the popularity of women's colleges, partly because most of these institutions do not offer the kinds of study options that women are increasingly being drawn to—such as economics, international relations, political science, and law—because employment prospects for graduates from those fields are better, and also because women's colleges have come to be viewed as somehow old-fashioned and lacking in any special merit. The decline in enrollment at these institutions has resulted in the closing of a number of them, while others have turned coed; still others have tried to survive as a women's institution by changing or adding new programs to the curriculum. My own view is that women's colleges, particularly those that have a relatively high proportion of female faculty who are committed to the task of teaching women and are serious about nurturing women with strong career and professional aspirations, have a vital role to play today and in the years to come.

One very positive development within women's colleges has been the appearance of nontraditional students, that is, women who are beyond the traditional eighteen- to twenty-two-year-old college population. While the presence of such women on college campuses has long been taken for granted in the United States, for example, in Japan this is a very new phenomenon, though one that is likely to become increasingly evident in the years to come, as the population of eighteen- to twenty-two-year-olds begins to take a sharp decline. We have several such students at my institution, and nearly all the faculty members are impressed by their enthusiasm and seriousness. In my own classes I have found that these women, many of whom are in their forties, are married and have children, and are also engaged in some type of work (e.g., as nurses, part-time teachers in private tutoring schools, independent entrepreneurs), serve as valuable role models and stimulate the younger students. In my courses that deal with women, especially, the different perspectives and insights these women are able to offer, based on their own personal experiences, provide a valuable dose of reality to many of the discussions:

> Honestly speaking, when I was young, I never thought about my life at age forty. Since I liked English in my high school days, I wanted to study English literature at a famous first-class university in Tokyo. But my parents were opposed to my going to Tokyo alone because I was an only child. And so I gave up my plans and went to work for a bank for a while. . . . In accordance with custom, I got married at the age of twenty-three. I have a nice, understanding husband, two pretty daughters, and a beautiful house.
>
> Some people say that I am very happy. However, I could not be satisfied with my life. I wanted to study more. Therefore I joined English classes at the Asahi Culture Center. I had a pleasant time, and, fortunately, I made many good friends there. But I thought I should study at a college, since I think a degree is necessary in order to get into a specialized occupation. Luckily, I passed the entrance examination for this college. It is a lot of fun for me to listen to the different lectures. After graduating, I hope to be able to go to England to teach Japanese.

These statements, written by a student in her forties and shared with the younger students, are able to convey much more directly the sense of discontent—of wanting to do "something more" with their lives and seek out their own, individual self-definition—which has become more and more widespread among relatively well-to-do, outwardly contended Japanese housewives (much like the American housewives of the 1960s described by

Friedan [1963]) and is being manifested in a variety of different ways, including rising rates of employment among married women, and growing participation in a variety of community, voluntary, study-related activities. In addition, these women, who are by no means passive and who demand to be taken seriously, can also serve a valuable function in terms of forcing institutions and faculty members to reexamine their existing facilities, curricula, and teaching practices in light of the evolving demands and needs of women.

NOTES

1. These and subsequent quotes are taken from assignments written by freshmen students in my introductory course on women's studies in the academic year 1991–92.
2. One very interesting study that confirmed this belief on the part of both female and male high school seniors is that by Yoshida (1988).

REFERENCES

Amano, Masako. 1985. "Shushoku gaidansu" (Employment guidance). In *Koza gendai: onna no issho 2: sotsugyo shushoku* (Contemporary lectures: women's lives, vol. 2: graduation and employment). Tokyo: Iwanami shoten.

"Arata na danjo 'kuwake' mo" (A new form male-female "division"). 1990. *Asahi shimbun* (Asahi newspaper). June 15.

Bando, Mariko. 1991. *Japanese Women: Yesterday and Today.* Tokyo: Foreign Press Center.

"Daisotsu saiyo konharu gekigen" (A sharp decrease in hiring of university graduates this spring). 1994. *Asahi (Asahi shimbun* (Asahi newspaper). 13 March: 1.

Friedan, Betty. 1963. *The Feminine Mystique.* New York: Dell.

Fujimura-Fanselow, Kumiko. 1985. "Women's Participation in Japanese Higher education." *Comparative Education Review* 29, no. 4 (November): 471–90.

Fukaya, Kazuko. 1991. "Kokusai hikaku chosa no naka de no katei to katei kyoiku" (Family and family education as seen through international comparison surveys). *Kyoiku to joho* (Education and Information), no. 402 (September): 16–19.

Kurokawa, Toshio. 1991. "Josei katsuyo no rodoryoku seisaku no nerai to doko" (The aim and trend in of policies on the utilization of the female labor force). In *Fujin hakusho 1991* (The 1991 white paper on women), ed. Nihon Fujin Dantai Rengokai. Tokyo: Horupu shuppan.

Kyoto Daigaku Kyoikugakubu, Kyoiku Shakaigaku Kenkyushitsu (Kyoto University, Faculty of Education, Seminar in the Sociology of Education). 1982. *"Gakushu fudo" to "Kakureta karikyuramu" ni kansuru shakaigakuteki kenkyu—"Chishiki no haibun" no kanten kara* (A sociological study of "learning climates" and the "hidden curriculum" from the standpoint of "distribution of knowledge"). No. 1 (October).

Machung, Anne. 1989. "Talking Career, Thinking Job: Gender Differences in Career and Family Expectations of Berkeley Seniors." *Feminist Studies* 15, no. 1: 35–55.

Mombusho (Ministry of Education). 1991. *Mombu tokei yoran* (Digest of educational statistics). Tokyo: Mombusho.

————. 1990. *Gakusei seikatsu jittai chosa* (Survey on college students' lives). Tokyo: Mombusho.

NHK (Japan Broadcasting Corporation). 1988. *Nihonjin no ishiki chosa* (The consciousness of the Japanese). Tokyo: NHK.

Nihon Fujin Dantai Rengokai, ed. 1991. *Fujin hakusho 1991* (1991 white paper on women). Tokyo: Horupu shuppan.

Nihon Rikuruto Senta (Japan Recruit Center). Annual. *Shingaku doki chosa* (Survey on motivations for going on to higher education). Tokyo: Nihon Rikuruto Senta.

Nijuisseiki Shokugyo Zaidan (Twenty-first century employment foundation). 1990. *Josei kanrishoku chosa* (Survey of women in administrative and managerial positions). Tokyo: Nijuisseiki Shokugyo Zaidan (formerly Josei Shokugyo Zaidan).

Rich, Adrienne. 1979. "Taking Women Students Seriously." *On Lies, Secrets, and Silence.* New York and London: W. W. Norton.

Rodosho Fujinkyoku (Ministry of Labor, Women's Bureau). 1993. *Fujin rodo no jitsujo* (Status of female workers). Tokyo: Rodosho.

"Shigoto yori katei no Bei, shigoto mo katei mo no Nihon" (United States: Family rather than work, Japan: family and work). 1992. *Asahi shimbun* (Asahi newspaper). 27 February, 16.

Sorifu (Office of the Prime Minister). 1987 and 1990. *Fujin ni kansuru yoron chosa* (Public opinion survey on women). MS. Tokyo: Sorifu.

Takano, Kazuko. 1991. "Koto kyoiku" (Higher education). In *Fujin hakusho* (White paper on women), ed. by Nihon Fujin Dantai Rengo-kai. Tokyo: Horupu shuppan.

Takeuchi, Kiyoshi. 1985. "Joshi no seito bunka no tokushitsu" (The special characteristics of the female student culture). *Kyoiku shakaigaku kenkyu* (Research in the sociology of education), no. 40.

"Tekireiki wa kigyo no teki" ("Marriageable age" is the enemy of industry). 1991. *Tokyo shimbun* (Tokyo newspaper). 30 September.

Tomoda, Yasumasa. 1972. "Educational and Occupational Aspirations of Female Senior High School Students." *Bulletin of the Hiroshima Agricultural College* 4 (December): 247–62.

Yoshida, Kiyomi. 1988. "Onna no ikikata o kangaeru" (Thinking about how women should live their lives). *Joseigaku nempo* (Annual report of the Women's Studies Society of Japan) 9:74–83.

Women's Studies: An Overview

❖ ❖ ❖

Mioko Fujieda
and Kumiko Fujimura-Fanselow

While the presence of gender ideology is universally observed, the ways in which it is constructed, reproduced, and reinforced, or even hidden, vary from culture to culture. Therefore, women's studies, which is primarily concerned with gender issues, must in effect be culture specific in many ways, although it shares commonalities across cultures. It means that the ways in which women's studies develops and is taught in each country are greatly affected by the historical, economic, political, social, and sometimes religious factors that operate in a particular country. To talk about women's studies in Japan is, therefore, to shed light on the situation of women and Japanese society at large.

As evidenced by many surveys and international comparisons that have been conducted by private and government agencies, one outstanding characteristic of Japanese society lies in the exceptional degree to which stereotyped conceptions of gender role division are ingrained in the minds of both men and women. That this is the case is obviously not a "natural" phenomenon as many would believe; rather, it is something that is politically maintained and reinforced in order to meet the needs of a corporate society whose aim is the pursuit of maximum economic efficiency. Without this "hidden" discrimination against women, Japan's so-called economic prosperity would not have been so successfully achieved. Moreover, many of the difficulties facing women's studies today arise from these same forms of structural discrimination.

The Meaning of *Women's Studies* in Japanese: A Semantic Problem

One confusion that arises when we talk about women's studies in Japan is that there are two terms that are used in Japanese to refer to what is generally called "women's studies" in English: one, *joseigaku*, literally meaning "womanology" or "feminology," and the other, *fujin mondai kenkyu,* which means "research on the woman question." These two terms correspond to the ways in which women have been viewed in Japanese society, and perhaps it would be appropriate to give some explanation of the differences between *fujin* and *josei* before proceeding further.

Translated into English, *fujin* and *josei* (as well as *joshi* and *onna*) all mean "woman" or ("women") or "female(s)." While the other terms have an equivalent term that refers to men or males (*josei-dansei, joshi-danshi, onna-otoko*), however, there is no such equivalent for *fujin.* Historically, the word *fujin,* when first adopted by the socialist thinker Sakai Toshihiko in the early part of the Meiji period (late nineteenth century), had a revolutionary meaning, in that it recognized the need to grant the right of women, who had been held in contempt for many ages, to be full human beings. It projected a new image of women possessing pride and dignity. But over the course of time the term was co-opted into the official language, in which the word was used euphemistically to put women on a pedestal and to cover up their actual position in society. *Josei,* literally meaning "female," began to be commonly used after World War II and used in reference to married women. *Josei* had a more neutral or even a modern and fresh connotation and was not as denigrating as *onna,* whose usage was taboo, at least in public, until the women's liberation movement reclaimed the word in a positive sense in the early 1970s.

Even though *fujin* has become old-fashioned, the term *fujin mondai* (the woman question) had, and in a way still has, a positive meaning. It is quite likely that it was a translated version of *the woman question* in English, *la question féminine* in French, and *die frauenfrage* in German, terms extensively used by many nineteenth-century writers when stressing the women's position. Instead of putting the blame on women for their inferior position, this term emphasizes the fact that the social order created problems for women, thus challenging entrenched and prevailing views on women's position and calling for action to improve their position.

Fujin mondai kenkyu, or research on the woman question, has a tradition dating back to the turn of the century.[1] This research tended to cover rather limited areas such as the education of girls and women, working women, and the history of women (mostly Japanese) from more or less socialist/reformist perspectives and to seek economic explanations for the oppression of women. In its long years of existence *fujin mondai kenkyu* accumulated a wealth of knowledge about women in each specific area and laid the groundwork on which future development could be built. Its rigid subdivisions, however, prevented it from developing interdisciplinary approaches aimed at arriving at a more complete understanding of the realities surrounding women. Although it did look for political and economic explanations for the oppression of women, it did not raise the fundamental issue of gender roles; rather, it accepted them as natural, with biological determinism as an unquestioned frame of reference. Much of its research tended to be based on the assumption that all the problems faced by women would be solved when socialism was achieved (see Box 1).

Box 1.

Debate over the Protection and Support of Motherhood

This first and most well-known debate among prewar feminists took place at the end of World War I, just at the time the so-called New Women appeared on the scene demanding social freedom and political rights for women, including suffrage and the abolition of prostitution. It was a time when, in addition to the large numbers of women already working in factories, women increasingly became employed in urban centers as clerical and department store employees, telephone operators, and typists. The debate, which was carried on primarily by three prominent feminists of the time— Hiratsuka Raicho, Yamakawa Kikue, and Yosano Akiko—concerned the issue of how best to enable women to achieve equality and economic independence and how to reconcile the need for women to achieve equality and economic independence with the special needs of women stemming from their role as mothers. The debate was published from 1918 to 1919 in the pages of the popular magazine *Taiyo* as well as in *Fujin koron*.

Poet and critic Yosano Akiko, who strongly advocated economic independence and social advancement for women, argued that women must be totally independent of both the state and of men and, therefore, rejected having the state accord protection and special treatment to women in their capacity as mothers. The position espoused by Hiratsuka Raicho was that, while economic independence was vital to women, children did not belong only to the mother but also to society, and, therefore, the state had an obligation to provide protection for motherhood. Indeed, the state had an obligation to give such protection, and women had a natural right to such protection. She insisted, moreover, that protection of motherhood was one means for women to realize the goal of economic independence. Her attitudes pertaining to the rights of motherhood were strongly influenced by her reading of the Swedish feminist author Ellen Key's *Love and Marriage*. (1903). Yamakawa Kikue, who was involved in the socialist movement in Japan, criticized both positions—Yosano's as "bourgeois" and Hiratsuka's as attaching excessive emphasis on the motherhood function of women. She insisted that the two, economic independence for women and protection of motherhood, cannot be simultaneously realized under a capitalist system; true liberation of women was possible only through the establishment of a socialist society.

Joseigaku, on the other hand, is generally understood to be the product of the new consciousness of the 1970s. It puts more emphasis on sociocultural and psychological issues that have their basis in the sexual division of labor and criticizes the needs of the corporate society itself. It raises several questions that *fujin mondai kenkyu* did not. These questions, which have definite political implications, include: the "invisibility" of women in the traditional disciplines, male orientation and methodology in traditional subject areas, sex-role relationships, and basic assumptions about society itself. They make interdisciplinary approaches indispensable. One problem associated with the term *joseigaku* is that, since it is tantamount to *womanology* or *feminology*, it sounds as if it is a single discipline, such as biology, psychology, or some other *-ology*. This often leads to bewilderment and skepticism among people who ask whether or not it is just an addition to traditional academic disciplines.

In the early years of women's studies there was tension between women's studies and *fujin mondai kenkyu*, and it took a while for academics and researchers associated with the two groups to come together. There was, in addition, a generational difference between the groups, with *fujin mondai kenkyu* representing the first phase of feminism and *joseigaku* the second. In recent years *joseigaku* has become the more common of the two terms used in the discussions of women's studies.

Sources of Influence on the Development of Women's Studies

We can point to three major factors that played a significant role in the development of women's studies in Japan:

1. The women's liberation movement in Japan that sprang up in the early 1970s.

2. The impact of the International Women's Year, the United Nations (UN) Decade for Women, the UN Convention on the Elimination of All Forms of Discrimination against Women, and other measures taken by the United Nations and its agencies.

3. The development of women's studies in the United States and Europe.

Let us consider, first of all, the relationship of women's studies to the women's liberation movement, called *uman ribu*, or simply *ribu*, in Japanese. In the West practically no one casts doubt on the fact that the women's liberation movement was the mainspring of women's studies. It is generally accepted that women's studies came into being as the academic arm of the women's liberation movement. In Japan, however, while some of us view women's studies as a direct response to the women's movement that occurred in Japan and elsewhere, this view is not necessarily shared by all.

The effect of the short-lived women's liberation movement in Japan is still a controversial subject even among practitioners of women's studies.[2] Some even try to ignore the fact that it did indeed exist, let alone acknowledge its influence. The *uman ribu* movement strongly condemned the sexist structure of Japanese society and pointed to the need for change. It was severely criticized and derided by the male-dominated media, which treated it as no more than "a spree by some crazy young women." While, on one hand, this movement provoked the enmity of the male world, on the other, it horrified the majority of women. Its language, strategies, and organization—everything about it—were unacceptable to those who defended the prevalent conventional attitudes and ideologies. The existing women's movement, which saw itself as "respectable," became defensive and often expressed its distaste for the proponents of *uman ribu*, labeling them as "deviant" or "disruptive."

Another criticism directed against members of this movement was that they were merely imitating Western, especially American, models. Although undeniably inspired and influenced by its American counterpart, it must be made clear that the women's liberation movement in Japan was not a spree nor composed of deviants nor a mere imitation. While it was a seriously radical movement, made up mostly of younger women, it was quite distinct from similar movements in other countries in many ways. It was, moreover, the socioeconomic circumstances of Japanese society itself which gave rise to to the Japanese women's liberation movement.

It may take some time before the legacy it has left is given full and rightful recognition. It should be noted, however, that most of the fundamental questions the movement raised about Japanese society—its norms and values—are still valid. Even if the liberation movement per se was short-lived, something of its spirit and consciousness still permeates the present women's movement. As Kuninobu points out, many of the women who participated in that movement have subsequently become involved in research on women and contributed valuable work in the field of women's studies. "The consumers of information and knowledge about feminism have gone on to become producers [of such information and knowledge]" (qtd. in "Takamaru 'joseigaku'" 1991).

Turning to the second set of influencing factors, one cannot overemphasize the importance that the International Women's Year, the World Plan of Action, and the UN Decade for Women have had for Japanese women. The International Women's Year, in fact, helped activate the present women's movement starting in 1975.[3] The most important contribution of these events is that they have provided a worldwide definition of sex-based discrimination and the need for promoting human rights for women. These UN-sanctioned initiatives provided women with a mandate to engage in work that previously would not have been permitted or considered legitimate by society at large.

As Tachi notes, the international meetings held in Mexico City, Copenhagen, and Nairobi provided an opportunity for many Japanese women—government officials and leaders of nongovernmental organizations (NGOs) at various local levels—who had previously had few such opportunities, to go abroad (1988a, 2–3). At these meetings, moreover, they gained more knowledge about feminism in other countries and became aware of similarities as well as differences in the situations faced by women in various countries.

In 1980 Japan became a signatory to the UN Convention on the Elimination of All Forms of Discrimination against Women. Before the National Diet could ratify the convention, however, it was necessary to undertake reforms in various areas, such as the family, education, media, and employment. Many scholars were summoned to join committees at various government levels to help formulate and implement domestic action programs. In the process they began to recognize the need for a much more direct approach to the investigation of women's issues through the development of a multidisciplinary approach. Researchers who stressed the importance of research in women's studies which integrated theory with practice emerged from a wide range of disciplines.

With regard to the third point, the example provided by the U.S. and European experience inspired and encouraged Japanese women academics. The greatest influence no doubt came from the women's studies movement in the United States. Books on the U.S. women's movement and research in the field of women's studies, translated into Japanese in many instances by young scholars who had studied in the United States and encountered women's studies there, provided the necessary academic rhetoric and theoretical framework for addressing the issues of sexual oppression and discrimination in Japan. Many of these same scholars were instrumental in pushing for the establishment of women's studies courses in Japan.

Many Japanese continue to look to the United States for encouragement as well as a source of information. But, of course, simply copying the experience of other countries is not feasible or adequate. What the Japanese women's studies movement is attempting to do is to develop its own approach and strategies within the historical, socioeconomic, and cultural contexts of Japanese society.

The progress of the women's studies movement in Japan would undoubtedly have been much slower had it not been for the impact of the two latter factors. Its course of development would likewise have been quite different in the absence of the women's liberation movement of the early 1970s, which marked the dawn of the second phase of feminism in Japan as well as elsewhere in the world.

Current Status of Women's Studies in Academia

It was in the mid-1970s that women's studies courses began to make their appearance in Japanese colleges and universities. Thus far, very few studies have actually looked closely at the types of courses offered; the content and methodology of the courses; how they are perceived and evaluated by students, faculty, and administrators; and their impact—both short and long term—on students as well as on the institutions themselves. An annual survey of women's studies course offerings in higher institutions nationwide conducted by the Kokuritsu Fujin Kyoiku Kaikan, or the National Women's Education Centre (NWEC), since 1983 is one of few such sources.

According to its 1994 report, in 1992, 268 institutions of higher education (junior colleges and four-year universities) offered courses in women's studies out of a total of 1,101 institutions—in other words, about 24 percent. At the graduate level, the number of institutions that reported offering such courses was just six; the total number of courses offered was eight (Kokuritsu Fujin Kyoiku Kaikan 1994, 3). The number of courses taught at junior colleges and four-year universities totaled 512 (table 1). There is no question that this represents a significant increase compared to the late 1970s, when only a handful of institutions offered such courses, or even the mid-1980s; 58 percent of all the courses offered have been started, in fact, since 1988. Yet, looking again at the courses again at the proportion of institutions offering courses in the field (24 percent), it must be pointed out that this figure is deceptive.

Even in cases in which courses are offered, usually just one or two courses are taught at each institution. For example, at a large private university with a student population of about 150,000, of which less than one-fifth is female, and which has 500 full-time faculty, of whom only around 10 are women, there is only one women's studies–related course, entitled "Human Rights and Discrimination." The number of registered students is about 50, with regular attendance close to 30. The number of students enrolled in such courses in 1992 nationwide amounted to roughly 57,000, or a mere 2 percent of all students enrolled in higher institutions. And, of the 57,000 students, just 9,200 were male.

Another questionable point concerns the extent to which the various courses are taught from a feminist perspective. The NWEC survey gives no definition for the term *women's studies*. The questionnaire asks whether the respondent runs any "women's studies–related courses," by which is meant basically any course that is labeled "women," such as "Women's Studies," "Women's Issues," and "Women's History" as well as courses in any of the various disciplines which deal with the subject of women or give special attention to women. Our estimate is that courses with explicitly feminist perspectives make up about one-third of all courses offered. The rest seem to consist at best of an "add women and stir" type of approach, as it were. Thus, the instructor of a course on Korean history

Table 1

Number of Colleges and Universities Offering Women's Studies and Related Courses

	No. of Institutions				No. of Courses Offered			
	1983	1985	1990	1992	1983	1985	1990	1990
Four-year universities:								
National	10	17	27	37	13	31	54	79
Public	5	4	10	9	5	7	13	16
Private	34	35	86	88	45	66	167	195
Junior colleges:								
National	0	0	1	1	0	0	1	1
Public	3	6	10	14	3	13	20	24
Private	23	34	117	119	28	49	208	197
Total	75	96	251	268[a]	94	166	463	512[b]

a. This figure represents 24 percent of all the four-year colleges and universities and junior colleges in Japan, which numbered 1,115 in 1992. Of the 268 institutions, 147 (55 percent) represented women's colleges and 121 (45 percent), coeducational institutions.
b. Of the 512 courses, 317 (62 percent) were offered at women's colleges and 195 (38 percent) at coeducational institutions.

Sources: Kokuritsu Fujin Kyoiku Kaikan. *Heisei ninendo koto kyoiku kikan ni okeru joseigaku kanren koza kaisetsu jokyo chosa kekka hokoku* (Survey of courses on women's studies and related subjects in institutions of higher education in Japan [fiscal 1990]) (Saitama-ken: Kokuritsu Fujin Kyoiku Kaikan, 1991); Kokuritsu Fujin Kyoiku Kaikan, *Koto kyoiku kikan ni okeru joseigaku kanren kamokuto no jokyo—Heisei gonen dochosa hokoku* (Status of courses on women's studies and related subjects in institutions of higher education in Japan—1993 survey report) Saitamaken: Kokuritsu Fujin Kyoiku Kaikan, 1994).

whose theme is "The History of Korean Family and Women" makes the comment: "The course is not from the perspective of women's studies but rather to fill a gap in Japanese research on Korean history" (Kokuritsu Fujin 1991, 21). This is not surprising in light of the fact that, in the NWEC survey, only 26 out of 499 instructors teaching women's studies–related courses—all of whom were women—claimed their field of specialization to be that of women's studies per se.

The 1994 Report of the National Women's Education Centre reveals several other features of women's studies in Japan. First, women's colleges and universities are much more likely to offer courses in women's studies than are coed institutions: in 1992, forty-five out of the ninety-one women's four-year universities offered such courses, compared to just eighty-nine out of the more than four hundred coed universities (ibid., 4, table 1). The fact that women's junior colleges and universities have been much more active in setting up women's studies–related courses reflects in part a growing appreciation by them of their potential role in promoting changes in young women's consciousness and a conviction that courses in women's studies should be an essential component of the curriculum at a women's institution. At the same time, one cannot help but also get the impression that many women's institutions, especially, are establishing such courses because it is the latest trend, and they see these courses as one way of attracting female students and of emphasizing their unique and special existence as women's institutions in the face of a growing trend in recent years away from women's colleges.

Second among the NWEC's features is that 40 percent of the courses are taught as part of general education subjects for first- and second-year students, the remainder as part of specialized subjects for third- and fourth-year students.[4] Courses offered as professional or specialized courses have increased in comparison to earlier years.

Third, about 80 percent of the courses are in the "general" category, with the remainder labeled "comprehensive." By general, it is meant that usually one person conducts the course for a semester or a year; in contrast, comprehensive courses (*sogo koza*) are taught by several instructors from different disciplines who take turns lecturing on a specific subject from the perspective of their own particular specialized fields. Comprehensive courses appear to have become more prominent in recent years with the growing recognition that an interdisciplinary approach might be better suited to addressing women's issues, which are, after all, multifaceted.

Fourth, there is often controversy, even among the female faculty, over the concept of women's studies as something that ought to be "for women, about women, and by women" (see box 2). What is rather unique in the Japanese case is that one out of three instructors teaching courses related to women's studies is male; in addition, male instructors are more likely to be teaching full-time compared to female instructors, although the number of full-time female instructors increased from 356 to 423 between 1990 and 1992 (see table 2). Women's studies courses are offered either at the instructors' own initiative or, in the case of *sogo koza*, or comprehensive courses, at the request of the coordinators. In the latter case, as described, several instructors from different disciplinary areas take turns lecturing, and this is where most of the male instructors come in. Thus, in the Japanese case we cannot necessarily assume that women's studies is a form of feminism or that those who teach such courses are committed to the feminist goals of identifying oppression and promoting women's liberation, as opposed to simply teaching on the subject of women. In terms of background, of the 594 instructors teaching women's studies–related courses, just 45 (of whom 43 were women) claimed women's studies as their primary field of specializaton, and 68 identified it as their secondary field of specialization (Kokuritsu Fujin 1994, 8). Sociology, literature, history/geography, education, home economics, and law are the disciplines most commonly identified by the instructors as their primary field of specialization (Kokuritsu Fujin 11, table 9).

Box 2.
Controversy Concerning the Nature and Goal of
Women's Studies: Inoue versus Hara and Iwao

From the very beginning of the birth of women's studies in Japan, feminist scholars have expressed conflicting views concerning the proper direction and goal of women's studies as an academic discipline. Very briefly, on the one side Inoue (1980, 1987) has argued forcefully for the position that women's studies ought to be an independent field of discipline that is about women, pursued primarily by women, and intimately linked to the women's movement and tied to the political goals of bringing about social change and reform and promoting women's equality and liberation. In contrast is the position represented by Iwao and Hara (Iwao and Hara 1979; Hara 1987), who downplay the political agenda and stress, instead, the scholarly contribution of women's studies in terms of infusing a new and valuable *approach*—that is, a feminist perspective—to the study of already existing disciplines. Their position, therefore, is that, if and when the day comes when this approach has become incorporated into the various disciplines, the need for women's studies as an independent discipline will no longer be present.

Table 2
Women's Studies and Related Course Instructors
by Sex and Employment Status

	1985			1990			1992		
	F	**M**	**All**	**F**	**M**	**All**	**F**	**M**	**All**
Full-time instructors	97	40	137	356	218	574	423	192	615
Part-time instructors	54	1	55	203	47	250	137	26	163
Total	151	41	192	559	265	824	560	218	800*
(%)	(78.6)	(21.4)	(100.0)	(67.8)	(32.2)	(100.0)	(72.0)	(28.0)	(100.0)

* This figure of 800 includes, in addition to full- and part-time instructors, the category of "other" and 7 "unknown."

Sources: From Kokuritsu Fujin Kyoiku Kaikan. *Heisei ninendo koto kyoiku kikan ni okeru joseigaku kanren koza kaisetsu jokyo chosa kekka hokoku* (Survey of courses on women's studies and related subjects in institutions of higher education in Japan [fiscal 1990]). 1991;
Koruritsu Fujin Kyoiku Kaikan, *Koto kyoiku kikan ni okuru joseigaku kanren kamokuto no jokyo—Heisei gonen do chosa hokoku* (Status of courses on women's studies and related subjects in institutions of higher education in Japan—1993 survey report (Saitama-ken: Kokuritsu fujin kyoiku kaikan, 1994).

Finally, it is important to point out that despite the increase in the number and variety of courses in women's studies offered at institutions of higher education throughout Japan, the position occupied by women's studies in Japanese higher institutions, as well as in society at large, is still very much a peripheral one. Women's studies has yet to be fully recognized and appreciated by the majority of students, both female and male, in our higher institutions as well as by the academic community as a whole.

The situation at the precollege level is even more backward. As Kameda points out (see her essay in this volume), up until just recently, gender issues have been largely ignored both in the elementary and secondary school textbooks, which are inspected and distributed by the Ministry of Education, and in training programs for teachers. As a result, little classroom teaching from the perspective of rectifying gender inequality can be seen at the elementary and secondary school levels. When such approaches are made, they are done by a handful of courageously committed teachers, most of whom are women. Some schools have recently begun to offer elective courses in women's studies at the high school level, and a few of the instructors have written extremely valuable accounts of their experiences (see Yoshida 1988; and Hino 1986). Such efforts are still rare, however, and, as a result, the overwhelming majority of students lack exposure to gender issues prior to entering college or university.

Evaluating the Impact of Women's Studies

While women's studies–related courses have become more visible, apart from a handful of studies (e.g., Hino 1986; Shima 1987; Yoshida 1988; Fujimura-Fanselow 1989; Tagawa 1992), there has been little assessment made of the impact of such courses on the attitudes, perceptions, and behaviors of students who have taken these courses, on the instructors, or on the institutions. The survey reports by the National Women's Education Centre, to which reference has already been made, are valuable sources, in that they include comments by instructors from several junior colleges and universities regarding the impact of their courses on students and on the institutions.

Impact of Women's Studies Courses on Students

In both the 1990 and 1992 NWEC surveys the instructors in charge of running women's studies–related courses generally offer a positive assessment of the impact of the courses on their students. Several of them point out that the courses have encouraged students to challenge the established, traditional image of sex roles and to provide a more realistic understanding of the nature of sexual discrimination that exists in contemporary society. Another point frequently mentioned is that many female students are stimulated by their study to think about pursuing careers and seek a more independent way of life. On the other hand, a few of the instructors pointed out in the 1990 survey that, in an atmosphere of an increasing trend toward conservatism at some women's universities, it is often difficult to interest female students in women's studies.

> Many students give a positive evaluation of the course. . . . They comment that they have come to realize the necessity of reconsidering what they had previously taken for granted to be women's role in society and to look at their future life course from a wider perspective. (Kokuritsu fujin kyoiku kaikan 1991,116)

> A comment that many women students make is that the course has made them realize that sexual bias is at the basis of many things that they have in the past simply put up with or endured because they thought that was just the way things were and nothing could be done about them, and that this realization has encouraged them to express their feelings and speak up. (110)

> A great many of the students seem to have gone through life without giving much thought to the fact that they are women. The course has made many of these same women aware of the importance of thinking seriously about future employment, marriage and other matters. Its influence does not, however, seem to have extended to the point where it has made them think about how they might try to influence society. (124)

> More and more male students are commenting that the course has made them realize that women's issues are, in fact, men's issues as well. (36)

> Some students have formed study circles to conduct research into women's issues. . . . In addition women's demands have begun to be taken up more positively by the [presumably teachers'] union. (20)

> We see a big contrast between those who don't seem to undergo any changes and those who show a dramatic change in attitudes. . . . In choosing jobs, more students have begun to take into consideration such factors as the working conditions a particular company offers to female employees and the extent to which it allows women to continue working on a long-term basis. . . . In terms of their attitudes regarding marriage and sex roles, these women have begun to realize the importance and necessity for drastic changes in men's attitudes. . . . And they have also begun to realize the ways in which the images of women have been shaped by society. (216)

At the same time, however, some instructors note a negative reaction against feminism and expressions of fear and uncertainty on the part of some male students.

> Many of the male students become more open in their thinking as they gain a better understanding of how women view or react to different situations and become aware of sexual discrimination. At the same time, there are always some who become even more set in their anti-feminist views. (Kokuritsu fujin kyoiku kaikan 1994, 50)

One of the conclusions reached from a survey by Shima (1987) of students enrolled in a comprehensive course entitled "Society and the Family— From the Standpoint of Women and Men" at Daito Bunka University, taught by her and three other instructors, was that, while those who took the course became more aware of social issues confronting women, they continued to be troubled and to feel conflicted over how to reconcile this new awareness and understanding with attitudes regarding gender roles and appropriate life-styles for women and men which they had until now taken so much for granted.

My (Fujimura-Fanselow) experience over the last five years of teaching a required introductory course in women's studies for first-year students and also a course on women and education has been that these courses offer a novel challenge for most students, not only in terms of their content but also, perhaps more significantly, in terms of the way the classes are conducted and kinds of classroom interactions—between teacher and students and among students—I have tried to foster. Thus, whereas throughout most of their Japanese schooling they have been called upon primarily to absorb material presented as indisputable facts and truths by the teacher or the textbook, these courses challenge them to raise questions and doubts regarding many customs and daily practices that they have always taken for granted as normal and right. Moreover, instead of sitting passively in class listening to the teacher lecture and copying notes from the chalkboard, they are required to assume an active role, almost as partners with the teacher, in the process of discovery and learning by asking questions and giving their own thoughts and opinions on issues being discussed. For many students this experience revealed to them their capacity for critical thinking:

> At first I wondered, "Is it really all right to give my own opinions?" But what was strange was that it was through the process of expressing my views that I realized I actually had my own personal thoughts and views on various matters. I was surprised by own ability to think and to express myself.
>
> I was given many opportunities to think about what seem very obvious and natural but really aren't and to see that there are too many things we take for granted that we shouldn't. I am glad I am now able to stop and question, "Is this OK?" instead of just thinking, "This is the way things are." My perspective has expanded.

The concept of sharing personal experiences and emotions and having those experiences and emotions validated and integrated into the learning process is also something quite new and different for most students. For older, returning female students who potentially have much to contribute in terms of prior experiences, the opportunity to share those experiences in class may be empowering, as the following comment by a student with a background in nursing shows: "The recognition and understanding I have gotten from the other students in the class for my ideas and for the way I have tried to live my life has given me tremendous confidence. I also gained confidence from being able to talk to the younger women about my experiences in terms of working as a nurse, marriage, and child raising."

At the same time, some of the returning students appear uncertain about to what extent they should bring their prior experience and accumulated insights into an environment in which they do not yet feel completely at home, in which their presence has yet to gain full acceptance:

> One important aspect of "women's studies" is to value personal experience and emotional reaction. It is amazing that something so individualistic as personal experience or emotions should be valued and considered important in academia. I had a prejudiced view that such things should not be revealed in public. But at the same time I also believed that they are an important component in the decisions we make. When I think of my position as a returning student in my mid-forties, I am not yet decided as to whether I should try to bring my past experiences into the classroom or instead just try to be like the other, younger students and avoid standing out or calling attention to ourselves, which is the position taken by another older student in a similar position. But if we do that, then we are nothing more than simply "older" students, rather than adult women from a variety of backgrounds who have had experiences that are in many ways unique and different from those of the typical younger students.

Behind this student's hesitancy about responding to the invitation to share her experiences is the fact that it is only within the last ten years or so that colleges have begun to admit returning students, and it is still done on a very limited basis, so that many professors, accustomed as they have been to dealing almost exclusively with eighteen- to twenty-two-year-olds, still feel uncomfortable about having nontraditional students in their classes and are not quite sure about how to deal with them. While some of the male professors at my institution have expressed admiration for these women—most of whom have families and/or full- or part-time jobs—for their high motivation and commitment to their studies, others appear not to appreciate the fact that these students also tend to be more demanding; for example, they are more apt to ask questions in class or complain about class cancellations. Some male professors are clearly intimidated by the very presence of strong-willed, middle-aged women in their classrooms, and it is very likely that, realizing this, many of these women decide it is safer to try to blend in with the younger students and refrain from making references to their past achievements or experience. Nevertheless, the impact of these women on younger women students is, in my view, invaluable, particularly in women's studies courses in which the older women can contribute important insights based on their experiences and at the same time serve as visible role models for the young undergraduate women.

Institutional Impact

The impact the introduction of women's courses into the curriculum of Japanese colleges and universities has had on the institutions themselves and on the faculty and administration is also something that has not been explored very much. We can, however, make some observations based on the comments provided by various women's studies course instructors in the NWEC survey. Perhaps the most noticeable impact has been a heightened awareness of women's issues and of the fact that such a thing as women's studies exists, particularly on campuses on which women's studies courses are offered. That is not to say, however, that most faculty and administrators necessarily share the view that women's studies courses are important or necessary or that they have a place in a college or university curriculum. As noted earlier, at least some faculty and administrators advocate offering such courses primarily for the reason that this is what is in vogue today. At the same time, in some cases, positive reactions and responses on the part of students to such courses seem to have the effect of getting other faculty members and administrators to adopt a more positive stance with respect to those courses. The following comments illustrate these points:

The course doesn't seem to have had much of a visible impact within the institution, but quite a few professors have learned about the existence of such a thing called women's studies for the very first time from seeing this course listed in the catalog. (Kokuritsu fujin kyoiku kaikan 1991, 110)

A women's studies perspective has been incorporated into other courses offered at the institution. The faculty and staff as a whole seem to have come to the realization that such a perspective and way of thinking must be a part of the total educational endeavor at this institution which has an exclusively female student body. Many of our college-wide lectures are also related to women's studies. (52)

When the course was first offered I was frequently called upon at faculty meetings to explain the meaning of "women's studies" and the rationale of such studies. Today, the course is offered as a general education subject and the number of people who are sympathetic to it has increased to the point where some are saying we ought to make the course available to all students throughout the junior college rather than simply in one department, which is now the case. (172)

It's difficult to assess the impact of the women's studies course on the college as a whole. One reason is the instructors teaching women's studies do not necessarily share a common view (regarding the goals and purposes of such studies). . . . There is as yet no indication that the women and men teaching in various fields recognize the need to incorporate a women's studies perspective in their teaching and research. (4)

When the course was first offered (in 1984), at a faculty party several people came up to me with questions and comments that were totally off-base or else mocking, such as, "What in the world is 'women's studies'?" "Wouldn't it be nice if we had 'men's studies' as well?" These days I don't come across such reactions. On the other hand, I can't say that we have made much of an impact on others within the college. Or perhaps I should rather say that most professors don't seem to have much intellectual interest in other fields. (198)

When I initially brought up the idea of starting a course in women's studies to the administration, the reaction was "We can't have you waving the flag of women's lib!" I was told that the course title should be changed to "sociology," although I was free to teach what I wanted in the course. . . . Three years have passed since then; this year in a series of ten public lectures being offered at the college, I have been give an opportunity to present one lecture on women's studies. (287)

The subject of changes in students' attitudes has been discussed at faculty meetings and in seminars sponsored by the academic affairs division and has been taken up in connection with discussions centering on curriculum reform, teaching methodologies and goals, and orientation for incoming students. (172)

Other points mentioned by the instructors in the survey include, for example, the fact that instances of faculty members expressing discriminatory views toward women have lessened, that the number of students—particulary women—writing about issues related to women for their senior theses in such areas as economics and sociology has been increasing, and that other faculty members have come to sit in on some classes in women's studies courses.

Issues Surrounding the Teaching of Women's Studies

Our discussion has alluded to several of the issues that confront those of us who are involved in the teaching of women's studies in Japanese colleges and universities. Foremost among these issues is the fact, noted earlier, that there still is not a single faculty or department devoted to women's studies, and there is no university that awards a bachelor's or higher degree in women's studies. While many institutions offer one or more courses dealing with women, there has been little effort to move on to the next stage of designing a curriculum and organizing the courses in such a way that they have some coherence. Many of the respondents in the NWEC survey point out the need to strengthen women's studies courses both in the category of general education subjects and professional education subjects and to link these two areas.

To bring together hitherto scattered courses in women's studies into a cohesive program requires cooperation and coordination among instructors so that they can arrive at some shared understanding of the unique and distinctive goals, perspectives, methodologies, and content of their particular women's studies program. Thus, several of the respondents in the NWEC survey call for the need to provide more opportunities for instructors to share and exchange ideas and information and to create a network of people on campus who share common interests and concerns. One of the difficulties involved in achieving such coordination is the fact that many of those teaching courses in women's studies are adjuncts, particularly in the case of women, as we noted above, so that opportunities for coming together are limited.

The Need for Developing Feminist Pedagogy

The issue of teaching methodologies is one that many of the respondents in the NWEC survey pointed to as requiring urgent attention and exploration. Many of them mentioned the need to develop methods or processes for teaching which will increase student awareness of women's issues and get them to see how those issues are related to their own lives (or, in other words, to see the relationship between theory and practice), to encourage students to take a more active role and assume initiative in the learning process, and to promote more discussions and the exchange of views and opinions among students.

These concerns regarding the issue of pedagogical practices are readily understandable in view of the fact that little attention is paid to teaching (as opposed to research) and to exploring alternative methods of teaching in Japanese higher education. The quality of teaching at Japanese universities, even at the most prestigious ones such as Tokyo University, is generally thought to be very poor. The dominant method of teaching is the lecture, with a heavy emphasis on top-down knowledge transmission and little emphasis on promoting active involvement and participation by students. At the larger universities it is pretty much taken for granted that students can and often do cut classes and still manage to pass a course by getting the lecture notes from a classmate in order to take the final exam (which is often the only basis on which students are graded). Classes are very much teacher centered; students rarely ask questions or express their opinions, nor are they expected to or encouraged to do so by teachers. It is only within the past few years that, faced with the prospect of a severe competition among colleges and universities for survival, resulting from a projected drastic drop in the population of eighteen-year-olds in the next decade, university professors and administrators have begun to turn attention to the issue of how to improve the quality of teaching.

It is questionable to what extent most instructors in the field of women's studies realize the fact that teaching women's studies calls for a very different type of attitude with respect to the role of teacher and student and a different style of interaction between the instructor and students as well as among students. Even those who do have such an awareness and a desire to adopt different kinds of pedagogical strategies—and who want to create an atmosphere and structure their classes in such a way that students can, for example, contribute their own knowledge and experiences—do not necessarily know how to bring this about, since they themselves have never been exposed to alternative teaching/learning models in their own school experience. Another problem that confronts many instructors in this regard is that classes tend to be very large at Japanese colleges and universities; this is equally true of many courses in women's studies, particularly introductory general education courses. Needless to say, such large classes greatly inhibit discussions and the sharing of personal experiences.

Even in small classes, however, I (Fujimura-Fanselow) have found that it is extremely difficult to get students to understand that they are being asked to assume a very different role from that which they have been accustomed to playing in most classrooms throughout their academic careers and more difficult still to get them to put that understanding into practice. The challenge facing Japanese teachers of women's studies is, indeed, a major one. As Schniedewind and Maher astutely point out, "Changing the process of how we teach is often more difficult and risky than changing the content of what we teach" (1987, 4). But, unless we start paying more attention to the issue of how women's studies is to be taught, we risk the danger of allowing women's studies to become simply another discipline and passing up a unique opportunity to introduce a radically different notion of teaching and learning into Japanese schools and universities.

Research in the Field of Women's Studies

Women's Studies Professional Organizations

By the end of the 1970s four women's studies groups had been formed (three local groups, one in Tokyo and two in the Kyoto-Osaka area, and one national). All four groups incorporated the term *joseigaku* in their official names—Kokusai josei gakkai (International group for the study of women), Nihon joseigaku kenkyukai (Women's studies society of Japan [WSSJ]), Joseigaku kenkyukai (Society for women studies—Japan), and Nihon joseigakkai (Women's Studies Association of Japan). What is interesting to note is that these groups did not represent some natural outgrowth of a proliferation of women's studies courses; instead, they were established by those people who saw a need for such groups as a means, first of all, of making women's studies more visible and, second, in order to seek new ways in which women's studies might be implemented in Japanese society. Some groups devote themselves exclusively to research in an academic setting behind closed doors, while others are more open, providing a forum in which a variety of experiences are exchanged and discussed and encompassing not only academics but also housewives, students, and women in a variety of occupations.

The Women's Studies Society of Japan, based in the Kyoto-Osaka area, is of the latter type. It is particularly interesting and unique in that, as Junko Wada Kuninobu (1990), one of its founding members explains, it exemplifies the nontraditional, nonhierarchical-type of organizational structure that developed and became popular among many women's groups that were organized in the late 1970s and early 1980s. In the very beginning the WSSJ was organized under a chair, director, and board committee, whose members were university professors, including male professors. After three years the membership of WSSJ reached three hundred. The policies of the organization and the projects it undertook were decided upon by the board committee, in which most of the general members could not participate. The housewives within the organization were consistently excluded from the decision-making process, working instead as secretaries and receptionists at the meetings. This organizational system came under criticism by graduate students and junior and senior high school teachers within the organization. After two years of struggle and debate it was decided that the position of chair, director, and board committee be abolished, to be replaced by a steering committee, in which any member could participate. Today there is no representative or chair. Tasks are divided among those who volunteer for them, and persons in charge are selected on a rotation basis. Any member can propose a new project to the steering committee as long as she or he can find three other members to support it.

Research in the area of women's studies has become increasingly more fruitful, in terms of the volume of data accumulated and the scope of subject areas covered. The women's studies groups described here are, one after another, publishing the results of their research. In 1980 the Women's Studies Society of Japan began publishing an annual report; this publication is now in its thirteenth volume. The Society for Women's Studies—Japan (Joseigaku kenkyukai), made up of academics in the Tokyo metropolitan area, has published four volumes of collected essays entitled *Koza joseigaku* (Lectures on women's studies), and since 1990 it has also put out a journal, *Joseigaku kenkyu* (Women's studies research). Japan Women's Studies Association also joined the publishing arena with its own journal, *Joseigaku* (Women's studies), in 1992. In addition, a number of women's universities have women's studies centers and institutes on their campuses (the 1994 National Women's Education Centre report cited earlier lists 10) which conduct research projects, put out newsletters, and host seminars and workshops. Writings by individual women as well as groups have become numerous and now fill the shelves of major bookstores. There are now a number of women's bookstores as well.

Several outstanding scholars and researchers have emerged on the scene, espousing a variety of theories regarding the nature of femininity, how liberation and equality for women ought to be defined, the direction feminism ought to take in order to reform the existing social order, among others. Many lively debates on ecological feminism, socialist feminism, radical feminism, postfeminism, and other theories have been carried on through books and scholarly journals and at conferences (see Ehara 1990). In some cases a much wider audience of women, who are neither scholars nor researchers, has been drawn into these discussions, largely as result of the fact that women's issues have increasingly become "hot" and "salable" and, therefore, more widely reported in the mass media. Recent examples are the controversy over work versus life, or "living" and the so-called Agnes Debate, both of which trace their roots to the Debate on Housewives which surfaced in the mid-1950s (see boxes 3, 4, and 5).

Box 3.
The Housewife Debate
The so-called Housewife Debate has gone through several phases since it first appeared in the mid-1950s. The debate started with an article by Ayako Ishigaki which appeared in 1955 in a major women's monthly magazine, *Fujin koron*, entitled "The Secondary Occupation Called Homemaking." In it Ishigaki, who had lived in the United States prior to the World War II and witnessed the movement of more and more American women into the labor force, resulting from the diffusion of labor-reducing household devices, foresaw a similar development eventually taking place in Japan in the coming years, although at the time the growing legion of Japanese women married to white-collar, salaried workers were retreating into the home as full-time housewives. Warning women that soon homemaking would be reduced to a secondary occupation, she urged women to seek economic independence through participation in the paid labor force. Her argument was countered by those who emphasized the importance of the housewife's role in the family and in the community, insisting that it is precisely because many women do not hold jobs that they can take part in various community activities and peace movements. Later, in the 1960s, as Japan entered a period of high economic growth and more and more married women entered the labor market as part-time workers, some women began to argue for a reassessment of the economic value of household labor. Lacking from these debates, however, was a questioning of assumptions about gender roles.

Box 4.
Controversy over "Work" versus "Living"
This issue, which emerged in the decade of the 1980s, was about whether the liberation of women is to be sought through participating in the labor market and attempting to function more or less like men or, instead, through trying to realize to the fullest extent those values associated with "living" rather than work (i.e., concerns relating to home and community). Seeing that working women were increasingly becoming treated merely as a source of labor and incorporated into the sexist, discriminatory structure of the workplace, many women began to question the validity of the notion that participation by women in paid employment was the path to women's liberation. One writer, Kano Mikiyo (1985), called for a total withdrawal of women from the labor market. Her sentiments have been reflected in the appearance of new types of business ventures started by women and based on principles that are quite different from those traditionally managed by males, for example, workers' collectives and retail shops selling box lunches made from organically grown food, for which profit is not the primary motive. Among those who have argued against this position are the members of the Women's Action Group, who firmly support women's advancement into the labor market, insisting that the real obstacle to working women in their quest for liberation is the persistence of traditional gender roles. They have emphasized the need to create a new environment in which both men and women participate in both paid employment and in the maintenance and care of the home and family.

Box 5.
The Agnes Debate
Agnes Chan, a well-know television personality, sparked wide debate in
the late 1980s in the mass media and among feminists and scholars as well
as women across the nation, particularly working women, when she
insisted on taking her newborn child to her studio workplace. Of course,
it was only because of her celebrity status that her action attracted such
wide attention. Many women, especially those who had had no choice but
to place their children in daycare centers in order to continue their careers,
criticized Chan for lacking professionalism and seeking special privileges
as a woman. Others criticized her for being bound to the traditional notion
that mothers must always be at the side of their children. However, just as
many women sympathized and identified with her strong desire to continue working but without denying herself close daily contact with her
infant child. What this debate revealed was that, while more and more
women now accept work as a natural component of their lives, there is a
split between those who favor pursuing a full-time career and those who
want to lead a more balanced life that takes into account the needs of
home, motherhood, and family. At the same time, it called attention to the
inadequacy of institutional support for working women in the form of
child daycare centers and workplace arrangements.

As a side note, it is interesting to observe that, amid these discussions, one
rarely finds women calling into question the desirability or necessity of
maintaining the modern institutions of marriage and family or the value
for women of bearing and raising children. Although most feminists are
critical of the traditional division of gender roles, the assumption generally
held is that the family and motherhood will continue to be central and vital
in the lives of women. Whether this assumption continues to retain validity in the future is an interesting question.

Areas Calling for Future Research

By and large, the focus of women's studies research, regardless of subject
area or discipline, has been on the ways in which gender roles are constructed and reinforced in Japanese society. Such issues, however, as the
commoditization of female sexuality, as represented by prostitution, trafficking in women, and pornography, which are currently being taken up by
various women's groups, have not yet been explored and researched fully by
academic scholars. This commoditization phenomenon is one that has
become increasingly rampant during the past twenty years, and it represents
a serious, common concern for Japanese women and women in Southeast
Asia, since it involves the degradation and exploitation of both groups of
women.

The issue of domestic violence is also one that has received little attention
on the part of Japanese researchers. On this point some of the participants

at the Asian Women's Conference, hosted jointly by several Japanese women's groups in April 1992, voiced the view that, so long as Japanese women continue to bear in silence violence perpetrated against them by Japanese men, they will in effect be guilty of condoning violence inflicted by Japanese men against women of other Asian countries. The fact that these issues are not properly addressed by women's studies scholars illustrates to some extent a lack of connection between academics and activists, and also between Japanese researchers and those of other Asian countries.

As noted, the central concern of women's studies in Japan has been primarily directed at domestic problems, with very little attention paid to the situation of women elsewhere in Asia, in spite of Japan's economic supremacy in this region. There is a definite need for Japanese women's studies to broaden its horizons in order to forge a community with women's studies researchers and practitioners in other Asian countries.

In addition to broadening its horizons beyond Japan, women's studies needs to broaden its horizons within the country as well. A particular case in point concerns the Korean women and women of Korean ancestry living in Japan, whose difficulties are compounded by circumstances of politics, history, culture, and ethnicity. Another issue in need of work is to forge closer links between feminists within academe and those outside. Thus, for instance, although there are persistent, ongoing campaigns by female teachers at the primary and secondary levels to make the curriculum nonsexist, many women in academia tend to remain indifferent to those developments.

Women's Studies Outside of Academe

In the last ten to fifteen years seminars in women's studies for a general audience, particularly housewives, have increased considerably, partly as a result of adult education programs for women provided by local governments.[5] Such courses have, to some extent, replaced classes in flower arrangement, tea ceremony, cooking, and other accomplishments, which used to be the main feature of these programs.

In addition, during this same period women's centers have been established at the national, prefectural, and local levels: for example, at the national level the National Women's Education Centre is located in Saitama Prefecture; at the prefectural level there are the Tokyo Women's Information Center and the Kanagawa Women's Center; and at the local level there is the Women's Forum, located in Yokohama City. These centers serve not only to make resources available—including books, magazines, and videos—but they also provide a meeting place for various women's groups, hosting seminars and meetings, offering workshops for women seeking employment, and training in specific skills such as word processing and computing.

The National Women's Education Centre has hosted an annual seminar on women's studies since 1980 which has attracted participants from abroad as well as within Japan and has served as a valuable forum for the exchange of information and data. The prefectural and local women's centers offer programs and activities that are closely linked with the local communities. In many cases seminar participants have set up study groups on the history of women in their particular regions and have initiated research activities. Additionally, NGOs such as the Ichikawa Fusae Memorial Association sponsor seminars on women's studies–related topics and also offer a library service.

"Grassroots" Women's Studies

Another significant phenomenon has been the emergence of many women's groups, including study groups outside of academe. In the case of these grassroots groups, women who share common concerns regarding some particular issue come together, study the issue, then take action. Among these groups are Yuseihogoho kaikaku soshi rengokai (Group fighting against restrictions on the abortion law), which has since 1970 continued to campaign against restrictions on the current abortion law, and Kodo suru onnatachinokai (Women's action group), which has taken up action against a variety of issues, including the display of pornographic ads on trains and subways and the curriculum requirement that girls, but not boys, study home economics in high school. Other groups include the Asian Women's Association and the Japanese-French Women's Information Center. Women have also formed groups to present films made by female directors, to publish newsletters for women, and to set up women's health clinics (Hisada 1987). Also prominent has been the emergence of local women's history study groups, which have unearthed valuable data and materials pertaining to women's history in various parts of Japan.

Conclusion

The past fifteen to twenty years has seen the establishment of women's studies and related subject courses both within and outside academia. At the same time, however, there is not a single faculty or department devoted to women's studies, and there is no university that awards a bachelor's or higher degree in women's studies. Moreover, personal involvement in the women's movement continues to be a controversial matter, at least on an institutional level, for the traditional attitude that scholarship and any form of political activity should remain separate weighs heavily on these groups as well as on their members. It seems that this whole situation illustrates the limitations faced by women's studies and raises questions concerning the extent to which it can exert an impact both on the academic world and society at large.

Another important point is that, in spite of dedication and commitment on the part of women's studies practitioners, and their growing involvement in various governmental bodies, the extent to which such involvement can be effective in bringing about changes in the status quo appears to be limited. This is largely due to the fact that the formulation and implementation of policies—including those that concern women—continues to be predominantly in the hands of males, at both the national and local levels.

As we look to the future, our agenda is twofold. On the domestic front we need to continue in the struggle to bring about changes through combining research, teaching, and action. Simultaneously, we must promote understanding of the interconnectedness of the situation of women in Japan and that of women in other countries, particularly Asian countries. The ways in which sexism manifests itself varies from culture to culture—according to the societal, economic, and political conditions within the society. Feminist ideology generation in the West, translated to the Asian context, could form the basis for solving some of the common issues faced by Asian women. Yet, because of the specificity of culture, religion, and varying degrees of industrial development, Western ideas evidently cannot provide a total solution to the problems of Asian women. Therefore, while we need to take that which is applicable to our situation in Asia, we also need to seek our own theoretical approaches. For this purpose more and more cross-cultural studies, as well as joint research projects among women's studies practitioners in the region, must be encouraged. Such research will, we hope, yield a better understanding of both differences and commonalities among women in various Asian countries, which will, in turn, help us in working together to promote the well-being of women in the region.

NOTES

Parts of this essay are based on the following writings by Fujieda: "An Overview of Women's Studies in Japan," in *Women in a Changing Society: The Japanese Scene*, comp. National Women's Education Centre (Bangkok, UNESCO, 1990); "Women's Studies in Japan—Its Past, Present and Future" (paper presented at the Asian Women's Conference, Tokyo April 1992.

1. See Tachi Kaoru, "A Historical Sketch of Some Pioneers in Women's Studies in Japan" (paper presented at the Center for Women's Studies, Tokyo Woman's Christian University, 10 September 1988).

2. For a discussion of the women's liberation movement of the early 1970s in Japan, see Kazuko Tanaka's chapter ("The New Feminist Movement in Japan, 1970–1990") in this volume.

3. Many of the younger generation of women view the second wave of Japanese feminism as having started in 1975, with the International Women's Year, rather than with the women's liberation movement of the early 1970s.

4. The Ministry of Education requires students in four-year colleges and universities to take generation education courses during the first two years as a prerequisite for proceeding to the specialized curriculum in the third and fourth years. The Ministry has, however, recently changed this requirement.

5. This section is based on Tachi Kaoru's "Current Trends of Women's Studies in Japan"(paper presented at the Center for Women's Studies, Tokyo Woman's Christian University, 10 September 1988), 11–14.

REFERENCES

Ehara, Yumiko, ed. 1990. *Feminism ronso—nanajunendai kyujunendai e* (Controversies within feminism—from the 1970s to the 1990s). Tokyo: Keiso shobo.

Fujimura-Fanselow, Kumiko. 1989. "Feminist Pedagogy: Its Goals, Principles and Implementation." *Toyo Eiwa Journal of the Humanities and Social Sciences* 1.

Hara, Hiroko. 1987. "Joseigaku no shimei" (The mission of women's studies). In *Koza joseigaku 4: Onna no me de miru* (Lectures in women's studies, vol. 4: looking through women's eyes), ed. Joseigaku Kenkyukai. Tokyo: Keiso shobo.

Hino, Reiko. 1986. "Onna o kangaeru—joshikosei to tomoni (II)" (Thinking about women together with female high school students (pt. 2.) *Joseigaku Nenpo* (Annual report of Women's Studies Society of Japan) 7:94–103.

Hisada, Megumi. 1987. *Onna no Networking—Onna no Group Zenkoku Guido* (Women's networking—a guide to women's groups nationwide). Tokyo: Gakuyo shobo.

Inoue, Teruko. 1980. *Joseigaku to sono shuhen* (Women's studies and related studies). Tokyo: Keiso shobo.

———. 1987. "Onna no 'koza' o tsukuru" (Establishing a women's "discipline"). In *Koza Joseigaku 4: Onna no me de miru* (Lectures in women's studies, vol. 4: looking through women's eyes), ed. Joseigaku Kenkyukai. Tokyo: Keiso shobo.

Iwao, Sumiko, and Hiroko Hara. 1979. *Joseigaku koto hajime* (Introduction to women's studies) Tokyo: Kodansha.

Kano, Mikiyo. 1985. "Shaen shakai karano sotettai o" (Toward a total withdraw from society). *Shinchihei* (New horizons) (November).

Kokuritsu Fujin Kyoiku Kaikan. 1994. *Koto kyoiku ni okeru joseeigaku kanren kamokuto no jokyo—Heisei gonen do chosa hokoku* (Status of courses on women's studies and related subjects in institutions of higher education in Japan—1993 survey report). Saitama-ken: Kokuritsu Fujin Kyoiku Kaikan (National Women's Education Centre).

———. 1991. *Heisei ninendo koto kyoiku ni okeru joseigaku kanrenkoza kaisetsu jokyo chosa kekka hokoku* (Survey of courses on women's studies and related subjects in institutions of higher education in Japan [fiscal 1990]. Saitama-ken: Kokuritsu Fujin Kyoiku Kaikan (National Women's Education Centre).

Kuninobu, Junko Wada. 1990. *Women's Networks: Organizing for Change.* MS.

Schniedewind, N., and F. Maher. 1987. Editorial. "Feminist Pedagogy" issue, *Women's Studies Quarterly* 15, nos. 3 and 4: 4.

Shima, Yoko. 1987. "Daigaku ni okeru 'joseigaku' no genjo to kadai" (The present status of and issues in women's studies in universities). *Daito Bunka Daigaku kiyo* (Research bulletin of Daito Bunka University) 25.

Tachi, Kaoru. 1988a. "Current Trends in Women's Studies in Japan." Paper presented at the Center for Women's Studies, Tokyo Woman's Christian University, 10 September.

———. 1988b. "Historical Sketch of Some Pioneers in Women's Studies in Japan." Paper presented at the Center for Women's Studies, Tokyo Woman's Christian University, 10 September.

Tagawa, Kenzo. 1992. "Daigaku ni okeru joseigaku no jugyo—Osaka Joshi Daigaku ni okeru jissen rei" (Teaching of women's studies in universities—the example of Osaka Women's University). *Joseigaku kenkyu* (Research in women's studies) 1 (March): 41–61 (journal published by Osaka Women's University).

"Takamaru 'joseigaku' e no kanshin—daigaku tandai nado koza kaisetsu sakan"

(The growing interest in "women's studies"—many universities and junior colleges setting up such courses). 1991. *Chunichi shimbun* (Chunichi newspaper), 26 September.

Yoshida, Kiyomi. 1988. "Onna no ikikata o kangaeru—koko kokugo de no jugyo jissen" (Thinking about women's lives—based on teaching a Japanese language arts course in high school). *Joseigaku nenpo* (Annual report of the Women's Studies Society of Japan), 9:74–83.

❖ 3 ❖

Marriage, Family, and Sexuality: Changing Values and Practices

Marriage and Family: Past and Present

❖ ❖ ❖

Kyoko Yoshizumi

The Japanese concept, ideology, and form of marriage and family has changed dramatically from that which prevailed up until the end of World War II. One manifestation of this change is that, whereas marriage used to be the only socially acceptable life choice for women, so that they were pressured to marry by a certain age, today marriage has increasingly become a matter of personal choice. At the same time, the family structure itself has undergone transformation in postwar society, giving rise to several variant forms, including the "pseudo–single-mother family," in which the father, though legally present, is in fact too busy to spend much time with his family, and the "latent-disorganization family," or "domestic divorce," in which a husband and wife continue to remain legally married in spite of the fact that a conjugal relationship no longer exists.

This essay begins with a description of marriage and family patterns in contemporary Japanese society and some of the ways in which they differ from those found in Western societies, after which it presents a historical look at the Japanese family system up to World War II. What I will try to demonstrate is that, although, indeed, many changes have taken place, remnants of the earlier patterns are present both in the consciousness of the Japanese people and in legal provisions that obstruct the realization of marriage and family based on true equality between women and men. Moreover, while many women and men are strongly attracted to a model of marriage which puts primary value on the couple's companionship based on romantic love, the reality is that the persisting impact of various historical and cultural factors is such that, in fact, priority is still placed on a couple's role as parents—yet in most cases they are not even conscious of the discrepancy between their professed ideal of marriage and actual practice. At the same time, I will highlight efforts being made by concerned feminists to overhaul such restrictive legal provisions.

Current Status of Marriage and Family in Japan

Marriage as One Possible Lifestyle

The ideal Japanese woman used to be one who married and raised children. Women's happiness was thought to lie in marriage. Until recently a so-called marriageable age existed apart from human maturation and lifestyle. If a woman wanted to marry prior to the "marriageable age," it was opposed on the grounds that she was "too young," yet, when she reached the marriageable age, she was urged to marry soon or else remain "an unsold good." There was strong social pressure on all women to marry within the marriageable age. In the past, when women faced difficulties in achieving economic independence, marriage was a form of social security for many women. After World War II women's status showed considerable improvement, yet, with the exception of a select few, women continued to find it difficult to maintain stable, financially sustaining jobs throughout their lives. In general, a woman had an easier life within the status of a wife supported by a husband than of living a single life. For those who wanted to have children, particularly, strong social support for the principle of legitimacy and the lack of an adequate system of social security for mothers and children served to make marriage almost a social necessity, rather than a matter of individual choice. Many young women rushed into marriage, regardless, in many cases, of their partners' suitability.

In recent years marriage for women has become one of many variant lifestyles. Though men are still socially and economically dominant, women can live fairly good lives on their own as working members of society. A survey by the Japan Institute of Life Insurance conducted in 1986 revealed that, among women ages twenty-five to twenty-nine, about 50 percent responded, "It is natural for women to marry," while the other 50 percent responded, "Women do not necessarily have to marry" (Seimei Hoken Bunka Senta 1987). The notion that women's happiness lies in marriage seems to be dying out or at least losing force. In another study of single Japanese women and men between ages eighteen and thirty-five conducted in 1986 by the Ministry of Health and Welfare, the percentage of female respondents who said they thought "a single life is advantageous" exceeded those who felt "marriage was advantageous" by twenty percentage points—90 versus 70 percent (Koseisho, Jinko Mondai Kenkyujo 1987). In 1972 the mean age of women's first marriage was 24.2; by 1986 it had risen to 25.6, and to 25.9 in 1990. The more educated a woman is, the later she marries. Some women postpone marriage, saying they want to enjoy their single lives a little more or they want to establish their careers first, while others question: Is marriage really a good thing? Isn't a single life more enjoyable than married life?

On the one hand, many women no longer seem to feel that they want to or have to marry at any cost; on the other hand, women's ideals and expectations regarding marriage have become higher. A career-oriented woman who wants to continue working after marriage wants a marriage partner who will understand and respect her work and share both housework and child care. But it is not easy to find such a man, even among today's young men. Most Japanese men are apt to think, "If my wife wants to work outside, I still want her to come home earlier than me to prepare supper," and "A man should occupy the primary position within marriage, both socially and economically." Even at the present, with more than half of all married women working in some capacity outside the home, most men continue to regard housework and child raising as "women's work" and want wives who will follow and be devoted to them as well as cater to them. Most Japanese men, it appears, have not been able to keep pace with the changes that have been taking place in women's attitudes and behavior. Single women lament that they want to marry but that there are no suitable men around.

Today's Variant Family Structures: The "Pseudo–Single-Mother Family" and "Latent-Disorganization Family"

Recently, particularly in the cities, the nuclear family—consisting of the father, mother, and child(ren)—has become increasingly dominant. In reality, however, many Japanese husbands place priority on their career as "company man," leaving their homes early in the morning and coming home late at night, so that they actually spend very little time with their wives and children.

A typical middle-class Japanese white-collar husband spends mosts of his waking hours working, even on weekends and holidays, when he has to socialize in bars and restaurants or on the golf course "for business"; often comes home after midnight, uttering only "supper," "bed," and "bath"; reads the newspaper, even when his wife is talking about their children or about what she did that day; and avoids matters concerning the children by saying, "Wives are responsible for the education of the children." This typical Japanese husband in no way senses that he is neglecting his family. Rather, he believes he is fulfilling the role of husband and father by earning wages to support his wife and children. In reality, however, he has very little time or emotional energy to give to his wife and children, and, as a result of this, his presence or position within the family has come to assume increasingly less importance.

More and more Japanese wives are beginning to question the validity of a conjugal relationship devoid of emotional and mental interaction and to seek deeper and more egalitarian relationships with their husbands. Increasingly, middle-aged and elderly wives are initiating divorce in order to escape the control of tyrannical husbands or a marriage that exists only in form, in

185

order to start new lives. The Japanese divorce rate, however, is lower than that of other developed countries.[1] The reason for this is that, even when the conjugal relationship has not lasted, many Japanese couples continue to maintain the outward form of marriage. The lower incidence of divorce does not mean that there are fewer problems among Japanese couples. Okonogi Keigo, a psychiatrist, points out that, while the so-called porcupine dilemma described by Leopold Bellak (1970) leads, in the U.S. case, to divorce, in Japan troubles are avoided by turning the dilemma into an illusion. The porcupine dilemma describes one inherent in human relationships whereby, "the closer the psychological distance between two human being becomes, the more their interests become bound to those of one another and the greater the likelihood is that their egoism—that is, the porcupine's quills—will hurt one another and lead to more conflict and suffering" (Okonogi 1983, 40). That is to say, whereas in an agrarian society extended family members worked together in order to maintain their livelihood, the small nuclear families that are predominant in modern industrial societies no longer function as units of production. The family has, instead, become the focus primarily of emotional life. Moreover, the habit of restraining individual emotions has weakened, thus aggravating the porcupine dilemma. In Japan this dilemma has been overcome by avoiding emotional relationships. Okonogi states that the Japanese have managed to maintain a more or less stable family life by creating and maintaining the illusion that "the family is important for us, and I have a good family" (Okonogi 1983, 69, 94).

Why does the porcupine dilemma lead to the creation of an illusion in Japan, while in Western countries it leads to divorce? The difference arises from conceptual differences regarding marriage and the family. To gain a better understanding of the context of our present situation, it is important to review the history of the Japanese family system.

The Japanese Family System prior to the End of World War II

The Family, or *Ie*, System

Prior to the enactment of the current Civil Code following World War II, Japanese society was characterized by a family, or *ie*, system. The *ie* connotes a family group as well as a household that continues and is carried forth from generation to generation. It continues successively from past to future through ancestors and descendants; moreover, it is a conceptual and abstract family that continues on even when family members all die away. Sometimes an *ie* is resurrected by relatives, and it can exist even in the absence of actual family members and succeeding generations.

Under this family system the heir among many children remained in the family and inherited all of the property in order to maintain the lineage and the family business. Among the feudal governing warrior, or samurai, class, the oldest male became the family successor as a basic principle. In rural areas this principle was not strictly followed, and the heir was not always the oldest son. Sometimes, in order to gain family labor, the oldest daughter or the youngest child inherited the family title.

The head of the family or the patriarch—generally, the father or husband—exercised a tremendous degree of power and authority, and other family members were required to be totally obedient and to assume a posture of allegiance to him. Any family member who behaved independently was severely sanctioned. The relationship was one of inequality, since power resided in the head, while other family members had little power, only duties. Such a relationship was far removed from a democratic one based on equality and mutual respect in which both sides have rights and duties.

Within this family system family members thought only of superficially fulfilling their assigned roles and avoided emotional relationships and expressions of feeling. The only affectionate expression was "serving." Filial piety on the part of children toward their parents and devotion of a mother to her children profiled the family emotional structure. This structure was applied to the entire society, as expressed in the notion of the "family state." The governance-obedience relationship of the family was applied to the relationship between landlord and tenant farmer, employer and employee, and even the emperor and the people.

The Meiji Civil Code and the System of Family Registration

The family system embodied in the Meiji Civil Code was based on a system of family registration called *koseki*. It was essentially a system of identification. Whereas in Western countries people are registered individually, however, the Japanese system of *koseki*, which exists to this day in a modified form, requires registration by family. Under this system one person, the family head, is central, and all other family members occupy their respective positions in relation to the head.

The *koseki* system had had a long tradition, but under the Meiji government the system was made universal and all-encompassing, and every Japanese was required to be registered within her or his family register. Two reasons for this were to eliminate tax evasions and avoidance of military service. The family register contained a record of every family member from birth to death, including any change of status. Instead of the earlier custom of recognizing a marriage at the time of the wedding, it was now mandatory to register marriages, and only those marriages that had been reported to the person in charge of one's register were officially recognized.

Under the Meiji Civil Code an individual's life was totally ruled and regulated by the family system. Every person had to belong to a family or household unit ruled by the head, who was called the *kacho*. The *kacho* was often also the *koshu*, the designated head of the family register, and he had the authority to govern the behavior of all family members, including marriage and place of residence. A family member who did not obey the orders of the *koshu* could be expelled from the family. Up until the age of twenty-five in the

187

case of women and thirty in the case of men, one had to obtain parental permission in order to marry. Moreover, consent of the *koshu* was required for all marriages regardless of the couple's age. The position of *koshu* was inherited by the eldest son from one generation to another, and it entailed also the inheritance of genealogy, the family altar, and the family tomb. The heir had exclusive rights to manage property and perform various rituals. It is important, however, that the patriarchal right given the head of the family was accompanied at the same time by his duty to notify the village or town master regarding changes in the status of all family members, such as marriages. Failure to fulfill these duties was punished according to the Criminal Law. Thus, the head of a family functioned as a terminal organ of the administrative machinery within the emperor system.

Women and men occupied positions of extreme inequality under the Meiji Civil Code. Men had priority in all areas. Husbands exercised legal control over their wives, who were not legally recognized persons and therefore enjoyed no rights. The former could, for example, dispose of any assets that their wives brought with them at the time of marriage. In fact, women were regarded as lacking in the ability to manage property. In addition, fathers always had superior rights over mothers in matters concerning children; the only cases in which the mother had parental rights was when the father died, abandoned the family, or became disabled.

Marriage under the Japanese Family System

Within this system marriage was regarded primarily as a means of perpetuating the family line. In selecting a spouse, priority was placed on the interests of the family, rather than the will of the two individuals involved. Most marriages were arranged by parents or relatives. At marriage the wife left her family of orientation and became part of her husband's household; her registration was listed in her husband's family register, and her surname was changed to that of her husband's surname, or *uji*. Marriage did not mean creating a new family; rather, it meant that a wife entered her husband's family. Fulfilling the role of bride and daughter-in-law within the family was the most important criterion for a wife, and she was expected to serve her parents-in-law and give birth to a male successor.

Divorce was likewise treated in terms of the interests of the family. Even if the conjugal relationship was perfect, if the wife could not get along well with the parents-in-law or could not bear a child, she was often divorced against her will.

It was considered socially acceptable and even necessary for a man to keep one or more mistresses as a way of ensuring a successor. Keeping mistresses also symbolized wealth, high status, and authority. Initially, the Meiji government officially recognized the concubine (*saisho*) system. In 1879 a new provision recognized both wives and concubines as a husband's legal relatives in the second degree. A cabinet proclamation in 1873 recognized both children born to a wife and those born to a concubine as legitimate.

Such a system, however, though quite natural in the earlier feudal society, was condemned as barbarous by Westerners. Therefore, with the enactment of the Old Criminal Law in 1882, concubines lost their legal status, and their children were considered illegitimate. The Meiji Civil Code legally adopted monogamy, but, as a matter of social practice, mistresses continued to be accepted. Children born to mistresses were divided into two categories: those that were acknowledged by the father, called *shoshi*, and those that were not, called *shiseiji*. Male children in the *shoshi* category had a higher rank in the succession line than legitimate female children.

In this way a husband was socially and legally allowed to have mistresses. A wife's adultery, however, was a criminal offense and constituted grounds for divorce. Thus, in prewar Japanese society monogamy was prescribed for women only.

Changes in Marriage and Family Following World War II

Legal Changes Pertaining to Marriage and Divorce

After World War II, the Constitution was revised, and the current Civil Law was enacted in 1947, based on the principles of family life grounded in respect for individual dignity and equality of both sexes. The old family system was abolished, and the conjugal relationship became the cornerstone of the family. Legal equality of wife and husband was recognized. The wife could now exercise individual legal rights based on her own free will. The right of a husband to manage and gain profit from his wife's assets was abolished; a wife and husband could now separate their finances. Parental rights became cooperative in marriage, and after divorce either parent could seek custody of the child(ren). Children were now expected to support their parents cooperatively when necessary. With respect to inheritance, upon the death of the husband the wife was to be granted one-third of the total inheritance, with the remainder to be divided equally among the children. A later provision enabled wives to inherit one-half of the property.

Marriage came to be viewed as the pursuit of the happiness of the husband and wife and their children. Marriage was to be entered into based on the will of the two individuals involved, and all regulations concerning marriage, such as that requiring the consent of the family head for all marriages, were abolished. Moreover, monogamy was made binding on the husband as well as the wife. Adultery on the part of either spouse was made a legitimate ground for divorce, and it was no longer to be considered a criminal offense.

A Comparison of Japanese and Western Views Regarding Marriage and Family

Concomitant with these postwar changes in legal provisions pertaining to marriage and family, the dominant view regarding marriage has undergone a change from one centered on the family to one that places priority on the

emotional relationship of the two individuals involved. So-called love marriages have become socially accepted and increasingly popular, although
there are still couples who rely on introductions arranged by third parties
(omiai). In modern Japanese society single women and men can freely associate with one another, but, unfortunately, there seem not to be sufficient
opportunities for them to meet. Therefore, relatives, friends, and neighbors
frequently act as traditional go-betweens *(nakodo)*. More recently, however,
many young people take advantage of private and public marriage advisory
institutions.

Despite the fact that the family system was legally abolished, the mentality of many Japanese remains embedded in that system. This is exemplified by the fact, noted earlier, that, whereas in U.S. society, failure of the
conjugal relationship frequently leads to divorce, in Japan many couples
continue to stay legally married even under such circumstances. Okonogi
(1983) attributes this to various historical and cultural differences between
Japan and Western societies pertaining to marriage and family. In
Okonogi's view, first of all, whereas in Western societies monogamy has its
roots in Christianity, in Japan monogamy has a short history, and polygamy
is still acceptable. Extramarital affairs carried on by husbands are tacitly
ignored, with wives saying, "I can live with it as long as he isn't in love
with the other woman"—or ". . . as long as the other woman is someone
who's in the entertainment business" or ". . . so long as the affair is only
temporary." Second, in many Western societies companionship between a
man and a woman or husband and wife is often given greater importance
than that between those of the same sex, and many social affairs call for
participation as couples. In Japan, on the other hand, the relationship
between a mother and child(ren) or companionship between people of the
same sex tends to be viewed as more important, whereas companionship
between wife and husband has yet to be fully established. In other words,
Western societies, such as the United States, tend to be "couple oriented,"
and Japan is a same-sex-oriented society.

Expounding on this point, I would say that, while, on the one hand, it
is difficult in Japanese society for friendship between those of opposite
sexes to develop, on the other hand, there is something in the culture which
is conducive to the development of strong emotional bonds and feelings of
solidarity between those of the same sex. Unlike Christian-influenced cultures, in which homosexuality has been viewed as sinful, quite the opposite has been the case in Japan, in which going far back in history there has
been a disposition to glorify homosexuality, particularly in the form of love
between an adolescent and an older male, even to regard it as something
surpassing and more noble than the love between a man and a woman.
This tendency became pronounced during the so-called period of the War-
ring States (fifteenth–sixteenth centuries), when the country was plunged
in a perpetual state of warfare in a struggle for the redistribution of feudal
power, as those values connected with military affairs and masculinity

came to be revered while, at the same time, women were denigrated. Later, in the Meiji period, the government sought to propagate among the common population the Confucian value system, which had, prior to that time, prevailed only among the ruling warrior class. Thus, whereas previously young women and men in farming and fishing villages had been permitted to socialize rather freely prior to marriage, as exemplified by the custom of *neyado,*[2] the Meiji government prohibited these traditional practices and sought to suppress love between men and women and promoted, instead, a social separation of the sexes. Thus, from the lower years of elementary school contact between the sexes was carefully avoided by having them study in separate classrooms and not play together. This effort by those in power to maintain a separation of the sexes was strengthened during World War II, when the values of sacrifice and stoicism were particularly extolled, and during that time a married couple, let alone a pair of lovers, seen walking alone together was reprimanded.

This notion of a strict social separation of, or a distance between, the sexes has become an integral part of the Japanese people's mentality, so that even today there is a tendency for those of the same sex to come together to form groups, even into adolescence. Whereas in the United States or European countries it is quite common for girls and boys to play in mixed groups, in Japan it is by far more common for children to play with those of the same sex. This tendency continues into adulthood, so that many Japanese feel much more comfortable, psychologically, being with those of the same sex rather than the opposite sex.

In terms of the relationship between Japanese wives and husbands, many husbands seek emotional satisfaction through male companionship, and many men go out to drink with colleagues after work on an almost daily basis, often coming home late. At the same time, wives tend to pay more attention to child raising and associating with female friends and prefer going out with female friends rather than their husbands. Several years ago there was a television ad that said, "Husbands are lovable as long as they keep earning money, stay healthy, and stay away from home." It seems to represent the feelings of many wives. In short, in Japan, even when husband and wife are not emotionally bonded, they rarely feel lonely because they feel such bonding with friends of the same sex.

Solidarity among men has tended to be glorified, and there is a generally tolerant attitude with respect to cultural expressions of homosexuality. Thus, for example, the Kabuki theater, which consists exclusively of male actors who play both male and female roles, and the more modern Takarazuka opera company, with its all-female cast, enjoy much popularity, and there is little opposition to gay bars. This is is not to say, however, that the right of individuals to freely choose a homosexual lifestyle is publicly or officially recognized. Spiritual closeness between individuals of the same sex is accepted, but sexual relations between such individuals is repudiated, and homosexuals are viewed as perverts and treated in a discriminatory manner.

191

It seems to be the case that, even among individuals who prefer to be with someone of the same sex and have a strong emotional attachment to that person, so long as no physical relationship exists between them, the fact of their homosexual tendency does not surface to the level of self-awareness.

While the women's movement in Europe and the United States has had to struggle to build and affirm a sense of solidarity among all women, and lesbianism has been a polarizing issue, in the Japanese case, in which this sense of solidarity has been achieved more readily, lesbianism has thus far not been taken up as an issue. In fact, it is only just recently that groups championing lesbian and gay rights and liberation have surfaced.

Third among the differences Okonogi notes is that in modern Western countries the relationship between wife and husband based on mutual romantic love is thought to be the primary and central component within a marriage, and priority is placed on their role as man and woman rather than their role as parents. While in postwar Japanese society love marriages have gained social acceptance, love is not regarded as essential in maintaining or sustaining a marriage. Whereas in U.S. society, for example, it is common for a married couple to go to a movie or a party leaving their children in the care of a babysitter, in Japan such behavior is likely to be viewed as abandoning the children.

A Japanese wife and husband are expected to act more as parents than as a couple, or, in other words, to place priority on their role as parents rather than as a couple. One illustration of this is that many husbands, when transferred to a position in another city or overseas, make the move alone and leave their families behind so as not to interrupt the children's schooling. Another manifestation of this is that, even after their children are grown, many partners continue to call each other "Mother" and "Dad." Even if a husband and wife cease to love each other, that alone is not usually viewed as a sufficient reason for divorce, so long as both continue to meet their parental obligations. This is one important reason why the divorce rate has been low in Japan until now.

In addition to the various historical and cultural factors, there are, of course, economic and social factors that have also played a significant role in maintaining a relatively low divorce rate in Japan. Women's low position in the labor market and lack of sufficient social security for children are critical factors. As discussed elsewhere in this volume, many women are forced to discontinue outside employment once they have children because of the lack of adequate child care facilities and lack of help with child care and household chores from their husbands, who tend to put in long hours on the job. Moreover, opportunities for married women to reenter the labor market on a regular, full-time basis are extremely limited. Therefore, for the majority of women it is a virtual certainty that, should they divorce, they would be unable to maintain their current living standard. In addition, in cases of divorce, even if a court orders the husband to pay child support, there is no mechanism for forcing compliance, and many men do not pay. Many women have been deterred from seeking divorce due to these financial reasons. They have, instead, endured their marriages by rationalizing to themselves, "Divorce is bad for children" or "This is simply the way most marriages are."

In recent years, however, more and more women are seeking and demanding more meaningful emotional relationships with their husbands. Particularly noticeable is the rise in the number of divorces initiated by middle-aged and older women. These women, who have finished raising their children and thereby fulfilled their parental responsibilities, seek a new start in life, often taking with them their share of the husband's lump-sum retirement payment. At the same time, among younger women there is a tendency to place greater importance on individual self-fulfillment, rather than the parental role, and they show a stronger willingness to take steps to end a marriage that is no longer based on love, even if they have small children.

Feminist Challenges to the Family Institution

Despite the significant changes that have been made with respect to the system and institution of marriage and the family in Japan, the fact remains that, in several ways, women continue to be hindered from exercising freedom of choice and independence in various matters relating to marriage and family. The feminist movement, which has become increasingly more active in recent years, has sought to address these issues.

The Movement for Separate Surnames

In Japan marriage is legally approved when a couple fills out a marriage license form and submits it to the municipal office; it is not necessary to go through a wedding ceremony. Under the current Civil Code (Art. 750), a couple must register under one family name, that of either the husband or the wife. While either name may be chosen, in reality most people seem to uphold the notion that the man must carry on the family name, and so it is habitual for couples to choose the husband's name. Ninety-eight percent of women change their surname to that of their husband. There is no way for both partners to continue using their own surnames; they are forced to choose one name. The reason is that, although the family system was done away with, the system of family register has been maintained under the Civil Code. The family register contains data on two generations, the wife and husband and their unmarried children. When a child becomes grown and gets married, she or he and the spouse establish a new family register under one common surname. The surname cannot be totally new.

Recently, with many women continuing to work after marriage, changing one's surname has come to be seen as causing various inconveniences, and therefore some women continue to use their maiden name for professional purposes. Others resist changing their surnames because they regard their surnames as an essential aspect of their identity or because taking the husband's name implies that the wife is being taken into the husband's family, an idea they dislike. Therefore, some women refuse to change their surnames and choose cohabitation rather than legal marriage.

At present the movement to allow independent surnames is very active among those advocating women's independence. There are, however, women as well as men who support independent surnames for other reasons that are based on traditional values, such as to perpetuate the family name or to ensure the maintenance of the family tomb. The existing Civil Code does not specify that the successor to a family tomb must have the same surname as that inscribed on the tombstone. Temples and offices in charge of cemeteries, however, tend to refuse to allow any person with a different surname into the tomb.

A woman who has changed her surname to that of her husband at marriage naturally enters the tomb of her husband's family, and thus, it is difficult for her to care for the tomb of her natal family. When a couple has only daughters and they all change their surnames, there is no one to take over their tomb. Moreover, as couples have fewer children, we find more and more cases in which an only son and only daughter marry, which leaves the parents of only daughters with no one to succeed to their tomb. For these reasons, too, there are couples who desire to maintain their individual surnames.

Legal Issues Concerning Children of Single Mothers

Another legal obstruction to freedom of choice with regard to marriage and family in contemporary Japanese society is the discrimination in treatment accorded to children born to single mothers. The birthrate of children of unwed couples has increased rapidly in recent years in various industrialized countries. In the case of Japan, however, the figure is very low—just 1 percent. How can this be explained?

Quite simply, there are few children of unwed couples because such children and their mothers face strong discrimination within Japanese society and are likely to find it very uncomfortable living in this closely knit society. Moreover, social security and social welfare institutions for assisting such women and children are insufficient. The dominant thinking in most contemporary Western countries is that it is unfair to discriminate against children on the basis of their parents' marital status. All children have the right of succession or the right to take the father's surname, regardless of whether or not their parents are legally married. In Sweden, for example, cohabitation is recognized as part of the social system in the same way as a legal marriage. There is no discrimination or prejudice toward unwed mothers or their children, and even the word *illegitimate* has been deleted from legal documents. On the contrary, in Japan discrimination against children of unwed mothers still persists in the legal provision (Art. 900 of the Civil Law) which grants illegitimate lineal descendants one-half the portion of an inheritance granted to legitimate descendants.

A Japanese teenager who becomes pregnant is very like to resort to abortion. Should an unwed woman decide to have a child out of wedlock, relatives and friends, as well as members of public institutions such as hospitals or municipal offices, are apt to try to dissuade her with the words "A fatherless child will surely be unhappy." There is a strong tendency to judge a child's happiness not in terms of the actual relationship between its parents or the parent-child relationship but, rather, on the basis of whether her or his father is legally registered. This notion tends, in fact, to lead to unhappiness and discrimination toward single mothers and their children.

The Struggle to Overcome Discrimination against Unwed Mothers and Their Offspring

Although, as noted, the principle of legitimacy has been strongly supported in Japan, in the midst of the feminist movement that sprang up in the 1970s some women began to criticize the modern system of marriage and actively chose to cohabit without registering their marriage or to have children out of wedlock. The principal view of such women is that they don't feel that the government should have the right to exercise control over private sexual relationships or to decide on their legitimacy by requiring marriage registration. At present sex between married couples is approved, indeed, marital sex is considered to be a wife's duty, even when she doesn't want to engage in sex. In the case of unmarried couples, however, sex is condemned as immoral even when partners love each other.

Another position held by many feminists is a rejection of the traditional conception of the bride *(yome)*. As mentioned, the prewar concept of the family still remains, and marriage for a woman implies not only that she becomes someone's wife but also the bride in the husband's family. The expectation remains that in her role as bride, or daughter-in-law, a woman will take her husband's surname; give birth to a male child, who will succeed to his family; take care of the family tomb; and care for the parents-in-law. Many feminists reject legal marriages precisely because they want no part of the obligations and expectations attached to the role of bride, and they repudiate the traditional ideology of sex roles, which limits women's sphere of activity to the home.

Recently, several organizations have sprung up expressing criticism of the current marriage system and seeking to put an end to discrimination against illegitimate children—for example, Kongaishi sabetsu to tatakau kai (Group to fight discrimination against children born out of marriage), "Shiseiji" sabetsu o nakusu kai (Association for eliminating discrimination against "illegitimate children"), and Juminhyo tsuzukigara saiban koryukai (Association in support of lawsuits against discriminatory expressions on the resident registration card). On the birth notification form, which is filled out at the local city office, under the column headed "Relationship to Parents," one is required to check off whether the child is legitimate or illegitimate. Clerks at these offices explain the terms *legitimate* and *illegitimate* to those who do not fully understand their meaning. Needless to say, this procedure puts considerable psychological pressures on unwed mothers registering the birth of their children. In this way discrimination against illegitimate children is reinforced. Currently, some women are seeking to abolish this column on the form and leave the column blank at the time of registration.

In addition, some women have brought litigation to protest the requirement that one indicate the nature of the parent-child relationship on the family register and on the resident registration form. On both the family register and the resident registration form illegitimate, or nonacknowledged, children are distinguished from legitimate, or acknowledged, ones. Legitimate children are listed as "first daughter," "second daughter," "first son," and so on. On the other hand, illegitimate children are listed only as "female" or "male" on the family register and as "child" on the resident registration form. This is a remnant of the earlier system of male primogeniture, in which birth order was very significant. Under that system an illegitimate child not acknowledged by the father had no right of succession, and therefore the order of birth had no relevance in her or his case. While this system no longer formally exists, the thinking behind it is still prevalent. A family register or resident form must be submitted at the time of registration to school, upon being hired for a job, and when applying for various licenses, so that the possibility that one may face discrimination on this basis is very real; therefore, many are calling for the abolishment of this system as soon as possible.[3]

Conclusion

"To marry" has been regarded as a natural way of living, and "not marrying" has been considered unnatural. Some Japanese women feel it is impossible to have an equal relationship with men in a society in which sex discrimination is still predominant, and so they have begun to choose the option of singlehood or cohabitation with a partner. Singlehood has, at last, so it seems, become partially recognized as a possible lifestyle, marriage being simply another option.

The institution as well as the concept and ideology of marriage and family have undergone a dramatic change in Japan since the end of World War II. Marriage in modern Japanese society no longer represents a linking of one family with another. Instead, it implies, at least theoretically, a free and equal relationship between two individuals; neither possesses the other, and neither can govern the other according to her or his will. Even though the husband and wife are a couple, each is an individual entitled to retain her or his own personality and will.

Despite these facts, however, there are still numerous psychological and cultural, as well as legal, residues of the prewar family system which stand as obstacles to the realization of a truly egalitarian relationship between wife and husband. Feminists in Japan have been in the forefront of the ongoing struggle to revise outdated laws such as those pertaining to surnames and birth registration. At the same time, many women have begun to assert their own preferences and to choose various alternative lifestyles beyond the traditional one of marriage.

NOTES

1. The number of divorces per 1,000 people in 1985 was: Japan, 1.30; France, 1.95; West Germany, 2.10; Sweden, 2.37; England, 3.20; U.S.S.R., 3.36; U.S., 4.96. Inoue Teruko and Ehara Yumiko, eds. *Women's Data Book* (Tokyo: Yuhiaku, 1991), p. 21, fig. 10–1. Data compiled from United Nations, *Demographic Yearbook*.

2. *Neyado*, literally "sleeping lodges," were communal lodges in which young women and men would sleep overnight until they found an appropriate marriage partner. Both single-sex and coed *neyado* existed, while still others had separate facilities for women and men within the same site. In some cases the young people were supervised by an older member of the village or community, but in most cases supervision was left up to the young people themselves. Once they chose a partner the couple moved into the home of one or the other and embarked on married life. *Neyado* can still be found in some fishing villages, particularly in the western part of Japan.

3. Efforts to bring about changes in the system have yielded some results. The Ministry of Home Affairs announced in December 1994 that, as of 1 March 1995, on the resident registration form both legitimate and illegitimate children would be entered simply as "child" under "relationship to household head," so long as the child is acknowledged by the household head—namely the father.

REFERENCES

Bellak, Leopold. 1970. *The Porcupine Dilemma: Reflections on the Human Condition*. New York: Citadel Press.

Kawashima, Takenobu. 1950. *Nihon shakai no kazokuteki kosei* (Family structure in Japanese society). Tokyo: Nippon hyoronsha.

Koseisho, Jinko Mondai Kenkyujo (Institution of Population Problems, Ministry of Health and Welfare). 1987. *Dokushin seinenzo no kekkonkan to kodomokan* (Attitudes toward marriage and the family among unmarried Japanese youth). Tokyo: Koseisho.

Okonogi, Keigo. 1983. *Katei no nai kazoku no jidai* (The age of family members without a home). Tokyo: ABC Shuppan.

Seimei Hoken Bunka Senta (Japan Institute of Life Insurance). 1987. *Josei no seikatsu ishiki ni kansuru chosa* (Survey on women's attitudes toward life). Tokyo: Seimei Hoken Bunka Senta.

The Mystique of Motherhood: A Key to Understanding Social Change and Family Problems in Japan

❖ ❖ ❖

Masami Ohinata

Translated by Timothy John Phelan

I n a basic sense family problems develop within the very relationships of which families are composed—the relations between husbands and wives, parents and children, brothers and sisters; increasing the number of relationships, of course, compounds the dynamics involved. The family is also a part of society, and so its configurations and the functions of the relationships within it are prescribed and given direction by the particular cultural values and socioeconomic demands within which it exists.

An increase in working mothers and nuclear families, the tendency to have fewer children, the accompanying decline in home child care, and an increase in divorces leading to single-parent families—these and other problems now confront the family in Japan. Conspicuous changes have thus occurred both in the way relationships within the family develop and in the structure of the family itself. Some even say that the problems confronting American families—divorce, remarriage, and the attendant problems of child rearing—will one day be problems in Japan as well. A careful consideration, however, of both the actual functions the Japanese family is made to serve and the broad influence of the symbolic meaning attached to it by society show such ideas to be superficial. They overlook the real problems involved.

In expecting the family to serve an enlarged symbolic function, Japanese society determines the direction in which these problems develop (problems that initially seem to be changing in diverse ways) and modifies them such that they ultimately function to maintain and preserve the social order. One function that has been repeatedly emphasized and which is being further emphasized today is that of the mother's role vis-à-vis her children. I believe an understanding of this motherhood concept can help us better grasp why various social changes and family problems confront Japanese society. While focusing on the concept of motherhood, this essay will thus consider how Japanese society, with the family at its center, has changed and how these changes have impacted the family.

Social Change in Japan and the Emphasis on Motherhood

Starting in the Meiji period and continuing until today, the family has been a target of Japanese governmental policy. An examination of the emphasis on motherhood in Japan in modern times, indeed, reveals that governmental policies toward the family have always been in the background. Specifically, this history can be broken into the five following periods.

The first period is the ten-year period following the enforcement of the Civil Law in 1898. During this time the enlightened policies of the early Meiji were set aside in favor of policies created in support of the idea of *fukoku-kyohei* (rich country, strong army). The principle was to develop a strong nation-state able to stand up to the countries of the West. Women, responsible for bearing children (future soldiers), thus took on increased importance, albeit an importance limited to their childbearing potential. Yet it wasn't just women who were singled out. The family itself came to be seen as the basic servant of the state.

To become a strong nation it was considered vitally important that the country be thoroughly organized into a controllable hierarchy with clear chains of command. The family was chosen as a unit to support the government. To reach this goal it was also deemed necessary that relations within the family be hierarchically ordered. Until that time it had been the government's policy that a family structure based on the Confucian morality of the old samurai class pervade families (Kawashima 1950; and Fujii 1975). Motherhood was thus emphasized within the context of a social hierarchy structured to support the state. The responsibility for developing a "rich country and strong army" was shifted first from the state to the family and then within the family to women.

This emphasis on motherhood would eventually lead to a sanctifying of "motherly love" and to an idealistic emphasis on the idea that motherly love and devotion are the keys to a child's development and education. This change corresponds to the second stage of the emphasis on motherhood in Japan and can be dated to the beginning of the 1920s in the Taisho period.

It was at this time that various magazines about child care first began to appear. One of these, *Report of the Japan Children's Association* (first published in 1920; for vols. 5–9 the name was changed to *Childcare Magazine*), is a good example of this new trend. The titles of articles published in the magazine are quite revealing in their use of the words *mother* and *motherhood:* "Mother-hood," "Mother's Love How Great!" "Motherly Love—a Living Thing," "The Evolution of a Mother's Love," "Training for Motherhood." One also finds that numbers 9 and 10 of the ninth volume are titled "Model Mothers" and "Motherly Love," respectively.

A typical example of what was meant by "a mother's love" can be found in an article by the doctor of literature, Shimoda, entitled, "Whether Children Turn Out to be Wise or Foolish Depends on the Education of Mother." In it he writes: "When it comes to the education of our children, we must keep uppermost in mind not the education they receive from society, nor the education they receive at school, but rather the education they receive at home. And the one most responsible for this is, of course, the mother . . . it is the mother who decides whether her children will live or die." Also, "If a mother neglects her child's education, the child will not grow up to be anything commendable or respectable."

Other articles share this emphasis on the mother's responsibility for the education children receive at home. Mothers considered worthy to be role models were the mothers of Napoleon, Yoshida Shoin, Nakae Toji, Nogi Shogun, and Shonan Ko. In other words, the mothers of Confucian scholars and military leaders were sanctified, evidence of the continuing influence of the first period, discussed previously, when an emphasis on motherhood was seen as key to realizing the Confucian ideal of "rich country, strong army." Why, however, did this particular type of motherly love receive so much praise and adoration at this time? Two reasons can be offered.

First, the tendency for mothers to devote themselves to caring for their children had become diluted at this time. Indeed, instead of parents taking care of their children, one finds that nursemaids, godparents, and wet nurses were being given parental-type responsibility. Indeed, communities provided places for children such as the *kodomo-gumi, wakamono-gumi,* and *musume-yado* outside the home.[1] It was expected that the entire village community, in other words, would participate in bringing up the children. The principal aim of the emphasis on motherhood during this second period, thus, seems to have been a negative, or critical, reaction to the growing numbers of mothers who were no longer devoting themselves to child care. On the one hand, there were songs of praise about great models of motherly love; on the other hand, there was lamenting over mothers who no longer saw themselves as indispensable to the child care process. A Dr. Kubota wrote in "Teach Mothers How to Raise Their Children": "In present-day Japan one finds half-witted fifteen and sixteen year olds, noses running, being hired to play with our precious children. Our utter blindness to this is truly abominable." Though severely critical of the nurses who had been put in charge of taking care of the community's children, he realized, however, that it was impossible for education about infancy to occur in the home and so proposed the establishment of "Centers for Infant Education."

Sano, in an article titled, "Discontentment Concerning Mothers with

Babies," had one section titled "I Am a Baby," in which he wrote critically—from a baby's point of view—about mothers unable to distinguish the different ways their baby cries and about mothers who only occasionally change their baby's diaper and who don't breastfeed at fixed times. An examination of these articles allows one to see what type of attitudes people at the time had toward both education at home and the way mothers should raise their children.

Another reason for the stress on the importance of motherly love at this time is the fact that, as part of the development of capitalism, working-class families began to appear in the cities. These families were usually nuclear families, a type of family different from that which had existed in the villages. This situation gave people a good reason to argue that families and mothers must take responsibility for their own children's upbringing.

If one looks at what these arguments were based upon one finds that it was primarily a stress upon the woman's role as "breastfeeder." Inoue's article, "The Spirit of Motherly Love Flows through the Milk of a Mother's Breast" and Yoshioka's "True Motherly Love Starts with the Breast" are two examples of this. It was felt that "Children raised with the milk from their own mother's breast, even if they have to live in miserable conditions, will still be children swimming, as it were, in the bliss of motherly love." Stressing that children can be brought up as long as they are provided the necessary natural nutrients from their mother was not only one way of criticizing a materialistic scientific culture and its artificial baby milk but also a lament over the fact that the use of wet nurses pulled mothers and children apart and did not allow them to establish proper affection for each other.

Most of the articles and papers written at this time were penned by men who were either doctors of medicine or doctors of literature. What they wrote, however, was usually not based upon their specialized fields of scientific study and research; such articles were rare. Rather, one finds that the articles usually contained arguments based on sentiment and moral idealism.

The third period started with the breakout of the Sino-Japanese War in 1937 and continued into the period following the beginning of the Pacific War in 1941. It was a time when everything seemed to emphasize "Mothers for a country at war." Indeed, under the governmental policy, "Have More Babies! Prosper!" the Patriotic Women's Association (Aikoku jido kyokai) began its annual congress, proclaiming, "Mothers, return to your homes!"

Mothers were to give birth to the "emperor's babies" (tenno no sekishi) and, as the phrase "the ones who will raise the boys and girls of the empire" illustrates, were considered an extremely important asset. Throughout Japan politicians, soldiers, scholars, and writers couldn't say enough in praise of "Mother." Takamure Itsue is a good example: "The Emperor's will is the mother's will. The mother's will is the Emperor's will. And it is our sacred duty, in 'the spirit of universal brotherhood, desiring to have all the corners of the world under one roof *(hakko ichiu)'* to see that this one will of mother and emperor extend beyond Japan, beyond Asia, and to the whole world" (Kano 1979).

It was also believed that the spirit of motherhood in Japan which led women to sacrifice themselves joyfully for the sake of their children was without parallel. It held the nation together and provided the country with a moral foundation (Miyamoto 1967). Under the Meiji government's policy of "rich country and strong army" it was the government's goal that the family function as a prime supporter of the nation-state. It can be argued that the concentration on motherly love exemplified by these various writers was a sign that the government had attained its goal.

Though the family system thus formed broke down after Japan's defeat in World War II, the various political and economic demands made upon it meant it continued to remain a target of governmental policy. Indeed, the fourth period of development in the emphasis on motherhood began in the middle of the 1950s and continued through the 1960s.

During this period of high economic growth, the family became the center of consumer activity and a place for the reproduction of energy. People expected the family to play a foundational role by assuming responsibility for the country's economic growth. With governmental policy elevating economic growth as the supreme good, male workers were expected to function in the workplace at their fullest potential. This meant the home had to be a place where they could rest and regain the energy needed for the next day's work. It was the wife's role to make sure this happened. Another important role for the family was that of producing tomorrow's labor force. The role of making the family an oasis, a place in which "good children" could be born and raised, was thus placed on women, and songs in praise of motherhood were sung all the more loudly. People also began to argue that the amount of time spent on housework, when calculated in terms of a wage, contributed more to family finances than work done outside the home.

The final period to be mentioned began in 1973, as Japan entered into a period of slower economic growth. It was at this time that the government presented various budgetary policies in line with the idea of a "Japanese-style welfare society." One finds, however, that the main aim of these policies was to cut back the amount of money allocated for child and elderly care. It was decided that the family should take over these functions. A policy of "strengthening the family's foundation" was announced, and women in the home were expected to bring up their children themselves and to take care of any elderly family members. The importance of motherhood was, thus, again being stressed.

Also at this time, caught up in the spirit of the International Year of Women being felt around the world, women began to rethink their ideas about both the place of women in society and the necessity of gender-based role divisions. On the one hand, women groped after new lifestyles. On the other hand, the government, however, enhanced its emphasis on motherhood by making welfare budget reductions. For a number of years, indeed, these two contradictory trends existed together. Yet in the middle of the 1980s, along with a general trend toward conservatism, old ways of thinking about gender-based role divisions came to the fore; the idea that women should take care of children and the elderly again gained influence. And today, as the birthrate drops, we are confronted with even more subtle attempts to emphasize motherhood (Ohinata 1991).

Though the slogans changed with the socioeconomic demands of each age—from "rich country, strong army" to "maintaining men's ability to provide quality labor" to "making up for cuts in the welfare budget"—it is distinctive that the concept of motherhood as expressed in "nothing surpasses a mother's love" and "women have an innate ability to raise children" has continually been emphasized in Japan. The specific role of an individual mother vis-à-vis her children is transcended and motherhood crafted into a symbol of great social value.

Of course, during the various political and economic situations Japan has faced since the Meiji, the concept of motherhood has not always been emphasized. The Confucian-based emphasis on educating women to be good wives and wise mothers propagated during the period of "rich country, strong army," for example, took a backward step during the liberalism that prevailed in the prosperous period of the Taisho democracy following World War I. There were economic demands for women to enter the labor force, an increase in the level of women's education, and a general mood encouraging women to become economically independent. It is at this time, indeed, that we see the working woman *(shokugyo fujin)* appear for the first time. The emphasis during World War II (with its slogans encouraging people to unify the nation's spirit) on married women finding their raison d'être in being mothers was also supposedly done away after Japan's defeat. Under the laws of the new Constitution and Civil Code, in which the old family system was abolished, women were again called upon to become free and economically independent, this time within the framework of a democratically run family.

But before the images of women which had emerged during the Taisho period and after the promulgation of the new Constitution could become rooted in people's consciousness—in the first case, the start of World War II and, in the second case, the beginning of the period of high economic growth—meant an unavoidable retreat to the traditional motherhood concept. As soon as women were encouraged to advance into society, counterarguments appeared in support of the importance of motherhood, and before women's participation in activities outside the home could become normalized, the importance of the woman's role as childbearer was again emphasized. This squaring of accounts, as it were, has been repeated since the Meiji era and can be seen as an established pattern in Japan.

Special Characteristics of the Motherhood Concept in Japan

As long as the family is regarded as the foundational unit of society, it is inevitable, from one point of view, that the family become the object of government policy—policies formed according to the social conditions of each age. A characteristic of governmental policy toward the family in Japan, however, has been that one function of the family—namely, "motherhood"—has always been targeted. Furthermore, the motherhood that has been emphasized has been of a particular kind: motherly love characterized by selfless devotion.

According to Yamamura's (1971) cultural analysis of the meanings Japanese give to the idea of mother, "the 'mother' in Japan exists as more than just the mother of children. She is a symbol imbued with much value." In other words, when Japanese hear the word *mother* they do not call to mind the real, flesh-and-blood mother of their personal experiences but, rather, see a personification of "devotion to children, parental affection, and self-sacrifice." For Japanese this image of mother exceeds money and honor in its ability to control behavior. People's devotion to the concept comes close to that of a religious faith.

It is certainly no mistake to say that, as often as opportunity allows, people in Japan stress the image of a mother who is devoted to her children, always shows them affection, and is willing to sacrifice her own plans and desires on their behalf. Without exception, when a famous person's accomplishments are lauded, the devotion and hard work of "Mother" are stressed. Inversely, when someone is admonished or punished for some socially deviant behavior, the tears and sorrow of Mother are referred to. When the various top members of each profession talk about their lives, they always attribute their success to the love and devotion of their mothers. A businessman reminiscing about his youth says that the driving force that keeps him going is Mother, who raised their family even though there had hardly been any food to eat. As a way of discharging his filial duties, he now always makes sure she has enough to eat and takes her to a hot spring or the theater.

There is the story of a man falsely charged with a crime who was incarcerated for many years. After his request for a retrial was allowed and he cleared himself of the charges, he talked of the joy he felt upon being found not guilty. He said that though he'd been abandoned by everyone and had daily trembled in fear because of the death sentence, his mother's fervent belief in his innocence had given him the will to live. The newspapers ran headlines proclaiming, "Hitasura haha no tame ni" (I owe everything to my mother) and included photographs of the man hugging his elderly mother. For Japanese the headline and photos couldn't have spoken more eloquently.

It can't be denied that having someone love you unconditionally certainly brings joy and happiness. This is even more true if one is going through a time of deep suffering or distress. Indeed, making it through—living or dying—often depends on whether one is loved in such a way.

But the kind of love that can save and encourage is not limited to motherly love. Another man also falsely charged and imprisoned was "saved" by a group of supporters made up of people from all over the country. It is said that the functioning of the group was quickened by the man's parents, whose sacrificial devotion led them to walk throughout Japan proclaiming their son's innocence. Many people saw them and were touched by their earnestness. The day after the man was proclaimed innocent, however, a newspaper headlined the story, "Machiwabita haha no me ni namida" (After waiting so long—tears in his mother's eyes) (*Asahi shimbun*, 27 July 1990). The father who had walked together with his wife, pleading on behalf of their son, was nowhere to be seen. This is how a society devoted to the ideology of motherhood performs.

It is certain that both the mother of the businessman mentioned earlier and the mothers of the men who had been sentenced to die loved their sons deeply. To think that such love issues forth from all mothers, however, would be a mistake. If there is a mother devoted to her children, there is also a mother whose love for her children amounts to less than what might be considered a minimum. And there are always devoted fathers. Unfortunately, society holds up *mothers* as symbols of love and devotion and proclaims that this stereotype should apply to *all* mothers everywhere. Newspapers write, with no apparent feelings of discomfort, of "mother's love being part of human nature and the same in all times and places." In a word, people are so convinced in their beliefs about motherhood that they are unable to see that in a different country, culture, or time the feelings and attitudes of mothers toward their children might very well be different.

Merits and Demerits of the Japanese Concept of Motherhood

Japanese mothers, quite apart from their actual family relationships, have thus been bestowed with the function of serving as symbols of great social value. This, in turn, has functioned in women's consciousness and emotions as a type of sociocultural standard informing them about both how they ought to live and how they ought to raise their children.

On the positive side this conception of motherhood helped establish a common understanding regarding the importance of child rearing. A responsive, warm, affectionate, and responsible relationship with children, in which they are provided appropriate amounts of stimulus in the form of cuddling, smiling, and talking, is indispensable in guaranteeing their physical and mental development. Alleged as being a maternal way of raising children—and though one might consider the idea to be a negative aspect of the traditional notion of motherhood, in which everything is made the wom-

206

en's responsibility—it is nevertheless a fact that, by limiting the responsibility for children to women, the issue of responsibility was clarified. Women were thought to possess an intrinsic aptitude, and child rearing came to be considered of self-evident importance.

Another point is that, since women were held responsible for this maternal way of raising children, and notwithstanding the fact that they were narrowly confined to the household and local community, it was still true that they were thus able to guarantee themselves a place in society. Though this wasn't an aggressive approach, for it left many problems untouched, nevertheless, considering there was a time when women were unable to secure a place in society, the emphasis on motherhood can still be seen to have helped them achieve at least this goal.

Though the issue of historical necessity can't be ignored when appraising the traditional concept of motherhood, still, with regard to our present sociocultural context, the following points can be made concerning its negative effects. First, the concept of motherhood which once helped to guarantee women's position in society now restricts them from fully participating in that society. The participation of women in society is indeed no longer simply something a few women are concerned about but, rather, given the prevailing social and political facts, a common concern for many. Since the mother-child relationship continues to be emphasized and women continue to be seen to possess an innate aptitude for child rearing, however, most cases of child care remain, as before, unchanged. Women are left in charge. Though it is claimed that we are now living in the age of the woman, many women have to choose between work and raising a family. Many problems have arisen concerning the quality and shape of women's participation in society and, even with the Equal Employment Opportunity Law enacted in April 1986 (aimed at eliminating discrimination of women based on gender), given the continued emphasis on motherhood and the distribution of roles in the family according to sex, women are faced with the contradiction that in the end their participation in society does not allow them to secure equality with men. For example, the flexibility of the regulations concerning working hours, enacted as a set along with the Equal Employment Opportunity Law, are such that a married woman with children has a more difficult time than before working in a full-time position. Indeed, since the weekly average under flex-time is set at forty hours, it is now possible for someone to actually work more than eight hours a day (i.e., he or she might work four hours one day and twelve hours the next.)

Second, under the traditional conception of motherhood and its attendant ideas about women's role concerning child rearing, little effort has been made to see that people other than the mother participate in the child-rearing process. For example, although 50 percent of all working women have children, the government has made cutbacks in its support for child care centers. This fact is not even recognized as a contradiction, however, since the logic of "Nothing surpasses a mother's love," and

"Children should stay at home with their mothers until they are three or go to school" still remains strong.

Third, the emphasis on the mother-child relationship has meant people have been very slow to understand the dynamics involved in the relationships children have with other people and society. In other words, even though children grow up both directly and indirectly influenced by a variety of human and societal relationships, it is often the case that, as soon as a problem arises, the mother is immediately held responsible. Also, the separation of children from men has meant that not only has the child-rearing environment lacked a male presence but also that the mode of thought in the Japanese workplace has been overwhelmingly masculine. Whereas men are unable to experience the influence of child rearing upon their own psychological development, women, on the other hand, their social relations limited almost exclusively to children, are apt to have trouble in their relations with other adults. Also, it is not enough that women are seen as having an innate aptitude for child rearing and come from homes in which the division of housework according to gender remains unchanged. Once in the workplace they experience discrimination (albeit in a different form) and find they are precluded from improving their positions as working professionals.

The fourth problem relates to the content of the traditional motherhood concept. If one mentions maternal love, for example, it suggests a person who expresses devotion toward children; one who is affectionate, self-sacrificing, and, in ignoring herself, spends as much time as possible with her children; and one who is esteemed. But this is no more than a manifestation of self-love, and one must take into consideration the danger that such mothers often become too attached to their children. In idealizing one side of the feelings experienced by mothers, the negative side has been ignored. Worry, exasperation, and depression are the problems that plague people who deal with children. To truly care about motherhood is to face such problems squarely and to take measures to develop appropriate child-rearing support systems. In Japan, a country that supposedly esteems motherhood, however, there is a strong tendency for motherhood to be respected only by turning the feelings of mothers into idealized images. The number of facilities to help support mothers perplexed by the task of raising children is far from adequate.

Topics for Future Discussion

The gap between the stress on motherhood and the actual lives of women in Japan today is great. As we have seen, this has resulted in numerous problems. That it is considered axiomatic for women to love their children and devote themselves to their upbringing and also that the presumption that this is an unchanging truth from old obstructs attempts to respond realistically to the problems at hand are both facts that must be recognized.

These problems have risen because of the tendency to emphasize a direct link between female reproductive functions and child-rearing ability—that is, being a women/mother equals raising children. As advances have been made in medical science, psychology, and related disciplines, the tendency to introduce a physiological perspective into discussions of the mother-child relationship has become more vigorous. Today attempts to illuminate the mother-child bond by studying the beginning stages of growth and the pre-natal period are quite common. The innate and physiological abilities pos-sessed by mother and child are said to guarantee that they will establish a bond between them.

This research differs from the older maternal instinct theory and, when presented as something founded upon scientific evidence, is very persuasive. It mustn't be overlooked, however, that the innate and physiologically based ability of humans to rear children is only one part of their child-rearing behavior. This physiological ability is limited to the early stages of the parent-child relationship and shouldn't be seen as continuing on for many more years. Also, one mustn't exclude from consideration the great variety of mother-child relationships and the various other factors that play a part in child development. One must also not neglect to consider the point of view and research methodology used in reaching these conclusions. In present-day research on the mother-child bond there are studies that limit the object of the child's early attachment to the mother, studies that fail to compare the child-rearing ability of the actual mother to that of other caretakers (male or female), and research that does not follow the elementary procedure of estab-lishing multiple variables. As long as such research is presented under a scholarly and scientific guise, the danger of concealing the real problem areas is great.

Similar problems occurred in the 1960s, when research on hospitalism was introduced into Japan. Delays and impediments in the development of children in child care institutions, claimed by Bowlby (1979) in his theories on mother-child relations to be the result of a lack in maternal care, focused the issue on the importance of the actual mother's presence during the rear-ing process. It was found, however, that a deterioration in the conditions of child care institutions could not be attributed simply to the fact that the real mother was absent. In the end psychological associations in Europe and the United States criticized the theory as, among other things, placing unwar-ranted emphasis on the mother-child relationship. The theory underwent a prompt reconstruction. Though reexamined in Japan as well, this trend failed to become the norm, and the theory that child rearing was a women's natural duty conspired to support the emphasis on the mother-child relationship. Introduced in Japan in the 1960s just as the period of high economic growth was picking up speed, hospitalism was used in governmental policies to make it the women's obligation to manage the home and rear children. This prevented working women from improving their position in society.

Japanese society's peculiar emphasis on motherhood can become a men-tal blind spot for the researcher. Research methodology and the interpretation of results can easily become one-sided and serve to support whatever governmental policies are then in vogue. This also eventually has a powerful impact on the lifestyles of women. The reason an emphasis on the mother-child relation based on physiological research has become increasingly conspicuous has been discussed. This emphasis has received even further support of late because of government cuts in the welfare budget and, to keep pace with these changes, the plan to revitalize the family as the foundation of society.

Even if it is a woman's peculiar destiny to be responsible for giving birth, child *rearing* is not something limited to them. The participation of men is necessary. When considering such things as the aspirations of women for personal independence and the need to broaden the environment within which children develop, restricting child rearing to the home clearly fails to meet the realities of our present day and age. The need to improve the social functions of preschools and other child care institutions grows stronger each year. Yet an image of motherhood, seemingly headed in the opposite direction, still exists.

The first step to be taken to right the many contradictions that have resulted from this separation of notions about motherhood from the facts is for women, the ones responsible for most of society's child rearing, both to refuse to be shackled to a uniform concept of motherhood and to take a long, hard look at the joys, the pains, and the problems of child rearing. The ability to raise children, as a learned, relational skill, ought to be objectively reexamined and the support of others (men and women) accessed to make improvements. Family relationships in which neither men nor women put limits on the other's participation in child rearing should be joyfully welcomed and advocated by society. Though child rearing is the private function of the family, social systems that support this function are necessary. In this regard, many issues related to the image of motherhood in Japan require further investigation.

NOTES

This essay is a revised and expanded version of the following papers by the author:
"Nihon ni okeru bosei gainen no tokusei—Nihon no shakai hendo to kazoku mondai wo toku kiiwaado toshite" (The special quality of "motherhood" in Japan: motherhood as a keyword for understanding social changes and family problems in Japan), *International Seminar on Women's Studies*. National Women's Education Centre (1989), 311–26; and *Bosei wa onna no kunsho desu ka? Kodomo no inai joseitachi no uttae. Sosa sareru bosei no jisshoteki kaimei* (Is motherhood a medal to be worn by women? Complaints from women without children: shedding light on being manipulated by motherhood) (Tokyo: Sankei shimbunsha hakko, Fusosha hatsubai, 1992).

1. These three groups functioned in Japanese villages as groups for young people. The *kodomo-gumi* (children's group) was made up of the youngest children. One of its

responsibilities was to participate in the village's yearly festivals. The *wakamono-gumi* (young men's group) was made up of young men who had yet to come of age. These groups would often gather at night at a selected home *(wakamono yado)* in the village to do some handiwork, to talk, and to stay overnight. The *musume-yado* was the home of a respected villager in which the *musume gumi* (young girl's group; a group of unmarried girls of the same age) would gather to talk, develop friendships, and stay overnight. The lodge-parents *(yado-oya)* would often become the girls' temporary or adopted parental guardians. These relationships often lasted for the girls' lifetimes.

REFERENCES

Bowlby, John. 1979. *The Making and Breaking of Affectional Bonds.* London: Tavistock. Trans. Tsutomu Sakuta under the title *Boshi kankei nyumon.* Tokyo: Seiwa Shoten, 1981.

Childcare Magazine. All volumes from 1920 to 1928. Tokyo: Oosorasha.

Fujii, Harue. 1975. *Gendai hahaoyaron* (Modern arguments about motherhood). Tokyo: Meiji tosho.

Kano, Mikiya. 1979. Bosei to tennosei (Motherhood and the emperor system). In *Josei to tennosei* (Women and the emperor system), ed. Kano Mikiya. Tokyo: Shisono kagakusha.

Kawashima, Takeyoshi. 1950. *Nihon shakaino kazokuteki kosei* (The family-like structure of Japanese society). Tokyo: Nihon hyoronsha.

Miyamoto, Tsuneichi. 1967. *Kakyo no oshie* (Lessons from my birthplace). In *Miyamoto Tsuneichi chosakushu 6* (The works of Miyamoto Tsuneichi, vol. 6). Tokyo: Miraisha.

Ohinata, Masami. 1991. *1.57 shokku o bunsekisuru* (Analyzing the shock produced by the announcement of Japan's 1.57% annual birthrate). In *Josanpu zasshi* (Magazine for midwives) 45, no. 5: 8–16.

———. 1988. *Bosei no kenkyu—sono keisei to henyo no katei—dentoteki boseikan e no hansho* (The study of motherhood—its formation and process of change: counter-evidence for the traditional understanding of motherhood). Tokyo: Kawashima shoten.

Yamamura, Yoshiaki. 1971. *Nihonjin to haha* (Japanese and mothers). Tokyo: Toyokan shuppan.

Care of the Elderly: A Women's Issue

❖ ❖ ❖

Takako Sodei

Care of the elderly has long been primarily a women's issue. Everywhere in the world the majority of caregivers at home as well as in institutions are women. In Japan the normal life course of women has been to care for their parents-in-law and their husbands and then to be cared for by their daughters-in-law. In recent years, however, this care cycle has become difficult to maintain. The purpose of this essay is to clarify the causes of this difficulty and to find its solution.

Women as Care Recipients

In advanced industrial societies women generally live longer than men. In Japan the average life expectancy at birth in 1993 was 82.51 for females and 76.25 for males, which is the longest in the world. The Research Institute of Population Problems, Ministry of Health and Welfare, estimated in 1991 that life expectancy will reach 83.85 for females and 77.87 for males by the year 2025. According to the 1990 national census, the ratio of females to males was 1.42 among people sixty-five years or older and 2.17 among people eighty-five or older.

As is shown in tables 1 and 2, the ratio of bedridden elders and of senile elders increases with age. Among people seventy-five years or older it exceeds 10 percent, and the ratio of females is higher than that of males. Therefore, it is estimated that there are more female bedridden or senile elders than male.

The proportion of people sixty-five years or older in the total population was about 13 percent in 1992, which was lower than that in Western nations. The rate

Table 1
The Ratio of Bedridden Elders, by Age and Sex

	Total	Female	Male
65–69	1.75	1.37	2.22
70–74	2.92	2.76	3.14
75–79	4.79	5.10	4.38
80–84	8.77	11.94	9.51
85–over	15.65		
Average	4.22	4.41	3.69

Source: Koseisho Tokeijoho-bu (Ministry of Health and Welfare, Division of Statistics and Information). *Kosei gyosei kiso chosa* (Basic Survey of the Health and Welfare Administration). Tokyo: Koseisho, 1984.

Table 2
The Ratio of Senile Elders, by Age and Sex

	Total	Female	Male
65–69	1.2	1.0	1.6
70–74	3.1	2.6	3.6
75–79	4.7	5.6	3.7
80–84	13.1	16.1	8.5
85–over	23.4	26.9	18.9
Average	4.6	5.1	3.9

Source: Tokyo-to fukushi kyoku (Tokyo Metropolitan Government, Bureau of Welfare). *Koreisha no seikatsu jittai oyobi kenko ni kansuru chosa* (Survey on the life and health status of elderly people). Tokyo: Tokyo-to fukushikyoku, 1980.

of aging, however, is particularly fast in Japan. The rise in proportion of people aged sixty-five or over from 7 percent to 14 percent took 115 years in France, 85 years in Sweden, and 75 years in the United States, while it has taken only 25 years in Japan. The Research Institute of Population Problems estimated in 1986 that in the year 2020 nearly one out of four people in Japan will be sixty-five years old or over, which is the largest percentage in the world.

We should also pay attention to the age distribution among old people. The number of "old-old,"—that is, people over seventy-five—is increasing rapidly. It is estimated that in the year 2025, when the "baby boom" generation reaches "old-old" age, the ratio of people over seventy-five will exceed that of people between sixty-five and seventy-four. The rate of aging is faster among females than males. As is shown in table 3, the number of "old-old" females will exceed that of "young-old" females in 2020, which is five years earlier than for males.

Improvements in sanitation, nutrition, and medical treatment will lower the percentage of elders who are bedridden or senile. Nonetheless, the num-

Table 3
Population of Japan by Age and Sex: 1990–2025
(Unit: 1,000 and the ratio to the total population)

	Male		Female	
	65–74	75–over	65–74	75–over
1990	3,752(6.18)	2,231(3.67)	5,166(8.21)	3,750(5.96)
1995	4,936(8.02)	2,575(4.19)	6,108(9.58)	4,537(7.12)
2000	6,008(9.63)	3,105(4.98)	6,895(10.68)	5,505(8.52)
2005	6,426(10.16)	4,046(6.39)	7,320(11.19)	6,585(10.07)
2010	6,862(10.78)	4,952(7.78)	7,798(11.86)	7,654(11.64)
2015	7,888(12.45)	5,575(8.80)	8,858(13.53)	8,455(12.91)
2020	7,813(12.53)	6,158(9.87)	8,737(13.54)	9,260(14.35)
2025	6,655(10.91)	7,042(11.55)	7,419(11.75)	10,394(16.46)

Source: Koseisho jinko mondai kenkyujo (Research Institute of Population Problems, Ministry of Health and Welfare). Projection based on the 1990 National Census.

ber itself will increase because the size of the oldest segment of the older population will be quite large.

Today it is estimated that there are about 800,000 bedridden elders and slightly more than 900,000 senile elders in Japan. If the ratio does not change, the estimates will reach 1,000,000 for each group around the turn of the century. The care recipients are increasingly aging females.

Women as Caregivers

Care of the elderly, like housework and care of the young and the infirm, has long been women's work. Graham stated that caring is a labor of love. It demands both love and labor, both identity and activity, with the nature of demands being shaped by the social relations of the wider society. In gender-divided societies caring tends to have particular consequences for the identity and activity of women (Graham 1983, 14–15).

The Basic Survey of the Health and Welfare Administration in 1984 indicated that the primary caregivers for the male bedridden elders at home were wives (73.6 percent), daughters-in-law (14.6 percent), and daughters (6.4 percent). Those for the female bedridden elders were daughters-in-law (58.7 percent), daughters (17.9 percent), and husbands (10.2 percent). In the United States wives came first and daughters came next for males, while daughters came first and husbands came next for females. Unlike in Japan, the chance of daughters-in-law being caregivers is quite slight in the United States (Stone, Caferate, and Sangl 1987).

Though both are unpaid work and take place within the small world of the family, care of children and care of the elderly are not the same. Care of children by the mother is based on love and affection, but care of the elderly by the daughter or the daughter-in-law is based on both love and obligation. Dependency of children does not last long, but caregivers for the elderly cannot see a bright future. The frail elders are getting weak and will become more dependent. At the end death will await them. Today child rearing seems to be regarded as a kind of constraint for women who want to be active outside the home, but child rearing comes to an end after a few years. One never knows, however, when caring for the elderly will end. Compared with care of children, care of the elderly is a heavier burden to the caregivers not only physically but also psychologically.

Why do women take on the role of caregivers? The reasons seem to be as follows: (1) the sex role differentiation in society, (2) the ideology of the patriarchal stem family, (3) the role expectations of others, and (4) the feminine role identification of women.

We often use the term *traditional sex role differentiation*—that is, men earn the money, and women manage the household. Women's alienation from productive work has rather a short history. In the preindustrial society both production and consumption took place at home. The family was a unit of production. Husbands and wives, including children, had to work together in order to survive. Women's alienation from productive work began only after the industrial revolution. Productive functions were transferred from the home to the factory, and the rise in productivity allowed women to stay at home, just doing housework.

In the Edo period (from the seventeenth to nineteenth centuries) there was a common saying that "the husband is responsible for things outside the home, and the wife is responsible for things inside the home." This was the ideal type of division of labor between husband and wife in the upper-class samurai family. Such sex-related role differentiation was not found among common people.

In Japan is was only after World War I that the rise of capitalism took productive functions out of the home. Men came to be employed, and women stayed at home. Then the husband became a breadwinner, and the wife became a full-time homemaker. Care of children and of the elderly came to be concentrated in the hands of the women. Women's work at home was not highly valued, because it took place privately without being evaluated by others and because, of course, they could not make any money. In a capitalist society nonremunerative work could not be valued.

The ideology of the patriarchal stem family *(ie)*, based on Confucianism which gives men the status of the family head and gives women the status of dependents, remains even in highly industrialized societies. In Japan, although the *ie* was legally abolished after World War II, the ideology still survives.

The idea that women's place is in the home and that women should be dependent on the male household head has been affecting our lives formally and informally. Our systems of wages, promotion, tax, and social security are based on the household in which the head is always a male. Women are not allowed to enjoy the same privileges as men because the normal position of women at home is that of dependency. Thus, it is always women who are supposed to stop working when someone in the family becomes sick or impaired.

In Japan the patriarchal family system—which stresses obedience of women to men, the young to the old, and the daughter-in-law to the mother-in-law—exerts strong pressure for the daughter-in-law to take on the role of caregiver.

Those who have internalized the value of the sex-segregated society and the ideology of the patriarchal stem family come naturally to expect women to be caregivers. When someone in the family is sick, relatives, friends, neighbors, employers, colleagues at work, doctors, and even social workers expect women to serve as caregivers. In Japan pressure from others is particularly strong when a woman is in the position of the daughter-in-law, because many people still believe that the daughter-in-law should be responsible for her parents-in-law.

Feminine identity, needless to say, is related to sex role differentiation, the patriarchal stem family ideology, and the role expectation from others. Even if there are no overt pressures, women voluntarily take on the role of caregivers. They know that they will feel guilty if they do not do so, or they feel it is a natural role for them. In order to escape from the role conflict between work and care, they give up their careers. As Graham stated, caring is "given" to women: it becomes the defining characteristic of their self-identity and their life's work. At the same time, caring is taken away from men: not-caring becomes a defining characteristic of manhood (1983, 18).

Recently, however, there has been a change in women's attitude toward caring for frail elders. A recent study indicates that, if the spouse of a bedridden elder is still alive, a daughter-in-law will not be a primary caregiver, even if she is living in the same house. Among caring daughters and daughters-in-law some said "*Shikataganai*" (There is no other way) or "I would prefer to escape from the present situation" (Center for Development of Welfare for the Aged 1987). Apparently, they do not identify themselves with caregiving roles. An increase in this type of sentiment will make family care more difficult.

Difficulties in Taking Care of Frail Elders at Home

In every society many people prefer to be cared for at home when they become old and weak, and their families often want to keep them at home as long as possible. Yet aging at home has been increasingly difficult because of the drastic changes at the societal level as well as at the family level.

There seems to be a myth that most frail elders in Japan are being cared for by their families at home. The ratio of old people staying at home, however, has been decreasing year by year; it was 95.4 percent in 1973, 95.0 percent in 1977, 94.4 percent in 1980, and 94.0 percent in 1983. The ratio of

217

people over eighty staying at home has been declining rapidly; it was 94.3 percent in 1973 and 88.8 in 1983 (Koyama 1986, 43–46). The Ministry of Health and Welfare estimated that in 1990, of 700,000 bedridden elders, 25 percent were in the hospital, 16 percent in nursing homes, 5 percent in intermediate-care facilities, and 24 percent at home. The following factors seem to be the causes of the difficulties in taking care of frail elders at home.

Demographic Change

Change in the Ratio of Caregivers to Care Recipients

Before World War II our population was characterized by a high birthrate and a high death rate. The average birthrate between 1933 and 1937 was 30.8 per 1,000, and the average death rate was 17.4 per 1,000. Just after the war a steep rise in the birthrate and a sudden drop in the death rate created the baby boom. The average birthrate between 1947 and 1949 was 33.6 per 1,000, and the death rate dropped to 12.7 per 1,000. Then both the birthrate and the death rate decreased. In 1991 the birthrate was 9.9 per 1,000, and the death rate was 6.7 per 1,000. A steep fall in birthrate will alter the ratio of potential caregivers to those in need of care. Before the war the average number of children per couple was five. There were many who did not have to take care of their parents because usually it was the wife of the first son who should assume the responsibility of caring for her parents-in-law, and parents-in-law did not live long at that time. Today the average number of children per couple is two, and there are many couples who have one child. If the only son and the only daughter get married, they will be responsible for their four parents. If their grandparents are alive, they will be responsible for their eight grandparents.

According to the Survey on Care for the Elderly (Somucho 1987), among those who were sixty years old or over 44.0 percent of male respondents and 66.5 percent of female respondents had some experience in caring for frail elders. Males usually took care of their parents, and females took care of their husband's parents as well as their own parents. Recently, it seems that in the female's life course a new stage of care for the elderly parents has appeared; if anything, her responsibility has increased. Care for frail elders used to be a problem for a small number of people, but now it has become everybody's problem.

Longevity of Frail Elders

Thanks to advanced medical treatment and improved nutrition and/or housing conditions, today even frail elders can live long. The Basic Survey of the Health and Welfare Administration in 1984 indicates that one-fourth of the bedridden elders have been in bed for more than five years and some more than ten years. It used to be difficult for frail elders to live long, but now some can live more than twenty years after they get sick. Apparently, the average age of bedridden elders and senile elders is increasing.

Longevity of frail elders makes it difficult for the family to take care of them at home, because the caregivers themselves grow old and become weak. The Survey of Old People Living Alone or Bedridden conducted by the National Association of Democratic Doctors in 1982–83 indicated that, among caregivers of the bedridden elders at home, 2.3 percent were seriously sick or impaired, 28.2 percent were sick and weak, and 9.2 percent did not feel well, yet they hardly found time to see a doctor. Sometimes it happens that caregivers die before frail elders.

Changes in the Family

Decrease in Shared Living Arrangements

Though two-thirds of people aged sixty-five or over are still living with children and/or grandchildren, the ratio has been decreasing steadily. According to the national census, the proportion of shared living arrangements among old people was 87.3 percent in 1960, 79.3 percent in 1970, 69.9 percent in 1980, and 60.6 percent in 1990. It is estimated that it will be about 50 percent at the beginning of the twenty-first century. The proportion of older married couples (i.e., one of them is sixty-five years old or over) to all households with persons over sixty-five was 7 percent in 1960, 11.3 percent in 1970, 18.0 percent in 1980, and 20.6 percent in 1990. The proportion of single-member households was 5.7 percent in 1960, 9.1 percent in 1970, 12.1 percent in 1980, and 15.1 percent in 1990. It is estimated that it will be about 30 percent for the former and about 20 percent for the latter at the beginning of the twenty-first century.

The decrease in the proportion of shared living arrangements was caused by: (1) a decrease in the number of children per couple; (2) an increase in geographical mobility from rural to urban areas, especially in the 1960s, the period characterized by technological innovation and high economic growth; (3) changes in attitudes toward living arrangements; and (4) a housing shortage in urban areas.

The average number of children per couple has fallen. It was five per couple in the Meiji era (1890s), three per couple in the Taisho era (1920s), and two per couple in the Showa era (1950s) (Economic Planning Agency 1983). Due to the smaller size, there are many elderly couples who have only daughters or whose children cannot live with them since their place of work is far away.

Rapid economic growth increased demand for labor in the manufacturing and service sectors. These sectors absorbed the labor that had become redundant in the primary industries, which accounted for 30.2 percent of the total workers in 1960. It has been reduced to less than 10 percent today. Young people moved from primary to secondary or tertiary industries and also moved from rural to urban areas. In the areas in which there were no such industries to attract young people, the first son or the only son even left home. Thus, in rural areas, old people came to be deserted.

Attitudes toward living arrangements seem to be related to industriali-

219

zation, modernization, and urbanization. In urban areas, especially among employees, an increasing number of elderly couples choose to live alone because they do not have to live with their sons' families in order to keep their family business and because they do not have to depend on their sons financially. Both the young and the older generations living in urban areas prefer more privacy and want to enjoy their own lifestyles without being disturbed by the other generation. Many old people, however, want to live with their children when they become weak or when their spouse has died.

In the households of childless married couples or of single people, there are no caregivers, or, if there are any, the caregivers themselves are old and weak. A decrease in the shared living arrangements among old people inevitably increases the need for social services.

The housing shortage is another reason why shared living arrangements have been decreasing in urban areas. The high cost of land makes it difficult for a young couple to own their own home. Low-rent public housing tends to be located outside of the city. Even if both young and old generations want to live together, it is not so easy to find the adequate size of house or apartment.

Recently, the housing industry began to sell so-called two-family houses, which enable two families to live under one roof with separate facilities. And the Japan Housing Loan Corporation offers a special loan called the "two generation loan" for which the term of redemption covers the father and the son.

These measures may encourage two generations to live together, but in metropolitan areas it is almost impossible to obtain new land. Therefore, those who already own land can build two-family houses. In a two-family house, there is a tendency to have separate entrances, separate kitchens, separate bathrooms, and so forth, even though the occupants are living under one roof. In some houses there is no pathway between the two households, and therefore parents have to go out of the house in order to visit their child's family.

Changes in Family Functions

Industrialization removed several functions from the home. For instance, the productive function was transferred to the factory, education to the school, and protection to the police. A drastic increase in the number of women working outside the home during and after the 1960s has also decreased or weakened family functions. Housework, which used to be managed at home, has been transferred to the service industry. Ready-made clothes and foods, eating out, dry cleaning and housekeeping services, and baby hotels have become common. Ways of housework and of child rearing have changed a great deal, which weakens a mother-in-law's power over her daughter-in-law.

Supporting elderly parents used to be the most important function of the family before World War II. Prior to the war older people were respected by their family members not only because their knowledge and skills were valued but also because the idea of filial piety based on Confucianism shaped the attitudes and behavior of Japanese people. Filial piety was emphasized repeatedly and internalized through moral education beginning in elementary school. The *ie*, as described in earlier essays in this volume, was the patriarchal family system that originated in the Edo period among upper-class samurai and was characterized by strong power vested in the family head, respect for the elders, low status for women, and ancestor worship.

Changes in Attitudes toward the Family

Although the *ie* system was legally abolished after World War II, until Japan reached a high economic growth, people still maintained the tradition of the patrilineal family system; that is, the first son inherited most of the family property, lived with his parents after marriage, and took care of them until they died. Many people, including the first son, believed that it was his obligation to live with his parents in order to perpetuate the family lineage.

Yet during the 1960s even the first son left home and moved to the city because it became difficult to support his family in an agricultural community. Through education and mass media people gradually came to realize that not only the first son but also other children have equal rights to inherit the family property as well as equal obligations to support elderly parents.

As people have become more concerned about the nuclear family, a sense of filial piety toward elderly parents appears to have weakened. Under the patriarchal family system it was the obligation of children to sacrifice themselves in order to meet the needs of their parents.

In addition to institutional changes after the war, industrialization, modernization, and influences from U.S. democracy changed people's attitudes from an emphasis on the family to an emphasis on the individual. Young people who have internalized the Western idea of individualism through education and mass media tend to express negative attitudes toward self-sacrifice or absolute obedience to the parents.

The family used to be a small cosmos that fulfilled most of its members' needs. Today, however, there are many places or agencies that can fulfill various needs. Many people still believe that the family is at the center of their lives, but sometimes they break their family relations in order to pursue their own needs or aspirations. Weakening family ties as well as family identification inevitably affects those who are relatively powerless, such as children or old people.

Changing Roles and Attitudes of Women

Today nearly 90 percent of caregivers are females. If the frail elders are males, their wives are the primary caregivers, and, if the frail elders are females, daughters-in-law or daughters take on the role of caregiver. Most caregivers are middle-aged housewives. Yet the rise in labor force participation by middle-aged women and changes in their attitudes toward the family and the elderly make family care increasingly difficult.

Our female labor force used to be characterized by the young and single. In 1955, 69 percent of employed women were under thirty years of age, and 65 percent were single. In 1990, however, 48.4 percent were over forty years of age; 58.2 percent were married, and 9.1 percent were divorced or widowed. A shortage of single young women caused by the drop in the birth-rate and by the rise in the educational level was the major factor in pulling the middle-aged housewives from the home. During the period of high economic growth, secondary and tertiary industries needed the soft hands of women as well as their cheap labor.

In addition to the strong "pull" factor from the labor market, there were "push" factors that encouraged middle-aged housewives to enter the labor market. Needless to say, inflation was the major cause. Inflation made their lives difficult, especially the high cost of educating children and of building or buying a house. These costs became a big burden to the household economy, and, thus, housewives had to work in order to help the household economy. The second reason that women began entering the work force was that they had enough spare time. Electric appliances like refrigerators, washing machines, and vacuum cleaners shortened the hours of housework considerably. Compared with their mothers, they spent less time and energy on housework and had time to work outside the home. The third reason that women moved into the labor market was the change in women's life cycle. Women born in 1905 married at the age of 23.1 and had five children until 38.0 years old; they died before their last child left home. Those born in 1927 married on the average at the age of 23.0 and gave birth to their third and last child at the age of 30.3; their last child started school when they were 37.3 years old. Those born in 1959 married at the age of 25.4 and gave birth to their second and last child when they were 29 years old (Ministry of Labor 1986). Apparently, the child-rearing period has become shorter and shorter, while the period after the last child goes to school has become longer and longer. It is quite natural, therefore, that many married women have begun to seek roles other than wife and mother. The fourth reason was the rise in the level of expectations. The rise of the educational level and the increase in information through mass media has widened the vision of housewives. They can no longer be satisfied with the roles of wife-mother. They try to find opportunities to use their abilities, or they want to have money they can spend at their own will.

Although many middle-aged married women are working part-time with low pay, they seem to enjoy their work as well as their association with colleagues. As long as their annual income does not exceed a million yen, they can keep the status of dependence on their husband. They do not have to pay any income tax and are covered by their husband's health insurance and pension.

During the period of high economic growth many daycare centers for children were built because employers needed female workers and also because various women's groups pressured local governments to create them. There are, however, not many daycare centers for the elderly. If there are any, they keep old people once or twice a week from 10 A.M. to 3 P.M.

Because of a shortage of adequate facilities and of strong pressures from others, many women stop working or take a leave of absence in order to take care of their parents or parents-in-law. Yet, recently, there appear to be changes in attitudes among working women. Some of them refuse to stop working despite the pressures from relatives or neighbors. The younger and the more highly educated women are reluctant to take care of frail elders at home and tend to rely on social services outside the home (Kokumin Seikatsu Senta 1981; and Yokohama-shi, Shimin koyoku 1984). On the other hand, the government is expecting housewives to take care of frail elders at home so that it may save expenditures for health and welfare.

A special tax deduction for full-time homemakers started in 1987. Some local governments offer a special allowance to caregivers or honor the daughters-in-law who have been taking care of bedridden elders at home for a long period of time. These measures, however, will have little impact on the present trend of women working outside the home. Other measures that enable family care to coexist with work will have to be sought.

Weakening Human Relations in the Community

In the traditional community in which the same families have been living for a long period of time, people know one another and help a great deal when someone needs help. Yet urbanization and geographical mobility have weakened the ties among people in the community. In Japan, especially during the 1960s, people moved from rural to urban areas, rural communities outside the city were urbanized, and people came to rely on money rather than human relations. When someone became sick, neighbors used to help by doing shopping or housework. Today, even in rural areas housewives go to work, and there is no one, or hardly anyone, who can offer a hand to a neighbor. Thus, more and more, frail elders have to depend on social services.

Reasons Specific to the Japanese Society
Dependence of Older People

Those brought up under the *ie* system still maintain the value that parents have the right to depend on children and that a daughter-in-law should take care of her parents-in-law. Women in their fifties or sixties often complain that they will never be able to depend on their children and that their daughters-in-law will not take care of them when they become bedridden, even though they are now taking care of their mothers-in-law at home.

It is often found that old people refuse to do things for themselves even though they can and that they demand their daughters-in-law do these things for them. Their daughters-in-law do everything because they are afraid to be criticized by their husbands' relatives and neighbors. Dependence by old people in Japan seems to be one of the reasons that contribute to the high ratio of bedridden elders—that is, 4.2 percent among people aged 65 or over, compared with 5 percent among people aged eighty or over in the United States (U.S. Senate Special Committee on Aging 1986).

Housing Conditions

Generally, Japanese houses are small and have many steps. Therefore, it is not so easy for people in wheelchairs to live independently. It is also difficult to provide a handrail inside a Japanese house with paper screens. Heating is also poor in many houses in which old people are living. Those specializing in housing problems point out that poor housing is the cause of poor health, which often leads to elders being bedridden.

The average length of a hospital stay in Japan was 44.9 days in 1990, which was three times as long as those in France or West Germany. Among elderly patients 50.8 percent had been in the hospital for more than six months in 1985.

Why are so many old people in the hospital? Hospital fees are covered by the National Health Insurance, though patients pay part of the fee. Second, while many people think it an embarrassment to send elderly parents to nursing homes, they feel better about hospitals. Third, because of poor housing, old people often have no choice: houses may be too small to include aged parents, and apartment owners may refuse to accept older people. Fourth, severe competition to enroll children in prestigious schools is another factor that keeps old people out of a family's home. Sometimes a grandparents' room turns into a study room for a grandchild. Young children, in this case, do not want to be disturbed by any noise and complain that old people often turn the television up to a high volume because of their hearing difficulties.

Are There Any Solutions?

In Japan it is widely believed that frail elders should be taken care of at home by housewives, especially daughters-in-law. Aging at home, however, is not the same as being cared for by a daughter-in-law. As mentioned, today many middle-aged women, including daughters-in-law, are working outside the home. Although many Japanese women still feel a strong sense of filial responsibility toward their aging parents and/or parents-in-law, they do not want to sacrifice themselves. The majority want to take care of old people with the help of community services. There are several ways in which the burden of caregiving can be relieved.

Social Services

In 1989, the Ministry of Health and Welfare issued the Ten-Year Strategy for Promoting Health and Welfare Services for the Elderly (the so-called Gold Plan), the purpose of which was to increase home care services. Home help services, visiting nurses, short-term stays at nursing homes, day-care services, and bathing services (found only in Japan), needless to say, help caregivers. Most of them are subsidized by the local government and/or the national government.

In order to expand the services without expanding the budget and to strengthen community ties, recently many local governments have started a so-called paid volunteer system, which is a kind of mutual help in the community. The system of paid volunteers is organized so that those who need help and those who want to work register in a membership organization. There is a full-time staff to manage the whole system. Their salaries and the cost of the office are usually financed by the local government. Payments vary: housekeeping is seven hundred or eight hundred yen (US$7.00 or $8.00) an hour, and bathing a frail elder is one thousand yen (US$10.00) an hour. Part of the payment goes to the organization, or else volunteers can save the hours so that they will receive help when they become in need.

This care work is not full-time, and it operates outside of the ordinary labor market. Paid volunteers, mostly middle-aged housewives, have no pensions and health insurance of their own, but, since their annual income is quite low, they can be covered by their husbands' pensions and health insurance. They are, however, insured against accidents. Sometimes payment to volunteers goes below the minimum wage of the area. The reason why it is low is that the work is not considered to be for earning money but, rather, to give fulfillment or meaning in life (especially to middle-aged housewives in the "empty nest" period).

It is quite difficult to encourage people to do this volunteer work in Japan. Since family ties and kinship ties used to be very strong, and many problems solved entirely within the family or within the kin group, it may be an embarrassment to disclose family problems outside the kin group. Whether volunteers should be paid has been debated. Needless to say, there is a danger in creating a cheap labor pool among women, which might lower the wage level of women as a whole. On the other hand, it may not be easy for housewives to get permission from their husbands or mothers-in-law, if they are not paid for their work. Voluntarism in Japan is still at a primitive state, and it is not valued socially.

Men's Participation in Care Giving

Caring is primarily women's task all over the world. Yet in the aged society of the near future, in which one out of four people will be sixty-five years old or older, it will be quite common for a couple to be expected to take care of their four parents, and perhaps even their eight grandparents. It will be impossible for one housewife to care for all the frail elders at home, and men's participation in caregiving will be inevitable. One of the barriers to this participation is our occupation system. Japanese salaried men work very long and very hard, few of them can enjoy full weekends, and many feel guilty using their paid vacations. These long hours make it difficult for men to participate in any housework. These men are usually alienated from their families because they have little time to spend with family members. In fact, Japanese salaried men are often called boarders or salary-earning robots. In order to encourage men to help their wives and to increase their involvement in family affairs, their working hours must be shortened.

Of course, shorter working hours would not automatically increase men's participation in caregiving unless their attitudes toward sex role differentiation changed as well. Some do not help their wives, even if they have the time, simply because they believe that men should not do women's work. Changing attitudes is much more difficult than changing institutions. It will take a long time to reach a society in which men and women equally share responsibilities for taking care of frail elders.

Changes in Women's Working Conditions

At the present moment many women give up their careers in order to take care of frail elders at home. According to the Survey on Working Women, a special leave for caregiving (46.0 percent) and flex-time (40.3 percent) were frequently mentioned by working women as conditions for continuing working while taking care of frail elders. Today a small number of companies and local governments offer a special leave for taking care of sick persons in the family; they range from three days to six months without pay. The Ministry of Labor issued guidelines for providing family care leave, and it has encouraged companies to introduce such a leave, but it will not be so easy because a special maternity leave policy up to one year after birth did not take hold even though the Ministry of Labor subsidized small companies to do this. Flex-time, short working hours, and special leave for caregiving will certainly help working women if or when they have frail elders at home.

Commercialized Services

Until the oil crisis in 1973 the government seemed to be moving in the direction of the welfare state, but, as soon as business slowed, government policy shifted social services from the public sector to the private sector. It is impossible for the government to provide adequate services to ever-increasing frail elders if we do not pay higher taxes.

Today the number of companies that provide such services as home help, visiting nurses, bathing, and selling or renting special beds, special bathtubs, and wheelchairs are increasing. At first most of them were small companies, but now big companies and some U.S. companies are participating in the so-called silver market. Even though reliance on the private sector is inevitable, the quality, standards, and prices of services must be controlled.

In 1987 the Ministry of Health and Welfare started a new section that deals exclusively with commercialized services for the elderly. Under the guidance of this section an association of private sector institutions began to promote and control services for the elderly.

Network of Caregivers

Caregivers are usually isolated from the community. They have no time to associate with neighbors, and it is commonly found that friends, neighbors, and even relatives rarely visit the home of frail elders.

Recently, people have come to realize the importance of providing support for the caregivers. Welfare of caregivers has long been ignored because many people, including women themselves, believed that caring was the destiny of women. Respite care or caring for the caregiver is now a big issue. A short-term stay by the frail elderly at a nursing home, bathing services, and daycare services are quite helpful in lifting some physical and emotional strain from caregivers. Today the Association of Families of Senile Elders has many branches, and the Association of Families of Bedridden Elders has been created. These informal networks new to Japan seem to be quite effective in giving information and emotional support to caregivers.

At the beginning of the twenty-first century the number of bedridden and/or senile elders will be quite large. It will be impossible for housewives to take care of the increasing number of frail elders even if they want to do so. It is probable that there will be more than two bedridden or senile elders at home if a family's only son and only daughter get married.

The burden of caring for the elderly should be shared within the family and the community as well as the society as a whole. While we now share the responsibility of support for the elderly through public pensions, we will also have to share the burden of caregiving. In order to establish a care-sharing society we will have to change our educational system, occupational system, and value system. In the twenty-first century caregiving will cease to be a women's issue and will become everybody's issue.

NOTE

An earlier version of this essay was presented at the symposium, "Who is responsible for my old age?" at the Mount Sinai Medical Center, New York, 28, 29, and 30 November 1988.

REFERENCES

Brody, E. M. 1981. "Women in the Middle and Family Help to Older People." *Gerontologist* 21, no. 5: 471–80.
Economic Plannung Agency. 1983. *Japan in the Year 2000*. Tokyo: Japan Times.

Graham, H. 1983. "Caring: A Labour of Love." In *A Labour of Love: Women and Caring*, ed. J. Finch and D. Groves. London: Routledge and Kegan Paul.

Kokumin seikatsu senta (National Life Center). 1981. *Shufu no rogokan ni kansuru chosa hokokusho* (Survey of housewives' attitudes toward their old age). Tokyo: Kokumin seikatsu senta.

Koyama, H. 1986. *Chukanshisetsu no choryu* (Trends of intermediate care facilities). Tokyo: Chuohoki shuppan.

Ministry of Labor. 1986. *The Present Status of Working Women*. Tokyo: Ministry of Labor.

Rojin fukushi kaihatsu senta (Center for the Development of Welfare for the Aged). 1987. *Zaitakujukaigo—rojin setai no kaigo to kakei ni kansuru jisshoteki kenkyu hokokusho* (Study on the care and household economy of the seriously impaired elderly at home). Tokyo: Rojin fukushi kaihatsu senta.

Somucho (Management and Coordination Agency). 1987. *Rogo no seikatsu to kaigo ni kansuru chosa* (Survey on care for the elderly). Tokyo: Somucho.

Sorifu (Prime Minister's Office). 1983. *Fujin no shugyo ni kansuru yoron chosa* (Survey on working women). Tokyo: Sorifu.

Stone, R., G. L. Caferate, and J. Sangl. 1987. "Caregivers of the Frail Elderly: A National Profile." *Gerontologist* 27, no. 5: 616–26.

U.S. Senate Special Committee on Aging. 1986. *Developments in Aging* 51.

Yokohama-shi, Shimin kyoku (Yokohama City Citizens' Bureau). 1984. *Yokohama-shi josei no rodo to seikatsu chosa* (Survey on the work and life of women in Yokohama City). Yokohama-shi: Yokohama-shi shimin-kyoku.

Zen-Nihon min'i-ren (National Association of Democratic Doctors). 1983. *Hitorigurashi/netakiri rojin jittai chosa hokokusho* (Report of survey of elderly people living alone and bedridden). Tokyo: Zen-Nihon min'i-ren kikanshi shuppan-bu.

The Changing Portrait of Japanese Men

The image many people have of the typical Japanese husband is a workaholic who toils long hours for Mitsubishi or Sony or some other large corporation, goes out drinking with his fellow workers or clients after work and plays golf with them on weekends, and rarely spends much time at home with his wife and children, much less does anything around the house, such as cleaning or changing diapers. In 1991 the average Japanese worker put in 2,044 hours of work—about 200 hours more than the average American or British worker and 500 hours more compared to a German or French worker ("Hatarakisugi kara" 1991, 2). This kind of lifestyle and the corporate structure and value system that sustains it has come under severe criticism by the feminist movement in recent years for maintaining a rigid division of gender roles, hindering the development of gender relations based on equality and sharing of family and community responsibilities, and creating what amounts to a father-absent family system.

One of the consequences of the women's movement and the discussions that have taken place has been that at least some men have begun to express doubts and misgivings about the kind of lives they lead. Thus, for example, we see the phenomenon of *"das sara,"* or salaried white-collar workers who quit their jobs after several years with one company and strike out in a new career. Such a thing, of course, goes totally against the concept of lifetime employment and loyalty to one's company which has been associated with the Japanese system of employment. An interesting development within the last three or four years has been the appearance of numerous books, often written by men, on such themes as the need for promoting men's independence and autonomy, sharing child care and housekeeping responsibilities, and making career changes in order to pursue a fulfilling personal life. Groups have been organized around such causes as pressing companies to provide child care leaves for men as well as women and decrying the distinctively Japanese phenomenon of *tanshin funin*—married men being assigned to posts that entail living away from their families for lengthy periods. The mystique of the Japanese male—personified by the workaholic "corporate warrior" and a system of values centered around success, ever-expanding economic growth, and pursuit of profit, which until now has been taken for granted—is undergoing a process of questioning and reexamination by at least some Japanese men.

What impact, if any, have the women's movement and the changes in women's attitudes and lifestyles had on Japanese men? To what extent are men changing in terms of their attitudes toward their own roles as husbands, fathers, and workers and in terms of their consciousness regarding gender equality? What are the forces impelling them toward change or, conversely, inhibiting them from change?

These and other questions are explored, first, through a dialogue among Charles Douglas Lummis, an American professor of political science at Tsuda College, the oldest women's college in Japan, who has lived and taught in Japan for more than twenty-five years; Satomi Nakajima, who has been active in women's causes for many years and has served as a member of the Tokorozawa City Assembly since 1991; and the two editors of this volume, Kumiko Fujimura-Fanselow and Atsuko Kameda. Another, somewhat different perspective on these issues is offered by Masanori Yamaguchi, a journalist with the *Yomiuri shimbun* newspaper, who has been reporting on changes in the family and in men, particularly, for the last several years and counts himself among those men who are seeking a new definition of masculinity and men's role in Japanese society. His reflections, based on many hours of conversation with men in various parts of the country and in many differing walks of life, offer valuable insights into the ongoing process of self-questioning and redefinition of the male role which is underway among a small but growing number of Japanese men today.

Dialogue

Charles Douglas Lummis and Satomi Nakajima with
Kumiko Fujimura-Fanselow and Atsuko Kameda

Translated by Kumiko Fujimura-Fanselow

Japanese Men and the Corporate Culture

Nakajima: Through many years of active involvement in community affairs
and as recently elected member of my local city assembly, I've had many
opportunities to observe what goes on in my community. One of the things
I'm concerned about is what often happens to Japanese men after retirement.
Most men leave for work early in the morning; on Sundays they might do a
little work in the garden or walk the dog. Aside from an occasional exchange
of greetings with neighbors, these men seem to lack the ability to communicate with other members of their community. I would personally like to see
more involvement by men in various community affairs and together try to
improve our local communities, but in fact, whereas women have many ave-
nues for building connections with other women through their children or
through involvement in such groups as food cooperatives, the men seem to
be cut off, or to cut themselves off, from the community. They seem to be like
robots who have lost their voices. My impression is that most men are able
to get by only because they have their wives to depend on. I can't help but
worry about how these men are going to cope in their old age, especially if
their wives die first. With couples having fewer children, going to live with
one's children in old age is becoming less and less feasible.

Lummis: We often hear about men in Japan dying soon after they retire from
work or withering away because they have nothing to do with their lives. I
think this shows how strongly they are rooted in a bureaucratic system of

management and control, are manipulated by it, and become psychologically dependent upon it. Since I teach at a women's university, I often hear things about Japanese men from students and graduates. And, because these women are very perceptive, I think that perhaps I can learn things about men from these women who associate with them which I could not learn from the men themselves.

I think college men have probably changed. Among university students the proportion of men who at least claim to recognize gender equality has increased. And many of them demonstrate this belief through action, for example, by cooking or washing dishes when they're with their girlfriends. However, if a woman marries such a man thinking that he will behave in the same way after marriage, she may be in for a rude surprise, for, from what I have heard, a common pattern is that a year or two after such a man enters a company, he reverts to being a typical Japanese husband.

I don't think it is necessarily the case that men personally choose to be this way or that they were deceiving their future wives when they professed to a belief in gender equality during their university days. Rather, it is because that's the organizational structure of Japanese business society. It is very difficult to assess to what extent the behavior of the individual salaried, white-collar employee stems from his own motives and to what extent it reflects the demands of the system. It's not necessarily the case that an office worker stays at work till late because he personally doesn't want to go home. He is enmeshed in a culture in which one simply doesn't go home early. The model employee is one who works overtime, while men who go home early to spend time with their wives and children are not "real" men or are "sissy" and of no use to the company. In the Japanese corporate workplace a man who puts into practice the concept of gender equality in his home is looked down upon. Not only that, but ultimately he is likely to end up in a position of little responsibility. So, it is the corporate system itself and the culture to which it has given birth which controls the men who work within it. And, unless a man is exceptionally strong, he is likely to be defeated by that system, even if he thinks he won't be.

Nakajima: A professor of political science at Chuo University recently said that young men today are rather choosy about jobs. Many of them say they want to go into work that is interesting. In other words, rather than thinking in terms of what company they want to work for, which has in the past been the major consideration, they're more concerned about what kind of work they want to do. This professor felt that this pointed to a possibility for change. While that is certainly a hopeful development, I think that the reality today is as you describe it: a man who leaves work early ends up being relegated to a less-important position.

A very interesting book came out recently called *Otoko to onna de 'ham-bunko' ism* (Men and Women Sharing Fifty-Fifty [1989]), compiled by a group that was organized around the issue of securing child care leave for both men and women. The contributors to the book are all women and men who have been either unable or unwilling to fit into the existing system and have either sought to change the system from within or else opted out of the system altogether and carved out a different kind of lifestyle for themselves. One of the contributors to the volume, Tambara Tsunenori, worked at one time in a civil service position. When his wife became pregnant he went home from work early, instead of putting in overtime, to prepare the evening meal since she wasn't well. His wife went back to work after giving birth, and the child was placed in a daycare center. Since his workplace did not allow men to take child care leave, Mr. Tambara decided to put his annual vacation days to use in fifteen-minute units for the purpose of taking his child to and from the daycare center every morning and afternoon. His employer's reaction was to assign him to a position of less responsibility. When he had used up all his vacation days, deductions were made from his monthly salary, and he was denied his annual promotion. The issue was taken up by his union, which at least verbally supported his cause. But there were no other men who followed his example. This went on for over four years, after which, due to a different set of family circumstances, Mr. Tambara left his job and became a reporter for a regional newspaper.

Another contributor to the book, Kawaguchi Haruo, who worked for a pharmaceutical company, brought suit against the company for forcing him to take a post in another city, leaving his family behind, despite his protest against the transfer because he wanted to stay with the family and bring up his child together with his wife and because his wife was also opposed to the transfer. The basis of his claim was that the company was infringing on the right of men to take part in the upbringing of their children and on the right of women to work and that this ran counter to the provisions set forth in the United Nations (UN) Convention on Elimination of All Forms of Discrimination against Women adopted by the Japanese government.

Gradually more and more people are showing support for men like Mr. Tambara and Mr. Kawaguchi. The practice of making workers take up posts in other cities alone while their families are left behind for varying lengths of time started about twenty-five years ago. Today this practice is accepted as a matter of course. It seems to be that it's because neither husbands nor wives have a strong conviction about what constitutes their own individual human happiness or about how one ought to live that they are so easily manipulated by the companies for which they work. Or it may be that it's because we have these powerful entities—that is, corporations—that people get that way. I think the cause is to be found in both.

The Dominance of a Male Culture in the Workplace

Lummis: It seems to me that a term such as *happiness* or *self-fulfillment* has no place within the corporate culture; such a quiet expression doesn't fit into company logic. Discourse within the corporation is carried on in a

233

harsher vocabulary: words like *success, efficiency, production, market share,* and so on.

Nakajima: I agree. I worked for a private corporation for six years. After encountering discrimination there, I became a schoolteacher, so I have a first-hand knowledge of how corporations operate. A corporation is really much like a nation. For example, companies have their own company song, which tries to instill loyalty to the company. There is competition of every kind at various levels—for example, between different sections—to see which can make the most profit. As you say, it is foremost a world of competition.

Lummis: Yes, and that's why I doubt whether significant improvements can be brought about within that system. I think it may be unreasonable to call for equality between men and women within such a system without questioning the nature of the system itself. It's often pointed out that the so-called miraculous economic growth of postwar Japan has been accomplished at the expense of women. If that's true, and I think it is, it means that gender inequality in the corporation is not an accident but is, rather, part of its essential structure.

The so-called Japanese style of management has recently come to be famous throughout the world and is said to be unique. But I think the organization of Japanese companies is not so unusual; it is essentially the same as that of military organizations, which is found everywhere. It is an essential characteristic of military organization that women are excluded from it. In ordinary societies men and women live and work together, not necessarily in equality, but at least in a relation of cooperation and dialogue. Military organization is an unnatural social formation that is historically based on the exclusion of women. Even today women formally in the military are excluded from combat units and kept in support roles. (The exception, of course, is genuinely defensive peoples' armies when they are actually defending the homeland.)

Japanese corporate organization resembles military organization very closely. All the things that are supposed to be peculiar to the Japanese company—the organization song, exercising together in the morning, the ethic of loyalty and putting the organization before the family, vertical hierarchy, interorganizational rivalry, no right to refuse overtime, respect language with different forms of address for superiors and inferiors, and profound contempt for women—are all commonplace in, say, the U.S. Marines.

If this is true, it means that Japanese corporations can't integrate women without threatening their very foundations. So, even though a company may hire women, it is done in such a way that the basic organization structure is undisturbed. The key positions—the "combat units"—are reserved for men only. Women are hired as support for the men, both functional and psychological. For example, they may hire only young, pretty women or assign women the job of pouring tea or put pressure on women to retire before the age of thirty or try to get around the Equal Employment Opportunity Law with various tricks. It's not that men are necessarily personally against women or against extending equal treatment on the job; rather, I think these practices stem from the fundamental structure of these organizations. Therefore, if women do become fully accepted into these organizations and begin to work under equal conditions, the organizations themselves will have to become something totally different from what they are now, with a very different culture, organizational logic, and way of functioning.

Nakajima: As you know, with the passage of the Equal Employment Opportunity Law in 1985 companies have gradually begun to hire women for positions previously reserved for men. While this is certainly a desirable trend, what we also hear is that such women are being made to work just like their overworked male colleagues. A former student of mine became the first female graduate from a four-year university to be hired by a film production company. According to her mother, though, she was expected to work until two or three in the morning. This is just one example of the limitless sacrifices Japanese companies demand from their employees in the pursuit of profit. Many companies now want to hire women because they feel they can offer certain perspectives and sensibilities that men don't have, but they are not giving thought to establishing a more comfortable working environment or one that better fits the needs of women. They simply want to utilize the talents of these women for company profits.

Despite certain changes, on the whole the dominant positions in society are occupied overwhelmingly by men. In the case of the mass media, those who write for the newspapers and television programs the Japanese read and watch daily are predominantly male. A 1990 survey of 111 newspaper publishing companies belonging to the Japan Newspaper Association found that women constituted just 3.5 percent of all reporters. What happens is that, even though female applicants generally score high on exams, the men who are doing the hiring reject them on the basis of various preconceived notions and biases, such as that women will quit if assigned a transfer or that they're unable to cover the police beat. We need to ensure more equality in hiring by making the process more open, such as by making the results of employment examinations public. Otherwise, women will continue to be subject to unequal treatment.

Back when I was a college student, in the 1950s, I didn't have a single female professor. Even today the vast majority of university professors are male, as are politicians, among whom only 2 percent are female, and newspaper reporters. In short, all the positions of influence are occupied by men. Since women occupy one-half of the population, 50 percent of these positions should be occupied by women. Unless this happens, we will continue to have a situation whereby women are always deliberately kept out.

Lummis: You made the point earlier that women have little voice in the mass media, but in the field of *mini-komi* (mini communications) women actually dominate, don't they? Although it's not an industry and doesn't produce profit, the network of *mini-komi* is very big. There are hundreds of little homemade publications being distributed through the mail. The majority of those who write for and read these "newspapers"—newsletters, actually—are women. The writers are actually doing the work of newspaper reporters.

Kameda: It seems there's a division here, with men being in control of the mass media and women, though present to some degree in the national mass media, engaging in the production of *mini-komi* in local communities. While each has its role, one wonders what kind of impact the *mini-komi* has on the more powerful mass media.

Lummis: Probably very little. But I think the *mini-komi* may be fostering a critical outlook among its readers about what is presented in the mass media. Those who read both the *mini-komi* and the mass-circulation newspapers discover a gap between the views presented and become more skeptical.

Nakajima: Those engaged in activities related to community life or children's education are for the most part women, as are those who go to local sites to gather material and write pieces for the *mini-komi*. In other words, women are the ones taking part in activities that are community based, and therefore they have a realistic grasp of what is going on. Yet, in fact, it is men who yield power and authority, and they do so without such a firm grounding in reality.

Lummis: There's a paradox here. Men occupy high positions and exercise authority in society as politicians, business executives, newspaper editors, principals, and university presidents. But at the same time, being enmeshed in bureaucratic structures, they are also more strictly managed. A few years ago I interviewed a man who is active in the antinuclear power movement. I asked him why it was that so many women were participating in the movement, particularly housewives. His response was that the question was why so many men were *not* taking part. The reason is that the daily lives of most Japanese men are controlled by the organizations for which they work. Nearly all of their time is spent working (including working overtime), sleeping, or getting drunk [laughter], so that they have no time left over for taking part in such movements. On the other hand, most women have more time, and more freedom. Even among those women who are employed, I don't think they are as caught up in their work lives. It is not as though their sense of identity or self-worth is dependent upon being part of a particular company, so that they are less fearful of doing something that might endanger their position in their company. As a result, paradoxically, they are much freer than men.

Related to this point is the fact that one of the characteristics of the women's movement in Japan from its inception, in contrast to that in the United States and Europe, has been that, while it has sought equality for the sexes, equality has not been associated with becoming like men or adopting the same lifestyles as men. I think that Japanese women, after taking a good look at male society, decided that it wasn't something worth imitating but that, instead, there was something valuable within the culture of women which was lacking in the male culture.

Nakajima: That's a point, but the problem with this is that it also reinforces the tendency for women to stay within the framework of the traditional view that women ought to stay at home and take care of children, without at the same time seeking to bring about equality in the workplace and allowing for the possibility that women can be politicians or business executives or whatever while at the same time maintaining a firm foothold in their personal lives and valuing their children.

Lummis: What you say is, of course, true. I do think that within the feminist movement in Japan there are many who favor seeking equality in the workplace while at the same time valuing and preserving that which might be different from the dominant male culture. An example that comes to mind is that in the United States the push for equality in the workplace has led at least some women to seek equal status in the armed forces. Such a demand would be unthinkable among Japanese feminists, who virtually are, without exception, I think, pacifists. Also, among those seeking to bring about equality in the Japanese workplace, many reject the idea of making women conform to the working conditions of men, insisting that those conditions are inhumane. Instead, they want to establish a new and different type of work environment, in which the pace is more relaxed. Of course, in reality, once women are hired they usually have no choice but to conform to prevailing working conditions; nevertheless, the desire for a different way of doing things is there.

Nakajima: There's no doubt about the fact that many Japanese men work under intolerable, inhumane conditions. Since the late 1980s several cases of *karoshi*, or death from overwork, have been documented. A much larger number come close to dying, refusing or neglecting to seek medical help even when they are ill and, instead, feeling that they have to go into the office everyday. The idea of loyalty—almost blind loyalty—to the organization of which one is a member, whether it be one's company or, in the case of prewar Japanese society, the nation as symbolized by the emperor, seems to be a powerfully propelling psychological force for Japanese men.

Changes in Men's Attitudes toward Work and the Impact of the Women's Movement

Fujimura-Fanselow: What you have described is the image of the typical Japanese working man which has been dominant up until now, but these days we hear that Japanese men are changing. Even around me I see examples of men who have left their companies after twenty or more years and struck out on a new venture. They are the so-called *dassara*, or "escaped (runaway) salaried workers." Such a thing was unthinkable a generation back. I get the impression that some men at least are beginning to break loose from the traditional notion of loyalty to one company and lifetime employment.

Nakajima: It's difficult to put a finger on the exact number, but there seem to be quite a number of people who contemplate changing jobs or careers or who want to start their own businesses. Young people these days, first of all, don't want to work for a company that doesn't give Saturdays and Sundays off or which makes people work overtime. Even after they're hired, they don't have many qualms about leaving if they find that the job doesn't suit them. Bosses are being cautioned not to talk to employees in such a way as to make them want to pick up and leave.

Lummis: Within the last four or five years several new weekly magazines have come on the scene devoted to advertising openings not only for part-time and temporary jobs but also regular openings for people who want to change jobs. Among recent college as well as high school graduates you find many people changing jobs or working for a time then quitting and taking up another job on a temporary basis. These days it's possible to earn quite a bit just working part-time. The attraction of working within one company for one's entire lifetime definitely is waning. The theory of "Japan, Inc.," which equates Japanese society as a whole with its large corporate society, is dangerous. Those who work for very large and powerful corporations, such as Mitsubishi or Sony or Toyota, constitute only part of the total labor force. There are still people engaged in farming or who work for medium- and small-sized companies or in small shops and stores. In the local shopping districts many husbands and wives work side by side in their shops and live in homes behind the shops. The children grow up seeing their mothers and fathers at work from the time they're born. Whether or not this symbolizes gender equality is another matter. The point is that not all Japanese families conform to the stereotypical pattern of the father who spends nearly all of his waking hours at his office, hardly ever spending time at home with his wife and children.

Fujimura-Fanselow: Going back to the point about the changes in men's attitudes toward work, what do you think has brought this about?

Lummis: The women's movement as well as various other movements that women have been involved in, such as the anti–nuclear power and the ecology movements, have definitely had an important impact. But the situation itself has also changed. In the years immediately following the end of World War II no one needed to ask why the Japanese ought to work hard. With the major cities of Japan in ruins and the people reduced to poverty, there was a clear and obvious goal: the country had to be rebuilt. The economy developed a terrific momentum, which soon carried it from rebuilding to excess. The economy became overdeveloped; it began invading the Third World and causing major ecological problems. Since the 1960s criticisms have been heaped upon Japanese society both from within and from outside the country—that something is awry with its educational system, that its people are overworked, and that its industrial policies are destroying the environment, among others. Whether or not everyone regards these criticisms to be justified, the corporate image and ideology has been weakened.

Nakajima: Of course, you still have plenty of men who are strongly committed to their work and their companies, but at the same time others are beginning to have doubts about the kind of work they're doing and the lives they're leading. The fact that you're finding more men leaving their jobs is symptomatic of this growing skepticism.

Fujimura-Fanselow: A significant development that has made it increasingly possible for men to make career changes or to turn their backs on the corporate culture is the fact that more women have careers. In the past families relied totally on the income of the father, and, therefore, men had little choice but to remain with their companies. Having a dual income makes it possible for men to exercise greater choice in terms of their careers. In that respect the women's movement may have helped to liberate men from the tyranny of the workplace and the psychological burden of feeling that they alone have to work to make the monthly loan payments on the house or to pay for children's college education.

Need for Promoting Sexual Equality in the Home and School

Fujimura-Fanselow: When we think about how Japanese men are changing or might change in the future, we, I think, need to consider the issue of the socialization of boys within the home and in the school.

Nakajima: Kodo suru onnatachi no kai (Women's Action Group), of which I am a member, has appealed to the Ministry of Education to allocate more funds—which at present are minimal—toward the promotion of gender equality in education. There are various private groups engaged in this effort, but it's vital at this point that such efforts be carried forth systematically within public schools. My view is that on the whole the level of consciousness among both men and women about the need for such an education is very low. The way it stands now, unless there happen to be enlightened teachers within a school who endeavor to promote mutual respect between the sexes, sexist attitudes continue to get reinforced in the educational process. I personally have been involved for the past eighteen years in the movement to make the study of domestic science (or home economics) mandatory for both boys and girls in junior and senior high schools. This finally became a reality starting in April 1994.

The aim behind having both female and male students study domestic science is to teach young people to value daily life. But then we run up against the fact that the overriding concern or value characterizing Japanese education today is competition—competition to get into the top high schools and top universities. Teachers are rewarded for their success in getting as many students as possible into the top schools at the next level. Given such a situation, schools see little merit in having boys study something like domestic science. Many of the mothers also would rather have their children, especially boys, spend their time and energy on scoring well on exams than on helping out with household tasks at home. And, of course, in the society as a whole the dominant male image is still that of those who place careers above all else in their lives. Never mind the fact that it's these very men who are regarded as nuisances by their wives once they retire, since they're totally incapable of doing anything for themselves!

Kameda: Speaking about the role of education, I teach at a women's junior college, which, like most colleges, has mostly male teachers. The expectations these male professors have of female students, as opposed to male students, are, I think, quite different. What is it like at the university where you teach?

Lummis: My institution, Tsuda College, is rather unusual in this respect. Just a few years back we celebrated the ninetieth anniversary of its founding in 1900 by Tsuda Umeko. Tsuda was not particularly a feminist, but she did feel strongly about the need for educating women, and she founded the college in order to train women to become teachers of English and thereby have a means of livelihood. The faculty of the Department of English Literature still consists in large part of women who themselves are graduates of Tsuda College. The Department of International Relations, where I am, has a more male faculty, but still about one-third are women.

As in the United States and other countries, there has been considerable argument, especially in recent years, about the desirability of women's colleges. Some say it's discriminatory to keep men out, others that it's overprotective or that it serves to perpetuate inequality. In an ideal society there might not be a need for an exclusively female college, but in today's Japanese society women's universities serve a valuable function. Many of my students, especially those who have gone to coed schools before entering Tsuda, tell me they've felt relieved by the absence of men at the college. In classes and seminars they can express what they really think without worrying about what males might think. In a society characterized by gender inequality in which men hold power, it's unavoidable that women tend to be concerned about the opinions or reactions of the males around them. They also tend to worry about how they look when men are around.

Another advantage of a women's college for women is that they can't sit back and depend on male students to carry on discussions, for example, in a seminar. At Tsuda it's a matter of course for the female students to take responsibility for everything and to work hard. That way they gain considerable self-confidence.

There might be a certain degree of bias on the part of some individual faculty members at women's colleges, but at least within the student culture there is, of course, no sex discrimination. What happens is that our students become so used to living in a bias-free environment that, when they graduate and get a job, they often suffer a tremendous culture shock. In the long run it's a good experience for them; little by little they can serve as agents for bringing about change in society. Not only Tsuda but other women's colleges as well perform the function of bringing pressure on society for change.

Nakajima: In my case I attended coed schools all the way through college, but that experience had the opposite effect of making me realize that it's ridiculous to discriminate against females, since I saw with my own eyes that boys didn't necessarily perform better than girls in all subjects.

Something that's related to what you just said is that very often, when men attend various local community meetings, they tend to monopolize the floor. They're not used to taking part in flexible, grassroots type activities and tend, instead, to have rigid minds.

Another problem is that there are women—not all women but still some—who are readily swayed by what men have to say, even if it makes little sense. There's a tendency on the part of some women to place greater weight on what men say, simply because it's coming from men. Of course, I still think it's important that women and men work out a way of working together for common causes. But we need to work toward creating an environment in which women are able to clearly state what's on their minds in the presence of men. At present, many housewives are so used to putting the head of the family at the center and deferring to him that they automatically nod their heads when a man speaks up at a local community gathering.

Kameda: You hear about retired men becoming involved in community activities and trying to take charge, as though they were still at their companies.

Nakajima: Yes, they like to advertise the fact that they used to be a section chief or department head, and, even when the women try to tell them that ranks and titles are irrelevant, these men try to assert their status. You also hear complaints that, in various gatherings of senior citizens, these retired men don't do their part in serving tea, for example. They're apt to think that the status they've enjoyed within their family or company can be transferred to the community. In this respect they need to be reeducated.

The Helpless Husband Syndrome/Absent Father Syndrome

Kameda: You made an interesting comment about the fact that so many Japanese men find themselves totally helpless in the home after they retire. We hear quite a bit about how these men can't even make a cup of tea for themselves and so become a burden and a nuisance to their wives, and we hear about women divorcing their husbands after they retire from work. To what extent do Japanese men perform various household chores?

Nakajima: Japanese men, in fact, spend very little time performing household activities. In a recent survey of three hundred married women with children living within a 30-kilometer radius of Tokyo, only 8 percent of the respondents said that their husbands performed household chores on a regular, daily basis. As many as 15 percent said their husbands never did anything around the house. The most common reasons cited were that the husbands were too busy with their work and too tired (56 percent), they regarded housework as a nuisance (49 percent), they simply didn't like to do housework (33 percent), and they thought housework was "women's work" (31 percent). The kind of chores they do are mostly limited to doing repairs and "Sunday carpentry," shopping, washing the car, and taking the garbage out.

Fujimura-Fanselow: But aren't there some women who regard the home as their domain and derive their sense of worth and status from single-handedly doing everything for their families and therefore don't want their husbands to "interfere"?

Nakajima: That's true; their attitude is, "Don't take my job away!"

Fujimura-Fanselow: Often, when I bring up the issue of sharing housekeeping chores, women say to me: "The reason you can ask your husband to do things around the house is because you have your own job. In the case of housewives like us, who are being supported by our husbands, we at least have to do all the housework; otherwise, we wouldn't be of any value." I think that this sense of "being supported," on the one hand, and "being the provider of support," on the other, definitely functions to sustain inequality within many Japanese marriages.

Nakajima: I've come across many such women in various gatherings of housewives. What happens is that when one day they decide they want to do something on their own—take on a job or become involved in some community activity—they realize that the habit, or pattern, they've gotten into of "doing for" their husbands (and children) has had the negative consequence of making them totally dependent on their wives (and mothers) and of making them feel that women are supposed to do everything around the house. Thus, for example, when I try to get housewives to come out on a Saturday or Sunday to take part in an election campaign or some other project, many of them say they can't because their husbands are home and need to be looked after.

Fujimura-Fanselow: You would think their husbands were helpless babies rather than grown men!

Nakajima: Exactly. The problem is that both parties lack independence and autonomy: women lack financial independence, while men lack the ability to fend for themselves in terms of meeting their daily needs. They've gotten into a rigid pattern that is very difficult to break. Imagine what would happen if one or the other should get sick or die.

Lummis: From the standpoint of a male, I think that a man who can't cook or clean or do the laundry or anything else is something to be pitied. A man who doesn't take part in the upbringing of his children and spend time with them leads a sad existence. I think the main reason many Japanese men don't want to perform chores around the house is not so much that they don't want to—I think it's natural to want to—but that they think it's somehow humiliating and beneath the dignity of a man to do such "women's work."

Fujimura-Fanselow: Doesn't this also have a lot to do with the fact that most Japanese fathers simply don't spend much time at home? If that's the case, how does this affect the socialization of children, especially boys?

Lummis: We have to remember that this absent father phenomenon is not a "tradition" at all. Prior to industrialization most of the people were engaged in agriculture or had small family shops in which husbands and wives worked side by side. Fathers had much more daily contact with their children compared to today.

Nakajima: In contrast, many fathers today have little daily contact with their children. It's only when a big decision has to be made—for example, about which high school or university to apply to—that the fathers suddenly appear on the scene.

Lummis: At my university we have a child daycare center on campus which is used mostly by children of graduate students and staff and faculty. Having such a facility at work creates, I think, a healthy environment. Of course, it's easier on a college campus, where there's space and trees around, but in principle there's no reason we couldn't have daycare centers in a bank or other workplaces. Shopkeepers manage to conduct their work while watching their children, so it's not impossible.

Nakajima: When I go and speak at various gatherings of women, a popular topic of discussion is, "How do we go about getting men to change?" A common complaint among women is that, when they try to speak to their husbands about various issues pertaining to changing gender roles, their husbands don't listen to them.

Fujimura-Fanselow: According to what Doug (Lummis) mentioned earlier, male university students seem to show support for the idea of equality between the sexes. At the same time, we hear that young people today are becoming more conservative in their thinking. How do we reconcile these conflicting pictures?

Lummis: I think many men are deathly afraid of being labeled "unmanly" or "sissy" by other men. I've had Japanese men, including some involved in the feminist movement, tell me this. Perhaps it's a fear of coming somehow under the control of women, a fear of again becoming a child under the control of a mother.

Nakajima: Until now men have been put one step higher simply by virtue of the fact that they're men. Parents have spoiled sons, given them special treatment, and pinned high hopes on their future careers. Because they've been propped up all along, many have doubts about their actual strength and ability.

Lummis: Yes, it's a fear of what might happen if the prop is removed. On a one-to-one basis a wife may well turn out to be much stronger than the husband.

The Future

Fujimura-Fanselow: What changes can we expect of Japanese men in the future, in terms of their role in the family and in the workplace and their role in relationship to women? My own view is that at the present time many Japanese still have conflicting attitudes about what ought to be the respective role of men and women or what constitutes the ideal husband or father. Many men themselves seem unsure about what's expected of them.

On the one hand, there's a growing pressure on men to stop putting their work above all else and to put more time and effort into cultivating their relationships with their wives and children and with their local communities. In a national poll of roughly 2,400 registered voters conducted in December 1991 by the *Asahi shimbun* newspaper, the percentage of respondents who answered yes to the question "Do you find men who place primary importance on their work attractive?" was 39 percent, in contrast to 56 percent who responded no. Among those in their twenties and thirties more than 70 percent said no ("Kawariyuku 'otoko'" 1992, 11).

At the same time, however, men seem to continue to be shouldered with the traditional social expectation that they have the primary responsibility for supporting their families financially as "the man of the house." Thus, in the same survey 55 percent of the respondents expressed agreement with the traditional notion of gender roles that "men should go out and work and women should stay home and care for the children"—as compared to 72 percent in a similar poll taken in 1980 ('Shigoto hitosuji'" 1992, 10). Moreover, fewer than 20 percent of both female and male respondents were in favor of having men take child care leave for awhile in order to share the responsibility of child care. Another interesting finding was that 72 percent of the female respondents and 63 percent of the male respondents agreed with the view that "the father is the central 'pillar' of the family" ("Kawariyuku 'otoko'" 1992, 11).

Such conflicting expectations reflect family arrangements in which men are the primary breadwinners. Of course, today more than half of all married women work outside the home, so that the full-time housewife is becoming more and more of a rarity, but the majority work part-time for relatively little pay. As Doug pointed out earlier, many or even most Japanese women show little eagerness to emulate the lifestyle of the typical Japanese working man. I think that many middle-class women are happy not to have to be tied to a full-time job and, instead, to be able to participate in leisure or various local community activities. But, of course, this attitude stems in large part from the fact that it is in fact very difficult for a woman in her late thirties or forties who has been staying home taking care of children to obtain a meaningful, full-time job that pays well. Perhaps in another generation or so, as more women begin to pursue full-time careers and acquire financial independence, we will begin to see more substantive changes in terms of gender role expectations as well as behaviors. Needless to say, at the same time, considerable changes will have to be brought about in the workplace so that women and men can comfortably combine dual careers with families.

Lummis: I think the signs are hopeful. Women are on the move in this country. It's not just a question of predicting change for the future; the process of change is already underway now, irreversibly. The fascinating question is, as women increasingly influence the corporation, what effect will that have on corporate ideology and culture? What effect will it have on the work ethic, the business ethic? Will the corporation still maintain its ideology of productivity, efficiency, rationalization, maximum exploitation of man and nature? Or, as the corporate society moves from a disfigured to a more natural form, will it also move away from these disfigured notions toward a healthier, more balanced way of thinking? To me this is one of the big questions for the twenty-first century.

NOTES

1. According to a survey by the Ministry of Labor, 30 percent of university graduates who entered employment in the spring of 1987 had left their jobs three years later (Kubota Izumi, "Dosuru shunto '92, chu: Nihonteki keiei, minaosu kiun" [The '92 annual spring wage bargaining round: what is to be done? part 2: time for reassessing Japanese-style management], *Asahi shimbun,* 18 February 1992, 3).

2. In a survey by the Japan Productivity Center of employees newly hired in 1991 by large corporations, just 15 percent indicated they "want to work until retirement," down nine percentage points compared to ten years ago (ibid).

REFERENCES

"Hatarakisugi kara nukedasutameni" (Escaping from overwork). 1991. *Asahi shimbun* (Asahi newspaper). 29 December, 2.

Ikujiren, ed. 1989. *Otoko to onna de "hambunko" ism* (Men and women sharing fifty-fifty). Tokyo: Gakuyo shobo.

Kawaguchi, Haruo. 1989. "Tanshin funin wa okotowari" (No thank you to posting away from the family). In *Otoko to onna de "hambunko" ism*, ed. Ikujiren. Tokyo: Gakuyo shobo.

"Kawariyuku 'otoko' no yakuwari" (The changing role of men). 1992. *Asahi shimbun* (Asahi newspaper), 1 January, 11.

Kubota, Izumi. 1992. "Dosuru shunto '92, chu: Nihonteki keiei, minaosu kiun" (The '92 annual spring wage bargaining round: what is to be done? part 2: time for reassessing Japanese-style management). *Asahi shimbun* (Asahi newspaper), 18 February, 3.

"'Shigoto hitosuji' ni hansei" (Reflecting on wholehearted commitment to work). 1992. *Asahi shimbun* (Asahi newspaper), 1 January, 10.

Tambara, Tsunenori. 1989. "Yonen to kyukagetsu no 'sotai'" (Four years and nine months of leaving work early). In *Otoko to onna de "hambunko" ism*, ed. Ikujiren. Tokyo: Gakuyo shobo.

Men on the Threshold of Change

❖ ❖ ❖

Masanori Yamaguchi

Translated by Kumiko Fujimura-Fanselow

On an evening in September 1991 I attended the opening session of a series of ten weekly lectures dramatically titled "A Course for Remodeling Men—1991: Men and Women Today," held at a women's center in Tokyo's Adachi ward. The course was initiated by several of the center's staff and based on the recognition that, since many of the so-called women's issues in Japan today have to do with men, those issues cannot be resolved unless Japanese men change their attitudes and way of life. The pamphlet advertising the course read: "Don't you find yourself imprisoned by the concept of 'masculinity'? Join us in seeking an alternative way of defining ourselves and living as men." Thirty-two men, ranging in age from nineteen to seventy-nine, responded to this invitation; the majority were corporate salaried workers, and their average age was forty-three. Here are some of the motivations they gave for coming to these lectures:

In ten more years I'll reach retirement age. What kind life will I lead after retirement? I want to leave the corporate world and discover my real self. (A forty-seven-year-old company employee)

The women we see around us are all active and full of life. On the other hand, the men, myself included, don't seem very happy. Through this course I want to discover my own direction for living. (A thirty-three-year-old civil service employee)

This series of lectures received widespread press coverage and created

247

quite a sensation. The lectures were published in a volume in 1993, which served as a springboard for similar courses organized by various local groups. Clearly, at least among some Japanese men, who have until now accepted without question the gender role definition that "men should go out and work and women should stay home" and been more or less contented with a society in which males enjoy superior status, are now beginning to waver and have doubts. These "quivers" are in the process of building up into a "movement" toward a new way of living among some Japanese men— granted, they are still a small minority at this point.

Stimulus for Change: Growing Revolt among Women

The conventional male response to the women's movement and the demands expressed by women for change up until now has been to suppress, ignore, and ridicule them and to dismiss them as a troublesome minority. The mass media, moreover, has served as a tool for this purpose. Since entering the decade of the 1990s, however, this kind of response has become increasingly untenable, and men themselves have begun to realize this. And the reason is that women's protest against the male-dominated society has spread to such an extent that it can no longer be ignored or dismissed as mere "whining" on the part of a "small group" of women.

The most pointed expression of this rising dissatisfaction by many "ordinary" women with the status quo is the growing phenomenon of the so-called retirement divorce, in which, simultaneous with the husband's retirement, wives in their fifties and sixties seek "retirement" from an unsatisfactory marriage. The following was written by a sixty-year-old woman in response to an invitation to readers of *Yomiuri shimbun* newspaper to send in contributions on the theme "A word from wives regarding husbands' retirement":

> For thirty-three years I have suffered alone with the burden of raising three children making ends meet. My husband has been occupied with his work and leisure activities and hasn't shown any concern when I or my son became ill. Retirement means only one thing to me: separation. He can go ahead and live the way he wants to from here on.

In this age, when the average life expectancy of Japanese women has risen to more than eighty-two years, more and more women are unwilling to remain in unhappy marriages with their retired husbands for the rest of their lives, twenty-four hours a day. According to the Welfare Ministry's data, the number of divorces in 1993 reached 189,000, the highest number in history. Couples married twenty or more years represented over 15 percent of the total figure; moreover, in the majority of these cases the divorces were initiated by the wife. The comparable figures were just 5 percent in 1970 and 8 percent in 1980. In other words, the rate of divorce among middle- and older-aged couples has tripled within the last twenty years. The sight of older men forced to accept divorce has become commonplace for Japanese men today.

Simultaneously, many young women are shying away from marriage. These women are disillusioned by the lives of married women around them, be it their own mothers who have led a life of self-renunciation, women exhausted from trying to juggle career and family with little help from their uncooperative husbands, or those who, having abandoned their careers and become full-time housewives, are no less dissatisfied. It is readily understandable that, seeing such models, more young women are choosing not to get married.

"Why," more women are asking themselves, "should I marry a man who not only doesn't help with housework and child care but can't even care for his own day-to-day needs? Why should I take on such a burden?" The expression "age of nonmarriage," which reflects this growing disillusionment with marriage on the part of women, is beginning to drive home to younger men the message that they cannot expect to act the way their fathers have until now if they hope to be accepted by today's young women.

Similarly, in the workplace, as women's presence has become more prominent in a variety of fields, it has become increasingly difficult to continue the kinds of discriminatory practices in pay, promotion, and so forth which have previously been accepted as a matter of course. Men who have been accustomed to regarding women not as equal colleagues in the workplace but, rather, as sex objects primarily, are being forced to change their perceptions. Thus, for example, women have begun to file lawsuits claiming sexual harassment in the workplace, and in some cases judges have ruled that sexual harassment is a violation of human rights and of women's right to work.

These manifestations of women's rebellion against existing practices in the family and in the workplace, together with various actions undertaken by feminists, have forced many Japanese men to question and examine anew their own lives.

Men Ask Themselves: What Are We Doing?

The emergence of self-questioning and doubt on the part of men is not only the result of external pressure from women. The growing expression of dissatisfaction on the part of women has resonated in the hearts of many men precisely because so many issues that need to be dealt with have been building up among men themselves. One such issue is that of *karoshi*, or "death resulting from overwork," which has become the focus of growing concern in society since the latter part of the 1980s. A well-known television commercial for a bottled drink that supposedly resuscitates energy contains this line: "Can you fight twenty-four hours?" Japanese businessmen have, in fact, survived in the corporate world by battling twenty-four hours a day. As Charles Douglas Lummis notes in the previous piece, for these "corporate warriors," putting in long hours of overtime has become the norm, while the home has become merely a place to sleep. Weekends and holidays are taken up with business trips and entertainment. Such a life leaves little time to spend with wives and children and little time for themselves. In extreme cases men in the prime of their lives have actually died as a result. Their pitiful example has made many men reexamine themselves and seek alternative life purposes apart from work.

Another increasingly pressing issue that has forced men to rethink the direction and purpose of their lives is that of how to live out the later stage of their lives, after retirement. The retirement age at many Japanese companies is sixty. Men who have known how to live only through their work are often baffled as they face twenty more years ahead of them. Many of them have not cultivated any hobbies apart from their work, nor have they established close friendships apart from those with colleagues at work. Not knowing what to do with their time, they tag along after their wives wherever they go and end up getting labeled *nureochiba* (wet fallen leaves) which cling to the ground and can't be swept away or else hang around the house all day and become a nuisance, earning such derogatory nicknames as *sodaigomi* (large-size refuse) and *sangyo haikibutsu* (industrial waste). In the worst cases their fate is "retirement divorce."

More and more men have come to learn about these cases through television dramas or reports in newspapers and magazines or else from actual examples in their midst, and they have begun to realize the need to think anew about how they should live, what the role of work should be in their lives, and how they should interact with their families.

In the summer of 1992 and again in the summer of 1993 I wrote a series of thirteen articles on retirement. Among those I interviewed for the series were several men in their fifties and sixties who had come to have strong doubts about their way of life thus far and were now groping for a different manner of living which would involve, to an important degree, acknowledging the needs of their wives, which they had tended to ignore in the past. Such a task would undoubtedly be a difficult and painful one, requiring a radical departure from current male-centered values; but these men were determined to undertake the challenge.

Men Who Have Started to Change

I have been interested in observing this phenomenon, both as a newspaper reporter and as a Japanese male who has come to share an aspiration to seek a way of life unencumbered by traditional notions of "masculinity" and "femininity" and gender roles. Let me present a few examples illustrative of this growing phenomenon.

Men Seeking a Greater Role in the Home

A group calling itself Men Concerned about Child Care was started a few years ago. Its members, numbering thirty or so, are made up of businessmen, civil service employees, teachers, and others in their twenties, thirties, and forties residing in the Tokyo area. They meet monthly to discuss ways for men to find a new meaning in life through taking on a greater role in activities related to the home and child care. In addition, they have an overnight "training camp" once a year and sponsor open lectures and symposia. The men who belong to this group take an active role in the home on an equal basis with their wives, and most appear to enjoy doing household chores and caring for children. Spending time with family and friends and doing what they personally enjoy is more important to them than work-related activities. Thus, they rarely put in overtime at work and do not hesitate to take vacations. As a result, they are apt to be viewed as deviants by many, but these men accept it.

One very unique means employed by the members of this group to convey their points of view at various gatherings is through the presentation of short, twenty- to sixty-minute skits that they themselves have written. The dominant theme generally revolves around men who, through encountering family problems and various other conflicts in their lives, begin to question their work-centered lives and to embark on new paths. Though the issues dealt with are serious, they are presented in a lighthearted way, with songs and laughter, and these skits are so popular that the group has gotten more than ten requests every year to perform them. These requests come from other men's groups, and the performances serve as a catalyst to widen the network of similar-minded men.

Another Tokyo-based group, called the Liaison Group for Granting Time for Child Care to Men and Women, includes both women and men. Like the previous group, this group rejects the concept of a gender-based division of labor, and it too holds symposia and meetings aimed at promoting changes in men's consciousness. The group undertakes joint activities with a similar group based in the Osaka region. It has gained media attention as a result of the actions taken by its members to bring about changes in working conditions so as to enable workers to have more time to devote to child care. Under the slogan "Four Hours of Work for Both Men and Women," the members conducted a "Time for Child Care Strike" for a couple of hours every day for four years. The group has also given active support to those who have brought lawsuits against employers for forcing them to accept job transfers that would result in their having to live apart from their families. Similarly, it is campaigning to revise the Child Care Leave Law, which went into effect in 1992, so that employees will be paid during the time they are on child care leave, in order to make it easier for men to take advantage of the system.

Growing Participation in Community-Based Activities

In some communities fathers have come together and organized activities for the local children. One such group, based in Kawasaki City, adjacent to Tokyo, was started by some fathers who had taken part in a city-sponsored course for fathers. Using the facilities of the civic center and public squares, they teach the children traditional games, make toys, cook together, put on plays, among other activities, and once a year they have an overnight excursion for fathers and children. As one businessman in his fifties commented:

> In the past I was interested only in my work. I started attending the course for fathers unwillingly and only because my wife insisted I go. But after listening to the lecturer and talking with the other participants, I came to value the relationships I formed with the people in my community, which are quite different from the kinds of relationship you have at work, and to enjoy being with the children.

Another interesting group was established in 1991 by the husbands of some of the women belonging to the Kanagawa branch of the consumer cooperative Seikatsu Club Seikyo. They issued the following invitation to the cooperative's male members:

> We've regarded with some envy our wives who seem to lead such full lives through their various activities and undertakings. The lives of most men, on the other hand, consist of days spent in a concrete jungle, coming home late at night, tired out, and just going to sleep. After we retire, there's no place where we can find peace of mind: we're treated as a nuisance at home, and we have no friends in the community. In order for each of us to live our one life fully, we must build a place for ourselves now.

More than one hundred men responded to this invitation, and the club now meets regularly for discussions, provides counseling for middle-aged men, and sponsors recreational activities. In the future it hopes to establish a workers' cooperative in which retired men can make use of the skills and knowledge they have acquired through their work in some type of undertaking which will benefit their communities and also provide some income for its members.

Reexamining Male Sexuality

Issues surrounding male sexuality, as exemplified by rape and prostitution, have also become a subject of debate among some men. The Association of Men Opposed to Prostitution in Asia, composed of about fifty men in the Tokyo area, has campaigned against prostitution tours by Japanese to Asian countries, and the group has also become active in the effort to make the Japanese government acknowledge responsibility for the military having forced Asian women to become "comfort women" for Japanese soldiers during World War II and to make an apology and pay compensation to them. The group was started by some men who met at a lecture given in 1988 by Filipina women denouncing prostitution tours to various Asian countries by Japanese men. The realization that prostitution is an issue that concerns men, and that it cannot be resolved unless men themselves become involved, led the men to form this group.

The group's representative, Taniguchi Kazunori, recalls: "Though I was concerned about pornography and the so-called entertainment industry, I felt I couldn't talk about these issues seriously with my male colleagues at work. But as I began to attend various gatherings sponsored by women's groups, I got to meet other men who shared my concerns." At about the time the group was started, Taniguchi quit his job with a publishing company and became a free-lance writer. From 1990 to 1991 he traveled to many parts of the world investigating Japanese men's participation in the prostitution industry, and he published a book on the subject in 1993. The group has put together slides and pamphlets and held symposiums and lectures on the status and background of prostitution in Asia. Its members claim that at the root of prostitution tours to Asia is the outrage committed by the Japanese military against Asian women during the World War II and the system of "comfort women" established to meet the sexual needs of Japanese soldiers. What their father's generation, wearing uniforms and wielding their guns, did to those women, their generation is doing, with the very same attitudes, only this time, they are wearing business suits and wielding their economic power."

Conclusion

The men I have introduced here still represent a small minority within Japanese society. They tend to be viewed by their colleagues at work as oddities, "dropouts" from the competition for success, or as traitors to the male sex who have gone over to the enemy camp. Nevertheless, they are beginning to have some impact on other men. The groups mentioned here have steadily increased their membership. Moreover, their activities are receiving increased coverage by the mass media, in large measure due to the efforts of the growing network of women who have become active in the mass media industry, in a variety of capacities, over the last ten years. Rising awareness of the existence of men who sympathize with many of the causes that women are advocating makes it more difficult for people to ignore or dismiss those claims. At the same time, the activities of these men serve as support and encouragement to the women's groups.

The impetus for these men to question and reexamine the present-day society in which men dominate has come from the women around them. Whether they had wives or not, when they turned their ears to the criticisms voiced by women, they felt their whole way of life was being questioned. And, when they turned their attention to themselves, they realized their lives were restricted and hampered by the values and norms associated with the dominant concept of masculinity prevalent in society and that, to discover and reclaim their own sense of self, it was necessary to abandon this concept of masculinity and to subject to examination society as a whole. Once they went through this process they could understand how women have had to struggle to break loose of the spell of "femininity" and to struggle against a male-dominated society that seeks to prevent them from breaking loose.

A society in which each individual can live in a way that allows one to be true to oneself values equally the human rights of all citizens. Men who have begun to move in this direction will be an important source for change in Japanese society in the future, and I hope to continue to be a part of this process.

Pornographic Culture and
Sexual Violence

❖ ❖ ❖

Kuniko Funabashi

Historically and culturally, the visual media have exercised an enormous effect in terms of creating sexual awareness and behavior. Images presented in advertisements, magazines, television, and video programs often have a binding impact on our perceptions, if unconsciously. A false mystique about sex and notions of femininity and masculinity are often produced by the media and then reproduced on a massive scale.

Ninety-nine percent of media programs are produced by men. Pornographic culture is but a symbol of male ideology reproduced on a vast scale by the visual media. We are overwhelmed in our daily lives by images and descriptions that treat women as sex objects. Female bodies separated from the character and personality of their owners flood the market. This generally degrading and discriminatory reference to woman and denial of her dignity as a person with an individual character is how I define pornography. Pornography may be defined, therefore, as the falsely perceived and abusive images of woman created by men.

Pornography does not stop at presenting familiar erroneous images of women, such as that "women are sexually passive," "women are men's possession," or "women want to be raped." It violates the female body by abusing her parts, especially the breasts and genitals. Pornography destroys her dignity as a human being and does injury to her identity and self-respect; it represents violence committed against her. Pornography, rape, sexual harassment, and woman beating are, without exception, violation of the female body based on the discriminatory view of woman as a mere sexual object.

This violence against the female is increasing worldwide in every country and on every continent.

As a result of the gaps that exist among national economies, prostitution—a trade offering the human body as a commodity of exchange—is also increasing. Economic disadvantages within a given nation can force women to take to prostitution as a job of last resort. The burgeoning sex industry is a product of commercialism, which exploits the female sex for profit. The growing objectification and commercialization of women's bodies cannot be viewed separately from the growing rate of violence and sexual crimes against women. According to Japan's National Police Agency, there is an average of 1.4 females murdered and 1.8 females raped daily in this country (Keisatsucho 1988).

I propose in this essay to discuss how pornographic culture is expressed in contemporary Japanese society through various types of mass-produced visual media, especially *manga*, or comic magazines, advertisements, and adult videos. I will also examine the impact of pornography on Japanese people's consciousness and attitudes toward women and the relationship between pornography and the growing incidence of sexual violence against women in Japan. Finally, I will introduce some of the concrete actions women's groups in Japan have taken in recent years to protest the present situation and to bring about change.

Sexual Expressions Seen in Comic Magazines

Manga, sometimes translated as comic books or magazines, are produced in enormous quantities at great speed. Dozens of them are published on a weekly or monthly basis. The Japanese *manga* is actually quite different from Western comic books.

The history of present-day pornographic *manga* can be traced back to the Edo period (seventeenth to nineteenth centuries), when a growing market for pornographic prints and advances in the technology of the printing press contributed to the development of this new genre for popular consumption. In the post–World War II period publishers have continued to expand their production of *manga*, targeting their products to specific audiences of readers based on sex, age, and so forth. Today, *manga* sales provide the greatest source of income for many publishers.

Manga bear great influence on the way teenagers live and the formation of their characters. Readers are often controlled and swayed by the whim of writers to such an extent that comics work to formulate rather than reflect the value judgments of the public. That the popular weekly youth comic magazine *Shukan shonen jump* enjoys a circulation of 4.85 million is evidence of its habitual and daily consumption by its youthful readership. Comics target not so much a particular "fan type" as a general reading public. Broadly speaking, it could be said that the comic culture is representative of the entire youth culture. How, then, do these comics, which young readers regard as a source of information about sexuality, portray sex?

Characteristic Features of Male Comics

Conquest, personal achievement, fighting, and sexual sadism are favorite themes in male comic magazines. The hero in this world of sex and violence is a male rather than a human person. To quote from one magazine: "When one begins with nothing, violence is all one has to rule with. In 1999, when the world is engulfed in a nuclear flame, it is the strong that will dominate the weak." "Be strong!" and "Be tough men!" are the themes forced on young minds. Just as modern times saw in nature an object for conquest by scientific civilization, modern rationalism regards woman as a part of nature and as the same object of conquest *(Hokuto no Ken)*.

Woman has been reduced to a sexual object, to be ogled and to be raped. Historically, it was the comic series "Harenchi gakuen" (Shameless school) in the weekly *Shukan shonen jump* published in 1968 which first treated the female body as purely an object. Sexual themes such as "touching the body" and "peeking under the skirt," which had been considered strictly taboo, were now exposed to broad daylight. This development in Japan coincided with the liberation of sex worldwide, and particularly with that in Western Christian societies, which was triggered by the student revolts in the late 1960s. The sexual revolution witnessed during the decade of the 1970s encouraged violence and exploitation of the female sex by increasing the availability of sexually stimulating information for men rather than promoting better communication between mutually respecting partners.

Today magazines for men of a type that in the 1970s were available only in special adult shops are sold in public bookstores or even in convenience stores. One million copies a month of these magazines are being sold today, expressing ever loudly the points of view of male ideology: "How to enjoy eating a girl"; "Sex is a man raping a girl. The wilder the rape, the better the sex." Such are the kinds of messages to be found on page after page of these magazines.

Since 1985 a new genre of sexually oriented literature has emerged called "Lolita eros." This style of comic magazines emphasizes sex with young girls and often features on its covers a cute young teenage girl in swimwear. From cover to cover the "Lolita" magazines abound in straightforward sex, exhibiting young girls in various positions and postures intended for visual rape. There is hardly any element of storytelling but, instead, portrayals of individual and gang rape, featuring violence and maltreatment of young girls. Furthermore, girls who have been raped are described as getting home not only unperturbed by their experience but even grateful for the ecstasy accorded them by their rapist. The writers completely ignore the fact that numerous girls who have actually been raped have suffered traumatic consequences for the rest of their lives. There are, moreover, numerous sadistic scenes in which girls are bound and beaten without any dialogue except suggestive onomatopoeic exclamations. And among the published letters to the editors, readers from fifteen to twenty-three years of age (mostly maie) commonly brag about their extensive sexual experiences and advertise with reference to their peculiar fetishes or sex partners.

The following features are characteristic of sexual descriptions contained in male-oriented comics:

1. Male writers describe the woman or girl's body as a commodity, as if it were a toy. Pictures of enlarged breasts and genitals are presented with no more respect than if they were pieces of meat.

2. Male and female roles are stereotyped, with the former as the rapist and voyeur and the latter the raped and the exhibit.

3. The female is portrayed as, by nature, a masochist. She is stimulated by being raped and awakened to her desires and becomes a "sex maniac." Her sexual passivity is emphasized.

4. The so-called "Lolita eros" magazines present the female body as the man's possession and young girls in particular as being at his mercy.

5. Sexual intercourse is repeatedly presented without apology as penetration and ejaculation. Sex for the man is portrayed as an invasion of the female body and the vagina as an object of conquest. There is no depiction of mutuality.

6. There is no reference to pregnancy or abortion as a result of sex nor to contraceptives. The concentration is only on techniques of violation.

Characteristics of Female-Oriented Comics

In contrast to the male-oriented comics, comics directed at a readership of girls and women present an altogether different world. There is a greater variety of topics about "life" and "sex," the latter being presented with a matter-of-fact touch. There is less emphasis on virginity today, and in its place is a new morality condoning sex if there is love between the partners. While the traditional idea of marriage as a consummation of love and sex is being eroded, there is still a strong commitment to marriage as an ideal way of life. Women are further portrayed as willing to sacrifice themselves for the sake of their loving partners. Heroines see themselves as objects of man's desire and at times expect to be loved for their provocative attitudes.

The titles demonstrate how much sex has become part of everyday life. These comics play on young women's fantasies and fears about sex. The girls in these stories begin sexual activity out of curiosity and do not exhibit any awareness about degrading their sexuality. Questions about relationships with others (mostly men) are a common theme, but the treatment is largely concerned with sex rather than the larger issues of life. Heroines are not allowed to choose their lives or sexual partners but are expected simply to be passive in these matters.

Adult Videos

Comics obstinately portray stereotyped images of femininity and masculinity which many readers come to accept. Serialized stories in weekly comics are published as monographs, produced as television programs, and end up eventually on shelves of video rental shops. The viewer can now watch the same rape scene over and over again.

Looking very briefly at the fast-growing world of adult videos, we find that this is as much a world of sex and violence as are "Lolita" erotica and comics for men. Porno videos represent a 100 billion yen market annually. Porno magazines of the 1970s are now losing ground against comics and videos for men in the 1980s and 1990s.

Pornographic videos are increasingly invading Japanese homes, 70 percent of which are equipped with video players. These videos, usually produced in two days, are marketed at a rate of two hundred fifty new products each month. Production costs are particularly low if there is no real plot or characterization, and a profit of fifteen million yen can be expected from an investment of three to four million yen. These films are produced because they sell. The number of video rental shops has also increased, and half of their sales are from adult porno video strips. Here, too, the female sex is treated as a commodity, with violence against women packaged for commercial profit.

Violence against Women as Seen in Advertising

Unlike comics or videos, advertisements posted in stations and trains are more public. They are violent because they force their message even on reluctant and disinterested passengers.

A survey conducted in 1988 and 1989 by the Ad Watching Project, a committee established by the Women's Studies Association of Japan, found that a common device used by advertisers was to picture women in swimwear or in the nude without any relation to the product advertised. Some portrayed bed scenes with women posing as though waiting for sex, obviously intended for visual rape.

One advertisement displayed in a large department store chain depicts a woman apparently kidnapped and dragged to a beach. Stripped to the waist and defenseless, but with her breasts hidden, she has her eyes closed and lips parted. Above her sand-covered face is a depiction of a hole in the ground. The headline is difficult to translate, but it refers to "pulling out" (her intellect) and pursuing sex and is obviously intended to provoke sexual association with the hole. One is led to recall director Abe Kobo's film *The Woman in the Dunes*, which depicts a woman with a womb but no face. All-Nippon Airways uses a similar concept. A young woman in a transparent party dress is lying on a bed, along with the words: "The morning that turns a girl into a woman."

Advertising has been harnessed by men for male consumption, abusing the female body to transmit sexual messages. A common message running through these advertisements is to abuse women as sexual objects so as to provoke sexual desires in the (mostly male) viewer. The passive poses adopted by the women are intended for visual rape. The use of the female body has been justified by the argument: "It is attractive because it is beautiful. Using bodies does not make for discrimination." Yet these are stereotyped images of women created by men which disregard the personality of the owner of the body. Women are deceived by this stereotyped flattery and manipulated as objects of appreciation.

Half of the advertisements in women's magazines are concerned with dieting and plastic surgery, suggesting that standards of beauty, which by nature are ambiguous, are being one-sidedly defined by the male-dominated culture. The use of the naked female body in advertising humiliates and discriminates against women. Given the inequality of male-female relations in contemporary society, the dictation of uniform standards of beauty results in the enslavement of every woman. If women feel obliged to diet and alter their faces and bodies because they are so conscious of men's gaze, it is tantamount to a violation of their bodies and thus is an act of sexual violence in itself.

Protest by Women against Pornographic Ads

While it is important to look at the great extent to which pornographic culture pervades contemporary Japan, it is also important to stress that women in Japan have been actively protesting the production of such images and are trying to change the situation. While, on the one hand, along with the privatization of the railways, stereotypical images of women have come to be seen everywhere, as if every corner of space has been cut up and sold as a commodity to then be filled with ads that use women's bodies freely, on the other hand, since 1985 women have become more vocal in their protest against images that are offensive and which they don't want to see but are forced to look at constantly.

Action was first taken by the Women's Action Group, which began a protest against sports newspapers in 1987, using the slogan "Rush Hour Is Porno Hour," referring to the fact that on crowded trains during rush hours male commuters often read sports newspapers, which contain explicitly pornographic images. At the spring meeting of the Women's Studies Association in 1988 we began the project of closely analyzing the images of women depicted in ads, looking at the power relations implied between the presumed male viewer and the women made the objects of his gaze. One outcome of this was the initiation of an "ad watching team": members of the group began both to watch for particularly offensive ads and to make organized protests against them. We printed large stickers with the clear message, "This Is Discrimination against Women." This enabled individual women to take guerilla-like action by giving expression to their feelings that certain ads were offensive. Through such actions women who had until then been passive consumers were able to assert their rights as active subjects.

In 1991 the Japanese Foundation for AIDS Prevention produced a set of posters to be displayed at train stations and city halls for World AIDS Awareness Day. These posters are interesting in terms of what they reveal about the prevailing attitudes concerning sexuality. One of these posters shows a businessman hiding his face with a Japanese passport, and the ad copy reads (both in Japanese and English): "Have a nice trip! But be careful of AIDS." Another poster features a naked woman enveloped in an enormous condom, with the caption, "Thin, but strong enough for [against] AIDS."

These posters clearly show that Japan's prostitution culture lives on in the attitudes and actions of Japanese men. It is these attitudes precisely which women's groups are fighting against. Through our efforts these posters were withdrawn, and we are working on producing our own versions.

Pornography and Sexual Violence

The theme of pornography in comics, videos, and advertising is the use of the nude or partly nude female body or disassociated parts of female bodies. Depictions of women bound, beaten, and raped are crude and highly suggestive. Apologists for pornography emphasize that it is not reality but, rather, fantasy, not fact but fiction. Men take to pornography to have their sexual fantasies provoked, and women respond by offering their bodies. As soon as her body is separated from her mind, a woman is "killed" by men's violence. What remains is mere flesh. Men refuse to accept this fact and insist that pornography is an illusion and not sexual crime.

The death of a john during a struggle with a prostitute in a hotel room in the Ikebukuro section of Tokyo in 1987, after he filmed her with his video camera, exemplifies the link between pornography and sexual crimes, the symbiosis of prostitution and pornography, and the difficulty of drawing a clear line between fiction and fact. While verbally abusing and physically torturing the woman, the man had forced her to repeat after him like a parrot, "A woman's vagina is a man's public toilet." Fearing for her life, the woman tried to break loose. They fought, and, as a result, he died. The film and tape recording made by the dead man were proof enough of the unequal power between the prostitute and the man who paid for her, yet the woman was arrested on charges of murder. Although the charges were later reduced to "excessive defense," that she was prosecuted at all is a clear indication of society's insistence that all women fulfill the passive, objectified role presented in pornography and advertising.

This incident is notable for several recurring characteristics: one, in most instances of prostitution there is coercion; two, pornography, claimed to be harmless fantasy, is based on the negation of women's existence as human beings; three, the mass media that report such incidents are owned by men. Had the incident resulted in the death of the prostitute, the pornographic film and tape would have been enjoyed and judged by men to have been a fabrication, and the newspapers would simply have reported that a woman had been found dead in a hotel room.

In a case that took place in 1989 some male high school students kept a teenaged girl prisoner for two months, repeatedly raping and torturing her. They eventually murdered her and hid her body in concrete. This case highlights the dangerous impact of the violence depicted in comics and adult video films. After seeing sexual violence in films, these boys went on to experience the real thing. It was a case of fiction becoming fact. Similarly, a man accused of a series of murders of young girls in 1990 reportedly found it hard to distinguish between illusion and reality. Many such cases prove the danger of violence in the media turning into reality. Men who fail to achieve the relations they want with real women satisfy themselves with comics and films that fantasize their sexual illusions.

"Sex is escalating in radical theater as well as in the hardcore sex videos industry. Today's fans are sophisticated, and half-hearted entertainment is not appreciated. The difference between what sells and what doesn't is the degree of hard core stimulation" (*Otoko no yuhogai*, September 1987). Sex is depicted as animal intercourse and without any consideration for living people. In every case the theme is of the domination of women by powerful men. Young people are surrounded from birth by mass media overflowing with pornography, which is a symbol of a male-dominated ideology.

Toward Building a New Self-Image

A very positive development in recent years is that Japanese women, like women elsewhere throughout the world, are beginning to say no to sexual violence and to all forms of violation of their being and their bodies. They are demanding their rights as a group and at the same time are learning to live independent lives by refusing to accept images that treat women as commodities. They are finding the courage to break the vicious cycle of allowing themselves to be victimized, invaded, and remodeled under the convenient guise of love while their self-respect and intelligence are destroyed.

The number of women's shelters operated by women for those escaping domestic violence is steadily increasing, and the network of courageous women supporting other women is expanding. We are also finding women protesting sexual harassment and even bringing such cases before the courts. Pressure brought to bear by various women's groups has forced city governments all over Japan to stop sponsoring local beauty contests. In addition, courses in women's studies have been started in colleges, universities, and community colleges to raise the consciousness of women. Finally, we find that Japanese men have also begun to examine their own sexuality, and several men's liberation groups have been organized, such as the Society of Men Raising Children (Otoko no kosodate kai) and the Society of Men Thinking about Asian Prostitution (Asia no baishun o kangaeru kai).

The male-dominated pornographic culture will exist only so long as women allow it to. And only when women are guaranteed physical and emotional safety and the freedom to define themselves will we be able to exercise equal rights with men. Until we reconstruct our society and change men's misconceptions about their own sexuality and their concepts of femininity, we cannot change our present pornographic culture.

NOTE

This essay is based on a paper that was presented at the International Seminar on Women's Studies held at the National Women's Educational Centre (Kokuritsu Kyoiku Fujin Kaikan) in Saitama Prefecture, Japan, in 1989, and printed in a report of its proceedings.

REFERENCES

Funabashi, Kuniko. 1988a. "Pornography no seijigaku" (The politics of pornography). In *Feminizumu nyumon* (Introduction to feminism), ed. Bessatsu Takarajima. Tokyo: JICC.

———. 1988b. "Manga zasshi no seibyosha" (The description of sexuality in comic books). *Seito shido*, no. 7 (July): 46–52.

Keisatsucho (National Police Agency). 1988. *Hanzai tokei* (Crime statistics).

Otoko no yuhogai (Men's pleasure town). 1987. September.

Domestic Violence

❖ ❖ ❖

Aiko Hada

Translated by Kumiko Fujimura-Fanselow

J apanese society has not yet grasped the true meaning of "gender-based violence." Since the rise of the second wave of the feminist movement, however, the steady work done by feminists has led to its gradual recognition as a social problem. In the mid-1970s, in the midst of this second wave, women's groups campaigned against prostitution tourism by Japanese men in various Asian countries. This led to the appearance of a new Japanese word for prostitution—namely, that for "buying sex"—as opposed to the hitherto accepted word for "selling sex," which stressed the female side of the act (both words have the same pronunciation in Japanese).[1] At about the same time, some feminist groups also called for the establishment of temporary shelters for battered women, leading to the movement for "temples of refuge."[2] Official response to this demand took the form of assigning to the Women's Guidance Centers (which had originally been established in each of the nation's forty-seven administrative divisions on the basis of the 1956 Anti-Prostitution Law) the new function of providing emergency temporary shelters for women. Yet this movement was not able to rouse public opinion to the point that the Japanese people recognized domestic violence as a significant social issue.

Later, in the early 1980s, emphasis was placed on fighting pornography and rape, while in the latter half of the decade sexual harassment began to draw attention. The first rape crisis center in this country—run by feminists—opened in Tokyo in 1983. The issue of sexual harassment in the workplace gained recognition and support among many women as well as at least some men as a result of a widely publicized "Poll of 10,000," which was conducted in 1989 by a suburban feminist group called the Santama Society (from the name of the satellite town where it originated) in order to ascertain the magnitude of this problem. Most effective in terms of promoting public awareness of this issue, however, has been the number of sexual harassment cases that have been won in court. Violence became, then, a recognized key concept within the Japanese feminist movement in the 1980s, but at the time it was still conceived of rather narrowly—that is, in terms mainly of sexual violence.

Sexual Violence, Domestic Violence, and Gender-Based Violence

The more broadly encompassing concept of gender-based violence, which includes not only various forms of sexually centered violence but, in addition, violence against women occurring in the home, did not gain public recognition until much later. The first national survey of domestic violence taking the form of child abuse was not done until 1983, and it was not until the 1990s that there appeared any kind of organized movement at the grassroots level to deal with this problem. Although we may conjecture that, historically, there has been a high incidence of wife battering in Japan, there is still a strong tendency to view this as a private matter, and Japanese society, including women, has yet to grasp the severity of this problem. No official body has yet conducted a national survey of wife battering, and there does not seem to be any plan to do so. The extent of the problem, as inferred from the only available official data, is as follows: "husband's violence" was the reason second most frequently cited by women filing for divorce arbitration, and "emotional abuse by husband" was the fifth (*Shiho tokei* 1990). Also, one-third of the women using the emergency temporary shelters at the Women's Guidance Centers mentioned earlier were running away from their husband's violence.

"Survey of Wife (Girlfriend) Battering"—1992

Domestic violence directed against women is overlooked in a number of ways. The most common pattern is to dismiss it as "something that occurs only in very rare, special cases." In an attempt to effect a breakthrough, a group of feminists (which included this writer) founded the Domestic Violence Action and Research Group in April 1992, and it proceeded to undertake a survey to determine the extent of domestic violence taking place in Japan. The self-reporting questionnaire was designed with the aim of ascertaining in as much detail as possible the physical, emotional, and/or sexual violence women had experienced. More concretely, the respondents were asked to check off however many items there were which applied to them in reference to the types of abuse they had received, the conditions under which the abuse took place, and the frequency of abuse as well as what they perceived to be the cause or reason behind the perpetrator's violence, how the victim felt when she was abused, what short- and long-term measures the victim took in the face of the abuse, and whether these were effective or not. Finally, the questionnaire also asked the respondents what social measures they would like to see implemented to deal with the problem.

Survey Results

The respondents were not chosen at random. The questionnaires were distributed nationwide to women's groups and adult education classes as well as to individual women, who were recruited through media announcements and social service agencies. All questionnaires were returned anonymously. Of the 4,675 questionnaires distributed, 809 were returned, a response rate of 17.3 percent. Of those 796 were valid, and of that number 613 (77 percent) indicated they had been victims of at least one form of abuse: physical (for example, getting hit, kicked, threatened or cut with knife, or burned with lit cigarette); emotional (including repeated ridicule, restriction against contacts with family of origin or friends, threat of divorce or harm, withholding adequate financial provisions); or sexual, (such as forced sex, refusal in cooperating with contraceptive use, forced sex with use of physical violence, forced abortion). Forty-four percent said they had simultaneously been subjected to all three types of abuse.

That our short-term, limited networking led to our collecting data from as many as 613 victims of domestic violence is proof that, although it may not be readily apparent or acknowledged, violence inflicted against women by husbands (and boyfriends) clearly does exist in Japan. The abuse is often severe and recurrent over long periods of time. More than half the victims in our survey were unable find a way out of their current situation and therefore continued to maintain their relationships with their husbands or boyfriends.

Future Tasks

Domestic violence in Japan has only recently begun to draw public attention, due to the efforts of feminist groups and victims of abuse. New laws are needed in order for the police and judiciary system to respond to the problem in an effective way, and better social measures are necessary to help victims and to provide them with medical care and emergency protection. The establishment of additional shelters for female victims of various forms of violence is vital in terms of promoting such measures as well as fostering greater public awareness of the problem. At present, there is but one public shelter specifically for battered women, located in Kanagawa Prefecture. This is supplemented by three very small shelters in Tokyo and its suburbs, which are run by feminist groups, and a Christian-affiliated shelter in Tokyo called

HELP.[3] The Women's Guidance Centers also provide temporary shelter to victims of domestic violence, but they are not actually equipped to function as shelters for battered women.

NOTES

1. Efforts by Japanese feminist groups to put a stop to these sex tours is discussed in the essay by Yayori Matsui, "The Plight of Asian Migrant Women Working in Japan's Sex Industry," in this volume.

2. The term "temples of refuge" *(kakekomidera)* is taken from the name given to temples that were established by nuns in the seventeenth century to which women seeking to sever a marriage (a difficult thing for women to do at the time) were able to flee.

3. HELP (House in Emergency of Love and Peace) is an emergency shelter for women of all nationalities which was established in 1986 by the Japan Christian Woman's Temperance Union, the oldest women's organization in Japan, on the one-hundreth anniversary of its founding.

REFERENCE

Shiho tokei (1990 Statistics of the Ministry of Justice.) 1991. In *Katei saiban geppo* (Family court monthly) 43, no. 1.

❖ 4 ❖

Women at Work

Women working at an office. Courtesy of Yomiuri News Photo Center, Tokyo.

Female Workers:
An Overview of Past and Current Trends

❖ ❖ ❖

Yoko Kawashima

In 1991, 26.5 million Japanese women were in the labor force, attaining a rate of labor force participation of 50.7 percent among all women of age 15 or over. Women constituted 40.8 percent of the total Japanese work force. Japanese women have come a long way from the times when being a "good wife and a wise mother" *(ryosai kenbo)* described their role in the family and society. The traditional division of "men at work and women at home" seems outdated.

Despite their importance in the labor force, contemporary working women in Japan reveal complex and contradictory characteristics. Ambitious career women claim a place equal to men in the business world. On the other hand, some working women view their responsibility at home as their primary occupation and their work outside as secondary. Surveys of working women have shown that the majority of Japanese women do not desire a job with great responsibility and consider earning supplementary income for the household as a primary reason for working.[1] Even among the younger generation many women still think that the primary caretakers of children are their mothers and, therefore, that women should stay at home while children are small.

Such contradictory portrayals and the apparent lack of a powerful women's movement often perplex overseas observers, who wonder whether Japanese women really want to achieve equality. One U.S. report surveying the status of women in ninety-nine countries ranked Japanese women's overall status as thirty-fourth and placed it at the bottom among the industrial countries surveyed (Population Crisis Committee 1988). The contrast between Japan's remarkable economic success and the apparent backwardness in women's status has recently drawn increasing attention and curiosity as well as criticism.

This essay will attempt to analyze the place and role of Japanese women in the labor market. I will first review Japanese women's work history. Second, I will examine the quantitative and qualitative changes in the female labor force over time. Finally, the impact of the Equal Employment Opportunity Law of 1985 on female workers will be my focus, with an emphasis upon current issues related to women.

Early Industrialization and Female Workers

The Japanese economy at the time of the Meiji Restoration (1868) was predominantly agrarian. Three-quarters of the total work force was engaged in agriculture, mostly small-scale family farming. With an abundant labor surplus agriculture was a main source of labor supply for wage employment in the nonagricultural sectors. One important initial event that triggered the disintegration of agriculture was the Land Tax Reform of 1873. The Meiji government, in order to raise the financial resources necessary to promote modern industry and the military system, introduced a tax reform that replaced tax-in-kind by tax-in-cash at high rates on the basis of land value. The reform's consequences were twofold: commercialization of agricultural products and partial disintegration of the peasant class, especially the poorest, who were unable to pay the tax. The disintegration took the following patterns: (1) second and third sons and daughters of peasants became wage employees, while the first son inherited the farm; (2) some farmers became *dekasegi* (short-term migrants who returned to their farms after some months or years of work outside); (3) farmers were partially employed in the factory (as semi–farm workers and semi–factory workers), especially after the 1930s; (4) the whole family moved from agriculture to urban areas. Among these the fourth pattern was rather marginal (see Okochi 1952; Okochi et al. 1961). Okochi (1952, 4) described the nature of wage employment in Japan as "household supplementary type" characterized by wages earned by *dekasegi* workers.[2]

The development of wage employment was rather slow. This was mainly because agriculture, which absorbed the largest proportion of the total labor force, consisted mostly of self-employed and family workers *(kazoku rodosha)* and had a very limited proportion of wage employment.[3] Taira (1970, 3) described Japan in the 1920s as predominantly a country of family farms, family workshops, and family stores.

The female participation rate in the labor force has been consistently high (53.3 percent in 1920, when the first nationwide population census was taken), as has been the female share in the total work force. The high female participation before World War II was due to the fact that Japanese agriculture, mostly small-size family farming, was highly dependent on female labor. In 1920, 62 percent of female workers were in agriculture, whereas the proportion of males in the agricultural labor force declined to below 50 percent in the same year. It was only in 1960 that the proportion for females fell below 50 percent (see tables 1 and 2).

The appearance of female wage workers in modern factories began with the Meiji era. The Meiji government built several model factories in the spinning and textile industry (e.g. Tomioka and Maebashi spinning factories), which were later sold to private interests (see Tsurumi 1990). The spinning and textile industry was the core industry during early industrialization and remained so until heavy industries developed rapidly after 1910. The spinning and textile industry mainly employed women. In 1915 the number of female workers in manufacturing industries reached 560,000; nearly 90 percent of them were employed in the spinning and textile industry (Hirota 1979, 95). The importance of women in total wage employment in manufacturing lasted until 1930, when heavy industries began to hire more workers, mainly men, than the spinning and textile industry.

During the 1870s, spinning and textile factories established by the national and prefectural governments recruited young girls, mostly from

Table 1
Distribution of Labor Force, by Sector and Sex, 1872–1990 (percent)

Sector	Female			Male		
Year	Primary	Secondary	Tertiary	Primary	Secondary	Tertiary
1872	77.2	22.8		69.3	30.7	
1890	74.3	25.7		63.3	36.7	
1900	71.6	28.4		60.4	39.6	
1910	70.9	12.7	9.1	60.0	18.3	19.7
1920	62.4	16.3	19.5	48.2	23.3	38.2
1930	60.8	14.1	25.0	43.1	23.9	32.7
1940	57.0	15.7	26.9	35.7	32.9	30.7
1950	61.2	13.2	25.5	40.2	27.4	32.3
1960	43.1	20.2	36.6	25.8	35.0	39.2
1970	26.5	26.2	47.6	14.9	39.3	45.8
1980	13.2	28.2	58.4	8.7	38.9	52.2
1990	8.5	27.3	63.8	6.4	38.1	56.5

Sources: Before 1920, Umemura Mataji, "Sangyobetsu koyo no hendo: 1800–1940" (Changes in employment by industry: 1800–1950, *Keizai kenkyu* (Research in economics) Vol. 24, no. 2: 112–13, 116; for 1920–70, Prime Minister's Office, Bureau of Statistics, *Nihon no jinko* (Japan's population), 1960, and *Kokusei chosa hokoku* (National census report), 1960 and 1970, cited in Ando Yoshio et al., *Kindai Nihon keizashi yoran* (Collection of data: modern Japanese economic history) (Tokyo: University of Tokyo Press, 1975); for 1980 and 1990, Somucho, Tokeikyoku (Management and Coordination Agency, Statistics Bureau), *Rodoryoku chosa* (Labor force survey) (Tokyo: Somucho, 1992).

Table 2
Distribution of Labor Force by Work Status, 1950–1990 (percent)

	Female			Male		
Year	Self-employed	Family workers	Wage employees	Self-employed	Family workers	Wage employees
1950	15.0	62.5	22.4	37.0	19.3	43.7
1955	14.7	57.7	27.6	34.0	18.8	47.2
1960	15.8	43.4	40.8	27.4	10.5	62.1
1965	14.5	36.8	48.6	23.4	7.8	68.8
1970	14.2	30.9	54.7	22.4	6.0	71.5
1975	14.3	25.7	59.8	20.1	3.9	75.8
1980	13.7	23.0	63.2	19.4	3.3	77.1
1985	12.5	20.0	67.2	17.9	2.8	78.9
1990	10.7	16.7	72.3	16.3	2.5	80.8

Sources: For 1950, Ministry of Labor, Yearbook of Labor Statistics, 1950 (Tokyo: Ministry of Labor); for 1955–90, Rodosho fujinkyoku (Ministry of Labor, Women's Bureau,) Fujin rodo jitsujo (Status of female workers) (Tokyo: Rodosho 1960 and 1992).

samurai or wealthy peasant families, who were encouraged to work for the nation. However, as the industry expanded and factories proliferated in many different parts of Japan, daughters of the poorest peasants became a major source of workers in these factories. According to Okochi, "to supplement their parents' impoverished income from farming, they worked in the remote factories as *dekasegi* for two to three years before marriage. Their pay was often paid to their parents in advance. As a result, they were obliged to work for the employers for a fixed number of years, usually two to three years" (1952, 4). The long hours of work under unhealthy factory conditions and malnutrition in the dormitory were detrimental to these young women's health. Many fell ill with tuberculosis.[4] The Factory Law of 1911 limited hours worked to twelve per day and required two days off each month. Even these minimal protections provided little immediate relief to factory workers, however, since the law was not enforced for another fifteen years.

Along with female factory workers, the tertiary sector grew in the Taisho era (1912–26), employing women as teachers, nurses, clerical workers, and retail workers. As the Showa era began in 1925, machinery and chemical industries expanded and employed a growing number of female workers. There were also a large number of women working as domestic servants, child care workers, or home-based workers doing piece work *(kanai rodosha)*.[5] (For an analysis of female workers during the period 1910–1930, see Tazaki 1990). Women from poor families were brought into work to supplement household income. The salient feature of the female labor force, however, was the predominance of family workers who worked on a farm or in a family enterprise for free or a small amount of payment. They were, in essence, a preindustrial type of worker, and their transformation into wage employment in the modern industrial sector lagged far behind male workers. It is only as recently as 1965 that the proportion of wage employment among women exceeded 50 percent.

The war economy during World War II brought about important changes in the female labor force. As men were recruited into the army, economic activities became heavily dependent on female labor. Women took over many jobs previously done by men in heavy industries. The outflow of women into the labor force was halted by the end of the war. The economic recession during and after the war, and the return of soldiers and repatriates from overseas, caused massive layoffs, leaving 14 million unemployed. Hirota (1979, 7) estimates that the number of female employees was reduced from over 4 million immediately before the end of the war to 2.8 million after the war. In contrast, the number of female family workers increased, absorbing part of the unemployed women.

Rapid Economic Growth: 1955–73

After the Korean War (1950), which provided an impetus for economic recovery after the defeat in World War II, the Japanese economy entered an era of rapid economic development; the economic boom continued until the onset of the recession caused by the "Nixon shock" (the devaluation of the dollar) in 1971 and the Oil Crisis in 1973. Rapid economic growth brought about a labor shortage. Until around 1965 the main labor supply had come from preindustrial-type workers such as peasants, small family enterprise owners, and family workers, but this labor pool was nearly exhausted. The labor shortage of new graduates from middle school was the most severe because more of them chose to continue their educations into high school. With the traditional labor pool diminished, women, especially housewives, were sought as a new labor supply.

Simultaneously, there were several changes both on the demand and supply sides of labor. Automation of production systems changed most of the jobs done by skilled workers into simple repetitive tasks, particularly in the electrical machinery and precision industries. Expansion of the tertiary sector as well as an increase of clerical work in manufacturing industries created a great number of clerical jobs requiring little skill. These changes offered increased job opportunities for women. There were changes on the supply side, too; mechanization and commercialization of some household work and development of child care in the community facilitated women's working outside the home. The perception of a need to increase the household income created by stronger aspirations for a better standard of living and the feeling of poverty due to soaring living costs drove women into the labor market. These together contributed to the expansion of the labor market for women and brought about important quantitative and qualitative changes in the female work force.

The shift of female labor in agriculture, particularly young women working as family workers, toward the secondary and rapidly growing tertiary sectors was accelerated after the 1960s. Female labor force participation rates in different age groups changed noticeably over time. In 1920 they were rather similar for all age groups, except for a decline at age fifty. Four major changes occurred thereafter: (1) the expansion of education resulted in a reduction in the participation rate of women under age twenty; (2) the rate for the age group from twenty to twenty-four increased; (3) the rate for the period of marriage and child rearing, ages twenty-five to thirty-four, declined; and (4) the rate increased again for the age group over thirty-five, when children reach school age, and attained a second peak for those forty to fifty years old. These changes were related to the decline in agricultural workers and small family enterprises, on the one hand, and, on the other, to the increase in wage employment. In farming, shopkeeping, or family enterprises the workplace is never distinctly separate from the household, enabling women to continue to work after marriage and childbirth, whereas wage employment tends to shape the female labor participation pattern by age. A female life cycle consisting of study, employment, retirement for child rearing, and reentry into the labor force, accommodating women's roles as mother and worker, became a common pattern (see Somucho 1990, Rodosho 1990).

Since the establishment of a modern employment system Japanese firms have preferred to employ persons directly out of school. The severe labor shortage after 1960, however, drove them to hire older workers, particularly an increasing number of married middle-aged women. Some of them were hired as "mid-point entrants" *(chuto saiyo)*, that is, workers who enter or reenter the labor market some years after they have left school.[6] Many were hired as part-time employees.[7] This was encouraged by the government's manpower policy, which was targeted at bringing middle-aged housewives into the labor force mainly as part-timers. The number of female part-timers increased from 4.4 million in 1955 to 10.7 million in 1970, representing 12 percent of female wage workers.

The number of female "nonpermanent regular workers"[8] also increased from 0.9 million in 1960 to 1.7 million in 1970. The distinction between "permanent regular workers" and "nonpermanent regular workers" is crucial in the Japanese employment system, as we will see. "Permanent" refers to the workers who are employed for an unspecified period or for a period of longer than a year, and "regular" to the workers who work the hours that the firm's internal regulations stipulate. "Temporary and casual workers" are those whose period of employment is specified be less than a year. There were, in 1970, 1.7 million female *kanai rodosha*, doing piecework in their homes, subcontracted mainly from small- or medium-sized firms in the textile, apparel, and electrical machinery industries.

The female labor force was transformed from one consisting predominantly of women who were young, unmarried, and working for a short period to one with older, married women working for a longer period. (The distribution of female workers by marital status in 1970 was 48 percent unmarried, 41 percent married and 10 percent widowed or divorced.) As the number of older women increased in the labor market, the age of employed women became closely connected with firm size and work status. Young women were hired by large firms and older women mostly by small firms. And young women were employed as permanent regular workers, whereas older women were more likely to work as part-timers, temporary workers, or home-based pieceworkers.

Takenaka (1989, 240) noted that after 1965 the use of part-timers spread from small-sized firms to large firms and generated a dualism among female workers through different hiring and working conditions and wages. The employment of male temporary workers by large firms, which was the custom after World War I, was replaced by the use of older female workers. Thus, pools of competing and substitutable labor—composed of housewives, home-based workers, and part-timers—were formed.

The increase in the number of middle-aged female workers did not help raise female wages but, instead, had the opposite effect. In fact, the ratios of the average female wage to the average male wage, which increased until 1965, remained around 0.55 during the second half of this period in terms of monthly contractual wages, excluding overtime pay and bonuses, and 0.50 in terms of total monthly earnings, including overtime pay and bonuses. (These figures are for permanent regular workers only.) The potentially favorable effect of the labor shortage, in pushing up the female wages, was offset by the influx of middle-aged women into the labor market. Further, there existed nearly eight million women who were not holding a job but were wishing to find one (31 percent of all women fifteen years or older were not holding a job) (Sorifu 1988). An abundance of housewives who wished to work when jobs were available to them, and who went back to the household when none were available, exerted a downward pressure on female wages.

Era of Slow Economic Growth after 1973

After the Nixon shock and the Oil Crisis (1973), the Japanese economy entered an era of slow economic growth and underwent a structural change from a manufacturing-centered to a service-oriented economy. Women's participation in the labor force declined immediately after the Oil Crisis but recovered quickly.

The participation rate showed a rise again for women at all age groups. Particularly, with more women postponing marriage and childbirth and also staying at work after marriage and childbirth, the great drop at ages 25 to 29 has recently become smaller. Among women with children who are newborn to age 3, 28.3 percent now work. Married women have continued to increase their share in wage employment relative to single women. (In 1991 there were 33.1 percent unmarried, 57.8 percent married, and 9.1 percent widowed or separated.) So, too, have women aged 30 or more increased their share relative to those under 30; 32.2 percent in 1991 were under 30 compared to 63 percent in 1960. The average age of employed women rose from 24 in 1950 to 35.8 in 1991 (the comparative figure for men being 39.7); the average length of stay in the same company grew from 4.0 years in 1960 to 7.4 years in 1991 for women (the male figure is 12.7 years).

Despite the big changes, both quantitative and qualitative, among female workers, male-female wage differentials have changed surprisingly little. A slight improvement was made only for the starting wages for workers directly out of school. In 1991 female workers, on average, earned 60.7 percent of the male average wage on the basis of monthly contractual wage but only 50.8 percent on the basis of total monthly earnings, including overtime pay and bonuses. (These figures are for permanent regular workers only and have not been adjusted for the difference in the hours worked nor the difference in work experience.) The ratio reached the peak of 61.4 percent (for contractual wages only), or 55.8 percent (for total earnings), in 1975 and declined thereafter.

The number and proportion of part-timers has continued to increase and accounted for 5.5 million, or 29.3 percent, of total female wage employment in 1991. Female temporary and casual workers reached 3.5 million, constituting 18.5 percent of total female wage workers in 1991.[10]

Although part-timers' average number of working hours was 6 hours daily, 22 percent of part-timers worked 6.5 to 7.4 hours, 16 percent worked 7.5 to 8.4 hours, and a small proportion worked more than 8.5 hours (Rodosho *chingin sensus* 1989). This means that a significant proportion of part-timers worked as long as full-time workers. Most of the part-timers, however, are a very different group of workers from permanent regular workers in all aspects. While permanent regular workers' average age was thirty-six, the part-timers' average age was forty-four in 1991. Half of the permanent regular workers were less than thirty years old, whereas only 14 percent of part-timers were less than thirty. In short, permanent regular workers are young women, whereas part-timers are mostly middle-aged women. Among female permanent regular workers, more younger women are employed by large firms and older women mainly by smaller firms.

The hourly regular contractual wage of part-timers is about 70 to 80 percent of that earned by female permanent workers. Their wages do not rise with the length of service, and the differences in bonuses are even larger. Part-timers earn, in total, only 60 to 70 percent of the female permanent workers' wage. Part-timers earn substantially less than female permanent regular workers, even less than the mid-point entrants whose wages are similar to those of recent graduates.

The number of female home-based workers (*kanai rodosha*) reached its peak of 1.8 million in 1973 and, thereafter, gradually declined to 0.84 million in 1991. The average age of home-based workers was forty-eight. Like part-timers, they are older than permanent workers. Home-based workers' average length of service for the same contracting firms was 8.4 years, considerably longer than part-timers' and almost the same as permanent workers'. They were, in effect, used as part of a firm's regular labor force, even though they were not employed by the firm under a labor contract. Due to the lack of bonuses and the absence of pay increases with the accumulation of years of service, home-based workers' hourly wage rate remained at about 60 percent of part-timers' and 35 to 40 percent of that of permanent workers. Furthermore, firms are exempt from all the costs involved in employing permanent workers, such as training costs and fringe benefits. Home-based pieceworkers are thus extremely cheap labor.

Recently, yet other types of workers have been emerging rapidly: contract workers dispatched by employment agencies *(haken rodo)*, temporary workers who are mostly students doing a variety of odd jobs *(arubaito)*, and workers on contract *(shokutaku)*. Whereas part-timers, mid-point entrants, and home-based workers are mostly middle-aged women, the new types of workers are mainly young women.

Among permanent regular workers, employment of women tends to fluctuate more than that of men. But the employment of part-timers fluctuates much more than that of permanent regular workers. When the economy turns up, a great number of part-timers are employed to increase production. When the economy falls into recession, they are laid off. Part-timers are cheap labor and unstable employment. Employers hire part-timers, mostly middle-aged women, to reduce labor costs and to be able to adjust the size of employment without provoking labor disputes.[11]

Theory of the Dual Economy and Labor Market in Japan

There is a well-established theory of the dual economic structure and labor market in Japan. The duality is focused on the differences between big firms and small firms. Since the appearance of wage differentials between large firms and small firms after World War I, the duality has been one of the conspicuous features of the Japanese economic structure and labor market. Shinohara (1970) defines the Japanese economic duality as: (1) the coexistence of modern large firms, which are equipped with high-level technology, and smaller firms, which lag technologically; (2) the importance of the share of the large-firm sector in the national economy; (3) the establishment of two extremes, the large-firm sector and the small-firm sector and their polarization.

Large firms have a highly structured internal labor market. Life long commitment to the same firm *(shushin koyo)* is a common practice. New graduates are hired to fill entry jobs, and other jobs in higher positions are filled through the internal promotion of workers. The *nenko joretsu* (seniority) wage has a low starting level and subsequently increases automatically and steeply with the worker's age and seniority in a given company. Promotion is regular, and the wage does not necessarily reflect a worker's productivity.

Small firms, in contrast, have many entry points and a high turnover rate. But labor mobility from small firms to large firms is restricted. Wages in small firms are directly influenced by the operation of the competitive labor market. There is an important difference in the power of unions within large firms and small firms; that is, workers in large firms have higher rates of unionization than workers in small firms.

The labor supply from agriculture declined after World War II, and recent graduates became the main source of labor supply under the lifelong commitment scheme. The fact that a large number of young, single recent graduates were all placed in the labor market at the same time in March and April contributed to keeping their wages low. The situation changed, however, after 1955. Rapid economic growth and labor shortages, particularly among recent graduates, buoyed their wages. The results were twofold. First, competition among firms for recent graduates led to a common competitive labor market and uniform wage rate. As a result, wage differences between big firms and small firms were partly eroded for this group of workers. Second, the wage differentials by age narrowed. During the recession from 1975 to 1978, caused by the Oil Crisis, interscale wage differentials widened again, because recession hit small firms much harder than bigger firms (Tachibanaki 1982).

The postwar labor unions, which were founded in the context of lifelong employment and the seniority-based wage system, were enterprise unions *(kigyo kumiai)*. The lifelong employment and seniority system establish strong ties between a firm and its employees and obstruct the formation of a common labor market beyond individual firms. Enterprise unionism, in turn, strengthens this vertical division and the isolation of labor markets within each firm. The membership is generally limited to permanent regular workers, excluding temporary and casual workers and part-timers.[12]

The rate of unionization varies greatly by size of firms, industry, and sex. Female workers are less unionized than male workers (17.7 percent compared with 28.5 percent, respectively, in 1991). This is due to three factors: first, a larger proportion of female workers are nonpermanent regular workers, who are excluded from unions; second, more female workers are employed in smaller firms in which the unionization rate is lower; and, third, they are employed in service industries, in which workers are less unionized. In fact, whereas the number of female wage workers nearly doubled in the last twenty years, the number of female union members has risen only slightly, pushing down the female rate of unionization from 29.4 percent in 1970 to 17.7 percent in 1991.

The lifetime commitment and seniority system make the large firm's employment practice and labor costs extremely rigid. Employers have used several means to adjust the amount of employment to the firm's business fluctuation and give flexibility to the labor cost. First, nonpermanent workers *(rinjiko)* have been commonly used. They are hired en masse during an economic boom and may be fired when the boom ends. They are paid less than permanent workers and are not entitled to various kinds of fringe benefits. They are not members of the enterprise union. The use of nonpermanent workers began at the same time as the lifelong employment system took root after World War I. It was a necessary safety valve for the system (Okochi et al. 1961). Second, the Japanese wage system contains flexible components. The wage is generally composed of monthly contractual pay (basic pay and some allowances), overtime pay, and special pay (bonuses). While the monthly contractual pay is a fixed cost, overtime pay and bonuses are more flexible costs to firms. In particular, the amount of the bonus, which often equals four to six months of monthly contractual pay, has a wide range of fluctuation according to the firm's business situation. Also, as automation reduced and standardized skill requirements, the importance of seniority as a measure of the skill specific to the firm declined, and the merit-based wage was gradually introduced into the *nenko* system after 1965.

Benefits of the system apply fully only to those who have worked a long time in the same firm since their graduation. It has been customary for women to work only for a few years, between the end of schooling and marriage, and to quit before they benefited from the wage increase under the *nenko* system. Some firms even had specific provisions for retirement upon marriage in the labor contracts. A series of court decisions beginning in 1966 made forced retirement upon marriage, and differential retirement age, illegal. Yet, women who remained longer in the firm were encouraged to quit upon marriage by being offered special allowances or were even forced to quit by explicit or tacit pressure. Since most women had jobs that did not require special skills, the replacement of senior women by recent graduates, part-timers, or mid-point entrants served as a means to reduce labor costs. Mid-point entry is a severe disadvantage for both men and women under the seniority system, but the disadvantages are much greater for women. Female entry-level wages, even for workers with permanent regular status, are almost the same as recent graduates' starting wages, while male entry wages are substantially higher than that of graduates. The older their entry age, the larger their disadvantage vis-à-vis the "standard worker" *(hyojun rodosha)*, or workers who have worked in the same firm without interruption (Kawashima 1987).

Another device for maintaining flexibility is the use of subcontract and home-based workers *(kanai rodosha)*. Big firms subcontract work to medium or small firms to adjust the amount of production to current demand and also to take advantage of cheaper labor. Medium and small firms subcontract the work to still smaller firms. The end point is the home-based workers. They are not employees of the firm and are, therefore, totally outside of any wage worker protection. Recently, the number of contract workers dispatched by employment agencies *(haken rodo)* has been increasing; most of them work in the tertiary sector.

In summary, workers have been divided between permanent regular workers and nonpermanent regular workers. Only the permanent regular workers benefit from the *nenko* wage, fringe benefits, stable employment under lifelong commitment practice, and union membership. They are the "core workers." The nonpermanent regular workers are outside the core labor market system. They are the "peripheral workers." The employment of permanent regular workers makes labor costs and the size of employment extremely rigid. Adjustment of the rigidity of the system to economic fluctuation has been mediated by the use of peripheral workers.

Women's Place in the Labor Market

The peripheral workers are further segmented into different subgroups of workers, who work under different labor conditions. A portion of "mid-point entrants"—temporary and casual workers, part-timers, and *kanai rodosha*—constitute separate subgroups. Even when female mid-point entrants are employed as permanent regular workers, most of them are faced with large wage disadvantages. They were employed as a cheap substitute for recent high school graduates during the 1960s labor shortage and, then, as a means to adjust the size of employment to the amount of production needed. Therefore, most female mid-point entrants are peripheral workers. Although home-based workers are classified as self-employed in the official statistics, we view them as peripheral workers because the substance of their labor is similar to wage employees in the peripheral labor market. Age functions as one of the determinants of women's work status: permanent regular workers are mostly young; contract workers dispatched by employment agencies are young to middle-aged women; part-timers are mostly middle-aged; and pieceworkers are older women.

Within the segmented labor market, the core workers and the peripheral workers are further divided into different subgroups by a variety of socioeconomic and institutional factors such as firm size, industrial sectors, occupation, sex, and age. Different groups of workers with different characteristics are faced with different wage structures, levels of employment, stability, promotion opportunities, and worker protection. Male permanent regular workers in large firms are the ones who benefit the most from the system; they are the core of the core workers.

During the period between 1960 and 1990, female temporary and casual workers substantially increased, both in number and proportion, in the total female wage employment, whereas male temporary and casual workers remained at the same number and declined in percentage in the total male wage employment. In 1960, 40 percent of temporary and casual workers were women, but in 1990 women's share increased to 68 percent. Similar changes occurred for part-timers; women's share increased from 43 percent in 1960 to 69 percent in 1990. By contrast, the number of home-based workers declined after 1970. In 1989 there were 0.84 million female home-based workers, or 94 percent of total home-based workers.

Regarding family workers, the number in the total labor force has decreased for both sexes since 1960, and the proportion of female family workers in the total female work force fell to 16.7 percent in 1990 (compared to 2.5 percent for men). This reduction was mainly in agriculture. In the non-agricultural sector the number of female family workers has remained unchanged, whereas the number of male workers declined. In 1990, 2.68 million, or 81 percent, of family workers were women. Although they are not directly placed in the labor market, their sizable numerical presence influences the operation of the labor market for female wage employment. In view of these figures, it is clear that the total number of peripheral workers has grown and that this is mainly due to the increase of female peripheral workers; further, female workers have become the major constituent of the peripheral work force.

In addition, attention should be paid to the fact that in 1988 there were 8 million women who were not working (non–job holders) but who wished to work, an increase from 3.9 million in 1962. The proportion of women who wished to work among all female non-job holders increased from 20.4 percent to 30.8 percent during this time. They are a potential labor supply consisting mostly of housewives. Among them 58 percent wished to have part-time, or *arubaito*, jobs, 17 percent home-based work, and only 14 percent permanent regular work (Sorifu 1988).

With an abundant labor surplus agriculture long constituted a source of cheap labor for the nonagricultural sectors. As the capacity of agriculture as a supplier of cheap labor declined, and the economy began to experience a labor shortage at the moment of rapid economic growth after the 1960s, firms turned to women. Many women entered the labor market to become peripheral workers. Many of those who stayed in the household wanted to work, and some of them sought jobs. Between households and the labor market female labor flows according to the job situation.

Moreover, the growth of the size of the potential labor supply pool among women functions to keep female wages low and to make women's bargaining position powerless vis-à-vis employers. They do not have any united power to strengthen their position.

The Passage of the Equal Employment Opportunity Law

The Equal Employment Opportunity Law (EEOL) was passed in 1985 and became effective in April 1986. Although there were women's movements during the 1970s and women's demand for equality in the workplace became stronger, the passage of the law was prompted by international circumstances. As Japanese economic success drew more interest overseas in the Japanese economic structure and labor customs, criticism was expressed about the discriminatory treatment toward Japanese women. The Japanese government was sensitive to foreign pressure. In 1980, in the middle of the United Nations (UN) Decade for Women (1975–85), the Japanese government signed the International Convention on Elimination of All Forms of Discrimination against Women. For the ratification of the convention the government was pressed to pass a new law eliminating discrimination in the workplace. The passage of the law was not easy; there were conflicts between the labor representatives and businesses and among government agencies and divisions among women too. Not surprisingly, the law was a product of the compromise among these different interests.

The law stipulates: (1) the firm shall "endeavor" to treat women equally to men regarding recruitment, hiring, placement (job assignment), and promotion; and (2) the firm shall not discriminate against women regarding training and education, employee welfare and benefits (housing benefit, loans and a variety of allowances), retirement, age limit, and dismissal. There is, however, no penalty for violation. The law's effectiveness was left to firms' goodwill and administrative guidance by the government bureaucracy.

Why does the law deal with these two areas differently? Owaki et al. (1985) explain that the law's passage was not a result of changes in prevailing social values and perceptions regarding women's roles in the work force but, instead, more a codification of the rules already established through a series of court decisions in the past, such as the illegality of forced retirement of women upon marriage or the differential retirement age clause by sex. Hanami and Shinotsuka (1987, 9) argue that the issues of recruitment, hiring, promotion, and placement (job assignment) touch firms' whole personnel and management policy, and, therefore, firms' resistance to quick changes was greater than in the other areas.

Has the law achieved any progress toward equality despite the lack of enforcement? It is generally viewed that equal treatment at "exit," that is, retirement, had already been realized to a great extent even before the law's passage and that women's gains from the law have been mainly at "entrance," that is, recruitment, hiring, starting wage, and training for new employees. Until 1985 sex-designated recruitment was common practice. After the law's passage more firms are reported to have adopted sex-blind recruitment as a principle (Rodosho, *Joshi koyo* 1993). Subtle discrimination remains, however. Many want ads specifying sex are still seen in major newspapers. Even at the exit level it is not uncommon for women to feel subtle pressure from employers and/or corporate custom to retire early.

The EEOL opened wider job opportunities to female four-year college graduates. For a long time firms showed a preference for female two-year college graduates over four-year college graduates. One of the reasons was that female four-year college graduates, who were paid more than two-year college graduates, often quit before they became productive, therefore making them unprofitable to hiring firms. In contrast, the two-year college graduates were paid less and tended to work more years and to quit upon marriage, just before their wages went up. Social pressure backed by the law, demanding that firms change their discriminatory hiring policies, has brought some improvement, and more firms now hire four-year university graduates.

The area in which improvement is minimal is the "middle area" between the entrance and the exit, that is, placement and promotion. Workers learn skills by working on the job. "Skill" likely includes not only dexterity directly related to a job but also organizational skills, human relations in the workplace, and knowledge about the overall work system in the firm. The latter aspect is particularly important for workers who have a chance to become managerial personnel. Such workers acquire the skill necessary to work in management by accumulating experiences in different fields of work as they climb the job ladder. Women are rarely given such opportunities; they often stay in the same field of work. Changes in this discriminatory job assignment and promotion system and differential opportunities for specific on-the-job training are still limited. Women occupied only 1.2 percent of total office director positions *(bucho)*, 2.3 percent of division chief positions *(kacho)*, and 6.4 percent of group chief positions *(kakaricho)* in 1992, practically no change in the last three years, except a 1.4 percent increase in group chiefs, the lowest-level management position (Rodosho, *Joshi koyo* 1993).

Firms' attitudes toward women are still strongly influenced by sexist stereotypes. Of the firms surveyed in 1988, 23 percent indicated that all the jobs were open to women, while 48 percent answered that they hired and assigned women to "the jobs which fit women's special attributes" (ibid). Improvement has been seen more among larger firms than small firms and more in the service industry than in manufacturing. As a whole, however, firms' policies are still quite distant from sex-blind, ability-based job assignment.

One of the most heated discussions during the drafting stage of the law revolved around the issue of equality versus protection, or special treatment of women. Businesses argued for the abolition of protection in exchange for equality. Some women also supported abolition of protection for the reason that protection is an obstacle to equality. The more prevalent feeling among working women, however, was that some protective measures should be maintained since the sociocultural norms still imposed primary responsibility for child care and household chores on women and also because work hours were very long. The new law, a consequence of compromises among conflicting interests, maintained the menstrual leave with modifications and extended maternity leave but introduced major changes in the restriction on work hours.

The menstrual leave, which is unusual among industrial countries and sometimes seen by overseas observers as a symbol of Japanese women's backwardness in the effort to achieve equality, was maintained with some modification in the EEOL; women can claim leave when menstruation makes working difficult. The number of women actually taking the leave, however, has gradually declined, from 26.2 percent in 1965 to 6.0

percent in 1988 (Rodosho 1989). Maternity leave was changed from six weeks preceding and six weeks following childbirth to six weeks before and eight weeks after. (The pay during the leave is about 60 percent of the worker's normal pay.)

The change that has had the most important consequences on the work conditions of female workers concerns work hours. The old Labor Standard Law restricted women's overtime to two hours a day, six hours a week, and 150 hours a year and forbade holiday work and late-night work, except in certain professions. Some modifications were introduced in these restrictions by the EEOL: for women in managerial positions and in some specialist/technical positions, all these restrictions were removed; for women in manufacturing, mining, construction, and transport, the restriction to a two-hour daily overtime was lifted; and, for women working mainly in the tertiary sector, restrictions were changed to twenty-four hours in four weeks (for some industries, twelve hours in two weeks) and 150 hours a year, while daily restrictions were dropped. One day of work on holidays was also allowed every four weeks. While these changes reflected some women's demand for equal working conditions, they also met firms' needs for greater flexibility in work schedules in the service-oriented economy. Service industries, more than manufacturing, require flexibility in work schedules to adjust to the demand for service. Takenaka (1989, 313) explains that this is because service cannot be stored like goods, and selling and buying takes place at the same time.

Restructuring the Labor Market

One of the most noticeable changes in firms' labor policies after the passage of the EEOL was that an increasing number of firms, mostly large, have introduced the two-track system, consisting of *sogoshoku* and *ippanshoku*. Among firms with employees of five thousand and over, 49 percent have introduced the track system. Only 1.4 percent of firms with thirty to ninety-nine employees have adopted the system. The *sogoshoku* track leads to managerial positions, but accepting possible overtime and transfer is a requirement. The *ippanshoku* track is a secondary track in which work is routinized and opportunities for promotion are limited. While all men are placed on the *sogoshoku* track, women are given a choice between the two, although many women feel pressured to choose the *ippanshoku* track. A small number of career-oriented women have opted for the *sogoshoku*. The outcome of this new system after five years is rather mixed. It has opened up to women some opportunities that had been closed to them in the past, especially to four-year university graduates—but many of those who venture into the male-dominated world quit their jobs, frustrated or worn out. The attrition rate among *sogoshoku* women is nearly 50 percent.

As the prospect of a labor shortage intensifies, firms feel it necessary to tap the resources of women. Mounting criticism has come from women that the track system keeps many women away from having careers, because they cannot accept geographic transfer and longer overtime working hours. Partly in response to such criticism, and partly from the need to reduce women's dropout rate, some firms introduced a third track, "*sogoshoku* without transfer."

Hanami and Shinotsuka (1987) state that the firms' move for changes was not specifically a response to the law but, rather, was a part of the necessary reorganizing process of firms' management policies in the context of Japan's changing economic structure after 1975—in particular, a shift from a manufacturing-centered economy to a service-oriented economy and intensification of international competition. The expansion of service industries has weakened the rationale of the lifelong employment and *nenko* wage systems that developed in manufacturing industries. In a search for an alternative personnel management system, merit-based wages have been introduced, especially in the tertiary sector. A change from the system in which seniority leads to a managerial position and wage increase to one based on ability was felt necessary for firms' survival. Some firms had introduced the two-track system even before the law came into effect. The new management system was, therefore, part of the firms' attempt to change the old system (18–20). In this sense, "the essence of the EEOL was well in line with the Japanese economy's effort to achieve efficiency" (ii).

In the finance and insurance industries 25 percent of firms, the highest proportion among all industries, have introduced the track system. For instance, city banks, which since the 1960s had adopted a single merit-wage system applied to all employees, male and female, introduced the two- or three-track system before or after the enactment of the EEOL. Since then they have employed five to ten women for the *sogoshoku* every year, about 10 percent of all *sogoshoku* positions. What was their aim in introducing the track system? The following explanation by Sakurai (1985) gives us an insight into the issue: the city banks' merit-wage system, in which the wage in principle is not a function of seniority, has in practice tended to be seniority based. Such a system has been sustained because women quit within a few years—in other words, before their wages increase. If the law raises women's consciousness as workers and encourages them to stay on the job to benefit from the seniority wage system, the system will not be sustained now that the firms' financial capacities are not large enough. An alternative personnel policy is needed to cope with the changing situation. This explanation indicates that the track system is aimed at dividing permanent regular workers into two groups, one consisting of all male workers and a small number of *sogoshoku* women who benefit from the seniority-based wage system and the other made up of the majority of *ippanshoku* women, who are excluded from this system. This enables firms to sustain the seniority-based wage system for core workers, holding the other group's wage at a lower level (see Kawashima 1994, for a discussion of the banking industry).

In essence the track system, seemingly gender neutral, was aimed at achieving three major purposes: first, to respond to the pressure, domestic as well as international, to change discriminatory treatment of female workers; second, faced with a labor shortage, to make use of career-oriented competent women; and, third, to divide female permanent regular workers into a small elite group separate from the rest, by offering differential job assignments, promotions, and wages.

A small number of women have chosen the *sogoshoku* and have joined firms' male core workers groups. The majority, however, have opted for *ippanshoku*. The dividing line between the two tracks apparently is not sex but, rather, workers' willingness to devote themselves to work; therefore, it is not ostensibly discriminatory against women and thus can be justified. Restriction on overtime, late-night work, and holiday work was removed or modified to treat the new female and male core workers equally. At the same time, *ippanshoku* meets the firms' needs for flexible use of the "other female workers" in the more service-oriented economy. It seems that the firms' recent efforts to reorganize the labor market have been more in accordance with economic efficiency than to achieve equality of the sexes. *Sogoshoku* women are expected to fit into a workplace created by men, one that includes long working hours and transfer if necessary. Their heavy share of responsibility at home, however, remains virtually unchanged. Under this circumstance it is not surprising that only a limited number of women have been able to join the male world. Those who have chosen this option are faced with many hardships in surviving in a world that does not yet welcome women. Lacking role models and a support system, they find themselves isolated. They are also paying heavily in terms of their mental and physical health and family lives.

Many women choose the secondary track. They have little expectation and aspiration for a position with greater responsibility or a promotion to a managerial position. Nevertheless, they often have a heavy workload. The Labor Standard Law was modified again in 1988 to reduce working hours from forty-eight hours a week to forty-six hours in 1988 and forty-four hours in 1990, a step toward the target of forty hours a week and also to give flexibility to work schedules according to the needs of the service-oriented economy. These changes allow firms, within the stipulated limit of total work hours, to adopt an "irregular work schedule" *(henkei rodojikan),* either on a weekly, monthly, or three-month basis. This system is aimed at adjusting daily, weekly, or seasonal fluctuations in a firm's need for labor, without hiring extra workers. It is convenient for firms because they can avoid overtime pay as long as an employee's total work hours remain within the stipulated limit. It was assumed that the flexibility would be convenient for women, too, yet the irregular work schedule not only means a reduction in overtime pay but, in practice, makes women's adjustment to their responsibilities at home even harder, because they might have to work overtime on a single day or for a longer period; also, the child care system generally does not accommodate such irregular schedules.

Further outside these *ippanshoku* workers there are also many women who work as peripheral workers. The most noticeable institutionalization of women's labor as a way to minimize employment fluctuation and save labor costs is the enactment in 1985 of the Temporary Workers' Law (temporary workers, or *haken rodosha*, refer to workers dispatched by employment agencies). The law was passed after the proposal by a business group alliance to create "a middle labor market" between firms' internal markets and external labor markets. The creation of such a labor market enables firms to use this group of workers as a stable labor force but one whose contract may be terminated any time if necessary. Employment agencies use mostly housewives who want to have shorter and flexible work hours. Their hourly wage is extremely low, except for those with highly specialized skills, and there is no opportunity for promotion. Some industries, mainly in the service sector, employ a large number of dispatched temporary workers. An example is the banking industry; in some banks temporary dispatched workers have replaced *ippanshoku* women to the extent that they now constitute 40 percent of the regular female work force. Although they are not bank employees, they perform many of the same tasks as *ippanshoku* women (Nakayama 1991; Kawashima 1994).

In sum, although peripheral workers have diverse work patterns, the fundamental nature of their work and place in the labor market has changed little since the passage of the Equal Employment Opportunity Law.

Conclusion

As more women enter the labor force, the traditional division of work by sex—"women at home and men at work"—has been eroding. Nevertheless, women's primary task is still considered to be housekeeping and child rearing. Employers view women as secondary, or supplementary, workers in the workplace and as secondary breadwinners in the household and, accordingly, pay them low wages. Women tend to accept low wages because they themselves often view their wages as supplementary to the household income. Even in 1989, as the reasons for their working, 49 percent of women cited "to supplement the household income," followed by "to gain an important proportion of the household income" (16 percent), "to improve the standard of living" (14 percent), and "to use leisure time" (14 percent) (Rodosho, *Koyo doko chosa* 1989).

As long as changes in the male-centered workplace culture and the share of responsibility at home by males stay minimal, Japanese women's ambivalent attitude toward work is likely to prevail. Firms, in turn, continue to view women as secondary workers and, thus, the cycle of inequality is not easily broken.

There are several factors, however, which might bring about important changes. Among those the passage in 1991 of the Child Care Leave Law is noteworthy. The law requires firms to allow workers with children less than a year old to take an unpaid child care leave of up to one year. Workers with preschool children may demand reduced work hours in place of a leave. Since 1976 female teachers, nurses, and child care workers in public institutions have been given child care leave. The new law covers workers, both male and female, in the private sector. This is an important step forward in a society in which child rearing has been viewed as a woman's primary occupation. The weakness of the law is that the leave is unpaid. Consequently, the wife is the one likely to take the leave in most households because the husband's income—and, therefore, opportunity cost—is greater than the wife's. Also, current corporate culture discourages men from using the system. The introduction of a paid-leave system will be necessary, as will the diffusion of a new attitude that fathers should take on an equal share in the care of children. In fact, some men, particularly among the younger generation, are now demanding a new corporate culture, shorter work hours, and more time for family life.

Major events revolving around women's lives, especially since the UN Decade for Women and the enactment of the Equal Employment Opportunity Law, have raised women's consciousness about equality. Many working women feel that the law has made their work conditions harder without achieving significant improvement in their work status and wages. They are demanding "equality of outcomes" beyond "equality of opportunity."

There have been a series of lawsuits brought by women challenging discriminatory firing, promotion and wage systems, and sexual harassment in the workplace (see Tsunoda 1993). One such case involved the family allowance payment. Firms often limit the family allowance to the "head" of the household, who is usually the husband, and deny the benefit to working wives. A court recently decided that limiting payment of this allowance to the husband was against the principle of equality in wages (see Nakajima 1994).

Severe labor shortages will also be an important element. Businesses are becoming more aware of the need to change the ways they have been treating female workers, in order to attract and retain them.

The younger generation, men as well as women, desiring more time for family and leisure, are demanding changes in the corporate culture. Additionally, cultural norms concerning gender roles have been changing: young women are demanding that men take greater responsibility for work at home, and more men, at least in principle, accept the idea of sharing more equally household chores and child rearing.

Finally, pressures from overseas for more equality in the workplace and shorter work hours has produced significant repercussions in the government's domestic policy and firms' labor policies. Japan's economic success has made all aspects of Japanese economic structure, including labor practices, an object of scrutiny abroad. Praise for its economic efficiency has been replaced by mounting criticism. These factors together may well contribute toward bringing about more rapid changes in the workplace, in the family, and in society.

NOTES

1. See Sorifu (Prime Minister's Office) 1984/1979, *Fujin ni kansuru yoron chosa* (Survey of public opinion regarding women); Rodosho (Ministry of Labor) 1990/1989, *Koyo doko chosa* (Survey on employment of female workers); Sorifu 1990/1983, *Fujin no shugyo ni kansuru yoron chosa* (Survey of public opinion on women and work); Sorifu 1992, *Danjo byodo ni kansuru yoron chosa* (Survey of public opinion on gender equality).

2. Okochi's "household supplementing-type labor" theory explains that second and third sons and daughters of poor farmers, short-term migrants from the farm, and semi-farmers became wage workers to supplement farm income; since they were supplementary earners to the farm household, the wage level was set below the subsistence level for a single person. The substance of this theory is pertinent to female workers.

3. Japanese labor statistics classify labor into three categories: wage employees, the self-employed, and family workers. Family workers are defined as those who work on a farm or in a business operated by their family members; they generally refer to unpaid family workers, but those who work for their family business with a small amount of payment are also included in this category (Sorifu 1988). This means that family workers are practically free labor.

4. The life of the female factory worker has been well documented by Hosoi Wakizo in *Joko aishi* (The pitiful history of female factory workers 1954).

5. Home-based workers *(kanai rodosha)* are those who perform contracted work at home or in the place of their choice and are paid piece wages. In the official statistics they are placed in the category of self-employed. The kind of work for home-based workers has recently shifted from those in apparel, textile, and sundry goods industries to work in the tertiary sector, especially the information industry.

6. Mid point entrants are those who are not recent graduates at the time of employment. While *midpoint entry* is descriptive of the point of view of the firm's organizational arrangement, *midlife entry* or *midcareer entry* is the expression from the workers' point of view.

7. *Part-timer* is an ambiguous term. Official statistics use different definitions: those who work less than thirty-five hours a week; employed workers whose number of work hours or workdays is less than the firm's regulations stipulate; or those who are employed as "part-timers" regardless of the number of hours of work. I use the first definition because of the availability of data in this category over a long period.

8. *Permanent workers* refers to those who are employed for an unspecified period or for a period longer than a year and *regular workers* to those who work hours stipulated by the firm's internal regulations. *Temporary* and *casual workers* are those whose period of employment is specified to be less than a year.

9. Since some part-timers are permanent workers while others are temporary and casual workers, the numbers of temporary and casual workers and part-timers cannot be added up as the total number of nonpermanent regular workers. Yet one can safely argue that the number of nonpermanent regular workers increased and that this is mainly due to the great increase of female workers.

10. Taira (1970, 180) states that "the union as a rule included all the employees of an enterprise except for the managerial personnel. But the 1949–50 deflation made it clear that it was not always practicable for the union to protect its members against the loss of jobs. The realization of this fact led to a union policy that limited membership to a size at which absolute security of uninterrupted employment could be possible at all times."

REFERENCES

Ando, Yoshio. 1975. *Kindai Nihon keizaishi yoran* (Collections of data: modern Japanese economic history). Tokyo: University of Tokyo Press.

Hanami, Tadashi, and Eiko Shinotsuka. 1987. *Koyo kinto jidai no keiei to rodo* (Management and labor in an era of equal employment opportunity). Tokyo: Toyo keizai shinposha.

Hirota, Hisako. 1979. *Gendai fujin rodo no kenkyu* (Study on contemporary female labor). Tokyo: Rodo kyoiku senta.

Hosoi, Wakizo. 1954. *Joko aishi* (The pitiful history of female factory workers). Tokyo: Iwanami shoten.

Kawashima, Yoko. 1995. "Rodo shijo kozo soshiki, kigyo bunka ni okeru jenda sayo to josei rodo" (Labor market, corporate organization culture, and gender). In *Jenda no nihonshi* (Japanese history of gender), eds. Wakita Haruko and Susan B. Hainley. Tokyo: University of Tokyo Press.

———. 1987. "The Place and Role of Female Workers in the Japanese Labor Market." *Women's Studies International Forum* 10, no. 6: 599–611.

Nakajima, Michiko. 1994. "Recent Legal Decisions on Gender-Based Wage Discrimination in Japan." *U.S.-Japan Women's Journal: English Supplement*, no. 6 (March): 27–43.

Nakayama, Toru. 1991. "Toshi-ginko ni okeru haken pato rodosha" (Temporary contract workers in city banks). In *Konnichi no haken rodosha* (Today's temporary contract workers), ed. Yuji Kato. Tokyo: Shin Nihon shuppansha.

Okochi, Kazuo. 1972. *Rodokankeiron no rekishiteki hatten* (Historical evolution of labor theories). Tokyo: Yuhikaku.

———. 1952. *Reimeiki no nihon rodo undo* (The early labor movements in Japan). Tokyo: Iwanami shoten.

Okochi, Kazuo, et al., eds. 1961. *Nihon no keiei to rodo* (Management and labor in Japan). Tokyo: Yuhikaku.

Owaki, Masako, et al. 1985. "Danjo koyo kikai kintohou no houteki impakuto" (The legal impact of the Equal Employment Opportunity Law). *Nihon rodo kyokai zasshi* (July): 2–24.

Population Crisis Committee. 1988. *Country Rankings of the Status of Women: Poor, Powerless and Pregnant.* Population Briefing Paper, no. 20 (July).

Rodosho (Ministry of Labor). 1989 and 1993. *Joshi koyo kanri kihon chosa* (Basic survey on employment and management of female workers). Tokyo: Rodosho.

———. 1989 and 1990. *Koyo doko chosa* (Survey on employment trends). Tokyo: Rodosho.

———. 1989. *Chingin sensus* (Survey on wages). Tokyo: Rodosho.

Rodosho, Fujinkyoku (Ministry of Labor, Women's Bureau), ed. Annual. *Fujin rodo no jitsujyo* (Actual status of female workers). Tokyo: Rodosho.

Sakurai, Minoru. 1985. "Haken ni chokumensuru kinyu kikan no jinji romu kanri"

(Banks' personnel management policy coping with changes). *Sogo ginko*. (October): 16–19

Sinohara, Miyohei. 1970. *Structural Changes in Japan's Economic Development*. Economic Research Series no. 11. Tokyo: Hitotsubashi University (Institute of Economic Research).

Somucho, Tokeikyoku (Management and Coordination Agency, Statistics Bureau). 1990. *Rodoryoku chosa* (Labor force survey). Tokyo: Somucho.

————. 1988. *Shugyo kozo kihon chosa*. (Employment status survey). Tokyo: Somucho.

Sorifu (Prime Minister's Office). 1992. *Danjo byodo ni kansuru yoron chosa* (Survey of public opinion on gender equality). Tokyo: Sorifu.

————. 1990 and 1993. *Fujin no shugyo ni kansuru yoron chosa*. (Survey of public opinion on women and work.) Tokyo: Sorifu.

————. 1979 and 1984. *Fujin ni kansuru yoron chosa* (Survey of public opinion regarding women). Tokyo: Sorifu.

Tachibanaki, Toshiaki. 1982. "Further Results on Japanese Wage Differentials: Nenko Wages, Hierarchical Position, Bonuses, and Working Hours." *International Economic Review* 23, no. 2: 447–61.

Taira, Koji. 1970. *Economic Development and Labor Market in Japan*. New York: Columbia University Press.

Takenaka, Emiko. 1989. *Sengo joshi rodoshiron* (The postwar history of female workers). Tokyo: Yuhikaku.

Tazaki, Nobuyoshi. 1990. "Josei rodo no shoruikei" (Female work and occupations). In *Nihon josei seikatsushi* (History of the lives of Japanese women), ed. Joseishi Sogo Kenkyukai. Tokyo: University of Tokyo Press.

Tsuda, Masumi. 1987. "Shin nijyukozo jidai wa toraisuruka?" (Is an era of new dual labor market coming?). *Nihon rodo kyokai zasshi* (January): 33–43.

Tsunoda, Yukiko. 1993. "Sexual Harassment in Japan: Recent Legal Decisions." *U.S.-Japan Women's Journal: English Supplement*, no. 5 (July): 52–68.

Tsurumi, E. Patricia. 1990. *Factory Girls: Women in the Thread Mills of Meiji*. Princeton, NJ: Princeton University Press.

Work, Education, and the Family

❖ ❖ ❖

Kazuko Tanaka

With the structural transformation of the Japanese economy over the last forty years, involving a shift from agriculture to manufacturing and service industries, employment opportunities outside the household for women have also expanded. Women have been increasingly drawn into the paid sector—initially young single women in the late 1950s and early 1960s and then middle-aged and older married women from the late 1960s. When a majority of Japanese women worked in the fields, in family-owned small-scale shops and factories, and at home doing simple assembling jobs, their economic activity rarely conflicted with their familial role. Rather, work for the family business and farm was a part of the wife's role. As paid employment became a dominant form of economic activity for married women, conflict between their economic and familial roles also increased. Since women, historically, have taken primary responsibility for household tasks and child care, they confront serious obstacles in working outside the home while also being a wife and mother at home. Mothers with small children generally are not engaged in the paid sector due to the difficulty of reconciling their competing roles.

The major goal of this essay is to examine changing features of Japanese employment behavior, especially focusing on the role of education. Access to educational resources has substantially increased for women. High school education has become universal, and more than two out of five women now continue on to higher education. In an industrialized society education is an important and usually decisive resource for individuals. Economic and social rewards are associated with levels of educational attainment. Previous studies, however, have consistently reported that education has a negative effect on Japanese women's employment (Umetani 1972; Hill 1982 and 1983; Osawa 1986; Tanaka 1987 and 1989b). Japanese women have not fully translated the potential benefits of their educational resources into their career development. This essay attempts to untangle the complicated relationship between education and employment.

Rapid social change differentiates the availability of opportunities and resources across birth cohorts, and successive birth cohorts experience changes in opportunities and accessibility to resources at different life stages. There are several important changes which have created a different social, economic, and familial context influencing women's approaches to combining family responsibilities and paid employment. These include employment opportunities and educational attainment, declines in fertility and a shorter period of intensive child care responsibility, an increase in cash demand for improving or maintaining a standard of living, and changing normative pressure with regard to being a full-time housekeeper or mother. Thus, it is important to understand women's employment behavior in terms of ongoing changes and the historical context.

In the next section changes in the larger social and economic structures are briefly described. This section provides the background to increase our understanding of Japanese women's employment behavior. The following section examines the relationship between education and employment, and the final section discusses the future direction of changes in women's life chances.

Changing Economic and Social Structures

Japanese society has experienced rapid structural transformation during the period after World War II, which can be divided into two stages, before and after the mid-1970s. Following the drastic changes in the Japanese economy concomitant with the shift out of agriculture, since the mid-1970s Japanese society has evolved into a more mature, developed economy. In this section changes in employment opportunities, educational attainment, and the family structure are briefly described.

Changing Employment Structure

The Japanese economy has rapidly shifted from agriculture to manufacturing and service industries over the past forty years. This shift out of agriculture was especially drastic during the period before the mid-1970s. The proportion of workers engaged in agriculture dropped from 32.6 percent in 1960 to 13.9 percent by the mid-1970s and has declined gradually since then. Meanwhile, the overall women's labor force participation rate declined up through the mid-1970s, from 56.7 percent in 1955 to 45.8 percent in 1975, only rising since then. In the 1950s the trend in the participation rate for family workers in agriculture dominated the overall trend in women's labor force participation. As a result of rapid transformation of the Japanese economy out of agriculture, women lost jobs in the agricultural sector more than they gained jobs in non-agricultural sectors. It is worth noting, however, that the importance of paid employment for Japanese women increased even during this stage, when the female labor force participation rate declined.

The expansion of employment opportunities outside the household has increasingly pulled women into the paid sector. Significantly, the economic activity of married women in the paid sector has continuously increased in the post–World War II era. In 1960 only 8.8 percent of married women worked as paid employees, rising to 35.7 percent in 1992. Consequently, the number of married women has exceeded that of single women among paid employees since the mid-1970s.

A massive influx of married women in the paid sector has changed the shape of the age-specific profile of paid employment from a single- to a bimodal peak. The 1965 profile, for example, showed a sharp peak at ages twenty to twenty-four, without a second peak, while the 1980 profile had a mild second peak at ages forty to forty-nine. During the 1960s, young single women had increased chances to work as paid employees, but quit their jobs at marriage. Middle-aged married women had few opportunities in the paid sector, and their economic activities were largely limited to home employment. Through the 1970s and 1980s an increasing number of married women reentered the labor market after intensive child care responsibilities had diminished.

Yet a sharp drop in the participation rates at ages twenty-five to twenty-nine and a further drop at ages thirty to thirty-four have not disappeared, even though the overall participation rates at these ages have increased. This is partly related to the timing of marriage and childbirth. The average age at the first marriage is relatively old, around twenty-six, but a majority of women marry and have their first child before age thirty. Thus, women aged twenty to twenty-four are most likely to be single and those aged twenty-five to thirty-four to be newly married or mothers with small children. For mothers with small children it is quite difficult to combine child care with work outside the home. In 1992, among mothers whose youngest child was younger than four years old, the paid employment rate was only 21.4 percent. After graduating from school, women work as paid employees at offices, factories, or shops until marriage. Soon after marriage, they give birth to two or three children on average while staying out of the labor market. This pattern is consistent among Japanese women born after World War II (Iwai, 1990).

Increased Educational Opportunity

Access to educational resources has increased rapidly, and children's average level of educational attainment has followed suit. In 1950 only one out of three girls (36.7 percent) and one out of two boys (48.0 percent) could receive high school educations. More than half of all Japanese children started working by helping with family-owned shops, factories, or farmers or by doing paid work soon after graduating from compulsory education. As educational opportunities increased, high school education has become universal. Since the mid-1970s almost all children have continued on to high school education (93 percent of girls and 91 percent of boys in 1975). In a similar manner, the enrollment rates in higher education have also increased until the mid-1970s, leveling off thereafter. Two out of five female high school graduates and two out of five male graduates now continue with higher education.

Equal educational opportunity has been achieved through the compulsory level and to a large degree at the secondary level, but at the college level substantial gender differences in educational opportunities still persist. Among those with a higher education, almost all men receive a four-year university education, while more than half of the women receive their further education at a two-year, junior college. (For further discussion of gender differences at the college level, see the essay by Kumiko Fujimura-Fanselow in this volume.) In 1989 the enrollment rate in four-year universities was 34.1 percent for eighteen-year-old males and 14.7 percent for females, while that in two-year colleges was 1.7 percent and 22.1 percent, respectively.

Changing Family Structure

The Ministry of Health and Welfare's *Vital Statistics* of Japan for 1989 reported that the average number of children born had dropped to an all-time low of 1.57 (Kosheisho tokeijohobu 1989). At the same time, the average age at first marriage rose to a record high: 28.5 years for men and 25.8 years for women. The current phenomena of delayed marriages and low fertility rates are important indicators of ongoing changes within the Japanese family.

The decline in fertility and the delay of marriage during the last forty years are not linear trends. People postponed their marriage to later ages and had fewer children during the 1950s; thereafter, the timing of marriage and fertility patterns stabilized until the early 1970s. Since then there has been a reemergence of delaying marriage and a consequent decline in fertility.

Japanese faced unstable and unpredictable social and economic conditions following World War II, and under these circumstances they could not afford to have large families. After a baby boom period for a few years just after World War II, fertility rates dropped sharply. Postponing marriage was also common. As noted, delayed marriages were related to the lower fertility rate, to some extent, but it is clear that during this period, couples were also choosing to have fewer children in their fecund years.

Thereafter, Japan moved into the stage in which marriage and fertility patterns generally stabilized. In the late 1950s and through the 1960s, the average age of first marriage was twenty-four years for women and twenty-seven years for men. The total fertility rates were consistently above 2.1, exceeding the replacement level.

It is interesting that, in general, the delay of marriage is explained in terms of prolonged schooling and increased employment opportunities outside the household. Yet, despite these changes, marriage timing was rather stable during this period. One reason might be that Japanese society had already established a relatively late age for marriage. Typical patterns in transition to marriage and parenthood can be described as follows: women marry around age twenty-six and men around twenty-eight; upon marriage women quit their jobs and give birth to two or three children before age thirty. The firmly engrained concept of the so-called prime ages of marriage had operated to control the timing of marriage. The social pressure to marry in the prime ages was especially severe on women, and women's "value" in the marriage market was considered to decline rapidly after age twenty-five.

It has only been since the mid-1970s that we detect an increased delay in marriage and a drop in fertility. Interestingly, despite the delaying of marriage since the mid-1970s, the notion of a prime age is still widely shared by young Japanese. At the same time, the importance of children to marriage has remained consistently high as a social virtue. The recent decline in the total fertility rate is mainly due to the delay of marriage. There is no increase in the proportion of couples with no children or with one child. More than one-half of married couples have two children, and about one out of four have three children (Atoh et al. 1988). For a majority of Japanese marriage is largely conceptualized as a step toward forming a family with children.

The delay of marriage since the mid-1970s indicates that opportunities outside the family have increased for Japanese women. Japanese society appears to have moved from a stage in which women's adulthood is defined solely by marriage and motherhood to one in which women can be accepted as social beings outside marriage. Although this transition has not been completed, traditional marriage has become a less attractive option for young Japanese women. There has been an increase in those who remain single in their thirties, especially among women with higher education. In 1987 the average age of first marriage was 25.7 years for women. According to the 1987 *Basic Survey on Employment Structure,* (Somucho Tokeikyoku 1987), marriage rates among women aged twenty-five to twenty-nine was 70.4 percent for high school graduates, 59.4 percent for junior college graduates, and 49.9 percent for four-year university graduates. Women who postpone marriage to their thirties are most likely to be pursuing careers. Singlehood for them can be understood as a result of the choice between marriage and work. Marriage is more costly for women than men because only women are called upon to reconcile the competing demands of work and family responsibilities, whereas men have come to rely on their wives to take primary responsibility for family obligations, freeing them to concentrate on work responsibilities.

We have examined the trends of structural transformation of Japanese society for the last forty years. Employment opportunities outside the household and educational attainment have substantially increased, while the family structure has undergone rapid changes. It appears that changing features before and after the mid-1970s differ, and Japanese society has moved into a new stage. In the next section Japanese women's employment behavior is examined in relation to education.

Education and Employment

In the framework of female labor supply theory, education is one of the most important human capital investments. Since education raises productivity (and trainability), higher wages are usually paid to more educated workers. Theoretically, women with higher levels of education stand to earn more and therefore are more likely to be in the paid labor market.

Although education is strongly related to wage rates, the effect of education on women's employment cannot be totally explained by wage rates only. In addition, education is a resource in the marriage market in which women with higher education are more likely to marry men with higher education, who in turn receive higher earnings. The higher the educational level, then, the higher the family income level. Thus, women with higher educations have access to greater economic resources, enabling them to choose to stay out of the paid labor market.

In Japan education is related to both wage rates and family income. The net effect, however, of education on employment, after controlling wage rates and family income level, is negative, while it is positive in the United States (Tanaka 1989b). Tanaka argues that education is related to two other factors besides employment: one is the quality of child care and the other is career orientation.

Some evidence suggests, however, that education only recently has come to have a strong positive effect on women's employment in the United States. The gross correlation between education and employment was only weakly positive in the 1950s and 1960s, and has become strongly positive only since the 1970s (Oppenheimer 1982). Furthermore, prior to 1960 the effect of education appeared to be either nonsignificant or significantly negatively related to women's employment, net of wage rate, and family income (Waite 1976; Long and Jones 1980). A strong positive relationship between education and American women's propensity to work in recent decades appears to be due to an emerging long-term career orientation and the increased importance of education for career advancement.

Tanaka (1989a) has reported that at each life cycle stage education has a negative effect on Japanese women's employment, after controlling for wage rates and husband's income. This finding suggests that education has not been fully translated into career advancement for Japanese women, which is largely due to the limited employment opportunities for married women.

One specific feature of the Japanese employment structure is that a relatively large proportion of married women still engage in economic activities as family workers or self-employed workers (home employment) in nonagricultural industries. It has been consistently about 14 percent through the 1970s and 1980s. Small-scale businesses are prevalent in the Japanese economy, and wives are expected to work for the family business as part of their family duties. In the paid sector educational background is one of the important determinants of wage scales and promotion opportunities, while it is not required when women work for family businesses or work on their own. Thus, less-educated women are more likely to be found in home employment (Nakano 1984; Tanaka 1987; Iwai 1990).

Another feature of Japanese women's employment is that a large part of the increase of married women in the paid sector has been due to the increase in part-time employment among middle-aged and older women. In 1960 only 8.9 percent of female paid employees worked on a part-time basis. This percentage has continuously increased, rising to 30.7 percent by 1992 (Rodosho fujinkyoku 1993, app. p. 68; app. tab. 66). A majority of part-time workers are married women who want to combine their family responsibilities and gainful work. In 1990 more than half of all female part-time workers were aged thirty-five to forty-nine.

Part-time jobs are typically low-paid, low-status, unstable jobs. More than eighty-five percent of part-time workers are concentrated in manufacturing, sales, and service industries, and more than one-half of all part-time workers are in small-scale firms with less than thirty employees. Occupational distribution of part-time workers is also skewed. More than eighty percent of part-time workers are sales workers, production process operatives, and service workers. Access to clerical occupations is very much limited for part-time workers. In 1988 only 14.2 percent were in this occupational category. A majority of part-time jobs are manual, sales, or service jobs, which do not require a high educational background.

Before marriage almost all female workers engage as full-time paid employees regardless of their educational background. At marriage a majority of women leave paid work, while the importance of home employment increases. This pattern can be observed among high school graduates and junior college graduates but not among four-year university graduates. They are rarely engaged in home employment, as family workers and self-employed workers or as part-time workers (Nakano 1984; Iwai 1990). Nakano (1984) reports that, among women who worked as paid employees before marriage, highly educated women are more likely to keep working as paid employees after marriage on a full-time basis and not work as part-time workers or self-employed workers, while less educated women are more likely to withdraw from the labor market after marriage but usually return to work as part-time or self-employed workers. Thus, education is not only related to home versus paid employment; it is also related to part-time versus full-time paid employment.

More-educated women delay marriage and keep working until later ages and continue to work even after marriage. Yet, once they withdraw from the labor market, they are less likely to return to work (Tanaka 1987, 1989a). In the birth cohort analysis of life cycle employment patterns across educational background, Tanaka (1989a) has reported that reentry to the paid sector occurred at the earlier life cycle states after childbirth for those with less education, and this reentry pattern became more distinct for more recent cohorts. For women with higher educations, however, life cycle employment patterns show little change across cohorts, and there was no increase in re-employment rates.

Using more recent data collected in 1985, Iwai (1990) has examined

Table 1

Changing Occupational Distribution among Women Born between 1946 and 1965 by Educational Background (in percentage)

Women with Only Compulsory Education						
Age	19	20	23	25	30	35
Professional	3.5	7.0	3.5	1.8	2.0	3.1
Managerial	0.0	0.0	0.0	0.0	0.0	0.0
Clerical	1.8	5.3	5.3	7.1	5.9	3.1
Sales	22.8	19.3	17.5	12.5	5.9	12.5
Skilled laborer	12.3	10.5	7.0	7.1	11.8	15.6
Semi-skilled laborer	29.8	24.6	17.5	12.5	15.7	15.6
Unskilled laborer	3.5	3.5	0.0	0.0	0.0	0.0
Farmer, gardener	0.0	0.0	5.3	7.1	9.8	12.5
Out of labor force	22.8	26.3	43.8	51.7	47.1	34.3
Others	3.6	3.6	0.0	0.0	2.0	3.1
Sample number	57	57	57	56	51	32

High School Graduates						
Age	19	20	23	25	30	35
Professional	4.3	4.3	7.4	5.8	3.9	3.9
Managerial	0.0	0.0	0.0	0.0	0.0	0.0
Clerical	47.2	48.5	34.6	19.2	13.3	15.6
Sales	7.4	8.6	7.4	8.3	7.8	14.3
Skilled laborer	4.9	7.4	6.8	7.1	11.7	15.6
Semi-skilled laborer	8.0	8.0	5.6	7.1	5.5	7.8
Unskilled laborer	0.0	0.0	0.0	0.0	0.0	0.0
Farmer, gardener	0.6	1.2	0.6	1.3	0.8	2.6
Out of labor force	26.4	21.4	36.4	50.0	56.3	37.7
Others	1.2	0.6	1.2	1.3	0.8	2.6
Sample number	163	163	162	156	128	77

changing occupational distribution until age thirty-five for women born between 1946 and 1965 (see table 1). First, as education increased, occupation has shifted from manual to nonmanual work and from clerical to professional work, especially for women in their early twenties. Second, women withdraw from the labor market regardless of education to give birth and raise their children. In their early thirties, however, high school and two-year college graduates have a high tendency to return to work, while such a reentry pattern is not observed for four-year university graduates. Third, changes in

Table 1 (continued)

Changing Occupational Distribution among Women Born between 1946 and 1965 by Educational Background (in percentage)

	Junior College Graduates				
Age	20	23	25	30	35
Professional	30.0	30.0	20.3	9.3	11.1
Managerial	0.0	0.0	0.0	0.0	0.0
Clerical	33.3	26.7	15.3	14.0	7.4
Sales	1.7	1.7	1.7	7.0	3.7
Skilled laborer	5.0	0.0	1.7	2.3	14.8
Semi-skilled laborer	1.7	1.7	1.7	0.0	3.4
Unskilled laborer	3.3	3.3	3.4	4.7	7.4
Farmer, gardener	1.7	3.3	5.1	7.0	11.1
Out of labor force	21.7	30.0	47.5	53.5	37.0
Others	1.7	3.3	3.4	2.3	3.7
Sample number	60	60	59	47	27

	Four-Year University Graduates			
Age	23	25	30	35
Professional	45.5	36.4	36.7	28.6
Managerial	0.0	0.0	0.0	0.0
Clerical	27.3	27.3	3.3	7.1
Sales	6.1	3.0	0.0	0.0
Skilled laborer	0.0	0.0	6.7	7.1
Semi-skilled laborer	0.0	0.0	0.0	0.0
Unskilled laborer	0.0	0.0	0.0	0.0
Farmer, gardener	0.0	0.0	0.0	0.0
Out of labor force	21.3	30.3	53.3	57.1
Others	0.0	3.0	0.0	0.0
Sample number	33	33	30	14

Source: Data from Iwai 1990, tables 7.7, 7.8, 7.10, and 7.11.

occupational distribution by ages reflect changes caused mainly by women's withdrawal from the labor market to give birth and raise families and only secondarily by job changes along the life course. Over time patterns of correspondence between education and occupation become similar for high school and two-year college graduates. Occupational distribution for four-year university graduates, however, is quite distinctive. They are less likely to quit jobs if they have a professional occupation, but most quit by the age of thirty if their jobs are clerical.

The negative relationship between education and employment is strongly related to limited opportunities, especially for reentry after women leave the labor market to take on child care responsibilities. Recent delay of marriage among more educated women is quite suggestive of how difficult it is for women to combine family and work responsibilities.

In the past fifteen to twenty years, occupational choices for women with a university education have been diversifying. While in the past a large proportion went into teaching, as Table 2 shows, the proportion of teachers has declined sharply, partially reflecting a sharp decline in the number of school-age children. During the same period, the proportion of professional technicians, sales workers, and clerical workers has increased. In general, increased occupational diversification provides better career and life choices for women. However, women in clerical and sales occupations are largely discouraged for seeking long-term careers, face limited promotions, and tend to withdraw from work upon marriage and childbirth. In contrast, clerical and sales jobs are usually stepping stones to managerial positions for male university graduates.

Table 2

Occupational Distribution among Four-Year University Graduates by Sex, 1977 and 1992 (in percentage)

	1977		1992	
	Females	**Males**	**Females**	**Males**
Professional, technical occupations	54.4	35.0	39.5	37.6
Technicians	3.6	25.7	14.7	30.6
Teachers	37.7	6.1	15.0	3.9
Health, medical	7.0	1.2	4.8	1.2
Others	6.0	1.9	5.0	1.9
Clerical	38.8	38.7	47.0	37.7
Sales	3.5	20.2	10.0	20.6
Others	3.4	6.0	3.6	4.1
Total	100.0	100.0	100.0	100.0

Source: Mombusho (Ministry of Education), *Gakko kihon chosa* (School basic survey) for various years. Tokyo: Mombusho, annual.

In general, women who withdraw from the labor market have little chance to return to jobs with prospects for career advancement. They are largely peripheral from the core labor market and tenure-related promotions. Referring to the dual labor market, Wada (1988) argues that the labor market for married women who interrupt their careers to raise a family is distinctive from that for young new graduates. Women with lower levels of educational attainment tend to be the most disadvantaged in resuming their careers, while college and university graduates have moderately better opportunities for reentering the labor market. Those with higher education usually can draw on greater financial resources, enabling them to stay out of the labor market if they wish and thus allowing them to be more selective about resuming their careers.

Summary and Discussion

Both access to educational attainment and employment opportunities outside the household have rapidly increased. Japanese women can draw on greater resources than before to be active outside the household. To some extent, we can say that Japanese women have gained sufficient educational resources to be on a more equal footing with men. Yet women's position is still circumscribed. Compared to the pre–World War II period, differences in the content of education between men and women have greatly diminished in the basic educational curriculum. Education for women in the pre–World War II period was explicitly designed to prepare them to become a *"ryosai-kenbo,"* a "good wife and wise mother" (Fukuya 1969; Murai 1969; Nolte 1983; Smith 1987). According to Smith (1987), this ideal feature of women was not based on Confucian precepts evident in Japanese ideology at that time, but rather was the Japanese version of the nineteenth-century Western "cult" of "true womanhood."

Nolte (1983) points out that "the theme of educated motherhood gradually came to be predominant as female factory labor diminished in relative economic importance during the early years of this century" (9). In the 1920s and 1930s the Japanese economy rapidly shifted from light to heavy industries and the modern middle and working classes started to emerge (Cole and Tominaga 1976). Contrary to the Western industrialized nations, in which a large proportion of women were already housewives in the nineteenth century, housewives became a pervasive phenomenon in Japan only after World War II.

During the pre–World War II period the importance of education beyond the compulsory level for a daughter grew popular, although education for girls, especially at the girls' high school, was viewed as a resource to facilitate marriage to white-collar, middle-class men. Under the new educational system after World War II the girls' high schools were transformed into two-year junior colleges for women, bastions of traditional gender-specific education for women which emphasized the need to become good wives and wise mothers. Higher education, especially two-year college education, is still considered to be a more valuable resource in the marriage market than in the labor market.

In the labor market, women workers have had limited access to "good" jobs that are stable and offer a room for growth. Although employment opportunities have increased for middle-aged and older married women, what are available for them are generally low-paid, low-status, and unstable jobs. Less-educated women are more likely to be movers between the home and the labor market. Four-year university graduates are more likely to be polarized into two groups, career seekers and full-time housewives. Once a woman withdraws from the labor market because of household and child care responsibilities, she rarely has a chance to resume her career in her previous workplace.

Japanese society is largely organized based on a rigid gender division of labor. Thus, it is difficult for women to have both career and family. Men are expected to devote, and are accustomed to doing so, their time and energy to the workplace. Long working hours have not been reduced much. Wives are supposed to take the primary responsibility for family affairs and cannot expect husbands to share in the household tasks and child care. Thus, a woman who wants to pursue a career has good reasons to, and is more likely to, postpone marriage.

Singlehood for women has become more accepted as an alternative lifestyle among Japanese. Increased employment opportunities allow women to be more independent and to refuse undesirable marriages. In Japanese society norms for women's roles are no longer so rigid or narrowly defined. Along with the development of alternatives to motherhood for women, marriage may someday no longer be exclusively viewed as merely a transition to parenthood. A variety of family formation strategies can be developed in the future. In this process the gender division of labor needs to be relaxed within the family and the workplace.

REFERENCES

Atoh, Makoto, and others. 1988. "Kekkon to shussan no doko: daikyuji shussanryoku chosa no kekka kara" (Marriage and fertility in present-day Japan: major findings of the Ninth Japanese National Fertility Survey). *Jinko mondai kenkyu* (Journal of population problems), no. 187: 1–28.

Brinton, Mary C. 1984. "Nihon ni okeru josei no rodo sanka: sono shakai/seidoteki kontekusuto" (Women's labor force participation in Japan: its social-institutional context). *Nihon rodo kyokai zasshi* (Monthly journal of the Japan Institute of Labor), no. 306 (November): 25–35.

Cole, Robert E., and Ken'ichi Tominaga. 1978. "Japan's Changing Occupational Structure and Its Significance." In *Japanese Industrialization and Its Social Consequences*, ed. Hugh Patrick. Berkeley: University of California Press. 53–95.

Cook, Alice H., and Hiroko Hayashi. 1980. *Working Women in Japan: Discrimination, Resistance, and Reform.* Ithaca: New York State School of Labor and Industrial Relations, Cornell University.

Fukaya, Masashi. 1969. "Sei to shakai ido" (Sex and social mobility). *Kyoiku shakaigaku kenkyu* (Journal of sociology of education), no. 24: 62–76.

Hill, Anne M. 1982. "Joshi rodoryoku no nichibei hikaku" (A comparison of female labor participation in Japan and the United States). *Nihon rodo kyokai zasshi* (Monthly journal of the Japan Institute of Labor), no. 274: 14–25.

————. 1983. "Female Labor Force Participation in Developing and Developed Countries—Consideration of the Informal Sector." *Review of Economic Statistics* 65: 459–68.

Iwai, Hachiro. 1990. "Josei no raifukoosu to gakureki" (Life course and educational attainment for women). In *Gendai Nihon no kaiso kozo ido* (Stratification structure of contemporary Japan), ed. Joji Kikuchi. Tokyo: Tokyo Daigaku shuppankai. 155–84.

Kameda, Atsuko. 1985. "Shokugyo seikatsu no renzokusei: saishushokugata shokugyo keireki no jittai" (Continuity of working life: reality of working history with intermittency). *Fujin kyoiku joho* (Information on women and education), no. 11: 15–19.

Koseisho, Tokeijohobu (Ministry of Health and Welfare, Statistics and Information Department). 1989. *Jinko dotai tokei* (Vital statistics of Japan). Tokyo: Koseisho.

Lebra, Takie Sugiyama. 1984. *Japanese Women: Constraint and Fulfillment.* Honolulu, Hawaii: University of Hawaii Press.

Long, James E., and Ethel B. Jones. 1980. "Part-Week Work by Married Women." *Southern Economic Journal* 46:716–25.

Morgan, Philip S., Ronald R. Rindfuss, and Allan Parnell. 1984. "Modern Fertility Patterns: Contrasts between the United States and Japan." *Population and Development Review* 10:19–40.

Murai, Minoru. 1969. *Gendai Nihon no kyoiku* (Education in contemporary Japan). Tokyo: Nihon hoso kyokai.

Nakano, Eiko. 1984. "Kyoiku suijun kara mita yuhaigu joshi no rodoryoku kyokyu kodo" (Labor supply of married women and its relation to their educational attainment). *Jinko mondai kenkyu* (Journal of population problems), no. 171: 36–51.

Nolte, Sharon H. 1983. "Women, the State, and Repression in Imperial Japan." Women in International Development Working Paper, no. 33, Michigan State University.

Oppenheimer, Valerie K. 1982. *Work and Family: A Study in Social Demography.* New York: Academic Press.

Osako, Masako Murakami. 1978. "Dilemmas of Japanese Professional Women." *Social Problems* 26:15–25.

Osawa, Machiko. 1986. "Nichibei hikaku de mita keizai hatten to josei no shugyo kikai no henka" (Economic development and changing women's employment opportunities: U.S. and Japan). *Nihon rodo kyokai zasshi* (Monthly journal of the Japan Institute of Labor), no. 322: 14–23.

Shiozaki, Chieko. 1984. "Gakureki to kikon josei no shugyo kodo" (Education and employment behavior of married women). *Kokuritsu kyoiku kenkyujo kenkyu shuroku* (National Institute of Education, study collection) September: 87–98.

Smith, Robert J. 1987. "Gender Inequality in Contemporary Japan." *Journal of Japanese Studies* 13, no. 1: 1–25.

Somucho, Tokeikyoku (Management and Coordination Agency, Statistics Bureau).

1987. *Shugyo koyo kihon chosa* (Basic survey on employment structure). Tokyo: Somucho.

Tanaka, Kazuko. 1987. "Women, Work and the Family in Japan: A Life Cycle Perspective." Ph.D. diss., University of Iowa.

———. 1989a. "Determinants of Paid and Home Employment—Life Cycle Stage Perspective." *Shakai kagaku jaanaru* (Journal of social science) 28, no. 1: 85–117. Tokyo: International Christian University.

———. 1989b. "Education and Changing Life Cycle Employment of Japanese Women." *Shakai kagaku jaanaru* (Journal of social science) 27, no. 2 (March): 55–80. Tokyo: International Christian University.

Umetani, Shunichiro. 1972. "Kikon joshi rodoryoku no bunseki" (Analysis of labor force participation rates of married women). In *Joshi rodo no keizaigaku* (Economics of female labor supply), ed. Yoko Sano. Tokyo: Japan Institute of Labor. 108–26.

Wada, Shuichi. 1988. 1988. "Shokugyo keireki o chushin ni shita shokugyo seikatsu" (Working life, focusing on working history). In *Kogakureki josei no raifukoosu* (Life course of women with higher education), ed. Aoi Kazuo. Tokyo: Keiso shobo. 39–82.

Waite, Linda J. 1976. "Working Wives: 1940–1960." *American Sociological Review* 41: 65–80.

The Plight of Asian Migrant Women Working in Japan's Sex Industry

❖ ❖ ❖

Yayori Matsui

I n the four decades since its defeat and devastation in World War II Japan
has developed into an economic giant. On the surface such rapid economic growth does indeed seem like a miracle. A less-publicized fact is
that this rise in economic prosperity has been accompanied by an expanding
sex industry that has exploited countless women both inside and outside
Japan. This is one of Japan's most serious social problems and one that various women's groups have increasingly sought to bring to national and international attention. A related issue, which I will not take up in this discussion,
concerns the many problems faced by the growing number of Asian women
who have come to Japan in recent years as brides in order to meet the growing demand for wives in the farming districts of the country, since young Japanese women are reluctant to marry farmers and live in the country (see
Shakuya 1988).

In the 1970s Japan drew international criticism because numerous Japanese men were going on "sex tours," often arranged and paid for by their
employers, to neighboring Asian countries. In more recent years a different
form of sexual exploitation has become prominent as Japan has become the
largest recipient of Asian migrant women: estimates place this figure at
nearly 100,000 every year. These women come to Japan seeking to earn and
save money to send or take back home. While some of them enter the country
with legitimate work visas, the majority enter on tourist visas and stay on,
working illegally. Many of them end up working in Japan's booming sex
industry as hostesses, striptease dancers, other sex service–related entertain-

ers, and, finally, as prostitutes. The sad fact is that, because these women are in a highly vulnerable position due to their illegal visa status, almost without exception they fall victim to various forms of exploitation. The purpose of this essay is to describe this very serious issue, analyze it within the context of the growing phenomenon of international trafficking in women for sexual exploitation, and finally discuss some of the efforts being made by concerned Japanese women to stem such abuse.

The Growing Problem

The number of women who come to Japan from Asia seeking work is well over 100,000. While these women come from nearly all countries of Asia, more than 90 percent originate from three countries: the Philippines, Thailand, and Taiwan. The number of Filipinas accounts for 80 percent of that total, but the number of Thai women is increasing at a rapid rate.

Japan places very stringent restrictions on the entry of foreign workers; only those falling into certain categories are granted work permits; unskilled workers are not allowed in. There is a special six-month work visa granted to those coming to Japan to work on contract as artists and entertainers. Another type of work visa is granted to those employed as domestic helpers (maids, chauffeurs, etc.) by foreign embassies and employees working for foreign-based companies with offices in Japan. Those who come to Japan under the latter type of arrangement are primarily Filipinas, who are most likely to speak English. The majority of women who want to come to Japan in order to earn money are unable to obtain legitimate working visas, so they enter the country on short-term tourist visas.

Many of the women who come to Japan as migrant workers are not in the position of being able to raise their own travel expenses to Japan or find jobs there on their own. What usually happens is that they are signed up by brokers in their own countries, given an advance in the form of a round-trip plane ticket, and sent to Japan with a promise or contract stating that they will work as receptionists, waitresses, models, or ordinary bar hostesses (not engaging in prostitution). In reality, however, they are often sold by brokers to promoters in Japan, many of whom are connected to organized crime syndicates, better known as *yakuza*. For each woman a broker receives between US$2,400 and US$8,000. The women are then sold again, by the Japanese promoters, to clubs or other sex business owners, at double the price. Sometimes they are simply "rented" at a monthly charge of US$1,600 to US$6,400. In order to cover such expenses the owners frequently force the women into prostitution.

Prostitution is clearly a most profitable means of exploiting Asian women, who are victims in the international flesh trade. Without the protection visa status affords, there is no limit to the abuse and exploitation that these women may face. In addition, these women are usually young, under thirty, with many in their late teens or early twenties. Not surprisingly, they cannot speak Japanese, and, in the case of Thai women, neither can they speak English. Further, they have little idea of how to cope with living in a foreign country with such a completely different culture and climate. On top of all that, they carry with them a strong sense of obligation to earn and send money to their poor families back home. Obviously, they are in no position to resist their employers' demands or to fight for their rights.

In most instances these women are deliberately kept ignorant of the names of their employers or the owners of their workplace. Moreover, they are forced to live under the close supervision of these anonymous "masters," often in shabby, cramped quarters. The women are virtually kept prisoner, as they are systematically locked in the "cells." In addition, their passports and return air tickets are confiscated, and they are not paid the wages fixed by the contract (which is probably unintelligible to the women anyway). Nor are they given any holidays.

The Lapin Case

A number of tragic cases of victimized migrant women have been reported over the last few years. The Lapin case in Nagoya is one such case that was recently tracked by women's groups. Four Filipina women aged twenty-one to twenty-six were employed by a snack bar called "Lapin," which was in actuality a brothel, in 1988, and forced to engage in prostitution daily. They attempted to escape, only to be punished brutally. Toward the end of 1988 one of the four women secretly managed to hand a letter to a customer asking for help, "Please rescue us from here!" This letter somehow reached a support group in Nagoya, and two volunteers were sent to the snack bar to investigate the situation. The two were beaten up by employees of the snack bar, which in turn led to a police investigation. The case then became known to the public.

In early January of 1989 the support group filed a suit against the owner and employees of the snack bar on eight charges, including multiple rape, physical injuries, illegal confinement, forced prostitution, nonpayment of wages, abduction, and illegal possession of weapons. The prosecutor's office, however, filed only two charges, violence and illegal confinement. The support group suspected that it was because all four women were illegal migrant workers that the authority did not give them fair treatment.

Groups of concerned Japanese and Filipina women then launched a joint campaign to demand justice from the court by collecting signatures and holding a rally in Tokyo. In July the court handed down sentences ranging from fourteen months of imprisonment to a one-year suspended sentence to the owner and four employees. The court issued a special statement saying in effect that, even though the victims were residing in Japan illegally, nevertheless, their status did not allow anyone to exploit or abuse them and that their human rights should be protected. In August the four women were deported back to the Philippines without getting any results on the other six charges that had been pressed on their behalf by the support group but which the prosecutor's office had declined to file. Clearly, these women were denied full justice by the Japanese judicial system.

This case is but one of several similar ones that have occurred recently. Following is a sample of other cases:

• A Filipina hostess was beaten up by her employer because she refused to sleep with customers; she subsequently died from brain damage.

• A Filipina woman was left nearly unconscious near the gate of the Philippine Embassy in Tokyo; she died of tuberculosis in the hospital five days later.

• Two Filipina dancers burned to death as a result of being confined to their room on the second floor of their club in Okinawa when a fire broke out.

• A Filipina stripper in the city of Nagoya tried to commit suicide after one of her customers forced her to perform a sadistic sexual act.

• A Filipina hostess refused to sleep with a customer and jumped out of the second floor of a club; she broke both of her legs and was sent back to Manila in a wheelchair.

The growing number of Asian migrant women who have sought help in shelters all over Japan—such as House in Emergency of Love and Peace (HELP)[1]—is further indicative of the scale of human rights violations, inhumane and humiliating treatment, and sexual abuse taking place. Over the three-year period from 1987 to 1990, twelve hundred women sought refuge and assistance as a result of having been subject to physical violence, psychological threats, nonpayment of wages, or forced prostitution. While migrant women suffer from this gross exploitation, those who take part in their exploitation, including brokers, promoters, club owners, and pimps, all make enormous profits at their expense; the returns from forced prostitution are particularly high. At the same time, these people have managed for the most part to escape prosecution for their crimes.

Most recently, allegations by the Philippine government that the actual cause of death in the case of a Filipina woman who had been working in Japan as a dancer had been covered up by Japanese authorities prompted President Aquino, in November of 1991, to approve a proposal for greatly restricting the number of Filipinos allowed to go to Japan and other countries as migrant workers ("Nihon dekasegi jijitsujo kinshi" 1991). Recognizing that a majority of women who go to Japan as "entertainers" in fact end up working as nightclub "hostesses," this plan, arrived at through consultations with civic and labor groups and promoters, called for raising the minimum age for women leaving the country as migrant workers from eighteen to twenty-three and requiring those seeking visas under the category of "entertainers" to demonstrate that they have had a minimum of one-year experience as singers, dancers, magicians, etc. It also called for cooperation in placing stricter regulations upon recruiters and having employers of these workers cooperate by practicing stricter self-regulation.

The Case of Thai Women

Although the number of Filipinas working in Japan far surpasses that of other Asian women, Thai women are coming to Japan in rising numbers, and these Thai women are even more vulnerable to the kinds of exploitation, abuse, and violence that I have described. This is attested to by the fact that the number of Thai women taken to shelters such as HELP in Tokyo now surpasses that of Filipina women.

Why are Thai women more likely to be victimized? Unlike Filipina women, they rarely speak English; second, since they are mostly Buddhists, they do not feel they can ask for help at Catholic churches, as Filipinas do; third, they are sent to Japan by well-organized recruiting agencies often connected with underground mafia-type organizations; and, last, Thai women cannot easily turn to the Thai community in Japan for help because it is much smaller than the Filipino community.

Thai women are not only likely to be forced into prostitution and abused in many ways in Japan, but in addition, if they are deported back to their home country, they often face imprisonment for using fake passports, which were provided by their brokers. It often happens that on their arrival at Bangkok airport their passports are checked, and, if they are found to be fake, the women are taken to a nearly police station and interrogated. Unless they can prove that they did not know the passports were fake, they may be sentenced to a term of one and a half years in prison. On the other hand, if such women somehow manage to run away from a brothel and make their way back to Thailand by themselves, they have to remain in hiding to avoid revenge from their brokers. It is very difficult for these women to return to a normal life once they have been sent to Japan. In early 1990 a feminist group in Bangkok called Thai Friends of Women set up a project to protect Thai migrant women who are deported back to Thailand. A feminist group in Japan, the Asian Women's Association, has supported the project through the Thai Migrant Women's Support Fund.

Why Do Asian Women Come to Work in Japan?

Why are such huge numbers of Asian women flooding into Japan? This phenomenon, essentially, is a manifestation of the unequal economic imbalance between the North and the South—that is, the wealthy, industrialized nations of the northern hemisphere versus the poorer, less economically developed nations of the southern hemisphere. In other words, it is a symptom of deeply rooted economic problems that prevail on a global scale.

If we look at the countries from which women come to work in Japan, we find that they are all facing deteriorating economic conditions. The burden of having to pay back huge foreign debts, the failure of land reform, continued corruption, intensified militarization, and other problems have made peoples' lives harder than ever. Unemployment and below-subsistence wages force both men and women to migrate and seek jobs elsewhere in order to survive and support their families. The legacy of exporting manpower and womanpower overseas for the purposes of relieving the unemployment problem and also earning much needed foreign currency continues.

On the side of the receiving country, Japan, we need to examine why the sex industry flourishes, creating such a high demand for female workers. The answer to this question is inextricably tied to Japan's economic system. Japanese men are probably the hardest workers among the advanced industrialized countries. Some may even go so far as to say that they are virtually enslaved by the companies that employ them. Under the so-called Japanese-style management system—based on the three pillars of lifelong employment, seniority, and cooperative management-labor relations—employees are treated as family members of the company-family and are in turn expected to be loyal and devote their lives to their companies.

The average number of working hours per year for employed Japanese workers is still over 2,000 hours, compared to 1,500 to 1,800 hours in Western European countries, and the average number of paid holidays taken is only nine days. Many men work on Saturdays and even on Sundays. These businessmen "warriors" seek outlet and relief from their demanding work lives by frequenting entertainment facilities together with their colleagues or business clients. Companies themselves officially provide their employees and clients opportunities to drink and enjoy entertainment in the company of women. In some cases companies themselves organize sex tours abroad for their employees as a reward for hard work or successful business deals.

Up until about fifteen or twenty years ago "hostesses" working in the so-called night industry—bars, nightclubs, and snack bars—catering to these men were mostly young, single women. More recently, as the level of education attained by Japanese women as well as the demand for young women workers in offices, factories, and retail businesses has increased, these establishments have found it increasingly difficult to recruit young women. Those who work in these establishments today are mostly middle-aged women. Within the structure of Japan's employment system, in which pay and promotion are generally based on length of continuous employment on a job, middle-aged women, who generally lack experience and skills and have not worked continuously, find it very difficult to obtain jobs that pay well. Women who find themselves in the position of suddenly having to support their families because of a husband's illness, death, or accident are often forced to work in the night industry in order to earn enough money. To make up for the shortage of young women, who are more likely to draw customers, these establishments have increasingly turned to "importing" young female workers from other Asian countries who can be exploited for low wages.

Japanese Attitudes Regarding Prostitution

To understand why the sex industry is so widespread and lucrative in Japan we need to look at certain historically formed cultural and ideological factors. Prostitution has a long history in Japan, one that is based on deeply rooted sexist and patriarchal attitudes derived from Confucian ideology; it has, indeed, long been socially accepted in Japan.

During its feudal period Japan was ruled by the warrior class (samurai), and a strict Confucian ethic was imposed on those who belonged to this ruling class. As for women, they were expected to follow the Confucian rule of the three obediences: as a daughter, obey the father; as a wife, obey the husband; and, as a mother, obey the son. Marriage was regarded not as a union of an individual man and woman based on love but, rather, a means of forging political alliances between families and preserving the feudal family, or *ie*. The vital role of women was to give birth to a son, a successor to the head of the family; in other words, they were regarded primarily as breeding machines. Love was not an essential ingredient in a marriage, and, in the matter of sex, it was in fact considered immoral for a married couple to enjoy sexual pleasure.

There was, however, another type of woman in society whose role was to provide sexual pleasure for men outside the home. As far back as 1528, Japan's feudal rulers had established an official system of prostitution and designated authorized prostitution districts, called *kuruwa*. By 1720 twenty-five such *kuruwa* existed throughout Japan. It was in these *kuruwa* that prostitutes, called *"yujo"* and, later, *"geisha,"* served men sexually. *Yujo* and geisha originated from the ranks of impoverished farming families, who resorted to selling their daughters to these establishment to relieve their economic hardship.

Women were thus divided into those with wombs and those with sexual organs. Both types of women were treated as mere objects or means, not as human beings, persons with human dignity. This dichotomy in the division of women has carried over into the present day. Many Japanese divide women into the categories of "good women," or housewives, and "bad women," or prostitutes. It is common thinking in this society that bad women are necessary in order to protect the good women. Men who buy the services of prostitutes are never socially condemned; even women will remark, "If my husband goes to a 'professional' woman, it's not a problem, but if he is attracted to an ordinary, respectable woman, I feel hurt and get jealous." Such a double standard regarding women is deeply rooted among Japanese, and they consider prostitutes as a special kind of women, failing to treat them as human beings and to accord them their human rights.

Although licensed prostitution was legally banned following the enactment of the 1956 Anti-Prostitution Law, in fact the government has continued to sanction state-regulated prostitution to exist in the form of "massage parlors." Although several prefectures have banned massage parlors from their areas, many others have allowed them to conduct business in designated prostitution areas, or "amusement centers."

Trafficking in Women as a Global Issue

While Japan is guilty of taking part in and profiting from the traffic in women for purposes of prostitution, this is, in reality, a phenomenon that is becoming increasingly conspicuous in nearly all Asian countries. The primary factor promoting the sex industry in several countries has been the expansion of international tourism. Most Third World countries suffer from the burden of heavy foreign debts, and many of their governments have promoted tourism as a means of obtaining foreign currency. The desire to attract foreign tourists has, in turn, promoted the traffic in young girls and women.

Yet, prior to prostitution tourism, military base prostitution was flourishing as the R&R (rest and recreation for U.S. military servicemen) industry in Thailand and Taiwan until the end of the Vietnam War. Still today, in several location in Asia—for example, Okinawa, Japan, Isan, South Korea, and, most notably, Olongapo, the Philippines, home of the U.S. Subic Naval Base, and Angeles, the location of Clark Air Base—prostitution is a serious problem.

At present Manila and Bangkok, among other Asian capitals, are known as international sex cities, with a vast number of entertainment facilities for tourists. In addition, a number of tourist resorts have been newly developed in Third World countries to sell the "three S's"—sun, sea, and sex—to male tourists from affluent countries.

One of those resorts, Phuket Island in southern Thailand, advertised as "Paradise," turned into hell in late January 1984 when a fire destroyed a brothel there and five girls perished in the flames. They were young prostitutes aged nine to twelve years old who had been locked in the basement and were unable to escape. They had been sold out by poor peasants from depressed rural villages in northern Thailand. A similar example can be found in Taiwan, where young aboriginal girls from mountain villages are sold to red-light districts in the capital city of Taipei. The number of aboriginal people is less than 2 percent of the entire population, but among prostitutes in Taipei 40 percent are tribal mountain girls, according to a survey done by Rainbow Project, an organization that aids these girls.

From my observations after visiting most of the red-light districts in Asia and talking with prostitutes from many countries, I can sum up several features of trafficking in women in our times. First, the average age of prostitutes is getting younger and younger in most countries. In some places young virgin girls who have not yet menstruated are traded, because trafficking in women is such a profitable business. As a result, the competition is becoming more fierce, and traders seek fresh young girls in their early teens, who can be easily controlled. The fear of AIDS is another reason why virgin girls are in high demand. Child prostitution in Third World countries, linked with tourism, is a most urgent issue to be tackled. Second, it is an entirely new phenomenon since the 1970s that trafficking in women has become a multinational business on a global scale. Thai women are sent to Western Europe, Japan, and many other countries. Filipina women also migrate to countries of all continents as entertainers, Japan being the largest receiving country. In nearly all cases of trafficking in women there are close linkages among underground crime syndicates in both the sending and receiving countries. Third, trafficking in women is a part of the consumer culture that has been created and promoted by transnational corporations. Everything is regarded as a commodity to be sold and bought, and even women are treated as commodities and traded to satisfy men's desires, which are stimulated in part by all forms of mass media. In this context Asian women, possessed of "oriental charm," are a favored commodity, an exoticism for Western and Japanese men. Thus, countless women in the Third World are victimized by poverty, racism, colonialism, commercialism, and sexism.

Taking Action to Stop Exploitation of Asian Women

Clearly, all means must be utilized to stem this continued wave of sexual exploitation. What kinds of actions should we take? Here I would like to talk about some of the actions we, Japanese women in alliance with other Asian women, have been taking. I will present first a brief account of the campaign we have been mounting against sex tours since the mid-1970s.

It was shocking news for Japanese women when in 1973 Korean women protested against sex tours to their country by Japanese men. At first Christian women's groups published a very strong statement condemning wealthy Japanese men who dehumanized their sisters. Then a handful of female Korean university students demonstrated at Kimpo Airport in Seoul with placards reading, "We Are Against Prostitution Tourism!" and "Don't Make Our Motherland a Brothel for Japanese Men!" Some of these women were arrested because the dictatorial government did not like such protests.

Responding to the courageous action of these Korean women, Japanese feminists organized demonstrations at Haneda Airport in Tokyo, distributing leaflets to tourists bound for Seoul, inscribed with words such as "Shame on You!" and "Stop the Shameful Behavior!" It was during this first demonstration against "Kisaeng Tourism" that I coined a new Japanese word for prostitution. In Japanese prostitution is called "*baishun*," and it is written using two Chinese characters that mean "to sell spring (body)." I substituted the first of the two characters, that is, *to sell*, for another that has the same pronunciation but has the meaning "to buy," so that the word connotes the meaning "to buy spring." I did this because I wanted to change the traditional attitude toward prostitution which condemns women for selling their bodies yet places no blame on the men who buy their services. It may seem like a rather small thing, but it is revolutionary to shift the responsibility from women to men. Those who buy sex are surely to be condemned more than those who engage in its sale.

Another example of our effort to stop sex tours was a solidarity action undertaken by Filipina and Japanese women in 1981 on the occasion of the visit to Manila by then Japanese prime minister, Suzuki Zenko. The Asian Women's Association, which had long been campaigning against sex tours, had published a special issue on prostitution tourism, exposing their exploitative structure. Just one hour after Prime Minister Suzuki's arrival, a large protest rally was held in the heart of the tourist area in Manila. About one thousand participants adopted a resolution condemning sex tours as a form of economic exploitation of women in poor countries by men of rich countries and a form of sexual exploitation as well.

This was the first mass protest action organized jointly by Filipina and Japanese women. It drew much attention from the media in the Philippines and served to discredit the image of Japanese men. As a result, Japanese travel agents began to refrain from sending tourists to Manila, and the number of Japanese visitors decreased by 25 percent following the spring of 1981. An anti–sex tour campaign was launched in Bangkok also when the prime minister visited there following his Manila trip. Thai women and students delivered a protest letter to the Japanese Embassy and performed street dramas and held placards reading "No More Sex Tours!"

Although our campaigns have achieved some results, the root causes of the traffic in women and their sexual exploitation and abuse—that is, poverty and sexism—remained unresolved. The result, as described, has been the phenomenon of Filipinas and other Asian women coming to work in Japan's sex and entertainment industry in rising numbers. The rapid growth in the trafficking in women is a worldwide phenomenon, and therefore global solidarity and cooperation among concerned women are urgently needed. To tackle this issue we need to apply both long- and short-term strategies. The long-term strategy is to attack the root causes—namely, poverty and lack of employment opportunities—which are to a large extent imbedded in unequal and unjust international and national economic systems. One of our tasks is to maintain a check on transnational corporations of the First World and to monitor the kind of official development aid extended to Third World countries. We need to work out alternative forms of development which will terminate trafficking in women for sexual exploitation and abuse. We must also change the sexist culture that regards women as sex objects and thereby dehumanizes them.

We cannot, however, just sit and wait for structural changes to be brought about, since those changes will take a very long time. We must take what actions we can within our power now to protect the human rights of victimized women. We need shelters, drop-in centers, telephone counseling, legal aid, medical care, and many other support facilities in both the receiving and sending countries. To respond to the frightening realities of international trafficking in women, networking of concerned women, especially between receiving and sending countries, is vitally needed.

NOTES

This essay is based on a report presented at the International Conference against Global Flesh Trade in New York, October 1988, organized by the Coalition against Pornography, and later in a revised, updated form at the In God's Image Advisory Committee Meeting in Kuala Lumpur, Malaysia, November 1989, and published in the book *In God's Image* (June 1990).

1. HELP is an emergency shelter for women of all nationalities which was established in 1986 by the Japan Christian Woman's Temperance Union, the oldest women's organization in Japan, on the one hundredth anniversary of its founding.

REFERENCES

Matsui, Yayori. 1987. *Onnatachi no Asia* (Women's Asia). Tokyo: Iwanami shinsho. (English trans. published as *Women's Asia* by Zed Books Ltd., 1989).

———. 1985. *Tamashii ni afureru Asia* (Asia—a continent overflowing with spirits). Tokyo: Asahi shimbunsha.

Matsui, Yayori, and Aiko Utsumi 1988. *Asia kara kita dekasegi Rodoshatachi* (Migrant workers from Asia). Tokyo: Meiseki shoten.

"Nihon dekasegi jijitsujo kinshi" (A virtual ban on migrant workers going to Japan). 1991. *Yomiuri shimbun* (Yomiuri newspaper), 21 November.

Shakuya, Kyoko. 1988. *Asia kara kita hanayome* (Brides from Asia). Tokyo: Akashi shoten.

Tanaka, Hiroshi, and Ayako Miko, eds. 1988. *Gendai no espuri*, no. 249 (April).

❖ 5 ❖

Women's Future:
Asserting New Powers

Eighty university students organized by a group calling itself Shushokunan ni
nakineirishinai joshigakusei no kai *(Association of female students who won't
give up in spite of the tough job market) demonstrated in Tokyo to protest sex
discriminition in job hiring. Dressed in their dark "recruit suits" the young
women carried placards that read "We want to work too!" "Government and
industry must guarantee our right to work," and "Don't discriminate against
women students!" Asahi shimbun Newspaper, July 28, 1994. Courtesy of
Asahi shimbun Newspaper Company, Tokyo.*

Carrying a banner with the words, "We will change politics through women's power!" a group of women demonstrate in support of their candidates in the election for the Tokyo Metropolitan Assembly. Mainichi shimbun Newspaper, *July 2, 1989. Courtesy of Mainichi Shimbun Information Center, Tokyo.*

Japan's First Phase of Feminism

❖ ❖ ❖

Mioko Fujieda

I n 1868 the new Meiji government was established in Japan, replacing the Tokugawa shogunate, whose rule had lasted for 260 years. A new Japan, with the emperor as head of state, abolished feudalism,[1] introduced a capitalist system, and pursued a path toward modernization, following the models of Western countries. Japan's start as a capitalist country lagged behind the Western countries by more than a century. To catch up with the West the political leaders of the time embarked on militaristic expansionism with the slogan "Enrich the nation, strengthen the army." Under this policy Taiwan and Korea were colonized successively.

Internally, the Emperor system and the feudalistic patriarchal family system, which formed the fundamental basis for achieving this political end, were placed on a firm ground by the end of the nineteenth century with the promulgation of the Meiji Constitution in 1889 and the Civil Code in 1898. Thus, total subjugation of women to the head of the household, and to men in general, was given legal justification. Women were placed, so to speak, outside the hierarchical order of society, regardless of the social class to which they belonged.

Women had to wait until the end of World War II in 1945 to see restrictions on their rights as human beings removed in all spheres. In the meantime, however, many women continued to struggle for their emancipation from all the miseries and injustices inflicted upon them by society and the state, through speeches, writings, and actions. Their struggle began in the earlier years of the Meiji period, often inspired and encouraged by the struggles and achievements of their sisters in the West.

It seems that outside Japan very little is known about Japanese women today, let alone about Japanese consciousness of "the Woman Question" in the past. This lack of knowledge about Japan's "First Phase," or "First Wave," as it is called in the West, holds true among most Japanese also, as the history of early feminism is totally absent from school curricula, except for a few women who are occasionally mentioned here and there, such as Yosano Akiko, poet and essayist (1878–1942), and Hiratsuka Akiko Raicho (1886–1971), who started the *Bluestocking* magazine (*Seito* in Japanese) in 1911.

Although such international developments in recent years as the International Women's Year and the United Nations (UN) Decade for Women have had an impact on the Japanese government, school textbooks, subject to rigorous inspection by the Ministry of Education prior to publication, are still filled with gender bias and sexual stereotyping and ignore the contributions made by women. Gender issues, including those having to do with the "hidden curriculum," are simply absent as a category from this inspection procedure, and thus textbooks function as an important vehicle for the perpetuation of gender bias with the Ministry's authorization. This is further compounded by the fact that for the most part textbook publishers are unaware of gender issues.

In this essay it is impossible to undertake a comprehensive discussion of the hundreds of notable women who were active in different ways during the First Phase. Therefore, what I will do here is to portray briefly the lives of the following six women: Kishida Toshiko, later known as Nakajima Shoen (1864–1901),[2] Kageyama (later Fukuda) Hideko (1865–1927), Shimizu (later Kozai) Toyoko/Shikin (1868–1933), Kanno Suga (1881–1911), Yajima Kajiko (1833–1925), and Ichikawa Fusae (1893–1981). This list is not intended to be all-inclusive but, rather, a selective illustration of different areas of commitment, persuasion, and inclination. One characteristic common among these women, however, though in different ways, is that they were all rebels.

A Real First: Kishida Toshiko

Kishida Toshiko (1864–1901) was a real first: she was the first woman to give public addresses in support of the Popular Rights Movement. Born to a wealthy merchant family in Kyoto, in 1879, at the age of fifteen she was called up to Tokyo to give lectures on Chinese classics to the empress.[3] Having grown up in a merchant family, however, she found the court life too conventional, superstitious, and unbearably hierarchical. After two years Kishida resigned, citing poor health as an excuse.

After resigning from her post, Kishida traveled extensively with her mother all over Japan, meeting people. It was a time when the Popular Rights Movement, which had lasted from the 1870s to the 1880s, was at its height.

Among the people she met during her travels were leaders in this movement, and she immediately became involved in it.

In 1882 Kishida made her appearance before the public as the first female speaker for the cause of women's rights, giving a speech entitled "Fujo no michi" (The way for women). She seems to have been a very good speaker, with an electrifying effect on the audience. In addition to being brilliant, articulate, and beautiful, the fact that she had served at the imperial court probably gave her a special aura. Her appearance on the political scene definitely had an impact on many women across the country, who were drawn to the popular rights ideas, many of them joining the movement.

This was the period immediately after the start of Japan's modernization, and feudal conventions prevailed. Life was based on Confucianist moral principles, a convention in which women were held to be biologically inferior to men. They were there to serve men and to maintain the family line. Kishida criticized this situation and called for its amelioration.

Alarmed by the heightening influence of the Popular Rights Movement, which attracted not only men but also quite a few women, the government embarked on a campaign of harsh repression. A speech Kishida made in 1883 titled "A Girl in a Box, or the Imperfection of Marriage," which criticized marriage based on a hierarchical relationship, led to her arrest and indictment on grounds of violating the Ordinance on Meeting.

It may seem extraordinary that a daughter from a merchant class could do such things, escaping the pressures from the family, but it was a period of transition and social change. Things were moving very fast in many directions. Prior to the Meiji Restoration of 1868 the samurai, or warrior class, had been the ruling class, followed by peasants and artisans, with the merchant class at the very bottom, in spite of their wealth. Toward the end of the feudal era, however, it was the merchants who controlled the whole economy. The samurai class was impoverished and in debt to the merchants. Among the merchant class one could say that there was considerable liberalism as well as criticism of the feudal system. In addition to these factors, in the case of Kishida, her mother's supportive role was extremely important in terms of her intellectual development. It was her mother who encouraged her to study and pursue her thinking.

Kishida's most representative article is one entitled "I Tell You, My Fellow Sisters," which appeared in a Liberal Party newspaper in 1884.[4] In it she refutes the commonplace argument that "men are strong and women are weak, therefore they can't be equal," saying that, if this contention refers to difference in physical strength, it reflects nothing but barbarism on the part of the speakers, whereas if it means differences in mental capabilities, it is only a distinction between the educated and uneducated. While urging women to be more self-confident, she turns to men, saying, "You men, alas, when you open your mouth you talk about reform or change, but then why are you so obstinately attached to old conventions when it comes to the issue of equal rights [between the sexes]?" Kishida continues to argue that the primary happiness for any human being will be realized only in a relationship built on love and compassion between equal men and women and that an imperious attitude on the part of men is sure to destroy this happiness.

To Kishida, however, the rights of the state (*kokken,* meaning "nationalism/patriotism"), people's rights (*minken*), and women's rights (*joken*) were all identical, and they coexisted without any contradictions in her mind. This attitude was not unique to her but was shared commonly by most of the People's Rights activists and theorists, for whom the rights of the state and those of the people were indistinguishable from each other. In Kishida's article, for instance, she explains why she wants to call to her fellow sisters, saying: "There are good reasons for this. . . . I do this from a deeply felt concern for the state and the country." Also, toward the end of the article, speaking about equal rights between the sexes, she says, "It should be a duty for any patriot concerned with our country's fate to make our country more civilized by adopting what is good from the West and making up for our shortcomings."

In 1884 Kishida married a politician, a Liberal Party leader, and withdrew not only from speaking engagements but also from direct involvement in politics.[5] Around this time Kishida and her husband were baptized and became Christians. Though in later years her writing lost the sharp edge it had in her earlier works, her rational and critical thinking did not wither until the end of her life. Their marital relationship seems to have been quite close to what she held as ideal—a relationship based on mutual love and respect. Kishida died of tuberculosis when she was thirty-seven (or forty, if she was born in 1861), two years after her husband also died of tuberculosis.

From a Popular Rights Advocate to a Socialist: Kageyama (later Fukuda) Hideko

One young woman who was very much inspired by Kishida Toshiko was Kageyama Hideko (1865–1927). She heard Kishida give a fiery speech in Okayama on the emancipation of women when she was about seventeen, and the speech made her determine that she would follow Kishida as a popular rights advocate.

Feeling the need for women's economic independence and an education that would enable them to achieve it, Kageyama founded a private school (of a family business nature) for girls and women from ages six through the sixties, but it was closed down by the authorities within a short time. Her involvement in a subversive plot, a planned putsch in Korea in 1885, which has come to be known as the Osaka Incident, resulted in her arrest, trial, and imprisonment. As she was the only woman among all those involved, this incident made her famous as "Japan's Joan of Arc." This incident only reveals how narrow and superficial her popular rights ideas were, however, as this putsch conspiracy was a manifestation of chauvinistic, interventionist nationalism. It took quite some time for Kageyama to abandon her narrow patriotism.

Her own financial predicaments drove her to become more acutely aware of women's need for economic independence, and this brought her to the Christian faith at one time. Later, her association with the then emerging socialist groups led her to socialism. In 1907, with the help of some of her male friends, she issued *Sekai fujin* (Women of the world) under the banner of women's emancipation. In a front page editorial of the first issue, she described the purposes for publishing this newspaper: "When we look at the conditions currently prevailing in society, we see that virtually everything is coercive and oppressive to the true nature of women. This necessitates that we women rise up and form a social movement of our own."[6] And in the third anniversary issue (no. 32, 5 January 1909) she claimed that the paper was meant for a readership of neither "good wives and wise mothers" nor "the successful" but, rather, for "the losers, the weak and the so-called hoodlums" for whom the paper wished to be a friend.[7] The paper was not, however, an undertaking exclusively of women, as was to be the case of *Seito (Bluestockings)* published about four years later.

In 1890 the government had prohibited women from attending political meetings. This was in response to the growing campaign by women against licensed prostitution as well as to their increasingly active participation in political discussions. And in 1900 the Police Security Regulations were introduced. The notorious Article 5 of the Regulations placed a total ban on every sort of political activity by women. This made it impossible for women to hold meetings, make speeches, and attend meetings and conferences, let alone form political organizations. All women working for the improvement of women's status became involved in a campaign against Article 5. Kageyama's journal, *Sekai fujin*, also took up this issue. While Kageyama's argument was based on the "different but equal" theory, in one of her articles she referred to a "dual struggle." According to this argument, women are subject to the rule of the "male class" and the "aristocrat and rich class," and this dominance is founded on "the society's class structure itself" (no. 4, 15 February 1907). In the meantime, she discussed elsewhere, the male-centered legal system "holds us women in contempt and abuses us," and men, who greatly benefit from this system, are dead set against women's rights. In order to change this she urged that women courageously stand up (no. 30, 4 November 1908).[8] Yet she did not elaborate on this argument. It was her dedication and commitment to her paper that made it possible for it to continue publication for two years in spite of severe repression by the government authorities.

Kageyama was a woman of action rather than a deep thinker. Her life was always a financially difficult one, as she was the main supporter of her family most of her life—her parents, her children, and her sick husband who died of syphilis in 1900, after eight years of marriage. She "always fought, never wavering because of any setback," as she triumphantly writes in her autobiography.[9] She died in extreme poverty at the age of sixty-three.

Independence versus Marriage: Shimizu (later Kozai) Toyoko/Shikin

From the same generation as Kishida and Kageyama there is Shimizu (later Kozai) Toyoko, also known by the pen name Shikin (1868–1933), who was influenced by the popular rights ideas, though she came upon the scene a little later than Kageyama. Known as a woman's rights advocate, journalist, and novelist, Shikin was a feminist pioneer in the earlier half of her life. "A Broken Ring," her earliest story, published in 1891 and believed to be based on her own life experience, is strikingly feminist in that she portrays a woman who leaves her marriage out of her own will when she finds out that her husband had been married to another woman with whom he had continued to maintain a relationship.[10] The story was literally a feminist declaration of independence, very much advanced for the period.[11]

As in the story, in her real life, in 1899, she walked out of her first marriage, which had been arranged by her father, because of her husband's involvement with other women. This unhappy experience helped awaken her to the cause of women's rights, and she joined the Popular Rights Movement. The way in which she developed her own thinking distinguishes her from her predecessors such as Kishida Toshiko and Kageyama Hideko.

In 1890 Shikin moved from Kyoto to Tokyo and worked as a journalist for *Jogaku zasshi* (Journal of women's education), and that was where she wielded her critical pen against the repressive government and against the society's "common sense," which backed the government's contemptuous attitude toward women. All her editorials, such as "Why are not women allowed to attend political meetings?" and "In tears I call you, my sisters," were written along this line.[12]

Her best novel, *Imin gakuen* (School for migrants), published in 1899, dealt with the issue of the Burakumin, or the "untouchables," for the first time in the history of Japanese literature. Although the story was idealistic, the ways in which she described society and the relationship between men and women reveal how accurate and farsighted her observations were.[13]

Earlier, around 1891, while she was engaged in the Popular Rights Movement, Shikin was proposed to by one of its leaders. It turned out that this same man had also seduced Kageyama Hideko with a promise of marriage, keeping silent about his wife. Both women, without knowing this and trusting what he had told each of them, became pregnant and gave birth to a child out of wedlock. The two women, who had been close friends at one time, were agonized. A striking difference between them, however, was that Kageyama reviled and slandered Shikin in her autobiography, whereas Shikin remained completely silent.[14]

Around 1892 Shikin again received a proposal of marriage from an extraordinary man, a natural scientist, who was later to become president of Tokyo University. He proposed to her with passion and wrote beautiful love letters in which he talked about his own feelings, something that was quite rare for that period. Obviously, she was moved, but she did not want to fall into the trap again. So she told him everything—not of her feelings but of the facts in the past. This man accepted her history, saying: "I'm not interested in your past. I love you as you are now." This rational approach and respect for their own feelings rather than for conventions and other people's feelings—such independence was remarkable for the period.[15]

The marriage did not work out, however, because she suffered within it. Shikin had to retreat from her writing. She stopped writing in her early thirties. She retreated into oblivion completely, only to be reread in the 1970s. She suffered all through the rest of her life because of the lack of a social life of her own. Her writing career was a brief ten years, and, ironically, she ended up being a model of a good wife and mother.

One of their sons, a well-known Marxist philosopher and editor of his mother's works, recalled his mother in the 1970s, saying that his parents got along perfectly well, except on one point. His father never understood how frustrated his mother felt about giving up her writing career. He writes how his father would tease her, while his mother kept silent, her eyes full of tears, saying: "You are now a fool. You who used to be a genius are now a fool."[16]

Japanese Women and the Influence of Christianity

Christianity, particularly in the form of Protestantism, greatly contributed to Japan's modernization, particularly in the early years of Meiji. This was especially notable in the area of education for girls and women and advocacy of improved status for women. Most of the girls' schools established in the early Meiji years were started by either foreign missionaries, quite often American women, or by Japanese Christians. The kind of education they sought for girls was to create "modern women," replacing Confucian values, which had been the guiding principle of education for women. What was meant by *modern women* was the type of women who would have independence of mind, which would allow them to think and act as freely and actively as men. In particular, Protestantism provided a moral support for the monogamous marriage, a union between two equal and free persons.

Protestantism emerged as a progressive ideology in support of the development of a modern society at a time when the creation of a new social order and culture following the dissolution of the feudal system was set as a prioritized task for the new nation, in the early Meiji period. As the Emperor state system became firmly entrenched, however, toward the end of the nineteenth century, with the promulgation of the Imperial Constitution (1889) and the Civil Code (1898), there was a reaction against Westernization, and Protestantism gradually lost its impact as a reformist and progressive force. Nevertheless, directly or indirectly, it had a great impact on the thinking of the Meiji intellectuals, becoming an impelling force for various social movements, developing into humanitarianism, or human emancipatory ideas, and socialism. Among leading female believers were Kishida Toshiko and Yajima Kajiko (who will be referred to later), and among those who were directly influenced by Christianity one can cite Fukuda Hideko, Shimizu Shikin, Kanno Suga, the "first political martyr," and many others.[17]

The First Female Political Martyr: Kanno Suga

Kanno Suga (1881–1911), an anarchist and political martyr,[18] was the only woman among the twelve people who were executed in 1911. Kanno, together with eleven men, were hanged on the charge of attempted assassination of the Emperor Meiji, known as the Great Treason Incident, which was trumped up by the state power determined to crush the socialist/anarchist movement. Until the very last moment of her life she is said to have remained calm as well as firm. At the time of her death she was twenty-nine years and seven months old.

It is quite often the case that a woman's reputation is affected by men's words, a reflection of the power relationship between women and men, and this is exactly what happened to Kanno. For she is described even to this day as a seductress, even to the point of being called a prostitute, an image far removed from what she really was. Even serious studies on her, including those by women writers, mostly follow this pattern, not to mention the novels about her: all bring disgrace upon her.

Where does this distortion come from? One finds that Kanno's allegedly degrading reputation originates in the autobiographies of a highly respected socialist, Arahata Kanson (1887–1981), who was married to her for a very short period. He was a dedicated socialist whose autobiographies are considered to provide valuable testimony about socialist ideas and the socialist movement in Japan from the Meiji through the Taisho and Showa periods. These works are also regarded as masterpieces of autobiographical literature. This is why his reminiscences about Kanno have been taken as truthful and dependable. Her case presents an excellent example of how male bias can affect a woman's reputation and honor.

As a result of the fact that Arahata kept republishing his autobiography, there are several versions of it. The first was *Kanson jiden* (The autobiography of Kanson), published in 1947, and subsequent ones were published in 1954, 1961, 1965, and 1975.[19] Every version contains a section on Kanno, but a careful examination of these versions reveals significant changes between the first and second versions in the ways she is described. In the second version, titled *Hitosuji no michi* (Earnestly on the way), one finds that there are additions to, and deletions from, the first version, and the subsequent versions more or less follow the line of the second version. What is to be noted here is that Arahata's revisions emphasize that he was just "a novice to the world of eroticism (or love)" and was seduced and driven mad by Kanno, who, according to him, was "a veteran in these matters." And, important, all these alterations were made in order to make this assertion sound more truthful.

In the first version Arahata writes that to get money Kanno turned to Udagawa Bunkai in return for sexual favors and that, after separating from Bunkai and becoming a journalist, she had affairs with one man after another. In short, "such a licentious life" became "second nature" to her, and she continued to repeat the same error. But in the later versions changes in wording, additions, or deletions are made in such a way that the examples he lists to demonstrate her "immoral" conduct are used to reinforce the impression on the readers' part that she became a Christian seeking salvation from her sinful life.

Much more significant was an addition Arahata made to the second version explaining Kanno's approach to socialism. He relates the story that, when Kanno was in her early teens, her stepmother arranged to have Kanno raped by a miner who worked for her father and that this traumatic experience was chiseled in her mind as an indelible memory, leading to a loss of her own self-respect. Much later, according to Arahata, she read a response by Sakai Toshihiko to a letter from an agonized rape victim which was printed in the newspaper *Yorozu choho* (All-Out morning paper), in which Sakai said, "It is nothing but an accident, just like a person attacked by a rabid dog on the street; though the victim is definitely unfortunate, it's not something for which the victim should be held responsible." Arahata conjectures that Kanno was deeply moved by the sympathy exhibited by Sakai for women and that it was a main motive for her interest in socialism. In this way her involvement with socialism is explained in the context of emphasizing a sexual experience in Kanno's life, and the "loose morals" she displayed in her later years are traced back to the assault she suffered earlier.

Except for Arahata's accounts, however, there is no evidence to indicate that her "wicked" stepmother schemed to have her raped. Also, no article, such as Arahata claims Sakai wrote, has been found. And nowhere in Kanno's own writings, in which she quite frequently refers to her family life and her own life, as well as in the police records drawn up at the time of her trial is there evidence to prove that she harbored any resentment toward her stepmother.

Later, when he learned that Kanno had begun to live with Kotoku Shusui, a senior socialist/anarchist, who was later executed together with Kanno in the same frame-up incident, the infuriated Arahata tried to kill both Kanno and Kotoku with a pistol but failed. Obviously, what consumed him was jealousy, possessiveness, and intensely ambivalent feelings of love and hatred toward Kanno.

In any case, all these accounts of Kanno by Arahata seem to be based on hearsay and rumors, the sources of which are unidentifiable or based merely on his own conjectures. Nevertheless, most of the biographical accounts of Kanno have relied, and still rely, on his words, quite often embroidering his stories further.

331

What, then, is the truth concerning Kanno? Born in Osaka, she grew up in a wealthy family as a brilliant, tomboyish daughter. After her father, originally from the samurai, or warrior, class, failed in his mining business, the family suffered hardship and misery, and Kanno was forced to give up plans for continuing education beyond primary school, despite her desire to do so. The pride and spirit she held as a samurai's daughter seem to have sustained her through all the difficulties she endured in her life. Her mother died when she was eleven years old, and she had to take care of various members of her family who fell sick—her grandmother and her brother, followed by her father and sister.

In 1899 she married Komiya Fukutaro, a Tokyo merchant. But this marriage did not give her a sense of fulfillment, and her father's illness gave her an excuse to walk out. She returned to Osaka in 1902 and, in the same year, was hired as a reporter for the newspaper *Osaka choho* (Osaka morning paper) on the recommendation of Udagawa Bunkai (1848–1930), an important figure in the world of journalism and literature in Osaka in the early and middle period of Meiji, under whom Kanno's younger brother was studying as a houseboy. Kanno respected Bunkai highly, and he in turn recognized talent in her and encouraged her to pursue a writing career. But, as already mentioned, Arahata conjectured that she had become Bunkai's mistress.

Writing for *Osaka choho*, Kanno mounted a strong campaign against licensed prostitution and the political circles that publicly sanctioned and were closely connected with it as well as social conventions that accepted it as a necessary evil, instead of denouncing it. To appeal to a much wider audience, she worked with eminent Christian and socialist figures, one of whom was the Christian socialist Kinoshita Naoe, and organizations, including the Osaka Women's Reform Society, a local branch of the Japan Women's Reform Society, which was founded in Tokyo by Yajima Kajiko and others in 1886.

Kanno's success in persuading the Osaka Reform Society, which up until then had been active primarily in the cause of temperance, to take a stand on the issue of prostitution led to her becoming an important figure within the organization. In November 1903 she was baptized a Christian, and in December she was elected to serve as one of the officers of the Osaka Women's Reform Society, responsible for documents and materials.

Kanno's involvement with and commitment to the activities of the Reform Society led her to contacts with socialists, because at the time socialists and Christians were seeking ways to forge unity in their work—though this proved to be impossible by the end of 1907. Her meeting with the socialist leader Sakai Toshihiko had an especially great impact on the subsequent course of her life.

In 1906, on Sakai's recommendation, Kanno moved to Tanabe, in the Wakayama Prefecture, in order to work for *Muro shimpo* (Muro news), a socialist and antiwar newspaper. This is where she met Arahata Kanson, who had already been working there as a reporter. After her assignment was over she returned to Kyoto with her sister, who was ill, in May 1906, and in the summer Arahata came to see her. To fulfill her promise to marry him, she moved to Tokyo later that year, again with her sister, and was hired by another newspaper, the *Mainichi Dempo* (Mainichi telegraph). The following year, her sister died. After her funeral Kanno collapsed, and her own tuberculosis was diagnosed. The relationship between Kanno and Arahata collapsed several months after they began living together.

Her worsening tuberculosis, the loss of her job with the newspaper as a result of the Red Flag Incident (though she was found innocent and later acquitted),[20] the increasingly reactionary stance of the government, which was determined to annihilate socialists, and her anger at all of this drove her to commit herself even more strongly to the socialist/anarchist cause.

Kotoku Shusui, an advocate of anarchism who was also suffering with tuberculosis, tried, with Kanno, to rebuild the socialist movement, which had been crushed by the Red Flag Incident. Kanno and Kotoku needed each other's support, and they became lovers. Their alliance was not welcomed by the socialist community because of the misunderstanding about Kotoku having stolen Kanno from Arahata during the latter's confinement in jail. Kanno and Kotoku were left isolated, both ideologically and personally. (It can easily be surmised that Arahata's accounts of Kanno had very much to do with his jealousy.) The situation worsened for them, almost to a point of suffocation. Kanno (and also Kotoku, at least in the initial stage) was pushed to be part of a scheme devised by Miyashita Takichi to manufacture explosives with the aim of assassinating the Emperor Meiji. But their plot was no match for the efficient police authorities, and it was uncovered. The incident was blown up as a major conspiracy to bring about a wholesale revolution. Charges were trumped up against Kanno and others, eventually leading her, Kotoku, and ten other men to the gallows.

Kanno Suga, sustained by lifelong pride in her own integrity and spirit as a woman from the former samurai class and led by new ideas, first Christianity and later socialism/anarchism, challenged head-on the state power as well as the society that cared not a farthing about the human rights of women and men.

An Outstanding Organizer of Women's Social Work: Yajima Kajiko

One of the most notable among the Christian women of the time was Yajima Kajiko (1833–1925). Yajima was the first president of both the Tokyo kyofukai (Tokyo Women's Reform Society), founded in 1886, and the Japan Christian Women's Society, founded seven years later, which were, in fact, the starting point of the women's movement seeking emancipation and respect for women's rights as human beings in modern Japan. It was she who pioneered in organizing the women's movement and developing women's social work.

After ten years of marriage, during which she gave birth to three children, Yajima divorced her drunken husband and moved from Kumamoto Prefecture in Kyushu to Tokyo, where she studied hard to obtain a teaching license. When she was promoted to principal of a Christian girls' high school she was forty-six years old, and it was from this point that her second life began. She was a woman possessed of an exceptionally independent mind and vitality, standing resolute when necessary; at the same time, she was patient and far-sighted.

One of her nephews, also a Christian and a well-known literary figure, did not hide his dislike of his aunt, calling her a haughty woman who did not have the heart to sympathize with her poor old husband. But his brother, also a very famous writer, had to admit that she was a woman "who does not fail to do what has to be done, and who does not do what needs not be done."[21]

Since its inception the Japan Women's Reform Society, under her leadership, actively campaigned against drinking and for the abolition of licensed prostitution. It was also actively engaged in petition campaigns for the revision of the Criminal and Civil Codes. While undertaking a campaign, together with other groups and individual women, to repeal the notorious Police Security Regulations, which prohibited women from participating in any form of political activities, the society organized petition campaigns for the abolition of licensed prostitution, organizing speech meetings and establishing refuge centers to which prostitutes could go for help. Other issues it took up included abuses inflicted upon factory women, a campaign against large-scale pollution of the Ashio Copper Mines area, the first of this kind brought about by industrial development, as well as aid projects extended to women in the polluted area.

The matrix of the Alliance for Obtaining Suffrage for Women, in which Ichikawa Fusae played a leading role, was in fact the Japan Women's Suffrage Association, which was founded by the Japan Christian Women's Reform Society in 1921 and headed by Kubushiro Ochimi in pursuance of its platform of action adopted in 1893.[22] In 1921, at the age of eighty-nine, Yajima traveled to Washington, D.C., where the Naval Arms Reduction Conference was being held, and she submitted signatures collected from more than ten thousand Japanese women petitioning for peace. She never ceased to work for the cause of women up until the very end of her days, at the age of ninety-three.

From Suffrage to the Second Phase of Feminism: Ichikawa Fusae

Since 1918, when she founded the New Women's Association, together with Hiratsuka Raicho and others, until the end of her long life, Ichikawa Fusae (1893–1981) continued to remain a leading figure in the women's movement and in the movement for suffrage. Ichikawa went to the United States in 1921, and during her three-year stay she met a number of people, including female leaders. Her meeting with Alice Paul of the National Woman's Party had a particularly great impact on her.[23]

Upon her return to Japan in 1924 Ichikawa opened a branch office of the International Labor Organization in Tokyo and also founded the Alliance for Obtaining Suffrage for Women. She led the campaign for women's suffrage over the following sixteen years, until the Alliance was forced to dissolve under militarist pressures just prior to the outbreak of World War II. What made her distinctly different from other suffragist leaders in the prewar days was her pragmatic strategy. Her primary goal was to improve the status of women by obtaining suffrage, and she sought to realize this goal by working on and through all the political parties, irrespective of their political directions.

Universal suffrage—ironically so called, even though women were excluded from it—was finally promulgated in Japan in 1925. And the first election under this law was carried out in 1928. Ichikawa headed the Election Campaign Committee of the Alliance for Obtaining Suffrage for Women for this election. The committee decided, first of all, to request all political parties and their candidates to explicitly include suffrage for women on their platforms, and, second, to send speakers from the Alliance in support of the particular candidates who placed women's suffrage on their platforms and to issue letters of recommendations from the Alliance to such candidates, if so required. Requests for female speakers came from all corners, from conservative parties to proletarian ones. The number of speeches women gave in support of various candidates amounted to 276. Especially when Ichikawa was the speaker, the halls were filled with audiences anxious to hear her speak.

This policy of the Alliance created quite a stir. Many suffragists, particularly those who argued that women should stand at least on the side of proletarian parties, bitterly criticized Ichikawa's position. Oku Mumeo, another suffragist leader, for instance, criticized her severely, saying: "In the morning they speak for the conservative party, and in the evening they speak for the socialist party. They behave themselves just like a prostitute."[24] But Ichikawa remained unperturbed because, for her, it was purely a matter of strategy.

In an essay titled "The Suffragist Spirit" (1934) Ichikawa writes:

> What I mean by the suffragist spirit is our attitude, our faith. We detest time-serving attitudes. We will not support the policies or the claims of the government or the municipal authorities. We will put them to careful scrutiny as we understand them, and then direct our effort toward what we believe to be right. I believe this is exactly the attitude that suffragists, those of us who demand women's political participation, must assume . . .
>
> Our job is to struggle through all the difficulties, and to open up a thorny path. Only then, time-servers, so-called ladies of high ranks and the masses, will follow after us along the path we have opened. Our job is to sow the seeds and to fertilize the land, and harvesting is done by those who come later. We are the ones who make efforts and spend our own money, and even so we are ill-spoken

of, and the result thus achieved is carried off by others. In this sense, we have not much to gain, but who cares . . .

Speak ill of us if they want to. As long as we have this suffragist spirit, our campaign will keep moving on.

Her pragmatism with regard to women's suffrage turned out to be all too naive in the face of the state's mounting interventionist/expansionist policy. This policy, which had been pursued since the Meiji period, entered a new phase in 1931, with the outbreak of the so-called Manchurian Incident. In July 1937 Japanese troops invaded China. In September, Ichikawa wrote in her autobiography:

I felt deeply depressed when I saw the [Japan-China] incident develop into a total war. . . . Now we are forced to choose one of three alternatives. The choices are: to go to prison by publicly opposing the war, to withdraw completely from the [women's] movement, or to cooperate with the state to a certain extent by acknowledging things as they are.

And then she quotes an article in which she wrote the conclusion she had reached at the time:

Under the present circumstances, there's no denying that obtaining women's suffrage—a legal reform campaign—will become even more difficult than ever before. However, the objective of our demand for suffrage is to enable women to cooperate with the government as fully as men, so that women can be of service to the state and society at large from the women's point of view. Therefore, when women demonstrate their merits with their own abilities in the face of the most serious national emergency the country has ever experienced, it would be a way to achieve the ultimate goal of suffrage, and it can be a step forward toward obtaining suffrage in legal terms. Let's take up the post women are expected to assume, overcoming sorrow and pain.[25]

It was a decision Ichikawa made in deep anguish. Not only Ichikawa but also other eminent leaders of the women's movement—such as Kubushiro Ochimi, Kora Tomiko, Kaneko (Yamataka) Shigeru, Maruoka Hideko, Gantoretto (probably Gauntlet) Tsuneko, Yamada Waka, and Hani Motoko—were all co-opted by the government and the military through clever maneuvering. They were all swallowed up in some way or another into a war footing called "Kokumin seishin sodoin taisei" (System for an all-out mobilization of the national spirit), though not necessarily actively or willingly. These women were all products of the era of Taisho democracy—Taisho being a brief period from 1912 to 1926, when liberal sentiments prevailed in Japanese society. How, then, could they have collaborated with the war effort? one might ask.[26]

They were made to collaborate with the war effort partly by political maneuvering by the military and the government, which were well aware that, without involving women in their scheme, it would be impossible to carry out the war. These female leaders at the same time harbored an illusionary hope. As Ichikawa's article, quoted in her autobiography, illustrates, they were made to think that their cooperation with the government and men might help improve women's social position, which had been kept deplorably low, with little improvement made since the Meiji period. While the extent of their deception was remarkable, the way they felt was, in a way, understandable, though not justifiable.

As soon as World War II ended, with Japan's surrender to the Allied Powers, Ichikawa went to the prime minister and other cabinet members, persuading them that women should get the vote immediately. That was before the American Occupation forces ordered the granting of general suffrage as part of their strategy to demilitarize and democratize Japan. Ichikawa immediately established the Women League of Voters but was expelled from public office by the Occupation forces on grounds that she had cooperated with the country's war efforts.[27] As soon as the purge was lifted in 1950, she made a comeback to the League's presidency.

In 1953 Ichikawa ran for the House of Councilors (the Upper House of the Diet) with the slogan of "An Ideal Election," meaning an election campaign that would be carried out in strict observance of the Election Law, and she was successfully elected. Since then she was successively elected to the House (one term of office lasting six years), developing a grassroots campaign for cleaning up elections and politics. And since the International Women's Year in 1975, she represented the Liaison Committee for the International Women's Year, a non-governmental organization consisting of forty-eight women's groups. In this way her commitment to the cause of women continued up until the last days of her life.[28]

Conclusion

In the days prior to World War II the women's movement was characterized essentially by rebellion, or resistance against conventions, to the way society was structured and run. During the early 1940s, as Japanese forces advanced into Asia, an all-out war effort was undertaken. The women's movement was either prohibited or co-opted, with the exception of a patriotic campaign by women to collaborate with the nation's war efforts. A large number of women were successfully mobilized, as exemplified by the case of Ichikawa Fusae.

Yet, when the war ended with Japan's surrender, the women's movement was suddenly out in the open, recognized as an indispensable part of the effort to democratize the society. With equality between the sexes declared in the Constitution, the change was so dramatic that many women felt there was not much to be learned from the past. This may partially account for the fact that the history of women in the prewar period was not given much attention until recently. And, of course, in a male-dominated society, it is the history of men that is taught and remembered.

As in many other countries, Japan saw a women's liberation movement emerge in 1970 which questioned the issue of gender division, a question the First Phase was not able to ask. Although, contrary to what happened in many other countries, the women's liberation movement per se lost its visibility as early as the first half of the 1970s, the emergence of the women's liberation movement marked the beginning of the so-called Second Phase.

And it is in the Second Phase that the history of Japanese women is being reexamined with new interpretations and that efforts to reevaluate and restore to their rightful place the past contributions and achievements of women have been made. As seen in the case of Kanno Suga, however, much has yet to be done to straighten out the historical records.

NOTES

1. Although feudalism as a political institution was officially abolished, the feudalistic patriarchal values in society remained intact, keeping women bound to traditional conventions.

2. Kishida's year of birth is generally believed to be 1864, but there are some differing views. Nishikawa Yuko recently came up with new evidence showing that Kishida was born in 1861, instead of 1864. Nishikawa Yuko, *Hana no imoto—Kishida Toshiko-den* (Flower's sister—a biography of Kishida Toshiko) (Tokyo: Shinchosha, 1986).

3. If Kishida was born in 1861, as Nishikawa Yuko argues, then it was at the age of eighteen that she was summoned to the Tokyo Imperial Court. This sounds more plausible.

4. "I Tell You, My Fellow Sisters" was published serially (in ten installments) in "Jiyu no tomoshibi" ("The light of freedom," a Liberal Party paper) from May to June 1884. Incidentally, this article is translated as "To My Brothers and Sisters" in Sharon L. Sievers's *Flowers in Salt—The Beginnings of Feminist Consciousness in Modern Japan* (Stanford, Calif.: Stanford University Press, 1985), 37. Judging from the text, however, it is evident that Kishida was specifically addressing women.

5. The period during which Kishida was politically active was very brief. The period in which she spoke publicly on women's issues was even more brief, limited only to three years, 1882 through 1884. But her public speeches were the first ever delivered by a woman with such logical and persuasive power that they had a great impact on many women who followed her path.

6. *Sekai fujin* (Women of the world), the first issue, 1 January 1907. Reprinted in *Josei—hangyaku to kakumei to teiko to* (Women—rebellion, revolution, and resistance: an anthology of works by women pioneers), ed. Hiroko Suzuki. (Tokyo: Shakai hyoronsha, 1990).

7. See Yamada Ko, *Joseikaiho no shisokatachi* (Thinkers of women's emancipation) (Tokyo: Aoki shoten, 1987).

8. Ibid.

9. Fukuda Hideko, *Warawa no hanseigai* (Half my life) (Tokyo: Iwanami shoten, 1983).

10. Shimizu Shikin, *Koware yubiwa* (A broken ring), in *Shimizu Shikin zenshu, zen*

ikkan (Complete works of Shimizu Shikin in one volume), ed. Kozai Yoshishige (Tokyo: Sodo bunka, 1983).

11. Ibid. Also refer to Takeda Kiyoko, *Fujin kaiho no dohyo* (Some signposts for women's emancipation) (Tokyo: Domesu shuppan, 1985). In the story the heroine relates that, inspired and encouraged by Western thoughts on women's rights, she came to ponder the deplorable conditions of Japanese women, whom she thought should be able to enjoy human rights as well as their happiness. Incidentally, the first translation of John Stuart Mill's *The Subjection of Women* appeared in Japan in 1878 as *On the Equal Rights between Men and Women*.

12. Kozai, *Shimizu Shikin zenshu.*

13. It is alleged that Shimazaki Toson's *Hakai* (Broken commandment) (1906), highly acclaimed as the first novel dealing with the issue of discrimination against the Burakumin, was actually an adaptation of Shikin's *Imin gakuen*, though Shimazaki did not give any acknowledgment to it. See Takeda, *Fujin kaiho.*

14. Ibid. See also Murakami Nobuhiko, *Meiji joseishi chukan zenpen—joken to ie* (History of Meiji women, the first part of the middle volume—women's rights and *ie*) (Tokyo: Rironsha, 1970).

15. Takeda, *Fujin kaiho*; and Murakami, *Meiji joseishi 1—bunmei kaika* (History of Meiji women, vol. 1—Westernization) (Tokyo: Rironsha 1969).

16. Takeda, *Fujin kaiho*; and Kozai, afterword, *Shimizu Shikin zenshu.*

17. Takeda, *Fujin kaiho*; and Murakami, *Meiji joseishi 1*. Also see Tanaka Sumiko, ed., *Josei kaiho no shiso to kodo, senzen hen* (Ideology and action of women's emancipation—the prewar period) (Tokyo: Jijitsushinsha, 1975).

18. See Itoya Toshio, *Kanno Suga* (Tokyo: Iwanami shinsho, 1970); and many others. Among thse works that help straighten out the record on Kanno are: Shimizu Unosuke, ed., *Kanno Sugako zenshu* (Collected works of Kanno Suga), vols. 1–3 (Tokyo: Koryusha, 1984); Suzuki Hiroko, ed., *Shiryo heiminsha no onnatachi* (Documents: women of the Commoners' Association) (Tokyo: Fuji shuppan, 1986); Suzuki, ed., *Josei—hangyaku to kakumei to teiko to* (see n. 6). I am particularly indebted to Oya Wataru, *Kanno Suga to Isonokami Tsuyuko* (Kanno Suga and Isonokami Tsuyuko) (Osaka: Toho shuppan, 1989). Oya's detailed examination of Arahata Kanson's autobiographies provide a valuable contribution in terms of shedding a new light on the life of Kanno Suga.

19. Arahata Kanson, *Kanson jiden* (The autobiography of Kanson) (Tokyo: Itagaki shoten, 1947); *Hitosuji no michi* (Earnestly on the way) (Tokyo: Keiyusha, 1954); *Kanson jiden* (The autobiography of Kanson) (Tokyo: Ronsosha, 1961); *Shimpan Kanson jiden* (The autobiography of Kanson—a new version) (Tokyo: Chikuma shobo, 1965); *Kanson jiden* (The autobiography of Kanson) (Tokyo: Iwanami Pocket Library, 1975).

20. At a gathering of socialists from all over the Tokyo area, some members of a group called the Friday Society brought banners reading "Anarchism" and "Anarcho-Communism," which they sought to carry into the streets at the close of the meeting. The police took this as an opportunity to arrest several socialists for allegedly violating the Police Security Regulations. Kanno was one of four women picked up and jailed in this incident, which came to be called the "Red Flag Incident." See Sharon L. Sievers, *Flowers in Salt—The Beginnings of Feminist Consciousness in Modern Japan* (Stanford, Calif.: Stanford University Press, 1985), 135–36.

21. Tanaka, *Josei kaiho.*

22. Takeda, *Fujin kaido.* Incidentally, the Anti-Prostitution Law was won in 1956

at long last. Takeda emphasizes that here, also, long years of struggle carried out by the Japan Christian Women's Reform Society since its inception cannot be overlooked.

23. In her autobiography Ichikawa writes that Alice Paul persuaded her to "devote herself to the cause of women's suffrage." Paul repeatedly said to her: "Leave the labor movement business to men. Women's issues are something that only women can take up. You cannot do [two] different things at one time." Ichikawa recalls this, saying, "This advice of Alice seems to have had a great impact upon my later campaign" (Ichikawa Fusae, *Ichikawa Fusae jiden—senzen hen* [The autobiography of Ichikawa Fusae—the prewar period] [Tokyo: Shinjuku shobo, 1974], 118).

24. Ibid., 171.

25. Ibid., 339, 433, 434.

26. Ichikawa describes herself in her autobiography as "one of the liberals baptized by Taisho democracy" (*Ichikawa Fusae jiden*).

27. The reasons for Ichikawa's expulsion from public office are, in fact, uncertain. According to a surmise of Takeda Kiyoko (*Fujin kaido*), it might have been because of Ichikawa's involvement with Dai nihon Genron Hokokukai (The Greater Japan Association for Patriotism through Speech). Emma Kaufman (of Canadian origin) of the Tokyo YWCA was one of those who wrote letters in defense of Ichikawa to the General Headquarters (GHQ) of the Occupation forces. According to Takeda, Ichikawa was very grateful to Emma Kaufman and often talked about her even in her later life. This episode is one more indication of the fact that Ichikawa worked closely with Christian women and that her work was highly respected by them.

28. Ichikawa Fusae remained single throughout her life.

REFERENCES

Arahata, Kanson. 1975. *Kanson jiden* (The autobiography of Kanson). Tokyo: Iwanami bunko.

———. 1965. *Shimpan Kanson jiden* (The autobiography of Kanson—a new version). Tokyo: Chikuma shobo.

———. 1961. *Kanson jiden* (The autobiography of Kanson). Tokyo: Ronsosha.

———. 1954. *Hitosuji no michi* (Earnestly on the way). Tokyo: Keiyusha.

———. 1947. *Kanson jiden* (The autobiography Kanson). Tokyo: Itagaki shoten.

Fukuda, Hideko. 1983. *Warawa no hanseigai* (Half my life). Tokyo: Iwanami shoten.

Ichikawa, Fusae. 1974. *Ichikawa Fusae jiden—senzen hen* (The autobiography of Ichikawa Fusae—the prewar period). Tokyo: Shinjuku shobo.

Itoya, Toshio. 1970. *Kanno Suga*. Tokyo: Iwanami shinsho.

Kozai, Yoshishige, ed. 1983. *Shimizu Shikin zenshu, zen ikkan* (Complete works of Shimizu Shikin in one volume). Tokyo: Sodo bunka.

Murakami, Nobuhiko. 1970. *Meiji joseishi chukan zenpen—joken to ie* (History of Meiji women, the first part of the middle volume—women's rights and *ie*). Tokyo: Rironsha.

———. 1969. *Meiji joseishi 1—bunmei kaika* (History of Meiji women, vol. 1—Westernization). Tokyo: Rironsha.

Nishikawa, Yuko. 1986. *Hana no imoto—Kishida Toshiko-den* (Flower's sister—a biography of Kishida Toshiko). Tokyo: Shinchosha.

Oya, Wataru. 1989. *Kanno Suga to Isonokami Tsuyuko* (Kanno Suga and Isonokami Tsuyuko). Osaka: Toho shuppan.

Shimizu, Unosuke, ed. 1984. *Kanno Sugako zenshu* (Collected works of Kanno Suga), vol. 1–3. Tokyo: Koryusha.

Sievers, Sharon L. 1985. *Flowers in Salt—The Beginnings of Feminist Consciousness in Modern Japan.* Stanford, Calif.: Stanford University Press.

Suzuki, Hiroko, ed. 1990. *Josei—hangyaku to kakumei to teiko to* (Women—rebellion, revolution, and resistance: an anthology of works by women pioneers). Tokyo: Shakai hyoronsha.

———, ed. 1986. *Shiryo heiminsha no onnatachi* (Documents: Women of the Commoner's Association). Tokyo: Fuji shuppan.

Takeda, Kiyoko. 1985. *Fujin kaiho no dohyo* (Some signposts for women's emancipation). Tokyo: Domesu shuppan.

Tanaka, Sumiko, ed. 1975. *Josei kaiho no shiso to kodo, senzen hen* (Ideology and action of women's emancipation—the prewar period). Tokyo: Jijitsushinsha.

Yamada, Ko. 1987. *Joseikaiho no shisokatachi* (Thinkers of women's emancipation). Tokyo: Aoki shoten.

The New Feminist Movement in Japan, 1970–1990

❖ ❖ ❖

Kazuko Tanaka

Background

On the evening of 21 October 1970 a major street in Tokyo was filled with female demonstrators carrying banners and placards asking, "What Is Womanliness?" "Let's Examine Our Feminine Consciousness!" "Mother, Are You Really Happy with Your Married Life?" "What Do Women Mean to Men? What Do Men Mean to Women?" and "A Housewife and a Prostitute Are Raccoons in the Same Den." This memorable event formally declared the start of a new feminist movement in Japan.

A teach-in entitled "Protesting Sexual Discrimination: A Discussion for Liberation" was held on 14 November, about a month after the demonstration. About seven hundred women participated in the movement, and enthusiastic discussions were carried on for eight hours on the nature of women's oppression and concrete experiences of sexual discrimination in various spheres.

What brought about the birth of the feminist movement in this period? During the 1960s Japan witnessed tremendous economic growth and rapid social change: between 1956 and 1970 Japan's gross national product increased eightfold. This economic growth was due to the accelerated process of industrialization in the 1960s which changed the industrial structure of Japan from one centered on primary industries to one centered on tertiary industries. In this period, the labor market expanded and there was a large increase in the demand for female labor. The number of employed women increased from 5.31 million in 1955 to 10.96 million in 1970.

Yet Japanese women's penetration into the labor market in the 1960s did not signify a real improvement in their status in society, for, despite rapid changes in other aspects of society, the traditional normative values had changed little in the 1960s. Employers' policies were shaped by traditional norms, which stipulated women's place and role as primarily in the home. Thus, the increasing numbers of women graduating from four-year universities as a result of expanded educational opportunities in the 1960s still found themselves subjected to inequitable pay scales and promotion schedules. In addition, married women who reentered the labor force after child rearing could still only obtain low-paying, part-time employment in the newly expanded sectors of the economy.

The fact that rising entry by women into the labor force in the decade of the 1960s resulted in limited progress for them had to do also with women's own self-restricting attitudes. Since women themselves had deeply internalized dominant social norms, such as "women's place is in the home" and "good wife, wise mother," in spite of the fact that more women were working for pay outside the home, the division of sex roles in the family changed little. Thus, the lives of working women were very difficult, since they bore the double burden of paid employment and household chores. Some women even felt guilty about working outside the home at this time. Due to these self-restricting attitudes, many women remained full-time housewives. The overall situation created a sense of discontent and oppression among Japanese women in the early 1970s.

The existing women's movement, however, could not respond usefully to the dramatic changes in the lives of women in the 1960s. As Inoue Teruko states, the women's movement that had existed in Japan prior to World War II was "a unified front of the middle class women's movement and the socialist-oriented women's movement, in spite of internal debates and conflicts" (1981 178). When the policy of democratization promoted by the Allied Occupation following Japan's defeat in World War II brought about constitutional equality for women and men, the middle-class women's movement lost its driving aim and "retreated to the goal simply of promoting the full utilization of each woman's ability in the work place" (Inoue 1981, 179). The socialist-oriented women's movement became the mainstream of the postwar women's movement in Japan. Yet this movement continued to adhere to the traditional Marxist idea that the oppression of women in capitalist society would disappear with the actualization of a classless society. Thus it continued to organize women into labor unions and neglected the complexities of new conditions.[1]

Hence, the new feminist movement of the 1970s was a response to these inadequacies in the postwar women's movements in Japan. The fact that quite a few of the older female activists who had supported the postwar women's movement could be seen among the participants in the first 1970 teach-in testified to the strong desire for a new movement.

This new feminist movement was motivated in addition by disillusionment with the New Left movements. Many activists in the new feminist movement had participated in the New Left movements of the late 1960s, which had attracted young workers and students. Many of these young persons, keenly critical of the bureaucratic and technological aspects of modern society and rejecting all forms of authority, were women. But many of the male participants continued to discriminate against women, even in the traditional manner of mainstream society, giving them only such tasks as housekeeping, typing, and fund-raising, and denying them access to decision-making positions. From such experiences, many women began to consider the need to establish their own movement, separate from men, in order to liberate themselves.

The Movement in the Early 1970s

The movement began by criticizing the postwar socialist-oriented women's movement, which had relied too heavily on the organization itself and had put most of its energy into broadening its membership. As a result, it had neglected to cultivate, and had even blunted, the self-awareness of individual members as active and creative agents of the movement. Thus, it could not make an effective attack on sexual discrimination, which had become more complicated because of rapid social changes and also more invisible because of the fact that the postwar democratization efforts had at least superficially established equality for women. Therefore, the new women's movement advocated nonreliance on any of the existing women's organizations and aimed at establishing a clear self-identity among individual women as the first step.

Second, in order to enable women to develop a clear self-identity, the new movement used consciousness-raising as a means not only of getting women to recognize themselves as victims of sexual discrimination but also to have them lay bare their own "inner feminine consciousness." This consciousness had been deeply imbedded in their spirits both through sex-role socialization and discriminatory experiences. Through consciousness-raising, women were to hack their way through the conservative views that had confined them in conventional sex roles and which were still widely disseminated through the various media. Women themselves had absorbed society's attitudes and consequently had unconsciously helped to propagate sexual discrimination.

Sexual discrimination had long been considered one of the contradictions of a class society. The new movement, however, emphasized the dual oppression of women: it insisted that women had been subjected both to the rule of the social class and to the rule of the men. The women's movement up to that time had relied heavily on the view that women and men were in the same situation insofar as they were both oppressed and that the abolition of social class would lead to the liberation of women. Yet, in fact, class rule had been carried out through the rule of men over women; men were the oppressors of women. Men had always been those in power, the patriarchs in the family system, which was the basis of the ruling system. Male workers sacrificed female workers to maintain their own vested rights. Male rule prevailed in the labor movement and in the socialist movement, and women's unique demands had been made light of until then. Further, the New Left movement, which had criticized the authoritarianism of the "Old Left" leaders, was also conservative with regard to its attitudes and behavior toward women, and women took part in the movement only as assistants to the men.

Thus, as its third point, the new feminist movement advocated challenging this male rule completely, claiming that women could not unconditionally cooperate with men, since women were oppressed in various spheres simply because they were women.

Fourth, the new feminist movement made "sexual liberation" the central point of its philosophy. It insisted that "the ruling power has been accomplishing its class will through male control and oppression of the female sex." In brief, the theoretical position claimed that "sex had existed as a fundamental means of human subordination" (Group Tatakau Onna 1971, 139). Thus, recovering, with their own hands, their sexual power that had been stolen from them and controlled by the system and by men, was a very important objective for women and for the new feminist movement. According to such an interpretation, some feminist groups tried to make knowledge about the female body available to a wider range of women; other groups promoted the diffusion of knowledge about contraceptives in order to enable women to manage their own sexual activities and agitated for the removal of the Japanese government's ban on the sale of contraceptive pills.

Last, but not least, the new feminist movement attacked the dominant cultural values of Japanese society of the previous decade. The rapid economic growth that Japan experienced in the 1960s went hand in hand with an uncritical positive evaluation of science and technology, especially the prevailing logic of productivity. According to this logic, women were seen as less productive than men in economic terms because of their reproductive functions. Thus, discrimination against women became assimilated into the entire prevailing cultural outlook connected with the rapid economic growth of the 1960s, which also undervalued such other groups as the handicapped and the aged. The new feminist movement sought to challenge this prevailing cultural frame of mind, oriented toward creating high commercial demand and at the same time promoting discrimination against the less productive—the cultural mind-set that produced such environmental destruction and human tragedies as Minamata.[2]

In a word, the aim of the new feminist movement of the early 1970s was to transform the entire cultural outlook from the standpoint of the oppressed segments of society through the consciousness-raising of women.

Changes by the Mid-1970s

Many *uman ribu* groups were formed in the early 1970s, most of which sought to establish a clear self-identity and a coherent vision of the social situation for women. Some of these groups also tried to set up collectives consisting solely of women and children in order to develop women's independence from men. At the same time, these groups tried to widen the scope of women's cooperation among themselves by holding such events as the First Women's Liberation Study-Work Camp in August of 1971, the First Women's Liberation Convention in May of 1972, and the Second Women's Liberation Study-Work Camp in August 1972. At the end of September 1972 the Shinjuku Women's Liberation Center was opened in Tokyo to serve as a focal point for the activities of different women's groups.

The high point in the effort of the various new feminist groups to achieve unity in the early 1970s occurred as a result of women's efforts to fight against a proposed revision of Japan's Eugenic Protection Law. Late in May 1972, soon after the First Women's Liberation Convention, a revision of the Eugenic Protection Law aimed at prohibiting abortions for economic reasons (which was allowed under the existing law) was proposed in the National Diet. This crisis served as the impetus to strengthen the unity of the early movement. Each of the groups that had been engaged in consciousness-raising undertook research on the law and protested against the proposed revision. The climax of this activity was the National Meeting for the Prevention of the Revision of the Eugenic Protection Law: Toward a Society Worthy of Giving Birth. Among the twenty-eight groups participating in the organizing committee for this meeting were members of the older postwar women's movements. As a result of this general protest , in which the *uman ribu* movement was at the center, the proposed bill was defeated in the Diet in May 1974.

This was the first concrete issue on which the different factions within the new feminist movement acted together, as a body. In addition, this protest marked the turning point at which the movement shifted its focus from consciousness-raising to action centered on specific social issues. Among the new women's groups that organized around specific issues were the Group to Protest Sexist Court Judgements against Working Women and Unmarried Women; the Group against Sex Tours to Korea for Japanese Men; the Group to Promote Coeducation in the Study of Home Economics in High School; and the Group Supporting Abortion and the Contraceptive Pill.

The most representative of the groups formed in the mid-1970s and one that focused on specific social issues was the International Women's Year Action Group, formed in 1975. This group was founded at the inititive of Fusae Ichikawa and Sumiko Tanaka, both members of the Diet, and was joined by members of women's groups of long standing. Rather than making consciousness-raising its central activity, this group worked on specific discriminatory conditions in areas such as employment, education, mass media, government, and administration and tried to make existing social institutions more egalitarian. As the booklet published by this group states:

> "Act, act, act" is the most conspicuous characteristic of our activities. We go to the Diet to eliminate sex discrimination in politics. We go to NHK [Japan Broadcasting Corporation] to protest against sexist programs. We go to law courts to support any woman who sues for sexual discrimination. We telephone, write letters, send telegrams, and set up signature-seeking campaigns in order to make society free of sex discrimination. (International Women's Year Action Group 1980, 2)

To summarize, the members of the groups that emerged in the middle of the 1970s were older, more likely to be professionals (including lawyers, Diet members, labor movement organizers, and activists within the established political parties), with some access to political channels. And the Japanese feminist movement changed its character from one that was targeted at bringing about changes in women's consciousness of themselves as women to one seeking visible changes in social institutions. The fact that the Shinjuku Women's Liberation Center, which had served as a communication center for *uman ribu* groups in the early period, went out of operation in 1977 is an indication of this alteration in the nature and direction of the new feminist movement.

In addition, the feminist movement underwent another change in the mid-1970s: that is, it attained a certain degree of legitimization. In the early 1970s public attitudes toward this movement and its members were negative,[3] and the movement was mostly ignored or regarded by the government as made up of troublemakers. However, the United Nations–sponsored 1975 International Women's Year forced the Japanese government to take seriously and act on the problem of sex discrimination. As a result, in November 1975 the Headquarters for the Planning and Promotion of Policies Relating to Women was set up in order to incorporate into national policy the decisions made at the World Conference of the International Women's Year. In the same month the Conference on Women's Problems for the International Women's Year was held, sponsored by the Japanese government. Although feminist groups criticized this conference as not reflecting women's real voice, on the other hand, the fact that it served "to attract wide public attention among both men and women who had been indifferent to women's problems" cannot be overlooked (Sato 1979, 27). Further, in the late 1970s, the Japanese government established the National Women's Education Center, and many other women's centers were established by local governments, including the Tokyo Metropolitan Women's Information Center.

As a result, the movement itself began to work harder on influencing governmental policies and actions. For example, women's groups, formed at the initiative of the International Women's Year Action Group, pressed their opinions and criticisms on the Japanese government's National Plan of Action and the Tokyo metropolitan government's Plan of Action.

Through these processes the feminist movement acquired a certain amount of access to institutional resources and legitimacy in the latter half of the 1970s.

The 1980s

The inclination toward issue-oriented activities of the feminist movement, which came to be obvious in the latter half of the 1970s, developed further throughout the 1980s. Diverse groups and organizations emerged in various parts of Japan. Among the core issues around which women's groups organized themselves were women's health and reproductive rights, sex discrimination in the workplace, alternative ways of working, child care, challenges to the marriage system, media sexism, feminist arts and publications, protest against war and environmental exploitation, representation in politics, aging, violence against women, and sexual harassment. The list of these activities can be extended to almost all aspects of women's lives.

Besides such grassroots activism, the Japanese feminist movement in the 1980s witnessed another development—namely, the advancement of women's studies. (See the essay by Fujieda and Fujimura-Fanselow in this volume for a fuller discussion of the development of women's studies.) Although there had been a relatively long tradition of research in women's history in Japan, women's studies based on a new feminist consciousness arose in the late 1970s and developed through the 1980s. By early in the 1980s major nationwide and regional women's associations and study groups were formed. Among the topics that underwent scrutiny were the sexist nature of academic disciplines, the nature of housework, gender and education, sexism in the mass media, and the specific character of women's oppression in Japanese society, to mention a few. Researchers in women's studies consisted in part of women who had been participants in the feminist movement, but there were also those who had had no direct involvement in or experience of the movement. Some of the latter even claimed the necessity of detaching women's studies from the movement in order to "make it relevant to all women." This claim led to a suspicion of women's studies by some *uman ribu* activists, who had been casting a doubtful eye on women's studies from the beginning as a form of appropriation of the movement by academic women. To some extent, an unfortunate animosity began to characterize the relationship between academics and activists.

In response to the statements in the World Plan of Action of the International Women's Year and the Convention on the Elimination of All Forms of Discrimination against Women, the government, at the national level and, more prominently, at the local level, also came to promote women's studies. While, on the one hand, the various government-supported activities contributed toward building a wider audience for women's studies, at the same time, we cannot ignore the fact that this kind of official recognition may also dilute the radical nature of women's studies to make it more "acceptable."

Accompanying the development and diffusion of women's studies have been ongoing "feminist debates" since the mid-1980s over strategies for women's liberation, the nature of women's oppression, issues surrounding work and family, and so on. Most of these debates have been led by scholars of women's studies and/or writers, rather than activists in the movement. In some cases these debates have attracted considerable media attention.

The most celebrated of these was the so-called Agnes Debate of the late 1980s, which drew broad media coverage. While the initial debate focused on women's individual attitudes and behavior—in this case, namely whether a professional woman like Agnes Chan (an entertainer) should bring her private life (i.e., her infant child) to her public life (i.e., her workplace, a recording studio)—it soon led to more institutional social issues such as the inflexible organization of the workplace and the lack of adequate child care facilities. That this debate captured a wide audience epitomized the social conditions of the 1980s, in which more and more women were entering paid work (in 1988 making up 37 percent of all employees, compared to 33 percent in 1970), while at the same time social and personal "infrastructures" to support these changes had yet to be developed. Thus, for example, the career paths for women continued to be very narrow relative to those for men, while government support for public daycare facilities remained inadequate, and no measures were undertaken to promote men's participation in the domestic sphere.

Another significant issue taken up by the feminist movement in the 1980s was the enactment of legislation ensuring equal opportunity in employment. Those in the feminist movement as well as the labor movement had been struggling for effective anti–sex discrimination legislation since the end of the 1970s. Efforts to introduce bills through the opposition parties were met by resistance on the part of the ruling party, but, as the deadline drew near for the ratification of the Convention on the Elimination of All Forms of Discrimination against Women, to which the Japanese government was a proposed signatory, the government proposed its own bill. Disagreement arose within the feminist movement, however, over whether protective measures designed specifically for women in the existing Labor Standards Law should be removed so that women could more readily penetrate various spheres of industry together with men or be kept intact, since, without certain regulations, such as limitations on overtime work, working conditions for most women, who in actuality bore most of the household responsibilities, would worsen. Although much discussion ensued, the movement could not reach a consensus over this issue, and this left it unable to organize a unified front against employers and the government. As a result, the bill that was passed in 1985 and came into effect in 1986 as the Equal Employment Opportunity Law was very weak, carrying no penalty and enforcement provisions.

Unresolved Issues and the Direction of the Feminist Movement in the 1990s

The Japanese feminist movement, which sprang up in the early 1970s, changed its nature in the course of its development over the next two decades from one that sought to transform the whole set of cultural values through raising the inner consciousness of individual women to one focused on attempting to change concrete social conditions surrounding the individual. Thus, the feminist movement became more single-issue oriented, because it perceived that, to borrow Jo Freeman's words, "the best way to be effective is to make demands for small changes, and to concentrate one's resources on a few specific areas" (1983, 203). As a result of this change in orientation, the Japanese feminist movement seems to have acquired more legitimacy and has been gradually succeeding in making its demands actualized, although progress has not necessarily been quick.

Is it, then, adequate for the Japanese feminist movement to maintain this orientation? The answer is not necessarily positive. Although the situation of women seems to have much improved on the surface, the improvement is a function of women's assimilation into the male-dominated system and culture rather than of the transformation of that system and culture. The oppression of women has, in fact, become more submerged and less visible. Women's situation has become worse in some aspects. For example, the commercialization of women's sexuality through magazines, television programs, and advertisements has become increasingly more visible over the last decade. What appeared to be an opening up of opportunities for women in the field of employment in the late 1980s, when the economy was booming, turned out to be a false reality once the recession hit Japan in 1991. Women have been the first to be let go, while women graduating from college have had much greater difficulty than their male counterparts in finding jobs. This is evidence of the fact that the deeply embedded gender role assumptions of Japanese society, which view women as second-class workers whose primary role is in the home, has hardly changed. Data showing that working wives continue to bear the major burden of the "second shift" also support this fact.

In order to break through this state of affairs, it will be necessary for the Japanese feminist movement to unify itself and pursue ways to transform the sociocultural system based on division of gender roles and the control and subjugation of women's sexuality. Women's studies in the 1990s must provide the movement with a lucid analysis of the mechanisms underlying women's oppression, often subtle and difficult to grasp, and also present viable strategies for confronting this oppression.

At the same time, in order to forge more solid unity and cooperation among various feminist groups, these groups must work out new ways to facilitate daily communication and discourse as well as channels for mobilization when crises, such as the controversy surrounding the Equal Employment Opportunity Law, present themselves. In this respect it is important to point out that the failure of the feminist movement to make that law more effective can be attributed, at least partially, to the lack of effectual communication and mobilization channels among the various women's groups. These tasks may not be easy, but they are surely challenging.

NOTES

1. For a description of the prewar and postwar women's movements in Japan, see Kazuko Tanaka, *A Short History of the Women's Movement in Modern Japan* (Tokyo: Femintern Press, 1977), chaps. 1–5.

2. Industrial waste dumped in the waters of Minamata Bay in the southern prefecture of Kumamoto was responsible for the so-called Minamata disease suffered by residents who consumed mercury-poisoned fish. This tragedy sparked nationwide concern regarding the environment as well as many civic action movements directed at the harmful effects of industrial pollution from the 1960s on.

3. For a discussion on the function of ridiculing to the women's liberation movement, see Ehara Yumiko, *Joseikaiho to iu shiso* (The ideology of women's liberation) (Tokyo: Keiso shobo, 1985), chap. 3: "Karakai no seijigaku" (The politics of ridiculing), 172–94.

REFERENCES

Ehara, Yumiko. 1985. *Joseikaiho to iu shiso* (The ideology of women's liberation). Tokyo: Keiso shobo.

Freeman, Jo. 1983. "A Model for Analyzing the Strategic Opinions of Social Movement Organization." In *Social Movements of the Sixties and Seventies*, ed. Jo Freeman. New York and London: Longman.

Group Tatakau Onna (Group of Fighting Women). 1971. "*Naze sei no kaiho ka*" (Why sexual liberation?). Editor's section in *Seisabetsu e no kokuhatsu* (Protest against sex discrimination), ed. Aki shobo. Tokyo: Aki shobo.

Inoue, Teruko. 1981. *Joseigaku to sono shuhen* (Women's studies and related studies). Tokyo: Keiso shobo.

International Women's Year Action Group. 1980. *Action Now in Japan*. Tokyo: International Women's Year Action Group.

Sato, Yoko. 1979. "Nanajunendai ni okeru joseitachi no tatakai" (Women's struggle in the 1970s). *Shiso no kagaku* (Science of ideas), no. 100 (January): 27.

Tanaka, Kazuko. 1977. *A Short History of the Women's Movement in Modern Japan*. Tokyo: Femintern Press.

Legal Challenges to the Status Quo

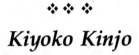

Kiyoko Kinjo

This chapter presents an overview of the legal status of women in Japanese society as well as the changes that have been brought about in recent years and the birth of feminist legal studies. Specific attention will be directed at recent legislative developments pertaining to women's employment, their status within the family, and the issues of nationality and abortion. What the discussion here will demonstrate is that while important advances in securing various legal rights for women have been made since the end of World War II, many forms of sex discrimination persist that have yet to be addressed in order to achieve true equality within Japanese society.

Legal Guarantees of Equal Rights for Women and Men

The Japanese Constitution, which was enacted in 1947 following the end of World War II, guarantees equal rights to both women and men as follows:

> Article 14 (1) All of the people are equal under the law and there shall be no discrimination in political, economic, or social relations because of race, creed, sex, social status, or family origin.

The Constitution contains another provision aimed specifically at abolishing the prewar patriarchal family system *(ie seido)* and securing equality of men and women within the family. Thus, Article 24 reads:

(1) Marriage shall be based only on the mutual consent of both sexes and it shall be maintained through mutual cooperation with the equal rights of husband and wife as a basis.

(2) With regard to choice of spouse, property rights, inheritance, choice of domicile, divorce, and other matters pertaining to marriage and the family, laws shall be enacted from the standpoint of individual dignity and the essential equality of the sexes.

The legal status of Japanese women before the end of World War II was similar to that of women in nineteenth-century Western societies. Their legal rights were severely restricted: they could not participate in political activities, vote, or control their own property. Moreover, it was difficult for women to obtain higher education since universities, both national and private, were totally closed to women.

Under the 1947 Constitution women were granted suffrage, and in the first postwar general election thirty-nine women were elected to the House of Representatives out of a total of roughly five hundred members. In addition, nearly every university opened its door to women. In line with the abolition of the patriarchal family system, the Family Law of Japan (book 4 of the Civil Code on Relatives and book 5 on Succession) was totally revised. The wife was given independent legal capacity, and separation of the marital property was established. Custody of children was to be exercised jointly by husband and wife during marriage and awarded to either according to the best interests of the children in the event of divorce. Although some discriminatory provisions remained, on the whole women acquired formal equal legal status in the area of family law.

As for employment, the Labor Standards Act of 1947 stipulated the equal treatment of women. Article 3 of the act prohibits differential treatment with respect to wages, working hours, or other working conditions by reason of nationality, creed, or social status. With regard to discrimination based on sex, however, Article 4 of the act prohibits only differential treatment in wages. This fact had the effect of depriving women of the equal right to work after marriage or childbirth or past a certain age and allowed employers to establish different retirement ages for female versus male workers. Many lawsuits were brought by women protesting such discrimination, and, finally, in 1981, the Supreme Court ruled that any differential treatment between the sexes concerning retirement age was void under the Constitution.[1]

Gap between Legal Equality and Reality

Once formal and legal equality was granted under the new Constitution and various legislation, it was at first supposed that substantive equality would be attained by the efforts of women newly conscious of their rights. The fact, however, has been totally different from this supposition. A huge gap between de facto equality and de jure equality persists in contemporary Japan. Table 1 gives some idea of the present status of women.

In Japan there are few women in decision-making positions, a fact that often mystifies visitors to Japan. Women active in top levels of government, business, and law are extremely rare, compared to countries in the West and even elsewhere in Asia. After Japan became a signatory to the United Nations (UN) Convention on the Elimination of All Forms of Discrimination against Women (CEDAW) in 1980, the government drew up a National Plan of Action to change this situation and attempt to make equality of the sexes a reality. The plan cites such specific targets as raising the proportion of women serving on government advisory councils to 15 percent by the year 1996. Such a figure might seem extremely low, but the actual figures attained thus far, as shown in table 1, have lagged far behind.

Most readers may have the impression that Japanese women stay at home caring for their husbands, children, and elderly parents. This is correct to some extent. Women do, in fact, shoulder the burden of housework and care giving. However, Japanese women's participation in the labor force, which is at a rate of around 40 percent, is as high as that of most Western countries. Under the current severe labor shortage women are urged to work outside the home, though as low-ranking part-timers. In spite of working hard to support Japanese society, however, women are virtually excluded from participating in vital decision-making processes. Although half of the population and more than one-third of the labor force is female, only men are engaged

Table 1
Women's Participation in Decision-Making Positions in 1991

	Number of Women	Percentage of Women (%)
Diet: House of Representatives	12	2.3
House of Councilors	33	13.1
Local assemblies	1,447	2.2
Advisory councils (national)	304	6.7
Public officials (national)	34,285	14.6
Management positions	53	0.6
Public officials (local)		
Management positions	152	1.0
Private business		
Management positions	189,100	8.5
Judges	115	4.0
Public prosecutors	35	1.7
Lawyers	725	5.3
Law professors	166	6.0

in the formulation of national and local governmental policies. The same is true of those who run the Japanese economy.

Recent Changes in Laws Relating to Women

The UN Decade for Women (1976–85) and the Convention on Elimination of All Forms of Discrimination against Women adopted in 1979 had a profound influence on Japanese women. Women saw laws as important vehicles for promoting their status and fuller participation in society.

I myself went to Harvard Law School in 1978 to study feminist legal theory, at that time called Women and the Law. Although the situation of women in Japan is different from that of women in the United States, my experience overseas helped me construct a theoretical framework for examining women and the law within the Japanese legal system. I published a book entitled *Ho joseigaku no susume* (A call for feminist legal studies) in 1983, and since then many books and articles have been written on law from women's perspectives (Kinjo et al. 1988; Sasano et al. 1989; Okubo and Goto 1990; Kinjo 1991). The theory and proposals put forth in these works have played a crucial role in challenging the status quo.

Many changes have taken place or are currently under way within the Japanese legal system as a result of pressures that have been brought to bear by broadly based women's movements as well as by initiatives, challenges, and demands as well as lawsuits brought forth by individual women.

Revision of the Nationality Law

What is meant by "nationality" is citizenship. Before the revision of the Nationality Law, children whose fathers were Japanese nationals automatically obtained Japanese nationality at birth, but those whose mothers were Japanese nationals but whose fathers were not could not do so. The law was discriminatory in its treatment of marriages between Japanese and non-Japanese individuals in that Japanese men could transmit their nationality to their children but women could not. Two cases were filed by married couples who claimed that the law discriminated against women. They sought to have this aspect of the law declared void under the Constitution. The Tokyo District Court in 1981 denied the claim, saying that the rule was intended to avoid the problem of dual nationalities and that it was not unconstitutional.

The UN Convention on Elimination of All Forms of Discrimination against Women stipulates that all signatory states agree to grant women equal rights with men with regard to their children's nationality. Japan's Nationality Law was clearly inconsistent with this goal. The government declared Japan would ratify the CEDAW by 1985 and revised the Nationality Law to be consistent with this provision in 1983. The revised law stipulates that a child shall be granted Japanese nationality when either the mother or father is a Japanese national (Art. 2). At the same time, the conditions for the naturalization of spouses of Japanese nationals were made equal.

The Equal Employment Opportunity Law

Notwithstanding the women's movement's active call for legislation to prohibit discrimination against women in employment, it was not until 1985 that the Equal Employment Opportunity Law (EEOL) was enacted. Companies that made enormous profits from the cost savings implicit in the existing discriminatory structure of employment strongly opposed the enactment of this act. In addition, opposition by the average man, who was happy to sit back comfortably and enjoy the benefits of the status quo; lack of interest on the part of ordinary people including women; the inability of women themselves to reach a consensus on the crucial issue of equality versus protection; and a lack of government leadership all were critical impediments. Outside pressure in the form of the CEDAW provided the crucial inducement for enactment of the act.

The Equal Employment Opportunity Law came into force in 1986. It is flawed, however, by the following shortcomings, which are obstacles to its effectiveness from a legal perspective:

1. The act prohibits discrimination on grounds of sex in the areas of on-the-job training, health and welfare benefits, compulsory retirement ages, and termination and dismissal (Arts. 9, 10, and 11), but it imposes on employers only the "duty to make efforts" to treat women equally with men in recruitment, hiring, job assignment and promotion (Art. 7 and 8). Therefore, the act cannot be called a law prohibiting discrimination in employment. Furthermore, it does not include any punitive provisions.

2. As relief measures to secure the effectiveness of the act, it provides for three measures: (1) voluntary resolution of employee complaints by a body consisting of labor and management representatives within the company (Art. 13); (2) the assistance of the director of the Prefectural Women's and Minor's Bureau in the resolution of disputes (Art. 14); and (3) conciliation by the Conciliation Committee on Equal Opportunity (Art. 18). None of these measures, however, imposes any obligations on employers. They merely encourage employers to comply with the act voluntarily. Revision of these provisions is urgently called for. (See Kawashima's essay in this volume for further discussion of the EEOL and its impact.)

Child Care Leave Law

In 1991 the Child Care Leave Act was enacted; it came into force in 1992. Under the act either the father or mother can take child care leave until one's child becomes a year old. A major impetus for the enactment of this law has been alarm over the continuing decline in birthrate over the recent years: the average number of births per woman in 1990 was just 1.53. The law represents a major new step in that it allows for men to take advantage of child care leave. On the other hand, the fact that the law makes no provisions for guaranteeing payment of salary during the period of leave makes it highly unlikely that men will, in fact, take such leave.

Revisions in the Civil Code

Continued Use of Married Name Following Divorce

Upon marriage a husband and wife must assume either the husband's or the wife's surname in accordance with Article 750 of the Civil Code; it is not permissible for each to retain his or her surname. In the event of divorce the wife or husband whose surname was changed at the time of marriage must revert to the use of the surname used prior to marriage (Art. 767).

In Japan today an overwhelming majority of couples—more than 98 percent—choose to use the surname of the husband, and in most instances of divorce the wife resumes use of her maiden name. Therefore, in reality, it is nearly always the woman rather than the man who suffers the considerable social disadvantages that result from changing one's name. In addition, it is not uncommon for children, who normally retain the surname of the father after divorce, to have a different surname from their mother's, even though in most cases the mother brings up the children.

In 1975, the International Women's Year, there were strong demands for the Civil Code to be amended in order to guarantee fuller equality between the sexes. Only one provision was revised, that allowing divorced women to continue to use their married names if an application is made within three months of the date of the divorce. In 1983 such applications were filed in 33 percent of all divorces.

Increase in the Spouse's Legal Share of Inheritance

Japan's inheritance system had not undergone any significant change since major amendments were carried out after World War II. During this period, however, Japanese society had changed significantly, mainly as a result of its rapid economic growth. The number of nuclear families increased, accompanied by a decline in the number of children per couple. Furthermore, the status of women, both in the home and in the larger society, underwent considerable improvement. As the wife's contribution to the marriage came to be evaluated more highly, demands for improvement of the spouse's (in practice, the wife's) legal status in the inheritance system came to be voiced more strongly. As a result, the wife's legal share in inheritance was raised in 1980, as shown in table 2.

Unresolved Issues Pertaining to the Civil Code

There remain some forms of differential treatment of men and women sanctioned by the Civil Code, such as the difference in minimum age requirement for marriage (eighteen for men and sixteen for women) and the provision that women may not remarry for six months after the dissolution or annulment

Table 2
Amendment Regarding the Legal Share of Inheritance in 1980

Cases of Joint Inheritance	Heirs	Shares of Inheritance Prior to Amendment	Shares of Inheritance Following Amendment
When both spouse and child are joint heirs	Spouse	⅓	½
	Child	⅔	½
When deceased's spouse and lineal ascendant(s) are joint heirs	Spouse	½	⅔
	Lineal ascendant(s)	½	⅓
When deceased's spouse and sibling(s) are joint heirs	Spouse	⅔	¾
	Sibling(s)	⅓	¼

of a previous marriage (supposedly in order to avoid confusion in specifying the paternity of a child born after remarriage), while men may do so. Women are currently concentrating their efforts, however, on the struggle to establish the right for couples to retain separate surnames following marriage.

As mentioned, the Civil Code requires the husband and wife to assume a single surname, decided by mutual agreement at the time of marriage. Since either the woman's or the man's name may be chosen, it has been said that this provision does not violate the constitutional guarantee of sexual equality. Yet, as already noted, in 98 percent of the cases the husband's name is chosen. Most women are forced by custom to change their surname upon marriage. Many women, claiming that this provision violates not only the Constitution but also the CEDAW, have called for an amendment to this provision. Responding to these demands, the Hosei Shingikai (Deliberative Council on the Legal System), which is considering the various revisions to the Civil Code prior to deliberation before the National Diet, began in 1991 to discuss this matter in order to open the way for couples to use separate surnames should they wish to do so.

Based on recommendations submitted by a subcommittee of the above-mentioned Deliberative Council on the Legal System, in July 1994 the Ministry of Justice made public a number of proposed changes in the Civil Code dealing with marriage and divorce. These proposals call for the most major changes in the Civil Code since 1947. Among the most significant proposals to legalize the use of separate family names by married couples and to make physical separation of five or more years a legal grounds for divorce, thereby recognizing failure of a marriage as a legitimate ground for either party to sue for divorce, regardless of which party is at fault (so-called no-fault divorce).

These proposals represent only a preliminary draft of possible revisions to the Civil Code. The next step in the process calls for the Ministry of Justice to solicit views and opinions on the proposed reforms from those in various fields, on the basis of which it will put forward its final recommendations. Whatever shape these proposed changes eventually take, a legislative bill embodying those changes will then have to win approval by the Diet.

Abortion

Japan was one of the first countries in the world to decriminalize abortion and contraception. Being relatively free from the kind of strong religious and medical opposition which has operated in Western countries, Japan moved to legalize abortion and contraception with the enactment of the Eugenic Protection Law in 1948. Following several revisions of the law, women are now able to obtain abortion virtually on demand. As Malcolm Potts and his colleagues (1977) point out in their influential book, *Abortion*, this early legalization of abortion was due largely to the fact that Western countries had not imposed their religious and medical traditions concerning abortion on Japan.

Legalization of Abortion as a Means of Population Control

In the Edo period (1603–1867) abortion and infanticide were commonly practiced throughout Japan, though they were officially denounced by both the central and local governments. After the Meiji Restoration of 1868 Japan undertook a process of modernization and was strongly influenced by the legal systems of the Western countries. The current Criminal Code, enacted in 1907, prohibits abortion. In order to modernize the country the Japanese government adopted the policy of *fukoku kyohei* (rich country, strong army) and undertook an all-out effort to increase the population. The prohibition of abortion was strictly enforced, and many women were severely punished for violating it. Women, the designated mothers of this militaristic country, were strongly urged to bear as many children as possible to provide future soldiers and a strong labor force.

After the end of World War II the nation faced an entirely different situation. Three million people from the territories Japan had formerly occupied and another three million soldiers from the front returned to their small island nation. Because the national economy had been destroyed by the war, many people starved. With the return of the young men a baby boom soon followed. Under these circumstances back-alley abortions thrived, and many women's health and lives were destroyed. In these new circumstances it was quite natural for the Japanese government to make a 180-degree turnaround concerning its policy of population control. The result was the enactment in 1948 of the Eugenic Protection Law.

Japan in fact succeeded in controlling its population through the legalization of abortion. Potts and his colleagues note that without abortion, legal or illegal, the rate of population increase in postwar Japan would have been twice the actual rate, and resources invested in economic growth would have been consumed to support the population (1977, 323).

Legal Framework of Abortion Regulation

The Criminal Code, as noted, prohibits abortion, and there is no likelihood that this prohibition will be repealed in the near future. The Draft Criminal Code Bill (Keiho Kaisei So-an) drafted in 1974 by the Deliberative Council on the Legal System to revise the outdated code contains basically the same provisions. The conditions under which abortion may be procured are governed by the Eugenic Protection Law. These conditions are as follow:

1. the abortion must be performed during the period when the fetus is unable to sustain its life outside the womb;

2. the husband's consent must be obtained; and

3. there must exist one or more eugenic or economic reasons.

In most cases women apply for abortions for economic reasons. Thus, on the surface it appears that women have the right to abortion on demand. Yet, from the standpoint of abortion as a woman's right, the legal framework contains many problems.

The first of these problems is that, because abortion is prohibited by the Criminal Code, it is considered, at least in principle, a crime. Abortion is permitted as an exception under the Eugenic Protection Law. It is possible for the state to prohibit abortion by repealing this law or by deleting *economic reasons* from the law. Such attempts were actually made twice, from 1972 to 1974 and in 1982. In 1982 a Diet member from the ruling Liberal Democratic Party, who was affiliated with a right-wing religious organization called Seicho no Ie (House of Growth), demanded the removal of the "economic reasons" clause from the law. Although on both occasions revision of the law was blocked by the active opposition of women's groups, the medical profession, and ordinary citizens, these events made it clear that the right to abortion has not yet really been established in Japan.

Second, the Eugenic Protection Law, as the name clearly shows, originated as the National Eugenic Law, which was copied from Nazi Germany's Hereditary Disease Prevention Law. Given these origins, the law not only has inherited outmoded eugenic thoughts demeaning to disabled persons but also stipulates an outdated list of hereditary diseases, such as leprosy. Japan must enact a new law that will place women's right to abortion on a sound basis.

Third, the law does not clearly stipulate a time limit for legal abortions. In 1953, in a circular issued by the Vice Minister of Health and Welfare, the limitation was set at eight months, and since then it has been shortened several times as medical technology has advanced; as of 1992, it stood at twenty-one weeks. Without borrowing medical concepts, the law itself should provide for a clear time limit for the procurement of a legal abortion.

Last, but by no means least, the law requires the consent of the husband in order for a woman to obtain an abortion. Thus, the state intervenes in order to give preference to the husband. When the man and woman disagree, however, the women's choice should prevail. Although no cases have come up before the courts challenging this clause, the husband's consent as a condition for abortion should be eliminated.

Future Prospects Regarding Abortion Rights

From the end of World War II until quite recently Japanese women have not experienced significant difficulties in obtaining abortion compared with their sisters in Western countries. That is not because the right to abortion is established in Japan but, rather, because the government, adopting a population control policy, has been tolerant of abortion. Circumstances in Japan, however, are changing. The birthrate has been dropping sharply each year (from 2.13 in 1970 to 1.75 in 1980, 1.53 in 1990, and 1.46 in 1993), and there is no indication of its bottoming out. In 1989 Japan's birthrate was the second lowest in the world, following West Germany's. The Japanese government began to study how this situation could be reversed. Raising the birthrate by prohibiting abortion would be not only ineffective, as the experience of Romania clearly shows, but would inherently infringe on human rights. One may well wonder whether Japanese women will have to confront adverse circumstances and struggle to firmly secure their right to abortion.

Conclusion

It is generally presumed that economic development promotes women's status. Although Japan is, economically, a highly developed country, the status of Japanese women resembles that of women in developing countries in many respects. Discrimination against women in the workplace has been a source of huge profit to companies; indeed, it has been a main source of economic power for Japan.

In order to attain not only de jure but de facto equality of the sexes in Japan, much will have to be done in the future. While it is important to raise women's awareness of various forms of sex discrimination that continue to prevail in Japanese society, at the same time it is imperative that the Japanese government assume a crucial role in eliminating sex discrimination and fulfilling the duty it undertook by ratifying the United Nations Convention on Elimination of All Forms of Discrimination against Women.

NOTE

1. Supreme Court Judgment, 24 March 1981 [Nakamoto. Nissan Motor Co.] 35.1 Minshu 300.

REFERENCES

Asakura, Mutsuko. 1992. *Danjo koyo byodoho-ron* (On the Equal Employment Opportunity Law). Tokyo: Domesu shuppan.

Fukushima, Mizuho. 1992. *Kekkon to kazoku* (Marriage and family). Tokyo: Iwanami shoten.

Kinjo, Kiyoko. 1991. *Ho joseigaku* (Feminist legal studies). Tokyo: Nihon hyoronsha.

———. 1985. *Kazoku to iu kankei* (Family relations). Tokyo: Iwanami shoten.

———. 1983. *Ho joseigaku no susume* (A call for feminist legal studies). Tokyo: Yuhikaku.

Kinjo, Kiyoko, et al. 1988. *Josei hogaku* (Feminist legal studies). Tokyo: Shogakusha.

Okubo, Kazunori, and Yasuko Goto. 1990. *Josei to ho* (Women and law). Kyoto: Horitsu bunkasha.

Potts, Malcolm, Peter Diggory, and John Peel. 1977. *Abortion*. Cambridge: Cambridge University Press (trans. C. Ikegami as *Bunka to shite no ninshinchuzetsu* [Tokyo: Keiso shobo, 1985]).

Sasano, Sadako, et al. 1989. *Josei hogaku no susume* (A call for feminist legal studies). Kyoto: Horitsu bunkasha.

From the Home to the Political Arena

❖ ❖ ❖

Yoko Sato

Translated by Kumiko Fujimura-Fanselow

Over the decade of the 1980s, and in particular the latter half of that decade, Japanese women underwent several dramatic transformations. Here I would like to focus specifically on the changes that have occurred among that group of women who have been described as the most conservative, namely, the *shufu*, or "housewives." I will describe how housewives, whose proper place has been regarded as being in the home, have emerged as an active force in society and have begun to channel their concerns into political involvement.

Out of the Home and into the Community

Married women in the twenties to the fifties age group are generally referred to as *shufu*. Those women who, upon marriage, discontinue working and devote themselves full-time to housekeeping and child rearing are called *sengyo shufu*, or "full-time housewives," while those who hold part-time employment or work on family farms or in family-owned business are called *kengyo shufu*, or "adjunct housewives."

Following the end of World War II Japanese women acquired equality in the realm of the family, education, political participation, and employment, and they proceeded to exhibit significant changes compared to women of the past. Nonetheless, a pattern emerged that once women married, aside from those engaged in farming or family businesses, the majority of them showed no qualms about leaving paid employment to take up the work of housewives. The most popular pattern included bearing two or three children and reentering the work force on a part-time basis to supplement the family income once these children entered school. The wide acceptance of this pattern demonstrates how firmly fixed is the sexual division of labor in Japan. In fact, the Japanese-style employment system, under which men are expected to devote nearly all of their waking hours to their employers, has operated on the premise that there is a wife at home to take care of the family.

Nevertheless, we have witnessed some dramatic changes through the 1980s in the attitudes and behavior of the hitherto "silent majority" of Japanese housewives. They have begun to look increasingly outward and to become involved in a variety of activities outside the traditional concern of the home. Indicative of this evolution was the birth in 1990 of a column entitled "From 'okusan' to 'sotosan'" in a women's magazine called *Wife*. The term *okusan*, which literally means "the one who resides in the inner part," was an honorific title used to refer to wives of the middle and upper classes who could afford the luxury of staying in the home. In post–World War II Japanese society, however, the term has come to refer to all housewives, as an alternative to the term *shufu*. *Sotosan*, which means "the one who is outside," is a play on the word *okusan* and was newly coined to describes housewives who are no longer content to stay at home. In this column housewives relate various experiences they have had while taking part in activities outside the traditional confines of the home.

Wife was originally started twenty years ago by a housewife living in a small town near Osaka. In the mid-1970s the magazine's headquarters were moved to Tokyo, and it gained a considerable readership among housewives as a forum for giving free expression to women's pent-up frustrations and grievances. Indeed, the magazine, which now has four thousand regular subscribers, has grown in step with changes in the lifestyles of urban Japanese housewives. While about 90 percent of the early readership consisted of full-time housewives, twenty years later the majority are engaged in some type of activity outside the home.

Manifestations of Housewives' Movement Out of the Home

Rising Participation in Paid Employment

This heightened shift in orientation on the part of housewives from the home to the outside in the decade of the 1980s has been manifested in their growing participation in paid employment. The desire on the part of women to work has been fueled by a growing demand for women's labor, resulting from a severe labor shortage from the mid-1980s. Thus, just from among the subscribers to *Wife* we find several women who have become semiprofessional workers in a variety of capacities—as writers, editors, consumer advisors, and so on.

The results of a national survey of twelve hundred married women between the ages of twenty and sixty undertaken by a major food manufacturer in 1988 underscore this trend (Ajinomoto Shokuhin Kaisha 1988). It found that married women holding full-time jobs (working forty or more hours), those working part-time (less than forty hours), and those in the so-called multi-activity group—women who do not have a job but are out of the house six or more hours a week—accounted for 44.5 percent of all those surveyed, exclusive of the elderly and those with infants. This figure represented a 4.8 percent increase over that found in a similar survey conducted in 1985. Particularly outstanding was the increase in full-time and part-time workers, centering on women in their forties.

Involvement in Local Community Causes and Movements

It is not only through increased participation in paid employment that traditionally home-bound married women have moved out into the larger society; active engagement in local community-based movements linked to a variety of causes is another significant manifestation of this trend. Among the myriad causes women have taken up in recent years are (1) those related to the environment, such as the effort to spread the use of soap bars in place of detergents that are harmful to the health as well as to the environment; protection of clean water; waste disposal, including collection of garbage by type and recycling of waste; and efforts to preserve forests, mountains, and green zones; (2) those that concern the welfare of children and the elderly such as nursing care and provision of meals for the elderly and the improvement and increase in child care and after-school centers and playgrounds; and (3) those in the cultural realm, such as promoting the establishment of libraries, civic centers, and women's centers. There are innumerable groups that are tied together through networks, and the various movements too are linked to one another.

The director of the Kanagawa Prefectural Women's Center, which has played a prominent role in sponsoring various activities as well as courses of study for women, explains women's involvement in local movements in this way:

> Up until the beginning of the 1980s, there were very few opportunities available to college-educated women who had given up careers to become wives and mothers to re-enter the job market. Many of these women, therefore, directed their time, energy and talents into involvement in local community movements and in self-study programs. (Kanamori 1989)

A survey of the content of courses offered to women at various civic and women's centers sponsored by community school boards shows a marked change over the decade of the 1980s. According to data compiled by the Women's Education Section of the Ministry of Education, the percentage of courses in the category of "hobbies" declined from 22.2 percent in 1978 to 2.9 percent in 1987; on the other hand, courses on "women's issues and women's history" jumped from a mere 4.3 percent to 30.1 percent (Mombusho fujin kyoiku-ka 1978 and 1987). In the United Nations Decade for Women, which followed the International Women's Year (1975), Japan faced the task of drawing up a national plan of action to put into practice the principles that had been adopted. Once we entered the decade of the 1980s efforts were undertaken at various levels throughout the country—prefectural, city, and local community—to draw up plans of action. In many cases the plans of action were formulated not by those in government exclusively but, rather, through the cooperation of government officials and women residing in the local communities. This experience also played an important role in awakening women's awareness of issues facing women in communities throughout Japan.

Although the discussion thus far has focused mainly on Japanese housewives and the process by which they have become increasingly involved in local community-level actions, it should be emphasized that nonemployed housewives are not the only segment of the female population that has begun to assume a more active role in community activities. A survey conducted by the *Asahi shimbun* newspaper in 1987 of over two thousand married women over the age of twenty in the greater Tokyo and Osaka area, for example, showed that 52 percent of those with jobs and 53 percent of those without jobs were involved in some type of community-related activity. A marked characteristic of Japanese women today is that they are taking an increasingly active part in local community movements irrespective of whether or not they are engaged in paid employment. Such involvement plays an important function for both types of women: for working women it represents an important channel for bringing about improvement in child daycare and after-school facilities; on the other hand, for many nonworking housewives such involvement may open up new job possibilities. The distance between these two groups of women has been increasingly closed over the past ten years.

Housewives Make Inroads into Politics

As women's awareness of their position in society deepened as a result of going out into the paid labor market and taking part in local community activities and study programs, they also became more conscious of other issues within Japanese society, and this in turn propelled them to take even more active roles in their communities. The knowledge and experience gained from such activities made women increasingly more confident of themselves, and by the latter part of the 1980s this newly acquired confidence was manifested in their advancement into the political realm. What seems to have occurred is that their experiences at the local community level spurred them to the realization that a solution to most of the issues affecting daily life which so concerned them could be arrived at only by bringing pressure to bear on the government and legislature at both the local and national levels.

From the mid-1980s we have seen for the first time since the immediate postwar period, when women first gained the right to vote and run for political office, a major increase in the number of female candidates both running for and getting elected to political office at the local, prefectural, and national levels. Moreover, these candidates, together with the female electorate as a whole, have demonstrated growing dissatisfaction with the record and policies of the conservative Liberal Democratic Party, which has ruled Japan throughout the postwar years, and have begun to shift their loyalties to the other national political parties as well as to newly established political groups.

The beginning of this new phase, and one that attracted national attention, was the movement opposing the destruction of the forests of Ikego in the city of Zushi in Kanagawa Prefecture (just south of Tokyo) for construction of housing facilities for military personnel and their families stationed in the U.S. military base located in that area. The women of this community, who were determined to preserve the forests for their children, ran up against the wall of a political establishment that was run by men. They decided, therefore, to try to get representatives from their own group elected to the local city assembly and to install as mayor someone who was sympathetic to their demands. Even though the group did not manage to win a majority in the city election of 1986, the top four candidates elected to the city assembly were women who were active in the movement to save the forests of Ikego.

In the unified local elections held the following year, 1987, thirty-one women affiliated with Seikatsu Club Seikyo, a nationwide network of women founded in 1965 and designed to help housewives to a better life through cooperatives that provide organically grown food, were elected to city assemblies within the greater Tokyo area. In the election for the House of Councilors held in 1989 the number of eligible female voters casting their ballots exceeded that of men by 2,370,000 (Nihon Fujin Dantai Rengokai 1990, 202). Moreover, 146 women ran for office in that election, compared to 82 in 1986, 55 in 1983, and many fewer in the preceding decades, and 22 won election to the Upper House, compared to 10 or fewer in the previous elections (210, fig. II-114). In contrast to the House of Councilors' election held in 1986, when support for the Liberal Democratic Party was high among women across age groups, in this election women in all age groups gave greater support to the other four main opposition parties—Socialist, Communist, Komei (Clean Government), and the Democratic Socialist parties. This was most prominent among women in the twenty-five to forty-nine age group—the very group among which a survey by NHK found the greatest opposition to the consumption tax instituted in 1989, the greatest degree of dissatisfaction with the manner in which the Recruit political scandal was being handled, and the strongest agreement with the view that "Our lives will not change unless changes are brought about in the social and political structures, and therefore those changes are necessary" (NHK Hoso Bunka Chosa Kenkyujo 1989). In the election for the House of Representatives which was held the following year, twelve women were elected to office, up from seven in the previous election.

The unified local elections held in April 1991 were a further demonstration of this growing involvement by women, as well as the growing significance of issues affecting female voters, in Japanese politics. In that election the number of women elected to various offices at the local and prefectural levels totaled 782, compared to 595 in 1987. As a result, the number of prefectures without any assemblywomen declined from nineteen to thirteen, and, for the first time since Japanese women gained the right to vote in 1947, a woman was elected to the office of mayor (in the city of Ashiya, near Osaka). Most striking was the fact that, while support by the opposition parties was an important factor, equally significant was the very strong showing of candidates not affiliated with any of the national political parties; more than two hundred of the women elected to office were in this category.

Many of these candidates ran on specific issues of immediate concern to ordinary Japanese citizens, such as those having to do with protection of the environment, care of the elderly, school improvement, and support of self-government, and were supported in their bids for election by various grass-roots groups and networks organized around those issues and often led by women. The most prominent of these, the Seikatsu Club Seikyo, alone succeeded in getting fifty-two of its members elected to various assemblies. Interesting as well as important to note are some of the unique principles and practices that radically sets this group apart from the traditional political parties. First of all, members from the club elected to political office are referred to as "proxies" to highlight the club's view that elected officials are indeed stand-ins, or representatives, of their constituents and in no way occupy a superior position. In addition the term of office is limited—in the case of Tokyo, to three terms—so as to provide opportunity for many of its members to serve as well as to prevent the establishment of a hierarchy and entrenchment of an elite within the organization. Democracy and equality are its guiding principles. This organization also forgoes the rituals commonly associated with the celebration of election victories among Japan's political parties—the rose corsage and the painting in of the eye of a Dharma doll by the victor.

Despite recent advances shown by Japanese women into the political realm, their presence in positions of political leadership is still very small: they constituted a mere 2.8 percent in prefectural assemblies in 1992, and 15.1 percent in the House of Councilors, and 2.7 percent in the House of Representatives in 1993. A recent international survey of 131 countries showed that Japan ranked in the 110th place in terms of the percentage women occupy in the lower house of national government assemblies—2.34 percent as compared to 11 percent on the average ("Kokkaigiin no josei hiritsu" 1992, 18). The developments since the mid-1980s are, nevertheless, very significant in that they demonstrate a new awareness on the part of ordinary Japanese housewives that they must and can take politics into their own hands.

Agenda for the Future

The women of Japan have thus undergone dramatic changes in recent years, but to what extent have the issues confronting them been resolved? As I have described, women have emerged from their homes and become active in their communities; however, they have done so only to find that they alone are the ones supporting and maintaining the home and the community. Many women have therefore come to the realization that, given the present arrangement in society, in which men are so involved in their work that they are for the most part absent from their homes and their communities, no matter how much women themselves change, there is a limit to how much improvement they can bring about, through their efforts alone, in terms of achieving equal partnership with men both in the family and in the larger society.

Japanese women, therefore, are now turning serious attention to the need to strive for both structural changes within society as well as changes in the way men think and behave. In the political sphere, for example, it implies a whole gamut of changes—from getting those in leadership of the governing Liberal Democratic Party to alter their ways of thinking to pressing for a reorganization of the processes by which candidates for political office are chosen. Within the realm of the family, it means bringing about changes in the relationship between wives and husbands and getting husbands—who, even in the case of those whose wives are employed, at present spend an average of twelve minutes per day performing housekeeping and child care activities and doing the shopping (Rodosho Fujinkyoku 1993, app. p. 63, app. table 6)—to reexamine and change their more tradition-bound attitudes and behavior. The first step toward getting men to assume a greater role in the day-to-day life of the home and family is a reduction in the number of hours Japanese men habitually put into work—which is over 2,000 hours on the average, compared to 1,500 to 1,800 hours in most Western industrialized countries. Through these and other fundamental changes in Japanese society today's women are seeking a better way of life for both women and men as well as more satisfactory relationships between them.

REFERENCES

Ajinomoto Shokuhin Kaisha. 1988, October. "Shufu no shokuseikatsu ishiki ni kan-suru chosa" (Survey of attitudes among housewives regarding dietary habits).
Asahi Shimbunsha. 1987, July. "Shufu no shugyo/shakai sanka to kateinai no shigoto ni kansuru chosa" (Survey of housewives' employment and social participation and work within the home). Tokyo: Asahi shimbunsha.
Kanamori, Toshie. Personal interview. 1989, November. Kanagawa, Japan.
"Kokkaigiin no josei hiritsu" (Ratio of women among national assembly members). 1992. *Asahi shimbun* (Asahi newspaper), 16 January, 18.
Mombusho fujin kyoiku-ka (Ministry of Education, Women's Education Section). 1978

and 1987. *Fujin kyoiku oyobi katei kyoiku ni kansuru shisaku no genjo* (Current status of policies regarding women's education and family education). Tokyo: Mombusho.

NHK hoso bunka chosa kenkyujo. 1989, October. *Hoso kenkyu to chosa* (Research on broadcasting). Tokyo: NHK shuppan kyoku.

Nihon fujin dantai rengokai, ed. *Fujin hakusho 1990* (White paper on women). Tokyo: Popuru shuppan.

Rodosho fujinkyoku (Ministry of Labor, Women's Bureau). 1993. *Hataraku josei no jitsujo* (Status of female workers). Tokyo: Rodosho.

Profiles of Two Assemblywomen

A 1991 study by the Center for the American Woman and Politics at Rutgers University revealed that, regardless of their party or ideology, women politicians have a different agenda than their male counterparts.* Among other things, they are more likely than their male counterparts to focus on issues pertaining to women's rights, child care, health care, and the family. These findings are very much applicable in the case of many Japanese women politicians, who have become increasingly more visible within the last fifteen years or so. The two Japanese politicians profiled here—Aokage Takako, from a newly established local political party affiliated with a consumer's cooperative association, and Mitsui Mariko, from the Socialist Party, both elected to local assemblies in 1987—have taken up issues relating to women, children, education, the elderly, and the environment which have hitherto received little attention among male politicians. The two women—both in their forties, members of the first post–World War II baby boom and brought up and educated under a newly democratized political, social, and educational system—exemplify a new generation of women who have come to play an increasingly vital and visible role in political and other spheres of public life in Japan.

---

*Center for the American Woman and Politics, *The Impact of Women in Public Office* (New Brunswick, N.J.: CAWP, Eagleton Institute of Politics, Rutgers, State University of New Jersey, 1991).

Aokage Takako: Housewife Turned Political Representative from Seikatsu Club Seikyo

❖ ❖ ❖

Naoko Sasakura

Edited and translated by Kumiko Fujimura-Fanselow

Seikatsu (Life) Club Seikyo is a nationwide network of women founded in 1965 in order to help housewives create a better life through cooperatives that provide organically grown food. In the unified local elections held in 1987 this organization succeeded in getting 31 of its members elected to city assemblies in the greater Tokyo area. Aokage Takako, a resident of Yokohama City, just south of Tokyo, and until then a full-time homemaker, was one of those thirty-one. In the 1991 election Aokage was once again reelected to office.

Background

Aokage was born in Hiroshima in August 1946, exactly one year after the first atom bomb was dropped on that city. Although she herself has no recollection of the horror of that event, she grew up hearing about it from family members and neighbors. She was of the generation that grew up and was educated under a newly democratized system of education. Although public schools were made coeducational following the postwar educational reforms, single-sex schools continued to exist in some areas of the country, and

This is an edited, translated version of a chapter titled by Naoko Sasakura "Onna ga chi'iki o kaeru" (Women bringing about change in the community), in *Onna ga seiji o kaeru* (Women bringing about change in politics), ed. Naoko Sasakura, Satomi Nakajima, and Kazuko Sugawara (Tokyo: Shinsensha, 1990). Permission has been granted by Naoko Sasakura and the publisher, Shinsensha.

Aokage attended an all-girls junior and senior high school and, later, a woman's university in Hiroshima. Reflecting on the influence of her schooling in an all-female student body environment and her subsequent career, Aokage comments:

> In the absence of boys, we girls assumed leadership and all the responsibilities. . . . The year I entered Hiroshima Women's College was the first year it had been elevated to a four-year university, [and]we had the sense that we were making history. Later, after I got married I got involved in the Seikatsu Club Seikyo and other local community activities, all of which were run by women. Come to think of it, all my life I have been working among women. (Qtd. in Sasakura 1990, 89)

Aokage married in 1972 and moved to a new housing complex located in the city of Yokohama. While today there are six thousand households and twenty thousand residents in the complex, at the time Aokage moved there, there were just a thousand households; very few public facilities existed, and shopping was inconvenient. As a newcomer to the area, the young housewife found herself very much alone and isolated. She discovered, however, that many of her neighbors belonged to the Seikatsu Club Seikyo food cooperative, and she joined up, not only so that she could have access to food that did not contain harmful additives but also to make friends with other women in her building. This turned out to be the first and decisive step toward her eventual involvement in politics.

Emergence of Seikatsu Club Seikyo as a Political Force

Seikatsu Club Seikyo grew out of a movement by two hundred Tokyo housewives who decided to organize a milk-purchasing cooperative in order to combat rising prices. Three years later the organization emerged as a consumers' cooperative union in Tokyo, and in 1971 it was also set up in Yokohama. Today the organization includes roughly 160,000 households from Tokyo and eight surrounding prefectures. Unlike many of the other consumers' cooperatives that exist in Japan, this one has no retail stores or outlets. Instead, units made up of roughly ten households make group purchases, which are then divided among unit members. Each member makes an investment in the association and participates in management, and there is an ongoing effort on the part of every member to increase membership.

In the latter part of the 1970s, a movement to ban the sale and use of synthetic detergents containing phosphates spread throughout the country, as more people began to learn about their harmful effect on sources of drinking water. Members of Seikatsu Club Seikyo took an active part in this movement, petitioning for the establishment of ordinances banning their use. Members of the group attended sessions of local assemblies and talked directly with individual assembly members, trying to get across their views to their representatives. For many of these women this was their first direct experience with the political process, and they realized how ignorant most politicians were about environmental issues. This realization awakened a determination among many members that they themselves must take a more direct and active role in electoral politics.

The first member of Seikatsu Club Seikyo to run for political office was Kitano Reiko, who was elected to the district assembly in Tokyo's Nerima ward in 1979, followed by others in 1983. Within the membership of the Kanagawa Prefecture branch of the association, a movement was started to try to get its representatives elected to governing bodies in each of the cities and towns within the prefecture in the next election. The result was the establishment in 1984 of a local political party made up largely of members of Seikatsu Club Seikyo, called the Kanagawa Prefecture Network Movement. Later several chapters of the party, all called "networks," were established throughout the prefecture to provide a springboard for candidates.

A defining characteristic of this political party and its chapter parties, or local networks (which numbered twenty-nine as of 1990), is that each of them is independent; the relationship between and among them is one of equality. Moreover, those elected to political office are referred to as "proxies," to highlight the fact that they are indeed stand-ins, or representatives, of their constituents and in no way occupy a superior position. In the unified local elections held in 1987 fifteen women ran for office from the Kanagawa Prefecture Network Movement, and nine were elected, of which Aokage was one.

Motivations behind Aokage's Decision to Run for Political Office

Normally, someone who stands for election as a representative from Seikatsu Club Seikyo counts on the association's membership within a particular electoral district as the base of support. In the case of Aokage there were only two thousand members in the ward in which she resided. She needed to obtain at least ten thousand votes in order even to come close to winning, which meant she would have to garner support among those outside its membership. What led to her decision to run for local assembly in spite of the uphill battle she faced?

> It was partly the climate of the times. Ms. Doi Takako had emerged on the political stage as the first female chairman of the Socialist Party. Moreover, protest against the proposed value-added tax had become heightened. The number of representatives from the ward in which I reside is restricted to seven. At the time, most of the seven were long-time residents of the area, who might be termed "local bosses." There was no one who represented the more recent residents who lived in the new housing projects and apartments. Given this situation, I had the rather naive feeling or hunch that I just might have a chance. (Sasakura 1990, 94–95)

Aokage goes on to emphasize the following point:

> I didn't look upon running for elected political office as something special or out
> of the ordinary. Rather, I regarded it as a logical extension of my involvement over
> the years in Seikatsu Club Seikyo and in other local community activities. I saw
> myself as simply doing my part toward creating greater participation on the part
> of local citizens in the process of self-government. (95)

Just about the time Aokage became a member of Seikatsu Club Seikyo,
the association had become active in the movement to stop the use of detergents containing phosphates and to promote the use of soap instead. Meanwhile, in the high-rise apartment complex in which she lived residents had
become increasingly concerned about the damage to the buildings' drainage
pipes caused by residents disposing of leftover cooking oil in the kitchen
drain. Aokage started a study group to look into both of these issues, which
then evolved into a much larger "free school" organized by Seikatsu Club
Seikyo. In addition, Aokage helped organize a "green market," which was
held periodically in order to promote the practice of recycling: local residents
would bring goods they no longer needed and exchange them for other
goods. She undertook many other projects as an active member of the housing projects' self-governing association. Over the fifteen years Aokage had
resided in her community she had come to forge close links with her neighbors through her many and varied voluntary efforts on behalf of the
community.

Following the announcement of her decision to run for Yokohama
City Assembly, Aokage and her supporters set about building support
within the community by holding bazaars and so-called home meetings,
small gatherings held in the homes of Aokage's supporters. At these gatherings Aokage spoke to local residents about her past efforts on behalf of
the community and what she hoped to accomplish as a member of the
assembly, and those gathered were in turn able to relate their concerns to
the candidate.

Aokage focused on three main issues: better care for the elderly, education, and environmental protection. Specifically, she advocated improved day
care and short-term residential care for the elderly, more emphasis on peace
education, and making the board of education more open to the public. On
the issue of the environment she proposed, as a means of protecting the
water supply and preserving greenery, banning the use of synthetic detergents in public facilities, collection of empty cans, and recycling of bottles
and used cooking oil.

Both Aokage and the women who supported her bid for election were
total amateurs to the field of electoral politics. While they had, of course, participated through the ballot, this was their first experience in putting up a
candidate and conducting a campaign. It was an experience, though, which
had a tremendous impact on their consciousness: "We realized that we, too,

have the power to shape politics" (qtd. in Sasakura 1990, 96). Aokage succeeded in winning election to the Yokohama City Assembly from her ward with slightly under ten thousand votes.

Issues Taken Up by Assemblywoman Aokage

Since getting voted into office, Aokage, along with the two other women from her party in the Yokohama City Assembly, has taken up several issues concerning the environment and also education.

Environmental Issues

One of the environmental issues to which Aokage has devoted her efforts has been the elimination of the use of detergents containing phosphates and their replacement with soap. Another issue, very much connected with the first, has been the preservation of clean water. She has also sought stricter inspection of food imported from abroad in order to check for radioactive contamination and greater protection against danger arising from accidents taking place in the process of transporting nuclear fuel.

Promoting the Use of Soap

Involvement by members of Seikatsu Club Seikyo in the campaign to ban the use of detergents containing harmful phosphates was the initial impetus for their entry into electoral politics. After the assembly of Shiga Prefecture passed a law regulating the sale and use of synthetic detergents in 1979, a petition movement to get similar laws enacted spread throughout the country. And in 1980 a petition was submitted to the Yokohama City Assembly. Although at the time, the petition was rejected, a resolution was adopted calling for the establishment of a deliberative council within the bureau for pollution control, and a policy was set forth advocating the elimination of phosphates and the use of soap instead.

Soon after her election to office Aokage pointed out that, despite the fact that a policy had been established to promote the use of soap in place of detergents, the city administration had not undertaken any positive efforts in this direction, apart from having setting aside 6 out of the 329 public schools that offer school lunches in the city of Yokohama as trial sites for the use of soap in place of detergents in their kitchens in 1987. She requested that a study be done of the trial schools to see how the new practice was being implemented, and she also called for greater promotion of the use of soap in public facilities. In the neighboring city of Kawasaki, elected representatives from Seikatsu Club Seikyo had been successful in instituting the use of soap in public facilities and school kitchens. Aokage's efforts bore some fruit when, in the proposed budget for 1990, funds were allocated for the pollution control bureau to conduct a survey on the use of soap among Yokohama residents.

Protecting the Community's Source of Water

Concern on the part of Seikatsu Club Seikyo with the issue of eliminating the use of phosphates and promoting the use of soap was based in large part on a desire to reduce environmental pollution and to protect the natural environment. In 1987 Kanagawa Prefecture (the prefecture in which Aokage resides) proposed building an industrial waste disposal plant in a town close to Sagami Lake, which supplied water to 60 percent of the residents in Kanagawa Prefecture. Fearing the possibility that dangerous waste material might seep underground and contaminate the water flowing into the lake, approximately thirty citizens' and labor groups united in opposition to the proposed plan, collecting more than 130,000 signatures. As a result, the plan was temporarily shelved.

Aokage had been very active in this opposition movement, and she took up the issue both during her election campaign and later in her role as assembly member. Aokage has cautioned that the plan has not been completely withdrawn, and we need to maintain a careful watch, given the prefectural government's apparent stance that, once the plan has been determined to be safe, it will go ahead and build such a facility, regardless of whether or not it is close to a source of drinking water. Similarly, Aokage has demonstrated opposition to the building of a golf course near a river in a neighboring prefecture which is also a source of water for Yokohama residents, since the large amounts of fertilizers used yearly would very likely contaminate the river.

Regulating Sale of Food Contaminated by Radiation

The nuclear plant accident that occurred in Chernobyl in 1986 led to a heightened movement in Japan against nuclear power plants. At the same time, many citizens were alarmed that some of the food imported from abroad might be contaminated by radiation and petitioned local governments to take necessary precautions.

In 1987 Seikatsu Club Seikyo petitioned the Yokohama City Council's Committee on Public Welfare, Health, and Pollution to conduct a study of radiation levels in imported foodstuffs sold in the city and to make their findings public. In addition, it called on the city government to demand that the national government set a lower limit on the acceptable level of radioactivity. In the process of debate over this issue Aokage was shocked to discover that many of the assembly members looked upon the issue of radioactivity as one of ideology (in other words, merely an extension of the political/ideological conflict over the desirability of building nuclear power plants). Aokage therefore went about meeting separately with representatives from the various parties and carefully explaining to them, "This issue is not one that has to do with ideology; it is, instead, one of protecting the safety of the food we consume" (qtd. in Sasakura 1990, 103). The outcome was that, in 1988, all of the different parties gave support for a petition to be submitted by the Yokohama City Assembly to the national government asking that it take stricter measures to control levels of radioactive contamination in food products.

Safety in the Transport of Nuclear Fuel

A related issue that Aokage took up in her first year in the city assembly concerned that of strengthening protection for citizens against possible accidents that might occur during the process of transporting nuclear fuel within the country. She pointed out the fact that existing regional disaster emergency plans did not contain any provisions for dealing with this type of accident and insisted that such provisions be included. Her argument was that the government had an obligation to protect its citizens. The Disaster Section of the Bureau of General Affairs responded by deciding to add such a provision to the regional disaster emergency plan. It was the first time that measures to protect people in the event of a disaster caused by radiation were included in the overall disaster emergency plan of a prefecture that did not itself have a nuclear power plant.

The head of the Disaster Section had this to say about Aokage's role in this matter:

> By bringing this issue up in the assembly, Aokage created an important opening. My impression is that the representatives from the Kanagawa Prefecture Network Party have brought concerns relating to the daily lives of community residents into politics. Instead of arguing over matters on the basis of ideology, as most politicians have tended to do, they approach issues from the standpoint of ordinary citizens, whose main concern is, "What are you going to do to make our lives and the lives of our children better and safer!" From this standpoint, there are several issues that those of us who work in government have failed to take note of and address in the past. (Qtd. in Sasakura 1990, 106)

Educational Issues

Along with environmental issues Aokage has also taken up several issues relating to education.

Reexamining School Regulations from the Standpoint of Students' Human Rights

In response to concerns voiced by teachers, administrators, students, and parents throughout the country over what they viewed as excessive regulation of students in many of the schools, the Ministry of Education in 1987 called on local boards of education to reexamine school regulations. The city of Yokohama began its own investigation, but, at the same time, Aokage, together with her staff, conducted an independent investigation of thirty lower secondary schools within Yokohama. Her research revealed that, indeed, many of the current regulations pertaining to such things as student dress and conduct were excessively strict (e.g., "the length of the skirt must be within 30 centimeters from the floor," "belts must be no wider than three centimeters").

When Aokage presented her findings before the city assembly, she emphasized the fact that the issue of school rules and regulations directed at students must be examined from the standpoint of human rights and that we need to ensure that the human rights of children are not violated through the imposition of such rules and regulations. She proposed, moreover, that a greater effort be made to promote student autonomy by having students themselves establish rules governing school life and see to it that those rules are followed.

Questioning the Use of the Personality Assessment Test

Another very important issue Aokage has raised concerns the use (or abuse) of the so-called Personality Assessment Test, which at the time she first raised the issue (in 1987) was administered to students in 74 percent of the lower secondary schools in Yokohama. Based on the results of the test, administered by an outside testing firm, students were categorized into one of several personality types and an assessment was made of their personality.

Aokage's main concern with regard to this test had to do with the dangers connected with the use(s) to which the test results might be put. She noted that in some schools they were being used as a means of detecting so-called problem children. There was a danger that, conversely, the data might be used as "evidence" to show that a particular student had a personality disorder. She insisted that, from the viewpoint of protecting the human rights of youngsters and their rights to privacy, schools have an obligation to ensure that the confidential data are carefully guarded. Aokage also questioned the purpose of conducting such a test in the first place as well as the validity of such a test:

> While it is suggested that the test is meant to benefit students, can it be totally denied that in fact the test is administered in order to provide certain data that the school bureaucracy deems important to obtain? . . . It seems unreasonable to try to place people into categories based on one measure and make judgments about their personality. Individuals have the potential of undergoing change through contact with other people and through the influence of environment. . . . Are you not denying this important role that education plays? (Qtd. in Sasakura 1990, 108)

After posing these questions to the superintendent of the Board of Education, Aokage proposed that a reassessment be made of the Personality Assessment Test itself.

At the time, the reply offered by the superintendent was simply: "The matter will be looked into with a forward-looking approach." Yet Aokage's impact can be discerned by the fact that, whereas the test had been administered in 74 percent of all lower secondary schools, a year later that figure had fallen to 45 percent. Apparently, the matter had been reexamined at a meeting of lower secondary school principals.

Conclusion

To emphasize once again the point made in the beginning, a defining feature of the issues Aokage has brought forth before the Yokohama City Assembly is that they all directly affect people in their roles as local community residents, consumers, and parents. She has focused attention on matters that previously had been ignored by the mostly male politicians, and at the same time she has, in many instances, offered a fresh perspective on both new as well as long-standing issues. Like other representatives from the Kanagawa Prefecture Network Movement, Aokage is basically a homemaker who found herself gradually drawn into politics as an extension of her involvement in various activities connected with Seikatsu Club Seikyo, such as the movement to recycle cooking oil or to promote the use of soap. Though she entered politics as an amateur, she has struggled to pursue her unique agenda through the established, male-dominated political organization. In the process, however, that organization itself, admittedly slowly, has begun to bend and to be more receptive to the concerns and viewpoints for which she stands.

The activities of Seikatsu Club Seikyo have in many ways responded to the desire felt by housewives to be involved in endeavors outside the home which have more meaning and value than working part-time for low hourly pay. Similarly, the people who have worked on behalf of Aokage's campaign and who have voted for her are largely women, most of them housewives. In the past these women showed little interest in local elections and constituted a floating electorate, having no strong allegiance to any particular party. For many of them the candidacy of Aokage and others like her spurred them to vote in the election for city assembly for the first time. The appearance of a new breed of politician speaking to the concerns of ordinary citizens seems to have encouraged voters to evaluate anew the importance of their individual ballots. At the same time, women have found a new means of asserting their political influence—through support for female candidates.

One of the biggest challenges facing this new political movement, if it seriously seeks to bring about significant change in politics, is to expand its base of support to embrace not only the traditional core of housewives but also men and young people. Yet, in order for the women who back Aokage and the others to be able to go out and convince a wider audience of voters of the importance of the values they stand for and the style of politics they have developed, they themselves must first undergo a change in their own consciousnesses; above all, they need to develop as individual women a strong sense of their own independence and autonomy.

Finally, there are a few issues that I would like to raise concerning this political movement. The first is that, while the relationship between the main political organization, Kanagawa Perfecture Network Movement, and its local "nets," is claimed to be nonhierarchical and based instead on the ideal of independence and equality, in reality this ideal seems not to have been totally achieved. A second issue concerns the fact that representatives are limited to two terms, or eight years, in order that many women can have the experience of serving as representative. While this practice has certain merits, it can also be argued that two terms may be too short a period in which to actually accomplish something in office, since it takes about that much time to gain sufficient experience on the job. A third issue is the question of to what extent women really do, in fact, occupy the central role within the movement. In the past it has often been pointed out that many of the activities of Seikatsu Club Seikyo, the parent organization of the Kanagawa Prefecture Network Movement, are led by men; there has been a similar criticism directed at the Network Movement itself. Many people are watching to see how the women respond to these challenges.

Mitsui Mariko: An Avowed Feminist Assemblywoman

❖ ❖ ❖

Emiko Kaya

Since she was elected a member of the Tokyo Metropolitan Assembly in April 1987, Mitsui Mariko has gained a reputation as one of the most vocal and energetic representatives and one who gives top priority to women's issues. As an avowed feminist, she has strived to examine the present conditions from an equal rights perspective and to demand that the government of Tokyo come up with effective measures to correct discriminatory practices against women. Mitsui served a second term in the assembly after being reelected to office in 1989. The issues she took up included those of gender inequalities in education, the depiction of women as sex objects in the mass media, sexual harassment, problems faced by working women, and welfare programs for the aged. All of these issues have, in fact, long been raised by the women's movement but received little attention from most politicians—largely male—until very recently, when women decided to try to secure seats in local as well as national legislative bodies and to tackle these issues themselves.

Background

When Mitsui won her victory as a candidate from the Socialist Party in the election to fill a vacancy in the Tokyo Metropolitan Assembly in 1987, the mass media described her as "a 'Madonna' who magnificently transformed herself from a mere high school teacher to an assemblywoman." Mitsui, however, completely rejects this view: "A 'mere high school teacher'? No, that's not an accurate characterization. Since the early 1970s I was continuously active in Women's Lib groups." After graduating from university, she worked as an "OL," or "office lady," for three years, during which she kept questioning why women are expected to pour tea as an extra duty or why they are not allowed to attend meetings or go on business trips. "Before I realized it, I found myself in and out of Ichikawa Fusae's Women's Suffrage Assembly Hall and began participating in meetings of a citizens' group that advocated making the study of home economics mandatory not just for girls but also boys."

Mitsui quit her job as an OL and became a high school teacher just around the time of the International Women's Year. In 1980, Tanaka Sumiko, a woman legislator in the House of Councilors, was appointed vice chair of the Socialist Party. The political climate in Japan in those days, however, was far from sympathetic toward a female political leader. "I was disgusted to learn that a male politician in the Socialist Party had stated, 'If a woman is going to be a vice-chair, then I'll resign.' In those days help wanted ads imposingly read 'Men Only,' 'Restricted to female junior college graduates commuting from their homes'. Although we pointed out the injustice of these practices, our protests were received as merely noisy complaints of aggressive women."

Her involvement with the women's movement continued throughout the early 1980s. In 1985 she went to the United States to study for a year and witnessed the political processes through which women's issues were dealt with at various political levels, national to local. By the time Mitsui returned to Japan she was firmly convinced of the need for women's active participation in politics. Or rather, in her words: "The activities I had been engaged in up until that time in Japan were, in fact, what is called 'politics.' My experience in the United States made me aware of this, and it seemed to me as though the Japan I found on my return had been waiting for me to make use of this experience" (Mitsui 1990a).

In the fall of 1986 Doi Takako became chair of the Socialist Party. Doi was Japan's first female party leader, and her presence gave great encouragement and confidence to Japanese women, who had become increasingly aware of their potential political power. It was in the following year that assemblywoman Mitsui Mariko made her political debut. That year a sweeping number of female candidates were elected in the regional elections held in April across the country, a phenomenon the mass media dubbed "the Madonna Whirlwind."

When Mitsui first spoke in the Tokyo Assembly in July of 1987 she did not forget to call everyone's attention to the fact that the traditional male monopoly of the political world was an aberrant phenomenon that ought to be done away with in the future:

Please imagine the following, everyone, that all the directors sitting here on this side of the podium were women, except for one man, and that 118 of the 127 peo-

385

ple sitting in the assembly were women and only nine were men. You would certainly think it was strange if all the members of the highest deliberative bodies with decision-making power in the government of Tokyo were women. Yet this strange phenomenon exists within the present assembly, only the situation is exactly the reverse. (Minutes of the Tokyo Metropolitan Assembly, 3 July 1987)

To make such a comment before a city assembly would have been unimaginable prior to Mitsui's appearance. Most women politicians, regardless of their political ideology, would have avoided taking such a strong feminist stand, for feminism had been viewed as somewhat too radical and dangerous, and it was thought to alienate not only most men but the majority of women, who prefer to take a moderate stand, leading to possible loss of popular votes. Political concerns of women have been accepted as long as they have remained within the realm of their traditional gender roles, that is, those of mothers and housewives, as often expressed in such slogans as "We, as mothers who give and bring up life, demand safe food products." Outright defiance about the male monopoly of politics had been very difficult.

The feminist movement, however, has been growing stronger since the United Nations (UN) Decade for Women. Both the national and local governments (especially the government of Tokyo) can no longer ignore, at least officially, the voices of women from various sectors demanding equality of the sexes, since Japan is one of the countries that has ratified the UN Convention on the Elimination of All Forms of Discrimination against Women. It may be said that the success of feminist assemblywoman Mitsui was made possible through the combination of many factors, her own political conviction and activities, the support of thousands of women who, like her, have been active in women's groups, and a change in the policy of Japan's Socialist Party toward greater cooperation with citizens' movements under the leadership of Doi Takako.

Issues Taken Up by Mitsui

After her election to the assembly Mitsui raised several questions regarding the metropolitan government's policies with respect to such issues as gender equality in the areas of education and employment and sexual exploitation of women in advertisements, among others.

Establishing a Mechanism for Handling Cases of Sexual Discrimination in Employment

In her first speech before the assembly Mitsui also proposed the enactment of a "sexual equality ombudsman regulation." The Committee for Processing Complaints about Sexual Discrimination had proved to be ineffective in resolving problems because it lacked both a legal basis for forcing companies to respond to complaints about sexual discrimination as well as the authority to enforce measures directed against eliminating discrimination. Mitsui proposed as three elements essential to an ombudsman system that its members be publicly recruited rather than appointed by the governor, be able to aid in litigation, and have penalties spelled out (Minutes of the Tokyo Metropolitan Assembly, 3 July 1987).

She later learned that, in the assembly, proposing a member's bill requires the support of one-eighth (16.7 percent) or more of all the assembly members, which was larger than the total number of Socialist Party members in the assembly at the time (12). In retrospect, speaking at a women's group two years later, she admitted that "proposing the ombudsman regulation as a member's bill was out of the question at the time, but I said what I had to say." She has found it very difficult to propose bills under present conditions but says: "It doesn't mean I can do nothing. I am given an equal right to speak up as the rest of the members. I have experienced firsthand the fact that the voice of one assemblyman is greater than that of many thousands of citizens. Therefore, if we want to bring up various issues pertaining to equality into the political scene in order to seek solutions, I'm convinced the most effective strategy is to send more women that women's groups can support to local and national legislative bodies" (Mitsui 1990b).

Issue of Gender Bias in Admission Quotas for High Schools

Mitsui has also questioned the metropolitan government's policies with regard to sexual equality in the field of education, using as a measuring stick the provisions called for in the preamble and Article 1 of the UN Convention on the Elimination of All Forms of Discrimination against Women.

> The place of learning is where equality should be carried through more than anywhere else. How on earth, then, can the Tokyo government allow public high school to discriminate against girls through the practice of setting recruitment quotas for girls? Because the so-called "numbered schools" (i.e., prestigious high schools which used to be boys' middle schools before the war) have a quota for girls that is about one-third that of boys, even girls who score the same as boys or higher on the entrance examinations end up not getting admitted.

Here Mitsui is referring to the fact that sex-segregated public secondary schools in Tokyo were made coeducational after World War II, but many of the top-rated boys' schools have persisted in setting a lower quota for girls, whereas most previously all-girls schools have achieved a fifty-fifty ratio of girls and boys. The result is that the admission quota for girls falls short of that for boys by three thousand for all the public high schools in Tokyo. Mitsui argued, "There is no clearer or more blatant manifestation of sexual discrimination than the quota system practiced by public high schools," and she demanded that the situation be corrected by 1990 (Minutes of the Tokyo Metropolitan Assembly, 3 July 1987). The Tokyo Bar Association concluded that differential quotas for boys and girls at public high schools violated the Japanese Constitution, the Basic School Education Act, as well as the spirit of the

Convention on the Elimination of All Forms of Discrimination against Women, and it strongly recommended equalizing the quota.

There have been some improvements, and since 1991 all of the thirteen numbered schools have a female enrollment of over 42 percent. In the meantime, the Committee for Considering the Selection of Entrants to Municipal High Schools was formed, and it has begun to shift toward the idea that sex-based quotas should be eliminated altogether. Does the abolition of quotas mean the elimination of sexual discrimination? No, not likely. Assemblywoman Mitsui points out the danger of such a change bringing about the opposite result. That is, because the gender role ideology is so strongly rooted in the consciousness of Japanese people and academic achievement is thought to be more important for males than females, the top-rated schools are likely to be flooded with male applicants.

> In several prefectures where sex-based quotas gave been eliminated, high schools which used to be all-male in the past still have an exceedingly high number of male students, while the former all-girls schools have mostly girls. Thus, unfortunately, the tradition of sex separation tends to be preserved. In addition, even though applications for technical and commercial programs in high school are open to both sexes, girls comprise a mere 4.6 percent of the students in the technical programs, while boys make up only 15 percent of those enrolled in commercial programs.

Mitsui insists that in order to achieve true equality between men and women it is urgent that, at the minimum, quotas be set for male and female students in accordance with the ratio of males and females in the general population (Minutes from the Tokyo Metropolitan Assembly, 8 December 1988).

Her concern is shared by many women's groups and the teachers' union. In the face of the continuing decline in the school-age population, a reorganization of public high schools is being considered. The Committee to Consider the Selection of Entrants to Municipal High Schools presented its final report in April 1990, in which it stated that, from the viewpoint of ensuring sexual equality, it would be appropriate to abolish the sex-based quota system, though certain measures must be taken to avoid extreme imbalances. Exactly what form of selection system is to be adopted is yet unknown, but Mitsui feels she cannot be too optimistic and that there is every possibility that the new nondifferentiated selection system will bring about biased results in the student population.

Issue of Sexual Exploitation in Ads and Beauty Contests

Another issue that Mitsui has been working on is that of the treatment of women as sexual commodities as witnessed in advertisement posters, beauty contests, and the practice of prostitution. Bringing in three posters in which a young woman's body or legs were displayed though they had no direct relation to the products being advertised, she called for a confirmation of the Tokyo Metropolitan Government's position on this matter, which is that social tolerance for the treatment of women as sexual commodities reinforces the deeply rooted tendency to view women as objects as well as a disregard for the humanity of women and that active countermeasures should be taken to eliminate such tendencies and to create a society free of sexual discrimination (Minutes no. 4 of the Special Budget Committee Meeting, 16 March 1990).

> We are faced with the reality in which women's naked bodies are used for advertisement posters of many companies, and the government of Tokyo is no exception. An example was a poster for Tokyo's Bureau of Transportation which featured a woman in bikini. . . . Also, the subway posters showing only legs in high-heeled shoes were terrible. Our protest led to the Bureau of Citizens and Cultural Affairs issuing a warning, though it was not in writing, to all departments of the metropolitan government that in advertisement posters the female body or its parts should never be used as objects or simply to attract attention. (Mitsui 1990b)

These two posters in which the Tokyo government was directly involved were removed immediately as a result of Mitsui's questioning, although the top official concerned never acknowledged in the meeting that the posters did, in fact, treat women as mere sex objects.

Mitsui also questioned the rationale for the Miss Tokyo Contest, which has been supported by the Tokyo Metropolitan Government for more than thirty years. "There has been protest that beauty contests are an example of the commoditization of sex, and that they are like a meat market for women. What is the relevance of a woman's bust, waist or hip measurements to the social service activities and the promotion of international friendship [which are the roles Miss Tokyo is supposed to fulfill]?" She also challenged the requirement that a contestant must be single and twenty-five years or younger by submitting her own name as a contestant, which was rejected. Mitsui publicized the decision by the prefecture and the city of Osaka to stop supporting beauty contests because of protests from women as well as the statement by Mayor Motoshima of Nagasaki that beauty contests are intricately related to discrimination against women (Minutes no. 4 of the Special Budget Committee of the Tokyo Metropolitan Assembly). Despite her failure to affect the policies of the Tokyo Metropolitan Government on this issue, her protest helped nonetheless to raise the consciousness of many Tokyo residents.

Other Issues

Other improvements for which Mitsui has worked include: (1) calling for the inclusion of sexual harassment among labor issues for which consultation is offered by the city to working women; (2) advocating extension of financial assistance to children of families headed by mothers at least until the children graduate from high school, that is, three years beyond the current limit; (3) eliminating the requirement that female, but not male, stenographers in the Tokyo Metropolitan Assembly wear uniforms; (4) including women's issues among those investigated by politicians and others taking part in city government–sponsored overseas study tours; (5) calling for a change in the architectural design of the Metropolitan Hall of Arts and Culture to create a nursery room; and (6) inviting a group of female interior designers to draw up plans for the new location of the Tokyo Women's Information Center.

> When politicians talk about their achievements in the assembly, male politicians will usually talk about having sponsored the building of a hall, a bridge, or a subway, which cost some hundreds of millions of yen. My accomplishments are totally different from those of traditional politicians, but if there existed a newspaper devoted to the cause of advancing gender equality, I'm sure I would appear on the front page. Most people, other than those who are committed to the women's movement, do not consider the kinds of things I have been doing as having much importance. . . . Traditional politics has neglected issues pertaining to culture, social welfare, education, and equality, and spent most of our tax money on buildings and subways. However, I will stick to my position to give top priority to human rights and equality issues in politics. (Mitsui 1990b)

Conclusion

In February 1992 the National Federation of Feminist Legislators was established as a network for nonpartisan assembly members, male and female, across the country. Not surprisingly, Mitsui was one of the main organizers. The group started with twenty members, including one male. The goal of this group is to create a society in which women's voices are reflected in politics. In order to bring this about they seek to increase to 30 percent (from the current figure of about 4 percent) the ratio of female assembly members at every level of government—prefectural, municipal, town, and village—and to promote policies to create an environment that will enable women to lead a full life ("Women's Share" 1992). Membership grew to about 130 as of July 1992. The organization has called for affirmative action programs of the type that exist in some European countries. So far, however, in Japan the concept of affirmative action has had very little support from the national or local governments, much less from private industry, although it has been recommended by advisory committees such as the Tokyo government's Council on Women's Issues as one of the most effective means to grapple with the problem of sexual inequality in present society. Mitsui has often referred to the kinds of changes that have been brought about in Norway, where not only is the prime minister a woman but eight out of eighteen cabinet members also are women, and she has expressed strong support for the enactment of an affirmative action program in order to increase female representation in legislative bodies.

Prior to the 1992 election for the House of Councilors, the federation requested that the major political parties list the names of male and female candidates alternately, instead of listing all of the male candidates' names before those of female candidates, as had always been the practice. Shortly before the election Mitsui made the following comment: "To women who have entered late into the political world, an alternate listing of male and female candidates has great significance. With the advancement of women's status, each party finds it necessary to pay lip service to equality, but in reality it seems the male-centered ways of thinking have not changed. I feel a sense of crisis and as well as anger." ("Josei koho" 1992). The results of that election proved to be a disappointment, with the number of women elected to the House of Councilors reduced to thirteen, compared with twenty-two in the prior 1989 election, although the total number of women members in the House of Councilors rose from thirty-five to thirty-seven. This clearly indicates that the so-called Madonna Whirlwind that swept the political scene in the latter part of the 1980s has lost its power. And, with the Japanese economy slowing down, the decade of the 1990s will further test the ability of women in Japan to break into the political world in substantial numbers and bring about long-awaited changes in the political decision-making processes. Nevertheless, as Mitsui has stated, "Women succeeded in bringing about a shift in politics from 'politics exclusively of men' to 'politics of women, too' in the 80s, and politics in the 90s should move towards 'politics of men and women'" (1990a).

Postscript

A great deal will have to be done if the 1990s is really to give birth to "politics of men and women." While efforts in this direction have been started under the leadership of Assemblywoman Mitsui and many other female politicians like her, the difficulty of accomplishing this goal was brought sharply to focus by Mitsui's announcement in January 1993 that she was leaving the Socialist Party. The reasons she cited were: "There is no democracy within the party. We cannot engage freely in discussion and debate" and "The Socialist Party does not value the voice of women and therefore is incompatible with my efforts to try to improve the status of women" ("Togisen hikae" 1993). She spoke of some male party leaders who denigrate the concept of gender equality and engage in sexual harassment of female assembly members, and she related some of her own experiences of sexual harassment ("Mitsui shato togi" 1993). Because Mitsui not only was the most well-known member among Socialist Party–affiliated assembly members but also had gained national prominence over the years, her decision to leave the Socialist Party and complete her term of office as an independent was seen as a serious blow to the party's image, particularly in light of upcoming elections.

Following completion of her term of office as assemblywoman in June of 1993, Mitsui ran, unsuccessfully, for the House of Representatives as an independent candidate in the July elections held the same year. Recognizing the difficulties facing candidates—particularly women such as herself—who are not affiliated with one of the major political parties in winning election to the

National Diet under the newly instituted single-member constituency system, Mitsui has decided to concentrate her efforts for the time being on trying to get as many women as possible elected to local assemblies throughout the country by providing support and assistance to female candidates as board member of the National Federation of Feminist Legislators.

REFERENCES

"Josei koho heru fuman" (Discontented with the decrease in the number of female candidates). 1992. *Asahi shimbun* (Asahi newspaper), 22 July.

"Josei no seikai she'a mokuhyo 30%" (Women's share in the political world aimed at 30 percent). 1992. *Asahi shimbun* (Asahi newspaper), 4 February.

Minutes of the Tokyo Metropolitan Assembly. 1987, 3 July.

———. 1988, 8 December.

Minutes No. 4 of the Special Budget Committee Meeting of the Tokyo Metropolitan Assembly. 1990, 16 March.

Mitsui, Mariko. 1990a. "Hey Mister Businessmen There Are No Mrs. Sazaes: So, Whatchya Gonna Do?" *Asahi journal*, 30 March. Trans. from the Japanese by Miya E. Gardner.

———. 1990b. "Josei ga seiji ni noridashita hi" (The day women launched into politics). *Nihon fujin mondai konwakai kaiho* (Bulletin of the Japan Women's Forum), no. 49 (March): 58–68.

"Mitsui shato togi ga rinto todoke" (Socialist party metropolitan assembly member Mitsui gives notice she is quitting the party). 1993. *Asahi shimbun* (Asahi newspaper), 14 January, 30.

"Togisen hikae tohombu konmei" (Party headquarters in turmoil in face of upcoming election for metropolitan assembly). 1993. *Asahi shimbun* (Asahi newspaper), 14 January, 27.

Selected Bibliography of English-Language Works since 1980

The following bibliography follows American custom, with authors listed in alphabetical order by family name.

Akamatsu, Ryoko. 1990. *Japanese Women.* Tokyo: Japan Institute of Women's Employment.

Asadori, Sumie. 1986. "Guide to Japanese Women's Organizations." *Ampo: Japan-Asia Quarterly Review* 18, nos. 2/3: 106–7.

Asahi shimbun. 1985. *Women in a Changing World.* Tokyo: Asahi shimbun.

Asian Women's Association. 1988. *Women from Across the Sea: Migrant Workers in Japan.* Tokyo: Asian Women's Association.

Bando, Mariko. 1991. *Japanese Women: Yesterday and Today.* Tokyo: Foreign Press Center.

———. 1986. "When Women Change Jobs." *Japan Quarterly* 33, no. 2: 177–82.

Bernstein, Gail Lee, ed. 1991. *Recreating Japanese Women, 1800–1945.* Berkeley: University of California Press.

———. 1983. *Haruko's World: A Japanese Farm Woman and Her Community.* Stanford, Calif.: Stanford University Press.

Bestor, Theodore C. 1985. "Gendered Domains: A Commentary on Research in Japanese Studies." *Journal of Japanese Studies* 11, no. 1: 283–87.

Bingham, Marjorie Wall, and Susan Hill Gross. 1987. *Women in Japan: From Ancient Times to the Present.* St. Louis Park, Minn.: Glenhurst Publications.

Birnbaum, Phyllis, comp. and trans. 1982. *Rabbits, Crabs, etc.—Stories by Japanese Women.* Honolulu: University of Hawaii Press.

Bowman, Mary Jean, and Machiko Osawa. 1986. *Developmental Perspectives on the Education and Economic Activities of Japanese Women.* Washington, D.C.: Office of Educational Research and Improvement.

Brinton, Mary C. 1993. *Women and the Economic Miracle.* Berkeley and Los Angeles: University of California Press.

———. 1989. "Gender Stratification in Contemporary Urban Japan." *American Sociological Review* 54, no. 4: 549–64.

Bryant, Taimie L. 1992. "'Responsible' Husbands, 'Recalcitrant' Wives, Retributive Judges: Judicial Management of Contested Divorce in Japan." *Journal of Japanese Studies* 18, no. 12: 407–43.

Buckley, Sandra, and Vera Mackie. 1986. "Women in the New Japanese State." In *Democracy in Contemporary Japan,* eds. Gavan McCormack and Yoshio Sugimoto. Armonk, N.Y.: M. E. Sharpe.

Chikap, Mieko. 1986. "I Am an Ainu, Am I Not?" *Ampo: Japan-Asia Quarterly Review* 18, nos. 2/3: 81–87.

Coleman, Samuel. 1983. *Family Planning in Japanese Society: Traditional Birth Control in Modern Urban Culture.* Princeton, N.J.: Princeton University Press.

Condon, Jane. 1985. *A Half Step Behind: Japanese Women of the '80s.* New York: Dodd, Mead.

Cook, Alice H., and Hiroko Hayashi. 1980. *Working Women in Japan: Discrimination, Resistance, and Reform.* Ithaca, N.Y.: New York State School of Industrial and Labor Relations, Cornell University.

Cornell, Laurel L. 1990. "Peasant Women and Divorce in Preindustrial Japan." *Signs: Journal of Women in Culture and Society* 15, no. 4: 710–32.

Edwards, Walter. 1989. *Modern Japan through Its Weddings: Gender, Person, and Society in Ritual Portrayal.* Stanford, Calif.: Stanford University Press.

Ehara, Yumiko. 1993. "Japanese Feminism in the 1970s and 1980s." *U.S.-Japan Women's Journal English Supplement,* no. 4 (January): 49–69.

English Speaking Society. 1992. *Japanese Women Now.* Kyoto: Women's Bookstore Shoukadoh.

Fister, Patricia. 1990. "Women Artists in Traditional Japan." In *Flowering in* *the Shadows: Women in the History of Chinese and Japanese Painting*, ed. Marsha Weidner. Honolulu: University of Hawaii Press.

———. 1988. *Japanese Women Artists, 1600–1900*. Lawrence: Spencer Museum of Art, University of Kansas.

Fraser, Mary Crawford. 1982. *A Diplomat's Wife in Japan: Sketches at the Turn of the Century.* New York: Weatherhill.

Fujieda, Mioko. 1989. "Some Thoughts on Domestic Violence in Japan." Trans. Julianne Dvorak. *Review of Japanese Culture and Society* 3, no. 1: 60–66.

Fujieda, Mioko, and Rebecca Jennison. 1985. "The UN Decade for Women and Japan: Tools for Change." *Women's Studies International Forum* 8, no. 2: 121–23.

Fujii, Harue. 1982. "Education for Women: The Personal and Social Damage of an Anachronistic Policy." *Japan Quarterly* 29, no. 3: 301–10.

Fujimura-Fanselow, Kumiko. 1991. "The Japanese Ideology of 'Good Wives and Wise Mothers': Trends in Contemporary Research." *Gender & History* 3, no. 3 (Autumn): 345–49.

———. 1989a. "Japan." In *International Handbook of Women's Education*, ed. Gail P. Kelly. New York, Westport, Conn., and London: Greenwood Press.

———. 1989b. "Women's Participation in Higher Education in Japan." In *Japanese Schooling: Patterns of Socialization, Equality and Political Control*, ed. James J. Shields, Jr. University Park and London: Pennsylvania State University Press.

Fujimura–Fanselow, Kumiko, and Anne E. Imamura. 1991. "The Education of Japanese Women." In *Windows on Japanese Education*, ed. Edward R. Beauchamp. New York, Westport, Conn., and London: Greenwood Press.

Fujimura–Fanselow, Kumiko, and Atsuko Kameda. 1994. "Changing Trends Related to Women in Education." In *Women of Korea and Japan*, ed. Joyce Gelb and Marian Lief Palley. Philadelphia: Temple University Press.

Fujita, Kuniko. 1987. "Gender, State and Industrial Policy in Japan." *Women's Studies International Forum* 10, no. 6: 589–97.

Fukutake, Tadashi. 1981. *The Japanese Family.* Tokyo: Foreign Press Center.

Fukuzawa, Yukichi. 1988. *Fukuzawa Yukichi on Japanese Women: Selected Works.* Ed. and trans. Eiichi Kiyooka. Tokyo: University of Tokyo Press.

Furuki, Yoshiko. 1991.*The White Plum: A Biography of Ume Tsuda.* New York: Weatherhill.

Garon, Sheldon. 1993. "Women's Groups and the Japanese State: Contending

Approaches to Political Integration, 1890–1945." *Journal of Japanese Studies* 19, no. 1: 5–41.

Gelb, Joyce. 1991. "Tradition and Change in Japan: The Case of the Equal Employment Opportunity Law." *U.S.-Japan Women's Journal English Supplement,* no. 1 (August): 51–77.

Gelb, Joyce, and Marian Lief Palley, eds. 1994. *Women of Korea and Japan.* Philadelphia: Temple University Press.

Hamabata, Matthews Masayuki. 1990. *Crested Kimono: Power and Love in the Japanese Business Family.* Ithaca, N.Y.: Cornell University Press.

Hane, Mikiso. 1988. *Reflections on the Way to the Gallows: Rebel Women in Prewar Japan.* Berkeley: University of California Press.

———. 1982. *Peasants, Rebels, and Outcasts: The Underside of Modern Japan.* New York: Pantheon.

Hanley, Susan B. 1993. "Introduction." Symposium on Gender and Women in Japan. *Journal of Japanese Studies* 19, no. 1: 1–3.

Hara, Kimi. 1984. "Women Workers in Textiles and Electrical Industries in Japan." In *Women on the Move: Women in a World Perspective.* Paris: UNESCO.

Hayakawa, Noriyo. 1990. "Biography, Autobiography and Gender in Japan." *Gender & History* 2, no. 1 (Spring): 79–82.

Hayashi, Yoko. 1992. "Women in the Legal Profession in Japan." *U.S.-Japan Women's Journal English Supplement,* no. 2 (February): 16–27.

Hendry, Joy. 1981/1986. *Marriage in Changing Japan: Community and Society.* New York: St. Martin's Press and Rutland, Vt: Tuttle.

Higuchi, Keiko. 1985. *Bringing up Girls: Start Aiming at Love and Independence.* Trans. Akiko Tomii. Kyoto: Women's Bookstore Shoukadoh.

———. 1982. "Japanese Women in Transition." *Japan Quarterly* 29, no. 3: 311–18.

Hiroki, Michiko. 1986. *In the Shadow of Affluence: Stories of Japanese Women Workers.* Kowloon, Hong Kong: Committee for Asian Women.

Hirota, H. 1988. *Japanese Women Today.* Tokyo: International Society for Educational Information.

Huber, Kristina Ruth. 1992. *Women in Japanese Society: An Annotated Bibliography of Selected English Language Materials.* Westport, Conn., and London: Greenwood Press.

Hunter, Janet, ed. 1994. *Japanese Women Working.* London and New York: Routledge.

Ide, Sachiko, and Naomi Hanaoka McGloin. 1990. *Aspects of Japanese Women's Language.* Tokyo: Kuroshio Publishers.

Imai, Yasuko. 1994. "The Emergence of the Japanese *Shufu:* Why a *Shufu* Is More than a 'Housewife.'" *U.S.-Japan Women's Journal English Supplement,* no. 6 (March): 44–65.

Imamura, Anne E. 1987. *Urban Japanese Housewife: At Home and in the Community.* Honolulu: University of Hawaii Press.

International Women's Year Action Group. 1980. *Action Now in Japan.* Tokyo: International Women's Year Action Group.

Ishimoto, Shidzue. 1984. *Facing Two Ways: The Story of My Life.* Stanford, Calif.: Stanford University Press.

Iwai, Tomoaki. 1993. "'The Madonna Boom': Women in the Japanese Diet." *Journal of Japanese Studies* 19, no. 1: 103–20.

Iwao, Sumiko. 1993. *The Japanese Woman: Traditional Image and Changing Reality.* New York: The Free Press.

Japan Headquarters for the Planning and Promoting of Policies Relating to Women. 1987. *New National Plan of Action toward the Year 2000: The Creation of a Society of Joint Participation by Both Men and Women.* Tokyo: Government Printing Office.

———. 1981. *Priority Targets for the Second Half of the Period Covered by the National Plan of Action for the Promotion of Measures Relating to Women.* Tokyo: Government Printing Office.

Japan Ministry of Education, Science and Culture. 1990. *Women and Education in Japan.* Tokyo: Ministry of Education, Science and Culture.

Japan Prime Minister's Office. 1990. *Japanese Women Today.* Tokyo: Prime Minister's Office.

———. 1985a. *The United Nations Decade for Women and the Women of Japan.* Tokyo: Prime Minister's Office.

———. 1985b. *International Comparison of Japanese Children and Their Mothers: Findings of a Survey Conducted in Commemoration of the International Year of the Child.* Tokyo: Prime Minister's Office.

———. 1984a. *A Public Opinion Survey of Women's Employment.* Tokyo: Foreign Press Center.

———. 1984b. *The Women of Japan.* Tokyo: Prime Minister's Office.

Japanese Association of University Women. 1985. *Attitudes of University Graduates toward Vocation and Family.* Tokyo: Committee for the Status of Women, Japanese Association of University Women.

Kakemi, Momoko et al., eds. 1988. *Women and Work: Annotated Bibliography 1970–1980.* Tokyo: International Group for the Study of Women.

Kaneko, Fumiko. 1991. *The Prison Memoirs of a Japanese Woman,* trans. Jean Inglis. Armonk, N.Y.: M. E. Sharpe.

Kato, Ryoko. 1989. "Japanese Women: Subordination or Domination?" *International Journal of Sociology of the Family* 19, no. 1: 49–57.

Kawashima, Yoko. 1987. "The Place and Role of Female Workers in the Japanese Labor Market." *Women's Studies International Forum* 10, no. 6: 599–611.

Kelsky, Karen. 1994. "Postcards from the Edge: The 'Office Ladies' of Japan." *U.S.-Japan Women's Journal English Supplement,* no. 6 (March): 3–26.

Cherry, Kittredge. 1987. *Womansword: What Japanese Words Say about Women.* Tokyo: Kodansha International.

Kodama, Mieko. 1991. *Women in Modern Journalism.* Trans. Norman Havens. Tokyo: Seikado.

Koh, Hesung Chun, comp. and ed. 1982. *Korean and Japanese Women: An Analytical Bibliographical Guide.* Westport, Ct. and London: Greenwood Press.

Kondo, Dorinne K. 1990. *Crafting Selves: Power, Gender, and Discourses of Identity in a Japanese Workplace.* Chicago: University of Chicago Press.

Koyama, Takashi, and Kiyomi Morioka, eds. 1980. *Family and Household in Changing Japan.* Tokyo: The Japan Society for the Promotion of Science.

Kubota, Kyoko. 1986. "Alcoholism and the Housewife." *Japan Quarterly* 33, no. 1: 54–58.

Kuninobu, Junko Wada. 1984a. "Bibliography of Contemporary Japanese Women (Materials in English)." *Women's Studies International Forum* 7, no. 4: 307–12.

———. 1984b. "The Development of Feminism in Modern Japan." *Feminist Issues* 4, no. 2: 3–21.

Kusano, Izumi, and Keiko Kawasaki. 1983. "Japanese Women Challenge Anti-Abortion Law." *Ampo: Japan-Asia Quarterly Review* 15, no. 1: 10–15.

Lam, Alice. 1992. *Women and Japanese Management: Discrimination and Reform.* London: Routledge.

Lebra, Takie Sugiyama. 1993. "Fractionated Motherhood: Status and Gender among the Japanese Elite." *U.S.-Japan Women's Journal English Supplement,* no. 4 (January): 3–25

———. 1984. *Japanese Women: Constraint and Fulfillment.* Honolulu: University of Hawaii Press.

————, ed. 1992. *Japanese Social Organization*. Honolulu: University of Hawaii Press.

Lemeshewsky, A. Kaweah. 1987. "Facing Both Ways: Japanese Lesbians in Japan and in the U.S." In *Between the Lines: An Anthology of Pacific/Asian Lesbians of Santa Cruz, California*, ed. C. Chung, A. Kim, and A. K. Lemeshewsky. Santa Cruz, Calif.: Dancing Bird Press.

Lo, Jeannie. 1990. *Office Ladies/Factory Women: Life and Work at a Japanese Company*. Armonk, N.Y.: M. E. Sharpe.

Lock, Margaret. 1993. "Ideology, Female Midlife, and the Greying of Japan." *Journal of Japanese Studies* 19, no. 1: 43–78.

————. 1988. "New Japanese Mythologies: Faltering Discipline and the Ailing Housewife." *American Ethnologist* 15:43–61.

Mamola, Claire Zebroski. 1989. *Japanese Women Writers in English Translation: An Annotated Bibliography*. New York and London: Garland Publishing.

Matsui, Yayori. 1989. *Women's Asia*. London and Atlantic Highlands, N.J.: Zed Books.

McClellan, Edwin. 1985. *Women in the Crested Kimono: The Life of Shibue Io and Her Family*. New Haven, Conn.: Yale University Press.

Meguro, Yoriko. 1985. "The Role of Women in Japanese Society." In *Perspectives on Japan: A Guide for Teachers*, ed. John J. Cogan and Donald O. Schneider. Washington, D.C.: National Council for the Social Studies.

Minamoto, Junko. 1993. "Buddhism and the Historical Construction of Sexuality in Japan." *U.S.-Japan Women's Journal English Supplement*, no. 5 (July): 87–115.

Mitsui, Mariko. 1985. "A Package for Sexism: Education in Japanese Senior High Schools." *The Japan Christian Quarterly* 51, no. 1: 6–18.

————. 1984. "Who Pays for Japan's Economic Miracle?" *Ms.* 13, no. 6: 23.

Mulhern, Chieko Irie. 1989. "Japanese Harlequin Romances as Transcultural Women's Fiction." *Journal of Asian Studies*, 48, no. 1: 50–70.

Muramatsu, Yasuko. 1990. "Of Women by Women for Women?" *Studies of Broadcasting*, no. 26 (March): 86–104.

————. 1986. "For Wives on Friday: Women's Roles in TV Dramas." *Japan Quarterly* 33, no. 2: 159–63.

————, ed. 1983. *Women and Work: Working Women and Their Impact on Society*. Tokyo: International Group for the Study of Women. Second Tokyo Symposium on Women, 1983.

Nakajima, Keiko. 1986. "Micro–electronics: For Women the Technology of Oppression." *Ampo: Japan-Asia Quarterly Review* 18, nos. 2/3: 42–7.

Nakajima, Michiko. 1994. "Recent Legal Decisions on Gender-Based Wage Discrimination in Japan." *The U.S.-Japan Women's Journal English Supplement*, no. 6 (March): 27–43.

———. 1985. "Women at Work." *Japan Echo* 12, no. 4: 58–65.

Nakamura, Hisashi. 1988. "Japan Imports Brides from Sri Lanka: A New Poverty Discovered." *Ampo: Japan-Asia Quarterly Review* 19, no. 4: 26–31.

Narumiya, Chie. 1986. "Opportunities for Girls and Women in Japanese Education." *Comparative Education* 22, no. 1: 47–52.

National Institute of Employment and Vocational Research. 1988. *Women Workers in Japan* (NIEVR Report No. 4). Tokyo: National Institute of Employment and Vocational Research.

National Women's Education Centre. 1991. *Survey of Courses on Women's Studies and Related Subjects in Institutions of Higher Education in Japan (Fiscal 1990).* Saitama-ken: National Women's Education Centre.

———. 1990. *Women in a Changing Society: The Japanese Scene.* Bangkok: UNESCO.

———. 1988. *International Seminar on Women's Information Network System.* Saitama-ken: NWEC.

———. 1986. *International Seminar on the Family.* Saitama-ken: NWEC.

———. 1985. *Women's Studies Programs in Japan.* Saitama-ken: NWEC.

Nishizawa, Emiko. 1987. "Rural Women Bear the Yoke of a Modern Economy." *Ampo: Japan-Asia Quarterly Review* 19, no. 2: 22–24.

Niwa, Akiko. 1993. "The Formation of the Myth of Motherhood in Japan." *U.S.-Japan Women's Journal English Supplement*, no. 4 (January): 70–82.

Oaks, Laury. 1994. "Fetal Spirithood and Fetal Personhood: The Cultural Construction of Abortion in Japan." *Women's Studies International Forum* 17, no. 5: 511–23.

Ochiai, Emiko. 1989. "The Modern Family and Japanese Culture: Exploring the Japanese Mother-Child Relationship." Trans. Masako Kamimura. *Review of Japanese Culture and Society* 3, no. 1: 7–15.

Ohshima, Shizuko, and Carolyn Francis. 1989. *Japan through the Eyes of Women Migrant Workers.* Tokyo: Japan Woman's Christian Temperance Union.

Omori, Maki. 1993. "Gender and the Labor Market." *Journal of Japanese Studies* 19, no. 1: 79–102.

Osawa, Machiko. 1988. "Working Mothers: Changing Patterns of Employment and Fertility in Japan." *Economic Development and Cultural Change* 36, no. 4: 623–50.

Osawa, Mari. 1992. "Corporate-Centered Society and Women's Labor in Japan Today." *U.S.-Japan Women's Journal English Supplement*, no. 3 (September): 3–35.

Parkinson, Loraine. 1989. "Japan's Equal Employment Opportunity Law: An Alternative Approach to Social Change." *Columbia Law Review* 89, no. 3: 604–61.

Paul, Dianna. 1985. *Women in Buddhism.* Berkeley: University of California Press.

Pharr, Susan J. 1984. "Status Conflict: The Rebellion of the Tea Pourers." In *Conflict in Japan*, ed. Ellis S. Krauss, Thomas P. Rohlen, and Patricia G. Steinhoff. Honolulu: University of Hawaii Press.

———. 1981. *Political Women in Japan: The Search for a Place in Political Life.* Berkeley: University of California Press.

———. 1980. "The Japanese Woman: Evolving Views of Life and Role." In *Asian Women in Transition*, ed. Sylvia A. Chipp and Justin J. Green. University Park: Pennsylvania State University Press.

Plath, David, ed. 1983. *Work and Life Course in Japan.* New York: State University of New York Press.

———. 1980. *Long Engagements: Maturity in Modern Japan.* Stanford, Calif.: Stanford University Press.

Reischauer, Edwin O. 1988. *The Japanese Today: Change and Continuity.* Cambridge: Belknap Press.

Reischauer, Haru Matsukata. 1986. *Samurai and Silk: A Japanese and American Heritage.* Cambridge: Belknap Press.

Rhim, Soon Man. 1983. *Women of Asia: Yesterday and Today (India, China, Korea, Japan).* New York: Friendship Press.

Roberts, Glenda S. 1994. *Staying on the Line: Blue-Collar Women in Contemporary Japan.* Honolulu: University of Hawaii Press.

Robertson, Jennifer. 1989a. "Butch and Femme On and Off the Takarazuka Stage: Gender, Sexuality, and Social Organization of Japan." *Working Paper on Women in International Development*, no. 181.

———. 1989b. "Gender-Bending in Paradise: Doing 'Female' and 'Male' in Japan." *Genders*, no. 5: 50–69.

Robins-Mowry, Dorothy. 1983. *The Hidden Sun: Women of Modern Japan.* Boulder, Colo.: Westview Press.

Saisho, Yuriko. 1981. *Women Executives in Japan: How I Succeeded in a Male-Dominated Society.* Tokyo: Yuri International.

Saso, Mary. 1990. *Women in the Japanese Workplace.* London: Hilary Shipman.

Shibamoto, Janet S. 1985. *Japanese Women's Language.* Orlando, Fla.: Academic Press.

Shiga-Fujime, Yuki. 1993. "The Prostitutes' Union and the Impact of the 1956 Anti-Prostitution Law in Japan." *U.S.-Japan Women's Journal English Supplement,* no. 5 (July): 3–27.

Shimada, Haruo, and Yoshio Higuchi. 1985. "An Analysis of Trends in Female Labor Force Participation in Japan." *Journal of Labor Economics* 3, no. 1, pt. 2: S355–74.

Shimizu, Yasuko. 1988. "Asian Perspective—Asian Brides for Rural Japan." *Japan Christian Quarterly* 54, no. 3: 179–81.

Shimazu, Yoshiko. 1994. "Unmarried Mothers and Their Children in Japan." *U.S.-Japan Women's Journal English Supplement,* no. 6 (March): 83–110.

Shinozuka, Eiko. 1989. "Japanese Women's Limited Job Choices." *Economic Eye* 10, no. 1: 27–8, 30.

Shiozawa, Mioko, and Michiko Hiroki. 1988. *Discrimination against Women Workers in Japan.* Tokyo: Asian Women Workers' Center.

Sievers, Sharon L. 1984. "The Future of Feminist Scholarship on Japanese Women." In *Women in Asia and Asian Studies,* ed. Barbara D. Miller and Janice Hyde. Syracuse, N.Y.: Committee on Women in Asian Studies of the Association for Asian Studies.

———. 1983. *Flowers in Salt: The Beginnings of Feminist Consciousness in Modern Japan.* Stanford, Calif.: Stanford University Press.

———. 1981. "Feminist Criticism in Japanese Politics in the 1880s: The Experience of Kishida Toshiko." *Signs: Journal of Women in Culture and Society* 6, no. 4: 602–16.

Smith, Robert J. 1987. "Gender Inequality in Contemporary Japan." *Journal of Japanese Studies* 13, no. 1: 1–25.

Smith, Robert J., and Ella Lury Wiswell. 1982. *The Women of Suye Mura.* Chicago: University of Chicago Press.

Sodei, Takako. 1985. "The Fatherless Family." *Japan Quarterly* 32, no. 1: 77–82.

Steinhoff, Patricia G., and Kazuko Tanaka. 1986/1987. "Women Managers in

Japan." In *International Studies of Management and Organization* 16 (Fall/Winter): 108–32.

Suzuki, Midori F. 1993. *Broadening Focus—Women and the Media in the Asia-Pacific Region: 1985–1993.* Commissioned by the United Nations ESCAP.

———. 1992. "Don't Be Afraid to Be Critical: A New Direction in Japan's Media Education." In *New Directions: Media Education Worldwide.* London: British Film Institute.

———. 1985. "Portrayal of Families and Gender Roles in Japan's TV Advertising." *Japan Christian Quarterly* 51, no. 1: 19–23.

Takahashi, Sachiko. 1986. "Weary Wives: A Glance into Japanese Homes through 'Wives of a Kingdom' and 'Housewives' Autumn.'" *Ampo: Japan-Asia Quarterly Review* 18, nos. 2/3: 65–69.

Tanaka, Yukiko. 1987. *To Live and Write: Selections by Japanese Women Writers, 1913–1938.* Seattle: Seal Press.

Tanaka, Yukiko, and Elizabeth Hanson, eds. 1982. *This Kind of Woman: Ten Stories by Japanese Women Writers, 1960–1976.* Stanford, Calif.: Stanford University Press.

Takeda, Kiyoko. 1984. "Ichikawa Fusae: Pioneer for Women's Rights in Japan." *Japan Quarterly* 31, no. 4: 410–15.

Takenaka, Emiko. 1992. "The Restructuring of the Female Labor Force in Japan in the 1980s." *U.S.-Japan Women's Journal English Supplement*, no. 2 (February): 3–15.

Takeuchi, Hiroshi. 1982. "Working Women in Business Corporations—The Management Viewpoint." *Japan Quarterly* 29, no. 3: 319–23.

Tokyo Metropolitan Government. 1983. *Stride by Stride: Women's Issues in Tokyo: The Current Situation.* Tokyo: Tokyo Metropolitan Government.

Tono, Haruhi. 1986. "The Japanese Sex Industry: A Heightening Appetite for Asian Women." *Ampo: Japan-Asia Quarterly Review* 18, nos. 2/3:70–76.

Toshitani, Nobuyoshi. 1994. "The Reform of Japanese Family Law and Changes in the Family System." *U.S.-Japan Women's Journal English Supplement*, no. 6 (March): 66–82.

Tsunoda, Yukiko. 1993. "Sexual Harassment in Japan: Recent Legal Decisions." *U.S.-Japan Women's Journal English Supplement*, no. 5 (July): 52–68.

Tsurumi, E. Patricia. 1990. *Factory Girls: Women in the Thread Mills of Meiji Japan.* Princeton, N.J.: Princeton University Press.

Ueda, Makoto. 1987. *The Mothers of Dreams and Other Short Stories: Portrayals of Women in Modern Japanese Fiction.* Tokyo: Kodansha International.

Ueno, Chizuko. 1988. "The Japanese Women's Movement: The Counter-Values to Industrialism." In *The Japanese Trajectory: Modernization and Beyond*, ed. Gavan McCormack and Yoshio Sugimoto. New York: Cambridge University Press.

———. 1987a. "Genesis of the Urban Housewife." *Japan Quarterly* 34, no. 2: 130–42.

———. 1987b. "The Position of Japanese Women Reconsidered" [with comments by D. P. Martinez]. *Current Anthropology* 28, no. 4: S75–S84.

Vernon, Victoria V. 1988. *Daughters of the Moon: Wish, Will, and Social Constraint in Fiction by Modern Japanese Women*. Berkeley: Institute of East Asian Studies, University of California.

Wakita, Haruko. 1993. "Women and the Creation of the *Ie* in Japan: An Overview." *U.S.-Japan Women's Journal English Supplement*, no. 4 (January): 83–105.

Walthall, Anne. 1994. "Devoted Wives/Unruly Women: Invisible Presence in the History of Japanese Social Protest." *Signs: Journal of Women in Culture and Society* 20, no. 1: 106–36.

Weidner, Marsha, ed. 1989. *Women in the History of Chinese and Japanese Painting*. Honolulu: University of Hawaii Press.

White, Merry I., and Barbara Molony, eds. 1978. *Proceedings of the First Tokyo Symposium on Women*. Tokyo: International Group for the Study of Women.

Yamakawa, Kikue. 1992. *Women of the Mito Domain: Recollections of Samurai Life*, trans. Kate Wildman Nakai. Tokyo: University of Tokyo Press.

Yamamoto, Itsuki, et al. 1992. "A Comparative Analysis of Gender Roles and the Status of Women in Japan and the U.S." *U.S.-Japan Women's Journal English Supplement*, no. 3 (September): 36–53.

Yamamoto, Kazuyo. 1980. "Women's Life-Long Education: Present Condition and Related Themes." *Feminist International*, no. 2: 9–12.

Yamashita, Katsutoshi. 1986. "Divorce, Japanese Style." *Japan Quarterly* 33, no. 4: 416–20.

Yamashita, Yasuko. 1993. "The International Movement toward Gender Equality and Its Impact on Japan." *U.S.-Japan Women's Journal English Supplement*, no. 5 (July): 69–86.

Yamazaki, Takako. 1989. "Tsuda Ume." In *Ten Great Educators of Modern Japan*, ed. Benjamin C. Duke. Tokyo: University of Tokyo Press.

Yamazaki, Tomoko. 1985. *The Story of Yamada Waka: From Prostitute to Feminist Pioneer*. Tokyo: Kodansha International.

Yoshi, Kuzume. 1991. "Images of Japanese Women in U.S. Writings and Scholarly Works, 1860–1990: Formation and Transformation of Stereotypes." *U.S.-Japan Women's Journal English Supplement*, no. 1 (August): 6–50.

Yoshida, Ritsuko. 1990. "Getting Married the Corporate Way." *Japan Quarterly* 37, no. 2: 171–75.

Yoshihiro, Kiyoko. 1987. "Interviews with Unmarried Women." *Japan Quarterly* 34, no. 3: 305–9.

Yuzawa, Yasuhiko. 1990. "Recent Trends of Divorce and Custody in Japan." *Journal of Divorce* 13, no. 1: 129–41.

Appendix

Significant Dates in the Recent History of Japanese Women

1871   Five young girls, including Tsuda Umeko—who later establishes the first private college for women in Japan—are dispatched by the Meiji government to study in the United States.

1872   The Fundamental Code of Education calls for the establishment of a national school system and requires four years of compulsory education for both girls and boys.
Women are for the first time granted permission to climb the sacred Mount Fuji following a proclamation that women are not "impure" because of menstruation and childbirth.

1875   Ishikawa Prefecture establishes a school for training female teachers; other prefectures follow suit.

1879   Coeducation is abolished beyond the third year of elementary school, and sewing and needlework is made a required subject of study for girls in elementary school.

1884   Ogino Ginko passes the examination to practice medicine and in the following year becomes the first woman to open a medical practice.

1886   One hundred female workers at a silk mill stage a strike, the first in Japan, protesting the owner's effort to increase working hours and at the same time lower wages. Japan's branch of the Woman's

Christian Temperance Union, called the Reform Society, is founded under the leadership of Yajima Kajiko; members seek to bring about the abolition of licensed prostitution and the concubinage system.

1899   The Higher Girls' School Law calls for the establishment of at least one girls' high school in each prefecture.

1900   Women are permitted to take examinations for medical licensing. The first medical school for women, Tokyo Women's Medical School, is established.

Tsuda Umeko founds the Girls' English School (later Tsuda College).

Under Article 5 of the Police Security Regulations women are prohibited from joining political organizations and from initiating, holding, or attending political meetings.

1902   Publication of *Socialism and Women* by Kotoku Shusui, who advocated socialism as a means to women's liberation. Later, in 1910, he, together with eleven other socialists, are executed on charges of plotting the death of the Meiji emperor.

The scientist Yasui Kono produces a textbook on biology which, despite its superior level of quality, is denied official approval by the Ministry of Education on the ground that it could not possibly have been written by a woman. Later, in 1927, she becomes the first woman to receive a doctor of science degree.

1911   First Japanese performance of Henrik Ibsen's *Doll's House*. Feminist Hiratsuka Raicho and others establish Seitosha (Bluestocking Society) and publish the magazine *Seito*.

1913   Tohoku University becomes the first national university to admit female students (as auditors only).

1916   *Fujin koron*, a magazine directed at urban women, is published, dealing with labor problems, the family system, marriage, and other issues.

1918   Issues relating to working conditions for women, including night work and length of shifts, become focus of attention.

204 housewives in Toyama Prefecture demonstrate against increase in rice prices, triggering a series of rice riots throughout the nation.

1920   Ichikawa Fusae, Hiratsuka Raicho, Oku Mumeo, and others establish the Shin Fujin Kyokai (New Women's Association) to gain political rights for women.

1922   Ministry of Education instructs female teachers to take two weeks' leave before and six weeks' leave after childbirth.

1925   The Universal Manhood Suffrage Law is passed, but women fail to win the franchise.

1926   Hitomi Kinue wins a medal in women's track and field at the Swedish Olympic games and sets new world records in the 1928 and 1930 Olympics. Although she receives little recognition back in Japan, she nevertheless performs an important role in promoting sports for women through lectures and other activities.

1928   Thirteen women's organizations in Tokyo submit a petition, backed by thirty-two thousand women, calling for women's suffrage.
The Women's Consumer Union Association is established. Oku Mumeo and others seek to heighten housewives' interest in economic and consumer-related issues.

1929   Late-night labor by women is banned in the spinning industry.

1930   The Women's Suffrage League holds its first conference.

1933   An amendment to the Attorneys-at-Law Act allows women to take the bar examination.

1937   Promulgation of the Mother and Child Protection Law.
Maruoka Hideko publishes *The Problems Faced by Japanese Farm Women*, in which she describes how farming women, who constituted 60 percent of all female workers at the time, suffered from the double burden of hard labor and the feudalistic family system.

1941   Japan enters World War II.

1945   The Allied Occupation authorities, under the leadership of the United States, call for five major reforms, one of which is the emancipation of Japanese women and their enfranchisement.
Coeducation is instituted at colleges and universities.

1946   The Allied Occupation authorities order the abolition of licensed prostitution.
Women stand for election and vote for the first time in history in the election for the House of Representatives. Of the seventy-nine women running for office, thirty-nine are elected (voter turnout: women 67.0 percent, men 78.5 percent).

1947   Japan's new Constitution is enacted, stipulating equality of the sexes.
In the first regular election for the House of Councilors, 10 women are elected. In the first nationwide local elections 798 women are elected.
The Ministry of Labor establishes the Women's and Minors' Bureau.
The National Diet approves the amended Civil Code, and Japan's

traditional family *(ie)* system is abolished; equality of the sexes is clearly stated.

The Fundamental Law of Education is passed by the Diet, establishing the principle of equality of opportunity in education for both sexes and coeducation at all levels through university.

1948   The Eugenic Protection Law is passed by the Diet, legalizing contraception, sterilization, and abortion in cases in which childbirth might endanger the health of the mother. (The next year the law is broadened to permit abortion when the mother's health might be endangered "for economic reasons.")

The Japan Housewives Association (Shufu rengokai), popularly called Shufuren and made up of regional consumer groups, comes into being with Oku Mumeo, now a member of the Diet, at its head. Housewives across the country, struggling to provide for their families amid postwar deprivations, take part in various actions, such as protest against the rise in public bath prices and against shoddy safety matches and textile goods.

1949   The reorganized system of higher education, which now includes thirty-one women's universities, goes into operation.

1951   The International Labor Organization (ILO) Convention Concerning Equal Remuneration for Men and Women Workers for Work of Equal Value (Convention 100) is adopted.

1956   Passage of the Anti-Prostitution Law.

1958   A course called "Industrial Arts and Homemaking" is established in lower secondary schools, with boys taking industrial arts and girls homemaking, a move regarded by many as promoting sex-differentiation in school curriculum.

1960   Nakayama Masa is appointed Minister of Health and Welfare, becoming Japan's first female cabinet minister.

1962   The growing presence of women in four-year universities gives rise to criticism by some male faculty that the trend will lead to the nation's demise (the so-called joshigakusei bokokuron debate).

1969   The Tokyo District Court declares invalid the system of early retirement for women (retirement at age thirty or so).

The percentage of females advancing to upper secondary school (79.5) overtakes that of males (79.2 percent).

The basic principles of "Education Suited for the Special Aptitudes and Abilities of Females and Males" are issued by the Ministry of Education and four credits of "general home economics" is made mandatory for girls in upper secondary school starting in 1973.

1970   Nakane Chie becomes the first female professor at Tokyo University.
        The first women's liberation conference is held, its theme "Emancipation: Farewell to Sexual Discrimination."

1971   Betty Friedan's *Feminine Mystique* appears in Japanese translation.

1975   The International Women's Year is observed.
        The Women's Action Group is formed, which initiates protest against sexism in commercials; another group is formed to look into problems faced by female university graduates seeking employment.
        A child care leave law for female teachers and nurses at public institutions and facilities is passed, guaranteeing them leave of absence until the child is a year old.
        The first public child care center specializing in the care of infants under the age of one is established in Tokyo's Nakano Ward.

1976   Ogata Sadako is appointed minister of the Permanent Mission to the United Nations, becoming the first female minister in the Diplomatic Corps.
        Revision of the Civil Code establishes the right of women to use their married surnames after divorce.

1977   A National Plan of Action for UN Decade for Women is announced.
        The National Women's Education Centre is opened.
        The International Women's Studies Association and the Japan Women's Studies Association are inaugurated.
        A revision of the Ministry of Education's Course of Study makes it possible for girls to take some industrial arts subjects and boys some subjects in homemaking in lower secondary school starting in 1981.

1980   Japan signs the United Nations (UN) Convention on the Elimination of All Forms of Discrimination against Women.
        Takahashi Nobuko is appointed ambassador to Denmark, becoming Japan's first female ambassador.
        Revision of the Civil Code increases the legal share of a surviving spouse's inheritance from one-third of the estate (with children splitting the remaining two-thirds) to one-half.

1981   The Supreme Court rules it is illegal for Nissan Motors Company to set a lower retirement age for female workers than for male workers.

1982   An interim report issued by the Ministry of Labor advises companies to abolish discriminatory retirement age standards for male and female employees.

Shoukadoh, the first bookstore to specialize in women's books and publications, opens in Kyoto.

1983   The Tokyo Rape Crisis Center is established.

The National Women's Education Centre initiates a periodic survey of courses on women's studies offered in institutions of higher education.

1984   The Women's and Minor's Bureau of the Ministry of Labor is reorganized, and an independent Women's Bureau is established.

The percentage of married women who are in the labor force reaches 50.3, overtaking that of full-time housewives for the first time.

The Nationality Law is revised, allowing Japanese women married to non-Japanese to pass on their nationality to offspring.

1985   The Equal Employment Opportunity Law is passed in the Diet.

The Japanese Diet ratifies the UN Convention on the Elimination of All Forms of Discrimination against Women.

1986   HELP (House in Emergency of Love and Peace), an emergency shelter for women of all nationalities, is established in Tokyo by the Japan Christian Woman's Temperance Union, the oldest women's organization in Japan, on the hundredth anniversary of its founding.

Doi Takako is appointed chair of the Japan Social Democratic Party, becoming the first woman to head a major political party in Japan.

1987   The high court rules for the first time that the person responsible for a marital breakup can initiate the divorce process if his or her request does not run counter to the principles of social justice.

The Eleventh Unified Local Elections produces a record number of female candidates (212) for prefectural assemblies, of which 52 are elected to office.

The so-called Agnes Debate becomes the subject of national controversy when novelist Hayashi Mariko criticizes singer-celebrity Agnes Chan for taking her infant to her workplace.

1988   Sekiguchi Reiko, who had been using her maiden name at her workplace even after marriage, sues the state and her new university employer for the right to continue such usage.

The Showa emperor's illness and the mass media's focus on it leads to heightened discussion and criticism of the Emperor system; a woman's group critical of the system is established.

1989 The Tokyo Lawyers' Association submits a report advocating the optional use of separate surnames for married couples.

Twenty-two female candidates win election to the House of Councilors, the largest number ever.

A women's group in the city of Sakai in Osaka initiates a campaign opposing women's beauty contests (so-called Miss Contests), sparking similar movements in various parts of Japan.

Chief Cabinet Secretary Moriyama Mayumi's attempt to challenge the traditional ban against women stepping into the sumo (traditional Japanese-style wrestling) ring in order to present a prize is rebuffed, sparking debate about sexism in many aspects of Japanese tradition.

Under the revised Course of Study announced by the Ministry of Education, general home economics is made a required subject for both sexes in upper secondary school starting in the 1994 academic year. The revision calls for allowing boys and girls to choose from a wider range of subjects in both industrial arts and homemaking at the lower secondary school level starting in 1993.

1990 The Tokyo District Court rules salary raises and advancement for men only as illegal.

The Association for Considering Work and Sexual Discrimination is established, and sexual harassment begins to gain recognition as a serious issue at many places of work as well as in society as a whole.

1991 Kitamura Harue becomes the first woman to be elected to the office of mayor (in Ashiya City, near Osaka).

The Diet passes the Child Care Leave Law, allowing either parent to take nonpaid child care leave until the child reaches one year of age.

1992 First sexual harassment won in April in Fukuoka Prefecture; victim is awarded $13,200.

The National Feminist Assemblywoman's League is founded. The group calls for affirmative action and other measures to increase female representation in national and local political assemblies.

All-Nippon Airways becomes the first Japanese airline company to announce plans to hire female pilots for regularly scheduled flights.

Thirteen groups, including the Japan YWCA and the Socialist Party's Japan's Women's Council, call on the prime minister to issue a formal apology and provide compensation in recognition of claims by so-called comfort women from Korea, the Philippines, and other countries.

1993   Doi Takako becomes the first woman chosen as Speaker of the House of Representatives.

The Tokyo Court rules against Sekiguchi Reiko (see 1988) in a suit against her employer, a national university, for the right to use her maiden name.

1994   Takahashi Hisako becomes the first woman appointed Supreme Court judge.

A noted professor at Kyoto University is charged with sexual harassment of a female student and a member of the office staff and resigns his post, though he later seeks to have the Ministry of Education nullify his resignation. Various women's and citizen's groups call for measures to deal with and prevent sexual harassment in school and universities.

The Deliberative Council on the Legal System (Hosei Shingikai) proposes changes in the Civil Code pertaining to divorce, inheritance rights for children born outside of marriage, and the use of separate surnames for married couples.

A group of women university students demonstrate in Tokyo to protest sex discrimination in hiring by corporations and to call for stricter enforcement of the Equal Employment Opportunity Law.

Home economics, which had been a required subject in high school for girls only, becomes mandatory for students of both sexes.

Notes on Contributors

Naoko Aoki (translator) holds a bachelor's degree in French literature from the Tokyo University of Foreign Studies and a master's degree in linguistics from Sophia University. An associate professor in the Faculty of Education at Shizuoka University, she teaches courses on the teaching of Japanese as a second language. Her writings have appeared in *Nihongo kyoiku* (Japanese language education) and *The Language Teacher* (for which she has served as the journal's Japanese language editor since 1991). In addition to her primary work in teaching and writing, she has also worked occasionally as an interpreter and translator for contemporary artists.

Chieko M. Ariga is associate professor of Japanese literature at the University of Utah. She received her Ph.D. from the University of Chicago. Her special research areas are Edo literature, women's literature, and feminist criticism. Her essays and translations have appeared in such journals as the *International Journal of Social Education, IRIS, Journal of Asian Studies, Manoa, Monumenta Nipponica,* and *Showa bungaku kenkyu.* Her *Jenda kaitai no kiseki: bungaku, seido, bunka* (Strategy of degendering: literature, institutions, culture) is forthcoming. She is associate editor of the *U.S.-Japan Women's Journal.*

Orie Endo, who holds bachelor's and master's degrees in Japanese literature from Ochanomizu Women's University in Tokyo, is professor of Japanese language education at Bunkyo University in Tokyo. She has written several articles (in Japanese) for such journals as *The Language Teacher, Kotoba*

(Language), and *Kokubungaku kaishaku to kansho* (Interpretation and appreciation of Japanese literature). She is the author of the book *Kininaru kotoba: Nihongo saikento* (Troubling words: a reevaluation of Japanese), a pioneering study that looks at many aspects of the Japanese language from a feminist perspective; a coauthor of *Kokugo jiten ni miru josei sabetsu* (Gender discrimination as seen in Japanese dictionaries); and editor of *Josei no yobikata daikenkyu* (Research on how women are addressed).

Mioko Fujieda, professor of women's studies and dean of the faculty of humanities at Kyoto Seika University, has written widely on Japanese feminism. She is the supervising translator into Japanese of the books *Sexual Politics*, by Kate Millet, and *The New Our Bodies, Ourselves*, by the Boston Women's Health Book Collective.

Kumiko Fujimura-Fanselow (coeditor) received a Ph.D. in comparative education from Columbia University and is associate professor of education and women's studies at Toyo Eiwa Women's University and its graduate school in Tokyo. Her articles on Japanese higher education and women's education have appeared in such journals as *Comparative Education Review* and *Gender & History,* and she has also contributed chapters to *International Handbook of Women's Education; Japanese Education: Patterns of Socialization, Equality and Political Control; Windows on Japanese Education; Women of Japan and Korea;* and *Higher Education in Asia: An International Handbook and Reference Guide.* She was coeditor with Denise Vaughn of a special issue of *The Language Teacher* on "Feminist Issues in Language Teaching" (July 1991).

Kuniko Funabashi, a feminist activist and researcher, received her B.A. in economics and geography from Ochanomizu Women's University. She is currently director of the Saga Prefectural Women's Center, as well as a member of the Asian Women's Research and Action Network (AWRAN) and a coordinator of the Asian Women's Network conference. She has contributed articles about sexual violence and pornography in *Joseigaku* (the journal of the Women's Studies Association of Japan), *Gendai shiso,* and the book *Feminizumu nyumon* (An introduction to feminism). She is also the translator into Japanese of the memoir *Facing Two Ways: The Story of My Life,* by Baroness Shidzue Ishimoto.

Aiko Hada, who holds an M.A. in sociology from Meiji Gakuin University, is currently with the Tokyo Institute of Psychiatry, Department of Sociopathology. She is the author of a chapter in the book *Joseirashisa no yamai* (Diseases of femininity), which she coedited, and she has also contributed to *Arukoru izon no shakai byori* (Sociopathology of alcohol dependence), *Josei shakaigaku o mezashite* (Toward a sociology of women), and *Joseigaku kenkyu* (the journal of the Society for Women's Studies—Japan). She is also a member of the Domestic Violence Action and Research Group and has recently founded a small shelter for battered women in Tokyo together with some recovered victims of battering.

Kimi Hara, who received a Ph.D. in the sociology of education and sociology from Michigan State University, is currently president of Okinawa Christian Junior College. Previously, she taught at many universities in Japan, including Tsuda Women's University, International Christian University, Shikoku Christian College, and Tokyo Union Theological Seminary. In addition, she served as director of the Japanese Studies Program at Ateneo de Manila University in the Philippines, visiting professor in the Japanese Studies Program at Padjadjaram University in Indonesia, and visiting professor of Japanese culture and education at the Philippine Women's University. She is the coauthor of *Kazoku mondai no shakaigaku* (The sociology of family-related problems), as well as several articles that have appeared in the journals *Contemporary Japan* and *Kyoiku shakaigaku kenkyu* (Journal of sociology and education), and the edited volumes *Women on the Move; Towards 2000 A.D.: Human Life and Resource Management;* and *Onnatachi no ima: koza joseigaku 2* (Women today: lectures on women's studies, vol. 2).

Atsuko Kameda (coeditor) holds an M.A. in the sociology of education from Ochanomizu Women's University. After working in the Women's Education Division of the Ministry of Education, she joined the faculty of Jyumonji Junior College in Tokyo, where she is currently associate professor of education. She has written widely (in Japanese) on the subject of women's studies and sexism in Japanese education and her work has appeared in such publications as *Josei no shogaikyoiku* (Lifelong learning for women), *Onna no me de miru: koza joseigaku 4* (Seeing through women's eyes: lectures on women's studies, vol. 4), *Joshi kotokyoiku no zahyo* (The status of women's higher education), and *Nihon no chichioya to kodomo—Nichibeidoku hikaku chosa* (Research report on father-child relationships in Japan, the U.S., and Germany). She also contributed a chapter to *Women of Japan and Korea.* She is also on the planning committee of the Society for Women's Studies—Japan and the planning committee for lectures on women's studies at the National Women's Education Centre.

Sachiko Kaneko has completed her course work for a Ph.D. in modern Japanese intellectual history at International Christian University in Tokyo and is currently working on her dissertation, which deals with the history of women's thought in modern Japan. She is a part-time instructor in women's studies at Toyo Eiwa Women's University and also teaches English at Musashi University. She is a coauthor of the three-volume *Nihon josei no rekishi* (A history of Japanese women), and she has also published numerous articles pertaining to the history of Japanese women in the early twentieth century in the journal *Kyoiku tetsugaku kenkyu* (Studies in the philosophy of education), and in *Asia bunka kenkyu* (Asian cultural studies) and *Shakai kagaku jaanaru* (Journal of social science), publications of International Christian University.

Yoko Kawashima, who holds a Ph.D. in education, an M.A. in economics from Stanford University, and a B.A. in law from the University of Tokyo, is a scholar of labor economics. She is the author (in Japanese) of *Hiyakusuru daigaku Stanford* (Stanford University: one example of a higher education institution in the U.S.A.), *Joshi rodo to rodo shijo kozo no bunseki* (Women workers and the labor market in Japan), and *Onnatachi ga kaeru America* (Women changing America). She has also contributed articles to the *International Journal of Industrial Organization* and *Women's Studies International Forum*.

Emiko Kaya holds an M.A. in behavioral sciences in education from California State University, Sacramento. During her stay in the United States she taught Japanese there and at Sacramento City College. Currently she is an instructor in English at Tokyo Metropolitan Ueno Senior High School. In addition to contributing chapters to *Onna no me de miru: koza joseigaku 4* (Seeing through women's eyes: lectures on women's studies, vol. 4) and *Josei shakaigaku o mezashite* (Toward a sociology of women), she has translated into Japanese Susan J. Pharr's *Political Women in Japan* and the chapter by Carolyn W. Sherif, "Bias in Psychology," in *The Prism of Sex*, edited by Julia A. Sherman and Evelyn Torton Beck. She is also a cotranslator of Lillian B. Rubin's *Intimate Strangers*.

Kiyoko Kinjo received her B.A. in law from Tokyo University and also studied at Harvard Law School. She is an attorney and professor of law at Tsuda College in Tokyo. In addition to having numerous articles published (in Japanese) in such journals as *Jurist*, *Horitsu Jiho*, and *Liberty and Justice*, she is the author of the books *Ho joseigaku* (Feminist legal studies), *Kazoku to iu kankei* (Family relations), *Ho no naka no josei* (Women's legal status), and *Ho joseigaku no susume* (A call for feminist legal studies), and coauthor of *Josei hogaku* (Feminist legal studies).

Charles Douglas Lummis, who holds a Ph.D. in political science from the University of California, Berkeley, is a professor at Tsuda College in Tokyo, where he has taught since 1974. He has published numerous books both in English and in Japanese, including, in English, *A New Look at the Chrysanthemum and the Sword*, *Boundaries on the Land, Boundaries in the Mind*, *Inside the Octopus Society*, *Peace and Democracy in Postwar Japan*, and, in Japanese, *Ideologii to shite no eikaiwa* (English conversation as ideology), *Uchinaru gaikoku* (The foreign land within us), *Kage no gakumon, mado no gakumon* (Scholarship of shadows, scholarship of windows), and (with Ikeda Masayuki) *Nihonjinron no shinso* (The deep structure of Japanology). He has also contributed articles to the *New York Review of Books*, *Alternatives*, *The Nation*, *AMPO*, and *Japan Quarterly*.

Yayori Matsui, a graduate of the Tokyo University of Foreign Studies, also studied at the University of Minnesota and the Sorbonne. An internationally known journalist, she was a reporter and senior staff writer for the *Asahi shimbun* newspaper from 1961 until 1994 and served as its correspondent in Singapore from 1981 to 1985. She is the author of several books, including *Josei kaiho to wa nani ka* (What is women's liberation?) and *Onnatachi no Asia* (Women's Asia) and coauthor of *Ajia kara kita dekasegi rodoshatachi* (Workers from Asia in Japan). Her English translation of *Women's Asia* was published in 1989. She is also a cofounder of the Asian Women's Association, which, among many other activities, campaigns against sex tours in Asia.

Satomi Nakajima received her B.A. from the Department of Literature at Chuo University in Tokyo. After teaching high school English for twenty-six years, she became a feminist organizer, participating in the Women's Action Group, Japan Women's Forum, and the International Women's Year conferences held in Copenhagen (1980) and Nairobi (1985). In 1991 she was elected to the Tokorozawa City Assembly. She has coauthored the books *Onnatachi wa chikyujin* (Women are members of the planet), *Onna ga seiji o kaeru* (Women bringing about change in politics), and *Kateika—naze onna dake* (Why should home economics be for girls only?).

Masami Ohinata, who received her Ph.D. in human culture from Ochanomizu Women's University, is a professor in the faculty of humanities at Keisen Women's University in Tokyo. She is the author of the books *Bosei wa onna no kunsho desu ka* (Is motherhood a medal to be worn by women?), *Bosei no kenkyu—sono keisei to henyo no katei: dentoteki boseikan e no hansho* (The study of motherhood—its formation and process of change: counterevidence for the traditional understanding of motherhood), and several other books and articles dealing with motherhood.

Haruko Okano holds a Ph.D. in comparative religion from the University of Bonn and is professor in the Department of Literature at Jissen Women's University in Tokyo. She is the author (in German) of *Die Stellung der Frau im Shinto Eine religionsphanomenologische und soziologische Untersuchung,* coauthor of the books *Wörterbuch der Feministischen Theologie, Japan—Ein Land der Frauen?* and *Theologie zwischen Zeiten und Kontinenten,* and coauthor (in Japanese) of the book *Shukyo no naka no joseishi* (Women's history in religion). She has also contributed chapters in *Nihon-Doitsu: josei no atarashi uneri* (Japan and Germany: the new surge of women) and *Das Gold im Wachs.*

Timothy John Phelan (translator), who holds a B.A. from Trinity College and an M.A. from Gordon-Conwell Theological Seminary, is assistant professor of communication studies in the Department of Japanese Studies at Keisen Women's College in Tokyo. He is the translator of the books *Nihongo and Foreign Students: A Personal Sketch,* by Sasaki Mizue, and *12 Months: Events and*

Persons, by Fujii Motokiyo; one of the translators of *The Complete Japanese Expression Guide*, by Sasaki Mizue; and the author of *A Shorter Course in Colloquial Japanese*. He spent five years as the translator of Sasaki Mizue's weekly column "Japanese Naturally" in the *Asahi Evening News*.

Naoko Sasakura, who attended Wako University, is a freelance writer. She is coauthor of the books *Onna ga seiji o kaeru* (Women bringing about change in politics) and *Abunai Nihongo gakko* (Questionable Japanese language schools).

Yoko Sato, a graduate of the Department of Political Science and Economics at Waseda University in Tokyo, was a reporter and staff writer in the arts and sciences department of the *Asahi shimbun* newspaper from 1964 until 1991, reporting extensively on issues concerning women. Since 1992 she has been head of the Sexual Equality Promotion Center in Tokyo's Toshima Ward. Among the books she has authored are *Onnanoko wa tsukurareru* (How girls are socialized), *Kodomo o azukete hataraku to iu koto* (Issues facing working mothers), *Jiyu to jiritsu e no ayumi—onna ga ikita nijusseiki* (Progress toward freedom and independence—women in the twentieth century), and *Shinbunkisha ni natte* (My life as a newspaper reporter).

Takado Sodei holds an M.A. in sociology from the University of California at Los Angeles and has completed course work for a doctorate at Tokyo Metropolitan University. She is currently a professor in the School of Human Life and Environmental Science at Ochanomizu Women's University in Tokyo. She has written extensively on issues pertaining to the family, women, and the elderly both in Japan and in other countries. Her publications include *Teinen kara no jinsei* (Life after retirement), *Kazoku ni totte teinen to wa* (What retirement means for the family), *Kazoku: daisan no tenkanki* (The family—the third turning point), *Gendai josei no chii* (The contemporary position of women), and *Chukonen joseigaku* (Middle-aged and older women's studies).

Midori Fukunishi Suzuki, who earned an M.A. in communications from Stanford University, is a professor of communications at the College of Social Science, Ritsumeikan University. She teaches courses in media literacy and gender and mass communications. She has also been a freelance journalist and has been active in the media reform movement since 1977, when she cofounded and became the spokeswoman for the Forum for Citizens' Television (FCT). She edited and contributed to the books *Terebi to kodomo* (Television and children) and *Terebi: dare no tame no media ka* (Television: Whose medium is it?), and contributed to *Imeji to shite no teikokushugi* (Image imperialism) and *Josei to media* (Women and media).

Kazuko Tanaka ("Work, Education, and the Family") received her M.A. and Ph.D. in sociology from the University of Iowa following her undergraduate studies at Ochanomizu Women's University. Currently, she is an associate professor in the Department of Comparative Society and Culture at International Christian University in Tokyo, and her articles have appeared (in English) in *Social Forces, Social Science Research*, and *Shakai kagaku jaanaru* (Journal of social science, a publication of International Christian University) and in *futuribles* (in French).

Kazuko Tanaka ("The New Feminist Movement in Japan, 1970–1990"), who holds an M.A. in sociology from the University of Hawaii and has completed her course work for a Ph.D. in sociology at the Tokyo Metropolitan University, is professor of sociology at Kokugakuin University in Tokyo. She is the author (in English) of *A Short History of the Women's Movement in Modern Japan*, and she has also written several articles in both Japanese and English, including chapters for *Competitive Frontiers: Women Managers in a Global Economy* and *Unresolved Dilemmas: Women, Work and the Family in the United States, Europe and the Former Soviet Union*. She is also the Japanese translator of *The Second Shift*, by Arlie Russell Hochschild, and *Female Sexual Slavery*, by Kathleen Barry, and a cotranslator of *The Prism of Sex*, edited by Julia A. Sherman and Evelyn Torton Beck.

Yoko Tsuruta (translator), assistant professor in Japanese as a second language teacher training at Toyo Eiwa Women's University, is currently completing her Ph.D. in the Department of Linguistics and Modern English at the University of Lancaster. Her research deals with Japanese linguistics communication, Japanese linguistic politeness, and linguistic communication failure in general, and she has coauthored (in Japanese) *Eigo no sosharu sukiru: Politeness systems in English and Japanese* and also contributed articles (in Japanese) to *The Language Teacher, International Journal of Pragmatics*, and the *SFC Journal of Language and Communication*.

Midori Wakakuwa pursued her undergraduate and graduate studies at the Tokyo National University of Fine Arts and Music and also studied at the University of Rome. She taught for many years as professor at the Tokyo University of Fine Arts and Music before taking up her current post as professor at Chiba University. She has written several articles pertaining to Renaissance art, particularly the works of Michelangelo, in both Japanese and Italian, and authored, among other books (in Japanese), *Gui to shocho no joseizo* (The female image in allegory and symbolism), *Manerisumu geijutsuron* (The artistic theory of mannerism), *Josei gaka retsuden* (The lives of women artists) , and *Kosai no kaiga—Michelangelo no Shisutiina reihaido tenjoga no zuzokaishakugakuteki kenkyu* (The picture of splendor—an iconological study of Michelangelo's painting on the ceiling of the Sistine Chapel).

Atsuko Watanabe (translator), who teaches English at Toyo Eiwa Women's University and at Obirin University, holds an M.A. in teaching English to speakers of other languages from Teachers College, Columbia University.

Her research interests include student autonomy and classroom dynamics, and she has contributed articles to the journal of the Japan Association for Current English Studies.

Masanori Yamaguchi, a graduate of Osaka Metropolitan University, has been a reporter for the *Yomiuri shimbun* newspaper since 1973. He has reported widely on such issues as men's participation in homemaking and child care, community action, sexual harassment, prostitution and the issue of "comfort women," and children's rights. He is also a leader of the Liaison Group on Human Rights and Reporting, which is concerned with issues surrounding press reporting and infringement of individual rights, and a member of the Association for the Elimination of Gender Discrimination in Newspaper Reporting. He has coauthored several books and essays, including *Tenno to masukomi hodo* (The emperor and mass communications reporting), *Hanzai hodo no genzai* (Current status of crime reporting), *Joshikokosei konkuriitozume satsujin jiken* (The case of the murder and concrete packing of a high school female student), and *Dansei kaiso koza* (A course on remodeling males).

Kyoko Yoshizumi, professor of sociology at Otemon Gakuin University in Osaka, holds an M.A. in the sociology of the family from the Osaka Metropolitan University. She is the author (in Japanese) of *Kongaishi no shakaigaku* (The sociology of unmarried women's children: a history of discrimination), editor of *Hikon o ikitai—kongaishi no sabetsu o tou* (Challenging discrimination against children born out of marriage), and a coeditor of *Home economics to josei* (Home economics and women) and *Datsu kekkon* (To wed or not to wed). She has also contributed chapters to *Kazoku to fukushi no mirai* (The future of the family and welfare) and *Gendai kazoku no runesansu* (The renaissance of the contemporary family).